Flex 3 Cookbook™

Flex 3 Cookbook™

Joshua Noble and Todd Anderson

O'REILLY®

Beijing · Cambridge · Farnham · Köln · Paris · Sebastopol · Taipei · Tokyo

Flex 3 Cookbook™

by Joshua Noble and Todd Anderson

Copyright © 2008 Joshua Noble and Todd Anderson. All rights reserved.
Printed in the United States of America.

Published by O'Reilly Media, Inc., 1005 Gravenstein Highway North, Sebastopol, CA 95472

O'Reilly books may be purchased for educational, business, or sales promotional use. Online editions
are also available for most titles (*http://safari.oreilly.com*). For more information, contact our corporate/
institutional sales department: (800) 998-9938 or *corporate@oreilly.com*.

Editor: Linda Laflamme	**Indexer:** Joe Wizda
Copy Editor: Sharon Wilkey	**Cover Designer:** Karen Montgomery
Production Editor: Michele Filshie	**Interior Designer:** David Futato
Proofreader: Nancy Bell	**Illustrator:** Jessamyn Read

Printing History:

May 2008:	First Edition.

The O'Reilly logo is a registered trademark of O'Reilly Media, Inc. *Flex 3 Cookbook*, the image of the
fringed gecko, and related trade dress are trademarks of O'Reilly Media, Inc.

Many of the designations uses by manufacturers and sellers to distinguish their products are claimed as
trademarks. Where those designations appear in this book, and O'Reilly Media, Inc. was aware of a
trademark claim, the designations have been printed in caps or initial caps

While every precaution has been taken in the preparation of this book, the publisher and authors assume
no responsibility for errors or omissions, or for damages resulting from the use of the information contained herein.

 This book uses RepKover, a durable and flexible lay-flat binding.

ISBN: 978-0-596-52985-7

[M]

1209583954

Adobe Developer Library

Adobe Developer Library, a copublishing partnership between O'Reilly Media Inc. and Adobe Systems, Inc., is the authoritative resource for developers using Adobe technologies. These comprehensive resources offer learning solutions to help developers create cutting-edge interactive web applications that can reach virtually anyone on any platform.

With top-quality books and innovative online resources covering the latest tools for rich-Internet application development, the *Adobe Developer Library* delivers expert training, straight from the source. Topics include ActionScript, Adobe Flex®, Adobe Flash®, and Adobe Acrobat® software.

Get the latest news about books, online resources, and more at *adobedeveloperlibrary.com*.

Table of Contents

Preface

Flex 3 is a powerful framework that provides enterprise-level components for the Flash Player platform in a markup language format recognizable to anyone with HTML or XML development experience. The Flex Framework provides components for visual layout, visual effects, data grids, server communication, charts, and much more.

To put a blunt point on it, the Flex Framework is massive, and any book attempting to cover the entire Framework in any depth will without question fail in some respect or another. With this in mind, we've made an attempt to cover the topics that most vex developers working with Flex 3—in a way that can illuminate how the Framework is structured as well as help solve common problems. The official Flex documentation is quite good at explaining in depth how particular methods or classes behave, so instead we explain how to tackle common tasks within the Flex Framework, how to get different components to work together, and how Flex can partner with other technologies to create Rich Internet Applications and more. With the help of Adobe AIR, for example, you can use the tools of Flex and the Flash Player to create deployable desktop applications. This complements the expansion of open source and commercial tools for Java, .NET, and PHP development, among others, making Flex a powerful solution for an ever wider range of development needs and challenges.

Bonus Chapters Online

The Flex framework is such a huge topic and we had so many recipes and so much information to cover that we simply couldn't fit it all into the printed book. Four chapters totaling 76 pages are available to you online that cover working with XML, the Charting components, working with SharedObjects, and Development Strategies for creating Flex applications. Go to www.oreilly.com/catalog/9780596529857 to read this bonus material.

Who This Book Is For

Flex 3 Cookbook is for developers who want to understand the Flex Framework more thoroughly or who need a reference to consult to solve particular problems. As such, this book assumes that you have some previous experience with Flex and ActionScript 3. The code samples and explanations likewise are geared toward intermediate developers familiar with the relationship between MXML and ActionScript, at least some of the components that make up the Flex Framework, and basic strategies of Flex development.

We have made a very deliberate decision to ensure that all the recipes contain usable components and functional, tested implementations of those components. This was not done with the intention of swelling the book unreasonably, but to ensure that this book is suitable for intermediate and advanced developers who simply need to see a small code snippet to understand a technique, as well as readers who are still learning how the Flex Framework can be used and the best practices for working with it.

Who This Book Is Not For

If you need to learn the Flex Framework from scratch, consult *Programming Flex 3* by Joey Lott and Chafic Kazoun (O'Reilly, 2008) to gain an understanding of the core concepts of Flex development before reading any further here. With a grounding in Flex and ActionScript basics, you'll be better prepared to take advantage of the techniques in this book. If you need a refresher course in ActionScript development, try *ActionScript 3.0 Cookbook* by Joey Lott, Darron Schall, and Keith Peters (O'Reilly, 2006) for techniques focused on core Flash ActionScript programming. Although *Flex 3 Cookbook* covers some areas of overlap between the Flex Framework and core Flash ActionScript classes, this book is very much focused on Flex development.

How This Book Is Organized

As its name implies, *Flex 3 Cookbook* is stuffed full with recipes for techniques that will help you get more from your Flex applications. To help you find the solutions you need faster, the recipes are organized by theme. Generally the recipes progress from simpler topics to the more complex throughout each chapter.

This book was not intended to be read from cover to cover but rather to be used as a reference for a particular problem, or to provide some insight into a particular aspect of the Flex Framework. The recipes also include complete component implementations to show you how to completely implement the concept discussed. You should be able to use the demonstrated code in your own applications or at the very minimum adapt relevant portions of the code to your needs.

Conventions Used in This Book

The following typographical conventions are used in this book:

Italic

Indicates new terms, URLs, email addresses, filenames, and file extensions.

`Constant width`

Used for program listings, as well as within paragraphs to refer to program elements such as variable or function names, databases, data types, environment variables, statements, and keywords.

`Constant width bold`

Shows commands or other text that should be typed literally by the user.

`Constant width italic`

Shows text that should be replaced with user-supplied values or by values determined by context.

Using Code Examples

This book is here to help you get your job done. In general, you may use the code in this book in your programs and documentation. You do not need to contact us for permission unless you're reproducing a significant portion of the code. For example, writing a program that uses several chunks of code from this book does not require permission. Selling or distributing a CD-ROM of examples from O'Reilly books does require permission. Answering a question by citing this book and quoting example code does not require permission. Incorporating a significant amount of example code from this book into your product's documentation does require permission.

We appreciate, but do not require, attribution. An attribution usually includes the title, author, publisher, and ISBN. For example: "*Flex 3 Cookbook* by Joshua Noble and Todd Anderson. Copyright 2008 Joshua Noble and Todd Anderson, 978-0-596-5298-57."

If you feel your use of code examples falls outside fair use or the permission given above, feel free to contact us at *permissions@oreilly.com*.

How to Use This Book

Think of this book like a friend and a counselor. Don't put it on a shelf. Keep it on your desk where you can consult it often. When you are uncertain as to how something works or how to approach a specific programming issue pick up the book and flip to the relevant recipe(s). We have written this book in a format so that you can get answers to specific questions quickly. And since it's a book you don't ever have to worry that it will laugh at you for asking questions. No question is too big or too small.

Although you can read the book from cover to cover, we encourage you to use this book when you need an answer. Rather than teaching you a bunch of theory, this book intends to help you solve problems and accomplish tasks. This book is meant for field work, not the research lab.

O'Reilly Cookbooks

Looking for the right ingredients to solve a programming problem? Look no further than O'Reilly Cookbooks. Each cookbook contains hundreds of programming recipes, and includes hundreds of scripts, programs, and command sequences you can use to solve specific problems.

The recipes you'll find in an O'Reilly Cookbook follow a simple formula:

Problem
> Each Problem addressed in an O'Reilly Cookbook is clearly stated, specific, and practical.

Solution
> The Solution is easy to understand and implement.

Discussion
> The Discussion clarifies and explains the context of the Problem and the Solution. It also contains sample code to show you how to get the job done. Best of all, all of the sample code you see in an O'Reilly Cookbook can be downloaded from the book's web site, at *http://www.oreilly.com/catalog/actscpt3ckbk*.

See Also
> The See Also section directs you to additional information related to the topic covered in the recipe. You'll find pointers to other recipes in the book, to other books (including non-O'Reilly titles), web sites, and more.

To learn more about the O'Reilly Cookbook series, or to find other Cookbooks that are up your alley, visit their web site at *http://cookbooks.oreilly.com*.

Safari® Enabled

Safari When you see a Safari® Enabled icon on the cover of your favorite technology book, that means the book is available online through the O'Reilly Network Safari Bookshelf.

Safari offers a solution that's better than e-books. It's a virtual library that lets you easily search thousands of top tech books, cut and paste code samples, download chapters, and find quick answers when you need the most accurate, current information. Try it for free at *http://safari.oreilly.com*.

How to Contact Us

Please address comments and questions concerning this book to the publisher:

O'Reilly Media, Inc.
1005 Gravenstein Highway North
Sebastopol, CA 95472
800-998-9938 (in the United States or Canada)
707-829-0515 (international or local)
707 829-0104 (fax)

We have a web page for this book, where we list errata, examples, and any additional information. You can access this page at:

http://www.oreilly.com/catalog/9780596529857

To comment or ask technical questions about this book, send email to:

bookquestions@oreilly.com

For more information about our books, conferences, Resource Centers, and the O'Reilly Network, see our web site at:

http://www.oreilly.com

Acknowledgments

This book truly does represent a product of the Flex community. Thanks belong to many developers and the community relations managers at Adobe, Amy Wong, Matt Chotin, Ely Greenfield, and Alex Harui in particular, as well as to the developers who work with Adobe products and contributed to the Flex Cookbook site or blogged about what they discovered. Without all of them, this book would not be conceivable.

Many, many thanks are due to the many people at O'Reilly who made this book possible. Many special thanks go to Steve Weiss, Linda Laflamme, and Michele Filshie for their hard work, flexibility, and patience throughout the writing and editing of this book.

The quality of the technical information within this book is not simply due to the knowledge of the many authors of this book. The technical reviewers for this book, Mark Walters (*http://www.digitalflipbook.com/*), Alfio Raymond, and Jen Blackledge, not only provided help debugging, correcting, and clarifying the code for this book, but also provided fantastic insight into ways to clarify explanations, structure chapters, alter recipes, and help the readers' understanding.

From Joshua

First and foremost, I need to thank Joey Lott for so graciously helping me get the opportunity to write this book and the one before this. I wouldn't be writing this without his encouragement and advocacy for my abilities, and I can't thank him enough for believing in me enough to recommend me for this book. The same goes to Steve Weiss, who took a chance on a somewhat unknown author and made it possible for the book to blossom to its current size. To my co-authors, Todd Anderson and Abey George, and also the people at Cynergy Systems, Andrew Trice, Craig Drabnik, Keun Lee, and Ryan Miller, for stepping in and helping when I needed them, to all of them I owe a huge debt. I also need to thank Daniel Rinehart, who did such a fantastic job writing the recipes that make up "Unit Testing with FlexUnit," simply to educate and share with the Flex community, completely unprompted. The same goes for everyone who participated in the Adobe Cookbook site and on forums like FlexCoders, making a vibrant, helpful community that helps us all.

I'd also like to thank my friends whom I've known from jobs and from life, for providing me with so much help, advice, support, and humor. Finally, I'd like to thank my family, and in particular my mother, for always providing me with encouragement and wisdom.

From Todd

I would first like to thank Josh Noble for asking me to participate in this book and for providing knowledge, patience, and humor throughout. I'd also like to thank Joey Lott for his huge encouragement and belief in people's abilities. I'd like to thank my friends and the Flash community for offering advice, a few laughs, and expertise. And finally to my family, I cannot thank you enough for the huge love and support.

Author Bios

Joshua Noble, a development consultant based in New York City, is the co-author of *ActionScript 3.0 Bible* (Wiley, 2007). He has worked with Flex and Flash on a wide range of web applications on a variety of platforms over the past six years as well as working with PHP, Ruby, Erlang, and C#. In his free time, he enjoys playing with C++ and OpenCV as well as using microcontrollers and sensors to create reactive environments. His website is *http://thefactoryfactory.com*.

Todd Anderson is a senior software engineer for Infrared5. With over five years of developing for the Flash platform in the areas of RIA and game development, Todd has delivered web and desktop solutions for the publishing and entertainment industries with companies including McGraw-Hill, Thomson, Motorola, and Condé Nast Publications. Currently residing in the Boston area, when he's not programming he likes to get back to his fine arts roots and build things on paper. Anderson runs *www.custardbelly.com/blog*, focusing on development of the Flash platform.

Contributor Bios

Abey George is a software engineer with expertise in architecting and developing Rich Internet Applications (RIAs). He has implemented a wide range of RIA solutions for both web and enterprise applications by using a combination of Flex, Flash, and C#. He holds an MS from Texas A&M University and has over six years of professional experience in the field of software engineering. Interested in effectively leveraging RIAs in the enterprise, Abey is currently a principal software engineer at Fidelity Investments and has worked previously for Yahoo, Keane, and Mindseye.

Daniel Rinehart is a software architect at Allurent, where he is helping to build a new generation of innovative online shopping experiences using Flex. He has worked in the field of software development as an engineer and architect for the past eight years. Prior to joining Allurent, Daniel worked at Ruckus Network, Towers Perrin, and Bit Group, where his clients included Cisco and Dell Financial Services. He can be reached on the Web at *http://danielr.neophi.com/*.

Andrew Trice is the principal architect for Flex and AIR for Cynergy Systems. He specializes in data visualization, client-server architectures, object-oriented principles, and rich application development. He has been developing for the Web for over 10 years, with over eight years of development for the Flash platform. Thriving on the creativity and flexibility that the Flex/Flash platform enable, Andrew has developed with Flex since version 1.5. Andrew also possesses over seven years' experience with ColdFusion, is a Microsoft Certified Application Developer, and has a wide range of knowledge regarding relational databases, Ajax/JavaScript, .NET, and Java web applications.

Keun Lee is a technical lead for Cynergy Systems. He specializes in technologies such as Adobe Flex and the Microsoft Windows Presentation Foundation. He has an extensive background in business intelligence, B2B application architecture, and Rich Internet Application development. In his spare time, he enjoys playing and composing music and in general building cool things with the abundance of available technology at his disposal.

Craig Drabik has been building web applications since 2000 by using DHTML, ColdFusion, Flash, and Flex. He currently works for Cynergy Systems, leading the implementation of customer Flex projects.

Ryan Taylor is an award-winning artist and programmer specializing in object-oriented Flash development and static/motion design. He currently serves as a senior developer on the Multimedia Platforms Group at Schematic. Ryan frequently speaks at industry events and shares all of his thoughts, experiments, and open source contributions on his blog at *www.boostworthy.com/blog*.

Marco Casario founded Comtaste (*www.comtaste.com*), a company dedicated to exploring new frontiers in Rich Internet Applications and the convergence of the Web and the world of mobile devices. He is the author of the *Flex Solutions: Essential Tech-*

niques for Flex 2 and Flex 3 Developers (Friends of ED, 2007) and Advanced AIR Applications (Friends of ED, 2008). Marco often speaks at such conferences as Adobe MAX, O'Reilly Web 2.0 Summit, FITC, AJAXWorld Conference & Expo, 360Flex, From A to Web, AdobeLive, and many others, details of which are on his blog at *http:// casario.blogs.com*.

Andrei Ionescu is a Romanian web developer who likes new technologies and making them interact. He enjoys making and implementing Rich Internet Applications in the best possible way and bringing to life all kinds of web applications. He is author of the Flex blog *www.flexer.info*, and his company site is *www.designit.ro*.

Ryan Miller has been developing web applications for more than seven years. Working for companies big and small, he's managed to get his hands all kinds of dirty over the years. Currently he works out of his Beaverton, Oregon home for Cynergy Systems doing Flex development, all day, every day, and loving every minute.

Colophon

The animal on the cover is a fringed gecko.

The cover image is from Wood's Animate Creation. The cover font is Adobe ITC Garamond. The text font is Linotype Birka; the heading font is Adobe Myriad Condensed; and the code font is LucasFont's TheSansMomoCondensed.

CHAPTER 1

Flex and ActionScript Basics

A Flex application consists primarily of code written in two different languages: ActionScript and MXML. Now in its 3.0 incarnation, *ActionScript* has gone from a prototype-based scripting language to a fully object-oriented, strictly typed, ECMA-Script language. *MXML* is a markup language that will feel comfortable immediately to anyone who has spent time working with Hypertext Markup Language (HTML), Extensible Markup Language (XML), or a host of newer markup-based languages.

How do MXML and ActionScript relate to one another? The compiler, after parsing through the different idioms, translates them into the same objects, so that

```
<mx:Button id="btn" label="My Button" height="100"/>
```

and

```
var btn:Button = new Button();
btn.label = "My Button";
btn.height = 100;
```

produce the same object. The major difference is that whereas creating that object in ActionScript (second example) creates the button and nothing else, creating the object in MXML adds the button to whatever component contains the MXML code. The Flex Framework handles calling the constructor of the object described in MXML and either adding it to the parent or setting it as a property of a parent.

MXML files can include ActionScript within an `<mx:Script>` tag, but ActionScript files cannot include MXML. Although it's tempting to think of MXML as the description of the appearance and components that make up your application, and of ActionScript as the description of the event handlers and custom logic your application requires, this is not always true. A far better way to think of their relationship is to understand that both languages ultimately describe the same objects via different syntax. Certain aspects of the Flash platform cannot be accessed without using ActionScript for loops, function declarations, and conditional statements, among many others. This is why the use of ActionScript and the integration between MXML and ActionScript is necessary for all but the very simplest applications.

This chapter discusses many aspects of integrating MXML and ActionScript: creating components in MXML, creating classes in ActionScript, adding event listeners, creating code-behind files by using ActionScript and MXML, and creating function declarations. Although it doesn't contain all the answers, it will get you started with the basics of ActionScript and MXML.

1.1 Create a Flex Project in Flex Builder

Problem

You want to create a project in Flex Builder.

Solution

Use the Create New Project wizard.

Discussion

Flex Builder is built on top of Eclipse, the venerable and well-respected integrated development environment (IDE) most strongly associated with Java development. Although Flex Builder certainly is not necessary for Flex development, it is the premier tool for creating Flex applications and as such provides a wealth of features to help you design and develop applications more effectively. You can use Flex Builder either as a stand-alone application or as a plug-in to an existing installation of Eclipse.

The first thing you need to do as a Flex developer is to create a Flex project. A Flex project is different from the other types of projects in Flex Builder because it includes theSWC (Flex library) Flex library SWC (unlike an ActionScript project) and is compiled to a SWF file that can be viewed in the Flash Player (unlike a Flex Library project). To create a project, right-click or Control-click (Mac) in Flex Builder's project navigator to display the contextual menu (Figure 1-1), or use the File menu at the top of the application. From either, choose New→Flex Project. A dialog box appears to guide you through creating a project.

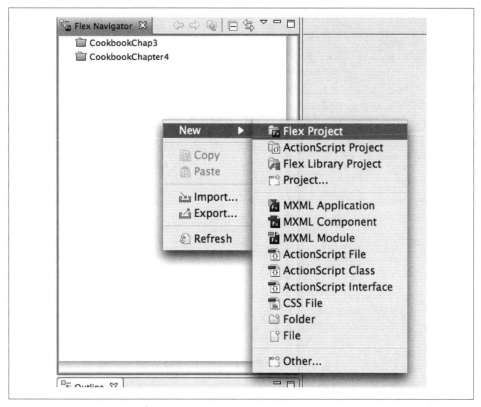

Figure 1-1. Creating a new Flex project

When prompted to specify how the project will get its data, choose Basic, which brings you to the New Flex Project dialog box (Figure 1-2).

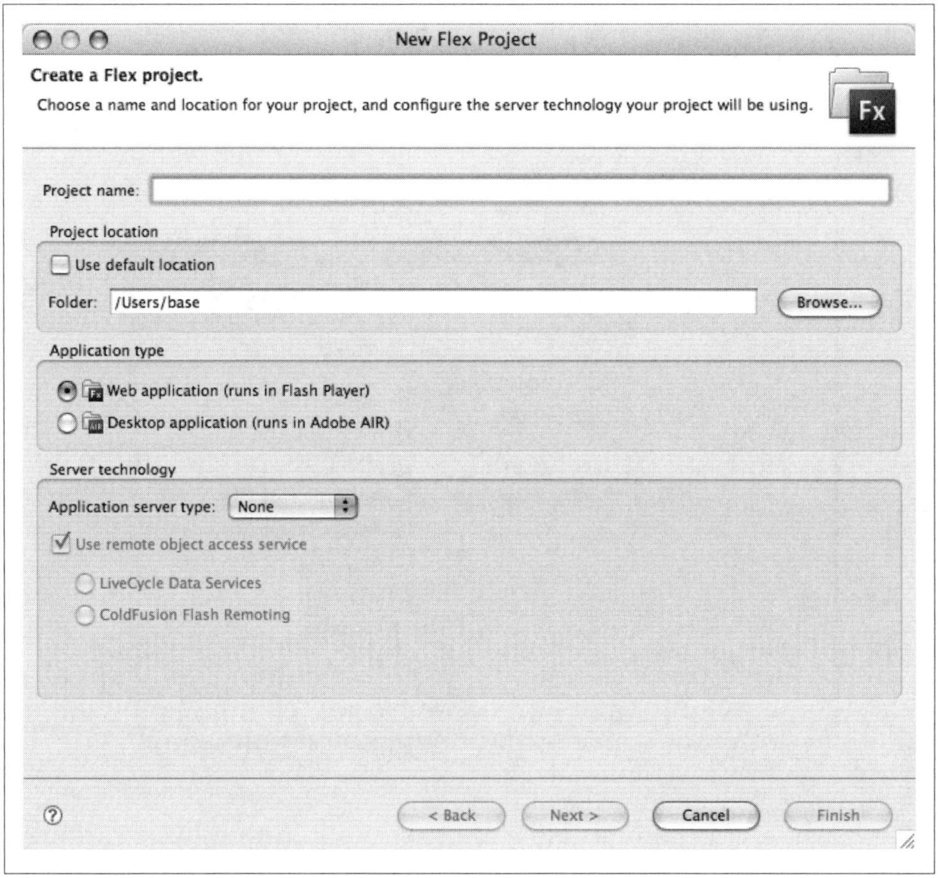

Figure 1-2. Creating a new project in Flex Builder

Enter an application name and below, a location where the files will be stored on your system. The default location is C:/Documents and Settings/Username/Documents/ workspace/Projectname on a Windows machine, and Users/Username/Documents/ workspace/Projectname on a Mac. You can of course, uncheck Use Default Location and store your files wherever you like. The name of the project must be unique. The Application Type section lets you select whether you are making an Adobe Integrated Runtime (AIR) application or an application that will run in a browser via the Flash Player plug-in. Finally, the Server Technology settings let you indicate whether the application will be connecting to a server, and if so, what server type and separate configuration type are needed.

If you have nothing more to add, click Finish. To change the location where the compiled SWF file will be placed, click Next to reach the screen shown in Figure 1-3.

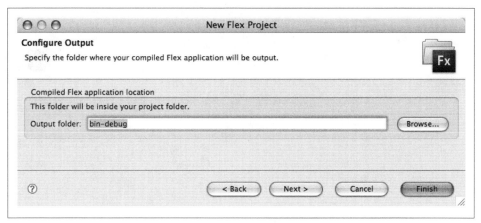

Figure 1-3. Setting the location where the compiled SWF will be placed

After the location of the generated SWF has been set, you can either finish or add source folders or SWC files to the project. To add another folder or set of folders, click the Source Path tab (Figure 1-4). To add SWC files to the project, click the Library Path tab (Figure 1-5). On this screen, you can also change the main MXML application file, which is by default the same name as the project.

Figure 1-4. Setting the source folder and main application file

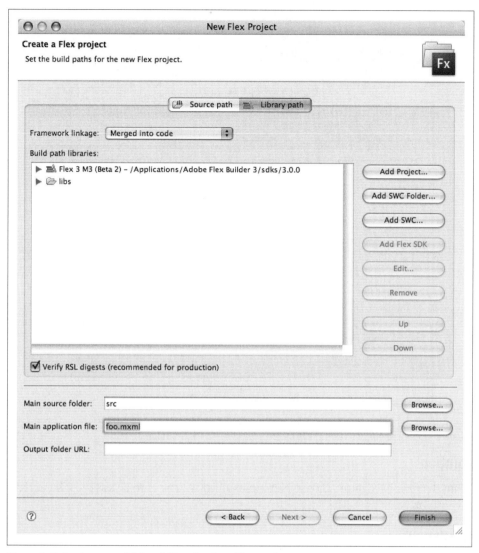

Figure 1-5. Setting any additional libraries for a Flex project

With all paths and names specified, click Finish. Your project is now configured, and you are ready to begin development.

1.2 Create a Flex Library Project in Flex Builder

Problem

You need to create a Flex Library project.

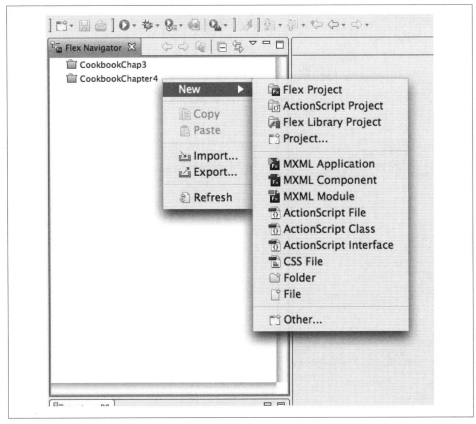

Figure 1-6. Creating a Flex Library project

Solution

From the Flex Navigator, choose New→Flex Library Project to access the Create New Project wizard.

Discussion

A Flex Library project does not have a main MXML file that it is compiled into a SWF. Instead the files are compiled into a SWC file that can be used in other applications or as the source for a runtime shared library (usually referred to as an RSL). The classes within the library are used to create a group of assets that can be reused in multiple projects at either compile time or runtime. To create a Flex Library project, right-click or Control-click (Mac) in the Flex Builder's project navigator to open the contextual menu (Figure 1-6) or use the File menu. In either case, then choose New→Flex Library Project.

In the resulting dialog box (Figure 1-7), specify a name for your project as well as its location.

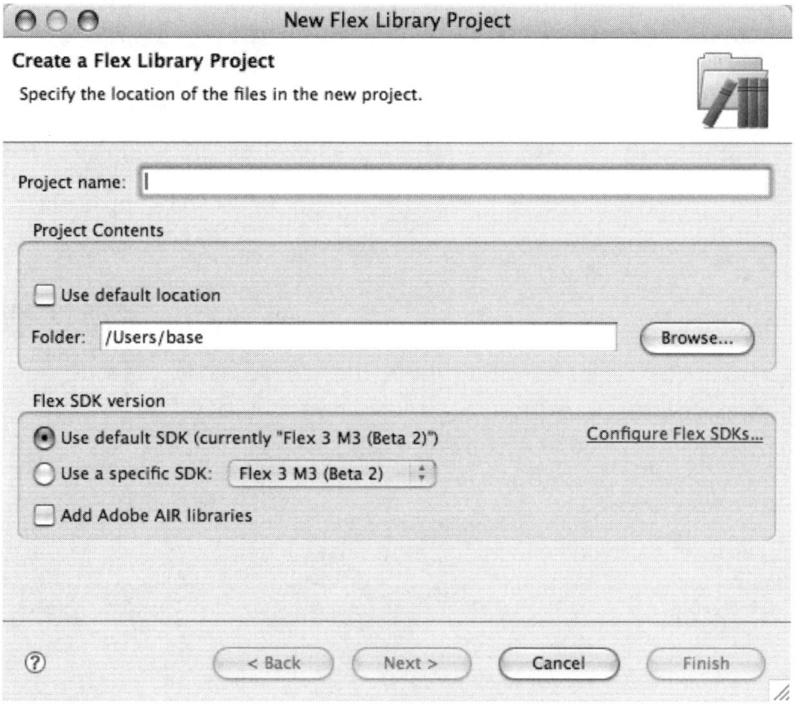

Figure 1-7. Setting the project location and SDK for the compiler

If you have nothing more to add, click Finish now. If you need to include files, assets, or other SWC files, including the Adobe AIR libraries, click Next and select them from the resulting screen. To set classes that can be selected and added into the recipe, first browse to a source path you would like to include and then set either classes or graphical assets that will be compiled into the library. Click Finish to create the project.

1.3 Create an ActionScript Project

Problem

You want to create an ActionScript project that does not use the Flex 3 libraries.

Solution

Use the Create New Project wizard and select ActionScript Project.

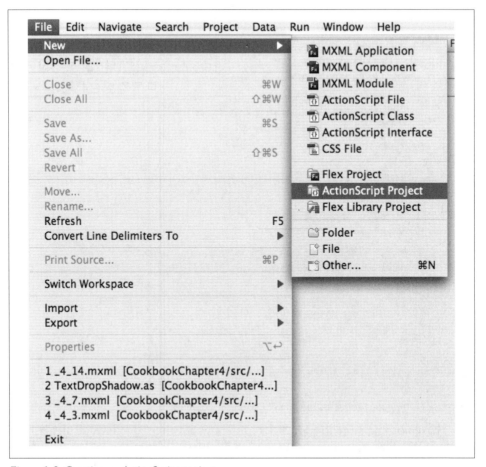

Figure 1-8. Creating an ActionScript project

Discussion

An ActionScript project is different from a Flex project in that it does not include the Flex Framework at all. ActionScript projects rely on the core ActionScript classes within the Flash code base and do not have access to any of the components in the Flex Framework. To create an ActionScript project, choose File→New→ActionScript Project (Figure 1-8).

In the resulting dialog box, specify a name for the project and a location where the files and compiled SWFs will reside. Click Finish to finalize the project with default settings, or click Next to add libraries or other source folders to the project, change the main file of the application, add SWC files that your code can access, or change the location of the output SWF. By default, the name of the main ActionScript file for the application will be set as the name of the project. The default output location of the SWF file will be the bin-debug folder in the project.

1.4 Set Compiler Options for the MXML Compiler in Flex Builder

Problem

You need to set specific compiler options for the MXML compiler.

Solution

Set the options for the compiler arguments in the Flex Compiler screen of the Project Properties dialog box.

Discussion

The *MXML compiler*, also called the *mxmlc*, is the application that compiles Action-Script and MXML files into a SWF file that can be viewed in the Flash Player. When you run or debug a Flex application in Flex Builder, the MXML compiler is invoked and the files are passed to the compiler as an argument to the application. When you debug the player, an argument to create a debug SWF is passed to the MXML compiler. Flex Builder lets you pass other arguments to the MXML compiler, as well; for example, you can pass arguments to specify the location of an external library path, allow the SWF to access local files, or set the color of the background.

To change the compiler settings for a project, right-click or Control-click (Mac) on the project and select Properties from the contextual menu (Figure 1-9), or choose Project→Properties from the menu bar.

In the resulting Project Properties dialog box (Figure 1-10), select Flex Compiler. Here you have several options to control how the SWF file is compiled. In the input field labeled Additional Compiler Arguments, you can add multiple options; simply type a hyphen (-) in front of each option and separate the options with spaces.

Some of the most commonly used options are as follows:

verbose-stacktraces
> Specifies whether the SWF will include line numbers and filenames when a runtime error occurs. This makes the generated SWF larger, and a SWF with verbose-stacktraces is different than a debug SWF.

source-path path-element
> Adds any directories or files to the source path to have any MXML or ActionScript files be included. You can use wildcards to include all files and subdirectories of a directory. Also you can use += to append the new argument to the default options or any options set in a configuration file, for example:
>
>   -source-path+=/Users/base/Project

include-libraries
> Specifies a SWC file to be compiled into the application and links all the classes and assets in the library into the SWF. This option is useful if the application will

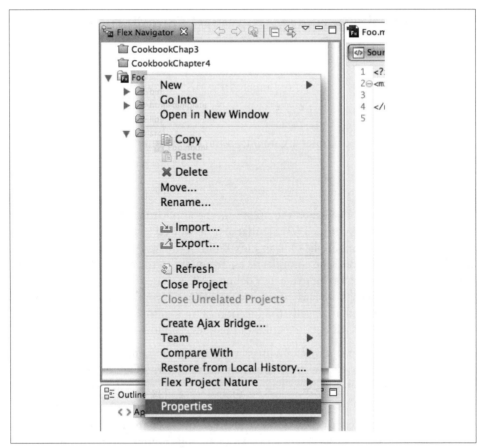

Figure 1-9. Changing the properties of a project

load in other modules that may need access to the classes in a SWC that the SWF will not be using.

library-path

Similar to the include-libraries option but includes only classes and assets that are used in the SWF. This lets you keep the size of the SWF file manageable.

locale

Specifies a locale to be associated with a SWF file. For example, use -locale=es_ES to specify that the SWF is localized for Spanish.

use-network

Indicates whether the SWF will have access to the local file system and is intended for use on a local machine, or whether the standard Flash Player security will apply. For example, use -use-network=false to specify that the SWF will have local file system access but will not be able to use any network services. The default value is true.

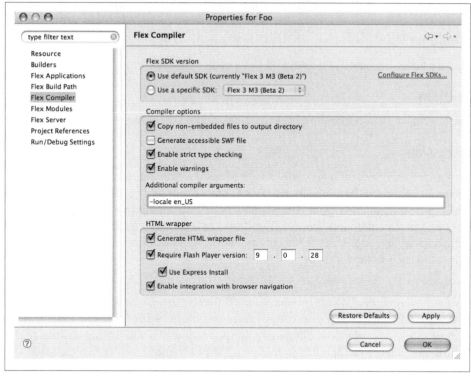

Figure 1-10. Setting compiler options

`frames.frame`

> Enables you to add asset factories that stream in after the application and then publish their interfaces with the `ModuleManager` class. The advantage of doing this is that the application starts faster than it would have if the assets had been included in the code, but does not require moving the assets to an external SWF file. One of the more difficult and more useful parameters.

`keep-all-type-selectors`

> Ensures that all style information, even if it is not used in the application, is compiled into the SWF. This is important if the application will be loading other components that require style information. The default value is false, which means that style information not used in the application is not compiled into the SWF.

After setting the options for the compiler, click the Apply button to save the options for that project.

1.5 Compile a Flex Project Outside of Flex Builder

Problem

You are not using Flex Builder for your Flex project and need to compile your project.

Solution

Use a terminal or command prompt to invoke the MXML compiler.

Discussion

Although Flex Builder is a powerful tool for Flex development, it is certainly not necessary for creating Flex applications. The MXML compiler (mxmlc) is free to anyone and can be downloaded from Adobe. To compile a Flex application outside of Flex Builder, open a command prompt (Windows) or a terminal (Mac OS X), invoke the MXML compiler, and pass the file containing the application as an argument, using a command such as the following:

```
home:base$ . /Users/base/Flex SDK 3/bin/mxmlc ~/Documents/FlexTest/FlexTest.mxml
```

This will compile the MXML file into a SWF that by default compiles into the folder where the MXML file is located. Any warnings or errors from the compiler will be displayed in the terminal or command-prompt window. To add further options to the MXML compiler, you append arguments to the call to the compiler. For example:

```
home:base$ ./mxmlc ~/Documents/FlexTest/FlexTest.mxml  -output=/Users/base/test/genera
ted/Index.swf -library-path+=/Users/lib/MyLib.swc
```

generates a SWF file named Index.swf, places it in the directory at /Users/base/test/generated/, and includes the SWC library /Users/lib/MyLib.swc.

To invoke the MXML compiler directly from the command line without providing the full path to your SDK installation (which in this example is C:\flex_sdk_3), you will need to add the /bin directory the compiler resides in to the Path systems variable.

On Windows:

1. Open System from the Control Panel.

2. Select the Advanced tab.

3. Click Environment Variables.

4. Within the System variables grid, navigate to and double-click Path.

5. In the Variable Value field, if the last character is not set to a semicolon (;), enter a semicolon and then the path to the /bin folder within your Flex SDK installation directory (Figure 1-11).

6. With the path to the MXML compiler directory set, open a command prompt, navigate to your project directory, and enter the following command:

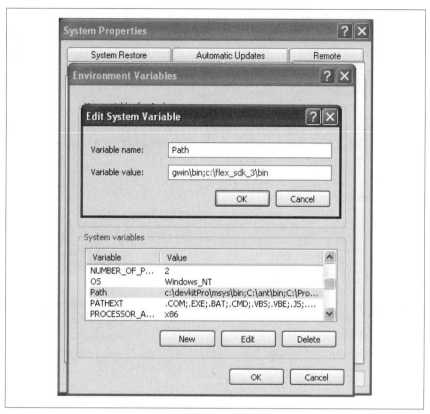

Figure 1-11. Setting the Flex SDK 3 Path variable

```
C:\Documents\FlexTest> mxmlc FlexTest.mxml
```

This generates the FlexTest.swf file within C:\Documents\FlexTest, just as the first command presented in this section does. Setting the path to the /bin directory of the Flex 3 SDK installation lets you invoke the compiler from any directory including, in this example, your current project directory.

7. If step 6 results in the following error message

```
Error: could not find JVM
```

you must manually enter the path to the directory in which the Java Runtime Environment (JRE) is installed on your machine. To manually enter the path, navigate to the /bin directory of your Flex 3 SDK installation. Open the jvm.config file in a text editor, and append the path to your JRE installation directory to the variable **java.home**. Assuming the Java installation is on the root of your drive, you enter the following:

```
java.home=C:/Java/jre
```

On Mac OS X or Linux:

1. Open your .bash_profile file (if you are using Bash) and edit the path variable by adding the location of the MXML compiler. Your .bash_profile file should look something like this:

```
PATH="${PATH}:~/flex3SDK/bin"
export PATH
```

   The .bash_profile will be located in your user home directory (which you can always access via a command line by typing **cd ~**). If you are using tsch, the path to the MXML compiler should be added to the .profile file.

2. If the Java runtime is not set properly, set the following path variable in your terminal shell:

```
PATH="${PATH}:~/flex3SDK/bin"
export PATH
```

1.6 Add an Event Listener in MXML

Problem

You need to add an event listener in MXML that will listen for any events dispatched by children within the MXML file.

Solution

Pass a method name to the event tag of the component either with or without an event object sent.

Discussion

Flex components dispatch events whenever an action occurs, such as a user clicking a button, the selected item in a combo box changing, or data loading. To listen to these events being broadcast, simply add a reference to a function that will handle the event. For example:

```
<mx:Canvas xmlns:mx="http://www.adobe.com/2006/mxml" width="400" height="300">

    <mx:Script>
        <![CDATA[

            private function buttonClick():void
            {
                trace(" Button has been clicked ");
            }

        ]]>
    </mx:Script>
```

```
        <mx:Button click="buttonClick()" label="Click Me"/>
    </mx:Canvas>
```

Adding `click="buttonClick()"` invokes the function `buttonClick` whenever the button dispatches a click event.

You can also pass the event object itself to the function. Every time a component dispatches an event, the component sends an object of type `Event` that any object listening to the event can receive. For example:

```
<mx:HBox xmlns:mx="http://www.adobe.com/2006/mxml" width="400" height="300">

    <mx:Script>
        <![CDATA[

            private function buttonClick(event:Event):void
            {
                trace(event.target.id);
                if(event.target.id == "buttonOne")
                {
                    trace(" button one was clicked")
        }
                else
                {
                    trace(" button two was clicked")
        }
            }

        ]]>
    </mx:Script>

    <mx:Button click="buttonClick(event)"
label="Click Me One" id="buttonOne"/>
        <mx:Button click="buttonClick(event)" label="Click Me Two" id="buttonTwo"/>
    </mx:HBox>
```

By telling the event listener to listen for an object of type `Event`, you can send the event to the event listener and then respond to that event in different ways depending on specified criteria. In this example, the response depends on where the event originated.

The event object and the event dispatching system in Flex are some of the most important things to understand. All events contain a type that is used when the event is being listened for; if an event is of type `click`, then the event-listening method will be added to the click event of the child:

```
<mx:Button click="trace('I was clicked')"/>
```

Notification for user interactions, messages sent to an application from a server, or timers are sent via events. The event object defines several properties that you can access in any listening function. They are as follows:

bubbles
    Indicates whether an event is a bubbling event, that is, whether it will be redis-
    patched from the object that has received the event to any listeners further up the
    event chain.

cancelable
    Indicates whether the behavior associated with the event can be prevented.

currentTarget
    The object that is actively processing the event object with an event listener.

eventPhase
    The current phase in the event flow.

Target
    The event target, which is the object that has dispatched the event.

Type
    The type of event.

You can also write event handlers in the MXML itself by using the binding tags {} to
indicate that the code inside of the braces should be executed when the event is fired.
For example:

```
<mx:Button click="{textComponent.text = 'You clicked the button}" label="Click Me"/
>
<mx:Text id="textComponent"/>
```

When it compiles this code, the Flex compiler creates a function and then sets `textCom`
`ponent.text = 'You clicked the button'` as the body of that function. It may look
different from the previous method, but the end result of this function is the same: It
listens for the event and executes its code. There's nothing inherently wrong with this
approach, but for anything more complex than setting a single property, use a defined
function to make your code easier to read and understand.

1.7 Set Properties of a Child Defined in MXML in ActionScript

Problem

You need to set the properties of a child defined in MXML in a script tag as a part of a
method.

Solution

Refer to the child component by its **id** property, and set properties or call methods by
using the **id** property.

Discussion

It's easy to think of the script part of a component as being somehow separate from the MXML part, but they are not separate at all. Consider an example:

```
<mx:HBox xmlns:mx="http://www.adobe.com/2006/mxml" width="400" height="300">
    <mx:Script>
        <![CDATA[

            private function changeAppearance():void
            {
                this.width = Number(widthInputField.text);
                this.height = Number(heightInputField.text);
            }

        ]]>
    </mx:Script>
    <mx:Image id="imageDisplay"/>
    <mx:Text text="Enter a width"/>
    <mx:TextInput id="widthInputField"/>
    <mx:Text text="Enter an height"/>
    <mx:TextInput id="heightInputField"/>
    <mx:Button click="changeAppearance()" label="Change Size"/>
</mx:HBox>
```

As you can see in the changeAppearance method, the use of this refers to the component itself, the HBox that contains the child components; that reference changes the width and height of the component. References to the two TextFields, widthInputField and heightInputField, are also being used to grab the text data from those TextInputs. Each TextInput is being referred to by its id, in much that same way that you would refer to the id of an element in Document Object Model (DOM) scripting. The id must be a unique name that can be used throughout the application to refer to the child components Within one component there is a single-level hierarchy, so no matter where a child is nested within the component (for example, within another child), the id still refers to that child. Look at a similar example of actively setting the property of a child:

```
<mx:VBox xmlns:mx="http://www.adobe.com/2006/mxml" width="520" height="650">
    <mx:Script>
        <![CDATA[

            private var fileName:String = "";

            private function saveResume():void
            {
                //....a service call to send the data and set the filename
                fileNameDisplay.text = "Your resume has been saved as "+fileName;
            }

        ]]>
    </mx:Script>
    <mx:Text id="fileNameDisplay" text="" width="500"/>
    <mx:RichTextEditor id="richTextControl" width="500" height="400"/>
```

```
            <mx:Button id="labelButton" label="Submit Resume" click="saveResume()"/>
        </mx:VBox>
```

In the preceding example, the child component is referenced by its id property and can have its properties set by using that id. All components added in MXML are by default visible to any component that has access to the parent component.

1.8 Define Arrays and Objects

Problem

You need to define an **Array** object or a hash table—style object to store values or other objects.

Solution

Use the ActionScript syntax for creating a new object or array with a constructor call, or define them in MXML.

Discussion

As with many things in Flex, arrays and objects, the two most commonly used types for containing data, can be defined in ActionScript or in MXML. To define an array in MXML, use the `<mx:Array>` tag to wrap all the items inside the array:

```
<mx:Array>
        <mx:String>Flex</mx:String>
        <mx:String>Flash</mx:String>
        <mx:String>Flash Media Server</mx:String>
        <mx:String>Flash Lite</mx:String>
        <mx:String>AIR</mx:String>
</mx:Array>
```

All the items in the array are accessible through their zero-based index. You can create multiple nested arrays in MXML by adding multiple **Array** tags within an array:

```
<mx:Array>
    <mx:Array>
        <mx:String>Flex</mx:String>
        <mx:String>Flash</mx:String>
    <mx:Array>
</mx:Array>
```

To create an object in MXML, use the `<mx:Object>` tag and add all the properties of the object and their values as attributes in the tag. For example:

```
<mx:Object id="person" firstName="John" lastName="Smith" age="50"
    socialSecurity="123-45-6789"/>
```

The limitation of creating an object in MXML is that you cannot create multiple nested objects. By creating your objects within a script tag, however, you can create objects containing multiple complex objects within them. You can create an object by creating a variable of type Object and calling the constructor on it and then attaching properties later:

```
var object:Object = new Object();
var otherObject:Object = new Object();
object.other = otherObject;
```

You can also create an object by simply using curly brackets to delimit the properties within the object. For example:

```
var person:Object = {name:"John Smith", age:22, position:{department:"Accounting",
    salary:50000, title:"Junior Accountant"}, id:303};
```

Note how for the Person object the position properties point to another object that contains its own distinct properties. Notice how you don't even need to declare a variable name for the object that the position property will point to.

To create an array in ActionScript, create a variable and call the Array constructor:

```
var arr:Array = new Array("red", "blue", "white", "black", "green", "yellow");
```

You can also create an array without using the constructor by using square brackets and supplying any objects that will populate the array, as shown:

```
var noConstructorArray:Array = [2, 4, 6, 8, 10, 12, 14, 16];
```

This is the same as calling the Array constructor and then passing the objects in the constructor.

1.9 Set the Scope of Variables in ActionScript

Problem

You need to make certain variables publicly accessible but protect others from external access.

Solution

Use the ActionScript scope modifiers for variables and methods.

Discussion

Within an ActionScript file or MXML file, there are different scopes of variables. *Private* variables and functions are visible only within the component itself; no other component can access them. This definition is useful for variables or methods that are used by a component only, that contain data only a single component should modify, or that are not modified except within the class. When you design complex classes, a good practice is to mark all properties that are not explicitly needed by outside components as private. *Public* variables are visible to any object that has a reference to the object of the class defining the property. Carefully considering which properties will be needed by outside classes and limiting access to those properties creates a far better class structure and frequently helps the programmer clarify the needs of a certain part of the application. Properties marked as private will not be visible to inheriting classes either, only the class or component in which they are defined. Finally, *protected* variables are accessible only to any object of a class that extends the class in which the property is defined, but not to any external objects.

Variables and functions marked private are visible only within the class or component in which they are defined and any inheriting class. For example, here is a class with protected and private properties:

```
package oreilly.cookbook
{
    public class Transport
    {
        protected var info:Object;
        private var speed:Object;
    }
}
```

By using the extends keyword, you can share the properties and methods of one class with another. In the following example, marking the Car class with the keyword extends the Transport class so that Car inherits all of its nonprivate properties and methods. Car does not have access to the private properties of the Transport class, however, and attempting to access them results in an error stating that the properties cannot be found.

```
package oreilly.cookbook
{
    public class Car extends Transport
    {
        public function set data(value:Object):void
        {
            info = value;
            speed = value.speed; /* this will throw an error because the speed
variable is private and access to it is not allowed to any other class */
        }
    }
}
```

The protected properties of the Transport class are available to the Car class, but they are not available to any class that has an instance of either of these classes as a property.

Any public properties of both classes, however, are available to any class that instantiates one of these objects. The static keyword indicates that any object that references the class can access the specified property without needing to instantiate an object of that class. In other words, the static keyword defines a variable for all instances of a class. Adding the following line to the Car class

```
public static const NUMBER_OF_WHEELS:int = 4;
```

means you can now access the NUMBER_OF_WHEELS property with a reference to the class without needing to instantiate an object of that class, such as

```
import oreilly.cookbook.Car;
public class CompositionTest
{
    private var car:Car;

    public function CompositionTest()
    {
        trace(" a Car object has "+Car.NUMBER_OF_WHEELS+" wheels");
    }
}
```

So far, this recipe has examined the scope of variables that are affiliated with classes. Variables, however, need not be properties of a class. They can be created and destroyed within a function, being meaningful only within a function body. For example:

```
private function processSpeedData():void
{
    var speed:int;
    var measurement:String = "kilometers";
}
```

Outside the body of this function, the variables speed and measurement are meaningless. ActionScript uses something called *variable hoisting*, which means that variables defined anywhere within a function are in scope throughout the function. Unlike languages that support block-level scoping, the following code traces the newCar object as being valid:

```
private function makeCars():void
{
    for(var i:int = 0; i<10; i++)
    {
        var newCar:Car = new Car();
        carArray.push(newCar);
    }
    trace(newCar);
}
```

The reference to newCar goes out of scope only when the function returns.

ActionScript also defines a final modifier that indicates to the compiler that the method cannot be altered by any classes that extend that class. This modifier enables you to define methods that are not private but that will not be altered or overridden. For example, defining this method in the Transport class

```
public final function drive(speed:Number):void{ /* final and cannot be overriden in
any other class*/ }
```

indicates that any class that extends Transport will possess this method. Its public scoping means any properties will be accessible to any object with access to that Transport object but that subclasses cannot redefine the method.

1.10 Create a Component in ActionScript

Problem

You want to create a component in ActionScript without using any MXML.

Solution

Create an ActionScript file and extend one of the Flex library components.

Discussion

In addition to creating components in MXML, you can create them in ActionScript without using any MXML at all. You just need to do a few things differently. The first is to ensure that your class is properly packed in relation to the main application file. In the following example, the component is from the application-level folder; specifically, it's within oreilly/cookbook/, which is reflected in the package name:

```
package oreilly.cookbook
{
```

The next difference is that any classes to be included or referenced in the component must be imported by using their full package name. This includes any class that the component will extend, in this case `mx.containers.Canvas`:

```
import mx.containers.Canvas;
import mx.controls.Text;
import mx.controls.Image;
import oreilly.cookbook.Person;

public class PersonRenderer extends Canvas
{
```

Any constants and variables for the components are listed just below the class declaration generally. In the following example, all the private properties of this class are listed. These are properties that the component can access but that no other component can access or alter. To access these properties, **get** and **set** methods will be provided so that if any processing is necessary when these properties are accessed, it can be done when the property is accessed. Getter and setter methods are common ways to provide access to private variables through functions.

```
private var _data:Object;
private var nameText:Text;
private var ageText:Text;
private var positionText:Text;
private var image:Image;
```

In ActionScript, the constructor function always must be public, not return a value, and have the same name as the class itself. For example:

```
public function PersonRenderer ()
{
    super();
```

Any components that will be added to the component need to have their constructors called and then passed as a parameter to the addChild method in order to be added to the display list and so that their properties can be altered by the component.

```
nameText = new Text();
addChild(nameText);
ageText = new Text();
addChild(ageText);
```

In the following example, the ageText Text component is manually positioned, a necessity because its component, PersonRenderer, is a Canvas and does not have any layout management, unlike a VBox or HBox component.

```
ageText.y = 20;
positionText = new Text();
addChild(positionText);
positionText.y = 40;
image = new Image();
addChild(image);
image.y = 60;
}
```

If a component already defines a method to set data, such as mx.containers.Canvas here, you must override the method if you want the component to perform any custom actions. To do so, use the override keyword to indicate to the compiler that you intend to override the method of the superclass. For example:

```
override public function set data(value:Object):void
{
    _data = value;
    nameText.text = value.name;
    ageText.text = String(value.age);
    positionText.text = value.position;
    image.source = value.image;
}

override public function get data():Object
{
    return _data;
}
```

A final method finishes the component; this one originates in the class and is publicly scoped:

```
public function retrievePerson():Person
{
    /* do some special employee processing */
    return null;
}
    }
}
```

To add this class to any other component, you can use ActionScript:

```
var renderer:PersonRenderer  = new PersonRenderer();
addChild(renderer);
```

Or you can use MXML:

```
<renderers:PersonRenderer id="renderer"/>
```

In ActionScript, the constructor is explicitly called, and in the MXML version it is called when the constructor for the component that the PersonRenderer object is nested inside of gets called.

1.11 Use Event Bubbling

Problem

You want to listen for events passed up from children components to parent components without adding a long chain of event listeners.

Solution

Use the event-bubbling mechanism in the Flash Player to listen for events passed up from children.

Discussion

Understanding bubbled events requires looking at several classes. Several types of events can be bubbled up: mouse-down events, click events, and keyboard events. The term *bubbling up* refers to the event working its way up through the display list to the application container, like a bubble rising to the surface through the water. When the user clicks on any component, that event is passed up through the hierarchy. This means that the parent of a component can listen on a component for a click event, and if one is dispatched anywhere within the child component, the parent will be notified. To have the parent listen for all events of a certain type within the child, the parent simply needs to add an event listener to that child to receive all bubbled-up events.

Consider this class defined in BubblingComponent.mxml:

```
<mx:HBox xmlns:mx="http://www.adobe.com/2006/mxml" width="400" height="200">
    <mx:Script>
        <![CDATA[
            private function sendClick():void
            {
                trace(" BubblingComponent:: click ");
            }
        ]]>
    </mx:Script>
    <mx:Button click="sendClick()"/>
</mx:HBox>
```

This component contains a button that will dispatch a click event up the display list to any component that contains an instance of the `BubblingComponent`. To listen to this event, use the click handler in a component that contains `BubblingComponent`:

```
<cookbook:BubblingComponent click="handleClick()" id="bubbler"/>
```

A `BubblingHolder` that contains a `BubblingComponent` could be defined as shown in the following code snippet:

```
<mx:Canvas xmlns:mx="http://www.adobe.com/2006/mxml" width="400" height="300"
xmlns:cookbook="oreilly.cookbook.*"
 creationComplete="complete()">
    <mx:Script>
        <![CDATA[
            private function handleClick():void
            {
                trace(" BubblingComponentHolder:: click ");
            }
        ]]>
    </mx:Script>
    <cookbook:BubblingComponent click="handleClick()" id="bubbler"/>
</mx:Canvas>
```

This component will dispatch an event up to any component listening, even to the application level. When we add the `BubblingHolder` to the main application file

```
<mx:Application xmlns:mx="http://www.adobe.com/2006/mxml" layout="vertical"
xmlns:cookbook="oreilly.cookbook.*">
    <mx:Script>
        <![CDATA[
            public function createName():void
            {
                name = "Flex Cookbook";
            }
        ]]>
    </mx:Script>
    <cookbook:BubblingComponentHolder click="handleClick()"/>
</mx:Application>
```

the click event from BubblingComponent.mxml will be broadcast all the way up to the application level.

The sequence of events in a `MouseEvent` sends the information about the event, such as a click and the location of the click, up the display list through all the children, to the child that should receive the event, and then back down the display list to the Stage.

The Stage detects the `MouseEvent` and passes it down the display list until it finds the target of the event, that is, the last component that the user's mouse is interacting with. This is called the *capturing phase*. Next, the event handlers within the target of the event are triggered. This is called the *targeting phase*, when the event is given an actual target. Finally, the *bubbling phase* occurs, sending the event back up the display list to any interested listeners, all the way back to the Stage.

1.12 Use a Code-Behind Model to Separate MXML and ActionScript

Problem

You want to use a code-behind model to keep ActionScript and MXML code separate.

Solution

Create a component in ActionScript that extends the Flex library class that provides any needed functionality and then add any properties and methods there. Then create an MXML file that extends that class you've created.

Discussion

If you're familiar with ASP.NET development, you've doubtless heard the term *code-behind*—likewise, if you're familiar with the notion of separating the controller and the view in any type of application that mixes markup and another language (Ruby on Rails, JavaServer Pages (JSP) developments, PHP, and so forth). Separating the actual layout elements from the code that controls them is a good strategy for keeping the different aspects of a view cleanly separated for readability and clarity. There are times when the sheer number of files required to use this approach throughout an application makes navigating a project difficult, because two files are created for each component. Moreover, separating business logic and view logic is frequently difficult and can lead to difficult-to-follow separations of code within a component. Many developers, however, prefer this approach, and sometimes it helps clarify an application and its workings.

To begin, first look at the *behind* part of the code-behind: a component that extends the class (`mx.containers.Canvas` in this example) and contains methods to listen for the component to be added to the stage, as well as a method that can handle any event but is intended to handle button clicks specifically.

```
package oreilly.cookbook
{
    import mx.containers.Canvas;
    import flash.events.Event;

    public class CodeBehindComponent extends Canvas
    {
        public function CodeBehindComponent()
        {
            super();
            addEventListener(Event.ADDED_TO_STAGE, addedToStageListener);
        }

        protected function addedToStageListener(event:Event):void
        {
```

```
        trace(" Added to Stage from Code Behind ");
    }

    protected function clickHandler(event:Event):void
    {
        trace(" Click handled from component "+event.target);
    }

    }
}
```

In this example, methods that would normally be marked as private are scoped as protected. This is because the code portion of the code-behind, the MXML, will inherit from the `CodeBehindComponent` class and to function, requires access to these methods. Here you have the MXML component of the component:

```
<cookbook:CodeBehindComponent xmlns:mx="http://www.adobe.com/2006/mxml" width="200"
height="400" xmlns:cookbook="oreilly.cookbook.*">
    <mx:Button click="clickHandler(event)"/>
</cookbook:CodeBehindComponent>
```

1.13 Make Properties of a Component Bindable

Problem

You are creating a component and would like to allow properties on that component to be bindable, for other components to bind to.

Solution

Create getter and setter methods, and mark those methods with a `Bindable` metadata tag that contains the name of the event that the methods will dispatch when the property is set.

Discussion

Any object can define bindable properties by dispatching an event when the property's changed and using the `Bindable` metadata tag above the property. The best practice is to use `get` and `set` functions to define these bindable properties. When the property is set, an event is dispatched using the same name indicated in the `Bindable` tag. For example:

```
package oreilly.cookbook
{
    import flash.events.EventDispatcher;
    import flash.events.Event;

    public class Person extends EventDispatcher
    {
        public static var NAME_CHANGE:String = "nameChange";
        private var _name:String;
```

```
[Bindable(event=NAME_CHANGE)]
public function get name():String
{
    return _name;
}

public function set name(value:String):void
{
    dispatchEvent(new Event(NAME_CHANGE));
    _name = value;
}
    }
}
```

The Bindable tag requires the name of the event that will be dispatched when the name property is set. This ensures that any component binding a property to the name property of the Person object is notified when the value changes.

Now that the bindable property has been set on the Person object, you can use all instances of Person in binding expressions:

```
<mx:Canvas xmlns:mx="http://www.adobe.com/2006/mxml" width="400" height="300">
    <mx:Script>
        <![CDATA[

        [Bindable]
        private var _person:Person;

        public function set person(person:Person:void
        {
            _person = person;
        }

        ]]>
    </mx:Script>
    <mx:Label text="{_person.name}"/>
</mx:Canvas>
```

1.14 Use Custom Events and Dispatch Data with Events

Problem

You want to dispatch data with an event by using a custom event class.

Solution

Create a class that extends the flash.events.Event class and create a property for the data that you would like to be available from the event.

Discussion

At times you may need to dispatch data objects with events so that listeners can access that data without accessing the object that dispatched the event. Renderers or deeply nested objects that are dispatching events up through multiple components to listeners will frequently want to send data without requiring the listening component to find the object and access a property. As a solution, create an event type and add any data types that you want to include to the constructor of the event. Remember to call the super method of the Event class so that the Event object is properly instantiated. For example:

```
package oreilly.cookbook
{
    import flash.events.Event;

    public class CustomPersonEvent extends Event
    {

        public var person:Person;
        public var timeChanged:String;

        public function CustomPersonEvent(type:String, bubbles:Boolean=false,
cancelable:Boolean=false, personValue:Person=null, timeValue:String="")
        {
            super(type, bubbles, cancelable);
            person = personValue;
            timeChanged = timeValue;
        }

        override public function clone():Event
        {
            return new CustomPersonEvent(type, bubbles, cancelable, personValue,
timeValue);
        }
    }
}
```

In this custom Event class, the inherited Event.clone method is overridden as well in order for the CustomPersonEvent to be able to duplicate itself. If an event listener attempts to redispatch this custom event, as shown here:

```
private function customPersonHandler(event:CustomPersonEvent):void {
    dispatchEvent(event);
}
```

the event that is dispatched is not the event that is received; instead, it is a copy of the CustomPersonEvent created using the clone method. This is done inside the flash.events.EventDispatcher class. If the clone method is not overridden to ensure that all properties of the CustomPersonEvent are carried into a clone of itself, then the event returned from the clone will be of type flash.events.Event and will not have any properties of the CustomPersonEvent.

1.15 Listen for a Keyboard Event

Problem

You need to listen for the user to press a key and determine which key was pressed and handle the event accordingly.

Solution

Add an event listener for the keyDown event either on the component or on the stage of the application and read the KeyboardEvents keyCode property.

Discussion

To listen for a KeyboardEvent, use the keyDown event handler, which all classes that extend UIComponent possess. The KeyboardEvent class defines a keyCode property which contains the code for the key that the user pressed. For example:

```
<mx:HBox xmlns:mx="http://www.adobe.com/2006/mxml" width="400" height="300"
keyDown="keyHandler(event)" backgroundColor="#0000ff">
    <mx:Script>
        <![CDATA[

            import flash.events.KeyboardEvent;

            private function keyHandler(event:KeyboardEvent):void
            {
                switch(event.keyCode)
                {
                    case 13:
                        trace(" Enter pressed ");
                    break;
                    case 32:
                        trace(" Space Bar pressed ");
                    break;
                    case 16:
                        trace(" Shift Key pressed ");
                    break;
                    case 112:
                        trace(" F1 pressed ");
                    break;
                    case 8:
                        trace(" Delete pressed ");
                    break;
                }
            }

        ]]>
    </mx:Script>
    <mx:Button label="One"/>
</mx:HBox>
```

A note about this component: It will listen only for events that occur while the button has focus. If you remove the button from this component, there is nothing left that can have focus, and the keyHandler function will never be called. To catch all KeyEvents that occur in the application, whether or not the component has focus, add the following to the opening tag of the component:

```
addedToStage="stage.addEventListener(KeyboardEvent.KEY_DOWN, keyHandler)"
```

This ensures that the keyHandler method will handle all KeyEvents that the stage catches, which would be all of them.

1.16 Define Optional Parameters for Methods

Problem

You want to define methods for a parameter that have default values or null values so that the method does not always need those values passed.

Solution

Use default values or null values in the method declaration by setting the parameter equal to a default value or equal to null.

Discussion

To define an optional method or multiple optional methods for a method, simply set the default value of an object to null in the signature of the event. The ActionScript primitives String, Number, int, and Boolean cannot be null values, however; you must supply a default value. For example:

```
        public function optionalArgumentFunction(value:Object, string:String,
    count:int = 0, otherValue:Object = null):void
        {
            if(count != 0)
            {
                /*if the count is not the default value handle the value the call
    passes in*/
            }
            if(otherValue != null)
            {
                /* if the otherValue is not null handle the value the call passes in */
            }
        }
```

Another strategy for providing not only optional parameters to the method but also an indeterminate number of arguments is to use the ... marker in front of a variable name. This is referred to officially as the ...(rest) parameter. This variable will contain an array of arguments that can be looped over and processed.

```
public function unlimitedArgumentsFunction(...arguments):void
{
    for each(var arg:Object in arguments)
    {
        /* process each argument */
    }
}
```

1.17 Determine the Type of an Object

Problem

You need to determine the type of an object that has been passed to a method.

Solution

Use the **is** operator to determine the object's type or the superclass of the object's type.

Discussion

To determine the type of an object, ActionScript provides the **is** operator, which tests the type of an object and returns true or false. The **is** operator returns true if the object is of the type tested against or if the object extends the type indicated. For example, because the Canvas object extends UIComponent, the **is** operator returns true if the Canvas object is tested as being of type UIComponent. A UIComponent however, will not return true if tested as being of type Canvas, because UIComponent does not inherit from Canvas. Consider this code:

```
public function TypeTest()
{
    var uiComponent:UIComponent = new UIComponent();
    var canvas:Canvas = new Canvas();
    trace(" uiComponent is UIComponent "+(uiComponent is UIComponent));
    trace(" uiComponent is Canvas "+(uiComponent is Canvas));
    trace(" canvas is UIComponent "+(canvas is UIComponent));
}
```

which produces the following output:

```
uiComponent is UIComponent true
uiComponent is Canvas false
canvas is UIComponent true
```

A common use of type testing is to determine the component that has thrown an event. This lets you use a single method for simple event handling and test the type of the object to determine appropriate actions.

```
private function eventListener(mouseEvent:MouseEvent):void
{
    if(mouseEvent.target is Button)
    {
        /* handle button specific actions */
```

```
        }
        else if(mouseEvent.target is ComboBox)
        {
            /* handle combobox specific things */
        }
        else
        {
            /* handle all other cases */
        }
    }
}
```

1.18 Define and Implement an Interface

Problem

You need to create an interface and then create a component that implements that interface.

Solution

Create an ActionScript file, declare that file as an interface, and define any methods you would like the interface to require. To implement the interface, use the `implements` keyword in the class declaration of the component that will use the interface.

Discussion

Interfaces are powerful tools that let you describe a contract that an object must fulfill: the interface must contain a specified set of methods with a certain scope, name, parameters, and return type; components using the object, in turn, will expect that this set of methods is present. This lets you create lightweight descriptions of a class without actually creating a new class that would clutter your inheritance trees. Classes that implement an interface are considered to be of that interface type, and this can be used to set the types for parameters of methods or to set the return types of methods as shown here:

```
public function pay(payment:IPaymentType):IReceipt
```

This method can accept any object that implements `IPaymentType` and will return an object that implements the `IReceipt` interface.

The interface cannot define the method body nor can it define any variable. In the following code snippet, `IDataInterface` is declared and defines five methods that any object that implements the interface must also possess and define:

```
package oreilly.cookbook
{
    public interface IDataInterface
    {
        function set dataType(value:Object):void;
```

```
            function get dataType():Object;

            function update():Boolean;

            function write():Boolean;

            function readData():Object;
    }
}
```

To implement the interface, declare the class and add the `implements` marker to the
class declaration. All methods defined in an interface must be implemented by the class.
In the following code snippet, all the methods of the preceding interface are included
and are given function bodies:

```
package oreilly.cookbook
{
    import flash.events.EventDispatcher;
    import flash.events.IEventDispatcher;

    public class ClientData extends EventDispatcher implements IDataInterface
    {

        private var _dataType:Object;

        public function ClientData(target:IEventDispatcher=null)
        {
            super(target);
        }

        public function set dataType(value:Object):void
        {
            _dataType = value;
        }

        public function get dataType():Object
        {
            return _dataType;
        }

        public function update():Boolean
        {
            //do the actual updating
            var updateSuccessful:Boolean;
            if(updateSuccessful)
            {
                return true;
            }
            else
            {
                return false;
            }
        }

        public function write():Boolean
```

```
    {
        var writeSuccess:Boolean;
        if(writeSuccess)
        {
            return true;
        }
        else
        {
            return false;
        }
    }

    public function readData():Object
    {
        var data:Object;
        //get all the data we need
        return data;
    }
  }
}
```

To implement an interface in MXML, use `implements`. in the top-level tag for the component. For example:

```
<mx:HBox xmlns:mx="http://www.adobe.com/2006/mxml" width="400" height="300"
implements= "IDataInterface">
```

CHAPTER 2

Menus and Controls

The Flex 3 software development kit (SDK) comes with an extensive library of prebuilt user interface (UI) controls that make application development a snap. You can easily configure the behavior of these controls through their properties by using ActionScript or MXML, as well as modify their visual appearance by using Cascading Style Sheets (CSS). Additionally, because ActionScript 3 is a full-fledged object-oriented programming (OOP) language, you can extend the default controls to provide custom functionality, through classical OOP constructs.

The controls available in the Flex 3 SDK are located in `mx.controls package`. At the time of this writing, the `mx.controls package` lists more than 50 controls that serve as building blocks for a rich user interface.

2.1 Listen to a Button Click

Problem

You need to perform a task in response to user interaction, such as output a list of names to the console when the user clicks a button.

Solution

Use the `click` event attribute of the `<mx:Button>` tag to assign a handler for the event in MXML. Alternatively, in ActionScript use the `addEventListener` method on the button instance to assign a listener for the click event.

Discussion

The following code shows how to listen to a button click by using MXML to assign a handler for the `click` event attribute of the `<mx:Button>` tag:

```
<mx:Application
    xmlns:mx="http://www.adobe.com/2006/mxml"
    layout="vertical">
```

```
<mx:Button id="btn" label="Show Names" click="showNames(event)"/>

<mx:Script>
    <![CDATA[

        private function showNames(evt:MouseEvent):void
        {
            var temp:Array = new Array("George","Tim","Alex","Dean");
            trace(temp.toString());
        }
    ]]>
</mx:Script>

</mx:Application>
```

The code creates an application that contains an instance of the button control btn. For the application to output a list of names to the console when the btn instance is clicked, the click event attribute of the btn instance is wired to the method showNames:

```
<mx:Button id="btn" label="Show Names" click="showNames(event)"/>
```

Every time a user clicks the button, the Flex Framework dispatches an event of type MouseEvent.CLICK. The preceding line of code assigns the method showNames to be invoked every time the click event is dispatched by the button. Within the showNames method, an array of names is created and output to the console. Notice that an event object of type MouseEvent is automatically passed into the handler function. Depending on the event being dispatched, this object can be queried for detailed information about the event itself. Run the application in debug mode (F11 in Eclipse), and you'll see the following output in the Console window:

```
George,Tim,Alex,Dean
```

Event listeners can also be assigned using ActionScript. The following example assigns the listeners showNames and showTitles to the btn instance, using ActionScript:

```
<mx:Application
    xmlns:mx="http://www.adobe.com/2006/mxml"
    layout="vertical"
    creationComplete="initApp(event);">

<mx:Button id="btn" label="Show Names"/>

<mx:Script>
    <![CDATA[
        import mx.events.FlexEvent;

        private function initApp(evt:FlexEvent):void
        {
            btn.addEventListener(MouseEvent.CLICK,showNames);
            btn.addEventListener(MouseEvent.CLICK,showTitles);
        }

        private function showNames(evt:MouseEvent):void
        {
```

```
        var temp:Array = new Array("George","Tim","Alex","Dean");
        trace(temp.toString());
    }

    private function showTitles(evt:MouseEvent):void
    {
        var temp:Array = new Array("Director","Vice-President","President",
"CEO");
        trace(temp.toString());
    }

    ]]>
  </mx:Script>

</mx:Application>
```

Note that the **creationComplete** event of the application is used to wire up the button's click event to two listeners, **showNames** and **showTitles**, as shown:

```
private function initApp(evt:FlexEvent):void
{
    btn.addEventListener(MouseEvent.CLICK,showNames);
            btn.addEventListener(MouseEvent.CLICK,showTitles);
}
```

Running this application in debug mode generates the following output in the Console window:

```
George,Tim,Alex,Dean
Director,Vice-President,President,CEO
```

The listeners are called in the same order as they are registered. Because **showNames** was registered before **showTitles**, the list of names is generated before the list of titles. To change the order of execution, either change the order in which they are registered with the button, or better yet, set the priority value while registering the listeners with the button, as shown here:

```
private function initApp(evt:FlexEvent):void {
    btn.addEventListener(MouseEvent.CLICK,showNames,false,0);
    btn.addEventListener(MouseEvent.CLICK,showTitles,false,1);
}
```

Running the application in debug mode, with the modified code, displays the following:

```
Director,Vice-President,President,CEO
George,Tim,Alex,Dean
```

Listeners registered with a larger priority value will be called earlier than those with a smaller priority value. If more than one listener has the same priority value, the order of execution will be based on the order of registration.

2.2 Create a Set of Buttons That Toggle

Problem

You need to present the user with a series of button choices.

Solution

Use the `ToggleButtonBar` control, and an `ArrayCollection` to create a series of buttons.

Discussion

To build a series of buttons, create an application with an instance of the `ToggleBut
tonBar` control. The `ToggleButtonBar` defines a horizontal or a vertical group of buttons
that maintain their selected or deselected state. Here's one approach:

```
<mx:Application
    xmlns:mx="http://www.adobe.com/2006/mxml"
    layout="vertical"
    initialize="initApp(event)">

<mx:ToggleButtonBar id="toggle"
    dataProvider="{dataProvider}"
    itemClick="setMode(event)"/>

<mx:Script>
    <![CDATA[
        import mx.collections.ArrayCollection;
        import mx.events.FlexEvent;
        import mx.events.ItemClickEvent;

        [Bindable]
        private var dataProvider:ArrayCollection;

        private function initApp(evt:FlexEvent):void {
            var temp:Array = new Array({label:"Show Labels",
                                        mode:"labels"},
                                       {label:"Show Titles",
                                        mode:"titles"});
            dataProvider = new ArrayCollection(temp);
        }

        private function setMode(evt:ItemClickEvent):void {
            switch (evt.item.mode) {
                case "labels":
                    trace("George, Tim, Dean");
                    break;
                case "titles":
                    trace("Vice President, President, Director");
                    break;
                default:
                    break;
            }
        }
```

```
                }
            ]]>
        </mx:Script>

    </mx:Application>
```

When the application initializes, the `initialize` event invokes the `initApp` method. The `initApp` method then sets up the `dataProvider ArrayCollection` with source data for the `ToggleButtonBar`. Because the `dataProvider` property of the `ToggleButtonBar` instance is bound to the `ArrayCollection`, it updates the display to reflect the new buttons.

By default, the `label` property of the items in the `ArrayCollection` shows up as the label of the button in the `ToggleButtonBar` instance. To set any other property (for example, `mode`) to be used as the button's label, use the `labelField` property of the `ToggleButton Bar` as follows:

```
<mx:ToggleButtonBar id="toggle"
        dataProvider="{dataProvider}" labelField="mode"
        itemClick="setMode(event)"/>
```

The `itemClick` event of the `ToggleButtonBar` instance is wired to the method `setMode`. Notice that an event object of type `ItemClickEvent` is passed into the `setMode` method. The `item` property of the `ItemClickEvent` instance holds a reference to the corresponding item in the `dataProvider ArrayCollection`.

A common use case when using a `ToggleButtonBar` is to have the buttons deselected on application startup until the user specifically selects a button. However, the default behavior is for the first button to be selected when the `dataProvider` is set. Fortunately, Flex 3 provides access to the SDK source code, and you can use this knowledge to extend the `ToggleButtonBar` to suit your needs. The source for the `ToggleButtonBar` can be found at the following location:

```
<Flex 3 installation dir>/sdks/3.0.0/frameworks/projects/framework/src/mx/controls/
ToggleButtonBar.as
```

The `highlightSelectedNavItem` method provides a clue on how to deselect a button. It obtains a reference to the currently selected button and sets its selection state to false:

```
child = Button(getChildAt(selectedIndex));
child.selected = false;
```

You can leverage this information from the Framework code to create a custom version of the `ToggleButtonBar` that matches your specific needs, which in this case is to have all the buttons deselected on startup.

The following example shows a `CustomToggleButtonBar` class that extends the `Toggle ButtonBar` with functionality required to deselect the buttons any time the `dataProvider` changes. Note that it overrides the `dataProvider` setter and uses a Boolean flag called `dataReset` to keep track of when the `dataProvider` is reset on the component. The `updateDisplayList` method of the component is overridden to deselect the currently-selected button every time the `dataProvider` is reset. After the display is updated, the `dataReset` flag is reset to the default state.

```
package {
    import mx.controls.Button;
    import mx.controls.ToggleButtonBar;

    public class CustomToggleButtonBar extends ToggleButtonBar     {
        public function CustomToggleButtonBar() {
                super();
         }

        private var dataReset:Boolean = false;
        override public function set dataProvider(value:Object):void {
            super.dataProvider = value;
            this.dataReset = true;
        }

        override protected function updateDisplayList(unscaledWidth:Number,
                                                unscaledHeight:Number):void {

            super.updateDisplayList(unscaledWidth,unscaledHeight);


            if(this.dataReset) {
                if(selectedIndex != -1) {
                    var child:Button;
                    child = Button(getChildAt(selectedIndex));
                    if(child) {
                        child.selected = false;
                        this.dataReset = false;
                    }
                }
            }
        }
    }
}
```

To use this new component, simply replace the `ToggleButtonBar` with the `CustomToggleButtonBar` in the application:

```
<mx:Application
    xmlns:mx="http://www.adobe.com/2006/mxml"
    xmlns:local="*"
    layout="vertical"
    initialize="initApp(event)">

    <local:CustomToggleButtonBar id="toggle" selectedIndex="-1"
        dataProvider="{dataProvider}"
        itemClick="setMode(event)"/>
```

As you can see, extending the default components to suit your application needs is relatively easy. Looking at the Flex SDK source code is not only a great way to learn more about the internals of the Framework, but it also provides a lot of power to extend the default component set. Exercise caution, however, while using any undocumented features or properties/methods in the mx_internal namespace, because they are likely to change in future versions of the SDK.

2.3 Use a ColorPicker to Set Canvas Color

Problem

You want to allow users to change the color of a component by using a color picker.

Solution

Use a color picker to provide the user with a color palette for selection, and use the change event of the ColorPicker control to set the background color of the canvas.

Discussion

To give users access to a color palette, create an application that uses a ColorPicker control to change the backgroundColor of a Canvas control. The ColorPicker control provides a way for the user to select a color from a color swatch. To achieve this, the change event of the ColorPicker control is wired to the method setColor. The set Color method receives a ColorPickerEvent as an argument that contains information about the currently selected color in the ColorPicker control's palette. Take a look at the code:

```
<mx:Application
    xmlns:mx="http://www.adobe.com/2006/mxml"
    layout="vertical">

    <mx:Canvas id="cnv" width="450" height="450"
                backgroundColor="#eeaeaea">
        <mx:ColorPicker id="pckr" right="10" top="10"
                change="setColor(event)"/>
    </mx:Canvas>

    <mx:Script>
        <![CDATA[
            import mx.events.ColorPickerEvent;

            private function setColor(evt:ColorPickerEvent):void
                {
                cnv.setStyle("backgroundColor",evt.color); }
        ]]>
    </mx:Script>
</mx:Application>
```

When the user selects a new color, the backgroundColor style of the Canvas is updated. Note that because backgroundColor is a style attribute rather than a property of the Canvas control, the setStyle method is used to update the style as shown:

```
private function setColor(evt:ColorPickerEvent):void
    {
        cnv.setStyle("backgroundColor",evt.color); }
```

2.4 Load a SWF by Using the SWFLoader

Problem

You want to load external SWFs created either with Flex 3 or Flash CS3 into the current Flex application at runtime.

Solution

Use the SWFLoader component to load external SWFs at runtime.

Discussion

To load external SWFs at runtime, use the SWFLoader component. The example code loads external SWFs into Canvas containers that are children of a TabNavigator. The source attribute of the SWFLoader references the path to the external SWFs to be loaded at runtime. Sub1.swf is a Flex 3 application; Sub2.swf is a SWF created in Flash CS3.

```
<mx:Application
    xmlns:mx="http://www.adobe.com/2006/mxml"
    layout="vertical">

    <mx:TabNavigator resizeToContent="true"
        paddingTop="0">
        <mx:Canvas>
            <mx:SWFLoader source="assets/Sub1.swf"/>
        </mx:Canvas>
        <mx:Canvas>
            <mx:SWFLoader source="assets/Sub2.swf"/>
        </mx:Canvas>
    </mx:TabNavigator>
</mx:Application>
```

The SWFLoader component can also load SWFs that are embedded in the Flex application. Use the Embed directive for this. In the following example, Sub2.swf will be compiled into the main application:

```
<mx:SWFLoader source="@Embed('assets/Sub2.swf')"/>
```

2.5 Set Tab Indexes for Components

Problem

You need to change the default tab order of the components in a Flex application.

Solution

Use the `tabIndex` property of Flex components to specify a custom tab order.

Discussion

By default, all tab-enabled Flex components have a tab order based on their onscreen layout. To change this default order and explicitly specify a custom tab order, use the `tabIndex` property on components. In the following example, the `tabIndex` property of the `TextInput` controls are set explicitly to achieve a left-to-right tab order:

```
<mx:Application
    xmlns:mx="http://www.adobe.com/2006/mxml"
    layout="horizontal">

    <mx:VBox>
        <mx:Label text="First Name : "/>
        <mx:TextInput tabIndex="1"/>
        <mx:Label text="Home # : "/>
        <mx:TextInput tabIndex="3"/>
    </mx:VBox>
    <mx:VBox>
        <mx:Label text="Last Name : "/>
        <mx:TextInput tabIndex="2"/>
        <mx:Label text="Work # : "/>
        <mx:TextInput tabIndex="4"
            text="978-111-2345"/>
        <mx:Button label="Submit" tabIndex="5"/>
    </mx:VBox>
</mx:Application>
```

If the tab indexes are not specified, the default order based on the layout would be top to bottom. The `tabIndex` property for components can also be set programmatically using ActionScript, and is useful when the tab order needs to be controlled in custom components that create children dynamically at runtime.

2.6 Set a labelFunction for a Control

Problem

You need to combine different fields from a data provider to customize the label displayed in a combo box.

Solution

Use the `labelFunction` property of the `ComboBox` control to assign a reference to a custom function that defines the label to be displayed.

Discussion

By default, list-based controls in Flex look for a `label` property in the `dataProvider` items for the display value. In some cases, however, the `dataProvider` may not have a `label` property, or you may need to show a display value that concatenates values from multiple fields in the `dataProvider` item. The `labelFunction` property allows a user-defined method to be invoked for each item in that list's `dataProvider` and return a display label for that item. In the example code, the `labelFunction` property of the `ComboBox` contains a reference to the `getFullName` function, which concatenates the values from the `fName` and `lName` fields of the `dataProvider` item to return the full name string. Take a look:

```
<mx:Application
    xmlns:mx="http://www.adobe.com/2006/mxml"
    layout="horizontal">

    <mx:ComboBox dataProvider="{myDP}" labelFunction="getFullName"/>

    <mx:Script>
        <![CDATA[
            import mx.collections.ArrayCollection;

            [Bindable]
            private var myDP:ArrayCollection = new ArrayCollection([{id:1,fName:
"Lucky", lName:"Luke"},
                                                                    {id:2, fName:
"Bart", lName:"Simpson"}]);

            private function getFullName(item:Object):String{
                return item.fName + " " + item.lName;
            }

        ]]>
    </mx:Script>
</mx:Application>
```

2.7 Provide Data for Menus

Problem

You need to create a menu bar from a data provider.

Solution

Assign a `Collection` object such as an `ArrayCollection` or an `XMLListCollection`, to the `dataProvider` property of the `MenuBar` control by using MXML.

Discussion

The simplest way to populate a `MenuBar` control with data is to use MXML to create an instance of type `XMLList` inside the control:

```
<mx:Application
    xmlns:mx="http://www.adobe.com/2006/mxml"
    layout="horizontal">

    <mx:MenuBar labelField="@label">
        <mx:XMLList>
            <menuitem label="File">
                <menuitem label="New"/>
                <menuitem label="Open"/>
                <menuitem label="Close" enabled="false"/>
            </menuitem>
            <menuitem label="Edit"/>
            <menuitem label="Source"/>
            <menuitem label="View">
                <menuitem label="50%"
                    type="radio" groupName="one"/>
                <menuitem label="100%"
                    type="radio" groupName="one"
                    selected="true"/>
                <menuitem label="150%"
                    type="radio" groupName="one"/>
            </menuitem>
        </mx:XMLList>
    </mx:MenuBar>
</mx:Application>
```

Because the `dataProvider` property is the default property of the `MenuBar` control, the `XMLList` object can be assigned as a direct child of the `<mx:MenuBar>` tag. The top-level nodes in the `XMLList` correspond to the buttons on the `MenuBar`, while the `menuitem` node corresponds to the hierarchy of menu entries under each of the top-level buttons. The nodes themselves can be named anything—for example, instead of `menuitem` it could have been `subnode`. The attributes on the nodes, however, have special meaning and affect the display and interaction of the menus. These attributes are as follows:

enabled
: Specifies whether the user can select this menu item.

groupName
: Applicable when the type is `radio` and acts as the group name for a set of menu items.

icon
: Specifies the class identifier of an image asset.

label
: Specifies display text for the menu item. Note that when the `dataProvider` is in ECMAScript for XML (E4X) format, as in the preceding code example, the `label`

Field property on the MenuBar must be specified explicitly even if an attribute called label exists.

toggled

Specifies whether menuitems of type check or radio are selected.

type

Specifies one of three possible types of menu items: check, radio, or separator.

2.8 Dynamically Populate Menus

Problem

You want to populate and modify a menu bar dynamically.

Solution

Assign a Collection object, such as an ArrayCollection or an XMLListCollection, to the dataProvider property of the MenuBar control by using ActionScript.

Discussion

The MenuBar control in Flex 3 supports the dynamic creation of menu items at runtime. This recipe creates an application with a MenuBar control that is populated when the application initializes using an ArrayCollection:

```
<mx:Application
    xmlns:mx="http://www.adobe.com/2006/mxml"
    layout="vertical"
    creationComplete="initApp(event)">

    <mx:MenuBar id="menu" dataProvider="{menu_dp}"/>

    <mx:Script>
        <![CDATA[
            import mx.collections.ArrayCollection;
            import mx.events.FlexEvent;

            [Bindable]
            private var menu_dp:ArrayCollection;

            private function initApp(evt:FlexEvent):void {
                var temp:Array = new Array();

                var subNodes:ArrayCollection = new ArrayCollection( [ {label:"New"},
                                                                      {label:"Open"},
                                                                      {label:"Close",
enabled:false}
                                                                    ]);
                temp.push(    {label:"File",children:subNodes});
                temp.push({label:"Edit"});
                temp.push({label:"Source"});
```

```
                    subNodes = new ArrayCollection( [    {label:"50%", type:"radio",
            groupName:"one"},
                                                          {label:"100%", type:"radio",
            groupName:"one",selected:true},
                                                          {label:"150%", type:"radio",
            groupName:"one"}
                                               ]);
                    temp.push({label:"View",children:subNodes});
                    menu_dp = new ArrayCollection(temp);
                }
            ]]>
        </mx:Script>

    </mx:Application>
```

The preceding code uses binding to bind the `menu_dp` `ArrayCollection` to the `dataProvider` property of the `MenuBar` component. On the `creationComplete` event of the application, the `menu_dp` `ArrayCollection` is initialized and populated with the menu items. As with the other data-driven components in Flex, using a collection such as the `ArrayCollection` or `XMLListCollection` ensures that any changes to the underlying data will cause the control's display to update accordingly.

The collection classes provide convenient methods for editing, adding, and deleting items from the menu. To demonstrate this, this example adds a simple `Form` control below the `MenuBar`, enabling you to edit the menu entries based on their indices within the `ArrayCollection`:

```
    <mx:Form>
        <mx:FormHeading label="Menu Editor"/>
        <mx:FormItem label="Menu Index">
            <mx:TextInput id="menuIdx" restrict="0-9" text="0" width="20"/>
        </mx:FormItem>
        <mx:FormItem label="Sub-Menu Index">
            <mx:TextInput id="subMenuIdx" restrict="0-9" width="20"/>
        </mx:FormItem>
        <mx:FormItem label="Menu Label">
            <mx:TextInput id="label_ti"/>
        </mx:FormItem>
        <mx:FormItem>
            <mx:Button label="Edit" click="editMenu()"/>
        </mx:FormItem>
    </mx:Form>
```

This is a basic `Form` with input controls that allow you to specify the array indices to get at a specific menu item. Entering 0 in the `menuIdx` text input and leaving the `subMenuIdx` input blank will refer to the top-level File menu. Entering 0 in the `menuIdx` text input and 0 in the `subMenuIdx` input will refer to the New submenu item.

When the user clicks the Edit button, the `editMenu` method is invoked, which uses the specified indices to get a reference to the menu item and change its label. Take a look:

```
    private function editMenu():void {
        var itemToEdit:Object;
```

```
    try {
        itemToEdit = menu_dp.getItemAt(int(menuIdx.text));
        if(subMenuIdx.text) {
            itemToEdit = itemToEdit.children.getItemAt(int(subMenuIdx.text));
        }
        itemToEdit.label = label_ti.text;
        menu_dp.itemUpdated(itemToEdit);
    }
    catch(ex:Error){
        trace("could not retrieve menu item");
    }
}
```

The editMenu code looks at the values entered in menuIdx and subMenuIdx to retrieve a specific menu item and then uses the value in label_ti to update the display value of that menu item. Note that in order to modify the menu display, the underlying data Provider associated with the MenuBar is modified and then a request is made for the view to be updated using the itemUpdated method of the ArrayCollection. In nested data structures such as this example, it is important to call itemUpdated to request a display update. Otherwise, the underlying data would change but the display would still show the old value. The example code uses a try...catch block for some basic error handling for array bounds.

2.9 Create EventHandlers for Menu-Based Controls

Problem

You need to act on user interaction with the menu bar.

Solution

Add event listeners for the itemClick event of the MenuBar control.

Discussion

To respond to menu bar interaction, assign a listener function, handleMenuClick, to the itemClick event of the MenuBar control. The itemClick event is dispatched whenever a user selects a menu item. A MenuEvent object is received by the listener function as its argument. The MenuEvent object contains information about the menu item from where this event was dispatched. The item property of the MenuEvent object contains a reference to the item in the dataProvider that is associated with that particular menu item. Here's the code you need:

```
<mx:Application
    xmlns:mx="http://www.adobe.com/2006/mxml"
    layout="vertical">

    <mx:MenuBar
        labelField="@label"
```

```
            itemClick="handleMenuClick(event)">
            <mx:XMLList>
                <menuitem label="File">
                    <menuitem label="New"/>
                    <menuitem label="Open"/>
                    <menuitem label="Close" enabled="false"/>
                </menuitem>
                <menuitem label="Edit"/>
                <menuitem label="Source"/>
                <menuitem label="View">
                    <menuitem label="50%"
                        type="radio" groupName="one"/>
                    <menuitem label="100%"
                        type="radio" groupName="one"
                        selected="true"/>
                    <menuitem label="150%"
                        type="radio" groupName="one"/>
                </menuitem>
            </mx:XMLList>
        </mx:MenuBar>

        <mx:Label id="disp0_lbl"/>

        <mx:Script>
            <![CDATA[
                import mx.events.MenuEvent;

                private function handleMenuClick(evt:MenuEvent):void {
                    this.disp0_lbl.text = evt.item.@label + " was selected";
                }
            ]]>
        </mx:Script>
</mx:Application>
```

Note that because the dataProvider is in E4X format, the example uses the E4X notation @label to retrieve the label attribute. The MenuBar control also supports other event types, such as change, itemRollOut, itemRollOver, menuHide, and menuShow.

2.10 Display an Alert in an Application

Problem

You want to show a modal message to the user and optionally present the user with action choices.

Solution

Use the Alert control to display a message to the user.

Discussion

The `Alert` control provides a modal dialog box with buttons that the user can click to respond to a message in the dialog box. The `Alert` control cannot be created using MXML. You need to use ActionScript instead. For example:

```
<mx:Application
    xmlns:mx="http://www.adobe.com/2006/mxml"
    layout="vertical">

    <mx:Button id="btn" click="showAlert(event)" label="Alert"/>

    <mx:Label id="lbl"/>

    <mx:Script>
        <![CDATA[
            import mx.events.CloseEvent;
            import mx.controls.Alert;
            import mx.events.MenuEvent;

            private function showAlert(evt:MouseEvent):void {
                var alert:Alert = Alert.show("Button was clicked","Alert Window
Title",Alert.OK|Alert.CANCEL|Alert.NO|Alert.YES,this,onAlertClose);
            }

            private function onAlertClose(evt:CloseEvent):void {
                switch(evt.detail) {
                    case Alert.OK:
                        lbl.text = "OK Clicked";
                        break;
                    case Alert.CANCEL:
                        lbl.text = "CANCEL Clicked";
                        break;
                    case Alert.NO:
                        lbl.text = "NO Clicked";
                        break;
                    case Alert.YES:
                        lbl.text = "YES Clicked";
                        break;
                }
            }
        ]]>
    </mx:Script>
</mx:Application>
```

When the user clicks the `btn` button, the example code creates an `Alert` control by using the static method `show` on the `Alert` class. The `show` method accepts the following arguments to configure the alert:

text
> The message to display to the user.

title
> The title of the `Alert` box.

---

flags
> The buttons to be shown on the `Alert`. Valid values are `Alert.OK`, `Alert.CANCEL`, `Alert.NO`, and `Alert.Yes`. More than one button can be shown by using the bitwise OR operator, as in `Alert.OK | Alert.CANCEL`.

parent
> The display object to center the `Alert` on.

closeHandler
> The event handler to be called when any button on the `Alert` control is pressed.

iconClass
> Asset class of the icon to be placed to the left of the display message in the `Alert`.

defaultButtonFlag
> The button to be used as the default button for the `Alert` control. Pressing the Enter key activates the default button. Valid values are `Alert.OK`, `Alert.CANCEL`, `Alert.NO`, or `Alert.Yes`.

The method `onAlertClose` is set as the `closeHandler` event handler for the `Alert`. The method receives a `CloseEvent` object as an argument, and uses the `detail` property of the `CloseEvent` to determine which button was clicked on the `Alert` control.

2.11 Use the Date from a Calendar Control

Problem

You want to allow the user to select dates from a calendar-like control.

Solution

Use the `DateField` control or the `DateChooser` control to provide the user with a convenient calendar-like control to pick dates.

Discussion

The Flex Framework provides two controls for calendar-like functionality: the `DateField` control and the `DateChooser` control. The `DateField` control provides a `TextInput` control with a calendar icon that when clicked opens a calendar. The `DateChooser`, on the other hand, provides a persistent calendar to the user. The following example is a simple trip calculator that illustrates both types of controls. The user selects a start date using `DateField`, and an end date using `DateChooser`. The program then calculates the duration of the trip on the `change` event of the controls in the `update` event handler. The `selectedDate` property of both controls returns a `Date` object representing the user's selection.

```
<mx:Application
    xmlns:mx="http://www.adobe.com/2006/mxml"
    layout="vertical">
```

```
<mx:Form>
    <mx:FormHeading label="Trip Calculator"/>
    <mx:FormItem label="Start Date">
        <mx:DateField id="startDate" change="update(event)"/>
    </mx:FormItem>
    <mx:FormItem label="End Date">
        <mx:DateChooser id="endDate" change="update(event)"/>
    </mx:FormItem>
    <mx:FormItem label="Trip Duration (days)">
        <mx:Label id="display"/>
    </mx:FormItem>
</mx:Form>

<mx:Script>
    <![CDATA[
        import mx.events.CalendarLayoutChangeEvent;

        private static const MILLISECONDS:int = 1000;
        private static const SECONDS:int = 60;
        private static const MINUTES:int = 60;
        private static const HOURS:int = 24;


        private function update(evt:CalendarLayoutChangeEvent):void {
            try {
                var diff:Number = endDate.selectedDate.getTime() -
startDate.selectedDate.getTime();
                // convert the millisecond into days
                var days:int = int(diff/(MILLISECONDS*SECONDS*MINUTES*HOURS));
                display.text = days.toString();
            }
            catch(ex:Error) {

            }
        }

    ]]>
    </mx:Script>
</mx:Application>
```

When performing date arithmetic, it is important to use the `getTime` method of the `Date` object, so that leap years are factored correctly. The `getTime` method returns the number of milliseconds that have elapsed since January 1, 1970.

2.12 Display and Position Multiple Pop-ups

Problem

You want to display additional messages to users by using pop-up windows.

Solution

Use `PopUpManager` to create `TitleWindow` component instances upon user interaction.

Discussion

The Flex Framework includes a `PopUpManager` class that contains static methods to manage the creation, placement, and removal of top-level windows in a Flex application. Take a look at the code:

```
<mx:Application
    xmlns:mx="http://www.adobe.com/2006/mxml"
    layout="absolute">

    <mx:Canvas horizontalCenter="0" verticalCenter="0">

        <mx:LinkButton label="Top" x="100" y="10" click="showDetail(event)"/>
        <mx:LinkButton label="Left" x="10" y="100" click="showDetail(event)"/>
        <mx:LinkButton label="Bottom" x="100" y="200" click="showDetail(event)"/>
        <mx:LinkButton label="Right" x="200" y="100" click="showDetail(event)"/>
        <mx:Canvas width="100" height="100" x="125" y="40"
            backgroundColor="#ff0000" rotation="45">
        </mx:Canvas>
    </mx:Canvas>

    <mx:Script>
        <![CDATA[
            import mx.managers.PopUpManager;

            private const POPUP_OFFSET:int = 10;

            private function showDetail(evt:MouseEvent):void {
                // create the popup
                var popup:CustomPopUp = CustomPopUp(PopUpManager.createPopUp(this,
    CustomPopUp,false));
                popup.message = "This is the detail for " + evt.target.label;

                // position the popup
                var pt:Point = new Point(0, 0);
                pt = evt.target.localToGlobal(pt);
                popup.x = pt.x  + POPUP_OFFSET;
                popup.y = pt.y  + evt.target.height + POPUP_OFFSET;
            }
        ]]>
    </mx:Script>
</mx:Application>
```

In this example, a series of `LinkButton` controls are created and placed inside a `Canvas` using absolute positioning. When the user clicks a `LinkButton`, a pop-up is displayed below it to present a detailed message to the user. To do this, the click event of the `LinkButton` controls is wired to the `showDetail` method. The `showDetail` method uses the `PopUpManager`'s `createPopUp` method to create an instance of a custom component called `CustomPopUp`. Next the `message` property of the pop-up is set to the value that

needs to be displayed to the user. Finally, the pop-up's positioned relative to the Link
Button that initiated the request. To do this, the top-left corner coordinates of the
LinkButton (x = 0, y = 0 in the LinkButton's coordinate space) are converted from the
component's local coordinate space to the global coordinate space by using the local
ToGlobal method. This is a convenience method available to all DisplayObjects and
their descendants. The CustomPopUp class is shown here:

```
<mx:TitleWindow xmlns:mx="http://www.adobe.com/2006/mxml"
    layout="vertical"
    width="300" height="50"
    styleName="customPopUp"
    showCloseButton="true"
    close="handleClose(event)">

    <mx:Style>
        .customPopUp {
            header-height:2;
            padding-left:5;
            padding-right:5;
            padding-top:5;
            padding-bottom:5;
            border-color:#000000;
            border-alpha:.5;
            border-thickness-left:5;
            border-thickness-right:5;
            border-thickness-bottom:5;
            border-thickness-top:5;
            background-color:#666666;
            color:#ffffff;
        }
    </mx:Style>

    <mx:Text width="100%" height="100%" text="{message}"/>

    <mx:Script>
        <![CDATA[
            import mx.managers.PopUpManager;
            import mx.events.CloseEvent;
            [Bindable]
            public var message:String;

            private function handleClose(evt:CloseEvent):void {
                PopUpManager.removePopUp(this);

            }
        ]]>
    </mx:Script>
</mx:TitleWindow>
```

The CustomPopUp class inherits from the TitleWindow class and adds a Text control to
display the messages. The close event of the TitleWindow is assigned to the handle
Close method, which closes the pop-up with the removePopUp method of the PopUpMan
ager. It also contains CSS styles to customize the appearance of CustomPopUp.

2.13 Create a Custom Border for a Pop-up Window

Problem

You want to customize the border of a pop-up window to show a callout pointing to the control that launched the window.

Solution

Convert the `PanelSkin` class to a subclass and override the `updateDisplayList` method to draw the callout arrow. Set the new skin as the `borderSkin` for the pop-up window.

Discussion

This technique builds on Recipe 2.12 by modifying the `CustomPopUp` component. To customize your window border, this time set the `borderSkin` style to a custom class called `CustomPanelSkin`:

```
<mx:TitleWindow xmlns:mx="http://www.adobe.com/2006/mxml"
    layout="vertical"
    width="300" height="50"
    styleName="customPopUp"
    showCloseButton="true"
    close="handleClose(event)"
    borderSkin="CustomPanelSkin"
    initialize="initPopUp()">

    <mx:Style>
        .customPopUp {
            header-height:2;
            padding-left:5;
            padding-right:5;
            padding-top:5;
            padding-bottom:5;
            border-color:#000000;
            border-alpha:.5;
            border-thickness-left:5;
            border-thickness-right:5;
            border-thickness-bottom:5;
            border-thickness-top:5;
            background-color:#666666;
            color:#ffffff;
        }
    </mx:Style>

    <mx:Text width="100%" height="100%" text="{message}"/>

    <mx:Script>
        <![CDATA[
            import mx.managers.PopUpManager;
            import mx.events.CloseEvent;
            [Bindable]
```

```
                    public var message:String;

                    private function handleClose(evt:CloseEvent):void {
                        PopUpManager.removePopUp(this);
                    }

                    private function initPopUp():void {
                        this.isPopUp = false;
                    }
                ]]>
        </mx:Script>
    </mx:TitleWindow>
```

The code for the `CustomPanelSkin` class follows. Note that setting the `isPopUp` property of the `TitleWindow` to false prevents users from dragging the pop-up.

```
package
{
    import flash.display.Graphics;

    import mx.skins.halo.PanelSkin;

    public class CustomPanelSkin extends PanelSkin
    {
        override protected function updateDisplayList(w:Number, h:Number):void {
            super.updateDisplayList(w,h);

            var gfx:Graphics = this.graphics;
            gfx.beginFill(this.getStyle("borderColor"),
                            this.getStyle("borderAlpha"));
            gfx.moveTo(this.getStyle("cornerRadius"),0);
            gfx.lineTo(15,-10);
            gfx.lineTo(25,0);
        }
    }
}
```

This simple class extends the `PanelSkin` class, which is the default border skin class for the `TitleWindow`. The `updateDisplayList` method is overridden to add the logic for drawing a callout arrow at the top-left corner of the `CustomPopUp` component.

2.14 Handle focusIn and focusOut Events

Problem

You want to show a pop-up window when the user focuses on a label and close the pop-up when the user focuses out.

Solution

Use the `focusIn` and `focusOut` events (available to all instances of classes inheriting from the `InteractiveObject` class) to invoke the appropriate methods on the `PopUpManager`.

Discussion

To launch a window based on user focus, you can repurpose the code from the two previous recipes. However, instead of launching the pop-up merely when the user clicks the LinkButton, create it on a focusIn event. The focusIn event is dispatched when the component receives focus, such as when the user tabs to it or clicks on it. The handler code for the focusIn event makes one addition to the previous recipe:

```
systemManager.removeFocusManager(IFocusManagerContainer(popup))
```

Here it is in context:

```
<mx:Application
    xmlns:mx="http://www.adobe.com/2006/mxml"
    layout="absolute">

    <mx:Canvas horizontalCenter="0" verticalCenter="0">
        <mx:LinkButton id="lbl" label="Top" x="100" y="10" focusIn="showDetail(event)"
 focusOut="closePopUp()"/>
        <mx:LinkButton label="Left" x="10" y="100" focusIn="showDetail(event)"
focusOut="closePopUp()"/>
        <mx:LinkButton label="Bottom" x="100" y="200" focusIn="showDetail(event)"
focusOut="closePopUp()"/>
        <mx:LinkButton label="Right" x="200" y="100" focusIn="showDetail(event)"
focusOut="closePopUp()"/>
        <mx:Canvas width="100" height="100" x="125" y="40"
            backgroundColor="#ff0000" rotation="45">
        </mx:Canvas>
    </mx:Canvas>

    <mx:Script>
        <![CDATA[
            import mx.managers.IFocusManagerContainer;
            import mx.managers.PopUpManager;

            private const POPUP_OFFSET:int = 10;

            private var popup:CustomPopUp;

            private function showDetail(evt:FocusEvent):void {
                // create the popup
                popup = CustomPopUp(PopUpManager.createPopUp(this,CustomPopUp,false));
                popup.message = "This is the detail for " + evt.target.label;

                // position the popup
                var pt:Point = new Point(0, 0);
                pt = evt.target.localToGlobal(pt);
                popup.x = pt.x  + POPUP_OFFSET;
                popup.y = pt.y  + evt.target.height + POPUP_OFFSET;

                systemManager.removeFocusManager(IFocusManagerContainer(popup))
            }
```

```
private function closePopUp():void {
    PopUpManager.removePopUp(popup);
}

    ]]>
  </mx:Script>
</mx:Application>
```

When any pop-up is created, the SystemManager, by default, activates the FocusManager associated with that pop-up. This allows the focus loop (what controls the tab order) to be based on the pop-up that was just created. In this recipe, a different behavior is desired. The pop-up window should close when the user focuses out of the link bar (for example, by tabbing out of it). This is achieved by removing the pop-up window's FocusManager from the SystemManager, thus reactivating the application's FocusManager. The focusOut event handler closePopUp includes the logic to close the pop-up. When this application is run and the Tab key is pressed repeatedly, the focus cycles between the LinkButtons and the appropriate pop-up windows will be created or removed.

CHAPTER 3

Containers

The term *containers* generally refers to all the classes held in the mx.containers package of the Flex Framework. Containers extend the UIComponent class, adding layout management functionality, methods to control the creation of children using creation policies, and automatic scrolling. The implementations of containers are quite distinct, but all share the ability to position children, lay out those children by using constraints or styles, and control scrolling and how those children respond to scroll events.

Constraints are new to Flex 3. They enable developers to create rules for positioning, in terms of both location and sizing, to which the children of containers can be assigned. Constraints work only with containers, such as the Canvas container, that have absolute positioning, which has much the same meaning as it does in CSS. Box and Tile containers provide automatic layout of children and methods for controlling which children are included in the layout management.

3.1 Position Children by Using Layout Management

Problem

You need to position multiple children vertically or horizontally and control the layout of those children.

Solution

Use the HBox or VBox container, and set the horizontalGap or verticalGap for the HBox or VBox, respectively, to set the distance between the components.

Discussion

Extending the common base class mx.containers.Box, the HBox and VBox components lay out their children horizontally or vertically, respectively, and can hold an unlimited number of children. When the size of the children is greater than the height or width of the Box component, Box adds scroll bars by default. To determine the distance between the children, VBox containers use the `verticalGap` property and HBox containers use `horizontalGap`. For example:

```
<mx:VBox width="400" height="300" verticalGap="20">
    <mx:Button label="Button"/>
    <mx:LinkButton label="Link Button"/>
</mx:VBox>
```

The HBox and VBox containers, however, do not respect the `bottom`, `left`, `right`, or `top` constraint properties. To add spacing between the children laid out in a Box container, use a Spacer as shown:

```
<mx:VBox width="400" height="300" verticalGap="20">
    <mx:Button label="Button"/>
    <mx:ComboBox top="60"/>
    <mx:Spacer height="20"/>
    <mx:LinkButton label="Link Button"/>
</mx:VBox>
```

To change the distance padding style or the distance between the border of the component and its children, add `paddingTop`, `paddingLeft`, `paddingRight`, or `paddingBottom` styles. This will affect all children added to the container. To move a single child to the left or right in a VBox, or up or down in an HBox, add an inner container and use that to position the child:

```
<mx:HBox x="400" horizontalGap="10" top="15">
    <mx:Canvas>
        <mx:Button top="50" label="Button" y="20"/>
    </mx:Canvas>
    <mx:Panel height="40" width="40"/>
    <mx:Spacer width="25"/>
    <mx:LinkButton label="Label"/>
    <mx:ComboBox/>
</mx:HBox>
```

This example uses both an HBox and VBox within a Canvas container to show both types of layouts:

```
<mx:Canvas xmlns:mx="http://www.adobe.com/2006/mxml" >
    <mx:VBox width="400" height="300" verticalGap="20">
        <mx:Button label="Button"/>
        <mx:ComboBox/>
        <mx:Spacer height="20"/>
        <mx:LinkButton label="Link Button"/>
    </mx:VBox>
    <mx:HBox x="400" horizontalGap="10" top="15">
        <mx:Canvas>
            <mx:Button top="50" label="Button" y="20"/>
        </mx:Canvas>
        <mx:Panel height="40" width="40"/>
        <mx:Spacer width="25"/>
        <mx:LinkButton label="Label"/>
        <mx:ComboBox/>
    </mx:HBox>
</mx:Canvas>
```

3.2 Position and Size Containers via Percentage Positioning

Problem

You need to size children according to the size of their parent component.

Solution

Use percentage sizing so that as the size of the component changes, the Flex Framework will automatically adjust the size of the children components.

Discussion

Percentage positioning is a powerful tool that enables you to easily define the size and location of a child with respect to its parent. For example, the `RelativePositioning Child.mxml` component that follows lays itself out to be 40 percent of the measured width and 70 percent of the measured height of its parent component:

```
<mx:VBox xmlns:mx="http://www.adobe.com/2006/mxml" width="40%" height="70%" background
Color="#0033ff">
    <mx:Image source="@Embed('../../assets/image.png')"/>
    <mx:Image source="@Embed('../../assets/image.png')"/>
</mx:VBox>
```

In the following example, multiple instances of `RelativePositioningChild` have been laid out in a parent container, which also has percentage sizing. Whatever parent this component is added to will determine the width and height of this component and consequently of its child components.

```
<mx:HBox xmlns:mx="http://www.adobe.com/2006/mxml" width="75%" height="50%" background
Color="#0099ff" alpha="0.3" xmlns:cookbook="oreilly.cookbook.*">
    <cookbook:RelativePositioningChild/>
    <cookbook:RelativePositioningChild/>
</mx:HBox>
```

To demonstrate the effects of the percentage resizing, the preceding code snippet has been saved as RelativePositioningParent.mxml and used here:

```
<mx:Application xmlns:mx="http://www.adobe.com/2006/mxml" layout="absolute"
xmlns:cookbook="oreilly.cookbook.*">
    <mx:Script>
        <![CDATA[

            private function changeWidth():void
            {
                this.width = slider.value*150;
            }

        ]]>
    </mx:Script>
    <cookbook:RelativePositioningParent/>
```

```
        <mx:HSlider id="slider" change="changeWidth()"/>
    </mx:Application>
```

As the slider changes the width of the application, `RelativePositioningParent` and `RelativePositioningChild` position themselves according to the width of the parent application.

3.3 Track Mouse Position Within Different Coordinate Systems

Problem

You need to track the user's mouse position relative to the parent container and relative to the children of that container.

Solution

Use the Stage and local positioning properties of the `MouseEvent` class and the `mouseX` and `mouseY` properties of the `UIComponent` class that all containers extend.

Discussion

The `MouseEvent` class has four properties that enable you to determine the mouse position. The `localX` and `localY` properties provide the position in relation to the component that has thrown the mouse event, while `stageX` and `stageY` provide the position in relation to the Stage itself.

In the following example, if the mouse is over the `LinkButton` component, the `localX` and `localY` properties will reflect the position of the mouse on the `LinkButton` component. If the mouse is not over the `LinkButton`, the properties indicate the mouse's position on the `VBox`:

```
<mx:VBox xmlns:mx="http://www.adobe.com/2006/mxml" mouseMove="traceMousePosition
(event)">
    <mx:LinkButton label="MyButton"/>
</mx:VBox>
```

To determine the mouse position on a particular component regardless of whether the mouse is over that component or not, use the `DisplayObject`'s `mouseX` and `mouseY` positions, which return the position of the mouse in relation to the 0,0 point of a container or component. Last, the `Container` class defines `contentMouseX` and `contentMouseY` positions that describe the mouse position in relation to the entirety of the content of a container. The following example returns the mouse position in relation to the two `Panel` children added to the `HBox`, rather than in relation to the upper left of the `HBox`:

```
<mx:HBox xmlns:mx="http://www.adobe.com/2006/mxml" width="500" height="300" mouseMove=
"trace(this.contentMouseX+' : '+this.contentMouseY);">
    <mx:Panel width="400">
        <mx:Label text="Center" horizontalCenter="200"/>
    </mx:Panel>
```

```
    <mx:Panel width="400">
        <mx:Label text="Center" horizontalCenter="200"/>
    </mx:Panel>
</mx:HBox>
```

Because the sum of the two children of the HBox is 812 pixels, when you scroll all the way to the right and mouse over the HBox, you will see x values beyond the set size of the HBox. The container defines a contentPane property, a private DisplayObject to which all children are added. The container then masks those children if their height or width exceeds the set height and width of the container. The contentMouseX and contentMouseY positions measure the position of the mouse on this protected content DisplayObject.

This final example puts all these methods to use:

```
<mx:VBox xmlns:mx="http://www.adobe.com/2006/mxml" width="300" height="500" paddingTop=
"10" paddingLeft="10" verticalGap="15" mouseMove="traceMousePosition(event)">
    <mx:Script>
        <![CDATA[

            private function traceMousePosition(event:MouseEvent):void
            {
                trace(" MouseEvent local position "+event.localX+" "+event.localY);
                trace(" MousePosition stage position "+event.stageX+" "+event.stageY);
                trace(" MouseEvent position from w/in component "+this.mouseX+"
"+this.mouseY);
                trace(" Content Mouse Position "+this.contentMouseX+"
"+this.contentMouseY);
            }

        ]]>
    </mx:Script>
    <mx:Image source="@Embed('../../assets/image.png')"/>
    <mx:Image source="@Embed('../../assets/image.png')"/>
    <mx:Image source="@Embed('../../assets/image.png')"/>
    <mx:Image source="@Embed('../../assets/image.png')"/>
</mx:VBox>
```

The function will be called when the mouse is moving over the VBox component and so will trace only positive values for the mouseX and mouseY positions.

3.4 Dynamically Add and Remove Children from a Container

Problem

You need to add and remove children from a container at runtime without using a Repeater or DataProvider control.

Solution

Use the `addChild` or `addChildAt` methods to add a child, and the `removeChildAt` or `removeAllChildren` methods to remove one.

Discussion

Flex methods make adding and removing children easy, but `UIComponent`s and containers follow slightly different rules.

The `addChild` method adds any child that extends `UIComponent` to the component on which the method is called. For example:

```
var component:UIComponent = new UIComponent();
addChild(component);
```

The `addChildAt` method differs in that it requires an index within the container at which the child should be added. In the case of containers that do not have layout management, such as `Canvas` objects, this means that the added child will appear at the z-index depth indicated. For containers that do have layout management, such as `HBox` and `VBox` components, the added child will appear at the index supplied. For example:

```
var component:UIComponent = new UIComponent();
addChildAt(component, 3);
```

To remove any child, call `removeChildAt`, which removes the child at the supplied index:

```
removeChildAt(2);
```

Containers and `UIComponent`s also possess a `removeChild` method that requires a reference to the child that you would like removed from the display list.

Flex provides different methods of accessing the children that have been added to a container. After you know how to access the children, you can use that reference to remove them. For example, any children added to an MXML container can be accessed by its `id` property. All the children of any container can be accessed by using the `getChildAt` method, as shown:

```
getChildAt(index:int);
```

They can also be accessed by the `name` property, if the child has been assigned a name. To determine the number of children that any component contains, use the `numChildren` property:

```
var i:int = 0;
while(i<this.numChildren)
{
    trace(getChildAt(i));
i++;
}
```

You can use a child's index or `id` as a reference when removing the child, as in

```
removeChild(getChildAt(2);
```

or

```
removeChild(this.childId);
```

Finally, there is also a `removeAllChildren` method, which removes all the children that have been added to a component.

3.5 Use Constraint-Based Layout for Containers

Problem

You want to define the size of child components based on the inner borders of the parent component.

Solution

Use the constraint properties: `left`, `right`, `top`, and `bottom`.

Discussion

The constraint properties of the `UIComponent` class let you define the height and width of a component in relation to a gutter on the parent component. A component with a width of 200 pixels and a child with `left` and `right` properties of 20 pixels each will have a width of 160 pixels. A child with a `bottom` constraint of 40 pixels within a component with a height of 200 pixels will be placed at 160 pixels within the parent. Constraints cannot be used with components that do not have an absolute layout, such as `HBox` or `VBox` components. Containers that can have children set to use constraints are `Canvas`, `Panel`, and `Application`.

In the following example, the `innerCanvas` component will be placed at 20 pixels from the top, right, and left and extend to 50 pixels from the bottom of the outer canvas, making the `innerCanvas` 360 pixels wide and 230 pixels tall. If the outer canvas is expanded or shrunk, the `innerCanvas` maintains the same gutters on the top, left, right, and bottom. The `Button` and `TextInput` controls within the component will be sized according to the size of the `innerCanvas` component, maintaining the gutters indicated in the constraint properties.

```
<mx:Canvas xmlns:mx="http://www.adobe.com/2006/mxml" width="400" height="300">
    <mx:Canvas left="20" right="20" top="20" bottom="50" id="innerCanvas ">
        <mx:Button label="Button Label" left="20" right="20" top="10"/>
        <mx:TextInput left="30" right="30" bottom="10"/>
    </mx:Canvas>
</mx:Canvas>
```

In the following code snippet, the two `Panel` components will each be rendered with 320-pixel widths because of the constraint properties that have been applied to the panels. The `topPanel` will be placed at 40 pixels, conforming to the `top` constraint that has been placed on that Panel, and the bottomPanel will be placed at 260 pixels, conforming to the bottom constraint.

```
<mx:Canvas xmlns:mx="http://www.adobe.com/2006/mxml" width="400" height="300">
    <mx:Panel left="40" right="40" top="40" id="topPanel ">
        <mx:Label text="Label text"/>
    </mx:Panel>
    <mx:Panel left="40" right="40" bottom="40" id="bottomPanel">
        <mx:Label text="Label text"/>
    </mx:Panel>
</mx:Canvas>
```

3.6 Set Maximum and Minimum Sizes for Children Within Containers

Problem

You need to add multiple children to a component and ensure that if the number of children extends beyond a certain width, the children will be added to another row within the container.

Solution

Use the maxWidth or maxHeight property to determine where to place children within a component.

Discussion

The maxWidth and maxHeight styles define the maximum height and width at which the component's parent will allow it to be displayed. In the following code snippet, the maxWidth style of the property is checked to ensure that the next component added will not cause the container to exceed the maximum width allowed by the parent container. If the maximum width is going to be exceeded, another HBox component is generated and the image is added to that component. The VBox container's layout management will take care of properly laying out the new, added children.

```
<mx:Canvas xmlns:mx="http://www.adobe.com/2006/mxml" height="400"
xmlns:cookbook="oreilly.cookbook.*" backgroundColor="#0000ff">
    <cookbook:AddConstraintChildren maxHeight="400" maxWidth="800" horizontalAlign=
"center" verticalScrollPolicy="off"/>
</mx:Canvas>

<mx:VBox xmlns:mx="http://www.adobe.com/2006/mxml">
    <mx:Script>
        <![CDATA[
            import mx.controls.Image;

            [Embed(source="../../assets/image.png")]
            public var image:Class;
```

```
        private var childCount:int = 0;
        private var currentHolder:HBox;

        private function addMoreChildren():void
        {
            var image:Image = new Image();
            image.source = image;
            if((currentHolder.width + image.width) >= this.maxWidth)
            {
                var holder:HBox = new HBox();
                addChild(holder);
                currentHolder = holder;
            }
            currentHolder.addChild(image);
        }
    ]]>
</mx:Script>
<mx:Button label="addMoreChildren()" click="addMoreChildren()"/>
<mx:HBox id="topHolder" creationComplete="currentHolder = topHolder"/>
</mx:VBox>
```

See Also

Recipe 3.5.

3.7 Specify Constraint Rows and Columns for a Container

Problem

You want to define distinct columns or rows of children with distinct constraint properties without defining the constraints on each child.

Solution

Use `ConstraintRow` and `ConstraintColumn` to define regions of a container where constraints can be added.

Discussion

`ConstraintRow` and `ConstraintColumn` objects let you define a grid of constraints that you can use to position components. You use these constraints in much the same way that you would define constraints by using the edges of the container. For example, the syntax

```
left="columnName:10"
```

positions a component 10 pixels to the left of the column indicated in the following example:

```
<mx:Canvas>
    <mx:constraintColumns>
```

```
            <mx:ConstraintColumn id="leftCol" width="200"/>
            <mx:ConstraintColumn id="rightCol" width="60%"/>
        </mx:constraintColumns>
        <mx:constraintRows>
            <mx:ConstraintRow id="topRow" height="80%"/>
            <mx:ConstraintRow id="bottomRow" height="20%"/>
        </mx:constraintRows>
    <mx:Button label="Click Me" left="leftCol:0" right="leftCol:0" top="row2:0" bottom=
    "row2:0"/>
    </mx:Canvas>
```

In addition, you can add sliders to let the user expand or shrink the amount of space assigned to each column, showing how the layout will change to respond to changing container sizes. For example:

```
<mx:Application xmlns:mx="http://www.adobe.com/2006/mxml">

<mx:Script>
    <![CDATA[
        [Bindable]
        public var txt:String = "Cortázar is highly regarded as a master of short
stories of a fantastic bent, with the collections Bestiario (1951)" +
                " and Final de Juego (1956) containing many of his best examples in
the genre, including the remarkable \"Continuidad de los Parques\"" +
                " and \"Axolotl.\" These collections received early praise from
Álvaro Cepeda Samudio, and selections from the two volumes were published" +
                " in 1967 in English translations by Paul Blackburn, under the title
End of the Game and Other Stories (in later editions, Blow-Up and " +
                "Other Stories, in deference to the English title of Antonioni's
celebrated film of 1966 of Cortázar's story Las babas del diablo).";

                private function changeColumnProportion():void
                {
                    this.leftCol.percentWidth = (10*c_slider.value);
                    this.rightCol.percentWidth = 100 - (10*c_slider.value);
                }

                private function changeRowProportion():void
                {
                    this.row1.percentHeight = (10*r_slider.value);
                    this.row2.percentHeight = 100 - (10*r_slider.value);
                }

    ]]>
</mx:Script>

<mx:Canvas width="100%" height="100%" horizontalScrollPolicy="off"
verticalScrollPolicy="off">
    <mx:constraintColumns>
        <mx:ConstraintColumn id="leftCol" width="50%" />
        <mx:ConstraintColumn id="rightCol" width="50%" />
    </mx:constraintColumns>
    <mx:constraintRows>
        <mx:ConstraintRow id="row1" height="20%"/>
        <mx:ConstraintRow id="row2" height="80%" />
```

```
        </mx:constraintRows>

        <mx:HSlider id="c_slider" change="changeColumnProportion()" value="5"/>
        <mx:HSlider id="r_slider" x="200" change="changeRowProportion()" value="5"/>

        <mx:Text text="{txt}" left="leftCol:0" right="leftCol:0" top="row2:0" bottom=
    "row2:0"/>

        <mx:Text text="{txt}" left="rightCol:0" right="rightCol:0" top="row2:0" bottom=
    "row2:0"/>

    </mx:Canvas>

    </mx:Application>
```

3.8 Create Layout Flows for Text Using Constraints

Problem

You want to create a layout flow for multiple sections of text.

Solution

Create and add `ConstraintColumn` and `ConstraintRow` objects to a `Canvas` Canvascomponent and use them to set constraints for the children.

Discussion

All containers that support constraints possess two arrays to keep track of the columns and rows added to that `Canvas`. Adding a created constraint to its respective array is all that's needed to ensure that any child component can access that constraint for its own properties. This recipe's example uses constraints to control layout flow. First, multiple `ConstraintColumn` and `ConstraintRow` objects are created, and then they're added to the `constraintRows` and `constraintColumns` properties of a `Canvas`.

To use a constraint for a dynamically generated `UIComponent` object, use the `setStyle` method to set the constraint. The example accesses the constraint dynamically from the array of `ConstraintColumn` objects, using

```
    text.setStyle("left", constraintColumn.id+":10");
```

or a slightly more convoluted syntax to ensure access of the correct column:

```
    child.setStyle("left", (constraintColumns[i-(constraintColumns.length/2)-2] as
    ConstraintColumn).id+":10");
```

In the full listing that follows, `ConstraintColumn` objects are generated and the new children are assigned style properties based on them. When the new rows are added, the children are restyled to modify their positions to use the new rows, and any unused

ConstraintColumn objects are removed from the `Container.constraintColumns` array by simply shortening the array.

```
<mx:Canvas xmlns:mx="http://www.adobe.com/2006/mxml" width="1000" height="800">
    <mx:Script>
        <![CDATA[
            import mx.core.UIComponent;
            import mx.controls.TextArea;
            import mx.containers.utilityClasses.ConstraintColumn;

            [Bindable]
            public var txt:String = "Cortázar is highly regarded as a master of short
stories of a fantastic bent, with the collections Bestiario (1951)" +
            " and Final de Juego (1956) containing many of his best examples in the
genre, including the remarkable \"Continuidad de los Parques\"" +
            " and \"Axolotl.\";

            private function addText(event:Event):void
            {
                var text:TextArea = new TextArea();
                addChild(text);
                text.text = txt;
                var constraintColumn:ConstraintColumn = new ConstraintColumn();
                constraintColumn.id = "column"+numChildren.toString();
                constraintColumns.push(constraintColumn);
                if(constraintColumns.length > 1)
                {
                    for each(var col:ConstraintColumn in constraintColumns){
                        col.width = (width / (numChildren-2));
                    }
                }
                constraintColumn.width = (width / (numChildren-2));
                text.setStyle("top", "row:30");
                text.setStyle("bottom", "row:30");
                text.setStyle("left", constraintColumn.id+":10");
                text.setStyle("right", constraintColumn.id+":10");
            }

            private function addRow(event:Event):void
            {
                var constraintRow:ConstraintRow = new ConstraintRow();
                constraintRows.push(constraintRow);
                constraintRow.id = "row"+constraintRows.length;
                for each(var row:ConstraintRow in constraintRows){
                    row.height = (height / (constraintRows.length-1));
                }
                var i:int = Math.round(numChildren - (numChildren-2)/constraintRows.le
ngth);
                while(i < numChildren){
                    var child:UIComponent = (getChildAt(i) as UIComponent);
                    child.setStyle("top", "row"+constraintRows.length+":30");
                    child.setStyle("bottom", "row"+constraintRows.length+":30");
                    child.setStyle("left", (constraintColumns[i-(constraintColumns.
length/2)-2] as ConstraintColumn).id+":10");
                    child.setStyle("right", (constraintColumns[i-(constraintColumns.
```

```
length/2)-2] as ConstraintColumn).id+":10");
                    i++;
            }
                constraintColumns.length = constraintColumns.length / constraintRows.
length;
        }

    ]]>
</mx:Script>
<mx:constraintRows>
    <mx:ConstraintRow id="row" height="100%"/>
</mx:constraintRows>
<mx:Button click="addText(event)" label="add text"/>
<mx:Button click="addRow(event)" label="add row" x="150"/>
</mx:Canvas>
```

3.9 Control Scrolling and Overflow Within Containers

Problem

You want to disable vertical scroll bars for a container and create regions on a component that the user can mouse over to control the scrolling.

Solution

Use the `horizontalScrollPolicy`, `verticalScrollPolicy`, and `verticalScrollPosition` properties.

Discussion

You control scroll bars through the `horizontalScrollPolicy` and `verticalScrollPolicy` properties. Use the `on` setting for either or both if you want one or both scroll bars to always appear, and use `off` if you never want scroll bars. The `auto` setting causes the scroll bar to appear when the container measures larger than its specified width or height. For example, setting `horizontalScrollPolicy` to `auto` means a scroll bar would appear when the container's width becomes wider than the `width` setting.

To scroll a component, use the `horizontalScrollPosition` and *verticalScrollPosition* properties. With these, you can set how far the component scrolls between the left or top edge of the component's content area and the visible top or left edge. For example:

```
<mx:HBox xmlns:mx="http://www.adobe.com/2006/mxml" width="600" height="200" horizontal
ScrollPolicy="auto" verticalScrollPolicy="off" mouseMove="autoScroll(event)">
    <mx:Script>
        <![CDATA[

            private var hasAddedScroll:Boolean = false;
```

```
            private function autoScroll(event:MouseEvent):void
            {
                if(mouseX > width - 50 && !hasAddedScroll)
                {
                    addEventListener(Event.ENTER_FRAME, scrollRight);
                    hasAddedScroll = true;
                }
                else if(mouseX < 50 && !hasAddedScroll)
                {
                    addEventListener(Event.ENTER_FRAME, scrollLeft);
                    hasAddedScroll = true;
                }
                else
                {
                    removeEventListener(Event.ENTER_FRAME, scrollRight);
                    removeEventListener(Event.ENTER_FRAME, scrollLeft);
                    hasAddedScroll = false;
                }
            }

            private function scrollRight(event:Event):void
            {
                if(horizontalScrollPosition < maxHorizontalScrollPosition)
                {
                    horizontalScrollPosition+=4;
                }
                else
                {
                    removeEventListener(Event.ENTER_FRAME, scrollRight);
                    hasAddedScroll = false;
                }
            }

            private function scrollLeft(event:Event):void
            {
                if(horizontalScrollPosition > 0)
                {
                    horizontalScrollPosition-=4;
                }
                else
                {
                    removeEventListener(Event.ENTER_FRAME, scrollLeft);
                    hasAddedScroll = false;
                }
            }
        ]]>
    </mx:Script>
    <mx:Image source="@Embed('assets/image.png')"/>
    <mx:Image source="@Embed('assets/image.png')"/>
    <mx:Image source="@Embed('assets/image.png')"/>
    <mx:Image source="@Embed('assets/image.png')"/>
    <mx:Image source="@Embed('assets/image.png')"/>
</mx:HBox>
```

3.10 Control the Layout of Box Components

Problem

You want to change the layout of a Box component from vertical to horizontal, as well as control the vertical and horizontal gap in components and centering of children.

Solution

Use the `verticalAlign` and `horizontalAlign` properties and set the layout direction of the Box by using the `direction` property.

Discussion

The `mx.containers.Box` class defines several properties that control the layout of the children within the Box. These are as follows:

direction
: Determines how the container lays out its children. Can be either `vertical` or `horizontal`.

horizontalAlign
: Determines the alignment of the children horizontally and can be set to `left`, `right`, or `center`.

horizontalGap
: Determines the gap between children if the `direction` property is set to `horizontal`. If `direction` isn't set to `horizontal`, the `horizontalGap` property is ignored.

verticalAlign
: Determines the alignment of the children vertically and can be set to `top`, `bottom`, or `center`.

verticalGap
: Determines the gap between children if the `direction` property is set to `vertical`. If `direction` is not set to `vertical`, then the `verticalGap` property is ignored.

In the following example, all the properties are bound to controls so they can be changed dynamically for demonstration:

```
<mx:HSlider change="{vbox.verticalGap = vSlider.value*10}" id="vSlider"/>
    <mx:VBox y="100" direction="{_direction}" id="vbox">
        <mx:Panel width="90" height="60">
            <mx:Label text="Some Text" />
        </mx:Panel>
        <mx:Panel width="90" height="60">
            <mx:Label text="Some Text" />
        </mx:Panel>
        <mx:Panel width="90" height="60">
            <mx:Label text="Some Text" />
```

```
        </mx:Panel>
        <mx:Panel width="90" height="60">
            <mx:Label text="Some Text" />
        </mx:Panel>
        <mx:Panel width="90" height="60">
            <mx:Label text="Some Text" />
        </mx:Panel>
    </mx:Box>
```

Because verticalGap is a bindable property and not a style, you can set it dynamically at runtime without needing a call to setStyle().

3.11 Use Containers for Initialization

Problem

To improve application responsiveness, you want to ensure that all the children of a container are created as soon as the application initializes.

Solution

Use the creationPolicy property of the Container class to determine when components will be created.

Discussion

All containers and in fact all UIComponents use a three-step process to create themselves, create all their properties, create their children, and lay themselves out. The first step for any container is to have its constructor called by the Framework and dispatch the preinitialize event. The second step is for any children of the component to be pre-initialized, all the way down until the deepest child is preinitialized. The third step is for the deepest child to be initialized, and this process repeats up to the parent container. After the parent container is initialized, the child dispatches the creationComplete event, the next child up dispatches the creationComplete event, and so on, all the way up to the last parent container. This briefly shows the initialization sequence:

```
<mx:HBox>
    <mx:VBox>
        <mx:Panel/>
        <mx:Panel/>
    </mx:VBox>
</mx:HBox>
```

initializes in the following order:

```
HBox preinitialize
    VBox preinitialize
        FirstPanel preinitialize
        SecondPanel preinitialize
```

```
        FirstPanel initialize
        SecondPanel initialize
    VBox initialize
HBox initialize
        FirstPanel creationComplete
        SecondPanel creationComplete
    VBox creationComplete
HBox creationComplete
```

When a component dispatches the `preinitialize` and `initialize` events, its children components have not yet been created. Therefore, to access all the children of a component, you must listen for the `creationComplete` event. After the `initialize` event has been dispatched, the component has been measured, drawn, and laid out, but the children may not yet have been fully instantiated. Finally, the `creationComplete` event indicates that all children within that component have been fully instantiated.

3.12 Create a TitleWindow

Problem

You want to create a `TitleWindow` component to display a dialog box and use the `PopUpManager` to remove a dialog box if certain criteria are met.

Solution

Use the `TitleWindow` component, which extends the `Panel` and adds additional functionality that enables you to set a title for the window and provide style information for the border.

Discussion

In this example, `TitleWindow` is used to create a login screen for an application. The `PopUpManager` class provides a way for a component to remove itself from the screen through the `PopUpManager.removePopUp` method:

```
PopUpManager.removePopUp(this);
```

This assumes that the `TitleWindow` component was added through the `PopUpManager`.

```
<mx:TitleWindow xmlns:mx="http://www.adobe.com/2006/mxml" borderColor="#0000ff"
backgroundAlpha="0.6" title="Title Window" x="168" y="86">
    <mx:Script>
        <![CDATA[
            import mx.managers.PopUpManager;
            import mx.controls.Text;

            // A reference to the TextInput control in which to put the result.
            public var loginName:Text;
                public var loggedIn:Boolean;

            // Event handler for the OK button.
```

```
        private function returnName():void {
            loginName.text="Name entered: " + userName.text;
            PopUpManager.removePopUp(this);
        }

        private function checkUserNameAndPass():void
        {
            /* Do some processing */
        }

        /* have this handle the event when the server has logged in */
        private function returnValueFromLogin(event:Event):void
        {
            if(loggedIn)
            {
                PopUpManager.removePopUp(this);
            }
            else
            {
                successText.text = "User/Pass not recognized";
            }
        }

    ]]>
</mx:Script>
<mx:HBox>
    <mx:Label text="Username "/>
    <mx:TextInput id="userName" width="100%"/>
</mx:HBox>
<mx:HBox>
    <mx:Label text="Password"/>
    <mx:TextInput id="password" width="100%"/>
</mx:HBox>
<mx:HBox>
    <mx:Button label="Enter" click="checkUserNameAndPass();"/>
    <mx:Button label="Cancel" click="PopUpManager.removePopUp(this);"/>
</mx:HBox>
<mx:Text id="successText" color="#ff0000"/>
</mx:TitleWindow>
```

3.13 Control a ViewStack via a LinkBar

Problem

You want to control a ViewStack by using a LinkBar component.

Solution

Use either the selectedIndex or selectedItem property of LinkBar to determine which
item in the ViewStack should be displayed.

Discussion

The LinkBar lets you pass an array as a data provider, or you can pass a container with multiple children (such as a ViewStack), and the LinkBar will interpret it as the data provider. The second case is the most useful for this recipe. When you pass a container, the selected item that will be displayed in the container is automatically bound to the selected item of the LinkBar control. This means that you can pass a container with multiple children to the LinkBar and have the children used to populate the LinkBar. The LinkBar automatically adds the correct number of buttons for children in the ViewStack and wires an event to each of those buttons to set the ViewStack's selected Child property correctly.

```
<mx:Canvas xmlns:mx="http://www.adobe.com/2006/mxml" width="800" height="600">
    <mx:LinkBar dataProvider="{viewStack}" direction="horizontal" labelField="name"/>
    <mx:ViewStack id="viewStack" y="60">
        <mx:Panel width="150" height="150" name="first" label="First Panel" title=
"First Panel">
            <mx:Label text="First label"/>
        </mx:Panel>
        <mx:Panel width="150" height="150" name="second" label="Second Panel" title=
"Second Panel">
            <mx:Label text="Second label"/>
        </mx:Panel>
        <mx:Panel width="150" height="150" name="third" label="Third Panel" title=
"Third Panel">
            <mx:Label text="Third label"/>
        </mx:Panel>
    </mx:ViewStack>
</mx:Canvas>
```

See Also

Recipe 3.16.

3.14 Bind the Selected Index of a ViewStack to a Variable

Problem

You need to bind the selectedIndex property of a ViewStack to an integer that can be changed elsewhere in the component.

Solution

Create a variable that is marked as bindable and bind the selected index of a View Stack control to that variable.

Discussion

In the case of the LinkBar control, the selected item of ViewStack is automatically bound to the selected item of the LinkBar. When you use other controls, the selected index or selected item of a ViewStack or other control that contains multiple children but displays them one at a time needs to bound to a bindable variable or set on an event. To control a ViewStack through another means, bind the selectedIndex of the ViewStack to a variable and change the variable at runtime as shown:

```
<mx:Canvas xmlns:mx="http://www.adobe.com/2006/mxml" width="400" height="300" click=
"changeViewStack()">
    <mx:Script>
        <![CDATA[

            [Bindable]
            private var selectedIndexInt:int = 0;

            private function changeViewStack():void
            {
                if(selectedIndexInt == 2)
                {
                    selectedIndexInt = 0;
                }
                else
                {
                    selectedIndexInt++;
                }
            }

        ]]>
    </mx:Script>
    <mx:ViewStack selectedIndex="{selectedIndexInt}">
        <mx:HBox height="{this.height}" width="{this.width}">
            <mx:Label text="First View Item"/>
            <mx:Label text="First View Item"/>
        </mx:HBox>
        <mx:VBox height="{this.height}" width="{this.width}">
            <mx:Label text="Second View Item"/>
            <mx:Label text="Second View Item"/>
        </mx:VBox>
        <mx:Canvas height="{this.height}" width="{this.width}">
            <mx:Label text="Third View Item"/>
            <mx:Label text="Third View Item" y="40"/>
        </mx:Canvas>
    </mx:ViewStack>
</mx:Canvas>
```

See Also

Recipe 3.17.

3.15 Use Delayed Instantiation to Improve Startup Time

Problem

You want to ensure that components are created only when they are needed for display on the screen.

Solution

Set the creation policy of the `Container` class to `queued` and use `creationIndex` for each child if necessary.

Discussion

The default behavior of the `Container` class is to create components only when they are displayed, because the default value of `creationPolicy` for the `UIComponent` is `auto`. In other words, when the view is set to visible, if it has not been created, the component will instantiate that view. The other possible values for `creationPolicy` are `none`, which means no components will be created, `all`, which means all components will be created, and `queued`, which means that components will be created according to their `creation Index`. The `creationIndex` is a zero-based array of the order in which the children of a component will be created.

In the following example, `creationPolicy` is set by using a `ComboBox`:

```
<mx:Canvas xmlns:mx="http://www.adobe.com/2006/mxml" height="600" width="600">
    <mx:Script>
        <![CDATA[

            private function changeViewStackCreation():void
            {
                viewStack.creationPolicy = (comboBox.selectedItem as String);
                viewStack.createComponentsFromDescriptors(true);
            }


            private function changeViewStack():void
            {
                viewStack.selectedIndex = comboBoxChangeIndex.selectedIndex;
            }
        ]]>
    </mx:Script>
    <mx:Fade alphaFrom="0" alphaTo="1" duration="4000" id="fadeIn"/>
    <mx:ComboBox dataProvider="{['none', 'all', 'queued', 'auto']}" change="changeView
StackCreation()" id="comboBox"/>
    <mx:ComboBox dataProvider="{[1, 2, 3, 4]}" change="changeViewStack()" id="comboBox
ChangeIndex" x="150"/>
    <mx:ViewStack id="viewStack" width="400" height="300" creationPolicy="none"
y="100">
        <mx:Canvas creationCompleteEffect="{fadeIn}" creationIndex="0" backgroundColor
="#0000ff" id="canvas1">
```

```
        <mx:LinkButton label="Link Button Number One"/>
    </mx:Canvas>
    <mx:Canvas creationCompleteEffect="{fadeIn}" creationIndex="1" backgroundColor
="#0000ff" id="canvas2">
        <mx:LinkButton label="Link Button Number Two"/>
    </mx:Canvas>
    <mx:Canvas creationIndex="2" creationCompleteEffect="{fadeIn}" backgroundColor
="#0000ff" id="canvas3">
        <mx:LinkButton label="Link Button Number Three"/>
    </mx:Canvas>
    <mx:Canvas creationIndex="3" creationCompleteEffect="{fadeIn}" backgroundColor
="#0000ff" id="canvas4">
        <mx:LinkButton label="Link Button Number Four"/>
    </mx:Canvas>
  </mx:ViewStack>
</mx:Canvas>
```

3.16 Create and Control Resizable Containers

Problem

You need to create a container that can be resized by dragging an icon in the corner.

Solution

Use the MouseEvent classes to listen for mouseDown, mouseMove, and mouseUp events on a drag icon. Reset the size of the container when the drag icon is released.

Discussion

By adding event listeners for these events both in MXML and ActionScript, you can listen for the mouseDown event on the Icon object. When the mouseDown event is captured, an event listener is added for any mouse movement on the Stage that will let the listener capture any mouse movement and determine when the user is resizing the Container. By using the startDrag and stopDrag methods of the UIComponent class, you can set when the UIComponent that represents the resizing icon is being dragged and not. In the following example, the position of the icon is used to set the new height and width of the Canvas via the explicitWidth and explicitHeight setters:

```
<mx:Canvas xmlns:mx="http://www.adobe.com/2006/mxml" width="400" height="300"
    backgroundColor="#ccccff" verticalScrollPolicy="off" horizontalScrollPolicy="off">
    <mx:Script>
        <![CDATA[

            private function startResize():void
            {
                stage.addEventListener(MouseEvent.MOUSE_MOVE, resize);
                resizeIcon.addEventListener(MouseEvent.MOUSE_UP, stopResize);
                resizeIcon.addEventListener(MouseEvent.ROLL_OUT, stopResize);
                resizeIcon.startDrag();
            }
```

When the user holds down the mouse button, all mouseMove events on the Stage are captured. When the user releases the mouse button, all the event listeners are removed and the stopDrag method of the resizeIcon is called. This prevents the icon from moving, and stops the resize method of this component from being called.

```
private function stopResize(mouseEvent:MouseEvent):void
{
    resizeIcon.removeEventListener(MouseEvent.MOUSE_UP, stopResize);
    resizeIcon.removeEventListener(MouseEvent.ROLL_OUT, stopResize);
    stage.removeEventListener(MouseEvent.MOUSE_MOVE, resize);
    resizeIcon.stopDrag();
}
```

The explicitHeight and explicitWidth properties of the component specify the size of the component in pixels irrespective of any measuring or resizing logic within the Flex Framework:

```
private function resize(mouseEvent:MouseEvent):void
{
    this.explicitHeight = resizeIcon.y + resizeIcon.height + 10;
    this.explicitWidth = resizeIcon.x + resizeIcon.width + 10;
}
```

```
        ]]>
    </mx:Script>
    <mx:Panel width="60%" height="60%" top="20" left="20"/>
    <mx:Image id="resizeIcon" source="@Embed('../../assets/Resize.png')" mouseDown=
"startResize()" x="360" y="260"/>
</mx:Canvas>
```

See Also

Recipe 3.9.

3.17 Create, Enable, and Disable TabControls Within a TabNavigator

Problem

You need to dynamically add and remove tabs from a TabNavigator, as well as occasionally disable tabs.

Solution

Use the addChild and removeChild methods of the TabNavigator to add or remove children, and set the enabled property on the child itself to enable or disable the tab in the TabNavigator.

Discussion

Any child added to a TabNavigator adds a new tab to the TabNavigator top navigation bar. Removing a child causes the tab to be automatically removed. Both of these work by using the binding properties of the dataProvider for the TabNavigator. Any changes to the dataProvider cause an update of the TabNavigator and the dynamic addition or subtraction of any children to the top navigation bar. Here, access methods have been created to provide access to the TabNavigator control within the component:

```
<mx:Canvas xmlns:mx="http://www.adobe.com/2006/mxml" width="400" height="300">
    <mx:Script>
        <![CDATA[
            import mx.core.UIComponent;

            public function addChildToNavigator(value:UIComponent):void{
                navigator.addChild(value);
            }

            public function removeNavigatorChild(value:int = 0):void{
                if(value == 0){
                    navigator.removeChildAt(navigator.numChildren-1);
                }
                else
                {
                    navigator.removeChildAt(value);
                }
            }

            public function disableTab(value:int = 0):void{
                if(value == 0){
                    (navigator.getChildAt(navigator.numChildren - 1) as UIComponent).
    enabled = false;
                }
                else
                {
                    (navigator.getChildAt(value) as UIComponent).enabled = false;
                }
            }

            public function get tabNumChildren():Number{
                return navigator.numChildren;
            }

        ]]>
    </mx:Script>
    <mx:TabNavigator id="navigator">

    </mx:TabNavigator>
</mx:Canvas>
```

To use the control, pass any instance of a Container object, in this case Canvas, to the component, calling the method name by using a reference to the id of the component. The label property of the Container passed to the TabNavigator will be used to set the title of the tab that will be added. The `Button` controls here add, remove, and disable the controls.

```
<mx:Application xmlns:mx="http://www.adobe.com/2006/mxml" layout="absolute"
xmlns:cookbook="oreilly.cookbook.*">
    <mx:Script>
        <![CDATA[
            import mx.controls.Label;
            import mx.containers.Canvas;

            private function addCanvas():void
            {
                var canvas:Canvas = new Canvas();
                cavas.title = "Tab "+this.tabNavigator.tabNumChildren.toString();
                var label:Label = new Label();
                label.text = "Hello Label "+this.tabNavigator.tabNumChildren.
toString();
                canvas.addChild(label);

                canvas.minHeight = 200;
                canvas.minWidth = 200;
                this.tabNavigator.addChildToNavigator(canvas);
            }

        ]]>
    </mx:Script>
    <cookbook:TabNavigatorDemo id="tabNavigator"/>
    <mx:HBox y="300">
        <mx:Button click="addCanvas()" label="add child"/>
        <mx:Button click="tabNavigator.removeNavigatorChild()" y="300" label="remove
child"/>
        <mx:Button click="tabNavigator.disableTab()" y="300" label="disable child"/>
    </mx:HBox>
</mx:Application>
```

3.18 Create a TabNavigator with Closeable Tabs

Problem

You need to create a `TabNavigator` that has closeable tabs, that is tabs with close buttons which when clicked will both remove the tab as well as the child at that index within the `TabNavigator`.

Solution

Use the `SuperTabNavigator` component from the flexlib library.

Discussion

The flexlib library is a set of open source controls developed by multiple Flex developers to provide components for use in any Flex project. The `SuperTabNavigator`, developed by Doug McCune and shown next, provides closeable tabs, tab reordering, and a drop-down list in the upper-right corner of the component.

```
<mx:Canvas xmlns:mx="http://www.adobe.com/2006/mxml" width="600" height="600"
xmlns:containers="flexlib.containers.*">
    <containers:SuperTabNavigator>
        <mx:VBox width="500" label="First Label">
            <mx:Label text="Label"/>
            <mx:TextInput/>
        </mx:VBox>
        <mx:VBox height="500" label="Second Label">
            <mx:Label text="Label"/>
            <mx:TextInput/>
        </mx:VBox>
        <mx:VBox label="Third Label">
            <mx:Label text="Label"/>
            <mx:TextInput/>
        </mx:VBox>
    </containers:SuperTabNavigator>
</mx:Canvas>
```

The flexlib library is available for downloading at *http://code.google.com/p/flexlib/*. Download the library and add the unzipped folder as a source folder in the project you've created in Flex Builder or as an option to the MXML compiler.

3.19 Create and Control an Alert

Problem

You need to create an Alert control and to control its display.

Solution

Use the show method of the mx.controls.Alert class and register a callback with that method.

Discussion

You can set all the properties of the Alert control by using the static reference to the mx.controls.Alert class, which will remain until overwritten by different values. For example, after you set the yesLabel property, all Alert controls with yes labels will use that property unless it is overwritten.

The show method of the Alert class requires a message for the alert, a title, a set of values to indicate whether respective Yes, No, or Cancel buttons will be displayed, the parent of the alert, a callback to handle when the alert is closed, and an icon to display in the alert. For example:

```
mx.controls.Alert.show("This is an alert", "title of the alert", 1|2|8, this,
alertClosed, iconclass);
```

All the parameters except the first two are optional. By default, the alert will display a button labeled OK, which will close the alert when clicked. A complete listing is shown here:

```
<mx:Canvas xmlns:mx="http://www.adobe.com/2006/mxml" width="400" height="300">
    <mx:Script>
        <![CDATA[
            import mx.events.CloseEvent;
            import mx.controls.Alert;

            [Embed(source="../../assets/4.png")]
            private var iconclass:Class

            private function createAlert():void
            {
                mx.controls.Alert.buttonHeight = 20;
                mx.controls.Alert.buttonWidth = 150;
                mx.controls.Alert.yesLabel = "Click Yes?"
                mx.controls.Alert.noLabel = "Click No?"
                mx.controls.Alert.cancelLabel = "Click Cancel?"
                mx.controls.Alert.show("This is an alert", "title of the alert",
1|2|8, this, alertClosed, iconclass);
            }

            private function alertClosed(event:CloseEvent):void
            {
                trace(" alert closed ");
                if(event.detail == Alert.YES)
                {
                    trace(" user clicked yes ");
                }
                else if(event.detail == Alert.CANCEL)
                {
                    trace(" user clicked cancle ");
                }
                else
                {
                    trace(" user clicked no ");
                }
            }

        ]]>
    </mx:Script>
    <mx:Button label="Create Simple Alert" click="createAlert()"/>
</mx:Canvas>
```

3.20 Size and Position a Dialog Box Based on Its Calling Component

Problem

You need to make a dialog box that's the same size and position as the component that called it.

Solution

Use the `MouseEvent target` property to determine information about the component that called the method and use the `mx.geometry.Rectangle` class to determine the actual height and width and Stage position of the calling component.

Discussion

To ensure that the dialog box will be added to the application and appear in the correct spot no matter whether the application layout is set to `absolute`, `horizontal`, or `vertical`, you need to create a `TabNavigator` that has closeable tabs that will remove the tab and the child at that index within the `TabNavigator`. Set the dialog box's `includeInLayout` property to `false` to ensure that the application does not modify the dialog box's position.

```
dialogue = new Dialogue();
mx.core.Application.application.rawChildren.addChild(dialogue);
dialogue.includeInLayout = false;
```

The `getBounds` method returns a rectangle with the x and y position and height and width of the `DisplayObject` in the bounds of the object passed into the method. In the example that follows, the Stage is passed as the `DisplayObject` for the `getBounds` method so that the position of the component will be returned in terms of the entire application.

```
<mx:VBox xmlns:mx="http://www.adobe.com/2006/mxml" width="700" height="500" left="50"
top="50" verticalGap="50">
    <mx:Script>
        <![CDATA[
            import mx.core.Application;
            import mx.core.UIComponent;

            private var dialogue:Dialogue;

            private function placeLabel(event:MouseEvent):void
            {
                if(dialogue == null)
                {
                    dialogue = new Dialogue();
                    mx.core.Application.application.rawChildren.addChild(dialogue);
                    dialogue.includeInLayout = false;
                }
                var rect:Rectangle = (event.target as UIComponent).getBounds
```

```
            (this.stage);
                        dialogue.x = rect.x;
                        dialogue.y = rect.y + (event.target as UIComponent).height;
                }
            ]]>
        </mx:Script>
        <mx:HBox horizontalGap="50">
            <mx:Label text="First label."/>
            <mx:Button label="Place First" click="placeLabel(event)"/>
        </mx:HBox>
        <mx:HBox horizontalGap="50">
            <mx:Label text="Second label."/>
            <mx:Button label="Place Second" click="placeLabel(event)"/>
        </mx:HBox>
        <mx:HBox horizontalGap="50">
            <mx:Label text="Third label."/>
            <mx:Button label="Place Third" click="placeLabel(event)"/>
        </mx:HBox>
        <mx:HBox horizontalGap="50">
            <mx:Label text="Fourth label."/>
            <mx:Button label="Place Fourth" click="placeLabel(event)"/>
        </mx:HBox>
    </mx:VBox>
```

3.21 Manage Multiple Pop-up Dialog Boxes

Problem

You need to access and alter multiple dialog boxes.

Solution

Use the `createPopUp` method of the `PopUpManager` class.

Discussion

Accessing and altering multiple dialog boxes requires a reference to the `PopUp` control, which the `PopUpManager.addPopUp` method does not provide. Instead, you need to use the `createPopUp` method of the `PopUpManager` class. This method returns a reference to the object created so you can then add the reference to an array. In a large application, this array should be globally accessible through a public static getter and setter so that any component can access generated pop-ups if necessary. For example:

```
            var pop:Panel = (PopUpManager.createPopUp(this, mx.containers.Panel,
        false, PopUpManagerChildList.POPUP) as Panel);
```

The `createPopUp` method requires a reference to a parent container, a class to generate the pop-up, and a Boolean value to determine whether the pop-up will be a modal dialog box and returns a reference to the object created. The object can then have properties set on it if necessary.

The following example uses an array to store all the pop-ups created by the PopUpManager so that they can be accessed later:

```
<mx:HBox xmlns:mx="http://www.adobe.com/2006/mxml" width="600" height="500"
creationComplete="addDialog()">
    <mx:Script>
        <![CDATA[
            import mx.managers.PopUpManagerChildList;
            import mx.controls.LinkButton;
            import mx.containers.Panel;
            import mx.managers.PopUpManager;

            public var popUpArray:Array = new Array();

            private function addDialog():void
            {
                var pop:Panel = (PopUpManager.createPopUp(this, mx.containers.Panel,
false, PopUpManagerChildList.POPUP) as Panel);
                pop.title = "First Pop Up";
                pop.y = 100;
                popUpArray.push(pop);
                pop = (PopUpManager.createPopUp(this, mx.containers.Panel, false,
PopUpManagerChildList.POPUP) as Panel);
                pop.title = "Second Pop Up";
                pop.y = 200;
                popUpArray.push(pop);
                pop = (PopUpManager.createPopUp(this, mx.containers.Panel, false,
PopUpManagerChildList.POPUP) as Panel);
                pop.title = "Third Pop Up";
                pop.y = 300;
                popUpArray.push(pop);
            }

            private function returnDialog():void
            {
                var link:LinkButton = new LinkButton();
                link.label = "Hello";
                (popUpArray[selectDialog.selectedIndex] as Panel).addChild(link);
            }

        ]]>
    </mx:Script>
    <mx:ComboBox id="selectDialog" change="returnDialog()">
        <mx:dataProvider>
            <mx:Array>
                <mx:Number>0</mx:Number>
                <mx:Number>1</mx:Number>
                <mx:Number>2</mx:Number>
            </mx:Array>
        </mx:dataProvider>
    </mx:ComboBox>
    <mx:Panel>
        <mx:LinkButton label="Button"/>
    </mx:Panel>
    <mx:Panel>
```

```
        <mx:LinkButton label="Button"/>
    </mx:Panel>
</mx:HBox>
```

3.22 Scroll to a Specific Child in a Container

Problem

You need to control the default scrolling behavior on a container and control the scrolling through a separate control.

Solution

Use the getChildAt method to get all the children up to the desired index of the child to which you wish to scroll and sum the heights of those children. Use that value to set the verticalScrollPosition of the container.

Discussion

In the following example, the VBox that contains the children has its verticalScrollPo licy set to off and an event listener bound to the change property of the ComboBox. When the change event is fired, the function loops through all the children of the VBox, summing the children until the desired child is found. This value is used to set the verticalScrollPolicy of the VBox.

```
<mx:Canvas xmlns:mx="http://www.adobe.com/2006/mxml" width="800" height="600">
    <mx:Script>
        <![CDATA[

            private function showScrollValue():void
            {
                trace(this.verticalScrollPosition+" "+this.horizontalScrollPosition);
            }

            private function changeScrollToShowChild():void
            {
                vbox.verticalScrollPosition = (returnChildrenHeights((comboBox.
selectedItem as Number)+1)) - vbox.height;
            }
```

The height of all the children within the VBox is calculated and used to determine the y value that the verticalScrollPosition will need to be set to in order to scroll to the correct child.

```
            private function returnChildrenHeights(index:int):Number
            {
                var i:int = 0;
                var sumHeight:Number = 0;
                while(i<index)                    {
                    sumHeight+=vbox.getChildAt(i).height;
                    i++;
```

```
                    }
                    return sumHeight;
                }

        ]]>
    </mx:Script>
    <mx:ComboBox id="comboBox" change="changeScrollToShowChild()">
        <mx:dataProvider>
            <mx:Array>
                <mx:Number>1</mx:Number>
                <mx:Number>2</mx:Number>
                <mx:Number>3</mx:Number>
                <mx:Number>4</mx:Number>
                <mx:Number>5</mx:Number>
            </mx:Array>
        </mx:dataProvider>
    </mx:ComboBox>
    <mx:VBox width="650" height="300" id="vbox" backgroundColor="#00ffff" y="50"
verticalScrollPolicy="off" scroll="showScrollValue()" paddingLeft="50">
        <mx:Panel height="150" width="550">
            <mx:LinkButton label="First"/>
        </mx:Panel>
        <mx:Panel height="160" width="550">
            <mx:LinkButton label="Second"/>
        </mx:Panel>
        <mx:Panel height="110" width="550">
            <mx:LinkButton label="Third"/>
        </mx:Panel>
        <mx:Panel height="150" width="550">
            <mx:LinkButton label="Fourth"/>
        </mx:Panel>
        <mx:Panel height="130" width="550">
            <mx:LinkButton label="Fifth"/>
        </mx:Panel>
    </mx:VBox>
</mx:Canvas>
```

3.23 Create a Template Using IDeferredInstance

Problem

You want to create a template component to handle multiple types of components passed to it as well as delay instantiation until the component is created to improve startup times.

Solution

Use the IDeferredInstance marker to specify that an array or property will handle any component type passed to it, creating its children when the component's instantiated.

Discussion

The IDeferredInstance interface is implemented by all UIComponents and allows the child to be added to an array and instantiated later when the parent component is initialized. All components passed to an array typed as IDeferredInstance will be stored until they are added to the display list, as the example demonstrates:

```
<mx:VBox xmlns:mx="http://www.adobe.com/2006/mxml">
    <mx:Script>
        <![CDATA[
            import mx.containers.HBox;
            import mx.containers.ViewStack;
            import mx.core.UIComponent;

            // Define a deferred property for the top component.
            public var header:IDeferredInstance;
            // Define an Array of deferred properties
            // for a row of components.
            [ArrayElementType("mx.core.IDeferredInstance")]
            public var leftDataRow:Array;

            [ArrayElementType("mx.core.IDeferredInstance")]
            public var centerDataRow:Array;

            [ArrayElementType("mx.core.IDeferredInstance")]
            public var rightDataRow:Array;

            public var layoutHBox:HBox;

            public var layoutWidth:int = 0;

            public function createDeferredComponents():void {
                addChild(UIComponent(header.getInstance()));

                layoutHBox = new HBox();

                if(layoutWidth != 0){
                    layoutHBox.setStyle("horizontalGap", layoutWidth);
                }

                if(leftDataRow.length > 0){
                    var leftVBox:VBox = new VBox();
                    layoutHBox.addChild(leftVBox);
                    for (var i:int = 0; i < leftDataRow.length; i++){
                        leftVBox.addChild(UIComponent(leftDataRow[i].getInstance()));
                    }
                }
                if(centerDataRow.length > 0){
                    var centerVBox:VBox = new VBox();
                    layoutHBox.addChild(centerVBox);
                    for (var i:int = 0; i < centerDataRow.length; i++){
                        centerVBox.addChild(UIComponent(centerDataRow[i].
getInstance()));
                    }
                }
```

```
                if(rightDataRow.length > 0){
                    var rightVBox:VBox = new VBox();
                    layoutHBox.addChild(rightVBox);
                    for (var i:int = 0; i < rightDataRow.length; i++){
                        rightVBox.addChild(UIComponent(rightDataRow[i].
getInstance()));
                    }
                }
                // Add the HBox container to the VBox container.
                addChild(layoutHBox);
            }
        ]]>
    </mx:Script>
</mx:VBox>
```

As you can see in the following example, you can pass any array of objects that extend IDeferredInstance to the component and then later call a method to add those children to the displayList. In this example, the method is called explicitly, though it could be wired to an asynchronous event or any other event.

```
<mx:Canvas xmlns:mx="http://www.adobe.com/2006/mxml" width="700" height="500"
xmlns:cookbook="oreilly.cookbook.*">
    <mx:Script>
        <![CDATA[

            private function createDeferredInstance():void
            {
                this.deferredInstance.createDeferredComponents();
            }

        ]]>
    </mx:Script>
    <mx:Button click="createDeferredInstance()" label="make components"/>
    <cookbook:DeferredInstance layoutWidth="30" id="deferredInstance">
        <cookbook:header>
            <mx:Label text="This will be the header of my templated component"/>
        </cookbook:header>
        <cookbook:leftDataRow>
            <mx:Array>
                <mx:Label text="data"/>
                <mx:Label text="data"/>
                <mx:Label text="data"/>
            </mx:Array>
        </cookbook:leftDataRow>
        <cookbook:centerDataRow>
            <mx:Array>
                <mx:Button label="press me"/>
                <mx:Label text="data"/>
            </mx:Array>
        </cookbook:centerDataRow>
        <cookbook:rightDataRow>
            <mx:Array>
                <mx:CheckBox label="click"/>
                <mx:Button label="press me"/>
                <mx:Label text="data"/>
```

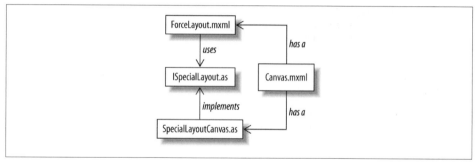

Figure 3-1. Relationships between containers and interfaces

```
            </mx:Array>
        </cookbook:rightDataRow>
    </cookbook:DeferredInstance>
</mx:Canvas>
```

3.24 Manually Lay Out a Container

Problem

You need to lay out the children of a container according to their type and properties of their type.

Solution

Override the `updateDisplayList` method of the `UIComponent` class to move the children.

Discussion

To override any layout or sizing logic in any `Container` or `UIComponent` object, override the `updateDisplayList` method and insert your own layout logic after the call to the `super.updateDisplayList` method. This recipe concentrates on how to lay out the children of an `HBox` by using custom properties on children to determine the layout.

The example consists of four files, three classes, and one interface, with distinct responsibilities and properties. The rough Universal Modeling Language (UML) diagram of Figure 3-1 describes the relationship.

The Canvas.mxml file adds the `ForceLayout` component and provides it with its children. The `ForceLayout` component can have any children, but if the child implements the `ISpecialLayout` interface, the `ForceLayout` component will lay out that component differently depending on whether it is selected. The `SpecialLayoutCanvas` simply defines methods to determine whether it has been selected.

First, look at the SpecialLayoutCanvas.as file:

```
package oreilly.cookbook
{
```

```
import mx.containers.Canvas;
import mx.controls.Label;
import mx.core.UIComponent;
import flash.events.MouseEvent;

public class SpecialLayoutCanvas extends Canvas implements ISpecialLayout
{
    private var titlelabel:Label;
    private var selectedlabel:Label;
    private var _isSelected:Boolean = false;

    public function SpecialLayoutCanvas()
    {
        super();
        titlelabel = new Label();
        addChild(titlelabel);
        titlelabel.text = "Label";
        this.addEventListener(MouseEvent.MOUSE_DOWN, setIsSelected);
        minHeight = 45;
        minWidth = 80;
        selectedlabel = new Label();
        //addChild(selectedlabel);
        selectedlabel.text = "Selected";
    }

    private function setIsSelected(mouseEvent:MouseEvent):void
    {
        _isSelected ? isSelected = false : isSelected = true;
    }

    public function set isSelected(value:Boolean):void
    {
        _isSelected = value;
        if(isSelected)
        {
            addChild(selectedlabel);
            selectedlabel.y = 30;
        }
        else
        {
            try{
            removeChild(selectedlabel);
            }catch(err:Error){}
        }
        if(parent != null)
        {
            (parent as UIComponent).invalidateDisplayList();
        }
    }

    public function get isSelected():Boolean
    {
        return _isSelected;
    }
```

```
        }
    }
```

This class simply defines a `selected` property by using a getter and setter and adds a label if the object is selected or removes the label if it is not.

Next, consider the `ForceLayout` component, which reads all its children to determine if any implement the `ISpecialLayout` interface, and if so, whether they're selected.

```
package oreilly.cookbook
{
    import mx.core.EdgeMetrics;
    import mx.core.UIComponent;
    import mx.containers.VBox;
    import mx.containers.Panel;
    import mx.containers.Canvas;
    import flash.display.DisplayObject;

    public class ForceLayout extends VBox
    {
        public var gap:Number;
        public function ForceLayout()
        {
            super();
        }
```

The `updateDisplayList` method is called by the Flex Framework whenever the component needs to be redrawn. Because one of the things that the component needs to do when redrawing is reposition all its children, any repositioning logic is performed here:

```
        override protected function updateDisplayList(unscaledWidth:Number,
    unscaledHeight:Number):void
        {
            super.updateDisplayList(unscaledWidth, unscaledHeight);
            var yPos:Number = unscaledHeight;
            // Temp variable for a container child.
            var child:UIComponent;
            var i:int = 0;
            while(i<this.numChildren)
            {
                // Get the first container child.
                child = UIComponent(getChildAt(i));
                // Determine the y coordinate of the child.
                yPos = yPos - child.height;
                // Set the x and y coordinate of the child.
                // Note that you do not change the x coordinate.
                if(child is ISpecialLayout)
                {
                    if((child as ISpecialLayout).isSelected)
                    {
                        yPos -= 20;
                        child.move(child.x, yPos);
                        yPos -= 20;
                    }
                    else
                    {
```

```
                child.move(child.x, yPos);
            }
        }
        else
        {
            child.move(child.x, yPos);
        }
        // Save the y coordinate of the child,
        // plus the vertical gap between children.
        // This is used to calculate the coordinate
        // of the next child.
        yPos = yPos - gap;
        i++;
    }
    i = 0;
    var amountToCenter:Number = yPos / 2;
    while(i<this.numChildren)
    {
        getChildAt(i).y -= amountToCenter;
        i++;
    }
    }
  }
}
```

The final listing puts both components to use, adding the ForceLayout container to a Canvas and adding SpecialLayoutCanvas children to it. Notice that because you're not requiring any special properties, only changing the layout if they're present, any child type can be added to the ForceLayoutCanvas, and in fact any child that implemented the ISpecialLayout interface could be used.

```
<mx:Canvas xmlns:mx="http://www.adobe.com/2006/mxml" width="800" height="600"
xmlns:cookbook="oreilly.cookbook.*">
    <cookbook:ForceLayout width="400" height="500" backgroundColor="#ffffff">
        <mx:HBox>
            <mx:Button label="button"/>
            <mx:LinkButton label="link"/>
        </mx:HBox>
        <cookbook:SpecialLayoutCanvas isSelected="false" backgroundColor="#c0c0cc"/>
        <mx:HBox>
            <mx:Button label="button"/>
            <mx:LinkButton label="link"/>
        </mx:HBox>
        <cookbook:SpecialLayoutCanvas isSelected="false" backgroundColor="#ccc0c0"/>
        <cookbook:SpecialLayoutCanvas isSelected="true" backgroundColor="#cc00cc"/>
        <cookbook:SpecialLayoutCanvas isSelected="false" backgroundColor="#ccc0c0"/>
    </cookbook:ForceLayout>
</mx:Canvas>
```

3.25 Measure and Alter Container Size

Problem

You need to alter the size of a container based on its children.

Solution

Override the container's `measure` property, which is called when the `updateDisplay List` method is called by the Flex Framework.

Discussion

The size of a container is determined by the `measure` method that the Flex Framework calls whenever it needs to determine how large a child is and how large it should be based on all style and constraint information. In much the same way that you overrode the `updateDisplayList` method in Recipe 3.24, you can override the `measure` method to perform any custom calculations that you might need for sizing.

First, you must define the `ExtendableCanvas` class in an MXML file:

```
<mx:HBox xmlns:mx="http://www.adobe.com/2006/mxml">
    <mx:Script>
        <![CDATA[
            import mx.core.Container;
            import mx.core.UIComponent;

            override protected function measure():void
            {
                super.measure();
                var childrenWidth:int = 0;
                var childrenHeight:int = 0;
                //loop through all children, and determine the height and width
                //of all the children components
                for(var i:int = 0; i<this.numChildren; i++)
                {
                    var obj:UIComponent = (getChildAt(i) as UIComponent);
                    if(obj is Container)
                    {
                        //here we are using the viewMetricsAndPadding
                        //so that we get any style information affiliated
                        //with the child as well as its actual width
                        childrenWidth += Container(obj).viewMetricsAndPadding.left+
Container(obj).viewMetricsAndPadding.right+obj.width;
                        childrenHeight += Container(obj).viewMetricsAndPadding.top+
Container(obj).viewMetricsAndPadding.bottom+obj.height;
                    }
                    else
                    {
                        childrenWidth += obj.width;
                        childrenHeight += obj.height;
                    }
```

```
            }
            //set this components measured height based on our calculations
            measuredHeight = childrenHeight;
            measuredWidth = childrenWidth;
        }

    ]]>
    </mx:Script>
</mx:HBox>
```

Next, use the ExtendableCanvas.mxml file in a Canvas, adding children to it to test that it expands properly:

```
<mx:Canvas xmlns:mx="http://www.adobe.com/2006/mxml" width="1400" height="500"
xmlns:cookbook="oreilly.cookbook.*">
    <mx:Script>
        <![CDATA[

            import mx.containers.Panel;

            private function addChildToExtendableCanvas():void
            {
                var panel:Panel = new Panel();
                panel.height = 100 + Math.random()*200;
                panel.width = 100 + Math.random()*200;
                extCanvas.addChild(panel);
            }

        ]]>
    </mx:Script>
    <mx:Button click="addChildToExtendableCanvas()" label="add child"/>
    <cookbook:ExtendableCanvas id="extCanvas" y="50" verticalScrollPolicy="off"
horizontalScrollPolicy="off"/>
</mx:Canvas>
```

As more children are added to the Container, the ExtendableCanvas instance will redraw and resize itself by using the height and width of all children plus the amount specified by the padding style information.

3.26 Control the Visibility and Layout of Children

Problem

You need to remove children from the layout of a container without destroying them.

Solution

Use the includeInLayout property of the UIComponent class and set the visibility to null.

Discussion

The `includeInLayout` property of a child of a container indicates whether that child will be included in whatever layout schema the parent is using to lay out its children: VBox, HBox, or a Canvas with centering set. If you were simply to set the child's visibility to false, it would still be included in the layout mechanism of the parent and be given the amount of space that its width and height require. Instead, set `includeInLayout` to false to ensure that the HBox will not lay out space for the child:

```
(event.target as UIComponent).includeInLayout = false;
```

To reinclude the child in layout, set `includeInLayout` to true. The following example uses the `includeInLayout` property to let the child be dragged. With the child included in the layout of the HBox, the layout management would change the position of the child to conform with its layout. Because the `includeInLayout` property is set to false, the child will be ignored when the HBox sets the x value of all its children components.

```
<mx:HBox xmlns:mx="http://www.adobe.com/2006/mxml" width="600" height="400">
    <mx:Script>
        <![CDATA[
            import mx.core.UIComponent;

            private function removeFromLayout(event:MouseEvent):void
            {
                (event.target as UIComponent).includeInLayout = false;
                (event.target as UIComponent).startDrag();
            }

            private function reincludeInLayout(event:MouseEvent):void
            {
                (event.target as UIComponent).stopDrag();
                (event.target as UIComponent).includeInLayout = true;
            }

            private function hideAndRemoveFromLayout(event:Event):void
            {
                (event.target as UIComponent).visible = false;
                (event.target as UIComponent).includeInLayout = false;
            }

        ]]>
    </mx:Script>
    <mx:VBox>
        <mx:LinkButton id="firstLabel" label="this is the first label" mouseDown=
"removeFromLayout(event)" mouseUp="reincludeInLayout(event)"/>
        <mx:LinkButton id="secondLabel" label="this is the second label" mouseDown=
"removeFromLayout(event)" mouseUp="reincludeInLayout(event)"/>
        <mx:Button id="button" label="My First Button" mouseDown="removeFromLayout
(event)" mouseUp="reincludeInLayout(event)"/>
    </mx:VBox>
    <mx:VBox>
        <mx:Button label="Remove from Layout and Hide" click="hideAndRemoveFromLayout
(event)" borderColor="#0000ff"/>
```

```
        <mx:Button label="Remove from Layout and Hide" click="hideAndRemoveFromLayout
(event)" borderColor="#00ff00"/>
        <mx:Button label="Remove from Layout and Hide" click="hideAndRemoveFromLayout
(event)" borderColor="#ff0000"/>
    </mx:VBox>
</mx:HBox>
```

3.27 Create a Tile Container with Simple Reorganization

Problem

You want to enable users to drag the tiles in a `Tile` container and have the container reorganize when the user drops the tile.

Solution

Use the `swapChildren`method of the `DisplayObjectContainer` class that the `Tile` extends to change the positions of children within the `Tile`.

Discussion

The `Tile` container lays out its children in much the same way as a `Box` container, except that if there is space for a second renderer to fit in the nonprimary direction, the `Tile` container adds multiple `itemRenderers`. If the `Tile` container's `direction` property is set to `horizontal`, for example, and the `Tile` is 400 pixels across, and the items added to the tile are 150 pixels wide, then the tile will add components two across until all the children have been added, providing vertical scroll bars if necessary. Tiles always create grid-like arrangements (Figure 3-2).

In the following example, the `Tile` component is used to arrange its children components. When a child is dropped after dragging, the `Tile` is marked for redrawing by calling the `invalidateDisplayList` method:

```
<mx:Tile xmlns:mx="http://www.adobe.com/2006/mxml" width="300" height="600" direction=
"horizontal">
    <mx:Script>
        <![CDATA[
            import mx.core.UIComponent;

            private function childStartDrag(event:Event):void
            {
                (event.currentTarget as UIComponent).startDrag(false, this.getBounds
(stage));
                (event.currentTarget as UIComponent).addEventListener(MouseEvent.
MOUSE_UP, childStopDrag);
                (event.currentTarget as UIComponent).addEventListener(MouseEvent.
ROLL_OUT, childStopDrag);
                swapChildren((event.currentTarget as UIComponent), getChildAt
(numChildren-1));
            }
```

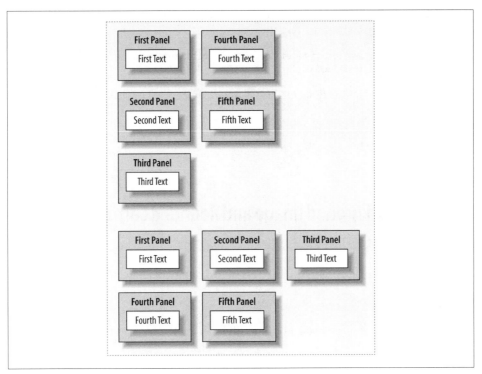

Figure 3-2. Tiles with vertical and horizontal directions

```
private function childStopDrag(event:Event):void
{
    swapChildren((event.currentTarget as UIComponent),
hitTestChild((event.currentTarget as UIComponent)));
    (event.currentTarget as UIComponent).stopDrag();
    this.invalidateDisplayList();
    this.invalidateProperties();
}

private function hitTestChild(obj:UIComponent):DisplayObject
{
    for(var i:int = 0; i<this.numChildren; i++)
    {
        if(this.getChildAt(i).hitTestObject(obj))
        {
            return getChildAt(i);
        }
    }
    return getChildAt(0)
}


    ]]>
</mx:Script>
```

```
        <mx:Panel title="First Panel" mouseDown="childStartDrag(event)">
            <mx:Text text="First Text"/>
        </mx:Panel>
        <mx:Panel title="Second Panel" mouseDown="childStartDrag(event)">
            <mx:Text text="Second Text"/>
        </mx:Panel>
        <mx:Panel title="Third Panel" mouseDown="childStartDrag(event)">
            <mx:Text text="Third Text"/>
        </mx:Panel>
        <mx:Panel title="Fourth Panel" mouseDown="childStartDrag(event)">
            <mx:Text text="Fourth Text"/>
        </mx:Panel>
    </mx:Tile>
```

3.28 Set a Background Image and Rounded Corners in an HBox

Problem

You need to create an HBox with rounded corners that has an image set as a background.

Solution

Load an image object and create a bitmap fill by using the `beginBitmapFill` method.

Discussion

Setting a `cornerRadius` for an HBox gives a rounded corner if the background is not an image. However, after an image is set for the background of the HBox, as shown here

```
<mx:HBox xmlns:mx="http://www.adobe.com/2006/mxml" width="400" height="300" backgroundI
mage="../../assets/beach.jpg" borderStyle="solid"
    borderThickness="0" cornerRadius="20">
```

the corners of the HBox show right-angle edges like the edges of the image. To round the corners of the image, you need to use the image as the fill instead. All UICompo nents possess a `graphics` property, an instance of the `flash.display.Graphic` object, which possesses low-level drawing routines. By using the `beginBitmapFill` method, you can create a fill to use for the **drawRoundRect** complex method, filling the rounded rectangle with the bits of the image that you've loaded. Calling the `endFill` method completes the drawing routine, as shown:

```
this.graphics.beginBitmapFill(bm, m, true, true);
            this.graphics.drawRoundRectComplex(0, 0, this.width, this.height, 20,
    20, 20, 20);
            this.graphics.endFill();
```

A loader loads the image, and then all the data from the loaded image is drawn into a BitmapData object:

```
var bm:BitmapData = new BitmapData(loader.width, loader.height, true, 0x000000);
bm.draw(this.loader);
```

Now you can use the `BitmapData` object to create the fill. The entire sample follows:

```
<mx:HBox xmlns:mx="http://www.adobe.com/2006/mxml" width="400" height="300"
creationComplete="createFill()" cornerRadius="20">
    <mx:Script>
        <![CDATA[

            import flash.net.URLRequest;

            private var loader:Loader;

            private function createFill():void
            {
                loader = new Loader();
                loader.contentLoaderInfo.addEventListener(Event.COMPLETE,
completeLoad);
                loader.load(new URLRequest("../../assets/beach.jpg"));
            }

            private function completeLoad(event:Event):void
            {
                var bm:BitmapData = new BitmapData(loader.width, loader.height,
true,0x000000);
                bm.draw(this.loader);
                var m:Matrix = new Matrix();
                m.createBox(this.width/loader.width, this.height/loader.height);
                this.graphics.beginBitmapFill(bm, m, true, true);
                this.graphics.drawRoundRectComplex(0, 0, this.width, this.height,
20, 20, 20, 20);
                this.graphics.endFill();
            }

        ]]>
    </mx:Script>
</mx:HBox>
```

3.29 Control Positioning and Scrolling of Child Components

Problem

You want to scroll a parent component and move all but one of the children components.

Solution

Reposition the child component based on the `verticalScrollPosition` during the `scrollChildren` method that the container defines.

Discussion

The `scrollChildren` method of the container measures the container's `contentPane`, measures the `DisplayObject`, which contains all the children that have been added to the container, and determines how much of what it measured will be shown by the container during scrolling. The contentPane is moved according to the horizontal ScrollPosition and verticalScrollPosition. The container itself acts as a mask to the contentPane, and the position of the contentPane is determined by the position of the relevant scroll bar and the ViewMetrics properties of the container.

The following code snippet stores the y position of the top component, allowing users to drag the component and still hold top in the correct place and set all other components normally:

```
<mx:Canvas xmlns:mx="http://www.adobe.com/2006/mxml" width="500" height="500">
    <mx:Script>
        <![CDATA[

            private var top:TopComponent;
            //store the y position
            private var topY:Number;

            private function showTop():void
            {
                top = new TopComponent();
                addChild(top);
                top.verticalScrollPolicy = "none";
                top.x = 200;
                top.y = 100;
                topY = top.y;
                top.addEventListener(MouseEvent.MOUSE_DOWN, dragTop);
            }

            private function dragTop(event:Event):void
            {
                top.startDrag(false, this.getBounds(stage));
                top.addEventListener(MouseEvent.MOUSE_UP, stopDragTop);
            }

            private function stopDragTop(event:Event):void
            {
                topY = top.y;
                top.stopDrag();
                top.removeEventListener(MouseEvent.MOUSE_UP, stopDragTop);
            }

            override protected function scrollChildren():void
            {
                super.scrollChildren();
                if(top){
                    top.y = verticalScrollPosition+topY;
                    //
                    top.verticalScrollPosition = this.verticalScrollPosition/height *
    top.height;
                }
            }

        ]]>
```

```
        </mx:Script>
        <mx:Panel>
            <mx:Label text="LABEL BABEL"/>
            <mx:Label text="LABEL BABEL"/>
            <mx:Label text="LABEL BABEL"/>
        </mx:Panel>
        <mx:Panel y="500" height="200">
            <mx:Label text="LABEL BABEL"/>
            <mx:Label text="LABEL BABEL"/>
            <mx:Label text="LABEL BABEL"/>
        </mx:Panel>
        <mx:Button click="showTop()"/>
    </mx:Canvas>
```

This is a little simplistic, and the same sort of logic could be extended to create custom scrolling for all the children of the container. If you knew that all container children within the container would be scrolled, you could override the scrollChildren method as shown here:

```
private var dir:String;
private function handleScroll(event:ScrollEvent):void {
    dir = event.direction;
}

override protected function scrollChildren():void {
    var i:int = 0;
    do{
        var comp:DisplayObject = getChildAt(i);
        if(comp is Container){
            trace( Container(comp).maxVerticalScrollPosition );
            dir == "horizontal" ?
            Container(comp).horizontalScrollPosition = horizontalScrollPosition *
(Container(comp).maxHorizontalScrollPosition/maxHorizontalScrollPosition) :
            Container(comp).verticalScrollPosition = verticalScrollPosition *
(Container(comp).maxVerticalScrollPosition/maxVerticalScrollPosition);
        }
        i++;
    } while (i < numChildren)
}
```

This example uses the maxVerticalScrollPosition and maxHorizontalScrollPosition to calculate the correct amount that each container should scroll. The container determines these properties by subtracting the actual height and width of the container from the height and width of all the children that it contains. In the preceding code snippet, each child's maxVerticalScrollPosition and maxHorizontalScrollPosition is divided by the parent's value to determine the amount that the child should scroll. This ensures that even if the parent is smaller or larger than the child, the corrected value amount will be passed to the child.

CHAPTER 4

Text

To work with text in a Flex application, use these components: `mx.text.Text`, `mx.text.RichTextEditor`, `mx.text.Label`, `mx.text.TextArea`, `mx.text.TextInput`, and `flash.text.TextField`. Each of these components performs different functions in the context of a Flex application. The `TextInput`, `TextArea`, and `RichTextEditor` controls all allow for user interaction and editing. The `TextArea`, `RichTextEditor`, and `Text` controls all handle display of multiline text. Finally, the `flash.text.TextField` class is a low-level class that gives you fine-grained control over the layout and manipulation of the text in the `TextField` but requires a `UIComponent` instance containing it to be used in a Flex application. In fact, each of the Flex controls in the `mx.text` package utilizes the `flash.text.TextField`, adding different functionality to this component.

Flex allows for the display of plain text and a subset of HTML, and the use of both text formatting and CSS styles to control the appearance of text. When using the subset of HTML that is supported by the Flash Player, images and other SWF files can be used to load content into the player. Text formatting, that is, controlling the font size and color, is done by setting properties on the `mx.text` components, through CSS, or for the `flash.text.TextField` component by using the `flash.text.TextFormat` object. Text can be selected by the user or set programmatically by using the `setSelection` method. The recipes in this chapter cover uses of all six of these components.

4.1 Correctly Set the Value of a Text Object

Problem

You need to correctly display HTML and simple strings that may be passed to a `Text` object.

Solution

Use the `htmlText` and `text` properties, depending on the input type, to render the text appropriately and analyze the string being passed to the `Text` object through the use of a regular expression.

Discussion

The Text and TextArea components do not display HTML correctly unless the HTML is passed to the htmlText property of the Text or TextArea component. Usually there is no problem with passing non-HTML text to Text or TextArea, unless there is a possibility that the text may contain HTML characters.

Regular expressions are powerful tools that let you parse text and text patterns quickly and efficiently without tedious string manipulation. The expression looks for a < followed by any number of alphabetic characters, followed by a >:

```
var regexp:RegExp = /<.+\w.>/;
```

This example uses a regular expression to determine whether the string being passed to the Text component contains HTML or XML:

```
<mx:VBox xmlns:mx="http://www.adobe.com/2006/mxml" width="400" height="300">
    <mx:Script>
        <![CDATA[

            private var htmlStr1:String = '<b>Header</b><br/>Hello.<i>Hello.</i>
<font color="#ff0000" size="15">RED</font>';
            private var htmlStr2:String = "<ul><li>Item 1</li><li>Item 2</li><li>
Item3</li></ul>";
            private var textStr1:String = "It is a long established fact that a reader
will be distracted by the readable content of a page when looking at its layout, if
say the amount of text > 100.";
            private var textStr2:String = " We can use <<String>> to indicate in
Erlang that the values being passed are Strings";

            private function setNewText():void
            {
                determineTextType(changeText.selectedItem.value.toString());
            }

            private function determineTextType(str:String):void
            {
```

Here the regular expression is used to determine whether any HTML tags are found in the text by testing for the pattern of a < symbol, followed by any letters, followed by another >:

```
                var regexp:RegExp = /<.+\w.>/;
                if(regexp.test(str))
                {
                    textArea.htmlText = str;
                }
                else
                {
                    textArea.text = str;
                }
            }

        ]]>
    </mx:Script>
```

```
    <mx:ComboBox id="changeText" dataProvider="{[{label:'HTML1', value:htmlStr1},
{label:'HTML2', value:htmlStr2}, {label:'Text1', value:textStr1}, {label:'Text2',
value:textStr2}]}" change="setNewText()"/>
    <mx:TextArea id="textArea" height="100%"/>
</mx:VBox>
```

4.2 Bind a Value to TextInput

Problem

You need to bind the value of a user's input in a TextInput control to another control.

Solution

Use binding tags to bind the text of the TextInput component to the Text component that will display the input.

Discussion

The TextInput control here is used to provide the text that will be displayed in the TextArea control. As the amount of text is increased, the width of the TextArea is increased by using the binding mechanism of the Flex Framework:

```
<mx:VBox xmlns:mx="http://www.adobe.com/2006/mxml" width="400" height="300">
    <mx:TextInput id="input" width="200"/>
    <mx:TextArea text="{input.text}" width="200" id="area" backgroundAlpha="0"
height="{(Math.round(input.text.length/40)+1) * 20}" wordWrap="true"/>
</mx:VBox>
```

TextInput can be bound to a variable and have its value bound as well. This will not set the variable that the TextInput text property is bound to when the user inputs any text, but it will change the text property of any component that is bound to the *TextInput*. For example:

```
<mx:Script>
    <![CDATA[

        [Bindable]
        private var bindableText:String = "Zero Text";

        private function setText():void
        {
            bindableText = String(cb.selectedItem);
        }

    ]]>
</mx:Script>
<mx:ComboBox id="cb" dataProvider="{['First Text', 'Second Text', 'Third Text',
'Fourth Text']}" change="setText()"/>
<mx:TextInput id="inputFromCB" width="200" text="{bindableText}"/>
<mx:Text id="textFromCB" width="200" text="{inputFromCB.text}"/>
```

4.3 Create a Suggestive TextInput

Problem

You want to create a predictive TextInput that will read from a dictionary of words and suggest choices to the user.

Solution

Use the change event of the TextInput component to listen for user input and use a regular expression to test the dictionary for matches to the input.

Discussion

The TextInput component defines a change event that is dispatched every time that the component's value changes. You can use this event to check the input and test it against all the words in the short dictionary. For example:

```
<mx:Canvas xmlns:mx="http://www.adobe.com/2006/mxml" width="400" height="300">
    <mx:Script>
        <![CDATA[

            [Bindable]
            private var probableMatches:Array;

            private var allWords:Array = ["apple", "boy", "cat", "milk", "orange",
"pepper", "recipe", "truck"];
            private var regexp:RegExp;

            private function checkInput():void
            {
                var i:int = 0;
                var temp:Array = allWords.filter(filter);
                input.text = temp[0];
            }

            private function filter(element:*, index:int, arr:Array):Boolean
            {
                regexp = new RegExp(input.text);
                return (regexp.test(element as String));
            }

        ]]>
    </mx:Script>
    <mx:TextInput id="input" change="checkInput()"/>
</mx:Canvas>
```

The filter function used here is a part of the Array class and lets you create a method that will take any object and, after performing any calculation, return a true or false that indicates whether the item should be included in the filtered array. The temp array created in the checkInput method includes all items that match the regular expression.

4.4 Create an In-Place Editor

Problem

You want to create an in-place editor component that will become editable when the user clicks on the text.

Solution

Use the `click` listener on a `Text` component to change the state of the component to display a `TextInput`. Use the `enter` and `focusOut` events on the `TextInput` to determine when the user has finished editing the component and revert to the `Text` component by using states.

Discussion

States are a powerful and convenient way to add multiple views to a single component. This recipe's example uses two states: a `display` and an `edit` state. The `display` state holds the `Label` that will display the value of the text, and the `edit` state holds the `TextInput` component that will enable the user to edit the value.

You change a state by setting the `currentState` property to the string value of the name of the state you wish to display. For example:

```
currentState = "display";
```

To ensure that you store the value of the user's input after the Enter button is clicked or after the user clicks away from the `TextInput`, the `TextInput` component sets focus on itself when it is created and listens both for the `enter` event and `focusOut` event to call the `changeState` method.

```
<mx:Canvas xmlns:mx="http://www.adobe.com/2006/mxml" width="250" height="40" top="10"
currentState="display">
    <mx:Script>
        <![CDATA[


            [Bindable]
            private var value:String;

            private function changeState(event:Event = null):void
            {
                if(this.currentState == "display")
                {
                    currentState = "edit";
                }
                else
                {
                    value = editInput.text;
                    currentState = "display";
                }
```

```
        }

    ]]>
    </mx:Script>
    <mx:states>
        <mx:State id="display" name="display">
            <mx:AddChild>
                <mx:Label text="{value}" id="text" x="{editorValue.x +
editorValue.width}" click="changeState()" minWidth="100" minHeight="20"/>
            </mx:AddChild>
        </mx:State>
```

When the edit state is set as the currentState of the component, the TextInput text
property will be set to the value of the Label in the display state. After the user presses
the Enter key, the state of the component returns to the display state and the value
from the TextInput is used to set the Label of the display state. The enter event of the
TextInput indicates that the user has pressed the Enter or Return key while the component has focus.

```
        <mx:State id="edit" name="edit">
            <mx:AddChild>
                <mx:TextInput creationComplete="editInput.setFocus()" focusOut=
"changeState()" id="editInput" x="{editorValue.x + editorValue.width}" text="{value}"
minWidth="100" minHeight="20" enter="changeState()"/>
            </mx:AddChild>
        </mx:State>
    </mx:states>
    <mx:Label text="Value: " id="editorValue"/>
</mx:Canvas>
```

4.5 Determine All Fonts Installed on a User's Computer

Problem

You want to determine all the fonts installed on a user's computer and let the user set
the font from that list for the Text component to display.

Solution

Use the enumerateFonts method defined in the Font class and set the fontFamily style
of a Text component with the fontName property of a selected font.

Discussion

The Font class defines a static method called enumateFonts to return an array with all
the system fonts on a user's computer. This method returns an array of
flash.text.Font objects, which define three properties:

fontName

> This is the name of the font as reported by the system. In some cases, such as Japanese, Korean, or Arabic characters, the Flash Player may not render the font correctly.

fontStyle

> This is the style of the font: Regular, Bold, Italic, or BoldItalic.

fontType

> This will be either Device, meaning that the font is installed on the user's computer, or Embedded, meaning the font is embedded in the SWF file.

In the following example, the fonts are passed to a ComboBox, from which the user can select the font type for the Text area. The call to setStyle

```
text.setStyle("fontFamily", (cb.selectedItem as Font).fontName);
```

sets the actual font in the Text component, using the fontName property of the Font object selected in the ComboBox.

Here is the complete code you need:

```
<mx:VBox xmlns:mx="http://www.adobe.com/2006/mxml" width="400" height="300"
creationComplete="findAllFonts()">
    <mx:Script>
        <![CDATA[

            private var style:StyleSheet;

            [Bindable]
            private var arr:Array;

            private function findAllFonts():void
            {
                arr = Font.enumerateFonts(true);
                arr.sortOn("fontName", Array.CASEINSENSITIVE);
            }

            private function setFont():void
            {
                text.setStyle("fontFamily", (cb.selectedItem as Font).fontName);
            }

        ]]>
    </mx:Script>
    <mx:ComboBox id="cb" dataProvider="{arr}" change="setFont()" labelField="fontName"
/>
    <mx:Text text="Sample Text" id="text" fontSize="16"/>
</mx:VBox>
```

4.6 Create a Custom TextInput

Problem

You need to create a custom `TextInput` component with a multiline field for entering text and to bind the output of that component to a `Text` display.

Solution

Use `UIComponent` and add a `flash.text.TextField` to the component. Then set a bindable `text` property and bind the `Text` component's `htmlText` property to the text of the new component.

Discussion

The `mx.controls.TextInput` component limits access to the inner `flash.text.TextField` component. To have more-complete access and control over the `TextField`, simply add a `TextField` to a `UIComponent`.

Any methods that you need to provide for access to the `TextField` should be defined in the component. If complete access to the `TextField` is needed, it might be easier to define the `TextField` as a public property. However, it may be convenient for the component to be notified whenever the properties of the `TextField` are accessed or altered. Take a look at this in practice:

```
package oreilly.cookbook
{
    import flash.events.Event;
    import flash.events.TextEvent;
    import flash.text.TextField;
    import flash.text.TextFieldType;

    import mx.core.UIComponent;

    public class SpecialTextInput extends UIComponent
    {

        private var textInput:TextField;
        public static var TEXT_CHANGED:String = "textChanged";

        public function SpecialTextInput()
        {
            textInput = new TextField();
            textInput.multiline = true;
            textInput.wordWrap = true;
            textInput.type = flash.text.TextFieldType.INPUT;
            textInput.addEventListener(TextEvent.TEXT_INPUT, checkInput);
            addChild(textInput);
            super();
        }
```

```
        private function checkInput(textEvent:TextEvent):void
        {
            text = textInput.text;
        }

        override public function set height(value:Number):void
        {
            textInput.height = this.height;
            super.height = value;
        }

        override public function set width(value:Number):void
        {
            textInput.width = this.width;
            super.width = value;
        }

        [Bindable(event="textChanged")]
        public function get text():String
        {
            return textInput.text;
        }

        public function set text(value:String):void
        {
            dispatchEvent(new Event("textChanged"));
        }
    }
}
```

To use the new component, bind the htmlText property of the Text to the new component's text property:

```
<mx:VBox xmlns:mx="http://www.adobe.com/2006/mxml" width="400" height="300"
xmlns:cookbook="oreilly.cookbook.*">
    <cookbook:SpecialTextInput id="htmlInput" height="200" width="300"/>
    <mx:TextArea htmlText="{htmlInput.text}"/>
</mx:VBox>
```

See Also

Recipe 1.18.

4.7 Set the Style Properties for Text Ranges

Problem

You want to set font information for a range of text without using HTML text.

Solution

Use the TextRange class to set properties for a range of characters.

Discussion

The TextRange class accepts a component that has a TextField within it, a parameter to indicate whether the component will be modified by the properties set in the TextRange object, and then two integers to determine the beginning and end of the range of characters in the TextField. The TextRange object is constructed as follows:

```
var textRange:TextRange = new TextRange(component:UIComponent, modify:Boolean,
startIndex:int, endIndex:int);
```

The properties of the TextRange object affect the component that is passed in. In the following example, the color and the letter spacing of the user-selected area are set when the check box is selected:

```
<mx:VBox xmlns:mx="http://www.adobe.com/2006/mxml" width="400" height="300">
    <mx:Script>
        <![CDATA[
            import mx.controls.textClasses.TextRange;

            private function alterTextSnapshot():void
            {
                var textRange:TextRange = new TextRange(area, true,
area.selectionBeginIndex, area.selectionEndIndex);
                textRange.color = 0xff0000;
                textRange.letterSpacing = 3;
            }

        ]]>
    </mx:Script>
    <mx:CheckBox change="alterTextSnapshot()"/>
    <mx:TextArea id="area" text="Lorem ipsum dolor sit amet, consectetuer adipiscing
elit." width="200" height="50"/>
</mx:VBox>
```

4.8 Display Images and SWFs in HTML

Problem

You need to use images and external SWF files in HTML text that is displayed in your Flex component.

Solution

Use the `<img>` tag that is supported by the Flash Player's HTML rendering engine and set the src attribute to the URL of the SWF or image you're loading.

Discussion

The `<img>` tag enables you to indicate the location of an image or SWF file that will be loaded into the Text component and displayed. The `<img>` tag supports the following properties:

src

> Specifies the URL to a GIF, JPEG, PNG, or SWF file. This is the only required attribute. All the others simply control the layout of the image in relation to the text around it.

align

> Specifies the horizontal alignment of the embedded image within the text field. Valid values are left and right. The default value is left.

height

> Specifies the height of the image, in pixels.

hspace

> Specifies the amount of horizontal space (containing no text) that surrounds the image. The default value is 8.

vspace

> Specifies the amount of vertical space that surrounds the image. The default vspace value is 8.

width

> Specifies the width of the image, in pixels.

In the following code snippet, a SWF file is loaded into the application by using the <src> HTML tag, and the vspace property of that <src> tag is set to 10, indicating that 10 pixels of white space will be on both the top and the bottom of the image:

```
<mx:Canvas xmlns:mx="http://www.adobe.com/2006/mxml" width="400" height="300">
    <mx:TextArea width="300" height="300" backgroundAlpha="0">
        <mx:htmlText>
            <![CDATA[
                <img src='../assets/fries.jpg' width='100' height='100' align='left'
hspace='10' vspace='10'>
                <p>This  is the text that is going to appear above the swf.</p><p>
<img src='../assets/test_swf.swf' width='100' height='100' align='left' hspace='10'
vspace='10'>
                Here is text that is going to be below the image.</p>
            ]]>
        </mx:htmlText>
    </mx:TextArea>
</mx:Canvas>
```

4.9 Highlight User-Input Text in a Search Field

Problem

You want to create a TextArea in which a user can search and to highlight text the user enters into a TextInput.

Solution

Use the `flash.text.TextField` object and set the `alwaysShowSelection` property to true. Then use the `setSelection` method to set the index and length of the selected text.

Discussion

The `mx.controls.TextArea` component needs to have its focus set in order to display text selections. To work around this, you can create a subclass of the `TextArea` component so you can access the `flash.text.TextField` that the `TextArea` contains:

```
public function createComp():void{
        textField.alwaysShowSelection = true;
}
```

Setting the `alwayShowSelection` property to true means that the `TextField` will show a selection whether or not it has focus. Now when the `setSelection` method is called, the `TextField` within the `TextArea` component will display and the `TextArea` will automatically scroll correctly to show the selection.

```
<mx:Canvas xmlns:mx="http://www.adobe.com/2006/mxml" width="1000" height="800"
xmlns:cookbook="oreilly.cookbook.*">
    <mx:Script>
        <![CDATA[

            [Bindable]
            private var text_string:String = "Aenean quis nunc id purus pharetra
pharetra. Cras a felis sit amet ipsum ornare luctus. Nullam scelerisque" +
                    " placerat velit. Pellentesque ut arcu congue risus facilisis
pellentesque. Duis in enim. Mauris eget est. Quisque tortor. ";
            private function searchText():void
            {
                var index:int = masterText.text.indexOf(input.text);
                masterText.verticalScrollPosition = 0;
                if(index != -1)
                {
                    masterText.setSelection(index, index+input.text.length);
                }
            }

        ]]>
    </mx:Script>
    <mx:TextInput id="input" change="searchText()"/>
    <cookbook:SpecialTextArea editable="false" id="masterText" text="{text_string}"
fontSize="20" width="600" height="200" x="200"/>
</mx:Canvas>
```

4.10 Manipulate Characters as Individual Graphics

Problem

You want to manipulate individual characters as graphics to create effects.

Solution

Use the `getCharBoundaries` method to return the actual height, width, and x, y position of the character in the `TextField`. Then create a bitmap from the `TextField` that contains the desired character.

Discussion

The `getCharBoundaries` method returns a rectangle that describes the x and y position as well as the height and width of the character index within a `TextField`. You can use this information to create a bitmap of the character, preserving all of its visual information, and animate those bitmaps. The key to the process is this code snippet:

```
char_bounds = addCharacters.getTextField().getCharBoundaries(i);
bitmapData=new BitmapData(char_bounds.width, char_bounds.height, true, 0);
matrix = new Matrix(1, 0, 0, 1, -char_bounds.x, char_bounds.y);
bitmapData.draw(addCharacters.getTextField(), matrix, null, null, null, true);
bitmap = new Bitmap(bitmapData);
```

The `char_bounds` object is a rectangle that will store all of the information about the character. This information is used to create the `flash.display.BitmapData` object that will appear in the bitmap object when it is created. The `BitmapData` object accepts four parameters in its constructor:

```
BitmapData(width:Number, height:Number, transparency:boolean,    fillColor:Number);
```

Now that you have the bitmap object, create the `Matrix` object to store information about the particular part of the `TextField` that you want to capture, namely, the area of the `TextField` bounded by the rectangle returned by the `getCharBoundaries` method. This `Matrix` is passed to the `BitmapData` draw method, which grabs the actual pixel data from the `DisplayObject` passed in. After you've drawn the actual bitmap data, you can create a `Bitmap` object, which is a `DisplayObject` and can be added to the display list, by using the newly populated `BitmapData` object.

The rest of the example takes care of looping through the characters in the `TextField`, performing the preceding operation for each character, and then animating each new bitmap object created:

```
<mx:Canvas xmlns:mx="http://www.adobe.com/2006/mxml" width="600" height="300"
xmlns:cookbook="oreilly.cookbook.*">
    <mx:Script>
        <![CDATA[
            import flash.display.Sprite;

            import mx.core.UIComponent;
            import flash.text.TextField;
            import flash.text.TextFormat;

            private var characterArray:Array = new Array();
            //set up our master character index we're going to use when animating the
    characters
            private var charIndex:int = 0;
```

```
            //keep track of the final position we're going to place all the
characters in
            private var finalX:Number = 0;

            private function addNewCharacters():void
            {
                render();
                invalidateDisplayList();
                invalidateProperties();
            }

            public function render():void
            {
                //define all the variables that we'll need
                var bitmapData:BitmapData;
                var bitmap:Bitmap;
                var char_bounds:Rectangle;
                var matrix:Matrix;
                var component:UIComponent;
                //get the text format and set the
                //tf.defaultTextFormat = addCharacters.getTextField().
defaultTextFormat;
                //tf.text = addCharacters.text;
                for each(component in characterArray)
                {
                    holder.removeChild(component);
                }
                characterArray.length = 0;
                for(var i:int=0; i<addCharacters.text.length; i++)
                {
                    char_bounds = addCharacters.getTextField().getCharBoundaries(i);
                    bitmapData=new BitmapData(char_bounds.width,char_bounds.height,
true,0);
                    matrix = new Matrix(1,0,0,1,-char_bounds.x,char_bounds.y);
                    bitmapData.draw(addCharacters.getTextField(), matrix, null, null,
null, true);
                    bitmap = new Bitmap(bitmapData);
                    component = new UIComponent();
                    component.width = bitmapData.width;
                    component.height = bitmapData.height;
                    component.addChild(bitmap);
                    holder.addChild(component);
                    component.x=char_bounds.x;
                    characterArray[i] = component;
                }
                holder.invalidateDisplayList();
                startEffect();
            }

            private function startEffect():void
            {
                addEventListener(Event.ENTER_FRAME, moveCharacter);
            }

            private function moveCharacter(event:Event):void
```

```
                    {
                        var comp:UIComponent = (characterArray[charIndex] as UIComponent);
                        if(comp)
                        {
                            if(comp.x < 200 - finalX)
                            {
                                (characterArray[charIndex] as Sprite).x+=2;
                            }
                            else
                            {
                                if(charIndex == characterArray.length - 1)
                                {
                                    removeEventListener(Event.ENTER_FRAME, moveCharacter);
                                    return;
                                }
                                finalX += comp.width+2;
                                charIndex++;
                            }
                        }
                    }

                ]]>
            </mx:Script>
            <mx:HBox>
                <cookbook:AccessibleTextInput id="addCharacters" fontSize="18"/>
                <mx:Button label="add characters" click="addNewCharacters()"/>
            </mx:HBox>
            <mx:Canvas id="holder" y="200"/>
        </mx:Canvas>
```

The example uses an `AccessibleTextInput` control, a simple extension of the `TextInput` control that gives access to the `TextField` control within the `TextInput`:

```
<mx:TextInput xmlns:mx="http://www.adobe.com/2006/mxml">
    <mx:Script>
        <![CDATA[

            public function getTextField():IUITextField
            {
                return this.textField;
            }

        ]]>
    </mx:Script>
</mx:TextInput>
```

This lets you simply pass the `TextFormat` object to the `TextField` you create to use in your bitmap manipulation and read directly from the `TextField` for the `getCharBoundaries` method.

4.11 Specify Styles for HTML in a TextField

Problem

You want to use CSS styles for the HTML displayed in `TextField` by using either a CSS file loaded externally or a CSS style written into the application.

Solution

Use the `StyleSheet parseStyle` method to parse the string and assign the style sheet to the `TextArea`.

Discussion

The `StyleSheet` object can parse any valid CSS as a string, process all that information, and assign it to a component or use it in HTML text. To set this up, you need to either load the file by using a `URLLoader` object, passing the loaded data to the `parseCSS` method as a string, or write the string out and pass it directly to the `StyleSheet` object. The following example writes the style in a string that is parsed when the `creationComplete` event is dispatched.

The `htmlText` property of the `TextArea` is set after the style is applied to ensure that the styles are properly applied to the HTML. The style of the `<span>` is set by using the style attribute:

```
"<span class='largered'>
```

This style is specified in the string that will be passed to the `StyleSheet.parseStyle` method:

```
.largered {  font-family:Arial, Helvetica; font-size:16; color: #ff0000; }
```

Here is the full example:

```
<mx:Application xmlns:mx="http://www.adobe.com/2006/mxml" width="1000" height="800"
creationComplete="createStyle()">
    <mx:Script>
        <![CDATA[
            //note even though names are camel cased here when used, all lowercase
            private var styleText:String = '.largered {  font-family:Arial, Helvetica;
font-size:16; color: #ff0000; }' +
                    '.smallblue { font-size: 11; color: #0000ff; font-family:Times New
Roman, Times; }' +
                    'li { color:#00ff00; font-size:14; }' +
                    'ul {margin-left:50px;}';

            [Bindable]
            private var lipsum:String = "<span class='largered'>Nulla metus.</span>
Nam ut dolor vitae risus condimentum auctor."+
                    " <span class='smallblue'>Cras sem quam,</span> malesuada eu, faucibus
aliquam, dictum ac, dui. Nullam blandit"+
                    " ligula sed arcu. Fusce nec est.<ul><li> Etiam</li><li> aliquet,</li>
```

```
<li>nunc</li></ul> eget pharetra dictum, magna"+
            " leo suscipit pede, in tempus erat arcu et velit. Aenean condimentum.
Nunc auctor"+
            " nulla vitae velit imperdiet gravida";

        [Bindable]
        private var style:StyleSheet;

        private function createStyle():void
        {
            style = new StyleSheet();
            style.parseCSS(styleText);
             text.styleSheet = style;
            text.htmlText = lipsum;
        }

    ]]>
    </mx:Script>
    <mx:TextArea id="text" width="200" height="300"/>
</mx:Application>
```

4.12 Use the RichTextEditor

Problem

You want to create a component that will let the user input rich text by using all the fonts on the user's computer and then use the HTML created in the rich text.

Solution

Create a RichTextEditor and read the htmlText property from the control. Set the data Provider of the fontFamilyCombo defined in the RichTextEditor to add all the results returned from Font.enumerateFonts.

Discussion

The RichTextEditor is a great convenience, enabling users to create HTML text that can then be read from the editor by using the htmlText property. The RichTextEditor contains several buttons to set the text style to bold, italicized, or underlined, a Combo Box to set the font, and a ColorPicker that sets the color of the selected text, all of which can be accessed from the RichTextEditor. The following example accesses the fontFamilyCombo ComboBox to add all the fonts that the user has installed so that the user can select any one of these for use.

To access the text with all the attributes that the user has created, use the htmlText property of the RichTextEditor. This property is both gettable and settable, so if you want to prepopulate the editor with HTML, simply set the htmlText property to a string of valid HTML.

```
<mx:Canvas xmlns:mx="http://www.adobe.com/2006/mxml" width="900" height="500"
creationComplete="addFonts()">
    <mx:Script>
        <![CDATA[
            import mx.collections.ArrayCollection;

            private function addFonts():void
            {
                var arr:Array = Font.enumerateFonts(true);
                richText.fontFamilyCombo.labelField = 'fontName';
                richText.fontFamilyCombo.dataProvider = Font.enumerateFonts(true);
            }

        ]]>
    </mx:Script>
    <mx:RichTextEditor id="richText" width="400" height="400" change="trace(richText.
htmlText+' '+richText.text)"/>
    <mx:TextArea height="100%" width="400" htmlText="{richText.htmlText}" x="410"/>
</mx:Canvas>
```

See Also

Recipe 4.5.

4.13 Apply Embedded Fonts with HTML

Problem

You need to use an embedded font in HTML text.

Solution

Use the `@font-face` tag within a style to embed the font and then use the `<font>` tag to
set the family attribute for the tag.

Discussion

Applying an embedded font to HTML text is much more difficult than using system
fonts. The standard method of applying a font is simply to set the font in a
`font-family` property within a style and then apply the style to a span. However, embedded fonts require that the `font` tag is used in the HTML to apply the embedded font.

```
<font size="20" family="DIN">Using the new font</font>
```

The `font` tag uses the `fontFamily` property set in the `font-face` declaration within the
`<mx:Style>` tag:

```
@font-face{
        src:url("../assets/DIN-BLAC.ttf");
        fontFamily:DIN;
        advancedAntiAliasing: true;
    }
```

Here is the full example:

```
<mx:Application xmlns:mx="http://www.adobe.com/2006/mxml" layout="absolute">
    <mx:Style>
        @font-face{
            src:url("../assets/DIN-BLAC.ttf");
            fontFamily:DIN;
            advancedAntiAliasing: true;
        }
        .embeddedFontStyle{
            fontFamily:DIN;
            fontSize:18px;
            color:#CCCCFF;
        }
        .white{
            color:#ffffff;
        }
    </mx:Style>
    <mx:VBox backgroundColor="#000000">
        <mx:Label text="This is some test text" styleName="embeddedFontStyle"/>
        <mx:TextArea id="ta" backgroundAlpha="0" width="250" height="150" styleName=
"white">
            <mx:htmlText>
                <![CDATA[
                    Not Using the New Font.<font size="20" family="DIN">Using the new
font</font>
                ]]>
            </mx:htmlText>
        </mx:TextArea>
    </mx:VBox>
</mx:Application>
```

4.14 Add a Drop Shadow to Text in a Text Component

Problem

You want to add a drop shadow to the actual text in a TextArea component.

Solution

Use a BitmapData object to get a copy of a TextField and add that bitmap to the parent component with an offset to simulate a shadow.

Discussion

When trying to show a shadow image of the actual contents of a TextArea or Text component, you simply need to get a bitmap representation of all the information in the text field and then add that bitmap to the parent component. Moving the image slightly off-center and dimming it by lowering the alpha value provides the correct look. Building a custom component by using the UIComponent class eases the development process in this case, letting you directly read and add the lower-level base ActionScript display components from the `flash.display` package.

The method for getting the `bitmapData` into a bitmap is described in Recipe 4.10.

```
package oreilly.cookbook
{
    import flash.display.Bitmap;
    import flash.display.BitmapData;
    import flash.events.TextEvent;
    import flash.text.TextField;

    import mx.core.UIComponent;

    public class TextDropShadow extends UIComponent
    {

        private var _useShadow:Boolean = false;
        private var _shadowHolder:Bitmap;
        private var _bitmapData:BitmapData;
        private var _textField:TextField;
```

Here the `Bitmap` is created and placed in the parent component at a slight offset, to simulate a shadow:

```
        public function TextDropShadow()
        {
            super();
            _shadowHolder = new Bitmap();
            addChild(_shadowHolder);
            _shadowHolder.x = 5;
            _shadowHolder.y = 5;
            _textField = new TextField();
            _textField.type = "input";
            _textField.addEventListener(TextEvent.TEXT_INPUT, inputListener);
            addChild(_textField);
        }
```

The `updateDisplayList` method is overridden to draw the `TextField` and all its visual information, including the text, into the `Bitmap`.

```
        override protected function updateDisplayList(unscaledWidth:Number,
    unscaledHeight:Number):void
        {
            super.updateDisplayList(unscaledWidth, unscaledHeight);
            if(_useShadow)
            {
                _bitmapData = new BitmapData(_textField.width, _textField.height,
    true);
                _bitmapData.draw(_textField);
                _shadowHolder.bitmapData = _bitmapData;
                _shadowHolder.alpha = 0.7;
            }
        }

        private function inputListener(event:TextEvent):void
```

```
        {
            invalidateDisplayList();
        }

        public function set useShadow(value:Boolean):void
        {
            _useShadow = value;
        }

        public function get useShadow():Boolean
        {
            return _useShadow;
        }
    }
}
```

See Also

Recipe 4.10.

4.15 Find the Last Displayed Character in a TextArea

Problem

You want to find the last displayed character in a `TextArea` component.

Solution

Use the `bounds` method of the `TextField` to return the size of the `TextArea` and use the `getLineMetrics` method to determine the actual heights of the lines. After determining the last visible line, use the `getLineOffset` and `getLineLength` methods to find the last visible character in the last visible line.

Discussion

Each line within a `TextField` can have its specific properties accessed by using the `getLineMetrics` method and using the `TextLineMetrics` object that is returned. The `TextLineMetrics` object defines multiple properties about a line of text: the height, width, baseline, and spacing between lines.

Figure 4-1 shows the properties of the line that the `TextLineMetrics` object defines.

The following example uses the `height` property to find the last displayed line in the `TextArea`. First, a rectangle that represents the height, width, and x, y information about the visible (unmasked) `TextArea` is retrieved by using the `getBounds` method. Then the height of the lines is added until the last visible line is found by using the `TextLineMetrics` objects. Finally, the last character in the line is found by using the `getLineOffset` method, which finds the index of the first character in a line, added to the length of the line:

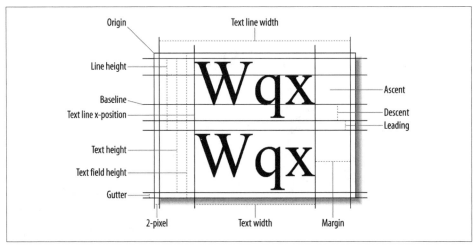

Figure 4-1. The properties of the TextLineMetrics object

```
changeArea.text.charAt(changeArea.getLineOffset(i-1)+changeArea.getLineLength(i-1))
```

Here is the code for the full example:

```
<mx:Canvas xmlns:mx="http://www.adobe.com/2006/mxml" width="400" height="300"
xmlns:cookbook="oreilly.cookbook.*">
    <mx:Script>
        <![CDATA[

            private function findLineMetrics():void
            {
                if(changeField.text.length > 1)
                {
                    var rect:Rectangle = changeArea.getBounds(this);
                    var visibleTextHeight:Number = 0;
                    var i:int = 0;
                    while(visibleTextHeight < rect.height && i < changeArea.numLines)
                    {
                        var metrics:TextLineMetrics = changeArea.getLineMetrics(i);
                        visibleTextHeight+=metrics.ascent+metrics.height;
                        i++;
                    }
                    trace(changeArea.text.charAt(changeArea.getLineOffset(i-1)+
changeArea.getLineLength(i-1)));
                }
            }

        ]]>
    </mx:Script>
    <mx:TextInput id="changeField" width="200" textInput="findLineMetrics()"/>
    <cookbook:SpecialTextArea id="changeArea" text="{changeField.text}" wordWrap=
"true" width="150" height="30" y="100"/>
</mx:Canvas>
```

CHAPTER 5

Lists, Tiles, and Trees

The three components covered in this chapter extend the `mx.controls.list classes.ListBase` class, and the methods for working with these data-driven controls are consistent in their implementation and use. Each of these data-driven controls has its children generated by a data provider and allows for sorting, filtering, reordering, and the setting of visual components to act as item renderers and item editors. These controls also allow for dragging and dropping.

The recipes in this chapter focus on working with item renderers, controlling selection, setting styles in `ListBase` controls, and working with data providers for different control types. This does not begin to exhaust the topics in working with these `ListBase` controls, though. For more recipes on working with drag-and-drop, see Chapter 10, "Dragging and Dropping." For recipes on working with skinning, see Chapter 9, "Skinning and Styling."

5.1 Create an Editable List

Problem

You need to create a list in which all the items are editable.

Solution

Set the `editable` property of the `List` control to true and listen for the `itemEditBegin` and `itemEditEnd` properties, or set the `editedItemPosition` by passing an object containing `columnIndex` and `rowIndex` properties.

Discussion

All `List` controls can be made editable by simply setting the list's `editable` property to true. This means that each renderer will become an editor control with a `TextInput` populated with the value currently in the `itemRenderer` that the user has selected. The `List` class also defines several events that notify the application when the user has begun and finished editing the value:

itemEditBegin

This event is dispatched when the `editedItemPosition` property is set and the item can be edited. When this event is fired, the `List` creates an `itemEditor` object by using the `createItemEditor` method and copies the `data` property from the item to the editor.

itemEditBeginning

This event is dispatched when the user releases the mouse button while over an item, tabs to the list or within the list, or in any way attempts to edit the list.

itemEditEnd

The list components have a default handler for this event that copies the data from the item editor to the data provider of the list control. By default, the `List` uses the `editorDataField` property of the `List` control to determine the property of the `itemEditor` containing the new data and updates the data provider item with that new data.

Using these different events and controlling the data that an `itemEditor` returns to the list data is covered in greater detail in Chapter 7, "Renderers and Editors."

The editable item can be set either by the user clicking on an `itemRenderer` in a list or by setting the `editedItemPosition` of the `List` control with an object that possesses `columnIndex` and `rowIndex` properties. In a `List`, the `columnIndex` will always be 0, and the `rowIndex` will be the index of the row where the editor will be created, for example:

```
listImpl.editedItemPosition = {columnIndex:0, rowIndex:2};
```

The complete example is as follows:

```
<mx:Canvas xmlns:mx="http://www.adobe.com/2006/mxml" width="400" height="300">
    <mx:Script>
        <![CDATA[

            [Bindable]
            private var dp:Array = [{name:"John Smith", foo:"bar"}, {name:"Ellen
Smith", foo:"baz"}, {name:"James Smith", foo:"eggs"}, {name:"Jane Smith", foo:"spam"}]
```

The `selectedItem` property returns the value of the item edited without any changes that the user has made to the renderer:

```
            private function editEnd(event:Event):void {
                trace(listImpl.selectedItem.foo+'  '+listImpl.selectedItem.name);
            }
```

Setting the `editedItemPosition` creates the editor at the position indicated by the `rowIndex` and `columnIndex` properties:

```
            private function setEditor():void {
                listImpl.editedItemPosition = {columnIndex:0, rowIndex:2};
            }

        ]]>
    </mx:Script>
    <mx:Button click="setEditor()"/>
```

```
          <mx:List y="30" width="200" selectedIndex="6" id="listImpl" selectionColor=
     "#CCCCFF" labelField="name" dataProvider="{dp}" editable="true" itemEditBegin=
     "trace(listImpl.editedItemPosition)"
               itemEditEnd="editEnd(event)" editorXOffset="5" editorYOffset="2"/>
     </mx:Canvas>
```

5.2 Set Icons for Items in a List

Problem

You want to set icons for a List control's itemRenderer based on the data provided from the list.

Solution

Use the iconFunction property of the List control and create a method to return the correct image as an embedded class.

Discussion

An iconFunction is any method that returns a Class object representing an embedded graphic for use by the itemRenderer in the List control requesting the graphic. The reference to the iconFunction is simply passed as a reference to the method name. Here, for example, setIcon is the name of the method that is typed to receive any value:

```
     iconFunction="setIcon"
```

The iconFunction is always passed the value of the object at that index in the dataProvider:

```
     private function setIcon(value:*):Class
```

In the body of the iconFunction method, any information about the data object at that index in the dataProvider should be processed. The iconFunction returns the class of the object that will be used to create the icon for the renderer. The complete example follows:

```
<mx:Canvas xmlns:mx="http://www.adobe.com/2006/mxml" width="400" height="300">
    <mx:Script>
        <![CDATA[

            [Bindable]
            private var dp:Array = [{name:"John Smith", position:"developer"},
{name:"Ellen Smith", position:"manager"}, {name:"James Smith", position:"accountant"},
{name:"Jane Smith", position:"designer"}];

            [Embed(source="../../assets/manager.png")]
            private var managerIcon:Class;

            [Embed(source="../../assets/designer.png")]
```

```
        private var designerIcon:Class;

        [Embed(source="../../assets/accountant.png")]
        private var accountantIcon:Class;

        [Embed(source="../../assets/developer.png")]
        private var developerIcon:Class;

        private function setIcon(value:*):Class
        {
            if(value.position != null)
            {
                switch(value.position)
                {
                    case "developer":
                        return developerIcon;
                    break;
                    case "designer":
                        return designerIcon;
                    break;
                    case "accountant":
                        return accountantIcon;
                    break;
                    case "manager":
                        return managerIcon;
                    break;
                }
            }
            return null;
        }

    ]]>
    </mx:Script>
    <mx:List width="200" selectedIndex="6" id="listImpl" selectionColor="#CCCCFF"
labelField="name" dataProvider="{dp}" editable="true" iconFunction="setIcon"/>
</mx:Canvas>
```

5.3 Add Effects to a List to Indicate Changes

Problem

You want to add effects to a list to be shown when the list's data changes.

Solution

Create a sequence of effects and pass them to the `itemsChangeEffect` property of the
List control.

Discussion

Data-change effects are a powerful new addition to Flex 3. In previous versions, you
could write data changes yourself and then dispatch and register events and event lis-

teners, but with Flex 3's addition of the `itemsChangeEffect` property, the `List` and any class that extends `ListBase` can dispatch an event when its `dataProvider` changes; that event then triggers any effect or sequence of events that are passed to the `List` in the new `itemsChangeEffect` property.

Because the `dataChange` event is fired from the `dataProvider` within the list, setting an array as a `List` control's `dataProvider` means that `itemsChangeEffect` events will not be dispatched when the array changes. Remember, events do not dispatch events when they change. The `ArrayCollection` class, however does dispatch events when they change, as will any class that extends `EventDispatcher` and is set to dispatch events when a set method is called to change the value of one of the objects in the underlying array.

By simply setting an `itemsChangeEffect` to be an instance of a `DefaultListEffect` with a 2-second fade-out duration, the following example applies an instance of an `mx.effects.Glow` effect to the list when it is changed:

```
<mx:VBox xmlns:mx="http://www.adobe.com/2006/mxml" width="400" height="900" top="20"
left="20">
    <mx:Script>
        <![CDATA[
            import mx.collections.ArrayCollection;

            //note that for this example to work, the dataprovider
            //must be an array collection
            [Bindable]
            private var dp:ArrayCollection = new ArrayCollection([{name:"John Smith",
position:"developer"}, {name:"Ellen Smith", position:"manager"}, {name:"James Smith",
position:"accountant"}, {name:"Jane Smith", position:"designer"}]);


            private function addItem():void
            {
                dp.addItem({name:"Jim Smith", position:"Janitor"});
            }

        ]]>
    </mx:Script>
    <mx:DefaultListEffect color="0xccccff" fadeOutDuration="2000" id="glow"/>
    <mx:List width="300" itemsChangeEffect="{glow}" dataProvider="{dp}" editable=
"true" labelField="name"/>
    <mx:Button click="addItem()" label="add item"/>
    <mx:List width="300" itemsChangeEffect="{glow}" dataProvider="{dp}" editable=
"true" labelField="name"/>
</mx:VBox>
```

For another example of `itemsChangeEffect` in action, consider the next example. Here a `Sequence` tag is used to create a sequence of events that will be fired when the data of the list changes:

```
<mx:VBox xmlns:mx="http://www.adobe.com/2006/mxml" width="400" height="900" top="20"
left="20">
    <mx:Script>
```

```
            <![CDATA[
                import mx.collections.ArrayCollection;
                import mx.effects.easing.*;

                [Bindable]
                private var dp:ArrayCollection = new ArrayCollection([{name:"John Smith",
    position:"developer"}, {name:"Ellen Smith", position:"manager"}, {name:"James Smith",
    position:"accountant"}, {name:"Jane Smith", position:"designer"}]);

            ]]>
        </mx:Script>
        <mx:Sequence id="itemsChangeEffect">
            <mx:WipeDown duration="500"/>
            <mx:Parallel>
                <mx:Move
                    duration="750"
                    easingFunction="{Elastic.easeOut}"
                    perElementOffset="20"/>
                <mx:RemoveItemAction
                    startDelay="400"
                    filter="removeItem"/>
                <mx:AddItemAction
                    startDelay="400"
                    filter="addItem">
                </mx:AddItemAction>
                <mx:Blur
                    startDelay="410"
                    blurXFrom="18" blurYFrom="18" blurXTo="0" blurYTo="0"
                    duration="300"
                    filter="addItem"/>
            </mx:Parallel>
        </mx:Sequence>
        <mx:List width="300" itemsChangeEffect="{itemsChangeEffect}" dataProvider="{dp}"
    editable="true" labelField="name"/>
        <mx:Button click="{dp.addItem({name:'Jim Smith', position:'Janitor'});}" label=
    "add item"/>
        <mx:Button click="{dp.removeItemAt(3)}" label="remove item"/>
        <mx:Button click="{dp.setItemAt(dp.getItemAt(1), 2)}" label="change item"/>
    </mx:VBox>
```

5.4 Set a Basic Item Renderer for a TileList

Problem

You need to set a custom itemRenderer for a TileList class that will attach a certain image depending on code in the data passed to the renderer from the TileList.

Solution

Create a VBox object and override the set data method to read from a hash that will match the images to the codes passed in when the data is set for the renderer.

Discussion

The item renderer for a list is passed a data object representing each item in the collection. This is used to create the renderer at the particular column and row. Any custom data processing that needs to be done in the `item renderer` should take place in the set method for the data property so that the `item renderer` will be kept in sync with its parent list.

For the following example, a list of images was stored as static public references in a separate file for access and is referenced here in a hash list for comparison with the `positionType` value that is expected in the `value` parameter passed to the data property:

```
<mx:VBox xmlns:mx="http://www.adobe.com/2006/mxml" width="400" height="300">
    <mx:Script>
        <![CDATA[

            [Bindable]
            private var type:String;

            [Bindable]
            private var imageClass:Class;

            private var typeToPositionHash:Object = {1:"Manager", 2:"Accountant",
3:"Designer", 4:"Developer"};
            private var typeToImageHash:Object = {1:Assets.managerIcon,
2:Assets.accountantIcon, 3:Assets.designerIcon, 4:Assets.developerIcon};

            override public function set data(value:Object):void {
                type = typeToPositionHash[value.positionType];
                imageClass = typeToImageHash[value.positionType];
                nameText.text = value.name;
            }

        ]]>
    </mx:Script>
    <mx:Text text="{type}"/>
    <mx:Image source="{imageClass}"/>
    <mx:Text id="nameText" fontSize="16"/>
</mx:VBox>
```

To use the `itemRenderer` shown here, you simply pass a reference to the fully qualified class name to the `List` component. Note that if the `dataProvider` objects do not possess a `positionType` property, the `itemRenderer` will not work as expected. In a larger application, all these data types should be represented by strongly typed data objects to ensure that this does not cause problems.

```
<mx:Canvas xmlns:mx="http://www.adobe.com/2006/mxml" width="400" height="300">
    <mx:Script>
        <![CDATA[

            import oreilly.cookbook.SimpleRenderer;
            import mx.collections.ArrayCollection;
```

```
        [Bindable]
            private var dp:ArrayCollection = new ArrayCollection([{name:"John Smith",
    positionType:1}, {name:"Ellen Smith", positionType:2}, {name:"James Smith",
    positionType:3}, {name:"Jane Smith", positionType:4}]);


        ]]>
    </mx:Script>
    <mx:List itemRenderer="oreilly.cookbook.SimpleRenderer" dataProvider="{dp}"/>
</mx:Canvas>
```

5.5 Set XML Data for a Tree

Problem

You need to use a Tree control to represent XML data that will be loaded from an external source.

Solution

Set the type of an HTTPService object to e4x and load the XML file, setting the result of the request to be the data provider for the tree. Ensure that the tree will display the correct label by using ECMAScript for XML (E4X) syntax to pass the property of the nodes that you would like to use as the labelField of the Tree leaf.

Discussion

The Tree control handles XML data very well as long as the labelField property of the Tree is set so the proper attributes are displayed. For the following example, the label property is an attribute called label:

```
<data label="2004">
    <result label="Jan-04">
        <product label="apple">81156</product>
        <product label="orange">58883</product>
        <product label="grape">49280</product>
    </result>
    <result label="Feb-04">
        <product label="apple">81156</product>
        <product label="orange">58883</product>
        <product label="grape">49280</product>
    </result>
</data>
```

Set the labelField property by using E4X syntax to indicate the location of the attribute or property that you want to use for the label:

```
labelField="@label"
```

This indicates that you would like to use an attribute called label that exists on every node in the XML. By default, if no labelField is provided, the Tree displays the value of the node. Here is the full example:

```
<mx:Canvas xmlns:mx="http://www.adobe.com/2006/mxml" width="400" height="300" left="20"
top="10">
    <mx:HTTPService id="xmlLoader" url="assets/data.xml" resultFormat="e4x"
contentType="application/xml" result="xmlReturned(event)"/>
    <mx:Script>
        <![CDATA[
            import mx.collections.XMLListCollection;

            [Bindable]
            private var xmlValue:XMLListCollection;

            private function xmlReturned(event:Event):void
            {
                xmlValue = new XMLListCollection(new XMLList(xmlLoader.lastResult));
            }

        ]]>
    </mx:Script>
    <mx:Button click="xmlLoader.send()" label="get XML"/>
    <mx:Tree dataProvider="{xmlValue}" y="100" labelField="@label" width="300"
showRoot="true"/>
</mx:Canvas>
```

5.6 Create an Item Renderer for a Tree

Contributed by Joan Lafferty

Problem

You need to change functionality of a Tree control.

Solution

Create an itemRenderer that extends the TreeItemRenderer class.

Discussion

Changing how a Tree control functions is a little trickier than it is for other list-based components. Unlike for DataGrid, TileList, or List controls, you cannot use a dropInItemRenderer for Tree. Instead, you must extend the TreeItemRenderer class with an itemRenderer. The TreeItemRenderer class defines the default item renderer for a Tree control. The default behavior of the TreeItemRenderer is to draw the text associated with each item in the tree, an optional icon, and an optional disclosure icon.

This recipe uses the TreeListData object that the TreeItemRenderer is passed by its parent. The TreeListData object defines the following properties:

depth : int
   The level of the item in the tree.

disclosureIcon : Class

A class representing the disclosure icon for the item in the Tree control.

hasChildren : Boolean

Contains true if the node has children.

icon : Class

A class representing the icon for the item in the Tree control.

indent : int

The default indentation for this row of the Tree control.

item : Object

The data for this item in the Tree control.

label : String

The textual representation of the item data, based on the List class's itemToLabel method.

open : Boolean

Contains true if the node is open.

The following example uses this method to change the text of branches to purple and bold. It also adds some text to each folder label that indicates how many objects are in that particular branch.

```
package oreilly.cookbook
{

import mx.controls.treeClasses.*;
import mx.collections.*;

    public class CustomTreeItemRenderer extends TreeItemRenderer
    {
        public function CustomTreeItemRenderer() {
            super();
            mouseEnabled = false;
        }
```

The listData property of the TreeItemRenderer references the data of the parent Tree object. Here this is used to determine whether the data object that this renderer contains has any children:

```
        override public function set data(value:Object):void {
            if(value != null) {
                super.data = value;
                if(TreeListData(super.listData).hasChildren) {
                    setStyle("color", 0x660099);
                    setStyle("fontWeight", 'bold');
                } else {
                    setStyle("color", 0x000000);
                    setStyle("fontWeight", 'normal');
                }
            }
        }
```

The `updateDisplayList` method is overridden to check whether the node that this renderer has been passed possesses any children using the `TreeListData` of the parent `Tree`.

```
        override protected function updateDisplayList(unscaledWidth:Number,
unscaledHeight:Number):void {
            super.updateDisplayList(unscaledWidth, unscaledHeight);
            if(super.data)
            {
                if(TreeListData(super.listData).hasChildren)
                {
                    var tmp:XMLList = new XMLList(TreeListData(super.listData).item);
                    var myStr:int = tmp[0].children().length();
                    super.label.text =  TreeListData(super.listData).label + "(" +
myStr + " objects)";
                }
            }
        }
    }
}
```

5.7 Use Complex Data Objects in a Tree Control

Problem

You want to pass complex data objects to the `Tree` control and have the `Tree` parse them properly.

Solution

Implement the `ITreeDataDescriptor` interface in a class and set an instantiated object of your new data descriptor class to the `dataDescriptor` property of the `Tree`.

Discussion

To use an object with a `Tree`, you need to pass the `Tree` an object that implements `ITreeDataDescriptor` to parse data and return correct information about the relationship of the objects within the data. XML data lends itself easily to this approach, but complex objects can be used as well with an object that defines the relationships for the `Tree`.

Consider the example, `ComplexDataType`, which is a typical complex data type:

```
package oreilly.cookbook
{
    import flash.events.Event;
    import flash.events.EventDispatcher;
    import flash.events.IEventDispatcher;

    public class ComplexDataType extends EventDispatcher
    {
```

```
        public static const NAME_CHANGED:String = "nameChanged";
        public static const OFFICE_CHANGED:String = "officeChanged";
        public static const RECORD_CHANGED:String = "recordChanged";

        private var _name:Name;
        private var _office:Office;
        private var _label:String;

        public function ComplexDataType(target:IEventDispatcher=null)
        {
            super(target);
        }

        [Bindable(RECORD_CHANGED)]
        public function set label(value:String):void
        {
            _label = value;
            dispatchEvent(new Event(RECORD_CHANGED));
        }

        public function get label():String
        {
            return _label;
        }

        [Bindable(NAME_CHANGED)]
        public function set name(value:Name):void
        {
            _name = value;
            dispatchEvent(new Event(NAME_CHANGED));
        }

        public function get name():Name
        {
            return _name;
        }

        [Bindable(OFFICE_CHANGED)]
        public function set office(value:Office):void
        {
            _office = value;
            dispatchEvent(new Event(OFFICE_CHANGED));
        }

        public function get office():Office
        {
            return _office;
        }
    }
}
```

The Office and Name objects are simple value objects consisting of the name and address
for the Office object, and firstName, lastName properties for the Name object. Without
an ITreeDataDescriptor object to describe the relationship between the ComplexData
Type and the Office and Name properties that it contains, the Tree would not be able to

properly display an `Array` or `ArrayCollection` of these objects. Instead it would show simply two objects in an `Array` that cannot be expanded.

The `ITreeDataDescriptor` interface defines the following methods:

`addChildAt(parent:Object, newChild:Object, index:int, model:Object = null):Boolean`

This method inserts a new object into your structure and determines where in the data structure any new additions should go.

`getChildren(node:Object, model:Object = null):ICollectionView`

For any node, this method determines whether the node or object has any children to display. If the node or object does, the method returns them in a `Collection View`; if the node or object does not have any children, the method returns `null`.

`getData(node:Object, model:Object = null):Object`

This method returns all the data for a given node.

`hasChildren(node:Object, model:Object = null):Boolean`

This method determines whether the node has any children and returns a Boolean value.

`isBranch(node:Object, model:Object = null):Boolean`

This method tests whether the node is a terminating node, that is, whether it has any children that could be displayed.

`removeChildAt(parent:Object, child:Object, index:int, model:Object = null):Boolean`

This methods removes an object from your structure and determines what should happen to the data structure after a node is removed.

The proper implementation of a data descriptor for the `ComplexDataType` follows:

```
package oreilly.cookbook
{
    import mx.collections.ArrayCollection;
    import mx.collections.ICollectionView;
    import mx.controls.treeClasses.ITreeDataDescriptor;

    public class ComplexDataCollection implements ITreeDataDescriptor
    {
        public function getChildren(node:Object, model:Object=null):ICollectionView
        {
            var col:ArrayCollection;
            if(node is Office){
                col = new ArrayCollection([node.officeAddress, node.officeName]);
                return col;
            }
            if(node is Name){
                col = new ArrayCollection([node.firstName, node.lastName]);
                return col;
            }
            if(node is ComplexDataType){
                col = new ArrayCollection([node.office, node.name]);
```

```
            return col;
        }
        return null;
    }

    public function hasChildren(node:Object, model:Object=null):Boolean
    {
        if(node is Office){
            if(node.officeAddress != "" && node.officeName != ""){
                return true;
            } else {
                return false;
            }
        }
        if(node is Name){
            if(node.firstName != "" && node.firstName != ""){
                return true;
            } else {
                return false;
            }
        }
        if(node is ComplexDataType){
            if(node.office != null && node.name != null) {
                return true;
            } else {
                return false;
            }
        }
        return false;
    }

    public function isBranch(node:Object, model:Object=null):Boolean
    {
        if(node is Office){
            if(node.officeAddress != "" && node.officeName != ""){
                return true;
            } else {
                return false;
            }
        }
        if(node is Name) {
            if(node.firstName != "" && node.firstName != ""){
                return true;
            } else {
                return false;
            }
        }
        if(node is ComplexDataType) {
            if(node.office != null && node.name != null) {
                return true;
            } else {
                return false;
            }
        }
        return true;
```

```
        }

        public function getData(node:Object, model:Object=null):Object {
            if(node is Office) {
                return {children:{label:node.officeName, label:node.officeAddress}};
            }
            if(node is Name) {
                return {children:{label:node.firstName, label:node.lastName}};
            }
            if(node is ComplexDataType){
                return {children:{label:node.office, label:node.name}};
            }
            return null;
        }

        public function addChildAt(parent:Object, newChild:Object, index:int,
model:Object=null):Boolean
        {
            return false;
        }

        public function removeChildAt(parent:Object, child:Object, index:int,
model:Object=null):Boolean
        {
            return false;
        }

    }
}
```

To use the data descriptor and have the Tree control properly display an array of ComplexDataTypes, simply set an instance of the ComplexDataCollection class listed in the preceding code to be the dataDescriptor property for the Tree:

```
dataDescriptor="{new ComplexDataCollection()}"
```

The full code is listed here:

```
<mx:Canvas xmlns:mx="http://www.adobe.com/2006/mxml" width="400" height="300"
creationComplete="initCmp()">
    <mx:Script>
        <![CDATA[
            import mx.collections.ArrayCollection;

            [Bindable]
            private var dataProv:ArrayCollection;


            private function initCmp():void
            {

                var compData:ComplexDataType = new ComplexDataType();
                compData.label = "13";
                var _name:Name = new Name();
                _name.firstName = "Joe";
                _name.lastName = "Smith";
```

```
        compData.name = _name;
        var office:Office = new Office();
        office.officeAddress = "544 Happy St. Anytown NY 01092";
        office.officeName = "Happy Town Branch";
        compData.office = office;

        var compData2:ComplexDataType = new ComplexDataType();
        compData2.label = "328";
        var _name2:Name = new Name();
        _name2.firstName = "Jane";
        _name2.lastName = "Doe";
        compData2.name = _name2;
        var office2:Office = new Office();
        office2.officeAddress = "544 Happy St. Anytown NY 01092";
        office2.officeName = "Happy Town Branch";
        compData2.office = office2;

        dataProv = new ArrayCollection([compData, compData2]);

    }

    ]]>
  </mx:Script>
  <mx:Tree dataDescriptor="{new ComplexDataCollection()}" dataProvider="{dataProv}"
labelField="label" width="300"/>
</mx:Canvas>
```

5.8 Allow Only Certain Items in a List to Be Selectable

Problem

You want to parse the `dataProvider` of a list to ensure that certain items are not select-able by the user.

Solution

Create a `filterFunction` property that can be set on a subclass of the `List` component. Use `mouseEventToItemRenderer` and `finishKeySelection` to check the user's selection via the `filter` function and allow or disallow the user's selection.

Discussion

To control the user's selection of certain items in a list, you need to control the items that the user can select with the mouse and the keyboard. Mouse selection is slightly easier to deal with: Simply override the `mouseEventToItemRenderer` method and return `null` if the `itemRenderer` contains data you want to be unselectable. The keyboard event handling is more complex because you want to send users to the next selectable item in the list if they try to navigate to an unselectable item by using the up or down arrow keys.

To provide custom filtering for what constitutes an unselectable item for each instance of your custom list class, simply create a disabledFilterFunction property that is publicly accessible, to which the user can pass a value, creating a custom filter. For example:

```
public var disabledFilterFunction:Function;
```

The rest of the work is done in overriding the mouseEventToItemRenderer method, which returns the itemRenderer to be selected by the MouseEvent, and the finishKeySelection key-selection method, which selects the itemRenderer selected by the keyboardEvent:

```
<mx:List xmlns:mx="http://www.adobe.com/2006/mxml" width="400" height="300">
    <mx:Script>
        <![CDATA[

            import flash.events.MouseEvent;
            import flash.ui.Keyboard;
            import mx.controls.listClasses.IListItemRenderer;
            import mx.controls.List;

            public var disabledFilterFunction:Function;
            private var selectionIsAbove:Boolean;


            // we need to catch all mouse events that could change the index
            override protected function mouseEventToItemRenderer(event:MouseEvent):
    IListItemRenderer {
                var listItem:IListItemRenderer = super.mouseEventToItemRenderer(event);
                if (listItem){
                    if (listItem.data){
                        if (disabledFilterFunction(listItem.data)){
                            return null;
                        }
                    }
                }
                return listItem;
            }
```

Here you catch all keyboard events that could change the index when the key selection is finished:

```
            override protected function finishKeySelection():void {
                super.finishKeySelection();
                var i:int;
                var uid:String;
                var rowCount:int = listItems.length;
                var partialRow:int = (rowInfo[rowCount-1].y + rowInfo[rowCount-1].
    height > listContent.height) ? 1 : 0;
                var item:IListItemRenderer = listItems[caretIndex -
    verticalScrollPosition][0];
                if (item) {
                    if (item.data) {
                        if (disabledFilterFunction(item.data)){
```

Here you use the `disabledFilterFunction` property to determine whether the particular item is allowed to be selected. If the currently selected item shouldn't be selected, the code simply locates another visible item that is enabled.

```
rowCount = rowCount - partialRow;
var currIndex:int = caretIndex - verticalScrollPosition;
if (selectionIsAbove){
    // look up;
    i = currIndex - 1;
    while(i>0){
        item = listItems[i][0];
        if (!disabledFilterFunction(item.data)){
            selectedIndex = i - verticalScrollPosition;
            return;
        }
        i--;
    }
    i = currIndex + 1
    while(i<this.rowCount){
        item = listItems[i][0];
        if (!disabledFilterFunction(item.data)){
            selectedIndex = i - verticalScrollPosition;
            return;
        }
        i++;
    }
} else {
    // look down;
    while(i<this.rowCount){
        item = listItems[i][0];
        if (!disabledFilterFunction(item.data)){
            selectedIndex = i - verticalScrollPosition;
            return;
        }
        i++;
    }
    while(i>0){
        item = listItems[i][0];
        if (!disabledFilterFunction(item.data)){
            selectedIndex = i - verticalScrollPosition;
            return;
        }
        i--;
    }
}
}
}
}
}
}
]]>
</mx:Script>
</mx:List>
```

5.9 Format and Validate Data Added in a List's Item Editor

Problem

You need to validate any data that the user enters in an item editor before committing the value to the list.

Solution

On the `itemEditEnd` event, retrieve the text from the item editor by using the `itemEditorInstance` property of the `ListBase` class and parse the results.

Discussion

To validate and format any data that is entered, you must listen to the item edit events that the `List` dispatches when the user begins and finishes editing an item in the list. The `List` control dispatches three events when the item editor is edited:

itemEditBegin

> This event is dispatched when the `editedItemPosition` property is set and the item can be edited. When this event is fired, the `List` creates an `itemEditor` object by using the `createItemEditor` method and copies the data property from the item to the editor. By default, the `itemEditor` object is an instance of the `TextInput` control. You use the `itemEditor` property of the `List` control to specify a custom `itemEditor` class and finally set the `itemEditorInstance`. To stop the editor from being created, you can call `preventDefault` as part of the default event listener.

itemEditBeginning

> This event is dispatched when the user releases the mouse button while over an item, tabs to the list or within the list, or in any way attempts to edit the list. The default listener for this event sets the `List.editedItemPosition` property to the item that has focus, which starts the item-editing session. You typically write your own event listener for this event to disallow editing of a specific item or items. Calling the `preventDefault` method from within your own event listener for this event prevents the default listener from executing.

itemEditEnd

> The list components have a default handler for this event that copies the data from the `itemEditor` to the data provider of the `List` control. By default, the `List` uses the `editorDataField` property of the `List` control to determine the property of the `itemEditor` containing the new data and updates the data provider item with that new data. Because the default `itemEditor` is the `TextInput` control, the default value of the `editorDataField` property is `text`, to specify that the `text` property of the `TextInput` contains the new item data and then calls `destroyItemEditor`, which destroys the `itemEditor`. In an event-listening function, you can modify the data returned by the editor to the list component. In your event listener, examine the

data entered into the `itemEditor`. If the data is incorrect, you can call the `prevent` `Default` method to stop Flex from passing the new data back to the `List` control and from closing the editor.

In the following example, the `preventDefault` method of the event is used to prevent the editor from closing and saving the value to the `dataProvider` if based on the regular expression. If the value passed in to the `itemEditor` is correct, then it formats the string into proper first and last names and saves the result.

```
<mx:Canvas xmlns:mx="http://www.adobe.com/2006/mxml" width="400" height="300">
    <mx:Script>
        <![CDATA[
            import mx.events.ListEvent;
            import mx.controls.TextInput;
            import mx.events.ListEvent;
            import mx.collections.ArrayCollection;

            [Bindable]
            private var dp:ArrayCollection = new ArrayCollection([{name:"John Smith",
positionType:1}, {name:"Ellen Smith", positionType:2}, {name:"James Smith",
positionType:3}, {name:"Jane Smith", positionType:4}]);
```

Here the event listener for the `itemEditEnd` event is defined. Note that the event is a `ListEvent` object that contains a **reason** property. This property will be used to determine whether the user has made a change to the value of the `itemEditor`.

```
        public function formatData(event:ListEvent):void {
            // Check the reason for the event.
            if (event.reason == "cancelled") {
                // Do not update cell.
                return;
            }

            // Get the new data value from the editor.
            var newData:String = TextInput(event.currentTarget.itemEditorInstance)
.text;

            // Determine if the new value is an empty String.
            var reg:RegExp = /\d/;
            if(newData == "" || reg.test(newData)) {
                // Prevent the user from removing focus,
                // and leave the cell editor open.
                event.preventDefault();
                // Use the errorString to inform the user that something is wrong.
                TextInput(listInstance.itemEditorInstance).setStyle("borderColor",
0xff0000);
                TextInput(listInstance.itemEditorInstance).errorString = "Enter a
valid string.";

                return void;
            }
            //test for FirstName LastName format
            reg = /\w+.\s.\w+/
            if(!reg.test(newData)) {
                event.preventDefault();
                TextInput( listInstance.itemEditorInstance ).setStyle
```

```
        ( "borderColor", 0xff0000);
                        TextInput(listInstance.itemEditorInstance).errorString = "Enter
        first name and last name";
                    } else {
                        //make sure the name is properly formatted
                        var firstName:String = newData.substring(0, newData.indexOf(" "));
                        var lastName:String = newData.substring(newData.indexOf(" ")+1);
                        firstName = firstName.charAt(0).toUpperCase() + firstName.substr
        (1);

                        lastName = lastName.charAt(0).toUpperCase() + lastName.substr(1);
                        TextInput(listInstance.itemEditorInstance).text = firstName+"
        "+lastName;

                        newData = newData.charAt(0).toLocaleUpperCase()+newData.substring(
        1, newData.indexOf(" "))+newData.charAt(newData.indexOf(" ")+1)+newData.substring
        (newData.indexOf(" ")+2);
                    }
                }
            ]]>
        </mx:Script>
        <mx:List id="listInstance" dataProvider="{dp}" editable="true" labelField="name"
        itemEditEnd="formatData(event)" width="300"/>
        </mx:Canvas>
```

5.10 Track All Selected Children in a TileList

Problem

You need a toggle in a renderer for a TileList and you want to track all children that have been selected.

Solution

Extend the TileList component and create a custom renderer to use as the itemRenderer. On the toggle event in the renderer, dispatch the uid unique identifier in an event to the TileList that will store all the IDs in an array.

Discussion

All itemRenderers have access to their parent ListBase component when their list Data property is set. When a renderer implements IDropInListItemRenderer, it implements methods to get and set listData, a BaseListData object. The BaseListData class provides access to the ListBase object that is setting the data in the itemRenderer via the owner property, as shown here:

```
public function set listData( value:BaseListData ):void
    private var listParent:ListBase;
    listParent = _listData.owner as ListBase;
}
```

After you have a reference to the ListBase that has created a renderer, any public properties of the ListBase are accessible to that renderer. This recipe's example makes an

ArrayCollection of all toggled buttons available to the itemRenderer, which is the SelectedChildrenTileListRender class in this case. The SelectedChildrenTileListRender class takes care of looking through the ArrayCollection and either adding or removing itself from the array depending on whether its button is toggled on or off.

The SelectedChildrenTileListRender uses the uid property that is passed into it with the BaseListData property to determine whether the itemRenderer is represented in the array of toggled renderers. This uid, or unique identifier, ensures that even if the data has duplicated items, the itemRenderer will always have a unique reference with which to identify itself.

The SelectedChildrenTileListRender defines the item renderer that will be used:

```
<mx:VBox xmlns:mx="http://www.adobe.com/2006/mxml" implements="mx.controls.listClasses.
IDropInListItemRenderer">
    <mx:Script>
        <![CDATA[
            import mx.controls.listClasses.BaseListData;
            import mx.controls.Button;
            import mx.controls.TileList;
            import mx.events.FlexEvent;
            import mx.controls.listClasses.IDropInListItemRenderer;

            private var _listData:BaseListData;
            [Bindable]
            public var key:String;
              //the list parent of this renderer
            private var tileList:SelectedChildrenTileList;

            override public function set data(value:Object):void {
                super.data = value;
                this.invalidateProperties();
                dispatchEvent(new FlexEvent(FlexEvent.DATA_CHANGE));
            }

            [Bindable("dataChange")]
            public function get listData():BaseListData {
                return _listData;
            }

            public function set listData( value:BaseListData ):void {
                //set the list data
                _listData = value;
                //get access to the tile list
                tileList = _listData.owner as SelectedChildrenTileList;
                //finally, track this item's unique ID that all items
                //in a BaseListData are assigned
                key=_listData.uid;
            }

            private function onToggle(event:Event):void
            {
                var i:int = tileList.toggledButtons.getItemIndex(key);
```

```
                    //if the key of this renderer appears in the list of toggled buttons,
          then remove it
                    if(i != -1 && (event.target as Button).selected==false){
                        tileList.toggledButtons.removeItemAt(i);
                    }
                    //if the key of this renderer doesn't appear in the list of toggled
          buttons, then add it
                    if(i == -1 && (event.target as Button).selected == true){
                        tileList.toggledButtons.addItem(key)
                    }
                    tileList.invalidateList();
                }

                override protected function updateDisplayList(unscaledWidth:Number,
          unscaledHeight:Number):void
                {
                    super.updateDisplayList(unscaledWidth, unscaledHeight);
                    if(key)
                    {
                        var i:int=tileList.toggledButtons.getItemIndex(key);
                        //sometimes putting your if/else on one line makes things neater,
          not always, but sometimes
                        if(i != -1){ toggleBtn.selected=true; } else { toggleBtn.selected
          = false; }
                    }
                }
            ]]>
        </mx:Script>
        <mx:Button id="toggleBtn" width="100%" label="{data.label}" toggle="true" change=
    "onToggle(event)"/>
    </mx:VBox>
```

The SelectedChildrenTileList shown in the following code uses the SelectedChildren TileListRender, extends TileList, and as mentioned previously, defines a toggledButton's ArrayCollection to store the uids of all items selected. You must also define a returnAllSelected method to find all the selected itemRenderers currently toggled.

```
    <mx:TileList xmlns:mx="http://www.adobe.com/2006/mxml" initialize="toggledButtons = new
    ArrayCollection()">
        <mx:Script>
            <![CDATA[
                import mx.collections.ArrayCollection;
                [Bindable]
                public var toggledButtons:ArrayCollection;

                public function removeAll():void{
                    toggledButtons.removeAll();
                    //use the invalidatList method to redraw the grid right away
                    this.invalidateList();
                }

                public function returnAllSelected():Array{
                    var arr:Array = new Array();
                    for(var i:int = 0; i < (dataProvider as ArrayCollection).length; i++)
```

```
                {
                    if(toggledButtons.contains((indexToItemRenderer(i) as
SelectedChildrenTileListRender).key)){
                        arr.push((indexToItemRenderer(i) as
SelectedChildrenTileListRender).data);
                    }
                }
                return arr;
            }
        ]]>
    </mx:Script>
</mx:TileList>
```

5.11 Use and Display Null Items in an Item Renderer

Problem

You want to display null items in a sparsely populated array.

Solution

Set nullItemRenderer for the List control.

Discussion

Use the nullItemRenderer property whenever a null object is encountered in the data Provider of any class that extends ListBase:

```
<mx:TileList nullItemRenderer="oreilly.cookbook.NullItemRenderer"/>
```

NullItemRenderer.mxml shows the complete listing for a typical nullItemRenderer:

```
<mx:Canvas xmlns:mx="http://www.adobe.com/2006/mxml" width="50" height="50">
    <mx:Image source="Assets.notAvailableImage"/>
    <mx:Text text="sorry, unavailable" y="30"/>
</mx:Canvas>
```

The NullItemRenderer class is passed into the nullItemRenderer property of the TileList as shown here:

```
<mx:Canvas xmlns:mx="http://www.adobe.com/2006/mxml" width="400" height="300">
    <mx:Script>
        <![CDATA[
            import mx.collections.ArrayCollection;
            [Bindable]
            private var dp:ArrayCollection = new ArrayCollection([null, {name:"Ellen
Smith", positionType:2}, null, {name:"Jane Smith", positionType:4}]);
        ]]>
    </mx:Script>
    <mx:TileList width="100%" columnWidth="150" rowHeight="150" dataProvider="{dp}"
labelField="name" nullItemRenderer="oreilly.cookbook.NullItemRenderer"/>
</mx:Canvas>
```

5.12 Create a Right-Click Menu for a List

Problem

You need to create a custom context menu to display when the user right-clicks or Control-clicks on a specific item.

Solution

Create `ContextMenu` and `ContextMenuItem` objects and assign those to the renderer that will be assigned to the list as the `itemRenderer`.

Discussion

The context menu is what appears for the user when she right-clicks or Control-clicks on your Flex application. By default, this menu shows Loop, Play, Print, Quality, Rewind, Save, and Zoom controls, as well as a link to an info screen about the Flash Player 9. You can easily customize this menu, however, by creating a new `ContextMenu` object. Simply call the constructor for the `ContextMenu` class and set the `contextMenu` property of any display object to be the object just created, as shown:

```
var menu:ContentMenu = new ContextMenu();
this.contextMenu = menu;
```

This code needs to be run within a `DisplayObject`, that is, any object with a visual display. The custom context menu created here will appear only if the user has right- or Control-clicked the `DisplayObject` or a component with the `contentMenu` property set.

To add new items to a context menu, use the `customItems` array defined by the `Context Menu`. Instantiate new `ContextMenuItem` objects and add them to the array by using the `push` method.

The constructor for the `ContextMenuItem` has the following signature:

```
ContextMenuItem(caption:String, separatorBefore:Boolean = false, enabled:Boolean =
true, visible:Boolean = true)
```

The `caption` property determines the title of the menu item—for example, Look Up Employees. The `separatorBefore` property determines whether a thin bar will appear above the `ContextMenuItem` to divide it from the items above it in the menu. Finally, the `visible` and `enabled` properties control whether the item is visible and able to be selected by the user, respectively.

The `ContextMenuItem` dispatches a `ContextMenuEvent` event of type `SELECT` when the item is selected by the user.

The example that follows creates a renderer for a `List` control that will create custom context menus based on the data type passed in from the `List`.

```
<mx:VBox xmlns:mx="http://www.adobe.com/2006/mxml" width="150" height="80" paddingLeft=
"10">
    <mx:Script>
        <![CDATA[

            import flash.display.*;

            override public function set data(value:Object):void
            {
                if(value is Name)
                {
                    text1.text = value.firstName;
                    text2.text = value.lastName;
                    var personMenu:ContextMenu = new ContextMenu();
                    var lookupRecord:ContextMenuItem = new ContextMenuItem("Look Up
Record");
                    var lookupPicture:ContextMenuItem = new ContextMenuItem("Look Up
Picture");
                    personMenu.customItems.push(lookupRecord);
                    personMenu.customItems.push(lookupPicture);
                    this.contextMenu = personMenu;
                }
                else if(value is Office)
                {
                    text1.text = value.officeAddress;
                    text2.text = value.officeName;
                    var officeMenu:ContextMenu = new ContextMenu();
                    var lookupMap:ContextMenuItem = new ContextMenuItem("Look Up
Map");
                    lookupMap.addEventListener(ContextMenuEvent.MENU_ITEM_SELECT, show
Map);
                    var lookupEmployees:ContextMenuItem = new ContextMenuItem("Look Up
Employees");
                    lookupEmployees.addEventListener(ContextMenuEvent.MENU_ITEM_SELECT
, showEmployees);
                    officeMenu.customItems.push(lookupEmployees);
                    officeMenu.customItems.push(lookupMap);
                    this.contextMenu = officeMenu;
                }
            }

            private function showMap(event:ContextMenuEvent):void
            {
                //do something with the map
            }

            private function showEmployees(event:ContextMenuEvent):void
            {
                //do something to look up all the employees
            }

        ]]>
    </mx:Script>
    <mx:Text id="text1"/>
```

```
    <mx:Text id="text2"/>
</mx:VBox>
```

5.13 Customize the Appearance of a Selection in a List

Problem

You want to attach a graphic to the selection in a List component.

Solution

Override the drawSelectionIndicator method of the ListBase class and modify the indicator sprite that is used by that method.

Discussion

The List control creates the appearance of the selected itemRenderer in a list through the drawSelectionIndicator method. The signature of this method is as follows:

```
override protected function drawSelectionIndicator(indicator:Sprite, x:Number, y:Number
, width:Number, height:Number, color:uint, itemRenderer:IListItemRenderer):void
```

Any offset and size and color information can set in the x, y, width, height, and color properties. The first parameter, indicator, is an instance of the flash.display.Sprite on which the graphical representation of the selection is drawn, and the last parameter, itemRenderer, is the item renderer that will be selected.

The recipe's example adds an image to the indicator sprite. Because the sprite is removed and destroyed when the itemRenderer is unselected, you don't need to worry about it reappearing later.

The drawHighlightIndicator method functions the same as drawSelectionIndicator, except that it is applied to any highlighted itemRenderer—that is, any itemRenderer being moused over by the user, but not selected. Take a look:

```
override protected function drawHighlightIndicator(indicator:Sprite, x:Number, y:Number
, width:Number, height:Number, color:uint, itemRenderer:IListItemRenderer):void
```

A separate image is used to represent the highlight, moved over to the edge of the itemRenderer, and shown any time the user mouses over an itemRenderer in the list.

Here is the complete listing for the technique:

```
<mx:List xmlns:mx="http://www.adobe.com/2006/mxml" selectionColor="#ffcccc">
    <mx:Script>
        <![CDATA[

            import mx.controls.listClasses.IListItemRenderer;

            [Embed("../../assets/outline_arrow.gif")]
            private var img:Class;
```

```
            [Embed("../../assets/in_arrow.gif")]
            private var highlight_img:Class;

            override protected function drawHighlightIndicator(indicator:Sprite,
x:Number, y:Number, width:Number, height:Number, color:uint, itemRenderer:IListItem
Renderer):void
            {
                var this_img:Object = new highlight_img();
                indicator.addChild((this_img as DisplayObject));
                (this_img as DisplayObject).x = itemRenderer.width - (this_img as Disp
layObject).width
                super.drawHighlightIndicator(indicator, x, y, width, height, 0xff0000,
itemRenderer);
            }

            override protected function drawSelectionIndicator(indicator:Sprite,
x:Number, y:Number, width:Number, height:Number, color:uint, itemRenderer:
IListItemRenderer):void
            {
                var this_img:Object = new img();
                indicator.addChild((this_img as DisplayObject));
                (this_img as DisplayObject).x = itemRenderer.width - (this_img as
DisplayObject).width
                super.drawSelectionIndicator(indicator, x, y, width, height, 0xffcccc,
itemRenderer);
            }

        ]]>
    </mx:Script>
</mx:List>
```

CHAPTER 6

DataGrid and Advanced DataGrid

The `DataGrid` control is a list-based control optimized to display large data sets in a multicolumn layout. The `DataGrid` control features resizable columns, customizable item renderers, and sorting capabilities, among other features. Flex 3 adds two new controls to the `DataGrid` family: `AdvancedDataGrid` and `OLAPDataGrid`. The `AdvancedDataGrid` control expands on the `DataGrid` control to add extra data visualization capabilities such as data aggregation, data formatting, multicolumn sorting, and so on. This is similar to the functionality of Pivot Tables in Microsoft Excel. The `Advan cedDataGrid` and `OLAPDataGrid` controls are available with the data visualization framework that is bundled with the Flex Builder 3 Professional Edition.

The two `DataGrid` controls are typically used to display arrays or collections of data objects with similar types. The `AdvancedDataGrid` control can also display `HierarchicalData` objects, show the parent-child relationships among complex data objects, and allow for the creation of specialized groupings of data.

6.1 Create Custom Columns for a DataGrid

Problem

You need to specify custom columns for a `DataGrid` and explicitly control the display.

Solution

Use the `DataGridColumn` tag to specify custom properties for columns in a `DataGrid`.

Discussion

This recipe adds three `DataGridColumn` tags to the `columns` property of a `DataGrid`. It uses the homesforsale.xml data file. The `DataGridColumn` tags specify the order in which to display the properties of the objects in the `dataProvider` and the title to use for the column headers. The `dataField` property of the `DataGridColumn` specifies the property of the object to be displayed in the cells of that column. In this example, the object's range property is not displayed in the DataGrid control because there is no DataGrid Column with a dataField associated to the range property. Here's the necessary code:

```
<mx:Application
    xmlns:mx="http://www.adobe.com/2006/mxml"
    layout="absolute"
    creationComplete="initApp()">

    <mx:HTTPService id="srv" url="assets/homesforsale.xml"
        resultFormat="object"
        result="onResult(event)"/>

    <mx:DataGrid id="grid"
        width="100%"
        height="100%"
        dataProvider="{homesForSale}">
        <mx:columns>
            <mx:DataGridColumn headerText="Total No."
                dataField="total"/>
            <mx:DataGridColumn headerText="City"
                dataField="city"/>
            <mx:DataGridColumn headerText="State"
                dataField="state"/>
        </mx:columns>
    </mx:DataGrid>
    <mx:Script>
        <![CDATA[
            import mx.collections.ArrayCollection;
            import mx.rpc.events.ResultEvent;

            [Bindable]
            private var homesForSale:ArrayCollection;

            private function initApp():void {
                this.srv.send();
            }

            private function onResult(evt:ResultEvent):void {
                this.homesForSale = evt.result.data.region;
            }

        ]]>
    </mx:Script>
</mx:Application>
```

The DataGridColumn supports further customization of the display through the use of itemRenderers. The following code sample adds a new DataGridColumn that uses a custom renderer, RangeRenderer, to render the range property in a more-meaningful way. The range property contains three values that indicate the percentage of houses for sale based on their price ranges: range1 contains the percent of houses on sale under $350,000, range2 is the percent of houses on sale between $350,000 and $600,000, and range3 contains the houses over $600,000.

```
<mx:Application
    xmlns:mx="http://www.adobe.com/2006/mxml"
    layout="absolute"
    creationComplete="initApp()">

    <mx:HTTPService id="srv" url="assets/homesforsale.xml"
        resultFormat="object"
        result="onResult(event)"/>

    <mx:DataGrid id="grid"
        width="100%"
        height="100%"
        dataProvider="{homesForSale}">
        <mx:columns>
            <mx:DataGridColumn headerText="Total No."
                dataField="total"/>
            <mx:DataGridColumn headerText="City"
                dataField="city"/>
            <mx:DataGridColumn headerText="State"
                dataField="state"/>
            <mx:DataGridColumn headerText="Price Ranges"
                dataField="range"
                itemRenderer="RangeRenderer"/>
        </mx:columns>
    </mx:DataGrid>
    <mx:Script>
        <![CDATA[
            import mx.collections.ArrayCollection;
            import mx.rpc.events.ResultEvent;

            [Bindable]
            private var homesForSale:ArrayCollection;

            private function initApp():void {
                this.srv.send();
            }

            private function onResult(evt:ResultEvent):void {
                this.homesForSale = evt.result.data.region;
            }

        ]]>
    </mx:Script>
</mx:Application>
```

The RangeRenderer shown in the following code uses the range percent values to draw
a color-coded bar that indicates the value of each range. This is done by overriding the
updateDisplayList method to draw the colored bars using the drawing API. For more-
detailed information regarding itemRenderers, see Chapter 7, "Renderers and Editors."

```
package {
    import flash.display.Graphics;

    import mx.containers.Canvas;
```

```
public class RangeRenderer extends Canvas {
    override public function set data(value:Object):void {
        super.data = value;
        if(value!= null && value.range != null) {
            this.invalidateDisplayList();
        }
    }

    override protected function updateDisplayList(unscaledWidth:Number,
unscaledHeight:Number):void {
        var g:Graphics = this.graphics;

        if(this.data) {
            var w1:Number = (this.data.range.range1 * unscaledWidth)/100;
            var w2:Number = (this.data.range.range2 * unscaledWidth)/100;
            var w3:Number = (this.data.range.range3 * unscaledWidth)/100;

            var x1:Number = 0;
            var x2:Number = w1;
            var x3:Number = w1 + w2;

            g.beginFill(0x0000ff);
            g.drawRect(x1,0,w1,unscaledHeight);
            g.beginFill(0x00ff00);
            g.drawRect(x2,0,w2,unscaledHeight);
            g.beginFill(0xff0000);
            g.drawRect(x3,0,w3,unscaledHeight);
        }
    }
}
```

Note that trying to sort the range column of the DataGrid still throws a runtime error.
You can resolve this by using a custom sort function as shown in the next recipe.

See Also

Recipe 6.2.

6.2 Specify Sort Functions for DataGrid Columns

Problem

You want to use custom sorting logic to sort complex objects within a DataGrid.

Solution

Use the sortCompareFunction property of the DataGridColumn tag to assign a reference
to a function that performs the custom sorting logic.

Discussion

You can modify the `DataGrid` used in the previous recipe to add a custom sorting function. This example uses a custom `itemRenderer` called `RangeRenderer` to add the sorting function `sortRanges` to the `DataGridColumn` that displays the `range` property:

```
<mx:Application
    xmlns:mx="http://www.adobe.com/2006/mxml"
    layout="absolute"
    creationComplete="initApp()">

    <mx:HTTPService id="srv" url="assets/homesforsale.xml"
        resultFormat="object"
        result="onResult(event)"/>

    <mx:DataGrid id="grid"        width="100%"        height="100%"
dataProvider="{homesForSale}">
        <mx:columns>
            <mx:DataGridColumn headerText="Total No."
                dataField="total"/>
            <mx:DataGridColumn headerText="City"
                dataField="city"/>
            <mx:DataGridColumn headerText="State"
                dataField="state"/>
            <mx:DataGridColumn headerText="Price Ranges [&lt;350K] [350K -600K]
[&gt;600K]"
                dataField="range"
                itemRenderer="RangeRenderer"
                sortCompareFunction="sortRanges"/>
        </mx:columns>
    </mx:DataGrid>
    <mx:Script>
        <![CDATA[
            import mx.collections.ArrayCollection;
            import mx.rpc.events.ResultEvent;

            [Bindable]
            private var homesForSale:ArrayCollection;

            private function initApp():void {
                this.srv.send();
            }

            private function onResult(evt:ResultEvent):void {
                this.homesForSale = evt.result.data.region;
            }

            private function sortRanges(obj1:Object, obj2:Object):int{
                var value1:Number = obj1.range.range1;
                var value2:Number = obj2.range.range1;

                if(value1 < value2) {
                    return -1;
                }
                else if(value1 > value2){
```

```
                return 1;
            }
            else {
                return 0;
            }
        }

    ]]>
    </mx:Script>
</mx:Application>
```

The `sortCompareFunction` property of the fourth `DataGridColumn` is assigned to `sortRanges`, which implements the custom logic to sort the ranges. The `sortCompare Function` property of the `DataGridColumns` expects a function with the following signature:

```
sortCompareFunction(obj1:Object, obj2:Object):int
```

The function accepts two parameters that correspond to two objects in the `dataProvider` being sorted at any given time, and it returns an integer value of –1, 1, or 0 that indicates the order in which the two objects were placed after the sort. When the user clicks the header for the `DataGridColumn`, the `DataGrid` runs the `sortCompare Function` for each item in the `dataProvider` and uses the return value to figure out where to order the items. The `sortRange` function looks at the nested `range1` property of the `dataProvider` item to calculate the sort order. Now when the user clicks the header of the Price Ranges column, the items are sorted based on their `range1` values.

6.3 Enable Multicolumn Sorting in a DataGrid

Problem

You need to enable support for multicolumn sorting capability in a `DataGrid`.

Solution

Use the `AdvancedDataGrid` control along with the `AdvancedDataGridColumn` to provide support for multicolumn sorting.

Discussion

The `AdvancedDataGrid` control introduced in Flex 3 has built-in support for multicolumn sorting. To demonstrate, the following example code modifies the previous recipe by replacing the `DataGrid` and the `DataGridColumn` controls with the `AdvancedDataGrid` and the `AdvancedDataGridColumn` controls, respectively. `AdvancedDataGrid` supports two modes of multicolumn sorting. The default mode, `sortExpertMode=false`, allows primary sorts by clicking on the column header, while secondary sorting can be achieved by clicking in the multicolumn sort area (the right side of the column header). The example code uses the expert mode, `sortExpertMode=false`, which allows primary sorting by clicking on the column header and secondary sorting by right-clicking (Windows) or Control-clicking (Mac) the column header.

```
<mx:Application
    xmlns:mx="http://www.adobe.com/2006/mxml"
    layout="absolute"
    creationComplete="initApp()">

    <mx:HTTPService id="srv" url="assets/homesforsale.xml"
        resultFormat="object"
        result="onResult(event)"/>

    <mx:AdvancedDataGrid id="grid"
        width="100%"
        height="100%"
        sortExpertMode="true"
        dataProvider="{homesForSale}">
        <mx:columns>
            <mx:AdvancedDataGridColumn headerText="Total No."
                dataField="total"/>
            <mx:AdvancedDataGridColumn headerText="City"
                dataField="city"/>
            <mx:AdvancedDataGridColumn headerText="State"
                dataField="state"/>
            <mx:AdvancedDataGridColumn headerText="Price Ranges [&lt;350K]
[350K -600K] [&gt;600K]"
                dataField="range"
                itemRenderer="RangeRenderer"
                sortCompareFunction="sortRanges"/>
        </mx:columns>
    </mx:AdvancedDataGrid>
    <mx:Script>
        <![CDATA[
            import mx.collections.ArrayCollection;
            import mx.rpc.events.ResultEvent;

            [Bindable]
            private var homesForSale:ArrayCollection;

            private function initApp():void {
                this.srv.send();
            }

            private function onResult(evt:ResultEvent):void {
                this.homesForSale = evt.result.data.region;
            }

            private function sortRanges(obj1:Object, obj2:Object):int{
                var value1:Number = obj1.range.range1;
                var value2:Number = obj2.range.range1;

                if(value1 < value2) {
                    return -1;
                }
                else if(value1 > value2){
```

```
                    return 1;
                }
                else {
                    return 0;
                }
            }

        ]]>
    </mx:Script>
</mx:Application>
```

6.4 Filter Items in a DataGrid

Problem

You need to provide "live" client-side filtering for a data set displayed in a DataGrid.

Solution

Use the filterFunction property of the ArrayCollection to assign a reference to a custom function that performs the filter matching.

Discussion

To demonstrate implementing client-side filtering, the following example adds a city-filtering feature to the previous recipe. The UI features a TextInput field that enables the user to type city names and filter out the records in the DataGrid that match the input. When the user types an entry into the cityFilter TextInput control, it dispatches a change event, which is handled by the applyFilter method. The applyFilter method assigns a function reference to the filterFunction property of the homesForSale Array Collection instance, if it wasn't assigned before, and proceeds to call the refresh method on the ArrayCollection. The filterCities method implements a simple check for a lowercase string match between the city property of the dataProvider item and the input text.

```
<mx:Application xmlns:mx="http://www.adobe.com/2006/mxml" layout="vertical"
creationComplete="initApp()">
    <mx:HTTPService id="srv" url="assets/homesforsale.xml" resultFormat="object"
result="onResult(event)"/>

    <mx:Form>
        <mx:FormItem label="City">
            <mx:TextInput id="cityFilter" change="applyFilter()"/>
        </mx:FormItem>
    </mx:Form>

    <mx:AdvancedDataGrid id="grid"          width="100%"          height="100%"
sortExpertMode="true"          dataProvider="{homesForSale}">
        <mx:columns>
            <mx:AdvancedDataGridColumn headerText="Total No."
```

```
                    dataField="total"/>
            <mx:AdvancedDataGridColumn headerText="City"
                dataField="city"/>
            <mx:AdvancedDataGridColumn headerText="State"
                dataField="state"/>
            <mx:AdvancedDataGridColumn headerText="Price Ranges [&lt;350K]
    [350K -600K] [&gt;600K]" dataField="range" itemRenderer="RangeRenderer" sortCompare
Function="sortRanges"/>
        </mx:columns>
    </mx:AdvancedDataGrid>
    <mx:Script>
        <![CDATA[
            import mx.events.FlexEvent;
            import mx.collections.ArrayCollection;
            import mx.rpc.events.ResultEvent;

            [Bindable]
            private var homesForSale:ArrayCollection;

            private function initApp():void {
                this.srv.send();
            }

            private function onResult(evt:ResultEvent):void {
                this.homesForSale = evt.result.data.region;
            }

            private function sortRanges(obj1:Object, obj2:Object):int{
                var value1:Number = obj1.range.range1;
                var value2:Number = obj2.range.range1;

                if(value1 < value2) {
                    return -1;
                }
                else if(value1 > value2){
                    return 1;
                }
                else {
                    return 0;
                }
            }
        }
```

Here the filter function is applied to the `dataProvider` of the `DataGrid`, and the `refresh` method is called to ensure that the grid will redraw all of its renderers:

```
    private function applyFilter():void {
        if(this.homesForSale.filterFunction == null) {
            this.homesForSale.filterFunction = this.filterCities;
        }
        this.homesForSale.refresh();
    }
```

The filter method used simply returns true if the item should be included in the filtered array, and false if it should not:

```
private function filterCities(item:Object):Boolean {
            var match:Boolean = true;

            if(cityFilter.text != "") {
                var city:String = item["city"];
                var filter:String = this.cityFilter.text;
                if(!city ||
                    city.toLowerCase().indexOf(filter.toLowerCase()) < 0) {
                    match = false;
                }
            }

            return match;
        }
    ]]>
    </mx:Script>
</mx:Application>
```

6.5 Create Custom Headers for an AdvancedDataGrid

Problem

You want to customize the header for a `DataGrid` by adding a `CheckBox`.

Solution

Extend the `AdvancedDataGridHeaderRenderer` class by overriding the `createChildren` and `updateDisplayList` methods to add a `CheckBox`.

Discussion

This recipe builds on the previous one by specifying a custom header renderer for the `city` `DataGridColumn`. Creating a custom header renderer is similar to creating a custom item renderer or item editor. A class reference that implements the `IFactory` interface is passed to the `headerRenderer` property of the `DataGridColumn`, and the column takes care of instantiating the object. This example uses a renderer class called `CheckBoxHeaderRenderer` to create a header with a `CheckBox` contained within it:

```
<mx:Application xmlns:mx="http://www.adobe.com/2006/mxml" layout="vertical"
    creationComplete="initApp()">
    <mx:HTTPService id="srv" url="assets/homesforsale.xml" resultFormat="object"
        result="onResult(event)"/>
    <mx:Form>
        <mx:FormItem label="City">
            <mx:TextInput id="cityFilter" change="applyFilter()"/>
        </mx:FormItem>
    </mx:Form>
```

```
        <mx:AdvancedDataGrid id="grid"        width="100%"        height="100%"
    sortExpertMode="true"       dataProvider="{homesForSale}">
            <mx:columns>
                <mx:AdvancedDataGridColumn headerText="Total No."
                    dataField="total"/>
```

Because the custom header renderer should be set for this particular column and not the others, you set the headerRenderer property on the AdvancedDataGrid column to the class name that will be used to create the headers:

```
        <mx:AdvancedDataGridColumn headerText="City"
            sortable="false"
            headerRenderer="CheckBoxHeaderRenderer"
            dataField="city"/>
        <mx:AdvancedDataGridColumn headerText="State dataField="state"/>
        <mx:AdvancedDataGridColumn headerText="Price Ranges [&lt;350K]
[350K -600K] [&gt;600K]" dataField="range" itemRenderer="RangeRenderer"
sortCompareFunction="sortRanges"/>
            </mx:columns>
        </mx:AdvancedDataGrid>
        <mx:Script>
            <![CDATA[
                import mx.events.FlexEvent;
                import mx.collections.ArrayCollection;
                import mx.rpc.events.ResultEvent;

                [Bindable]
                private var homesForSale:ArrayCollection;

                private function initApp():void {
                    this.srv.send();
                }

                private function onResult(evt:ResultEvent):void {
                    this.homesForSale = evt.result.data.region;
                }

                private function sortRanges(obj1:Object, obj2:Object):int{
                    var value1:Number = obj1.range.range1;
                    var value2:Number = obj2.range.range1;

                    if(value1 < value2) {
                        return -1;
                    }
                    else if(value1 > value2){
                        return 1;
                    }
                    else {
                        return 0;
                    }
                }

                private function applyFilter():void {
                    if(this.homesForSale.filterFunction == null) {
                        this.homesForSale.filterFunction = this.filterCities;
```

```
            }
            this.homesForSale.refresh();
        }

        private function filterCities(item:Object):Boolean {
            var match:Boolean = true;

            if(cityFilter.text != "") {
                var city:String = item["city"];
                var filter:String = this.cityFilter.text;
                if(!city ||
                    city.toLowerCase().indexOf(filter.toLowerCase()) < 0) {
                    match = false;
                }
            }
            return match;
        }

        ]]>
    </mx:Script>
</mx:Application>
```

The code for the custom header renderer class CheckBoxHeaderRenderer follows. Note that it overrides the createChildren method of the AdvancedDataGridHeader class to create a new CheckBox and add it to the display list. The updateDisplayList method forces the CheckBox to resize itself to its default size. The next recipe explains how to dispatch events from the custom renderer and handle them.

```
package {

    import flash.events.Event;

    import mx.controls.AdvancedDataGrid;
    import mx.controls.CheckBox;
    import mx.controls.advancedDataGridClasses.AdvancedDataGridHeaderRenderer;
    import mx.events.AdvancedDataGridEvent;

    public class CheckBoxHeaderRenderer extends AdvancedDataGridHeaderRenderer {

        private var selector:CheckBox;

        override protected function createChildren():void {
            super.createChildren();
            this.selector = new CheckBox();
            this.selector.x = 5;
            this.addChild(this.selector);
        }

        override protected function updateDisplayList(unscaledWidth:Number,
unscaledHeight:Number):void {
            super.updateDisplayList(unscaledWidth, unscaledHeight);
            this.selector.setActualSize(this.selector.getExplicitOrMeasuredWidth(),
                            this.selector.getExplicitOrMeasuredHeight());
        }
```

```
        }
    }
```

6.6 Handle Events from a DataGrid/AdvancedDataGrid

Problem

You need to manage events dispatched by the DataGrid and its item renderers.

Solution

Use the owner property inside the item renderer to dispatch an event from the parent DataGrid.

Discussion

In the previous recipe, a custom header renderer was created for a DataGridColumn by passing a class reference to the headerRenderer property of the column. In this recipe, the header renderer class used in that recipe will be extended. When the CheckBox in the header renderer is clicked, the class will dispatch an event up to the DataGrid that owns the column in which the headerRenderer is used.

```
<mx:Application xmlns:mx="http://www.adobe.com/2006/mxml"
    layout="vertical" creationComplete="initApp()">

    <mx:HTTPService id="srv" url="assets/homesforsale.xml"
        resultFormat="object"
        result="onResult(event)"/>

    <mx:Form>
        <mx:FormItem label="City">
            <mx:TextInput id="cityFilter" change="applyFilter()"/>
        </mx:FormItem>
    </mx:Form>

    <mx:AdvancedDataGrid id="grid"          width="100%"          height="100%"
sortExpertMode="true"          dataProvider="{homesForSale}"
        creationComplete="assignListeners()">
        <mx:columns>
            <mx:AdvancedDataGridColumn headerText="Total No." dataField="total"/>
            <mx:AdvancedDataGridColumn headerText="City" sortable="false"
                headerRenderer="CheckBoxHeaderRenderer2"
                dataField="city"/>
            <mx:AdvancedDataGridColumn headerText="State" dataField="state"/>
            <mx:AdvancedDataGridColumn headerText="Price Ranges [&lt;350K] [350K
-600K] [&gt;600K]" dataField="range" itemRenderer="RangeRenderer"
sortCompareFunction="sortRanges"/>
        </mx:columns>
    </mx:AdvancedDataGrid>
    <mx:Script>
        <![CDATA[
            import mx.events.FlexEvent;
```

```
import mx.collections.ArrayCollection;
import mx.rpc.events.ResultEvent;

[Bindable]
private var homesForSale:ArrayCollection;

private function initApp():void {
    this.srv.send();
}

private function onResult(evt:ResultEvent):void {
    this.homesForSale = evt.result.data.region;
}

private function sortRanges(obj1:Object, obj2:Object):int{
    var value1:Number = obj1.range.range1;
    var value2:Number = obj2.range.range1;

    if(value1 < value2) {
        return -1;
    }
    else if(value1 > value2){
        return 1;
    }
    else {
        return 0;
    }
}

private function applyFilter():void {
    if(this.homesForSale.filterFunction == null) {
        this.homesForSale.filterFunction = this.filterCities;
    }
    this.homesForSale.refresh();
}

private function filterCities(item:Object):Boolean {
    var match:Boolean = true;

    if(cityFilter.text != "") {
        var city:String = item["city"];
        var filter:String = this.cityFilter.text;
        if(!city ||
            city.toLowerCase().indexOf(filter.toLowerCase()) < 0) {
            match = false;
        }
    }

    return match;
}
```

Because the event bubbles up from the DataGridColumn to the parent DataGrid, you can simply add an event listener to the DataGrid itself to capture the event. The onColumn Select method will receive a custom event of type ColumnSelectedEvent that will contain information about the column in which the header renderer is used.

```
        private function assignListeners():void {
                    this.grid.addEventListener(ColumnSelectedEvent.COLUMN_SELECTED,
    onColumnSelect);
                }

            private function onColumnSelect(evt:ColumnSelectedEvent):void {
                trace("column selected = " + evt.colIdx);
            }

        ]]>
    </mx:Script>
</mx:Application>
```

The example code builds on the previous recipe by adding a new header renderer, CheckBoxHeaderRenderer2, for the city column of the AdvancedDataGrid. The code also assigns a listener to the ColumnSelectedEvent, which is a custom event dispatched by the AdvancedDataGrid. The listener function onColumnSelected merely traces out the selected column index to the console for display purposes. (As the next recipe demonstrates, this technique can be leveraged to provide more-useful functionality.) The following code demonstrates the CheckBoxHeaderRenderer2:

```
package {

    import flash.events.MouseEvent;

    import mx.controls.AdvancedDataGrid;
    import mx.controls.CheckBox;
    import mx.controls.advancedDataGridClasses.AdvancedDataGridHeaderRenderer;

    public class CheckBoxHeaderRenderer2 extends AdvancedDataGridHeaderRenderer {

        private var selector:CheckBox;

        override protected function createChildren():void {
            super.createChildren();
            this.selector = new CheckBox();
            this.selector.x = 5;
            this.addChild(this.selector);
            this.selector.addEventListener( MouseEvent.CLICK,
    dispatchColumnSelected);
        }

        override protected function updateDisplayList(unscaledWidth:Number,
    unscaledHeight:Number):void {
            super.updateDisplayList(unscaledWidth, unscaledHeight);
            this.selector.setActualSize(this.selector.getExplicitOrMeasuredWidth(),
                                this.selector.getExplicitOrMeasuredHeight());
        }

        private function dispatchColumnSelected(evt:MouseEvent):void {
            var event:ColumnSelectedEvent = new ColumnSelectedEvent(
    ColumnSelectedEvent.COLUMN_SELECTED, listData.columnIndex, selector.selected);
            AdvancedDataGrid(listData.owner).dispatchEvent(event);
        }
```

```
        }
    }
```

Note that although `ColumnSelectedEvent` is eventually dispatched by the `AdvancedData` `Grid`, it originates from the header renderer instance when the check box is selected. The `dispatchColumnSelected` method of the `CheckBoxHeaderRenderer2` class uses the `listData.owner` property to get a reference to the parent `AdvancedDataGrid` and subsequently dispatches the event from the "owner."

```
AdvancedDataGrid(listData.owner).dispatchEvent(event);
```

Finally, take a look at the code for the custom event class `CustomSelectedEvent`. This simply extends the `Event` class with two properties: `colIdx` to store the column index and `isSelected` to indicate whether the column is selected.

```
package {
    import flash.events.Event;

    public class ColumnSelectedEvent extends Event {

        public var colIdx:int;
        public var isSelected:Boolean;

        public static const COLUMN_SELECTED:String = "columnSelected";

        public function ColumnSelectedEvent(type:String,colIdx:Int,isSelected:
Boolean) {
                super(type);

                // Set the new property.
                this.colIdx = colIdx;
                this.isSelected = isSelected;
        }

        override public function clone():Event {
            return new ColumnSelectedEvent(type, colIdx,isSelected);
        }
    }
}
```

6.7 Select Items in an AdvancedDataGrid

Problem

You need to select multiple cells in an `AdvancedDataGrid` programmatically.

Solution

Set the `selectionMode` property of an `AdvancedDataGrid` to `multipleCells` and set the `selectedCells` property to an array of objects containing the `rowIndex` and `columnIndex` of the items to select.

Discussion

The `AdvancedDataGrid` control in Flex 3 provides several options for selecting items within the grid. You control the mode by the `selectionMode` property on the grid, and your choices are as follows:

- Multiple cells
- Multiple rows
- Single cell
- Single row
- None

To permit multiple cells to be selected, the `allowMultipleSelection` property also needs to be set to true.

In the following example, when the user selects the check box in the City column, all the items in that column are selected. The code builds on the previous recipe to handle cell selection. When the `CheckBox` in the `city` column header is selected, the `Advanced DataGrid` dispatches a `ColumnSelectedEvent`, which is handled by the `onColumnSelect` method. The `onColumnSelect` method constructs an array of objects, each containing the `rowIndex` and `cellIndex` of the cell to be selected. In this example, it selects all the items in the `city` column. This array of objects is then assigned to the `selectedCells` property of the grid. Note that to propagate display changes to the grid, a new array needs to be created and then assigned to the `selectedCells` property. Adding items directly to the `selectedCells` property by using `grid.selectedCells.push`, for example, will not work correctly, because the grid will not be able to detect the changes to the array.

```
<mx:Application xmlns:mx="http://www.adobe.com/2006/mxml" layout="vertical"
    creationComplete="initApp()">
    <mx:HTTPService id="srv" url="assets/homesforsale.xml" resultFormat="object"
result="onResult(event)"/>
    <mx:Form>
        <mx:FormItem label="City">
            <mx:TextInput id="cityFilter" change="applyFilter()"/>
        </mx:FormItem>
    </mx:Form>
    <mx:AdvancedDataGrid id="grid"          width="100%"          height="100%"
sortExpertMode="true"          dataProvider="{homesForSale}"          selection
Mode="multipleCells"
        creationComplete="assignListeners()">
        <mx:columns>
            <mx:AdvancedDataGridColumn headerText="Total No." dataField="total"/>
            <mx:AdvancedDataGridColumn headerText="City" sortable="false"
headerRenderer="CheckBoxHeaderRenderer2" dataField="city"/>
            <mx:AdvancedDataGridColumn headerText="State"
                dataField="state"/>
            <mx:AdvancedDataGridColumn headerText="Price Ranges [&lt;350K]
[350K -600K] [&gt;600K]"
                dataField="range"
```

```
                itemRenderer="RangeRenderer"
                sortCompareFunction="sortRanges"/>
        </mx:columns>
    </mx:AdvancedDataGrid>
    <mx:Script>
        <![CDATA[
            import mx.events.FlexEvent;
            import mx.collections.ArrayCollection;
            import mx.rpc.events.ResultEvent;

            [Bindable]
            private var homesForSale:ArrayCollection;

            private function initApp():void {
                this.srv.send();
            }

            private function onResult(evt:ResultEvent):void {
                this.homesForSale = evt.result.data.region;
            }

            private function sortRanges(obj1:Object, obj2:Object):int{
                var value1:Number = obj1.range.range1;
                var value2:Number = obj2.range.range1;

                if(value1 < value2) {
                    return -1;
                }
                else if(value1 > value2){
                    return 1;
                }
                else {
                    return 0;
                }
            }

            private function applyFilter():void {
                if(this.homesForSale.filterFunction == null) {
                    this.homesForSale.filterFunction = this.filterCities;
                }
                this.homesForSale.refresh();
            }

            private function filterCities(item:Object):Boolean {
                var match:Boolean = true;

                if(cityFilter.text != "") {
                    var city:String = item["city"];
                    var filter:String = this.cityFilter.text;
                    if(!city ||
                        city.toLowerCase().indexOf(filter.toLowerCase()) < 0) {
                        match = false;
                    }
                }
```

```
                return match;
        }

        private function assignListeners():void {
                this.grid.addEventListener(ColumnSelectedEvent.COLUMN_SELECTED,
onColumnSelect);
        }

        private function onColumnSelect(evt:ColumnSelectedEvent):void {
            var selectedCells:Array = new Array();
            var colIdx:int = evt.colIdx;

            if(evt.isSelected) {
                for(var i:int=0;i<this.homesForSale.length;i++) {
                    selectedCells.push({rowIndex:i,columnIndex:colIdx});
                }
            }
            this.grid.selectedCells = selectedCells;
        }

        ]]>
    </mx:Script>
</mx:Application>
```

6.8 Enable Drag-and-Drop in a DataGrid

Problem

You want to make items in a `DataGrid` drag-and-drop enabled, so that users can drag them from one grid to another.

Solution

Set the `dragEnabled` property to true on the source `DataGrid` and the `dropEnabled` property to true on the destination `DataGrid`.

Discussion

Enabling drag-and-drop in list-based controls, such as the `DataGrid`, is often as simple as setting the appropriate properties to true, because the Flex 3 Framework takes care of all the underlying work to support drag-and-drop. For example, the following example sets the `dragEnabled` property of the `AdvancedDataGrid` to true, which essentially enables the functionality to drag items outside this control. Notice that the `dropEnabled` property on the `DataGrid` is set to true, which enables the functionality for this control to accept items dropped inside it. An additional property that affects the drag-and-drop behavior is the `dragMoveEnabled` property on the source `AdvancedData Grid`. This property dictates whether items are moved out of the source or simply copied to the destination. The default value is false, which results in an item being copied to the destination.

For non-list-based controls or for custom drag-and-drop behavior, the Flex 3 Framework provides the `DragManager`, which is discussed in detail in Chapter 10, "Dragging and Dropping."

```
<mx:Application xmlns:mx="http://www.adobe.com/2006/mxml" layout="horizontal"
creationComplete="initApp()">
    <mx:HTTPService id="srv" url="assets/homesforsale.xml" resultFormat="object"
result="onResult(event)"/>
    <mx:AdvancedDataGrid id="grid" width="100%" height="100%" sortableColumns="false"
        dragEnabled="true"
        dataProvider="{homesForSale}">
        <mx:columns>
            <mx:AdvancedDataGridColumn headerText="Total No." dataField="total"/>
            <mx:AdvancedDataGridColumn headerText="City" sortable="false" dataField=
"city"/>
            <mx:AdvancedDataGridColumn headerText="State" dataField="state"/>
        </mx:columns>
    </mx:AdvancedDataGrid>

    <mx:DataGrid width="100%" height="100%"
        dropEnabled="true">
        <mx:columns>
            <mx:DataGridColumn headerText="Total No." dataField="total"/>
            <mx:DataGridColumn headerText="City" sortable="false" dataField="city"/>
            <mx:DataGridColumn headerText="State" dataField="state"/>
        </mx:columns>
    </mx:DataGrid>

    <mx:Script>
        <![CDATA[
            import mx.events.FlexEvent;
            import mx.collections.ArrayCollection;
            import mx.rpc.events.ResultEvent;

            [Bindable]
            private var homesForSale:ArrayCollection;

            private function initApp():void {
                this.srv.send();
            }

            private function onResult(evt:ResultEvent):void {
                this.homesForSale = evt.result.data.region;
            }
        ]]>
    </mx:Script>
</mx:Application>
```

6.9 Edit Items in a DataGrid

Problem

You need to make items in a `DataGrid` editable.

Solution

Set the editable property of an AdvancedDataGrid or DataGrid to true.

Discussion

In this example, an AdvancedDataGrid and a DataGrid control are bound to the same dataProvider. The editable property of each grid is set to true. Enabling the editable property allows the functionality to edit each cell within the grid. Because both controls are bound to the same source dataProvider, editing a cell in one grid propagates the change to the second grid. The code you need is as follows:

```
<mx:Application
    xmlns:mx="http://www.adobe.com/2006/mxml"
    layout="horizontal"
    creationComplete="initApp()">

    <mx:HTTPService id="srv"
        url="assets/homesforsale.xml"
        resultFormat="object"
        result="onResult(event)"/>

    <mx:AdvancedDataGrid id="grid" width="100%" height="100%" sortableColumns="false"
        editable="true"
        dataProvider="{homesForSale}">
        <mx:columns>
            <mx:AdvancedDataGridColumn headerText="Total No." dataField="total"/>
            <mx:AdvancedDataGridColumn headerText="City" sortable="false" dataField=
"city"/>
            <mx:AdvancedDataGridColumn headerText="State" dataField="state"/>
        </mx:columns>
    </mx:AdvancedDataGrid>

    <mx:DataGrid width="100%" height="100%"
        editable="true"
        dataProvider="{homesForSale}">
        <mx:columns>
            <mx:DataGridColumn headerText="Total No." dataField="total"/>
            <mx:DataGridColumn headerText="City" sortable="false" dataField="city"/>
            <mx:DataGridColumn headerText="State" dataField="state"/>
        </mx:columns>
    </mx:DataGrid>

    <mx:Script>
        <![CDATA[
            import mx.events.FlexEvent;
            import mx.collections.ArrayCollection;
            import mx.rpc.events.ResultEvent;

            [Bindable]
            private var homesForSale:ArrayCollection;

            private function initApp():void {
                this.srv.send();
```

```
        }
        private function onResult(evt:ResultEvent):void {
            this.homesForSale = evt.result.data.region;
        }
    ]]>
    </mx:Script>
</mx:Application>
```

6.10 Search Within a DataGrid and Autoscroll to the Match

Problem

You want to search for an item in a DataGrid and scroll to the match.

Solution

Use the findFirst method of an IViewCursor on an ArrayCollection to search for an item. Use the scrollToIndex method of the DataGrid to scroll to the index of the matching item.

Discussion

The keys to this technique are a DataGrid and a simple form that provides the user with a TextInput control to enter a city name, as well as a button to start the search process. When the user clicks the button (search_btn), the DataGrid's dataProvider is searched for an exact match, and the corresponding row is selected and scrolled into view if not already visible.

The two main aspects of this solution are finding the matching item and positioning the corresponding item in the DataGrid appropriately. To find the matching item, use an IViewCursor, which is an interface that specifies properties and methods to enumerate a collection view. All Flex collection objects support a createCursor method that returns an instance of a concrete IViewCursor class that works with that particular collection. In this example, the following lines create a cursor for the ArrayCollection instance that acts as the dataProvider for the DataGrid:

```
        private function onResult(evt:ResultEvent):void {
            var sort:Sort = new Sort();
            sort.fields = [ new SortField("city",true) ];
            this.homesForSale = evt.result.data.region;
            this.homesForSale.sort = sort;
            this.homesForSale.refresh();
            this.cursor = this.homesForSale.createCursor();
        }
```

Note that you also assign a Sort object to the ArrayCollection that defines the city property of the dataProvider's items as a sortable field. This is because the findFirst and other find methods of the IViewCursor can be invoked only on sorted views.

After a cursor has been created, it can be used to navigate through and query the associated view. The `searchCity` method that follows is invoked when the user clicks the Search City button:

```
private function searchCity():void {
    if(search_ti.text != "") {
        if(this.cursor.findFirst({city:search_ti.text})){
            var idx:int = this.homesForSale.getItemIndex(this.cursor.current);
            this.grid.scrollToIndex(idx);
            this.grid.selectedItem = this.cursor.current;
        }
    }
}
```

In this method, the user's entry for the city is used as a search parameter for the `find First` method of the `IViewCursor`. This returns true for the first occurrence of the match found within the `ArrayCollection` and also updates the `current` property of the cursor object to reference the matching item. After a matching item is found, the `getItemIndex` method of the `ArrayCollection` is used to figure out the index of that item within the `dataProvider`. Finally, the `DataGrid` display is updated by using the `scroll ToIndex` method to scroll to the matching index, and the `selectedItem` property of the grid is set to the matching item.

The complete listing is as follows:

```
<mx:Application xmlns:mx="http://www.adobe.com/2006/mxml" layout="vertical"
creationComplete="initApp()">

    <mx:HTTPService id="srv" url="assets/homesforsale.xml" resultFormat="object"
        result="onResult(event)"/>

<mx:Form>
    <mx:FormItem label="Search">
        <mx:TextInput id="search_ti"/>
    </mx:FormItem>
    <mx:FormItem>
        <mx:Button label="Search City" click="searchCity()"/>
    </mx:FormItem>
</mx:Form>

    <mx:DataGrid id="grid" width="300" height="150" editable="true" dataProvider="
{homesForSale}">
        <mx:columns>
            <mx:DataGridColumn headerText="Total No."dataField="total"/>
            <mx:DataGridColumn headerText="City"="false" dataField="city"/>
            <mx:DataGridColumn headerText="State" dataField="state"/>
        </mx:columns>
    </mx:DataGrid>

    <mx:Script>
        <![CDATA[
            import mx.collections.SortField;
            import mx.collections.Sort;
            import mx.collections.IViewCursor;
```

```
import mx.events.FlexEvent;
import mx.collections.ArrayCollection;
import mx.rpc.events.ResultEvent;

[Bindable]
private var homesForSale:ArrayCollection;
private var cursor:IViewCursor;

private function initApp():void {
    this.srv.send();
}

private function onResult(evt:ResultEvent):void {
    var sort:Sort = new Sort();
    sort.fields = [ new SortField("city",true) ];
    this.homesForSale = evt.result.data.region;
    this.homesForSale.sort = sort;
    this.homesForSale.refresh();
    this.cursor = this.homesForSale.createCursor();
}

private function searchCity():void {
    if(search_ti.text != "") {
        if(this.cursor.findFirst({city:search_ti.text})){
            var idx:int = this.homesForSale.getItemIndex(this.cursor.
current);

            this.grid.scrollToIndex(idx);
            this.grid.selectedItem = this.cursor.current;
        }
    }
}

            ]]>
    </mx:Script>
</mx:Application>
```

6.11 Generate a Summary for Flat Data by Using GroupingCollection

Contributed by Sreenivas Ramaswamy flexpearls *http://flexpearls.blogspot.com*

Problem

You need to generate summary values for flat data in a grid.

Solution

Use GroupingCollection to generate summary values for flat data and configure the AdvancedDataGrid such that it looks like you have summary for flat data.

Discussion

You can generate a summary for flat data by using `GroupingCollection` and configure `AdvancedDataGrid` to display it as flat data summary.

When generating the summary, you don't want to sort and group on any existing `dataField` because you want to display data as is from the flat data. Instead, the example code generates a dummy group using an invalid grouping field, specifically the code uses `fieldNameNotPresent` as the `dataField` value for `GroupingField`. Now the summary you require can be specified using the `SummaryRow` and `SummaryField` objects.

With the summary ready, you can take up the second task. When a `GroupingCollection` is fed to `ADG.dataProvider`, the data provider will try to display the collection in a tree view as `GroupingCollection` implements `IHierarchicalData`. Internally, `GroupingCollection` is converted into a `HierarchicalCollectionView` and `ADG.dataProvider` returns a `HierarchicalCollectionView` instance. (This is similar to feeding an array as `dataProvider`, which gets converted to an `ArrayCollection` internally.) You can control the display of the root node by using `HierarchicalCollectionView`'s `showRoot` property. By setting it to false, you can prevent the dummy group from getting displayed.

The `AdvancedDataGrid` by default uses the `AdvancedDataGridGroupItemRenderer` to display hierarchical data. This `itemRenderer` displays the folder and disclosure icons for parent items. By specifying the default `AdvancedDataGridItemRenderer` as `AdvancedDataGrid.groupItemRenderer`, you can prevent the group icons from getting displayed.

The complete listing follows:

```
<mx:Application xmlns:mx="http://www.adobe.com/2006/mxml" layout="absolute"
    width="460" height="428" >

<mx:Script>
    <![CDATA[
        import mx.controls.advancedDataGridClasses.AdvancedDataGridItemRenderer;
        import mx.collections.IGroupingCollection;
        import mx.controls.advancedDataGridClasses.AdvancedDataGridColumn;
        import mx.collections.GroupingField;
        import mx.collections.Grouping;
        import mx.collections.ArrayCollection;
        import mx.collections.GroupingCollection;
        var flatData:ArrayCollection = new ArrayCollection(
            [

                { Region:"Southwest", Territory:"Arizona", Territory_Rep:"Barbara
Jennings", Estimate:40000 , Actual:38865 },
                { Region:"Southwest", Territory:"Arizona", Territory_Rep:"Dana Binn",
Estimate:30000 , Actual:29885 },
                { Region:"Southwest", Territory:"Central California", Territory_Rep:"Joe
Schmoe" , Estimate:30000 , Actual:29134 },
                { Region:"Southwest", Territory:"Northern California" , Territory_Rep:
"Lauren Ipsum" , Estimate:40000 , Actual:38805 },
                { Region:"Southwest", Territory:"Northern California" , Territory_Rep:
```

```
"T.R. Smith" , Estimate:40000 , Actual:55498 },
            { Region:"Southwest", Territory:"Southern California" , Territory_Rep:
"Jane Grove" , Estimate:45000 , Actual:44913 },
            { Region:"Southwest", Territory:"Southern California" , Territory_Rep:
"Alice Treu" , Estimate:45000 , Actual:44985 },
            { Region:"Southwest", Territory:"Nevada" , Territory_Rep:"Bethany
Pittman", Estimate:45000 , Actual:52888 }

        ]);
```

Here the `styleFunction` property of the `AdvancedDataGrid` is used to format the `item
Renderer`s that possess the `summary` property within their data object:

```
        private function formatSummary(data:Object, col:AdvancedDataGridColumn):
Object
        {
            if (data.hasOwnProperty("summary"))
            {
                return { color:0xFF0000, fontWeight:"bold", fontSize:12 };
            }

            return {};
        }

        private function flatSummaryObject():Object
        {
            return { Territory_Rep:"Total", summary:true };
        }

    ]]>
</mx:Script>
```

The `AdvancedDataGridItemRenderer` is used here as the `groupItemRenderer` provider to
avoid displaying the icons in the first column. The `groupItemRenderer` property specifies
the renderer to be used for branch nodes in the navigation tree that appears for parent
nodes within the `dataProvider` for the `AdvancedDataGrid`. The `AdvancedDataGrid` also
defines a `groupLabelFunction` property that defines a method that the grid will use to
determine the label to be displayed for any parent node with its `dataProvider`.

```
<mx:AdvancedDataGrid id="adg" creationComplete="groupedData.refresh(); adg.dataProvider
.showRoot=false" groupItemRenderer="mx.controls.advancedDataGridClasses.
AdvancedDataGridItemRenderer" x="30" y="30" width="400" height="377" styleFunction=
"formatSummary">
    <mx:dataProvider>
        <mx:GroupingCollection id="groupedData" source="{flatData}" >
            <mx:Grouping>
                <!-- use some dummy field and set showRoot=false for the ADG
dataProvider -->
                <mx:GroupingField name="fieldNameNotPresent" >
                    <mx:summaries>
                        <!-- use the summaryObjectFunction to return a custom object
which can then
                        be used in the format function to detect a summary row -->
                        <mx:SummaryRow summaryPlacement="last" summaryObjectFunction=
"flatSummaryObject">
```

```
            <mx:fields>
                <mx:SummaryField dataField="Estimate" />
                <mx:SummaryField dataField="Actual" />
            </mx:fields>
        </mx:SummaryRow>
    </mx:summaries>
</mx:GroupingField>
        </mx:Grouping>
    </mx:GroupingCollection>

</mx:dataProvider>

<mx:groupedColumns>
    <mx:AdvancedDataGridColumn headerText = "Territory Rep"
        dataField="Territory_Rep"  />

    <mx:AdvancedDataGridColumnGroup headerText="Sales Figures" textAlign="center">
        <mx:AdvancedDataGridColumn headerText = "Estimate"  textAlign="center"
                    dataField="Estimate" width="100" />

        <mx:AdvancedDataGridColumn headerText = "Actual"  textAlign="center"
                        dataField="Actual"  width="100" />
    </mx:AdvancedDataGridColumnGroup>
    </mx:groupedColumns>
</mx:AdvancedDataGrid>
</mx:Application>
```

6.12 Create an Async Refresh for a GroupingCollection

Contributed by Sreenivas Ramaswamy

Problem

You want to asynchronously refresh the contents of a very large `GroupingCollection`'s grid so that it redraws only when called.

Solution

Use `GroupingCollection.refresh(async:Boolean)` with the `async` flag set to true.

Discussion

The `GroupingCollection.refresh` method takes a flag to indicate whether the grouping needs to be carried out synchronously or asynchronously. When the number of input rows is large, this flag can be set to true in the call to refresh the grouping result displayed earlier. This can be also used to avoid the Flash Player timing out when a `GroupingCollection.refresh` call is taking a long time.

This asynchronous generation of groups also helps in scenarios when users want to group items interactively. `GroupingCollection.cancelRefresh` can be used to stop an ongoing grouping and start a fresh grouping based on new user inputs.

In the following example, clicking the populateADGButton button generates random data and displays it in an `AdvancedDataGrid`. You can modify the number of data rows by using the numeric stepper. Clicking the Group button starts the asynchronous refresh, and `AdvancedDataGrid` starts displaying the results immediately. You can cancel grouping any time by clicking the Cancel Grouping button.

```
<mx:Application xmlns:mx="http://www.adobe.com/2006/mxml" layout="vertical"
    width="520" height="440">

<mx:Script>
    <![CDATA[
        import mx.controls.Alert;
        import mx.collections.IGroupingCollection;
        import mx.collections.GroupingField;
        import mx.collections.Grouping;
        import mx.collections.GroupingCollection;

        [Bindable]
        private var generatedData:Array = [];

        private var companyNames:Array = ["Adobe", "BEA", "Cosmos", "Dogma", "Enigma",
"Fury", "Gama", "Hima", "Indian", "Jaadu", "Karish", "Linovo", "Micro", "Novice",
"Oyster", "Puple", "Quag", "Rendi", "Scrup", "Tempt", "Ubiqut", "Verna", "Wision",
"Xeno", "Yoga", "Zeal" ];

        private var products:Array = [ "Infuse", "MaxVis", "Fusion", "Horizon",
"Apex", "Zeeta", "Maza", "Orion", "Omega", "Zoota", "Quata", "Morion" ];

        private var countries:Array = [ "India", "USA", "Canada", "China", "Japan",
"France", "Germany", "UK", "Brazil", "Italy", "Chile", "Bhutan", "Sri Lanka" ];

        private var years:Array = ["2000", "2001", "2002", "2003", "2004", "2005",
"2006", "2007", "2008", "2009", "2010", "2011", "2012", "2013", "2014", "2015",
"2016","2017", "2018", "2019", "2020", "2021", "2022", "2023", "2024"
                                ];
        private var quarters:Array = ["Q1", "Q2", "Q3", "Q4"];
        private var months:Array = ["Jan", "Feb", "Mar", "Apr", "May", "Jun", "Jul",
"Aug", "Sep", "Oct", "Nov", "Dec" ];

        private var sales:Array = [ 1, 2, 3, 4, 5, 6, 7, 8, 9, 10] ;

        private var costs:Array = [ 1, 2, 3, 4, 5, 6, 7, 8, 9, 10] ;

        private var dimNameMatch:Object = { Company:companyNames, Product:products,
    Country:countries, Year:years, Quarter:quarters, Month:months,    Sales:sales,
    Cost:costs};
```

The preceding arrays are randomly selected from to create a `dataProvider` with the correct number of rows:

```
        private function generateData():void
        {
            generatedData = [];
            var length:int = numRows.value;
            var dimNameMap:Object = dimNameMatch;
```

```
        for (var index:int = 0; index < length; ++index)
        {
            var newObj:Object = {};
            for (var prop:String in dimNameMap)
            {
                var input:Array = dimNameMap[prop];
                var inputIndex:int = Math.random()*input.length;
                newObj[prop] = input[inputIndex];
            }
            generatedData.push(newObj);
        }
    }

    private function populateADG():void
    {
        if (generatedData.length != numRows.value)
            generateData();
        adg.dataProvider = generatedData;
    }

    [Bindable]
    private var gc:GroupingCollection;
    private function groupData():void
    {
        var fields:Array = [];
        if (company.selected)
            fields.push(new GroupingField("Company"));

        if (product.selected)
            fields.push(new GroupingField("Product"));

        if (year.selected)
            fields.push(new GroupingField("Year"));

        if (fields.length == 0)
        {
            Alert.show("Select at least one of the items to group on");
            return;
        }

        gc = new GroupingCollection();
        gc.source = generatedData;

        gc.grouping = new Grouping();

        gc.grouping.fields = fields;

        //use async refresh so that we get to see the results early.
        gc.refresh(true);

        adg.dataProvider = gc;
    }

    private function handleOptionChange():void
    {
```

```
                //user has not started grouping yet
                 if (!gc)
                     return;

                //stop any refresh that might be going on
                gc.cancelRefresh();

                var fields:Array = [];
                if (company.selected)
                    fields.push(new GroupingField("Company"));

                if (product.selected)
                    fields.push(new GroupingField("Product"));

                if (year.selected)
                    fields.push(new GroupingField("Year"));

                //user might have checked off everything
                if (fields.length == 0)
                {
                    return;
                }

                gc.grouping.fields = fields;

                gc.refresh(true);
            }

        ]]>
    </mx:Script>

    <mx:AdvancedDataGrid id="adg" width="100%" height="260" >
        <mx:columns>
            <mx:AdvancedDataGridColumn dataField="Company" />
            <mx:AdvancedDataGridColumn dataField="Product" />
            <mx:AdvancedDataGridColumn dataField="Year" />
            <mx:AdvancedDataGridColumn dataField="Sales" />
        </mx:columns>
    </mx:AdvancedDataGrid>
    <mx:HBox>
        <mx:NumericStepper id="numRows" stepSize="1000" minimum="1000" maximum="10000" />
        <mx:Button label="Populate ADG" click="populateADG()" id="populateADGButton"/>
    </mx:HBox>
    <mx:VBox>
    <mx:HBox>
```

You can select different options for the Grouping fields here:

```
        <mx:Label text="Grouping fields:" />

        <!-- We can use cancelRefresh API to stop the refresh and immediately call refresh
    (true) in the change handler.-->
        <mx:CheckBox id="company" label="Company" selected="true" click=
    "handleOptionChange()"/>
        <mx:CheckBox id="product" label="Product" click="handleOptionChange()"/>
        <mx:CheckBox id="year" label="Year" click="handleOptionChange()"/>
```

```
    </mx:HBox>
    <mx:HBox>
        <mx:Button label="Group" click="groupData()" />
```

Here the `cancelRefresh` method of the `GroupingCollection` is invoked:

```
        <mx:Button label="Cancel grouping" click="gc.cancelRefresh()" enabled=
    "{gc != null}"/>
    </mx:HBox>
    </mx:VBox>
    </mx:Application>
```

The three check boxes allow different combinations of grouping to be performed. Users can change the grouping choice while refresh is going on. The `cancelRefresh` method of the `GroupCollection` is used to stop the `AdvancedDataGrid` from creating and displaying the new grouping.

CHAPTER 7

Renderers and Editors

The renderer, or `item renderer`, is a powerful and commonly used aspect of the Flex Framework that enables you to define components that will be used by data driven components to display arrays or collections of data. `DataGrid`, `List`, `Tile`, and `Combo Box` containers among others, use renderers, passing the data of each item in their `data provider` to a specified `item renderer` that then handles displaying and updating the data. Because Flex applications frequently make extensive use of tabular data and lists, understanding the most efficient way to display data and to edit that data once displayed is an important aspect of development with Flex.

The key to working with item renderers and item editors is understanding how the relationship between the `item renderer` and the parent component is defined by the Flex Framework. All item renderers must possess a `data` property that can be used by the parent component to set the relevant data item. How this data is displayed is entirely up to the developer; for example, you can use a simple "drop-in" `item renderer` or a custom component. Item renderers can also allow user edits of data, which will automatically update the `data provider` of the parent component.

The `item editor` functions quite differently, with the base `mx.controls.List` class creating an instance of the editor whenever an item renderer component is clicked. When that editor loses focus, the `List` attempts to read an `editorDataField` property that can be compared with the original data to determine whether the data has changed. If it has, the `dataProvider` of the `List` is updated, and then the `itemEditor` is destroyed and is replaced with the `itemRenderer`. This means that there is always only one class set as the `itemRenderer` for any `List` or `DataGrid` column.

7.1 Create Your Own Renderers

Problem

You need to create item renderers for a `List` or `DataGrid` component.

Solution

You can define an item renderer in MXML within the `List` component, passing the new item renderer as the `itemRenderer` property of the `List`. Or you can define an item renderer in a separate file and pass it to the `itemRenderer` using its qualified class name.

Discussion

Item renderers are simple to work with in their simplest incarnations, and there are many approaches to creating them. The easiest way is to pass the desired renderer to the `List` as its `itemRenderer` property:

```
<mx:List dataProvider="{simpleArray}">
    <mx:itemRenderer>
        <mx:Component>
            <mx:Label color="#007700"/>
        </mx:Component>
    </mx:itemRenderer>
</mx:List>
```

For each item in the `List`'s `dataProvider` `Array` or `ArrayCollection`, a new instance of the component used as the `itemRenderer` will be created and passed the information from that index in the array to the data property of the component being used as the item renderer. This works with the `Label` component being used in the preceding code because the data property of the `Label` automatically sets the value of the text contained within the `Label` to whatever data has been passed in. For this to work as expected, the data being passed to the item renderer needs to be simple strings. You'll see [Object object] in the `Label` if a complex object or other type of data is passed to the `Label`.

To use a complex data object or type of data other than **String**, you'll need to create a new item renderer and override the set data method for the item renderer to display the desired data properly. For example:

```
<mx:VBox xmlns:mx="http://www.adobe.com/2006/mxml" height="800">
    <mx:Script>
        <![CDATA[

            [Bindable]
            private var simpleArray:Array = new Array("one", "two", "three", "four",
"five");

        ]]>
    </mx:Script>
    <!-- this list can use an inline item renderer because the array that the List is
using as a dataprovider consists
        of simple object -->
    <mx:List dataProvider="{simpleArray}">
        <mx:itemRenderer>
            <mx:Component>
                <mx:Label color="#007700"/>
            </mx:Component>
        </mx:itemRenderer>
```

```
        </mx:List>
        <!-- the list component here requires a custom renderer because we're passing any
object to it, which
            means that the renderer will need to know how to handle each field in the
item -->
        <mx:List itemRenderer="oreilly.cookbook.SevenOneRenderer" dataProvider=
"{DataHolder.genericCollectionOne}"/>
        <!-- here we can use a proper drop in item renderer because the DataGrid handles
each field in the Object
            separately -->
        <mx:DataGrid dataProvider="{DataHolder.genericCollectionOne}">
            <mx:columns>
                <mx:DataGridColumn dataField="name"/>
                <mx:DataGridColumn dataField="age"/>
                <mx:DataGridColumn dataField="appearance" width="200">
                    <mx:itemRenderer>
                        <mx:Component>
                            <!-- note that any component placed here must extend
IDataRenderer and have a data property that properly displays any data passed to the data
setter method -->
                            <mx:TextArea/>
                        </mx:Component>
                    </mx:itemRenderer>
                </mx:DataGridColumn>
            </mx:columns>
        </mx:DataGrid>
</mx:VBox>
```

Of course, for any more-complicated data, you need to create a custom renderer. None
of the Flex components that can be dropped in within a Component tag can handle a
complex object as data. This is not frequently a problem because usually data objects
that possess multiple fields are handled by a DataGrid and each property of the object
is handled by a separate renderer. This isn't always the case, however. To properly
handle a data object with multiple fields, you need to override the data setter method
and handle each property of the object passed in. In the following code sample, the
data object passed in to the renderer by the list will be parsed and a Label created for
each of the fields present. This approach works well if data fields might not be present.

```
package oreilly.cookbook
{
    import mx.containers.HBox;
    import mx.controls.Label;
    import mx.core.IDataRenderer;

    public class SevenOneRenderer extends HBox
    {
        private var nameLabel:Label;
        private var ageLabel:Label;
        private var appearanceLabel:Label;

        private var _data:Object;

        public function SevenOneRenderer() {
```

```
        super();
    }

    override public function get data():Object {
        if(_data != null) {
            return _data;
        }
        return null;
    }

    override public function set data(value:Object):void {
        _data = value;
        if(_data.name != null) {
            nameLabel = instantiateNewLabel(_data.name);
        }
        if(_data.age != null) {
            ageLabel = instantiateNewLabel(_data.age);
        }
        if(_data.appearance != null) {
            appearanceLabel = instantiateNewLabel(_data.appearance);
        }
        setStyle("backgroundColor", 0xddddff);
    }

    private function instantiateNewLabel(value:*):Label {
        var label:Label = new Label();
        label.text = String(value);
        addChild(label);
        return label;
    }
}
}
```

7.2 Use the ClassFactory to Generate Renderers

Problem

You want to change the properties of the renderers being used by a List or a DataGrid Column at runtime, allowing different properties to be set for all the item renderers.

Solution

Use a ClassFactory object and pass it a class reference of an itemRenderer that implements the IFactory interface so that the class can return new instances of itself.

Discussion

This is a lengthy recipe and with good reason—it covers two things: using the Factory design pattern and using its built-in Flex Framework representation, the mx.core.Class Factory objects. Using the Factory pattern lets you set a class that will be used to create the item renderers for a data-driven control, and lets the ClassFactory instantiate and

---

destroy instances of that class as needed at runtime. The ClassFactory is passed a class reference like so:

```
var factory:ClassFactory = new ClassFactory(oreilly.cookbook.SevenTwoFactory);
```

As long as the SevenTwoFactory class extends the IFactory interface, this will work fine and can be passed to the PurgeList as shown here:

```
<cookbook:PurgeList id="list" itemRenderer="{factory}" width="300"/>
```

To demonstrate, here's a custom list that provides access to a single method, the protected purgeItemRenderers method of the ListBase class:

```
public function clearList():void{
    this.purgeItemRenderers();
    this.invalidateDisplayList();
}
```

Take a look at how the ClassFactory is passed a class reference and then set to be the itemRenderer of the List:

```
<mx:HBox xmlns:mx="http://www.adobe.com/2006/mxml" initialize="setType()"
xmlns:cookbook="oreilly.cookbook.*">
    <mx:Script>
        <![CDATA[

            [Bindable]
            private var factory:ClassFactory;

            private function setType():void
            {
                factory = new ClassFactory(SevenTwoFactory);
                factory.properties = {type:SevenTwoFactory.HORIZONTAL};
            }

        ]]>
    </mx:Script>
    <cookbook:PurgeList id="list" itemRenderer="{factory}" width="300"/>
    <!-- toggle between the horizontal and vertical item rendering -- >
    <mx:Button id="toggleStyle" toggle="true" click="toggleStyle.selected ?
factory.properties = {type:SevenTwoFactory.VERTICAL} : factory.properties =
{type:SevenTwoFactory.HORIZONTAL}" label="style"/>
    <!-- here we redraw the whole list to use our new renderers -- >
    <mx:Button id="toggleDP" toggle="true" click="list.clearList(), list.dataProvider
= DataHolder.genericCollectionOne, this.invalidateDisplayList()" label="generate"/>
</mx:HBox>
```

The properties object of the ClassFactory is passed to the new class object generated in the factory. The key to the factory method is the IFactory interface, which requires a newInstance method with the following signature:

```
public function newInstance():* {
    return new MyClass();
}
```

The ClassFactory object calls this method every time a new instance of the class is needed. The ClassFactory attempts to pass any properties passed into it to the new instance of the class created. In the preceding example, ClassFactory passes this object

```
factory.properties = {type:SevenTwoFactory.HORIZONTAL};
```

to the new instance of the class. The following item renderer, meanwhile, captures the value set in the properties with a setter function:

```
public function set type(value:String):void {
    _type = value;
    invalidateDisplayList();
}
```

For every property in the ClassFactory properties object, the ClassFactory will attempt to pass that property to each new instance of it's class that it generates. This is how new values can be added to the item renderer at runtime, and this will allow you to redraw all the item renderers and use the new information that you've set. For the item rendererused here, the UIComponent is used instead of one of the Container classes from the mx.containers package to ensure that the rendering is as fast as possible. For the same reason, the example uses the flash.text.TextField component instead of the mx.controls.Text or Label controls. When dealing with item renderers and in particular when redrawing them, speed is of the essence, and using lower-level components in ActionScript saves you a great deal of time and increases performance.

```
package oreilly.cookbook
{
    import flash.text.TextField;

    import mx.controls.Label;
    import mx.controls.listClasses.IListItemRenderer;
    import mx.core.IFactory;
    import mx.core.UIComponent;
    import mx.events.FlexEvent;
//the class implements IListItemRenderer to ensure that it will function
//properly with the List, and IFactory, to ensure that it can be used in
//a factory
    public class SevenTwoFactory extends UIComponent implements IFactory,
IListItemRenderer
    {
        //here are our two layout types that we'll use to the 'type'
        public static const HORIZONTAL:String = "horizontal";
        public static const VERTICAL:String = "vertical";
        //by default we'll go with horizontal
        private var _type:String = HORIZONTAL;

        private var _data:Object;
        //here are our three TextFields
        private var nameLabel:TextField;
        private var ageLabel:TextField;
        private var appearanceLabel:TextField;
        //this is the property we'll set in the properties of the
        //ClassFactory
```

```
public function set type(value:String):void {
    _type = value;
    invalidateDisplayList();
}

public function get data():Object {
    return _data;
}
// we need to do this to determine the correct size of the renderer
override protected function measure():void {
    super.measure();
    if(this._type == HORIZONTAL) {
        measuredHeight = nameLabel.height;
        measuredWidth = nameLabel.width + ageLabel.width + appearanceLabel.
width + 10;
    } else {
        measuredWidth = appearanceLabel.width;
        measuredHeight = nameLabel.height + ageLabel.height + appearanceLabel.
height + 10;
    }
    height = measuredHeight;
    width = measuredWidth;
    trace(" w "+this.measuredWidth+ "  "+ this.measuredHeight+" "+this.width+"
 "+this.height);
}
//set all the TextFields with the correct data by parsing out
// the data value. We create the TextField only if we need it.
  public function set data(value:Object):void {
    _data = value;
    if(_data.name != null && nameLabel == null) {
        nameLabel = instantiateNewLabel(_data.name);
    } else {
        nameLabel.text = _data.name;
    }
    if(_data.age != null && ageLabel == null) {
        ageLabel = instantiateNewLabel(_data.age);
    } else {
        ageLabel.text = _data.age;
    }
    if(_data.appearance != null && appearanceLabel == null) {
        appearanceLabel = instantiateNewLabel(_data.appearance);
    } else {
        appearanceLabel.text = _data.appearance;
    }
    setStyle("backgroundColor", 0xddddff);
    invalidateProperties();
    dispatchEvent(new FlexEvent(FlexEvent.DATA_CHANGE));
}
//Since the UIComponent doesn't possess any layout logic, we need to
//do all of that ourselves
override protected function updateDisplayList(unscaledWidth:Number,
unscaledHeight:Number):void {
    super.updateDisplayList(unscaledWidth, unscaledHeight);
    var sum:Number = 0;
    if(this._type == HORIZONTAL) {
```

```
            nameLabel.x = 0;
            sum += nameLabel.width;
            ageLabel.x = sum;
            sum += ageLabel.width;
            appearanceLabel.x = sum;
        } else {
            nameLabel.y = 0;
            sum += nameLabel.height;
            ageLabel.y = sum;
            sum += ageLabel.height;
            appearanceLabel.y = sum;
        }
    }

    private function instantiateNewLabel(value:*):TextField {
        var text:TextField = new TextField();
        addChild(text);
        text.text = String(value);
        text.width = text.textWidth + 5;
        text.height = text.textHeight + 5;
        return text;
    }
    // here, finally is the Factory method, that will return
    // a new instance for each renderer needed
    public function newInstance():* {
        return new SevenTwoFactory();
    }

    }
}
```

7.3 Access the Component That Owns a Renderer

Problem

You need to ensure that an item renderer has access to the component that created it.

Solution

Implement the IDropInListItemRenderer interface and access the **owner** property of the renderer.

Discussion

The IDropInListItemRenderer gives the renderer not only access to the data that has been passed into it—but via the **owner** property of the BaseListData type, also access to the List or DataGridColumn that the renderer belongs to. The mx.controls.list Classes.BaseListData type defines the following properties:

columnIndex : int

> The index of the column of the List-based control relative to the currently visible columns of the control, where the first column is at an index of 1.

owner : IUIComponent

> This is the List or DataGridColumn object that owns this renderer.

rowIndex : int

> The index of the row of the DataGrid, List, or Tree control relative to the currently visible rows of the control, where the first row is at an index of 1.

uid : String

> The unique identifier for this item. All items in an itemRenderer are given a unique id so that even if the data is the same for two or more itemRenderers, the List Base component will still be able to identify them.

When the itemRenderer is created, if it implements the IDropInListItemRenderer interface, the listData property of the renderer will be set and the renderer will have access to the BaseListData object passed in. After a renderer's data is set, the renderer checks the type of the owner component that has set the data, and depending on that type, either traces its name or calls a custom method on that owner. The example implements this process in a simple way to show how you can set the BaseListData and to show that the type of List that has created the renderer can be determined and methods called on that list.

```
<mx:VBox xmlns:mx="http://www.adobe.com/2006/mxml" width="400" height="50" implements=
"mx.controls.listClasses.IDropInListItemRenderer">
    <mx:Script>
        <![CDATA[
            import mx.controls.DataGrid;
            import mx.controls.List;
            import mx.controls.dataGridClasses.DataGridColumn;

            import mx.controls.listClasses.BaseListData;

            // store the list data item in case we want to do something with it
            // later on
            private var _listData:BaseListData;
            [Bindable("dataChange")]
            // a getter method.
            public function get listData():BaseListData
            {
                return _listData;
            }
            // a setter method,
```

After the BaseListData value is passed in to the control, the renderer will have access to the item that has created it via the owner property of the BaseListData object. This lets the renderer read additional data from and call methods on the parent component.

```
            public function set listData(value:BaseListData):void
            {
                _listData = value;
```

```
                if(value.owner is DataGridColumn) {
                    trace(" DataGridColumn ");
                } else if (value.owner is List) {
                    trace(" List ");
                } else if (value.owner is CustomDataGrid) {
                    trace(" CustomDataGrid ");
                    (value.owner as CustomDataGrid).checkInMethod(this);
                }
            }

            override public function set data(value:Object):void {
                nameTxt.text = value.name;
                appearanceTxt.text = value.appearance;
            }

        ]]>
    </mx:Script>
    <mx:Canvas backgroundColor="#3344ff">
        <mx:Label id="nameTxt"/>
    </mx:Canvas>
    <mx:Label id="appearanceTxt"/>
</mx:VBox>
```

Here is the IDropInListRenderer put to use using a simple custom DataGrid:

```
<mx:HBox xmlns:mx="http://www.adobe.com/2006/mxml" xmlns:cookbook=
"oreilly.cookbook.*">
    <mx:List itemRenderer="oreilly.cookbook.IDropInListRenderer" dataProvider=
"{DataHolder.genericCollectionOne}"/>
    <!-- note that creating a custom component with a new namespace, cookbook,
requires that our columns
        are declared w/in the cookbook namespace -->
    <cookbook:CustomDataGrid dataProvider="{DataHolder.genericCollectionOne}">
        <cookbook:columns>
            <!-- since we're not declaring a dataField, the entire data object
                is passed to the renderer -->
            <mx:DataGridColumn itemRenderer="oreilly.cookbook.IDropInListRenderer"/>
            <mx:DataGridColumn dataField="age"/>
        </cookbook:columns>
    </cookbook:CustomDataGrid>
</mx:HBox>
```

Here is the custom DataGrid with a single method that the renderer can call when its
data property is set:

```
<mx:DataGrid xmlns:mx="http://www.adobe.com/2006/mxml">
    <mx:Script>
        <![CDATA[

            public function checkInMethod(obj:*):void {
                trace(" hello from my renderer "+obj);
            }

        ]]>
    </mx:Script>
</mx:DataGrid>
```

7.4 Create a Single Component to Act as Renderer and Editor

Problem

You want to create a single component that can be used as both an item editor and an item renderer. Additionally, you want the item editor to receive an array of values that the user can edit with a combo box.

Solution

Create a component that implements the `IDropInListItemRenderer` and create two states within the component, one to act as an editor and one as a renderer. When the data is changed, dispatch an `ITEM_EDIT_END` event to the parent container so the parent container will set the value in the `dataProvider`.

Discussion

Item renderers can easily be used as item editors as well. The `List` class, which the `DataGridColumn` class extends, defines a `rendererIsEditor` property. This property, if set to true, indicates to the `List` that when the `itemRenderer` is double-clicked, the `List` is not to create a default item editor but simply to allow the `itemRenderer` to handle the editing itself.

All that is needed for the `List` to change the `dataProvider` when the user has finished editing is for the renderer to dispatch a `ListEvent` or `DataGridEvent` (depending on the parent) of the type `ITEM_EDIT_END`. The following example uses the `DataGridEvent` to send the column and row that are being edited to update the `dataProvider`. This `Data GridEvent` object is created and dispatched in the `setNewData` method that is called when the `ComboBox` used for editing is changed:

```
private function setNewData():void {
            _data.selected = selectCB.selectedItem;
            dispatchEvent(new DataGridEvent(DataGridEvent.ITEM_EDIT_END, true,
    true, _listData.columnIndex, 'selected', _listData.rowIndex));
        }
```

In the following example, the data type used by the data grid has a name, age, appearance, array of options that the user can edit, and a `selected` property that can indicate which of the items in the array is the selected:

```
{name:"Todd Anderson", age:31, appearance:"Intimidating",  extras:["bar", "foo",
"baz"], selected:"bar"}
```

Data types like this are fairly common. The relevant values for the multiple item renderers are the `extras` property, which defines the `dataProvider` of the `ComboBox`, and the `selected` property, which determines which item in the `ComboBox` is selected. Normally in a `DataGrid` the renderer is passed only a single value; however, if the `DataGridColumn` doesn't define a `dataField`, the whole data object is passed into the renderer as shown here:

```
<mx:DataGrid dataProvider="{DataHolder.genericCollectionTwo}" width="450" itemEditEnd=
"checkEditedItem(event)" id="dg">
    <mx:columns>
        <mx:DataGridColumn dataField="age"/>
        <mx:DataGridColumn dataField="appearance"/>
        <mx:DataGridColumn itemRenderer="oreilly.cookbook.ComboBoxRenderer"
editable="true" rendererIsEditor="true"/>
    </mx:columns>
</mx:DataGrid>
```

Note the `rendererIsEditor` property on the column. The renderer is shown here:

```
<mx:Canvas xmlns:mx="http://www.adobe.com/2006/mxml" width="400" height="100"
doubleClickEnabled="true" currentState="display" implements="mx.controls.
listClasses.IDropInListItemRenderer">
    <mx:Script>
        <![CDATA[
            import mx.events.DataGridEvent;
            import mx.events.ListEvent;

            import mx.controls.listClasses.BaseListData;

            // Internal variable for the property value.
            private var _listData:BaseListData;
            private var _data:Object = {};
```

After the data is set for the renderer, the component begins listening for the
`MouseEvent.DOUBLE_CLICK` event that will signal it to enter its editing state:

```
            override public function set data(value:Object):void {
                _data = value;
                if(_data.selected != null) {
                    addEventListener(MouseEvent.DOUBLE_CLICK, startEdit);
                }
            }
            override public function get data():Object {
                return _data;
            }

            private function startEdit(event:Event):void {
                if(currentState == "display") {
                    currentState = "edit";
                    addEventListener(FocusEvent.FOCUS_OUT, endEdit);
                }
            }

            private function endEdit(event:Event):void {
                currentState = "display";
            }

            // Make the listData property bindable.
            [Bindable("dataChange")]
            public function get listData():BaseListData {
                return _listData;
            }
```

```
                    // Define the setter method,
                    public function set listData(value:BaseListData):void {
                      _listData = value;
                    }

                    private function setNewData():void {
                        _data.selected = selectCB.selectedItem;
                        dispatchEvent(new DataGridEvent(DataGridEvent.ITEM_EDIT_END, true,
        true, _listData.columnIndex, 'selected', _listData.rowIndex));
                    }

                ]]>
            </mx:Script>
```

In this example, States are used to change the component from its item renderer state, in which the data is simply displayed, to the item editor state, in which the ComboBox can be used to edit the data of the renderer:

```
            <mx:states>
                <mx:State name="edit">
                    <mx:AddChild>
                        <mx:ComboBox id="selectCB"
                            addedToStage="selectCB.dataProvider = _data.extras;
        selectCB.selectedItem = _data.selected"
                            change="setNewData()"/>
                    </mx:AddChild>
                </mx:State>
                <mx:State name="display">
                    <mx:AddChild>
                        <mx:Text id="text" addedToStage="text.text = _data.selected"/>
                    </mx:AddChild>
                </mx:State>
            </mx:states>
        </mx:Canvas>
```

7.5 Create an Item Editor to Handle Data with Multiple Fields

Problem

You need to create an item editor that will allow the user to edit data types with multiple fields, such as custom objects.

Solution

Create an item editor that will return the edited items in the data property. Create an itemEditEnd event listener in the List that will cancel the event and access the data property of the itemEditorInstance of the List.

Discussion

The `List` provides an `editorDataField` that works perfectly well for dealing with a single field or property. Working with editors dealing with multiple fields, however, requires canceling the default behavior of the `List` and `DataGridColumn` and reading the fields back from the `itemEditorInstance`.

The `processData` method shown next is used to process the `itemEditEnd` event:

```
<mx:Canvas xmlns:mx="http://www.adobe.com/2006/mxml" width="700" height="300">
    <mx:Script>
        <![CDATA[
            import mx.events.ListEvent;
            import mx.collections.ArrayCollection;
            import oreilly.cookbook.MultipleDataTypeEditor;

            [Bindable]
            private var arr:ArrayCollection = new ArrayCollection([{age:12, name:"Joe"
}, {age:16, name:"Jorge"}, {age:19, name:"Jojo"}, {age:2, name:"James"},
{age:12, name:"Joaquin"}]);

                public function processData(event:ListEvent):void {
                    // Disable copying data back to the control.
                    event.preventDefault();
                    // Get new label from editor.
                    list.editedItemRenderer.data = MultipleDataTypeEditor
(list.itemEditorInstance).data;
                    // Close the cell editor.
                    list.destroyItemEditor();
                    // Notify the list control to update its display.
                    list.dataProvider.notifyItemUpdate(list.editedItemRenderer);
                }

        ]]>
    </mx:Script>
    <mx:List id="list" itemEditor="oreilly.cookbook.MultipleDataTypeEditor"
dataProvider="{arr}" itemEditEnd="processData(event)"
        itemRenderer="oreilly.cookbook.MultipleDataTypeRenderer" width="350" editable=
"true">
    </mx:List>
</mx:Canvas>
```

The `preventDefault` method of the event is used to cancel the normal behavior of the `itemEditor`. This ensures that the `List` doesn't attempt to read the `text` property from the `itemEditor`, the default behavior of the `List`. Instead, it reads the data from the `itemRendererInstance` and sets the `editedItemRenderers` data to that value. Finally, calling `notifyItemUpdate` on the `List` `dataProvider` ensures that the new data passed from the editor is reflected in the `dataProvider` of the `List`.

The `itemEditor` used in the preceding `List` simply returns the values of its two `TextInput` objects when the data property is accessed. The code listing for that item editor is shown here:

```
package oreilly.cookbook
{

    import mx.containers.Canvas;
    import mx.controls.TextInput;

    public class MultipleDataTypeEditor extends Canvas
    {

        private var nameField:TextInput;
        private var ageField:TextInput;

        public function MultipleDataTypeEditor() {
            super();
            nameField = new TextInput();
            ageField = new TextInput();
            addChild(nameField);
            nameField.focusEnabled = false;
            addChild(ageField);
            ageField.focusEnabled = false;
            ageField.x = 100;
            this.horizontalScrollPolicy = "none";
        }

        override public function set data(value:Object):void {
            super.data = value;
            nameField.text = value.name;
            ageField.text = value.age;
        }

        override public function get data():Object {
            return {name:nameField.text, age:ageField.text};
        }

    }
}
```

7.6 Display SWF Objects as Items in a Menu by Using an Item Renderer

Contributed by Rico Zuniga

Problem

You want to display SWF or image objects in the menu.

Solution

Use an `itemRenderer` object to load SWF files and customize the menu.

Discussion

The first step to customizing a menu is to create SWF files containing the fonts or graphics you want to display and save them in a folder. In this example, the folder is named swf. You can use Flash or Flex or any available authoring tool to create the files, and then save the files to a folder. For the example, the swf folder houses a SWF file containing a static text control with the font set to the desired typeface.

Next, create an item renderer component that is a `Canvas` and contains a `SWFLoader` component. The `Canvas` should implement the `IMenuItemRenderer` interface to be able to work with the custom menu. To accomplish this in MXML, set the `Canvas imple ments` property to the needed interface. You are also required to override the `IMenuItemRenderer`'s `get` and `set` methods for its `menu` property, but nothing is added to it here in the example. In the `SWFLoader` component, set its `source` property to `data.swf`, which represents the item in the `Menu`'s `dataProvider` that contains the path to the SWF files. Here's the code:

```
<mx:Canvas xmlns:mx="http://www.adobe.com/2006/mxml" width="100" height="25" verticalS
    crollPolicy="off" horizontalScrollPolicy="off" xmlns:external="flash.external.*"
    implements="mx.controls.menuClasses.IMenuItemRenderer">
    <mx:Script>
    <![CDATA[
    import mx.controls.Menu;

    public function get menu():Menu {
    return null;
    }

    public function set menu(value:Menu):void {
    }
    ]]>
    </mx:Script>
    <mx:SWFLoader source="{data.swf}" width="100" height="25" horizontalCenter="0"
    verticalCenter="0"/>
</mx:Canvas>
```

Next, you need to create the custom `Menu` in the main application. For the `Menu`'s `data Provider`, set `menuData`, which is an array of objects that represents the structure of the `Menu`. Add a `swf` property representing the path to the SWF file to display for each menu item object in the `Menu`. You must also set the `Menu`'s `itemRenderer` by creating a new `ClassFactory` object and passing in the item renderer component to its constructor; this is necessary because the `Menu`'s `itemRenderer` property needs to contain an object that implements the `IFactory` interface. Here's the code for the main application:

```
<mx:Application xmlns:mx="http://www.adobe.com/2006/mxml" layout="absolute"
creationComplete="init();" backgroundGradientColors="[#c0c0c0, #ffffff]">
  <mx:Script>
  <![CDATA[
  import mx.events.MenuEvent;
  import mx.controls.Menu;
```

```
    private var menu:Menu;

    private function init():void {
    var menuData:Array = [
        {swf:'swf/coolfonts.swf', children: [
        {label: "SubMenuItem A-1", swf:'swf/meridiana.swf'},
        {label: "SubMenuItem A-2", swf:'swf/virinda.swf'}
        ]},
        {swf:'swf/scriptfonts.swf', children: [
        {label: "SubMenuItem A-1", swf:'swf/monotypecorsiva.swf'},
        {label: "SubMenuItem A-2", swf:'swf/comicsansms.swf'}
        ]}
    ];

    menu = Menu.createMenu(this, menuData);
    menu.itemRenderer = new ClassFactory(FontItemRenderer);
    }

    ]]>
    </mx:Script>
    <mx:Button x="10" y="10" label="Show Menu" id="btnShowMenu" click="menu.show
    (btnShowMenu.x, btnShowMenu.y+btnShowMenu.height);"/>
    </mx:Application>
```

7.7 Select a DataGrid Column with a CheckBox Header Renderer

Contributed by Ben Clinkinbeard

Problem

You want to set up a DataGrid in which one column uses a CheckBox itemRenderer, and that column's headerRenderer is a CheckBox that serves as a Select/Unselect All control.

Solution

Create a class to serve as a headerRenderer. Then in that class, create a method that will bubble up an event to the parent DataGrid and set a property on each itemRenderer.

Discussion

Flex header renderers are different beasts than item renderers in both their creation and life cycle. During the life of a DataGrid, headerRenderers get reinitialized repeatedly as almost any action in any header of the DataGrid will cause the headerRenderers to reset themselves. As a result, you need to store outside the DataGrid anything that maintains state. To do this, use the mx.core.ClassFactory class, which ordinarily works behind the scenes. When you specify a class to use as an itemRenderer

```
    <mx:DataGridColumn itemRenderer="mx.controls.CheckBox" />
```

the MXML compiler converts that code for you into something that looks like this:

```
var temp : mx.core.ClassFactory = new mx.core.ClassFactory();
temp.generator = mx.controls.CheckBox;
return temp;
```

As you can see, the class you specified gets assigned to the `generator` property. When the rows for your `DataGrid` are created, the `newInstance` method of that `ClassFactory` instance is then called and a fresh copy of the class assigned to the generator property is created and returned. Although this is convenient in that you simply have to specify which class should be used to render your data, it does have its drawbacks. The main drawback is that you can't provide any constructor arguments, which can make it hard to create renderer classes that are generic enough to be used in more than one specific scenario. Thankfully, `ClassFactory` does provide a mechanism to aid in the creation of reusable renderers. The `properties` property is of type `Object`, and is used to set initial values on the instances of your renderer class. `ClassFactory` will loop over the properties exposed by the `properties` Object using a `for...in` loop, and set the same values on your renderer.

Using what you've just learned about `ClassFactory` and header renderers, you can create a few variables:

```
// var to hold header renderer's state
public var selectAllFlag:Boolean;

[Bindable]
public var hr:ClassFactory;
```

The `selectAllFlag` variable does just what its name says: It holds a value that specifies whether all our rows should be selected. The `hr` variable is assigned to the `headerRenderer` property of the `DataGridColumn` and is marked [Bindable] for convenience. The next step is to define the actual `ClassFactory` instance, which you can do in the `creationComplete` handler of the file your `DataGrid` lives in:

```
hr = new ClassFactory(CenteredCheckBoxHeaderRenderer);
hr.properties = {stateHost: this, stateProperty: "selectAllFlag"};
```

The first line here creates the instance and passes the renderer class to be assigned to the `generator` property. The second line specifies the values that should be set for two public properties of the `CenteredCheckBoxHeaderRenderer` class when it is created. Notice that `stateHost` refers to this, or the enclosing file/component, and `stateProperty` refers to the flag variable defined earlier. The last step before getting into the renderer code is to look at the `DataGridColumn` and how to assign the `ClassFactory` instance:

```
<mx:DataGridColumn width="30"
    sortable="false"
    dataField="addToCart"
    headerRenderer="{hr}"
    itemRenderer="CenteredCheckBoxItemRenderer" />
```

Notice that `sortable` is set to false, which is necessary to make sure mouse clicks are registered as `CheckBox` interactions and not column-sorting interactions.

On to the header renderer class:

```
package
{
    import flash.display.DisplayObject;
    import flash.events.MouseEvent;
    import flash.text.TextField;

    import mx.controls.CheckBox;
    import mx.controls.DataGrid;

    public class CenteredCheckBoxHeaderRenderer extends CenteredCheckBox
    {
        // these vars are used to reference the external property that stores our
selected state
        public var stateHost:Object;
        public var stateProperty:String;

        // this function will be called repeatedly as part of the (re)initialization
process
        // set selected state based on external property
        override public function set data(value:Object):void
        {
            selected = stateHost[stateProperty];
        }

        // this function is defined by mx.controls.CheckBox
        // it is the default handler for its click event
        override protected function clickHandler(event:MouseEvent):void
        {
            super.clickHandler(event);
            // this is the important line as it updates the external variable
            // we've designated to hold our state
            stateHost[stateProperty] = selected;
        }
    }
}
```

When the data setter is called, it ignores the value argument that is passed in (it's a reference to the DataGridColumn holding the renderer) and sets the selected state by looking at the external flag variable you pointed the renderer to in the properties property. Conversely, in the clickHandler function, you set the external flag variable to match the newly selected state.

Although this example is pretty straightforward, understanding how to use ClassFactory is a good skill to have because it is arguably the best way to create reusable renderers that have any sort of complexity to them. It can be used for itemRenderers as well by following the same methodology to specify properties and values to be set on instances of your renderer class.

The only thing left to do is to tie the action of clicking the check box in the header to selecting/deselecting all of the item renderer CheckBoxes. To do this, simply listen for MouseEvent.CLICK in the DataGrid's parent file, because those events will bubble, and take action from there. After verifying that the event came from the header renderer, loop over the data and set the appropriate data field to the correct value for each item.

You also need to call `itemUpdated` on each item because it will cause the associated renderers to be redrawn so that they accurately reflect the underlying data. For example:

```
// click events will still bubble
private function onCheckBoxHeaderClick(event:MouseEvent):void
{
    // make sure click came from header
    if(event.target is CenteredCheckBoxHeaderRenderer)
    {
        // loop over data
        for each(var obj:Object in dg.dataProvider)
        {
            // update value based on CheckBox state
            obj.addToCart = CenteredCheckBoxHeaderRenderer(event.target).selected;
            // notify collection item was changed
            ListCollectionView(dg.dataProvider).itemUpdated(obj, "addToCart");
        }
    }
}
```

7.8 Create a Self-Contained CheckBox itemRenderer for Use in a DataGrid

Contributed by Ben Clinkinbeard

Problem

You need to create a `CheckBox` `itemRenderer` for use in a `DataGrid` that will center the `CheckBox` in the renderer regardless of the size of the `DataGridColumn`.

Solution

Extend the `CheckBox` class and override the `updateDisplayList` method to properly center the `CheckBox`. In the `clickHandler` method of the `CheckBox`, set the data of the parent `DataGrid` to true or false based on the state of the `CheckBox`.

Discussion

The following class can be used as a completely self-contained item renderer and will center itself in its parent `DataGridColumn`. While this class provides all item rendering functionality by itself, a `MouseEvent` will still bubble up from the component should you need to capture it for other purposes. For instance, you could define a listener in the file that houses your `DataGrid` that catches the `MouseEvent` and updates a label to display a message stating how many `CheckBox`es are selected.

```
package
{
    import flash.display.DisplayObject;
    import flash.events.MouseEvent;
    import flash.text.TextField;
```

```
    import mx.controls.CheckBox;
    import mx.controls.dataGridClasses.DataGridListData;

    public class CenteredCheckBoxItemRenderer extends CheckBox
    {
        // this function is defined by mx.controls.CheckBox
        // it is the default handler for its click event
        override protected function clickHandler(event:MouseEvent):void
        {
            super.clickHandler(event);
            // this is the important line as it updates the data field that this
CheckBox is rendering
            data[DataGridListData(listData).dataField] = selected;
        }

        // center the checkbox icon
        override protected function updateDisplayList(w:Number, h:Number):void
        {
            super.updateDisplayList(w, h);

            var n:int = numChildren;
            for (var i:int = 0; i < n; i++)
            {
                var c:DisplayObject = getChildAt(i);
                // CheckBox component is made up of icon skin and label TextField
                // we ignore the label field and center the icon
                if (!(c is TextField))
                {
                    c.x = Math.round((w - c.width) / 2);
                    c.y = Math.round((h - c.height) / 2);
                }
            }
        }
    }
}
```

There are two notable aspects of this approach. First, it doesn't implement
ClassFactory, which means you can simply type its fully qualified class name into the
itemRenderer attribute of a DataGrid and it will work (just as with mx.controls.Check
Box), requiring one less bindable variable in your file. The reason you can do this is that
CheckBox, and by extension CenteredCheckBoxItemRenderer, implement
IDropInListItemRenderer. In the case of CheckBox, it knows how to set its selected state
based on a piece of data that is passed to it. The second major difference is closely
related to this fact: You no longer have to override the data setter because you get that
functionality for free.

The most important line in the itemRenderer class is essentially the other half of the
equation. Whereas you get data retrieval and rendering for free, you have to provide
the data setting functionality. The ability to correctly set the data is the only thing that
separates this CheckBox from a regular CheckBox other than the centering code, and this
is accomplished with this single line of code:

```
        data[DataGridListData(listData).dataField] = selected;
```

This line uses the `listData` property (defined by `IDropInListItemRenderer`) to locate and update the specific piece of data this `CheckBox` is rendering in the `DataGrid`.

7.9 Efficiently Set Images in a Renderer

Problem

You want to display images in an `itemRenderer` in the most efficient way, based on the data passed in to those images.

Solution

Create a new renderer class and use the `commitProperties` method to call the owner of the `itemRenderer` using the `listData` property of the `IDropInItemRenderer`. A method in the parent can return an embedded image object that can then be added to the display list of the renderer.

Discussion

As Alex Harui, one of the architects of the `List` and `ListBase` classes for the release of Flex 3, wrote on his blog, "You can stick an `Image` tag in a `Canvas`, but it's not the best way to do it." Why not? Because the Flex Framework simplifies our lives with a complex series of calls to measure the size of the component, redraw any children components, and redraw the component itself. The more you can work within the Flex Framework, the more you can allow the normal routines of the Framework to do your work for you and avoid adding unnecessary processing burdens on the Flash Player.

The renderer in this example implements both the `IListItemRenderer` and `IDropInListItemRenderer` interfaces to ensure that the renderer can be used flexibly and with a minimum of overhead. Because the component here extends the `UIComponent` tag, an override for the `measure` method is needed so that component will accurately report its size to the parent `DataGrid`. You implement the `measure` method by measuring the image and setting the `measuredWidth` and `measuredHeight` of the component using that value.

The other interesting approach that this recipe illustrates is how to access the `Image` class from the parent. The image isn't passed into the renderer itself. In this example, the renderer calls up to the parent with its data and receives a class reference to an embedded image that can then be accessed.

```
    if (listData) {
        // remove the old child if we have one
        if (img) {
            removeChild(img);
        }
        if(_imgClass == null) {
```

```
            var _imgClass:Class = UIComponent(owner).document[listData.label];
        }
        img = new _imgClass();
        addChild(img);
    }
```

The parent is accessed by using a reference to the listData owner document. The
document object of the listData is, in this case, the DataGridColumn using the renderer.
If a value is passed in to the renderer, that value is used to create the image. If not, the
DataGridColumn is accessed and the image class is retrieved from there. The code for the
renderer is shown here:

```
package oreilly.cookbook
{
    import flash.display.DisplayObject;
    import mx.events.FlexEvent;
    import mx.controls.listClasses.BaseListData;
    import mx.controls.listClasses.IDropInListItemRenderer;
    import mx.controls.listClasses.IListItemRenderer;
    import mx.core.UIComponent;

    public class SevenSixRenderer extends UIComponent implements
IDropInListItemRenderer, IListItemRenderer
    {
    private var _data:Object;
    private var img:DisplayObject;
    private var _listData:BaseListData;
    private var _imgClass:Class;

    [Bindable("dataChange")]
    public function get data():Object {
        return _data;
    }

    public function set data(value:Object):void {
        _data = value;
        if(_data.imgClass != null) {
            _imgClass =_data.imgClass;
        }
        invalidateProperties(); // invalidate properties so that we're certain that
they'll be updated.
        dispatchEvent(new FlexEvent(FlexEvent.DATA_CHANGE));
    }

    [Bindable("dataChange")]
    public function get listData():BaseListData {
        return _listData;
    }

    public function set listData(value:BaseListData):void {
        _listData = value;
    }

    override protected function commitProperties():void {
        super.commitProperties();
```

```
            // sometimes the listdata of the renderer can be null, in which case we
    certainly don't
            // want to throw runtime errors
            if (listData) {
                // remove the old child if we have one
                if (img) {
                    removeChild(img);
                }
                if(_imgClass == null) {
                    var _imgClass:Class = UIComponent(owner).document[ listData.label];
                }
                img = new _imgClass();
                addChild(img);
            }
        }

        /* create the image instance now that we know what it is */
        override protected function measure():void {
            super.measure();
            if (img) {
                measuredHeight = img.height;
                measuredWidth = img.width;
            }
        }

        /* make sure the image is positioned correctly */
        override protected function updateDisplayList(w:Number, h:Number):void {
            super.updateDisplayList(w, h);
            if (img) {
                img.x = (w - img.width) / 2;
            }
        }
    }
}
```

In the preceding overridden commitProperties method, if there is no Image passed in
the data, the renderer checks with the owner of the BaseListData to call its
labelFunction. This would be useful for creating default image settings in a DataGrid
or List. If a value is passed within the data passed to the renderer, the renderer uses
that value; otherwise, the renderer calls the getImage method, because it is set as the
labelFunction, and displays that image. The code to implement the renderer is shown
here:

```
<mx:HBox xmlns:mx="http://www.adobe.com/2006/mxml" width="700" height="300">
    <mx:Script>
        <![CDATA[

        import mx.collections.ArrayCollection;

        [Embed(source="../assets/foo.jpeg")]
        private var img:Class;

        [Embed(source="../assets/bar.jpeg")]
        public var img2:Class;
```

```
            //just a generic collection to store some plain old info
            [Bindable]
            private var genericCollectionOne:ArrayCollection = new ArrayCollection([{name:
"josh noble", age:30, appearance:"Somewhat wild"},
                {name:"Abey George", age:32, appearance:"Pretty tight", imgClass:img},
                {name:"Todd Anderson", age:31, appearance:"Intimidating"},
                {name:"Ryan Taylor", age:25, appearance:"Boyishly Handsome",
imgClass:img},
                {name:"Steve Weiss", age:36, appearance:"George Clooney-ish"}]);

            // for our itemRenderer we use the call into this method if the imgClass
property is null
            private function getImage(o:Object, c:DataGridColumn):String
            {

                return "img2";
            }

            ]]>
        </mx:Script>
        <mx:DataGrid dataProvider="{genericCollectionOne}">
            <mx:columns>
                <mx:DataGridColumn dataField="age"/>
                <mx:DataGridColumn dataField="name"/>
                <mx:DataGridColumn dataField="appearance"/>
                <mx:DataGridColumn itemRenderer="oreilly.cookbook.SevenSixRenderer"
labelFunction="getImage    " dataField="imgClass"/>
            </mx:columns>
        </mx:DataGrid>
    </mx:HBox>
```

7.10 Use Runtime Styling with itemRenderers and itemEditors

Problem

You need to be able to set information for itemRenderers or itemEditors within a Data
Grid.

Solution

Override the makeRowsAndColumns method of the ListBase that both the List and Data
GridColumn extend to set the style for each item renderer.

Discussion

Setting styles in the itemRenderers of a List or DataGridColumn involves simply looping
through the itemRenderers within the List or DataGridColumn and setting the style. This
should be done when the style is set and whenever the makeRowsAndColumns method of
the ListBase class that the DataGridColumn and List extend.

You can access each item renderer in a List through the indexToItemRenderer method of the ListBase class. Looping over all the item renderers by using the rowCount property of the ListBase ensures that you try to access only renderers that have been created. Simply looping through all the renderers when the style is set for the renderer is not sufficient. For performance, item renderers are created for the visible rows only. When a List or DataGrid scrolls, the data from the next visible item renderers are passed to the correct renderers to give the appearance of scrolling. This means that whenever the item renderers are redrawn, you need to check whether the styleName is correctly set, and if not, set the style and set the invalidateDisplayList flag for the item renderers:

```
<mx:List xmlns:mx="http://www.adobe.com/2006/mxml">
    <mx:Script>
        <![CDATA[
            import mx.core.UIComponent;
            private var _rendererStyle:String;
            //here's the most effective way to ensure that we draw
            //the item renderers only when we need them
            override protected function makeRowsAndColumns(left:Number, top:Number,
right:Number, bottom:Number, firstCol:int, firstRow:int, byCount:Boolean=false,
rowsNeeded:uint=0.0):Point
            {
                var pt:Point;
                pt = super.makeRowsAndColumns(left, top, right, bottom, firstCol,
firstRow, byCount, rowsNeeded);
                if(_rendererStyle != null) {
                    rendererStyle = _rendererStyle;
                }
                return pt;
            }

            public function set rendererStyle(styleName:String):void {
                _rendererStyle = styleName;
                if( collection != null ) {
                var i:int = 0;
                    do {
                        try{
                            var comp:UIComponent = (indexToItemRenderer(i) as
UIComponent);
                            if(comp.styleName == _rendererStyle){
                                comp.styleName = _rendererStyle;
                                comp.invalidateDisplayList();
                            } else { continue; }
                        } catch (err:Error){}
                        i++;
                    } while ( i < rowCount )
                }
            }

            public function get rendererStyle():String {
                return _rendererStyle;
            }

        ]]>
```

```
        </mx:Script>
    </mx:List>
```

To set the renderer style, simply update the `rendererStyle` property of the list on a button click, and the item renderers are updated through the `List`:

```
<mx:VBox xmlns:mx="http://www.adobe.com/2006/mxml" width="400" height="700"
xmlns:cookbook="oreilly.cookbook.*">
    <mx:Style>
        .firstStyle{
            color:#999999;
        }
        .secondStyle{
            color:#3344ff;
        }
    </mx:Style>
    <mx:Button toggle="true" click="list.rendererStyle == 'firstStyle' ? list.renderer
Style = 'secondStyle' : list.rendererStyle = 'firstStyle'" label="TOGGLE" />
    <cookbook:StylingRendererList id="list" dataProvider="{oreilly.cookbook.DataHolder
.simpleArray}" rendererStyle="firstStyle" width="200"/>
</mx:VBox>
```

7.11 Use States and Transitions with an itemEditor

Problem

You want to create effects to play when the user begins editing and when the user finishes editing.

Solution

Create a state in the `item editor` to play an effect by using a `Transition` when the user begins editing.

Discussion

Setting up an effect to play immediately after a user has finished editing data when using the item editor is quite easy to accomplish, by using a `DefaultListEffect` attached to the `List`. The `defaultChangeEffect` property of the `List` handles creating an effect for after the `itemEditor` of the `List` value has been committed:

```
<mx:List xmlns:mx="http://www.adobe.com/2006/mxml" width="400" height="300"
dataChangeEffect="{baseEffect}" editable="true">
    <mx:DefaultListEffect id="baseEffect" color="#ffff00" fadeInDuration="300"
fadeOutDuration="200"/>
</mx:List>
```

The preceding code will play an effect *after* the user has finished editing the value of the `itemEditor`. To display an effect when the user *begins* editing the data in the `itemEditor`, a custom item renderer that can double as an item editor will need to be created. The item renderer needs only to set the data for the `TextInput` component and define the Transition that will play when the editor is initialized. The effect will play when the editor is destroyed and the value is saved to the item renderer that is being edited.

```
<mx:Canvas xmlns:mx="http://www.adobe.com/2006/mxml" currentState="base" width="100"
height="20" creationComplete="currentState = 'init'" focusEnabled="true"
backgroundColor="#ffff00">
    <mx:Script>
        <![CDATA[

            [Bindable]
            private var _data:Object;

            override public function set data(value:Object):void {
                _data = value;
            }

            override public function get data():Object {
                return _data;
            }

            //so that the text of the input field can be set when we first start
            public function set text(value:String):void {
                input.text = value;
            }

            //this is needed so that the item editor will return the correct value
            //when the list reads that value back
            public function get text():String {
                return input.text;
            }

        ]]>
    </mx:Script>
    <mx:transitions>
        <!-- this transition will play when the component is ready to be displayed -->
        <mx:Transition fromState="*" toState="init">
            <mx:Fade alphaFrom="0" alphaTo="1" duration="500" target="{this}"/>
        </mx:Transition>
        <mx:Transition fromState="init" toState="*">
            <mx:Fade alphaFrom="1" alphaTo="0" duration="500" effectEnd="this.dispatch
Event(new Event('finishTransition', true))" target="{this}"/>
        </mx:Transition>
    </mx:transitions>
    <mx:states>
        <mx:State name="base"/>
        <mx:State name="init"/>
    </mx:states>
    <mx:TextInput id="input" creationComplete="input.text = String(_data),
input.setFocus()"/>
</mx:Canvas>
```

7.12 Create a CheckBox Tree Control

Contributed by Jeff Ploughman

Problem

You need to create a three-state `CheckBox` control to be used as the renderer of a `Tree` control.

Solution

There are three main aspects to the solution:

1. A `TreeItemRenderer` is created to place a `CheckBox` control at each node in the tree.

2. An image of a tiny black box is painted on top of the `CheckBox` when the `CheckBox` is in the third state.

3. The underlying data model for the tree needs to contain an attribute representing the state of the `CheckBox`.

Discussion

Trees are commonly used to represent file systems. Often the user needs to select several items within several folders and take an action on them, so there needs to be some visual mechanism for indicating that a node is selected. A check box is typically used to represent selection. What we need is a tree of three-state check boxes.

Selecting or deselecting a parent node should cause children nodes to be selected or deselected. To create a parent node that contains some children that are selected and some that are not, you need more than a simple two-state check box. You need a third state (in which some of a node's children are selected and others are not) that cannot be represented by a check box's Boolean `selected` property.

The solution is in the `TreeItemRenderer` class and a custom ActionScript class called `CheckTreeRenderer`. The `CheckTreeRenderer` class will extend the `TreeItemRenderer` and provide custom functionality to support the three-state checkbox:

```
<mx:Application xmlns:mx="http://www.adobe.com/2006/mxml" creationComplete="init();" >

<mx:Script>
<![CDATA[

    import mx.collections.*;

    [Bindable]
    public var folderList:XMLList =
        <>
        <folder state="unchecked" label="Marketing Collateral" isBranch="true" >
            <folder state="unchecked" isBranch="true" label="Media, PR, and
Communications" >
                <folder state="unchecked" isBranch="false" label="Article Reprint
```

```
        Disclaimers" />
                <folder state="unchecked" isBranch="false" label="Articles Reprints" />
                <folder state="unchecked" isBranch="false" label="Interviews and
Transcripts" />
                <folder state="unchecked" isBranch="false" label="Press Kits" />
                <folder state="unchecked" isBranch="false" label="Press Releases" />
                <folder state="unchecked" isBranch="false" label="Quick Hits" />
                <folder state="unchecked" isBranch="false" label="Rep Talking Points" />

                <folder state="unchecked" isBranch="false" label="Special Updates" />
                <folder state="unchecked" isBranch="false" label="White Papers" />
            </folder>
            <folder  state="unchecked" isBranch="true" label="Forms and Applications" >

                <folder state="unchecked" isBranch="false" label="Applications" />
                <folder state="unchecked" isBranch="false" label="Forms" />
            </folder>
        </folder>
        </>;

    [Bindable]
    public var folderCollection:XMLListCollection;

    private function init() : void
    {
        folderCollection = new XMLListCollection(folderList);
        checkTree.dataProvider = folderCollection;
    }

]]>
</mx:Script>
    <mx:Tree
            id="checkTree"
            itemRenderer="oreilly.cookbook.CheckTreeRenderer"
            labelField="@label"
             width="100%" height="100%" >
    </mx:Tree>
</mx:Application>
```

Here is the code listing for the CheckTreeRenderer that will be used to display the CheckBox within the Tree:

```
package oreilly.cookbook
{
    import mx.controls.Image;
    import mx.controls.Tree;
    import mx.controls.treeClasses.*;
    import mx.collections.*;
    import mx.controls.CheckBox;
    import mx.controls.listClasses.*;
    import flash.events.Event;
    import flash.events.MouseEvent;
    import mx.events.FlexEvent;
    import flash.display.DisplayObject;
    import flash.events.MouseEvent;
    import flash.xml.*;
```

```
    import mx.core.IDataRenderer;

    public class CheckTreeRenderer extends TreeItemRenderer
    {
```

Create a CheckBox and an Image:

```
    protected var myImage:Image;
    protected var myCheckBox:CheckBox;
    // set image properties
    private var imageWidth:Number    = 6;
    private var imageHeight:Number   = 6;
    private var inner:String     = "assets/inner.png";
    static private var STATE_SCHRODINGER:String = "schrodinger";
    static private var STATE_CHECKED:String = "checked";
    static private var STATE_UNCHECKED:String = "unchecked";

    public function CheckTreeRenderer ()
    {
        super();
        mouseEnabled = false;
    }
    private function toggleParents (item:Object, tree:Tree, state:String):void
    {
        if (item == null)
        {
            return;
        }
        else
        {
            item.@state = state;
            toggleParents(tree.getParentItem(item), tree, getState (tree, tree.get
ParentItem(item)));
        }
    }

    private function toggleChildren (item:Object, tree:Tree, state:String):void
    {
        if (item == null) {return;}
        else {
            item.@state = state;
            var treeData:ITreeDataDescriptor = tree.dataDescriptor;
            if (treeData.hasChildren(item)) {
                var children:ICollectionView = treeData.getChildren (item);
                var cursor:IViewCursor = children.createCursor();
                while (!cursor.afterLast) {
                    toggleChildren(cursor.current, tree, state);
                    cursor.moveNext();
                }
            }
        }
    }
```

The handler for the Image control delegates handling most of the selection logic to the
CheckBox handler. After all, the Image control is for handling only the third state.

For each node clicked, the CheckBox handler toggles the state of the node's children and then toggles the state of the node's parent(s). The children can be set to only a CHECKED or UNCHECKED state, whereas the parent(s) can be also be set to the third state. This third state, called the SCHRODINGER state, occurs when some of the parent node's children are in a CHECKED state, UNCHECKED state, and/or SCHRODINGER state.

The state that the parent will be set to is arrived at by looking at the state of its children. This is the job of the getState method:

```
private function getState(tree:Tree, parent:Object):String {
    var noChecks:int = 0;
    var noCats:int = 0;
    var noUnChecks:int = 0;
    if (parent != null) {
        var treeData:ITreeDataDescriptor = tree.dataDescriptor;
        var cursor:IViewCursor = treeData.getChildren(parent).createCursor();
        while (!cursor.afterLast) {
            if (cursor.current.@state == STATE_CHECKED){
                noChecks++;
            }
            else if (cursor.current.@state == STATE_UNCHECKED) {
                noUnChecks++
            }
            else {
                noCats++;
            }
            cursor.moveNext();
        }
    }
    if ((noChecks > 0 && noUnChecks > 0) || (noCats > 0 && noChecks>0)) {
        return STATE_SCHRODINGER;
    } else if (noChecks > 0) {
        return STATE_CHECKED;
    } else {
        return STATE_UNCHECKED;
    }
}
private function imageToggleHandlder(event:MouseEvent):void {
    myCheckBox.selected = !myCheckBox.selected;
    checkBoxToggleHandler(event);
}
```

Each child control, CheckBox and Image, needs to handle mouse clicks, so you must create an EventListener for each:

```
private function checkBoxToggleHandler(event:MouseEvent):void
{
    if (data)
    {
        var myListData:TreeListData = TreeListData(this.listData);
        var selectedNode:Object = myListData.item;
        var tree:Tree = Tree(myListData.owner);
        var toggle:Boolean = myCheckBox.selected;
        if (toggle) {
            toggleChildren(data, tree, STATE_CHECKED);
```

```
            } else {
                toggleChildren(data, tree, STATE_UNCHECKED);
            }
            var parent:Object = tree.getParentItem (data);
            toggleParents (parent, tree, getState (tree, parent));
        }
    }
```

Here you override the **createChildren** method, which is responsible for creating each node in the tree:

```
override protected function createChildren():void {
    super.createChildren();
    myCheckBox = new CheckBox();
    myCheckBox.setStyle( "verticalAlign", "middle" );
    myCheckBox.addEventListener( MouseEvent.CLICK, checkBoxToggleHandler );
    addChild(myCheckBox);
    myImage = new Image();
    myImage.source = inner;
    myImage.addEventListener( MouseEvent.CLICK, imageToggleHandler );
    myImage.setStyle( "verticalAlign", "middle" );
    addChild(myImage);

}

private function setCheckState (checkBox:CheckBox, value:Object, state:String)
:void
{
    if (state == STATE_CHECKED) {
        checkBox.selected = true;
    }
    else if (state == STATE_UNCHECKED) {
        checkBox.selected = false;
    }
    else if (state == STATE_SCHRODINGER) {
        checkBox.selected = false;
    }
}
override public function set data(value:Object):void {
    if(value != null) {
        super.data = value;

        setCheckState (myCheckBox, value, value.@state);
        if(TreeListData(super.listData).item.@type == 'dimension') {
            setStyle("fontStyle", 'italic');
        } else {
            if (this.parent != null) {
                var _tree:Tree = Tree(this.parent.parent);
                _tree.setStyle("defaultLeafIcon", null);
            }
            setStyle("fontStyle", 'normal');
        }
    }
}

override protected function updateDisplayList(unscaledWidth:Number,
```

```
unscaledHeight:Number):void
    {
        super.updateDisplayList(unscaledWidth, unscaledHeight);
        if(super.data)
        {
            if (super.icon != null) {
                myCheckBox.x = super.icon.x;
                myCheckBox.y = 2;
                super.icon.x = myCheckBox.x + myCheckBox.width + 17;
                super.label.x = super.icon.x + super.icon.width + 3;
            } else {
                myCheckBox.x = super.label.x;
                myCheckBox.y = 2;
                super.label.x = myCheckBox.x + myCheckBox.width + 17;
            }
            if (data.@state == STATE_SCHRODINGER) {
                myImage.x = myCheckBox.x + 4;
                myImage.y = myCheckBox.y + 4;
                myImage.width = imageWidth;
                myImage.height = imageHeight;
            } else {
                myImage.x = 0;
                myImage.y = 0;
                myImage.width = 0;
                myImage.height = 0;
            }
        }
    }
}
```

This item renderer now not only displays multiple check box states within the Check Box, but updates and reads data from the Tree component that makes use of it.

7.13 Resize Renderers Within a List

Problem

You want to create a renderer that resizes when the renderer is selected.

Solution

Create an item renderer that implements the IDropInListItemRenderer interface and use the listData to add eventListeners to the parent List for the Scroll and Change events. When the Change or Scroll events are fired, check whether the data property of the itemRenderer matches the data of the selectedItem in the List. If so, set the current state of the renderer. If not, reset the currentState to a base state.

Discussion

It is important to remember that the item renderer is reused by the List. When trying to set states in an item renderer when it is selected, the data of the item renderer must be compared with the selectedItem in the List or DataGridColumn rather than the selectedIndex, because the selectedIndex does not indicate which renderer is selected. In fact, the selected renderer could very well be scrolled away from in the List.

Because you have access to the List or DataGridColumn through the listData property, you can add event listeners and create a handler that will check the data and current state of the renderer as shown here:

```
private function resizeEventHandler(event:Event):void {
            if((_listData.owner as List).selectedIndex ==
ArrayCollection((_listData.owner as List).dataProvider).getItemIndex(this.data) &&
            currentState != "selected") {
                trace(" functions "+_listData.rowIndex+"  "+(_listData.owner as
List).selectedIndex);
                currentState = "selected";
            } else if((_listData.owner as List).selectedIndex !=
ArrayCollection((_listData.owner as List).dataProvider).getItemIndex(this.data) &&
            currentState == "selected") {
                currentState = "base";
            }
        }
```

There are different ways to extend this to be more general, but for a simple example, assuming that you'll always be using an ArrayCollection is sufficient. Take a look:

```
<mx:VBox xmlns:mx="http://www.adobe.com/2006/mxml" height="30" currentState="base"
    implements="mx.controls.listClasses.IDropInListItemRenderer" verticalScrollPolicy=
"off">
    <mx:Script>
        <![CDATA[
            import mx.controls.List;

            import mx.events.ListEvent;
            import mx.controls.listClasses.BaseListData;
            import mx.collections.ArrayCollection;

            private function resizeFocusInHandler(event:Event):void {
                if((_listData.owner as List).selectedIndex ==
ArrayCollection((_listData.owner as List).dataProvider).getItemIndex(this.data) &&
                currentState != "selected") {
                    trace(" functions "+_listData.rowIndex+"  "+(_listData.owner as
List).selectedIndex);
                    currentState = "selected";
                } else if((_listData.owner as List).selectedIndex !=
ArrayCollection((_listData.owner as List).dataProvider).getItemIndex(this.data) &&
                currentState == "selected") {
                    currentState = "base";
                }
            }
```

```
            override public function set data(value:Object):void {
                txt.text = value as String;
            }

            override public function get data():Object {
                return txt.text;
            }

            // Internal variable for the property value.
            private var _listData:BaseListData;

            // Make the listData property bindable.
            [Bindable("dataChange")]
            // Define the getter method.
            public function get listData():BaseListData {
                return _listData;
            }

            // set the event listeners for the Change and Scroll events
            // that the List or Column will dispatch
            public function set listData(value:BaseListData):void {
                _listData = value;
                _listData.owner.addEventListener(ListEvent.CHANGE,
resizeFocusInHandler);
                _listData.owner.addEventListener(Event.SCROLL, resizeFocusInHandler);
            }

        ]]>
    </mx:Script>
    <mx:transitions>
        <mx:Transition fromState="*" toState="selected">
            <mx:Resize heightTo="60" target="{this}"/>
        </mx:Transition>
        <mx:Transition fromState="selected" toState="*">
            <mx:Resize heightTo="30" target="{this}"/>
        </mx:Transition>
    </mx:transitions>
    <mx:states>
        <mx:State name="base"/>
        <mx:State name="selected">
            <mx:AddChild>
                <mx:HBox>
                    <mx:Label text="some text"/>
                    <mx:Label text="{'some text = '+txt.text}"/>
                </mx:HBox>
            </mx:AddChild>
        </mx:State>
    </mx:states>
    <mx:Text id="txt"/>
</mx:VBox>
```

CHAPTER 8

Images, Bitmaps, Videos, Sounds

Images, bitmaps, videos, and sounds is a mouthful and a far wider range of topics than could be adequately covered in a single chapter, so this one concentrates on answering the most common questions. As Flash becomes the primary method of delivering video over the Internet and the use of the Flex Framework in creating photo and MP3 applications increases, understanding how to work with all of these elements becomes more and more important.

The Flash Player offers multiple levels of tools for dealing with images and sound. The first avenue of control contains the `Image` and `VideoDisplay` classes, MXML classes that simplify much of dealing with images and video and enable you to quickly integrate these assets into your application. The next step down is the `flash.media` package, which houses the `Video`, `Sound`, `SoundTransform`, `Camera`, and `Microphone` classes; their corollaries, `Loader`, `NetConnection`, and `NetStream`, are in the `flash.net` package. These classes provide much finer control over the integration of sound, video, and images into an application and require slightly more time to perfect. Finally, you can reach down to the bytes that make up all data in the Flash Player: the `BitmapData` classes and the `ByteArray` classes. These enable you not only to manipulate the bitmap data of the images that you load into the Flash Player, but also to create new bitmaps and stream the data out.

Many of the examples in this chapter manipulate images and videos as bitmap data. This is not nearly as difficult as it sounds, because the Flash Player provides numerous convenience methods for working with the `BitmapData` class, and manipulating the bitmap data directly greatly increases the efficiency of your application. You'll also be working extensively with the `NetStream` class, for handling video and users' microphones and cameras. `NetStream` is an effective way of streaming information both to and from server-side applications.

8.1 Load and Display an Image

Problem

You need to display an image in a Flex component.

Solution

Use either an Embed statement to compile the image into the SWF file or load the image at runtime.

Discussion

Flex supports importing GIF, JPEG, PNG, and SWF files at runtime or at compile time, and SVG files at compile time through embedding. The method you choose depends on the file types of your images and your application parameters. Any embedded images are already part of the SWF file and so don't require any time to load. The trade-off is the size that they add to your application, which slows the application initialization process. Extensive use of embedded images also requires you to recompile your applications whenever your image files change.

Alternatively, you can load the resource at runtime by either setting the **source** property of an image to a URL or by using **URLRequest** objects and making the result of the load operation a **BitmapAsset** object. You can load a resource from the local file system in which the SWF file runs, or you can access a remote resource, typically through an HTTP request over a network. These images are independent of your application; you can change them without needing to recompile as long as the names of the modified images remain the same.

Any SWF file can access only one type of external resource, either local or over a network; it cannot access both types. You determine the type of access allowed by the SWF file by using the **use-network** flag when you compile your application. When the **use-network** flag is set to false, you can access resources in the local file system, but not over the network. The default value is true, which allows you to access resources over the network, but not in the local file system.

To embed an image file, use the **Embed** metadata property:

```
[Embed(source="../assets/flag.png")]
private var flag:Class;
```

Now this **Class** object can be set as the source for an image:

```
var asset:BitmapAsset = new flag() as BitmapAsset;
img3rd.source = asset;
```

Alternatively, you can set the property of the source to a local or external file system:

```
<mx:Image source="http://server.com/beach.jpg"/>
```

The full example follows:

```
<mx:VBox xmlns:mx="http://www.adobe.com/2006/mxml" width="400" height="300">
    <mx:Script>
        <![CDATA[
            import mx.core.BitmapAsset;

            [Embed(source="../assets/flag.png")]
            private var flag:Class;

            private function imgMod():void
            {
                var asset:BitmapAsset = new flag() as BitmapAsset;
                img3rd.source = asset;
            }

        ]]>
    </mx:Script>
    <mx:Image source="../assets/flag.png"/>
    <mx:Image source="{flag}"/>
    <mx:Image id="img3rd" creationComplete="imgMod()"/>
</mx:VBox>
```

8.2 Create a Video Display

Problem

You need to display an FLV file in your application.

Solution

Use the `VideoDisplay` class in your application and use `Button` objects to play and pause the application if desired.

Discussion

The `VideoDisplay` class wraps a `flash.media.Video` object and simplifies adding video to that object considerably. The `source` attribute of the `VideoDisplay` is set to the URL of an FLV file, and the `autoplay` parameter is set to true so that when the `NetStream` has been properly instantiated and the video information begins streaming to the player, the video will begin playing:

```
<mx:VideoDisplay source="http://localhost:3001/Trailer.flv" id="vid" autoplay="true"/>
```

In the following example, buttons are set up to play, pause, and stop the video by using the methods defined by the `VideoDisplay` class:

```
<mx:VBox xmlns:mx="http://www.adobe.com/2006/mxml" width="400" height="300">
    <mx:VideoDisplay source="http://localhost:3001/Trailer.flv" id="vid" autoPlay=
"false" autoRewind="true"/>
    <mx:HBox>
        <mx:Button label="Play" click="vid.play();"/>
```

```
            <mx:Button label="Pause" click="vid.pause();"/>
            <mx:Button label="Stop" click="vid.stop();"/>
        </mx:HBox>
    </mx:VBox>
```

8.3 Play and Pause an MP3 File

Problem

You want to allow a user to play a series of MP3 files.

Solution

Use the Sound and SoundChannel classes and load new files by using progressive down-load when the user selects a new MP3 file.

Discussion

The play method of the Sound class returns a SoundChannel object that provides access to methods and properties that control the balance or right and left volume of the sound, as well as methods to pause and resume a particular sound.

For example, let's say your code loads and plays a sound file like this:

```
var snd:Sound = new Sound(new URLRequest("sound.mp3"));
var channel:SoundChannel = snd.play();
```

You cannot literally pause a sound during playback in ActionScript; you can only stop it by using the SoundChannel stop method. You can, however, play a sound starting from any point. You can record the position of the sound at the time it was stopped, and then replay the sound starting at that position later.

While the sound plays, the SoundChannel.position property indicates the point in the sound file that's currently being played. Store the position value before stopping the sound from playing:

```
var pausePosition:int = channel.position;
channel.stop();
```

To resume the sound, pass the previously stored position value to restart the sound from the same point it stopped at before:

```
channel = snd.play(pausePosition);
```

The following complete code listing provides a combo box to allow the user to select different MP3 files, pause, and stop playback by using the SoundChannel class:

```
<mx:HBox xmlns:mx="http://www.adobe.com/2006/mxml" width="400" height="300">
    <mx:Script>
        <![CDATA[
            import mx.collections.ArrayCollection;
```

```
            public var sound:Sound;
            public var chan:SoundChannel;
            public var pausePos:int = 0;

            private const server:String = "http://localhost:3001/"

            private var dp:ArrayCollection = new ArrayCollection(["Plans.mp3",
"Knife.mp3", "Marla.mp3", "On a Neck, On a Spit.mp3", "Colorado.mp3"])

            private function loadSound():void {
                if(chan != null) {
                    //make sure we stop the sound; otherwise, they'll overlap
                    chan.stop();
                }
                //re-create sound object, flushing the buffer, and readd the event
listener
                sound = new Sound();
                sound.addEventListener(Event.SOUND_COMPLETE, soundComplete);
                var req:URLRequest = new URLRequest(server + cb.selectedItem as
String);
                sound.load(req);
                pausePos = 0;
                chan = sound.play();
            }
            //
            private function soundComplete(event:Event):void {
                cb.selectedIndex++;
                sound.load(new URLRequest(server + cb.selectedItem as String));
                chan = sound.play();
            }

            private function playPauseHandler():void
            {
                if(pausePlayBtn.selected){
                    pausePos = chan.position;
                    chan.stop();
                } else {
                    chan = sound.play(pausePos);
                }
            }

        ]]>
    </mx:Script>
    <mx:ComboBox creationComplete="cb.dataProvider=dp" id="cb" change="loadSound()"/>
    <mx:Button label="start" id="pausePlayBtn" toggle="true" click=
"playPauseHandler()"/>
    <mx:Button label="stop" click="chan.stop()"/>
</mx:HBox>
```

8.4 Create a Seek Bar for a Sound File

Problem

You need to create a seek control for a user to seek different parts of an MP3 file and a volume control to change the volume of the MP3 playback.

Solution

Pass a `time` parameter to the `Sound play` method to begin playing the file from that point. This creates a new `SoundTransform` object that should be set as the `soundTransform` of the `SoundChannel`.

Discussion

The `play` method of the sound file accepts a start-point parameter:

```
public function play(startTime:Number = 0, loops:int = 0, sndTransform: SoundTransform
= null):SoundChannel
```

This creates a new `SoundChannel` object to play the sound returns that object, which you access to stop the sound and monitor the volume. (To control the volume, panning, and balance, access the `SoundTransform` object assigned to the `SoundChannel`.)

To control the volume of the sound, pass the `SoundTransform` object to the `SoundChannel`. We create a new `SoundTransform` object with the desired values and pass it to the `SoundChannel` that is currently playing:

```
var trans:SoundTransform = new SoundTransform(volumeSlider.value);
chan.soundTransform = trans;
```

The `SoundTransform` class accepts the following parameters:

```
SoundTransform(vol:Number = 1, panning:Number = 0)
```

The `panning` values range from –1.0, indicating a full pan left (no sound coming out of the right speaker) to 1.0, indicating a full pan right. A full code listing is shown here:

```
<mx:VBox xmlns:mx="http://www.adobe.com/2006/mxml" width="400" height="300"
creationComplete="loadSound()">
    <mx:Script>
        <![CDATA[

            private var sound:Sound;
            private var chan:SoundChannel;

            private function loadSound():void {
                sound = new Sound(new URLRequest("http://localhost:3001/Plans.mp3"));
                chan = sound.play();
            }

            private function scanPosition():void {
                chan.stop();
```

```
                    //divide by 10 because the Slider values go from 0 - 10 and we want
    a value
                    //between 0 - 1.0
                    chan = sound.play(positionSlider.value/10 * sound.length);
            }

            private function scanVolume():void
            {
                    var trans:SoundTransform = new SoundTransform(volumeSlider.value,
    (panSlider.value - 5)/10);
                    chan.soundTransform = trans;
            }

        ]]>
    </mx:Script>
    <mx:Label text="Position"/>
    <mx:HSlider change="scanPosition()" id="positionSlider"/>
    <mx:Label text="Volume"/>
    <mx:HSlider change="scanVolume()" id="volumeSlider"/>
    <mx:Label text="Pan"/>
    <mx:HSlider change="scanVolume()" id="panSlider"/>
</mx:VBox>
```

8.5 Blend Two Images

Problem

You want to manipulate and combine multiple images at runtime and use filters to alter
those images.

Solution

Cast the images as `BitmapData` objects and use the `combine` method of the `BitmapData`
class to combine all the data in the two bitmaps into a new image.

Discussion

The `BitmapData` and `Bitmap` classes are powerful tools for manipulating images at runtime and creating new effects. The two classes are frequently used in tandem but are
quite different. `BitmapData` encapsulates the actual data of the image, and `Bitmap` is a
display object that can be added to the display list. The `BitmapData` object is created
and drawn into as shown here:

```
var bitmapAsset:BitmapAsset = new BitmapAsset(img1.width, img1.height);
bitmapAsset.draw(img1);
```

First, set the height and width of the `BitmapAsset`, ensuring that the object is the correct
size, and then draw all the data from an image. This captures all the data in the image
as a bitmap and allows you to manipulate that data. In the following example, the
`colorTransform` method manipulates the color data of the `BitmapData` object, and the

two bitmaps are merged via the `merge` method. The `colorTransform` method applies the data from a `ColorTransform` object to the `BitmapData` object. The `ColorTransform` object modifies the color of a display object or `BitmapData` according to the values passed in to the constructor:

```
ColorTransform(redMultiplier:Number = 1.0, greenMultiplier:Number = 1.0,
blueMultiplier:Number = 1.0, alphaMultiplier:Number = 1.0, redOffset:Number = 0,
greenOffset:Number = 0, blueOffset:Number = 0, alphaOffset:Number = 0)
```

When a `ColorTransform` object is applied to a display object, a new value for each color channel is calculated like this:

- New red value = (old red value * `redMultiplier`) + `redOffset`
- New green value = (old green value * `greenMultiplier`) + `greenOffset`
- New blue value = (old blue value * `blueMultiplier`) + `blueOffset`
- New alpha value = (old alpha value * `alphaMultiplier`) + `alphaOffset`

The `merge` method of the `BitmapData` class has the following signature:

```
merge(sourceBitmapData:BitmapData, sourceRect:Rectangle, destPoint:Point, redMultiplier
:uint, greenMultiplier:uint, blueMultiplier:uint, alphaMultiplier:uint):void
```

Its parameters are as follows:

`sourceBitmapData:BitmapData`
> The input bitmap image to use. The source image can be a different `BitmapData` object or the current `BitmapData` object.

`sourceRect:Rectangle`
> A rectangle that defines the area of the source image to use as input.

`destPoint:Point`
> The point within the destination image (the current `BitmapData` instance) that corresponds to the upper-left corner of the source rectangle.

`redMultiplier:uint`
> A hexadecimal `uint` value by which to multiply the red channel value.

`greenMultiplier:uint`
> A hexadecimal `uint` value by which to multiply the green channel value.

`blueMultiplier:uint`
> A hexadecimal `uint` value by which to multiply the blue channel value.

`alphaMultiplier:uint`
> A hexadecimal `uint` value by which to multiply the alpha transparency value.

A complete code listing follows with modifiable controls to alter the values of the `ColorTransform`:

```
<mx:VBox xmlns:mx="http://www.adobe.com/2006/mxml" width="500" height="550"
creationComplete="imgMod()">
    <mx:Script>
        <![CDATA[
```

```
        import mx.core.BitmapAsset;
        import mx.controls.Image;


        [Embed(source="../assets/bigshakey.png")]
        private var shakey:Class;

        [Embed(source="../assets/mao.jpg")]
        private var mao:Class;

        //superimpose the two images together
        //using the vslider data
        private function imgMod():void
        {
            var maoData:BitmapData = new BitmapData(firstImg.width,
firstImg.height);
            var shakeyData:BitmapData = new BitmapData(secondImg.width,
secondImg.height);
            maoData.draw(firstImg);
            shakeyData.draw(secondImg);
            maoData.colorTransform(new Rectangle(0, 0, maoData.width,
maoData.height), new ColorTransform(redSlider.value/10, greenSlider.value/10,
blueSlider.value/10,alphaSlider.value/10));
            var red:uint = (uint(redSlider.value.toString(16)) / 10) * 160;
            var green:uint = (uint(greenSlider.value.toString(16)) / 10) * 160;
            var blue:uint = (uint(blueSlider.value.toString(16)) / 10) * 160;
            var alpha:uint = (uint(alphaSlider.value.toString(16)) / 10) * 160;
            shakeyData.merge(maoData, new Rectangle(0, 0, shakeyData.width,
shakeyData.height), new Point(0, 0), red, green, blue, alpha);
            mainImg.source = new BitmapAsset(shakeyData);
        }

    ]]>
    </mx:Script>
    <mx:HBox>
        <mx:Image id="firstImg" source="{mao}" height="200" width="200"/>
        <mx:Image id="secondImg" source="{shakey}" height="200" width="200"/>
    </mx:HBox>
    <mx:HBox>
        <mx:Text text="Red"/>
        <mx:VSlider height="100" id="redSlider" value="5.0" change="imgMod()"/>
        <mx:Text text="Blue"/>
        <mx:VSlider height="100" id="blueSlider" value="5.0" change="imgMod()"/>
        <mx:Text text="Green"/>
        <mx:VSlider height="100" id="greenSlider" value="5.0" change="imgMod()"/>
        <mx:Text text="Alpha"/>
        <mx:VSlider height="100" id="alphaSlider" value="5.0" change="imgMod()"/>
    </mx:HBox>
    <mx:Image id="mainImg"/>
</mx:VBox>
```

8.6 Apply a Convolution Filter to an Image

Problem

You want to allow users to alter the colors, contrast, or sharpness of an image.

Solution

Create an instance of a `ConvolutionFilter` and bind the properties of the matrix within the `ConvolutionFilter` to text inputs that the user can alter. Then push the filter onto the image's filters array to apply the filter.

Discussion

`ConvolutionFilter` is one of the most versatile and complex filters in the `flash.filters` package. It can be used to emboss, detect edges, sharpen, blur, and perform many other effects. All the parameters are controlled by a `Matrix` object representing a three-by-three matrix that is passed to the filter in its constructor. The `ConvolutionFilter` conceptually goes through each pixel in the source image one by one and determines the final color of that pixel by using the value of the pixel and its surrounding pixels. A matrix, specified as an array of numeric values, indicates to what degree the value of each particular neighboring pixel affects the final resulting value. The constructor is shown here:

```
ConvolutionFilter(matrixX:Number = 0, matrixY:Number = 0, matrix:Array = null,
divisor:Number = 1.0, bias:Number = 0.0, preserveAlpha:Boolean = true,
clamp:Boolean = true, co
lor:uint = 0, alpha:Number = 0.0)
```

Its parameters are as follows:

`matrixX:Number` *(default = 0)*
> The x dimension of the matrix (the number of columns in the matrix). The default value is 0.

`matrixY:Number` *(default = 0)*
> The y dimension of the matrix (the number of rows in the matrix). The default value is 0.

`matrix:Array` *(default = null)*
> The array of values used for matrix transformation. The number of items in the array must equal `matrixX` * `matrixY`.

`divisor:Number` *(default = 1.0)*
> The divisor used during matrix transformation. The default value is 1. A divisor that is the sum of all the matrix values evens out the overall color intensity of the result. A value of 0 is ignored and the default is used instead.

`bias:Number` *(default = 0.0)*
> The bias to add to the result of the matrix transformation. The default value is 0.

`preserveAlpha:Boolean` *(default = true)*

A value of false indicates that the alpha value is not preserved and that the convolution applies to all channels, including the alpha channel. A value of true indicates that the convolution applies only to the color channels. The default value is true.

`clamp:Boolean` *(default = true)*

For pixels that are off the source image, a value of true indicates that the input image is extended along each of its borders as necessary by duplicating the color values at the given edge of the input image. A value of false indicates another color should be used, as specified in the color and alpha properties. The default is true.

`color:uint` *(default = 0)*

The hexadecimal color to substitute for pixels that are off the source image.

`alpha:Number` *(default = 0.0)*

The alpha of the substitute color.

Some common effects for the `ConvolutionFilter` are as follows:

`new ConvolutionFilter(3,3,new Array(-5,0,1,1,-2,3,-1,2,1),1)`

Creates an edge-detected image, where only areas of greatest contrast remain.

`new ConvolutionFilter(3,3,new Array(0,20,0,20,-80,20,0,20,0),10)`

Creates a black-and-white outline.

`new  ConvolutionFilter(5,5,new  Array(0,1,2,1,0,1,2,4,2,1,2,4,8,4,2,1,2,4,2, 1,0,1,2,1,0),50);`

Creates a blur effect.

`new ConvolutionFilter(3,3,new Array(-2,-1,0,-1,1,1,0,1,2),0);`

Creates an emboss effect.

The complete code listing is shown here:

```
<mx:VBox xmlns:mx="http://www.adobe.com/2006/mxml" width="450" height="550">
    <mx:Script>
        <![CDATA[
            import mx.core.BitmapAsset;

            [Embed(source="../assets/mao.jpg")]
            private var mao:Class;

            private function convolve():void
            {
                var asset:BitmapAsset = new mao() as BitmapAsset;
                var convolution:ConvolutionFilter =
new ConvolutionFilter(matrixXSlider.value, matrixYSlider.value,
                [input1.text, input2.text, input3.text, input4.text, input5.text,
input6.text],
                divisorSlider.value, biasSlider.value, true);
                var _filters:Array = [convolution];
                asset.filters = _filters;
                img.source = asset;
            }
```

```
            ]]>
        </mx:Script>
        <mx:Button click="convolve()" label="convolve away"/>
        <mx:HBox>
            <mx:Text text="Matrix X"/>
            <mx:VSlider height="100" id="matrixXSlider" value="5.0" change="convolve()"/>
            <mx:Text text="Matrix Y"/>
            <mx:VSlider height="100" id="matrixYSlider" value="5.0" change="convolve()"/>
            <mx:Text text="Divisor"/>
            <mx:VSlider height="100" id="divisorSlider" value="5.0" change="convolve()"/>
            <mx:Text text="Bias"/>
            <mx:VSlider height="100" id="biasSlider" value="5.0" change="convolve()"/>
            <mx:VBox>
                <mx:TextInput id="input1" change="convolve()" width="40"/>
                <mx:TextInput id="input2" change="convolve()" width="40"/>
                <mx:TextInput id="input3" change="convolve()" width="40"/>
                <mx:TextInput id="input4" change="convolve()" width="40"/>
                <mx:TextInput id="input5" change="convolve()" width="40"/>
                <mx:TextInput id="input6" change="convolve()" width="40"/>
            </mx:VBox>
        </mx:HBox>
        <mx:Image id="img"/>
    </mx:VBox>
```

8.7 Send Video to an FMS Instance via a Camera

Problem

You want to send a stream from the user's camera to a Flash Media Server (FMS) instance for use in a chat or other live media application.

Solution

Capture the user's camera stream by using the `flash.media.Camera.getCamera` method and then attach that camera to a `NetStream` that will be sent to the Flash Media Server instance. Use the `publish` method of the `NetStream` class to send the stream with a specified name to the application that will handle it.

Discussion

The `publish` method indicates to a Flash Media Server that has been connected to via the `NetConnection` class, that the `NetStream` will be sending information to the server. What the server does with that information depends on the application, but there are flags that can be set in the `publish` method that indicate to the server and the Flash Player what should be done with the streamed information. The `publish` method has the following signature:

```
publish(name:String = null, type:String = null):void
```

Its parameters are as follows:

name:String *(default = null)*
> A string that identifies the stream. If you pass false, the publish operation stops. Clients that subscribe to this stream must pass this same name when they call NetStream.play.

type:String *(default = null)*
> A string that specifies how to publish the stream. Valid values are record, append, and live (the default). If you pass record, Flash Player publishes and records live data, saving the recorded data to a new FLV file with a name matching the value passed to the name parameter. The file is stored on the server in a subdirectory within the directory that contains the server application. If the file already exists, it is overwritten. If you pass append, Flash Player publishes and records live data, appending the recorded data to an FLV file with a name that matches the value passed to the name parameter, stored on the server in a subdirectory within the directory that contains the server application. If no file with a name matching the name parameter is found, a file is created. If you omit this parameter or pass live, Flash Player publishes live data without recording it. If a file with a name that matches the value passed to the name parameter exists, the file is deleted.

When you record a stream by using Flash Media Server, the server creates an FLV file and stores it in a subdirectory in the application's directory on the server. Each stream is stored in a directory whose name matches the application instance name passed to NetConnection.connect. The server creates these directories automatically; you don't have to create one for each application instance. For example, the following code shows how you would connect to a specific instance of an application stored in a directory named lectureSeries in your application's directory. A file named lecture.flv is stored in a subdirectory named /yourAppsFolder/lectureSeries/streams/Monday:

```
var myNC:NetConnection = new NetConnection();
myNC.connect("rtmp://server.domain.com/lectureSeries/Monday");
var myNS:NetStream = new NetStream(myNC);
myNS.publish("lecture", "record");
```

If you don't pass a value for the instance name that matches, the value passed to the name property is stored in a subdirectory named /yourAppsFolder/appName/streams/ _definst_ (for *default instance*).

This method can dispatch a netStatus event with several different information objects. For example, if someone is already publishing on a stream with the specified name, the netStatus event is dispatched with a code property of NetStream.Publish.BadName. For more information, see the netStatus event.

In the following example, the connection to the server is established, and the data from the camera is streamed to the server:

```
<mx:Canvas xmlns:mx="http://www.adobe.com/2006/mxml" width="400" height="500"
creationComplete="setUpCam()">
```

```
<mx:Script>
    <![CDATA[

        private var cam:Camera;
        private var nc:NetConnection;
        private var ns:NetStream;

        private function setUpCam():void
        {
            trace(Camera.names.join(","));
            //I'm doing this only because it's the only way the
            //flash player will pick up the camera on my MacBook
            cam = flash.media.Camera.getCamera("2");
            vid.attachCamera(cam);
            nc = new NetConnection();
            nc.addEventListener(NetStatusEvent.NET_STATUS, netStatus);
            nc.connect("http://localhost:3002");
        }

        private function netStatus(event:NetStatusEvent):void
        {
            switch(event.info)
            {
                case "NetConnection.Connect.Success":
                    ns = new NetStream(nc);
                    ns.attachCamera(cam, 20);
                    ns.attachAudio(Microphone.getMicrophone());
                    ns.publish("appname", "live");
                break;
            }
        }

    ]]>
</mx:Script>
<mx:VideoDisplay id="vid" width="360" height="320"/>
</mx:Canvas>
```

8.8 Access a User's Microphone and Create a Sound Display

Problem

You want to access a user's microphone and use the sound level of the microphone to draw a sound level.

Solution

Access the microphone by using the `Microphone.getMicrophone` method. Access the sound level that this method detects by using the `mic.activityLevel` property of the `Microphone` class on a regular interval.

Discussion

The Microphone class provides access to a user's microphone and computer, and the user must allow the Flash Player application access for you to use the class. The Micro phone class shows the level of sound that the microphone is detecting, and dispatches events when sound begins and when there has not been any sound for a given period of time.

Three properties of the Microphone class monitor and control the detection of activity. The read-only activityLevel property indicates the amount of sound the microphone is detecting on a scale from 0 to 100. The silenceLevel property specifies the amount of sound needed to activate the microphone and dispatch an ActivityEvent.ACTIVITY event. The silenceLevel property also uses a scale from 0 to 100, and the default value is 10. The silenceTimeout property describes the number of milliseconds that the activity level must stay below the silence level, until an ActivityEvent.ACTIVITY event is dispatched to indicate that the microphone is now silent. The default silenceTimeout value is 2000. Although both Microphone.silenceLevel and Microphone.silenceTime out are read-only, you can change their values by using the Microphone.setSilenceLevel method.

The following example creates a Microphone object, which will prompt the user to accept or deny the Flash Player access to the microphone. Then, after microphone activity is detected via the Activity event, an enter frame event listener is added that will draw the soundLevel of the microphone into a Canvas.

```
<mx:VBox xmlns:mx="http://www.adobe.com/2006/mxml" width="400" height="300"
creationComplete="createMic()">

<mx:Script>
    <![CDATA[
    import flash.media.Microphone;
    import flash.events.ActivityEvent;
    import flash.events.Event;
    import flash.events.StatusEvent;

    public var mic:Microphone;

    public function createMic():void
    {
      mic = Microphone.getMicrophone();
      mic.setLoopBack(true);
      mic.addEventListener(ActivityEvent.ACTIVITY, activity);
      mic.addEventListener(StatusEvent.STATUS, status);
      mic.addEventListener(Event.ACTIVATE, active);
    }

    private function active(event:Event):void
    {
      trace(' active ');
    }
```

```
    private function status(event:StatusEvent):void
    {
      trace("status");
    }

    private function activity(event:ActivityEvent):void
    {
      trace("active ");
      addEventListener(Event.ENTER_FRAME, showMicLevel);
    }

    private function showMicLevel(event:Event):void
    {
      trace(mic.gain+" "+mic.activityLevel+" "+mic.silenceLevel+" "+mic.rate);
      level.graphics.clear();
      level.graphics.beginFill(0xccccff, 1);
      level.graphics.drawRect(0, 0, (mic.activityLevel * 30), 100);
      level.graphics.endFill();
    }

  ]]>
</mx:Script>
<mx:Canvas width="300" height="50" id="level"/>
</mx:VBox>
```

8.9 Smooth Video Displayed in a Flex Application

Problem

You need to control the smoothing of a video that is played back in an application.

Solution

Create a custom component that contains the `flash.media.Video` component, and then set Video's `smoothing` property to true.

Discussion

To smooth video—that is, to make the video look less pixilated—you need to access the `flash.media.Video` object. Video smoothing, like image smoothing, requires more processing power than un-smoothed playback and can slow video playback for large or extremely high-quality videos.

The Flex `VideoDisplay` component does not allow you to set the `smoothing` property of the `flash.media.Video` object that it contains, so you must create a separate component that adds the lower-level Flash `Video` component and set the `smoothing` property:

```
<mx:Canvas xmlns:mx="http://www.adobe.com/2006/mxml" width="400" height="300"
creationComplete="setup()">
    <mx:Script>
        <![CDATA[
```

```
                private var vid:Video;

                private var nc:NetConnection;
                private var ns:NetStream;
                private var metaDataObj:Object = {};

                private function setup():void {
                    vid = new Video(this.width, this.height);
                    vid.smoothing = true;
                    this.rawChildren.addChild(vid);
                    vid.y = 50;
                    this.invalidateDisplayList();
                }

                private function startVid():void {
                    nc = new NetConnection();
                    nc.addEventListener(NetStatusEvent.NET_STATUS, netStatusHandler);
                    nc.connect(null);
                }

                private function netStatusHandler(event:NetStatusEvent):void {
                    ns = new NetStream(nc);
                    metaDataObj.onMetaData = this.onMetaData;
                    ns.client = metaDataObj;
                    vid.attachNetStream(ns);
                    ns.play("http://localhost:3001/Trailer.flv");
                }

                private function onMetaData(obj:Object):void {
                    var i:int = 0;
                    for each(var prop:Object in obj)
                    {
                        trace(obj[i] + "  :  " + prop);
                        i++;
                    }
                    trace(obj.duration+" "+obj.framerate+" "+obj.bitrate);
                }

        ]]>
    </mx:Script>
    <mx:Button  click="startVid()" label="load" x="50"/>
    <mx:Button click="ns.resume()" label="resume" x="120"/>
    <mx:Button click="ns.pause()" label="pause" x="190"/>
</mx:Canvas>
```

8.10 Check Pixel-Level Collisions

Problem

You need to check whether images with alpha transparency regions are colliding with other images.

Solution

Draw the data of both images to a `BitmapData` object and use the `BitmapData.hitTest` method.

Discussion

The `BitmapData` object possesses a `hitTest` method that works similarly to the `hit Test` method defined by `DisplayObject` with one notable exception: whereas `DisplayObject`'s `hitTest` method returns true if the point given intersects with the bounds of the object, `BitmapData`'s `hitTest` method returns true if the pixel at the point given is above a certain threshold of alpha transparency. The signature of the method is shown here:

```
public function hitTest(firstPoint:Point, firstAlphaThreshold:uint, secondObject:
Object, secondBitmapDataPoint:Point = null, secondAlphaThreshold:uint = 1):Boolean
```

If an image is opaque, it is considered a fully opaque rectangle for this method. Both images must be transparent to perform pixel-level hit testing that considers transparency. When you are testing two transparent images, the alpha threshold parameters control what alpha channel values, from 0 to 255, are considered opaque. The method's parameters are as follows:

firstPoint:Point
> A position of the upper-left corner of the `BitmapData` image in an arbitrary coordinate space. The same coordinate space is used in defining the `secondBitmapPoint` parameter.

firstAlphaThreshold:uint
> The highest alpha channel value that is considered opaque for this hit test.

secondObject:Object
> A `Rectangle`, `Point`, `Bitmap`, or `BitmapData` object.

secondBitmapDataPoint:Point *(default = null)*
> A point that defines a pixel location in the second `BitmapData` object. Use this parameter only when the value of `secondObject` is a `BitmapData` object.

secondAlphaThreshold:uint *(default = 1)*
> The highest alpha channel value that's considered opaque in the second `Bitmap Data` object. Use this parameter only when the value of `secondObject` is a `Bitmap Data` object and both `BitmapData` objects are transparent.

In the following code sample, each corner of a rectangular image is checked for collisions against a PNG file with alpha transparency:

```
<mx:Canvas xmlns:mx="http://www.adobe.com/2006/mxml" width="1500" height="900">
    <mx:Script>
        <![CDATA[
            import flash.display.BlendMode;

            private var mainBmp:BitmapData;
```

```
                private var dragBmp:BitmapData;
                private var hasDrawn:Boolean = false;

                private function loaded():void{
                    if(!hasDrawn){
                    mainBmp = new BitmapData(mainImg.width, mainImg.height, true,
        0x00000000);
                    dragBmp = new BitmapData(dragImg.width, dragImg.height, true,
        0x00000000);
                    hasDrawn = true;
                    this.addEventListener(Event.ENTER_FRAME, showHits);
                    }
                }

                private function showHits(event:Event):void
                {
                    mainBmp.draw(mainImg);
                    dragBmp.draw(dragImg);
                    if(mainBmp.hitTest(new Point(0,0), 0xff, dragImg.getBounds(this).
        topLeft)){
                        trace(" true ");
                        return;
                    }
                    if(mainBmp.hitTest(new Point(0,0), 0xff, dragImg.getBounds(this).
        bottomRight)){
                        trace(" true ");
                        return;
                    }
                    if(mainBmp.hitTest(new Point(0,0), 0xff, new Point(dragImg.getBounds
        (this).left, dragImg.getBounds(this).bottom))){
                        trace(" true ");
                        return;
                    }
                    if(mainBmp.hitTest(new Point(0,0), 0xff, new Point(dragImg.getBounds
        (this).right, dragImg.getBounds(this).top))){
                        trace(" true ");
                        return;
                    }
                    trace(" false ");
                }

            ]]>
        </mx:Script>
        <mx:Image id="mainImg" source="../assets/alphapng.png" cacheAsBitmap="true"/>
        <mx:Image cacheAsBitmap="true" id="dragImg" mouseDown="dragImg.startDrag(false,
    this.getBounds(stage)), loaded()" rollOut="dragImg.stopDrag()"
    mouseUp="dragImg.stopDrag()" source="../assets/bigshakey.png"/>

    </mx:Canvas>
```

This code returns false when the pixels of the first image at the given points do not
possess alpha values greater than those set in the hitTest method. In Figure 8-1, the
two light blue squares are within a PNG file with alpha transparency. The shake is a
separate image that, at this moment, is not colliding with an area of the PNG with a

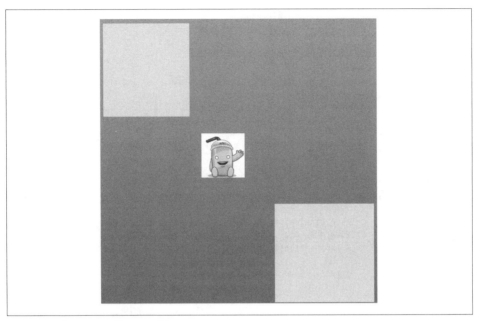

Figure 8-1. hitTest() will return false.

high-enough alpha. In Figure 8-2, however, the shake collides with a square and the method returns true.

8.11 Read and Save a User's Webcam Image

Problem

You want to read an image from a user's webcam and save that image to a server.

Solution

Create a `Camera` object and attach it to a `Video` object. Then create a button that will read a bitmap from the `Video` object and save the bitmap data to a server-side script that will save the image.

Discussion

To capture an image from a webcam, create a bitmap from the `Video` object that is displaying the camera image. The Flash Player doesn't provide any access to the stream of data that is read from the webcam, however, so you need to render the data as a bitmap before you can use it.

After the image has been captured as a `BitmapData` object, you can pass that data to an instance of the `JPEGEncoder` class to convert the image into JPEG data. Next, save the

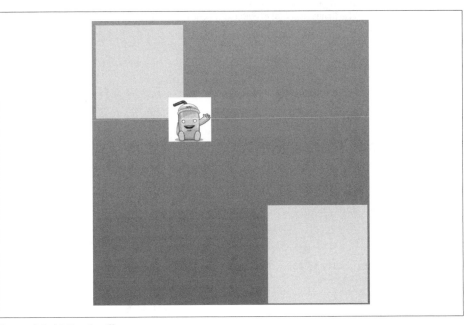

Figure 8-2. hitTest() will return true.

JPEG to a server by adding the data to a `URLRequest` object and sending it via the `navigateToURL` method. For example:

```
<mx:Canvas xmlns:mx="http://www.adobe.com/2006/mxml" width="400" height="500"
creationComplete="setUpCam()">
    <mx:Script>
        <![CDATA[
            import flash.net.navigateToURL;
            import flash.net.sendToURL;

            import mx.graphics.codec.JPEGEncoder;

            private var cam:Camera;

            private function setUpCam():void {
                cam = flash.media.Camera.getCamera("2");
                vid.attachCamera(cam);
            }

            private function saveImage():void {
                var bitmapData:BitmapData = new BitmapData(vid.width, vid.height);
                bitmapData.draw(vid);
                var encode:JPEGEncoder = new JPEGEncoder(100);
                var ba:ByteArray = encode.encode(bitmapData);
                var urlRequest:URLRequest = new URLRequest("/jpg_reader.php");
                urlRequest.method = "POST";
                var urlVars:URLVariables = new URLVariables();
                urlVars.pic = ba;
```

```
                urlRequest.data = urlVars;
                flash.net.navigateToURL(urlRequest, "_blank");
            }

        ]]>
    </mx:Script>
    <mx:VideoDisplay id="vid" width="360" height="320"/>
    <mx:Button label="Take Picture Now" click="saveImage()"/>
</mx:Canvas>
```

8.12 Use Blend Modes with Multiple Images

Problem

You want to blend multiple images.

Solution

Set the `blendMode` property of the images.

Discussion

Every `DisplayObject` defines a `blendMode` property that controls how that `DisplayObject` appears, controlling the alpha and how any `DisplayObject`s beneath that object in the `DisplayList` appear through that component. The blend modes should be familiar to anyone who has worked with Adobe Photoshop or After Effects:

`BlendMode.ADD ("add")`
　Creates an animated lightening dissolve effect between two images.

`BlendMode.ALPHA ("alpha")`
　Applies the transparency of the foreground to the background.

`BlendMode.DARKEN ("darken")`
　Superimposes type.

`BlendMode.DIFFERENCE ("difference")`
　Creates more-vibrant colors.

`BlendMode.ERASE ("erase")`
　Erases part of the background by using the foreground alpha.

`BlendMode.HARDLIGHT ("hardlight")`
　Creates shading effects.

`BlendMode.INVERT ("invert")`
　Inverts the background.

`BlendMode.LAYER ("layer")`
　Forces the creation of a temporary buffer for precomposition for a particular display object.

BlendMode.LIGHTEN ("lighten")
:   Superimposes type.

BlendMode.MULTIPLY ("multiply")
:   Creates shadows and depth effects.

BlendMode.NORMAL ("normal")
:   Specifies that the pixel values of the blend image override those of the base image.

BlendMode.OVERLAY ("overlay")
:   Creates shading effects.

BlendMode.SCREEN ("screen")
:   Creates highlights and lens flares.

BlendMode.SUBTRACT ("subtract")
:   Creates an animated darkening dissolve effect between two images.

The following example applies the various blend modes to the two Image objects:

```
<mx:Canvas xmlns:mx="http://www.adobe.com/2006/mxml" width="800" height="800">
    <mx:Script>
        <![CDATA[
            import flash.display.BlendMode;
        ]]>
    </mx:Script>
    <mx:Image id="img1" mouseDown="img1.startDrag(false, this.getBounds(stage)),
swapChildren(img1, img2)" rollOut="img1.stopDrag()" mouseUp="img2.stopDrag()"
source="../assets/mao.jpg"/>
    <mx:Image id="img2" mouseDown="img2.startDrag(false, this.getBounds(stage)),
swapChildren(img2, img1)" rollOut="img2.stopDrag()" mouseUp="img2.stopDrag()"
source="../assets/bigshakey.png"/>
    <mx:HBox>
        <mx:CheckBox id="chb" label="which one"/>
        <mx:ComboBox id="cb" dataProvider="{[BlendMode.ADD, BlendMode.ALPHA, BlendMode
.DARKEN, BlendMode.DIFFERENCE, BlendMode.ERASE, BlendMode.HARDLIGHT, BlendMode.
INVERT,BlendMode.LAYER, BlendMode.LIGHTEN, BlendMode.MULTIPLY, BlendMode.NORMAL,
BlendMode.OVERLAY, BlendMode.SCREEN, BlendMode.SUBTRACT]}"
            change="chb.selected ? img1.blendMode = cb.selectedItem as String :
img2.blendMode = cb.selectedItem as String"/>
    </mx:HBox>
</mx:Canvas>
```

8.13 Handle Cue Points in FLV Data

Problem

You need to work with cue points that are embedded in an FLV file while it plays.

Solution

Use the onCuePoint event of the NetStream class to create a handler method to be fired whenever a cue point is encountered.

Discussion

A *cue point* is a value inserted into an FLV file at a certain time within a video that contains either simply a name or a data object with a hash table of values. Usually cue points are inserted into an FLV when the file is being encoded, and any values are determined there. The Flex `VideoDisplay` object uses the `mx.controls.videoclasses.Cue Point` manager class to handle detecting and reading any data from a cue point. For a more-complete understanding of this, consider an example using the `flash.media.Video` object.

When the `NetConnection` object has connected and the `NetStream` is being instantiated, you need to set an object to relay any metadata and cue point events to handler methods:

```
var obj:Object = new Object();
obj.onCuePoint = onCuePoint;
obj.onMetaData = onMetaData;
ns.client = obj;
```

This needs to occur before the `NetStream play` method is called. Note in the following code that both the `onMetaData` and `onCuePoint` events accept an object as a parameter:

```
import flash.events.NetStatusEvent;
import flash.media.Video;
import flash.net.NetConnection;
import flash.net.NetStream;
import mx.core.UIComponent;

public class CuePointExample extends UIComponent
{
    private var ns:NetStream;
    private var nc:NetConnection;
    private var obj:Object = {};
    private var vid:Video;

    public function CuePointExample () {
        super();
        vid = new Video();
        addChild(vid);
        nc = new NetConnection();
        nc.addEventListener(NetStatusEvent.NET_STATUS, netStatusEventHandler);
        nc.connect(null);
    }

    private function netStatusEventHandler(event:NetStatusEvent):void {
        ns = new NetStream(nc);
        obj.onCuePoint = onCuePoint;
        obj.onMetaData = onMetaData;
        ns.client = obj;
        ns.play("http://localhost:3001/test2.flv");
        vid.attachNetStream(ns);
    }

    private function onCuePoint(obj:Object):void {
        trace(obj.name+" "+obj.time+" "+obj.length+" ");
```

```
            for each(var o:String in obj.parameters) {
                trace(obj[o]+" "+o);
            }
        }

        private function onMetaData(obj:Object):void{
        }
    }
```

Using the `mx.controls.VideoDisplay` simplifies working with a cue point object quite substantially. When using the `CuePointEvent` dispatched by the `CuePointManager`, unlike in the preceding case, the received event possesses only three properties: `cuePoint Time`, `cuePointName`, and `cuePointType`. If you need more or different information from the cue point, you can write a custom class to return the cue point data and set it to the `cuePointManager` property of the `VideoDisplay` object. The complete code listing is shown here:

```
<mx:VBox xmlns:mx="http://www.adobe.com/2006/mxml" width="400" height="300">
    <mx:Script>
        <![CDATA[
            import mx.events.CuePointEvent;

            private function onCuePoint(event:CuePointEvent):void {
                trace(event.cuePointName+" "+event.cuePointTime+"
"+event.cuePointType+" ");
            }

        ]]>
    </mx:Script>
    <mx:VideoDisplay id="vid" cuePoint="onCuePoint(event)"/>
</mx:VBox>
```

8.14 Create a Video Scrubber

Problem

You need to create a control that a user can use to scrub through a video as it plays.

Solution

Create a draggable `Sprite` object and listen for any `DragEvent` events dispatched from it. In the event handler for the `DragEvent`, set the amount to seek forward or backward in the `NetStream` that is streaming the video to the `Video` object.

Discussion

You can use any draggable display object to set the new position at which the video should be played. In this example, the `seek` method of the `NetStream` begins playback from the specified point in seconds from the beginning of the video:

```
ns.seek((playhead.x/timeline.width) * length);
```

To determine which second in the video that the user meant to seek, divide the position of the dragged Sprite by the width of the timeline area and multiply by the length of the video. The NetStream will take care of locating the appropriate frames in the video and restarting the streaming from that point.

```
import flash.display.Sprite;
import flash.events.MouseEvent;
import flash.events.NetStatusEvent;
import flash.media.Video;
import flash.net.NetConnection;
import flash.net.NetStream;

import mx.core.UIComponent;

public class Scrubber extends UIComponent
{

    private var playhead:Sprite;
    private var timeline:Sprite;
    private var ns:NetStream;
    private var nc:NetConnection;
    private var obj:Object = {};
    private var length:int;
    private var vid:Video;

    public function Scrubber () {
        super();
        playhead = new Sprite();
        addChild(playhead);
        playhead.graphics.beginFill(0x0000ff, 1);
        playhead.graphics.drawCircle(0, 0, 5);
        playhead.graphics.endFill();
        playhead.addEventListener(MouseEvent.MOUSE_DOWN, startSeek);
        timeline = new Sprite();
        timeline.graphics.beginFill(0xcccccc, 1);
        timeline.graphics.drawRect(0, 0, 200, 10);
        timeline.graphics.endFill();
        addChild(timeline);
        timeline.addChild(playhead);
        playhead.y = 4;
        vid = new Video();
        addChild(vid);
        vid.y = 100;

        nc = new NetConnection();
        nc.addEventListener(NetStatusEvent.NET_STATUS, netStatus);
        nc.connect(null);
    }

    private function netStatus(event:NetStatusEvent):void {
        obj.onMetaData = onMetaData;
        ns = new NetStream(nc);
        ns.client = obj;
        vid.attachNetStream(ns);
        ns.play("http://localhost:3001/test.flv");
```

```
    }

    private function onMetaData(obj:Object):void {
        length = obj.duration;
        trace(length);
    }

    private function startSeek(mouseEvent:MouseEvent):void {
        playhead.startDrag(false, timeline.getBounds(this));
        addEventListener(MouseEvent.MOUSE_MOVE, seek);
        playhead.addEventListener(MouseEvent.ROLL_OUT, endSeek);
        playhead.addEventListener(MouseEvent.MOUSE_UP, endSeek);
    }

    private function seek(mouseEvent:MouseEvent):void {
        ns.seek((playhead.x/timeline.width) * length);
    }

    private function endSeek(mouseEvent:MouseEvent):void {
        removeEventListener(MouseEvent.MOUSE_MOVE, seek);
        playhead.stopDrag();
    }
```

8.15 Read ID3 Data from an MP3 File

Problem

You want to read ID3 data from an MP3 file.

Solution

Use the Event.ID3 method that the Sound class will dispatch when the ID3 data has been parsed.

Discussion

The Sound class dispatches an event when the ID3 data has been parsed from a loaded MP3 file. That data is then stored as an ID3Info object, which defines variables to access all the properties written into the initial bytes of the MP3:

```
private var sound:Sound;

public function _8_16()
{
    sound = new Sound();
    sound.addEventListener(Event.ID3, onID3InfoReceived);
    sound.load(new URLRequest("../assets/1.mp3"));
}

private function onID3InfoReceived(event:Event):void
{
    var id3:ID3Info = event.target.id3;
```

```
    for (var propName:String in id3)
    {
        trace(propName + " = " + id3[propName]);
    }
}
```

The information from a song I was listening to while I wrote this recipe appears like this:

```
TCON = Alternative & Punk
TIT2 = The Pink Batman
TRCK = 2/9
TPE1 = Dan Deacon
TALB = Spiderman Of The Rings
TCOM = Dan Deacon
```

The ID3 info of an MP3 file is simply a grouping of bytes in a certain order that are read and turned into strings or integers. MP3 is the only file format that the Flash Player supports out of the box. Developer Benjamin Dobler of RichApps (www.richapps.de), however, has done some exceptional work with the WAV format. Getting the WAV file to play back in the Flash Player is slightly more tricky. If you're interested, go to Benjamin's site and take a look. If you want to parse the data from a WAV file, it looks like this:

```
public var bytes:ByteArray;
public var chunkId:String;
public var chunkSize:int;
public var chunkFormat:String;
public var subchunk1Id:String;
public var subchunk1Size;
public var audioFormat;
public var channels;
public var sampleRate;
public var bytesPersecond;
public var blockAlign;
public var bitsPerSample;
public var dataChunkSignature:String;
public var dataChunkLength;

public function read(bytes:ByteArray):void{
    this.bytes = bytes;
    // Read Header
    bytes.endian = "littleEndian";
    chunkId = bytes.readMultiByte(4,"utf"); //RIFF
    chunkSize = bytes.readUnsignedInt();
    chunkFormat = bytes.readMultiByte(4,"utf"); //WAVE
    subchunk1Id = bytes.readMultiByte(4,"iso-8859-1"); // 12 Header Signature
    subchunk1Size = bytes.readInt(); // 16 4 <fmt length>
    audioFormat = bytes.readShort(); // 20 2 <format tag> sample
    channels = bytes.readShort(); // 22    2 <channels> 1 = mono, 2 = stereo
    sampleRate = bytes.readUnsignedInt();// 24    4 <sample rate>
    bytesPersecond = bytes.readUnsignedInt(); //28 4 <bytes/second>    Sample-Rate *
Block-Align
    blockAlign = bytes.readShort(); // 32 2 <block align> channel * bits/sample / 8
    bitsPerSample = bytes.readUnsignedShort(); //34 2 <bits/sample> 8, 16 or 24
    dataChunkSignature = bytes.readMultiByte(4,"iso-8859-1"); //RIFF
```

```
        dataChunkLength = bytes.readInt();
    }
```

If you want to read the header info from an AU file, it would look like this:

```
public var bytes:ByteArray;
public var magicId;
public var header;
public var datasize;
public var channels;
public var comment;
public var sampleRate;
public var encodingInfo;

public function read(bytes:ByteArray):void{
    this.bytes = bytes;
    // Read Header
    bytes.endian = "bigEndian";
    magicId = bytes.readUnsignedInt();
    header = bytes.readInt();
    datasize = bytes.readUnsignedInt();
    encodingInfo = bytes.readUnsignedInt();
    sampleRate = bytes.readUnsignedInt();
    channels = bytes.readInt();
    comment = bytes.readMultiByte(uint(header)-24, "utf");
}
```

MP3 files may be the easiest format from which to read data, but they are certainly not the only format from which you can read.

8.16 Display a Custom Loader while Loading Images

Problem

You want to display custom animation while an image loads.

Solution

Create a custom graphic and listen for the `ProgressEvent.PROGRESS` event from the `Image` object loading the image. Then draw into the graphic by using the `bytesLoaded` and `bytesTotal` properties.

Discussion

There are two approaches to displaying an image when using the `Image` component: You can set the source for the `Image` class in MXML or you can pass a URL to load and use the `img.load` method:

```
img.load("http://thefactoryfactory.com/beach.jpg");
```

Before you load the image, though, you want to attach an event listener to ensure that each `ProgressEvent` is handled:

```
        img.addEventListener(ProgressEvent.PROGRESS, progress);
```

In the progress method, which is handling the ProgressEvent.PROGRESS event, a UICom
ponent is redrawn by using the bytesLoaded property of the Image:

```
<mx:Canvas xmlns:mx="http://www.adobe.com/2006/mxml" creationComplete="loadImage()">
    <mx:Script>
        <![CDATA[

            private var m:Matrix;

            private function loadImage():void {
                var m:Matrix = new Matrix();
                m.createGradientBox(450, 40);
                img.addEventListener(ProgressEvent.PROGRESS, progress);
                img.load("http://thefactoryfactory.com/beach.jpg");
            }

            private function progress(event:Event):void{
                grid.graphics.clear();
                grid.graphics.beginGradientFill("linear", [0x0000ff, 0xffffff],
[1, 1], [0x00, 0xff], m);
                grid.graphics.drawRect(0, 0, (img.bytesLoaded / img.bytesTotal) * 300,
40);
                grid.graphics.endFill();
            }

        ]]>
    </mx:Script>
    <mx:Canvas id="grid" height="40" width="300"/>
    <mx:Image id="img" y="40"/>
</mx:Canvas>
```

8.17 Enable Image Upload in Flex

Problem

You want to enable users to upload images via Flex to be stored on a server.

Solution

Create a FileReference object and attach the appropriate filters so that users can upload
the correct image types only. Then listen for the complete handler from the
FileReference object and send the uploaded image to a server-side script.

Discussion

Image upload in Flex as well as in Flash relies on the use of the FileReference class.
The FileReference object, when invoked, creates a window by using the browser's
normal upload window and graphic and sends the image through the Flash Player when

the user has selected a file for upload. Add an event listener to the FileReference object to indicate that the user has selected a file:

```
fileRef.addEventListener(Event.SELECT, selectHandler);
```

Then add a method to upload the file that the user has selected:

```
private function selectHandler(event:Event):void {
        var request:URLRequest = new URLRequest("http://thefactoryfactory.com/
upload2.php");
        fileRef.upload(request, "Filedata", true);
    }
```

After the file has been uploaded, send it to a PHP script to save the uploaded image:

```
package oreilly.cookbook
{
    import mx.core.UIComponent;
    import flash.net.FileFilter;
    import flash.net.FileReference;
    import flash.net.URLRequest;
    import flash.events.Event;

    public class _8_17 extends UIComponent
    {

        private var fileRef:FileReference;

        public function _8_17() {
            super();
            startUpload();
        }

        private function startUpload():void {
            //set all the file types we're going to allow the user to upload
            var imageTypes:FileFilter = new FileFilter("Images (*.jpg, *.jpeg, *.gif,
*.png)", "*.jpg; *.jpeg; *.gif; *.png");
            var allTypes:Array = new Array(imageTypes);
            fileRef = new FileReference();
            fileRef.addEventListener(Event.SELECT, selectHandler);
            fileRef.addEventListener(Event.COMPLETE, completeHandler);
            //tell the FileRefence object to accept only those image
            //types
            fileRef.browse(allTypes);
        }

        private function selectHandler(event:Event):void {
            var request:URLRequest = new URLRequest("http://thefactoryfactory.com/
upload2.php");
            fileRef.upload(request, "Filedata", true);
        }
        private function completeHandler(event:Event):void {
            trace("uploaded");
        }
    }
}
```

Because the file has already been uploaded, you can deal with the data on the server, moving the file to (in this case) a folder called images:

```
$file_temp = $_FILES['file']['tmp_name'];
$file_name = $_FILES['file']['name'];
$file_path = $_SERVER['DOCUMENT_ROOT']."/images";
//checks for duplicate files
if(!file_exists($file_path."/".$file_name)) {
    //complete upload
    $filestatus = move_uploaded_file($file_temp,$file_path."/".$file_name);
    if(!$filestatus) {
        //error in uploading file
    }
}
```

8.18 Compare Two Bitmap Images

Problem

You need to compare two bitmap images and display the differences between them.

Solution

Read the bitmap data from two images and use the compare method to compare the two images. Set the difference of the two images as the source of a third image.

Discussion

The compare method of the BitmapData class returns a BitmapData object that contains all the pixels that do not match in two specified images. If the two BitmapData objects have the same dimensions (width and height), the method returns a new BitmapData object, in which each pixel is the difference between the pixels in the two source objects: If two pixels are equal, the difference pixel is 0x00000000. If two pixels have different RGB values (ignoring the alpha value), the difference pixel is 0xFFRRGGBB, where RR/GG/BB are the individual difference values between red, green, and blue channels. Alpha channel differences are ignored in this case. If only the alpha channel value is different, the pixel value is 0xZZFFFFFF, where ZZ is the difference in the alpha value.

```
<mx:VBox xmlns:mx="http://www.adobe.com/2006/mxml" width="400" height="800">
    <mx:Script>
        <![CDATA[
            import mx.core.BitmapAsset;

            private function compare():void {
                var bmpd1:BitmapData = new BitmapData(img1.width, img1.height);
                var bmpd2:BitmapData = new BitmapData(img2.width, img2.height);
                bmpd1.draw(img1)
                bmpd2.draw(img2);
                var diff:BitmapData = bmpd2.compare(bmpd1) as BitmapData;
                var bitmapAsset:BitmapAsset = new BitmapAsset(diff);
```

```
                    img3.source = bitmapAsset;
            }

        ]]>
    </mx:Script>
    <mx:Image id="img1" source="../assets/mao.jpg" height="200" width="200"/>
    <mx:Image id="img2" source="../assets/bigshakey.png" height="200" width="200"/>
    <mx:Button click="compare()" label="compare"/>
    <mx:Image id="img3"/>
</mx:VBox>
```

CHAPTER 9

Skinning and Styling

The robust layout management of the Flex Framework combined with the default Halo Aeon theme provides you with a good-looking application right out of the box. The ease with which you can build an application's user interface by using containers and controls is matched by the ease with which you can customize the appearance of those components by using skins and styles.

The title of this chapter may be slightly misleading: Styles and skins are not separate concepts in Flex; they actually work in tandem to bring that visual uniqueness to your application. In fact, skins are assigned as style properties and have the ability to use other declared style values to their benefit. The practices of styling and of skinning components are different in their approach, and this chapter addresses how to use them to your advantage.

Styles are property settings, color, sizing, or font instructions, which modify the appearance of components and can be customized programmatically at both compile time and runtime. Style properties are defined in multiple ways: by setting them inline within a component declaration, by using the `setStyle` to apply a style, or by using Cascading Style Sheets (CSS). You can use CSS to define styles locally in an MXML file or in an external file.

Skins are applied as style properties and are used to modify the visual elements of a component. Those elements can be graphical, such as an image file or a SWF, or programmatic classes utilizing the drawing API. Skinning a control can modify or even replace visual elements of the component. As such, some style settings will be disregarded when applying a skin.

In addressing how these two processes work together to customize components, let's take a quick look at the visual makeup of a button. There are several style properties you can assign to a button, such as those related to font treatment and padding. Included in those properties are ones for defining the skin for each state of a `Button` instance.

To get a general understanding of what that means, consider a subset of the styles that can be applied to Button:

```
cornerRadius="4"
fillAlphas="[0.6, 0.4]"
fillColors="[0xE6EEEE, 0xFFFFFF]"
upSkin="mx.skins.halo.ButtonSkin"
```

The property values in this shortened list of styles available on a button are the default values set in the defaults.css file included in the Framework. The default upSkin value of a button instance is the mx.skins.halo.ButtonSkin class of the Halo skins package.

Utilizing the drawingAPI, this programmatic skin renders the up-state of a Button instance by using the other property values declared: cornerRadius, fillAlphas, and fillColors. Though the default value for the upSkin property is a programmatic class, the value could instead be a graphic file, which would effectively ignore utilizing the property values that a programmatic skin otherwise would.

This chapter addresses the processes of skinning and styling your components and how they can effectively be used to modify the look and feel" of your application.

 The online Flex Style Explorer lets you modify styles of various components at runtime and view the resulting CSS definitions. Visit the Flex Style Explorer at *http://www.adobe.com/go/flex_styles_explorer_app*.

9.1 Use CSS to Style Components

Problem

You want to skin components by using CSS.

Solution

Declare style properties by using either a class selector or a type selector.

Discussion

You can use CSS to style components of your user interface. If you are familiar with styling elements in an HTML document, you will find that the CSS syntax for Flex is largely the same. You can define class selectors to assign a style to multiple instances of a component and you can define a type selector for a component that will be applied to all instances of that component on the display list.

Class selectors can be declared and used multiple times on various components within your application. The syntax of a class selector is a period (or dot) followed by whatever name you wish to associate with the style, in camel caps starting with lowercase—for instance, .myCustomStyle. The following example creates a style locally in the

`<mx:Style>` tag and assigns that style to a `Label` component inline by using the `style Name` attribute:

```
<mx:Application
    xmlns:mx="http://www.adobe.com/2006/mxml"
    layout="vertical">

    <mx:Style>
        .labelStyle {
            font-family: 'Arial';
            font-size: 20px;
            font-weight: 'bold';
            color: #FFFFFF;
        }
    </mx:Style>

    <mx:Label text="Hello Flex!" styleName="labelStyle" />
</mx:Application>
```

The `.labelStyle` selector of this example defines style properties related to the font treatment to be applied to the label. The style is applied inline by assigning it as the value for the `styleName` attribute of the `Label` instance. You will notice that the preceding period/dot of the declaration is removed in assigning the style.

Type selectors can be used to apply their declared style across all instances of a particular component. To declare a type selector, you use the class name of the component you want to style, as shown:

```
<mx:Application
    xmlns:mx="http://www.adobe.com/2006/mxml"
    layout="vertical">

    <mx:Style>
        Label {
            font-family: 'Arial';
            font-size: 20px;
            font-weight: 'bold';
            color: #FFFFFF;
        }
    </mx:Style>

    <mx:Label text="Hello Flex!" />
</mx:Application>
```

Though you can declare type and class selectors for styling components, the properties defined can be overridden inline at compile time within the component declaration. In the following example, you see the style applied to two instances of a `Label` component, with the second one overriding the `fontSize` style property:

```
<mx:Application
    xmlns:mx="http://www.adobe.com/2006/mxml"
    layout="vertical">

    <mx:Style>
```

```
        Label {
            font-family: 'Arial';
            font-size: 20px;
            font-weight: 'bold';
            color: #FFFFFF;
        }
    </mx:Style>

    <mx:Label text="Hello Flex!" />
    <mx:Label text="Hello Flex!" fontSize="12" />
</mx:Application>
```

Assigning style property values inline at compile time is not limited to CSS declared locally in an `<mx:Style>` tag, as these examples have shown. Style property values declared inline can override defined styles from an external style file loaded at runtime and compile time as well.

You may notice that the inline `fontSize` property in this example is in camel caps while the `style` property is hyphenated in the CSS declaration. The hyphenated declarations follow CSS tradition, and can be used to declare style properties in external style sheets and within the `<mx:Style>` tag. The use of camel caps for style properties declared inline in MXML follow the ActionScript standard, which does not support hyphen characters. Internally, hyphenated style declarations from CSS are converted to camel caps and are used to retrieve available property declarations by using the `getStyle` method.

9.2 Override the Default Application Style

Contributed by Marco Casario

Problem

You want to change the default style assigned to your main `Application` container.

Solution

Set the `styleName` attribute of the main application to `plain`.

Discussion

The `Application` container is the root container for a Flex application and represents the area drawn by Flash Player.

It has default properties that define its style and appearance. For example, an `Application` tag has a `horizontalGap` value and a `verticalGap` value (the horizontal and vertical distance between child components) set to 8 and 6 pixels, respectively.

There may be a time when you want to reset all default properties for the `Application` tag. To reach this goal, you have to set the `styleName` attribute to `plain`:

```
<mx:Application
    xmlns:mx="http://www.adobe.com/2006/mxml"
    styleName="plain">
</mx:Application>
```

In setting this attribute to `plain`, you create the following scenario:

- All the paddings are set to 0.
- The background color is set to #FFFFFF.
- The background image is removed.
- The child components are left-aligned.

The `plain` style is available in the defaults.css file of the Framework. To learn how its property values are set initially, take a look at the `.plain` style selector from the default style sheet of the Flex Framework:

```
.plain
{
    backgroundColor: #FFFFFF;
    backgroundImage: "";
    horizontalAlign: "left";
    paddingBottom: 0;
    paddingLeft: 0;
    paddingRight: 0;
    paddingTop: 0;
}
```

The power of a class selector lets you assign the same style to different types of components and also enables you to assign different styles to the same type of component.

Flex also supports setting type selectors. The following example declares a type selector for the application in the `<mx:Style>` tag and styles the application the same as setting the `styleName` attribute to `plain`:

```
<mx:Application
    xmlns:mx="http://www.adobe.com/2006/mxml">
    <mx:Style>
        Application {
            backgroundColor: #ffffff;
            backgroundImage: '';
            paddingLeft: 0;
            paddingRight: 0;
            paddingTop: 0;
            paddingBottom: 0;
            horizontalAling: 'left';
        }
    </mx:Style>
</mx:Application>
```

9.3 Embed Styles by Using CSS

Problem

You want to embed styles for components by using CSS in your application.

Solution

Define styles in a local definition or use the `source` attribute of the `<mx:Style>` tag to embed a CSS rule from an external file.

Discussion

Styles can be embedded at compile time for your Flex application in many ways. This recipe addresses defining styles by using CSS syntax to be embedded in your application. By using CSS in Flex, you can do the following:

- Declare styles locally within the `<mx:Style>` tag of an MXML file.
- Set the `source` attribute of the `<mx:Style>` tag to an external style sheet.

The following example declares two class styles locally in the main application file that are applied to `Label` instances of the application display:

```
<mx:Application
    xmlns:mx="http://www.adobe.com/2006/mxml"
    layout="vertical">

    <mx:Style>
        .header {
            font-family: 'Arial';
            font-size: 15px;
            font-weight: 'bold';
            color: #FFFFFF;
        }
        .message {
            font-family: 'Arial';
            font-size: 12px;
            color: #336699;
        }
    </mx:Style>

    <mx:Label text="I have a header style!" styleName="header" />
    <mx:Text text="I have a message style!" styleName="message" />
</mx:Application>
```

In this example, the class selectors are defined locally and set inline to a `Label` component and a `Text` component. The property values defined in each selector will be applied to the appropriate element of the label instances and, specifically, modify the font treatment. Though this example declares styles local to the `Application` container, styles can be declared in a custom MXML component by using the `<mx:Style>` tag within that child component.

Alternatively, these style declarations can be held in an external CSS file and assigned to the **source** attribute of the **<mx:Style>** tag. The following code can be added to a file with the .css extension and made available for embedding:

```
.header {
    font-family: 'Arial';
    font-size: 15px;
    font-weight: 'bold';
    color: #FFFFFF;
}
.message {
    font-family: 'Arial';
    font-size: 12px;
    color: #336699;
}
```

To embed an external CSS file into your application, you assign the file's path to the **source** attribute of the **<mx:Style>** tag. The following snippet, which embeds the CSS file, results in the same visual display as the previous example:

```
<mx:Application
    xmlns:mx="http://www.adobe.com/2006/mxml"
    layout="vertical">

    <mx:Style source="assets/styles/label_styles.css" />

    <mx:Label text="Hello!" styleName="header" />
    <mx:Text text="Welcome to the example." styleName="message" />

</mx:Application>
```

Although the default styles for a Flex application are declared in a defaults.css file included with the Framework, there are many other themes that you can embed instead. Look for these in the directory *<flex sdk installation>*/frameworks/themes.

9.4 Override Base Style Properties

Problem

You want to modify a base style property in an instance of a component.

Solution

Assign a value to the specified style property inline by using either the attribute or a child tag of the component.

Discussion

You can assign style properties inline and within a child tag of the component declaration. Defining styles in either way overwrites any values already defined in the application locally and externally. Consider an example:

```
<mx:Application
    xmlns:mx="http://www.adobe.com/2006/mxml"
    layout="vertical">

    <mx:Style>
        Label {
            font-family: 'Arial';
            font-size: 20px;
            font-weight: 'bold';
            color: #FFFFFF;
        }
    </mx:Style>

    <mx:Label text="Hello Flex!" color="#336699" />
    <mx:Text text="Hello Flex!" fontStyle="italic">
        <mx:fontFamily>Verdana</mx:fontFamily>
    </mx:Text>
</mx:Application>
```

Here a type selector is declared locally in the main application and assigns style properties to the Label instances of the display. Essentially, the type selector declared in the <mx:Script> tag overwrites the default style defined in the defaults.css file of the Flex Framework, and the component elements overwrite specific style properties of that declaration inline and in child tags.

The Label component sets the font color to one different than that specified in the type selector for label instances. The Text component inherits all styles declared in the type selector because Text is a subclass of Label. As such, the font treatments defined for a label are set to child elements of the Text component. The Text instance assigns a value to the fontStyle property not defined in the selector and overwrites the fontFamily within a child tag; in this case, it changes the value from the Arial font to Verdana.

Using inline and child tag assignments to overwrite styles is a beneficial way to change the look and feel of individual components at compile time that share a common style from properties declared in a type selector or a class selector.

See Also

Recipe 9.3.

9.5 Customize Styles at Runtime

Problem

You want to customize style property values assigned to components at runtime.

Solution

Use the setStyle method to reset style property values.

Discussion

The setStyle method is inherited by any subclass of mx.core.UIComponent. By using setStyle, you assign property values to a defined style at runtime. The arguments for the setStyle method are the style name and the desired value:

```
myContainer.setStyle( "backgroundColor", 0xFFFFFF );
```

Although you can define styles for components at compile time by using local or external style sheets, CSS should refer to the language and assign styles upon instantiation by using the styleName property, the setStyle method lets you change those property values after compilation.

The following example uses the setStyle method to change color properties of components in response to the click event of a Button instance:

```
<mx:Application
    xmlns:mx="http://www.adobe.com/2006/mxml"
    layout="vertical">
    <mx:Style>
        VBox {
            backgroundColor: #CCCCCC;
            verticalAlign: 'middle';
            horizontalAlign: 'center';
        }
        .header {
            font-family: 'Arial';
            font-size: 15px;
            font-weight: 'bold';
            color: #FFFFFF;
        }
    </mx:Style>
    <mx:Script>
        <![CDATA[
            // reset color properties with random values.
            private function jumbleColors():void
            {
                holder.setStyle( "backgroundColor", getRandomColor() );
                labelField.setStyle( "color", getRandomColor() );
            }
            private function getRandomColor():uint
            {
                return randomValue() << 16 ^ randomValue() << 8 ^ randomValue();
            }
            private function randomValue():Number
            {
                return (Math.random() * 512) - 255;
            }
        ]]>
    </mx:Script>
    <mx:VBox id="holder"
        width="200" height="200">
        <mx:Label id="labelField" text="Hello Flex!" styleName="header" />
        <mx:Button label="jumble colors" click="jumbleColors();" />
```

```
        </mx:VBox>
    </mx:Application>
```

Upon instantiation of these components, their respective styles are applied: The VBox is styled by using the type selector, and the Label assigns the .header style through the styleName attribute. The click event handler for the button applies a new value for the color style properties of the VBox and Label instances. Though this example demonstrates overriding style properties that are declared locally to the application, styles declared in an external CSS file can also be overridden at runtime by using the set Style method.

The setStyle method is more expensive computationally than applying style sheets, yet affords you more control over how styles are applied and changed at runtime.

See Also

Recipe 9.3 and Recipe 9.4.

9.6 Load CSS at Runtime

Problem

You want to keep the file size of your SWF low by loading external CSS files at runtime instead of embedding them at compile time.

Solution

Use the mxmlc command-line tool available in the Flex 3 SDK to package your CSS file, and then load the external CSS file at runtime by using the mx.styles.StyleManager.

Discussion

Loading styles at runtime enables you to make changes to style definitions independent of having to recompile your application. To load a style SWF at runtime, you use the loadStyleDeclarations method of the StyleManager.

The StyleManager loads a style SWF as opposed to loading a CSS file. To create a style SWF, compile a CSS file into a SWF file by using the mxmlc command-line tool included in the Flex SDK. To begin, first create a file with the .css extension and add declarations such as the following:

```
VBox {
    backgroundColor: #CCCCCC;
    verticalAlign: 'middle';
    horizontalAlign: 'center';
}
.header {
    font-family: 'Arial';
    font-size: 15px;
```

```
        font-weight: 'bold';
        color: #FFFFFF;
    }
```

With the CSS file saved as MyStyles.css, open a command prompt. With a path to the /
bin directory of your Flex installation set in your System Path, enter the following
command in the prompt and press Enter:

```
> mxmlc MyStyles.css
```

This command will create a SWF file with the same name as the CSS file supplied. For
this example, MyStyles.swf will be found in the directory to which you were pointing
when invoking the compiler.

To load a style SWF and apply it to instantiated components, you use the `loadStyle`
`Declarations` method of `StyleManager` with the `update` argument set to `true`:

```
<mx:Application
    xmlns:mx="http://www.adobe.com/2006/mxml"
    layout="vertical"
    creationComplete="appComplete();">
    <mx:Script>
        <![CDATA[
            // load external style SWF and force update to display.
            private function appComplete():void
            {
                StyleManager.loadStyleDeclarations( "assets/styles/MyStyles.swf",
                                                    true );
            }
        ]]>
    </mx:Script>
    <mx:VBox id="holder"
        width="200" height="200">
        <mx:Label id="labelField" text="Hello Flex!" styleName="header" />
    </mx:VBox>
</mx:Application>
```

The declarations defined in the CSS file are applied to the components upon creation
of the application and successful load of the compiled style SWF file. Alternatively, you
can track the progress, success, and error of loading a style SWF by defining event
listeners to the `IEventDispatcher` instance returned from the `loadStyleDeclarations`
method:

```
private function appComplete():void
{
    // listen to the complete event of external style SWF load
    var dispatcher:IEventDispatcher = StyleManager.loadStyleDeclarations(
                                      "assets/styles/MyStyles.swf", true );
    dispatcher.addEventListener( StyleEvent.COMPLETE, styleCompleteHandler );
}

private function styleCompleteHandler( evt:StyleEvent ):void
{
```

```
        trace( "Styles Loaded!" );
    }
```

If you choose to use the IEventDispatcher instance returned from loadStyleDeclarations to monitor the load progress of a style SWF, you can set the update argument to false and programmatically assign style properties to components as you see fit in defined event handlers.

When you assign an external CSS file at compile time by using the source attribute of the <mx:Style> tag, the compiler runs a check to see whether that file exists. When loading a style SWF at runtime by using the StyleManager, that check is not made, enabling you to create that file at any time for your application, whether it is before or after you deploy your application.

9.7 Declare Styles at Runtime

Problem

You want to declare and customize styles for Flex components at runtime by using ActionScript.

Solution

Create mx.styles.CSSStyleDeclaration objects and associate them with a selector name to be stored by the mx.styles.StyleManager.

Discussion

A CSSStyleDeclaration object holds style properties and values that can be set and customized at runtime. When you define a CSS rule in an external file or locally by using the <mx:Style> tag, Flex automatically creates a CSSStyleDeclaration object for each selector declared at compile time. To create a style declaration at runtime, you use the StyleManager.setStyleDeclaration method, which takes a selector identifier string and a CSSStyleDeclaration object as its constructor arguments. You can access those CSSStyleDeclaration objects created at runtime or compile time by using the StyleManager.getStyleDeclaration method.

Associating selector names with a CSSStyleDeclaration created at runtime follows the same convention as that for style declarations embedded at runtime. Style rules for each instance of a class are applied by using a type selector, which is a string representation of the class name. For example:

```
    var vboxStyle:CSSStyleDeclaration = new CSSStyleDeclaration();
    vboxStyle.setStyle( "backgroundColor", 0xFF0000 );
    StyleManager.setStyleDeclaration( "VBox", vboxStyle, false );
```

You can associate a style declaration by using class selectors as well. Class selectors start with a period (or dot) and are applied to any component with the inline **style Name** property set to that value:

```
var redBoxStyle:CSSStyleDeclaration = new CSSStyleDeclaration();
redBoxStyle.setStyle( "backgroundColor", 0xFF0000 );
StyleManager.setStyleDeclaration( ".redBox", redBoxStyle, false );
```

Although setting declarations on the **StyleManager** at runtime follows the same rules as CSS converted at compile time, style properties cannot be created through the **set Style** method of a **CSSStyleDeclaration** instance by using hyphens (such as **font-family**), which are allowed in declarations in an external file or within the **<mx:Style>** tag.

 Setting style declarations at runtime by using the **StyleManager** will replace any declarations previously created and stored with the same selector name.

In the following example, **CSSStyleDeclaration** objects are created upon initialization of the application, and style updates are applied to child components:

```
<mx:Application
    xmlns:mx="http://www.adobe.com/2006/mxml"
    layout="vertical"
    initialize="init();">

    <mx:Script>
        <![CDATA[
            // create and store new style declarations.
            private function init():void
            {
                StyleManager.registerColorName( "cookbookBlue", 0x339966 );

                var headerStyleDeclaration:CSSStyleDeclaration =
                                        new CSSStyleDeclaration();
                headerStyleDeclaration.setStyle( "fontWeight", "bold" );
                headerStyleDeclaration.setStyle( "fontSize", 15 );
                headerStyleDeclaration.setStyle( "color",
                        StyleManager.getColorName( "cookbookBlue" ) );
                var msgStyleDeclaration:CSSStyleDeclaration =
                                        new CSSStyleDeclaration();
                msgStyleDeclaration.setStyle( "fontSize", 12 );
                msgStyleDeclaration.setStyle( "color",
                        StyleManager.getColorName( "haloSilver" ) );

                StyleManager.setStyleDeclaration( ".header",
                                        headerStyleDeclaration, false );
                StyleManager.setStyleDeclaration( ".message",
                                        msgStyleDeclaration, true );
            }
            // clear previously created styles.
```

```
        private function clickHandler():void
        {
            StyleManager.clearStyleDeclaration( ".header", false );
            StyleManager.clearStyleDeclaration( ".message", true );
        }

    ]]>
    </mx:Script>
    <mx:Label text="I'm a header styled through the StyleManager"
        styleName="header"
        />
    <mx:Text text="I'm a message styled through the StyleManager"
        styleName="message"
        />
    <mx:Button label="clear styles" click="clickHandler();" />
</mx:Application>
```

In this example, two class selectors are declared and stored in `StyleManager`. The style is applied to each respective component through the inline `styleName` property. The last parameter of the `setStyleDeclaration` method of `StyleManager` is a Boolean flag to update styles on components previously instantiated. Setting a new style declaration can be computationally expensive. As such, the call to update the display when adding styles to the `StyleManager` is generally deferred to the last style declared.

When a style is assigned to a component, such as through the `styleName` property, you are replacing the default style for that component. In this example, when the class style applied to the components is cleared from the `clickHandler` method, the components revert to having the default type style.

You can remove style declarations by using the `StyleManager.clearStyleDeclaration` method. Like `StyleManager.setStyleDeclaration`, this method has a parameter to force immediate update of styles in the application. In this example, updating the display after clearing the class styles is handled in the last call to the `StyleManager.clearStyle Declaration` method.

The `StyleManager` class also enables you to assign a color value with a key string through the `registerColorName` method. Using the `StyleManager.getColorName` method, you can access color values you create at runtime—and also those defined in the default styles of the Flex Framework—which is seen by assigning the color property of a `.message` class style to that of `haloSilver` in this example.

9.8 Create Custom Style Properties for Components

Problem

You want to create and expose custom style properties inline that are not inherently available in a component.

Solution

Add style metadata to your custom component and use the `getStyle` method to retrieve property values.

Discussion

Default style properties are available for components found in the Flex Framework, but you can declare additional style properties for custom components by using the [Style] metadata tag. Listing style definitions in the `<mx:Metadata>` tag lets you assign property values inline in MXML within the component declaration. You can also declare style property values for custom components by using CSS and the `setStyle` method. All these methods force an update to the display, just as setting the default property values do.

Adding additional style properties for custom components enables you to dictate which properties affect the visual makeup of a component. The following example is a custom component that is a subclass of the `mx.containers.Box` class and lists custom styles within the `<mx:Metadata>` tag used to customize its display:

```
<mx:Box
    xmlns:mx="http://www.adobe.com/2006/mxml"
    width="100%" height="100%"
    horizontalAlign="center" verticalAlign="middle"
    creationComplete="creationHandler();">

    <mx:Metadata>
        [Style(name="teeterAngle", type="Number")]
        [Style(name="activeColor", type="uint", format="Color")]
        [Style(name="idleColor", type="uint", format="Color")]
    </mx:Metadata>

    <mx:Script>
        <![CDATA[
            import mx.effects.easing.Bounce;

            [Embed("assets/fonts/verdana.TTF", fontName="MyFont")]
            public var verdana_font:Class;

            private function creationHandler():void
            {
                playAnim();
            }
            private function effectStartHandler():void
            {
                holder.setStyle( "backgroundColor", getStyle( "activeColor" ) );
                holder.enabled = false;
                field.text = "Wheeeee!";
            }
            private function effectEndHandler():void
            {
                holder.setStyle( "backgroundColor", getStyle( "idleColor" ) );
```

```
                    holder.enabled = true;
                    field.text = "Again! Click Me";
                }
                private function playAnim():void
                {
                    rotater.play( [this], true );
                }
        ]]>
    </mx:Script>

    <mx:Rotate id="rotater"
        effectStart="effectStartHandler();"
        effectEnd="effectEndHandler();"
        originX="{width}" originY="{height}"
        angleFrom="0" angleTo="{getStyle('teeterAngle')}"
        easingFunction="{Bounce.easeIn}" duration="500"
        />
    <mx:VBox id="holder"
        width="60%" height="60%"
        horizontalAlign="center"
        verticalAlign="middle"
        click="playAnim();">
        <mx:Text id="field" width="100%"
            selectable="false"
            fontFamily="MyFont"
            />
    </mx:VBox>
</mx:Box>
```

The angle at which to start the Rotate tween declared in this example is relative to the
teeterAngle style property, while the background color of the VBox child is updated
dependent on the state of the animation. The available custom style properties of this
component are listed in the <mx:Metadata> tag, and their corresponding property values
are accessed by using the getStyle method. By declaring the custom style properties
within the <mx:Metadata> tag, you can define their values inline during declaration of
the custom component.

```
<mx:Application
    xmlns:mx="http://www.adobe.com/2006/mxml"
    xmlns:cookbook="oreilly.cookbook.*"
    layout="vertical">

    <cookbook:ChompBox
        width="200" height="200"
        backgroundColor="#DDDDDD"
        textAlign="center"
        teeterAngle="45"
        activeColor="#FFDD33" idleColor="#FFFFFF"
        />

</mx:Application>
```

Though you can add custom style properties to a component, the inherent default style
properties are still available for customization, as can be seen when setting the

textAlign style in the declaration of the custom component. The ChompBox instance does not handle the textAlign property value and allows the base mx.containers.Box class to dictate its application to any child components through inheritance.

9.9 Use Multiple Themes in the Same Application

Contributed by Andrei Cristian

Problem

You want to apply multiple theme colors to separate controls in the same application.

Solution

Use the themeColor property of a container to assign a specified color value.

Discussion

Using the themeColor property of <mx:Canvas>, you can apply more than one Flex theme on controls in the same application. Applying a theme color affects the appearance of highlighting on rollover, selection, and similar visual treatments.

This recipe's example adds child components to <mx:Canvas> containers to show the look of three themes. The default theme color for a Flex application is set as haloBlue in the global style declaration of defaults.css of the Framework, but more are available and you can use as many themes as you like.

First, create the data provider, dp, and make it bindable. Then declare three Canvas instances containing the components on which the themeColor attribute will be set. Use the same dp data provider for the mx.controls.ComboBox and mx.controls.DataGrid child components of each Canvas instance. Take a look:

```
<mx:Application xmlns:mx="http://www.adobe.com/2006/mxml"
    layout="absolute"
    width="636" height="241">
    <mx:Script>
        <![CDATA[
            [Bindable]
            private var dp:Array =
            [
                    {label:'Carole King', Album:'Tapestry', data:1},
                    {label:'Paul Simon', data:2},
                    {label:'Original Cast', data:3},
                    {label:'The Beatles', data:4}
            ];
        ]]>
    </mx:Script>
    <mx:Label x="10" y="7" text="Standard Theme" fontWeight="bold"
        color="#ffffff"/>
    <mx:Label x="218" y="7" text="Green Theme" fontWeight="bold" color="#ffffff"/>
```

```
<mx:Label x="426" y="7" text="Silver Theme" fontWeight="bold" color="#ffffff"/>
<mx:Canvas x="10" width="200" height="200" verticalCenter="10.5">
    <mx:ComboBox x="10" y="10" dataProvider="{dp}" width="180"></mx:ComboBox>
    <mx:DataGrid x="10" y="40" width="180" height="120" dataProvider="{dp}">
        <mx:columns>
            <mx:DataGridColumn headerText="Id" dataField="data" width="30" />
            <mx:DataGridColumn headerText="Artist" dataField="label"  />
        </mx:columns>
    </mx:DataGrid>
    <mx:Button x="10" y="168" label="Button"/>
</mx:Canvas>
<mx:Canvas x="426" width="200" height="200" themeColor="haloSilver"
    verticalCenter="10.5" backgroundColor="#ffffff"
    cornerRadius="8" borderStyle="solid">
    <mx:ComboBox x="10" y="10" dataProvider="{dp}" width="180"></mx:ComboBox>
    <mx:DataGrid x="10" y="40" width="180" height="120" dataProvider="{dp}">
        <mx:columns>
            <mx:DataGridColumn headerText="Id" dataField="data" width="30" />
            <mx:DataGridColumn headerText="Artist" dataField="label"  />
        </mx:columns>
    </mx:DataGrid>
    <mx:Button x="10" y="166" label="Button"/>
</mx:Canvas>
<mx:Canvas x="218" width="200" height="200" themeColor="haloGreen"
    verticalCenter="10.5" backgroundColor="#ffffff" cornerRadius="8"
    borderStyle="solid" alpha="0.5">
    <mx:ComboBox x="10" y="10" dataProvider="{dp}" width="180"></mx:ComboBox>
    <mx:DataGrid x="10" y="40" width="180" height="120" dataProvider="{dp}">
        <mx:columns>
            <mx:DataGridColumn headerText="Id" dataField="data" width="30" />
            <mx:DataGridColumn headerText="Artist" dataField="label"  />
        </mx:columns>
    </mx:DataGrid>
    <mx:Button x="10" y="166" label="Button"/>
</mx:Canvas>
</mx:Application>
```

When applying a `themeColor` property value on a container instance, any child components on the display list for that container are styled with the theme color through inheritance. Though you can use a key string for color values available in the Flex Framework (such as `haloOrange`), you can assign any valid color value in hexadecimal format as well or use the `StyleManager.registerColorName` method at runtime to create custom key string values.

9.10 Compile a Theme SWC

Problem

You want to package your style files to be included in a theme SWC to compile into your application.

Solution

Use the command-line tools to create a theme SWC and compile the application by using the theme option of the mxmlc compiler.

Discussion

A Shockwave Component (SWC) file is an archive file packaged via the PKZIP format. SWC files enable you to exchange a single archive of multiple files among developers rather than the multitude of files themselves. Just as you may create and package MXML and ActionScript files into SWC files for custom components, so too can you package archive files for styles. To create a SWC file, you use the compc utility available in the /bin directory of your Flex SDK installation.

With a path to the /bin directory of your Flex installation set in your System Path, the following command-line entry shows how you can invoke the compc utility to generate a SWC file named MyTheme.swc:

```
> compc –include-file MyStyles.css C:/mystyles/MyStyles.css -o MyTheme.swc
```

The include-file option takes two arguments: the filename to refer to the style asset and the file system location of the asset. Multiple include-file options are possible for packaging all style assets needed for the application theme.

You can assign a theme during compilation of an application by using the theme option of the mxmlc compiler:

```
> mxmlc MyApplication.mxml -theme MyTheme.swc
```

For a better understanding of how to generate a theme SWC and compile the file into an application, try packaging one of the additional themes available in the Flex SDK.

Within a command prompt, navigate to the Smoke theme directory of your SDK installation: *<flex sdk installation>*/frameworks/themes/Smoke. With the /bin directory of your Flex SDK installation set in your System Path, enter the following command:

```
> compc –include-file Smoke.css Smoke.css –include-file smoke_bg.jpg smoke_bg.jpg
-o SmokeTheme.swc
```

This command generates a SmokeTheme.swc file in that directory. Move that SWC file to a new project directory and enter the following markup:

```
<mx:Application
    xmlns:mx="http://www.adobe.com/2006/mxml"
    xmlns:cookbook="oreilly.cookbook.*"
    layout="vertical">
```

```
<mx:Script>
    <![CDATA[
        [Bindable] private var dp:Array =
                                    [{label:"Josh Noble", data:0},
                                    {label:"Abey George", data:1},
                                    {label:"Todd Anderson", data:2}];

        private function clickHandler():void
        {
            messageField.text = "You chose: " + nameCB.selectedLabel;
        }
    ]]>
</mx:Script>

<mx:Panel title="Pick One:" width="50%" height="50%"
    paddingLeft="10" paddingTop="10">
    <mx:VBox width="100%">
        <mx:HBox width="100%">
            <mx:Text text="Choose:" styleName="windowStyles" />
            <mx:ComboBox id="nameCB" dataProvider="{dp}" />
            <mx:Button label="select" click="clickHandler();" />
        </mx:HBox>
        <mx:Text id="messageField" styleName="windowStyles" />
    </mx:VBox>
</mx:Panel>
</mx:Application>
```

Save the file as an MXML application. You may notice that there are no style declarations locally in the MXML file, nor any imports of external style sheets. However, the **styleName** property of each of the two **Text** components are given the selector value of **windowStyles**. The **.windowStyles** class selector is declared in the Smoke.css style sheet that was packaged into the SmokeTheme.swc previously.

When you compile the application with the **theme** option argument pointing to the SmokeTheme.swc, the styles are applied not only for the **Text** instances of the display, but for all components of the application.

Open a command prompt, navigate to the project directory that has the application MXML file and theme SWC previously created and enter the following command:

```
> mxmlc MyApplication.mxml -theme SmokeTheme.swc
```

This command generates the SWF file for your application with the theme SWC embedded. Open the generated SWF file from your project directory and you will see your application styled with the Smoke theme available from the Flex SDK.

Files that can be packaged into a theme SWC are not limited to CSS and graphic files, but can also include skin class files and font files, which are addressed in later recipes.

See Also

Recipe 9.2 and Recipe 9.6.

9.11 Use Embedded Fonts

Problem

You want to embed fonts into your application to ensure that the look and feel stays consistent on all machines without regard to users' system fonts.

Solution

Embed fonts by using either the [Embed] metadata tag in ActionScript or the @font-face directive in CSS.

Discussion

Embedding font outlines in your application ensures that style treatments assigned to text are intact without regard to the system fonts held on a user's machine. You can use ActionScript and CSS to embed fonts.

The following example illustrates how to use fonts for Flex components by embedding the font via ActionScript:

```
<mx:Application
    xmlns:mx="http://www.adobe.com/2006/mxml"
    layout="vertical">

    <mx:Script>
        <![CDATA[
            [Embed(source="assets/fonts/verdana.TTF", fontName="MyVerdana")]
            private var _verdana:Class;
        ]]>
    </mx:Script>

    <mx:Label text="i have no custom style." />
    <mx:Label text="i have verdana style!" fontFamily="MyVerdana" />
</mx:Application>
```

By using the [Embed] tag for a font, you can specify a fontName attribute to use as a reference when assigning the fontFamily style property during instantiation of a component. In this example, the font is embedded and an associative Class instance member is declared. That variable, however, does not need to be referenced when assigning the font family, but is added as a definition to associate with the embed directive.

The previous snippet embeds a font face with the plain, or normal, style. This font can be applied to any component and rendered to the display. However, you may notice that some components that render a child internally with a specified style, such as `mx.controls.Button` and its boldface label, will fail to render their text if the proper typeface has not been embedded. You can't apply bold typeface to a component unless you embed the typeface for that font and set the `fontWeight` attribute. For example:

```
[Embed(source="assets/fonts/verdanab.TTF", fontName="MyVerdana" fontWeight="bold")]
private var _verdanaBold:Class;
...
<mx:Button label="I have style" fontFamily="MyVerdana" />
```

Most fonts have four primary typeface styles: plain, bold, italic, and bold-italic. You can embed any of these typeface styles into your Flex application, but they need to be declared separately with the correct attributes.

Though using ActionScript to embed fonts is a viable solution, managing and creating multiple fonts for embedding with associative class members may become cumbersome. You can also embed fonts from CSS, both locally in an MXML file and externally, by using the `@font-face` directive as shown:

```
<mx:Application
    xmlns:mx="http://www.adobe.com/2006/mxml"
    layout="vertical">

    <mx:Style>
        @font-face {
            src: url('assets/fonts/verdana.TTF');
            font-family: MyVerdana;
        }
        @font-face {
            src: url('assets/fonts/verdanai.TTF');
            font-family: MyVerdana;
            font-style: italic;
        }
        @font-face {
            src: local('Verdana');
            font-family: MyVerdana;
            font-weight: bold;
        }

        Application {
            font-family: MyVerdana;
        }
        .italicStyle {
            font-style: italic;
        }
    </mx:Style>

    <mx:Text text="i have MyVerdana fontFamily styling." />
    <mx:Label text="i am in italics with MyVerdana styling."
        styleName="italicStyle" />
    <mx:Button label="i am a button. i am bold" />
</mx:Application>
```

Three typefaces for the Verdana font are embedded, and a default font is set for the application. Using the type selector for `Application`, all text within the application uses the embedded font. Because the default style for a `Button` instance has the `fontWeight` style property set to `bold`, you do not have to declare a style to apply to the button in this example because the bold font is embedded and the default `fontFamily` set in the `Application` selector.

You can also specify a font name rather than a location to embed a font by using the `local` function instead of the `url` function in the `@font-face` rule:

```
@font-face {
    src: local('Verdana');
    font-family: MyVerdana;
    font-weight: bold;
}
```

When using the `local` function, you do not specify the typeface name (such as `verdanab`, for this example), but rather the font family name. The bold, italic, and bold-italic typefaces can be embedded this way by adding the appropriate property in the declaration.

Embedding fonts into your application will increase the SWF file size. The previous examples demonstrate embedding font outlines for all available character sets of the font. You can decrease the size to which embedded fonts will bloat the application by declaring character ranges within the `@font-face` rule:

```
@font-face {
    src: local('Verdana');
    font-family: MyVerdana;
    unicodeRange: U+0041-U+005A, U+0061-U+007A, U+002E;
}
```

You can specify a range of characters and single characters to embed by using the `unicodeRange` property. Subsets are declared, separated by a comma. You can specify ranges by using a hyphen (-) and declare single characters. In this example, the upper-case and lowercase characters of the standard Latin alphabet (A to Z and a to z) and the period (.) character are embedded.

9.12 Embed Fonts from a SWF File

Problem

You want to embed fonts from a SWF file to be used in your application.

Solution

Create a SWF with embedded fonts and declare the typefaces you want to embed in your application by using the `@font-face` directive.

Figure 9-1. Create dynamic text fields and embed font ranges.

Discussion

You can embed multiple typeface font styles in your application from a single SWF file with embedded fonts. Using embedded fonts from a SWF, as opposed to embedding fonts from a font file, has the advantage of portability. You can embed fonts available on your system into a SWF file, and pass that file onto another developer who does not have to worry about having the specified fonts resident during compilation.

To embed fonts in a SWF file, create a new FLA file in the Flash IDE and add dynamic text fields to the Stage with the specified typefaces set and select the character ranges to include for embedding (Figure 9-1).

In this example, each dynamic text field is added with the Verdana font and typeface properties selected. As you can see, the bold-italic style is applied from the Properties panel. By selecting the Embed button from the panel, you can specify character ranges to cut down on file size. Save this FLA file with a name that you find appropriate for your project (this file was named Verdana.fla for this example) and publish the movie.

Declaring embedded fonts from a SWF file is similar to working with a font file. Instead of defining the font file location through the `url` function or the font name through the `local` function, you specify the SWF file location by using the `url` directive to embed fonts from the SWF, as shown:

```
@font-face {
    src: url("styles/fonts/Verdana.swf");
    font-family: Verdana;
}
```

This snippet will embed the plain typeface of the Verdana font seen in the topmost dynamic text field of Figure 9-1. To include the treatments of each typeface embedded in the SWF file, you declare the appropriate property values. Embedding the font typeface selected in Figure 9-1 includes setting the `fontWeight` property to `bold` and the `fontStyle` property to `italic`:

```
@font-face {
    src: url("styles/fonts/Verdana.swf");
    font-family: Verdana;
    font-weight: bold;
    font-style: italic;
}
```

Embedded fonts are a subclass of `flash.text.Font` from the ActionScript API. You can access a list of devices and embedded fonts from the static method `enumerateFonts` of the `Font` class. The argument for `enumerateFonts` is a flag to include device fonts within the returned array. The following example fills a data grid with the embedded fonts from the font SWF file declared within the `<mx:Style>` tag:

```
<mx:Application
    xmlns:mx="http://www.adobe.com/2006/mxml"
    layout="vertical" creationComplete="creationHandler();">

    <mx:Style>
        @font-face {
            src: url("assets/fonts/Verdana.swf");
            font-family: Verdana;
        }

        @font-face {
            src: url("assets/fonts/Verdana.swf");
            font-family: Verdana;
            font-weight: bold;
        }

        @font-face {
            src: url("assets/fonts/Verdana.swf");
            font-family: Verdana;
            font-style: italic;
        }

        @font-face {
            src: url("assets/fonts/Verdana.swf");
            font-family: Verdana;
            font-weight: bold;
            font-style: italic;
        }

        Label {
            font-family: Verdana;
            font-size: 15px;
        }
        .verdanaBoldStyle {
            font-weight: bold;
```

```
        }
        .verdanaItalicStyle {
            font-style: italic;
        }
        .verdanaBoldItalicStyle {
            font-weight: bold;
            font-style: italic;
        }

    </mx:Style>

    <mx:Script>
        <![CDATA[

            [Bindable] private var fontArray:Array;
            [Bindable] private var selectedFontStyle:String;
            [Bindable] private var selectedFontWeight:String;

            private function creationHandler():void
            {
                var embeddedFonts:Array = Font.enumerateFonts();
                embeddedFonts.sortOn( "fontStyle", Array.CASEINSENSITIVE );
                fontArray = embeddedFonts;
            }

            private function changeHandler():void
            {
                var italic:RegExp = /italic/i;
                var bold:RegExp = /bold/i;
                selectedFontStyle =
                        ( String( fontGrid.selectedItem.fontStyle ).match(italic) )
                                    ? 'italic'
                                    : 'normal';
                selectedFontWeight =
                        ( String( fontGrid.selectedItem.fontStyle ).match(bold) )
                                    ? 'bold'
                                    : 'normal';
            }

        ]]>
    </mx:Script>
    <mx:Label text="Select a font form the grid below:" />
    <mx:DataGrid id="fontGrid" dataProvider="{fontArray}"
        change="changeHandler();">
        <mx:columns>
            <mx:DataGridColumn headerText="Font Name" dataField="fontName"
                width="150" />
            <mx:DataGridColumn headerText="Font Style" dataField="fontStyle" />
            <mx:DataGridColumn headerText="Font Type" dataField="fontType" />
        </mx:columns>
    </mx:DataGrid>
    <mx:Label width="100%" textAlign="center"
        text="{fontGrid.selectedItem.fontName + ' : ' +
fontGrid.selectedItem.fontStyle}"
        fontFamily="{fontGrid.selectedItem.fontName}"
```

```
            fontStyle="{selectedFontStyle}"
            fontWeight="{selectedFontWeight}"
            />
    </mx:Application>
```

The `creationComplete` event handler accesses the array of embedded fonts in the application and updates the bindable `fontArray` member used as the `dataProvider` of the `DataGrid` instance. Upon selection of a typeface from the data grid, the font style properties of the label are updated at runtime.

See Also

Recipe 9.10.

9.13 Skin with Embedded Images

Contributed by Kristopher Schultz

Problem

You want to use custom images to skin the visual elements of a component.

Solution

Apply custom JPEG, GIF, or PNG images by using the style properties of a component. These attributes can be set directly on the component instance inline through MXML or as part of a CSS style definition.

Discussion

By default, the built-in Flex theme assigns programmatic skin classes to components. You can create custom programmatic skin classes or assign graphical elements as skins to modify the visual makeup of a component. Skinnable components generally have a set of skin *states*, or phases, shown during user interaction. As such, when creating custom graphical skins, it is beneficial to keep in mind the different interactive states of a component.

In the following example, custom images are applied to the various background states of a `Button` component. Specifically, the code sets the `upSkin`, `overSkin`, `downSkin`, and `disabledSkin` style properties directly on the `Button` instance inline:

```
<mx:Application xmlns:mx="http://www.adobe.com/2006/mxml"
    layout="horizontal" backgroundColor="#FFFFFF">

    <mx:Button label=""
        upSkin="@Embed('assets/images/text_button_up.png')"
        overSkin="@Embed('assets/images/text_button_over.png')"
        downSkin="@Embed('assets/images/text_button_down.png')"
        disabledSkin="@Embed('assets/images/text_button_disabled.png')"
    />
```

```
    </mx:Application>
```

Note the @Embed compiler directive forces the image assets to be bundled into the final application SWF file. It is important to embed the images this way so there is no loading delay when the button changes from one state to another.

Because the example supplies an empty string (' ') value for the label property, text will not be rendered on top of the graphical elements. The image files for this recipe, provided in the code samples accompanying this book, have their labels drawn within the graphic.

If you would like to display text on the Button instance and have the images scale to accommodate the varying length of label text, you can use the scale-9 feature of the Flex Framework to include scale grid information in your skin attributes. Scale grid values depend on the size and design of the graphical elements. The following example sets skin attributes in a CSS style definition and applies the style to multiple Button instances via the styleName attribute. When using the Embed directive in CSS, no preceding @ symbol is used, as is the case when embedding graphics inline.

```
<mx:Application xmlns:mx="http://www.adobe.com/2006/mxml"
    layout="horizontal" backgroundColor="#FFFFFF">

    <mx:Style>
        .customButton {
            color: #FFFFFF;
            text-roll-over-color: #FFFFBB;
            text-selected-color: #9999FF;
            disabled-color: #333333;
            up-skin: Embed(
                source="assets/images/button_up.png",
                scaleGridTop="15",
                scaleGridBottom="20",
                scaleGridLeft="15",
                scaleGridRight="28");
            over-skin: Embed(
                source="assets/images/button_over.png",
                scaleGridTop="15",
                scaleGridBottom="20",
                scaleGridLeft="15",
                scaleGridRight="28");
            down-skin: Embed(
                source="assets/images/button_down.png",
                scaleGridTop="15",
                scaleGridBottom="20",
                scaleGridLeft="15",
                scaleGridRight="28");
            disabled-skin: Embed(
                source="assets/images/button_disabled.png",
                scaleGridTop="15",
                scaleGridBottom="20",
                scaleGridLeft="15",
                scaleGridRight="28");
```

```
        }
    </mx:Style>

    <mx:Button label="This button is enabled"
        styleName="customButton"
    />

    <mx:Button label="This button is disabled"
        styleName="customButton"
        enabled="false"
    />

</mx:Application>
```

By using the scale-9 feature of the Flex Framework, you define nine sections of an image to scale independently of each other. The four corners of embedded graphics, which are deduced from the four scale grid attributes, do not scale and are positioned based on the horizontal and vertical scale size of the other grid elements. Using scale-9 by setting values for the scale grid attributes is beneficial when embedding graphics with borders you wish to keep sharp and intact, such as the rounded corners of the button graphics for this example.

9.14 Apply Skins from a SWF File

Problem

You want to hold a library of graphics in a SWF file to embed skins for components.

Solution

Create a SWF file with multiple symbols marked for export that represent the various states of the component.

Discussion

Creating a library of graphical skins within a SWF file is a convenient way to hand off designs to another developer. In addition, it opens the possibility of using vector graphics for skinning.

Using the Properties panel of a symbol from the Flash IDE library, you can select the class name and superclass linkage used for referencing the graphic symbol. Because you are using the class libraries available only to ActionScript-based projects when using the Flash IDE, you cannot select base classes that are available in the Flex Framework. That is fine, because the symbols are converted to their Flex counterpart when embedded into the application. For example, `MovieClip` instances marked for export in the library of a SWF file are converted to `MovieClipAsset` objects, which are then added to the display of a Flex application.

Creating assets that extend `MovieClip` are useful for graphics that have multiple states, but if you use static graphics, setting the base class of the symbol to the `flash.display.Sprite` class is sufficient. The `Sprite` object will be converted to a `SpriteAsset` object when embedded in the Flex application.

To begin creating static graphical skins in the Flash IDE, open a new FLA and create a new `MovieClip` symbol from the library. Import a graphic file to the stage of the `MovieClip` instance or use the drawing tools of the Flash IDE to create vector-based skins to use in your application. To enable the symbol for embedding in a Flex application, right-click on the symbol in the library to access the Symbol Properties panel from the context menu and select the Export for ActionScript check box. The Base class field will default to the value of `flash.display.MovieClip`. You can keep that value, but can also change it to `flash.display.Sprite` because the graphics are considered static—or do not have states that rely on the timeline.

Figure 9-2 shows the Symbol Properties panel's Advanced features set to create skins for the various states and elements of a scroll bar. From the Advanced features, you can set properties for embedding (also accessible from the Linkage panel) and have the opportunity to turn on draggable scale-9 grid lines within a symbol by selecting Enabled Guides for 9-Slice Scaling. If you manually set the scale-9 guides within a symbol, the Flex compiler automatically sets the style values for the scale grid properties (`scaleGridLeft`, `scaleGridRight`, `scaleGridTop`, `scaleGridBottom`).

With the skins created and each given a unique linkage identifier and marked for export, save the FLA file with a name appropriate for your project (in this example, that name is scrollbar_skins.fla) and publish the movie.

Embedding graphic symbols from a SWF file is similar to embedding singular graphic files. You set the `source` attribute to the SWF file within the `Embed` directive and set the `symbol` property value to that of the linkage identifier for the library symbol you want to embed. For example:

```
thumbUpSkin: Embed(source="styles/scrollbar_skins.swf", symbol="thumb_upSkin");
```

You can also set the `symbol` attribute value by delimiting the SWF location and the symbol linkage identifier with a pound (#) sign within the `source` definition, as shown:

```
thumbUpSkin: Embed(source="styles/scrollbar_skins.swf#thumb_upSkin");
```

The following example uses the generated style SWF (scrollbar_skins.swf, which can be found in the code examples for this chapter) to assign skins to an instance of the `ScrollBar` class. The `mx.controls.scrollClasses.ScrollBar` class of the Flex component architecture is made of multiple "stateful" elements. Each element of the scrollbar component has a visual representation of its current state. The state can relay the current user action and enablement. For instance, when a user hovers the mouse cursor over a child component of the scroll bar, the component enters an "over" state. Assigning symbol skins to each state phase of each element is achievable by using the corresponding style properties available on the `ScrollBar` class.

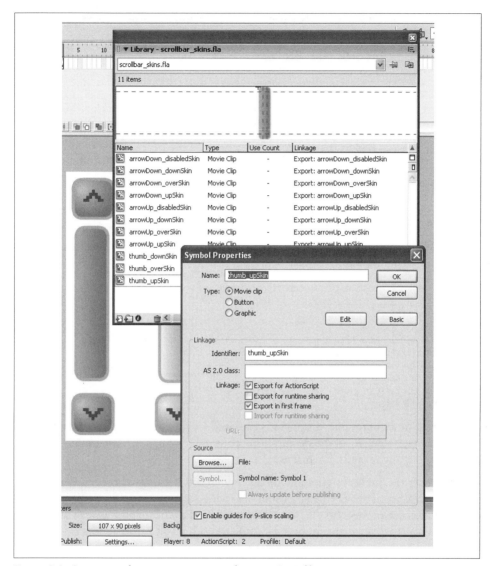

Figure 9-2. Creating and exporting vector graphics in a SWF file

```
<mx:Application
    xmlns:mx="http://www.adobe.com/2006/mxml"
    layout="vertical">
<mx:Style>
    ScrollBar
    {
        trackColors: #0099CC, #0099CC;
        borderColor: #99FFFF;

        thumbUpSkin: Embed(source="assets/styles/scrollbar_skins.swf",
            symbol="thumb_upSkin");
```

```
                    thumbOverSkin: Embed(source="assets/styles/scrollbar_skins.swf",
                        symbol="thumb_overSkin");
                    thumbDownSkin: Embed(source="assets/styles/scrollbar_skins.swf",
                        symbol="thumb_downSkin");

                    upArrowUpSkin: Embed(source="assets/styles/scrollbar_skins.swf",
                        symbol="arrowUp_upSkin");
                    upArrowOverSkin: Embed(source="assets/styles/scrollbar_skins.swf",
                        symbol="arrowUp_overSkin");
                    upArrowDownSkin: Embed(source="assets/styles/scrollbar_skins.swf",
                        symbol="arrowUp_downSkin");
                    upArrowDisabledSkin: Embed(source="assets/styles/scrollbar_skins.swf",
                        symbol="arrowUp_disabledSkin");

                    downArrowUpSkin: Embed(source="assets/styles/scrollbar_skins.swf",
                        symbol="arrowDown_upSkin");
                    downArrowOverSkin: Embed(source="assets/styles/scrollbar_skins.swf",
                        symbol="arrowDown_overSkin");
                    downArrowDownSkin: Embed(source="assets/styles/scrollbar_skins.swf",
                        symbol="arrowDown_downSkin");
                    downArrowDisabledSkin: Embed(source="assets/styles/scrollbar_skins.swf",
                        symbol="arrowDown_disabledSkin");
                }
            </mx:Style>

            <mx:Label text="Keep typing to see the scroll!" color="0xFFFFFF" />
            <mx:TextArea width="200" height="150"
                text="Lorem ipsum dolor sit amet..."
                borderColor="0x0099CC" />
            <mx:HScrollBar width="200" enabled="false" />
        </mx:Application>
```

A type selector for `ScrollBar` instances is declared locally to the application within the `<mx:Style>` tag. Defined in the declaration are stateful skins for three child elements: the thumb, up arrow, and down arrow.

The `mx.controls.TextArea` component displays scroll bars based on text length. To view a vertical scroll bar skinned by using the style SWF, type more text within the text area. An instance of `mx.controls.HScrollBar` is added to the display as well and is disabled to show that skins are applied the same to both scroll bar instances (`VscrollBar` and `HScrollBar`) and style properties are not dependent on direction.

See Also

Recipe 9.12.

9.15 Programmatically Skin a Component

Problem

You want more control over how visual elements are rendered in a component without assigning graphic skins.

Solution

Create a custom skin class that extends the `mx.skins.ProgrammaticSkin` class and over-rides the protected `updateDisplayList` method.

Discussion

Programmatic skinning, as opposed to graphical skinning, requires a higher level of understanding ActionScript but affords you more control over the visual presentation of a component. Programmatic skin classes are display objects that use the drawing API to render skin elements and enable you to use other style property values that may be negated if you were to assign a graphical skin.

Generally, Flex has two types of components: containers and controls. Containers have border skins representing the background display, whereas controls usually have a set of skins that represent state (up, down, over, and disabled). There are a few exceptions, such as the `TextInput` control, which uses a border skin, and, in general, it is important to be aware of the visual makeup of a component prior to creating a custom programmatic skin.

When creating a programmatic skin for a control, you extend the `mx.skins.ProgrammaticSkin` class. When creating a custom skin for a container, you can create a subclass of `ProgrammaticSkin`, but generally you create a subclass of either `Border` (which has a `borderMetrics` property) or `RectangleBorder` (which is a subclass of `Border` and has support for the background styles). Table 9-1 lists the base classes of the Flex API used to create custom programmatic skins.

Table 9-1. Base Classes of the Flex API Used for Creating Custom Programmatic Skins

Class	Usage
`mx.skins.ProgrammaticSkin`	Baseclass for all skin elements that programmatically draw themselves.
`mx.skins.Border`	Baseclass for drawing rectangular and nonrectangular borders. Contains a `borderMetrics` property. Subclass of `ProgrammaticSkin`.
`mx.skins.RectangularBorder`	Base class for drawing rectangular borders. Subclass of `Border`. Support for the `backgroundImage`, `backgroundSize`, and `backgroundAttachment` styles.

When you create subclasses of these base classes for your custom skins, you override the protected updateDisplayList method of ProgrammaticSkin to add drawing methods based on style property values. For example:

```
package
{
    import mx.skins.ProgrammaticSkin;
    public class MyCustomSkin extends ProgrammaticSkin
    {
        public function MyCustomSkin() {}

        override protected function updateDisplayList( unscaledWidth:Number,
                                                       unscaledHeight:Number ):void
        {
            // grab the value for the backgroundColor style property
            var backgroundColor:Number = getStyle( "backgroundColor" );
            // implement drawing methods.
        }
    }
}
```

The updateDisplayList method gets called internally within the class instance every time it needs to draw or redraw the skin elements based on updates to properties. As such, in overriding this method, you can access style properties through the getStyle method and use the drawing API to customize the display.

You also have the option of setting the default dimensions of a skin element by overriding the read-only properties of measuredWidth and measuredHeight, as shown:.

```
package oreilly.cookbook
{
    import mx.skins.ProgrammaticSkin;
    public class MyCustomSkin extends ProgrammaticSkin
    {
        private var _measuredWidth:Number;
        private var _measuredHeight:Number;

        public function MyCustomSkin()
        {
            _measuredWidth = 120;
            _measuredHeight = 120;
        }
        // return defaulted constant for width
        override public function get measuredWidth():Number
        {
            return _measuredWidth;
        }
        // return defaulted constant for height
        override public function get measuredHeight():Number
        {
            return _measuredHeight;
        }

        override protected function updateDisplayList( unscaledWidth:Number,
                                                       unscaledHeight:Number ):void
```

```
        {
            // grab the value for the backgroundColor style property
            var backgroundColor:Number = getStyle( "backgroundColor" );
            // implement drawing methods.
        }
    }
}
```

If you do not override the measuredWidth and measuredHeight read-only properties, their default value is set as 0. In the preceding example, a component assigned with the programmatic skin class will default to being 120 wide and 120 high. The dimensions can be modified during declaration of the component by using the width and height properties.

The following snippet creates a custom border skin that can be applied to the border Skin style property of a container:

```
package oreilly.cookbook
{
    import mx.graphics.RectangularDropShadow;
    import mx.skins.Border;

    public class CustomBorder extends Border
    {
        private var _dropShadow:RectangularDropShadow;
        private static const CNR_RAD:Number = 5;
        private static const POINT_POS:String = 'bl';
        private static const BG_COL:uint = 0x336699;
        private static const BG_ALPHA:Number = 1.0;

        public function CustomBorder()
        {
            super();
            _dropShadow = new RectangularDropShadow();
        }

        private function getCornerRadiusObj( rad:Number, pointPos:String ):Object
        {
            var pt:String = pointPos ? pointPos : POINT_POS;
            return {tl:rad, bl:0, tr:rad, br:rad};
        }

        override protected function updateDisplayList( unscaledWidth:Number,
                                                       unscaledHeight:Number ):void
        {
            super.updateDisplayList( unscaledWidth, unscaledHeight );
            var cornerRadius:Number = getStyle( "cornerRadius" ) ?
                                        getStyle( "cornerRadius" ) :
                                        CustomBorder.CNR_RAD;
            var backgroundColor:Number = getStyle( "backgroundColor" ) ?
                                        getStyle( "backgroundColor" ) :
                                        CustomBorder.BG_COL;
            var backgroundAlpha:Number = getStyle( "backgroundAlpha" ) ?
                                        getStyle( "backgroundAlpha" ) :
                                        CustomBorder.BG_ALPHA;
```

```
                var cnrRadius:Object = getCornerRadiusObj( cornerRadius,
                                        getStyle( "pointPosition" ) );
                graphics.clear();
                drawRoundRect( 0, 0, unscaledWidth, unscaledHeight,
                                cnrRadius , backgroundColor, backgroundAlpha );

                _dropShadow.tlRadius = cnrRadius.tl;
                _dropShadow.blRadius = cnrRadius.bl;
                _dropShadow.trRadius = cnrRadius.tr;
                _dropShadow.brRadius = cnrRadius.br;
                _dropShadow.drawShadow( graphics, 0, 0,
                                        unscaledWidth, unscaledHeight );
            }
        }
    }
```

Whenever the `updateDisplayList` method is called, the graphics layer is cleared and redrawn by using the inherited `drawRoundRect` method. In addition, a drop shadow filter is applied; this is an advantage of using programmatic skins over graphical skins because this technique allows you access to more low-level features such as filters.

You can assign a programmatic skin by using any of the methods you use for assigning other style property values: inline, using the `setStyle` method, or CSS. The following example demonstrates each of these techniques:

```
<mx:Application
    xmlns:mx="http://www.adobe.com/2006/mxml"
    layout="vertical"
    initialize="initHandler();">
    <mx:Script>
        <![CDATA[
            import oreilly.cookbook.CustomBorder;

            private function initHandler():void
            {
                myVBox.setStyle( "borderSkin", CustomBorder );
            }
        ]]>
    </mx:Script>
    <mx:VBox width="100" height="50"
        borderSkin="oreilly.cookbook.CustomBorder" />
    <mx:VBox width="50" height="20"
        borderSkin="{CustomBorder}" />
    <mx:VBox id="myVBox" width="80" height="20" />
</mx:Application>
```

When assigning the skin inline or using the `setStyle` method, you can import the class and use its shortened name or specify the skin by using the fully qualified class name. When using the shortened name to assign a skin class inline, curly braces ({}) are needed to evaluate the imported class.

Using CSS, you need to specify the fully classified class name wrapped in a `ClassReference` directive. Here the `CustomBorder` skin is assigned to the `borderSkin` property of an `mx.containers.VBox` instance by using a type selector:

```
<mx:Application
    xmlns:mx="http://www.adobe.com/2006/mxml"
    layout="vertical">

    <mx:Style>
        VBox {
            borderSkin: ClassReference("oreilly.cookbook.CustomBorder");
            cornerRadius: 30;
            pointPosition: 'bl';
            backgroundColor: #999933;
            backgroundAlpha: 1;
            paddingLeft: 5;
            paddingRight: 5;
        }
    </mx:Style>

    <mx:VBox id="myBox"
        width="120" height="100"
        verticalAlign="middle" horizontalAlign="center">
        <mx:Text text="i'm a styled VBox!" textAlign="center" />
    </mx:VBox>
</mx:Application>
```

In the override of the `updateDisplayList` method in `CustomBorder`, the other style properties (`cornerRadius`, `pointPosition`, and so forth) declared in the `VBox` selector are used to custom render the background display of a `VBox` instance.

See Also

Recipe 9.3 and Recipe 9.5.

9.16 Programmatically Skin a Stateful Control

Problem

You want to create a programmatic skin that can handle rendering different states of a control.

Solution

Create a subclass of `mx.skins.ProgrammaticSkin` and use the `updateDisplayList` method to update its display based on the `name` property value. Assign the custom programmatic skin by using the `skin` style property inline, using the `setStyle` method, or using CSS.

Discussion

In general, controls have states or child elements with states. Assigning a programmatic skin as a style to handle rendering the states of a control is the same as assigning a programmatic skin to render the background of a container: The style property values are defined by using the class name of the programmatic skin. Updating the visual elements of a skin for a control and a container differ, however, as most controls render their display based on a state.

In creating a programmatic skin class for a stateful component, you create a subclass of `ProgrammaticSkin` and override the protected `updateDisplayList` method. Within the `updateDisplayList` override, you can use a switch case statement to respond to state name values. The `name` property value for each skin phase is assigned internally by the control that you are skinning and is the same string value as that of a control's style property.

The following example creates a programmatic skin that updates its display based on the states `upSkin`, `overSkin`, `downSkin`, and `disabledSkin`:

```
package oreilly.cookbook
{
    import flash.filters.BevelFilter;

    import mx.skins.ProgrammaticSkin;

    public class CustomButtonSkin extends ProgrammaticSkin
    {
        private var _measuredWidth:Number = 100;
        private var _measuredHeight:Number = 100;
        // override measuredWidth and measuredHeight sets default size.
        override public function get measuredWidth():Number
        {
            return _measuredWidth;
        }
        override public function get measuredHeight():Number
        {
            return _measuredHeight;
        }
        // update display based on state phase name.
        override protected function updateDisplayList( unscaledWidth:Number,
                                            unscaledHeight:Number ):void
        {
            var backgroundAlpha:Number = 1.0;
            var bevelAngle:Number = 45;
            var backgroundColor:uint;
            // assign property values based on state name
            switch( name )
            {
                case "upSkin":
                    backgroundColor = 0xEEEEEE;
                    break;
                case "overSkin":
                    backgroundColor = 0xDDDDDD;
```

```
                break;
            case "downSkin":
                backgroundColor = 0xDDDDDD;
                bevelAngle = 245;
                break;
            case "disabledSkin":
                backgroundColor = 0xFFFFFF;
                backgroundAlpha = 0.5;
                break;
        }
        // clear the display and redraw with values assigned in switch
        graphics.clear();
        drawRoundRect( 0, 0, unscaledWidth, unscaledHeight, null,
                       backgroundColor, backgroundAlpha );
        // apply bevel filter
        var bevel:BevelFilter = new BevelFilter( 2, bevelAngle );
        this.filters = [bevel];
    }
 }
}
```

To assign a programmatic skin that responds to state phases within a control, you supply the class name as the value for the skin style property. The following uses CSS to supply the fully qualified class name of the CustomButtonSkin class wrapped in a ClassReference directive:

```
<mx:Application
    xmlns:mx="http://www.adobe.com/2006/mxml"
    layout="vertical">

    <mx:Style>
        .customButton {
            skin: ClassReference( "oreilly.cookbook.CustomButtonSkin" );
        }
    </mx:Style>

    <mx:Button id="skinnedBtn"
        styleName="customButton"
        label="click me"
        />
    <mx:Button label="toggle enabled"
        click="{skinnedBtn.enabled = !skinnedBtn.enabled;}"
        />

</mx:Application>
```

The skin style property is a new addition to the Flex 3 SDK. In Flex 2, each skin state needed to be defined even if each value was the same ClassReference directive. In Flex 3, you can assign a single skin property to be used for each state. After defining the skin property, you can still override specified state skin properties, such as overSkin, to have more control over customizing stateful components.

See Also

Recipe 9.14.

9.17 Create Animated Skins from a SWF File

Problem

You want to create a button that has different animations in the Flash IDE for each of its states.

Solution

Create an FLA and within that FLA create a MovieClip symbol marked for export that has multiple frame labels and animations. Using the name of the generated SWF and MovieClip, mark a MovieClip class as extending your animation by using the [Embed] metadata tag with source and symbol references. Assign a subclass of mx.core.UIComponent as the skin for an mx.controls.Button instance and use the inherited currentState property to control the current state and correct animation frame of the MovieClip within the Button instance.

Discussion

Assigning an animated skin from a SWF file is similar to assigning a programmatic skin to a component during its declaration. The creation of the skin differs in that tweens are applied between frames within a symbol as opposed to programmatically animating elements of a component.

To create an animated skin for embedding, use a MovieClip symbol from the library of an FLA document with frame labels defined corresponding to states. That symbol is then embedded within a class definition when you assign linkage properties to the symbol within the library of the FLA. You then add the animated skin to the display list by using the class reference, and animations are controlled by advancing to frames based on state phases of the component.

To begin creating animated skins, add a new MovieClip symbol in the Flash IDE and add multiple labeled frames and animations between those frames on its timeline, as shown in Figure 9-3.

Your animations can be considerably more complex than the ones included for this example if you wish. The important thing is that the frame labels are logical and correspond to the five main button states: up, down, selected, over, and disabled. In Figure 9-3's FLA, two frame labels were added for each of those states: one to mark the beginning of the animation for that state and one to mark the end (for example, Over Begin and OverEnd). A custom class responding to state phases will use these labels to

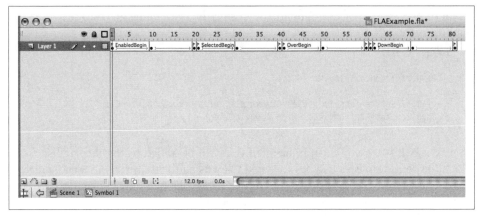

Figure 9-3. Create multiple labeled frames with animations in between.

Figure 9-4. Export the clip by using a unique class name.

advance to specified frames. The next step is to export the symbol from Flash so that the Flex compiler will be able to use it.

To allow access to the frames of a symbol in a SWF file, the *Base class* property is defined as an instance of the `flash.display.MovieClip` class and a class name assigned. In looking at Figure 9-4, the multiframe `MovieClip` symbol previously created is given the class name `ButtonClip` and marked for export.

To import the symbol from a generated SWF file, the `[Embed]` metadata tag is used during the class definition. The `source` attribute is defined as the location of the SWF file, and the symbol attribute is defined by using the class name given to the exported symbol, as shown:

```
package oreilly.cookbook
{
    import flash.display.MovieClip;

    [Embed(source="assets/styles/FLAExample.swf", symbol="ButtonClip")]
    public class ButtonClass extends MovieClip{}
}
```

This class will serve as a custom element that will be added to the display list, from which the defined tweens can be navigated to by using the frame labels. An instance of ButtonClass cannot be directly applied to the display list of a Flex application because it is a subclass of a Flash component that does not implement mx.core.IFlexDisplayObject. In order to add an instance of this class to the display, it must be a child of mx.core.UIComponent.

The custom UIComponent class that adds the ButtonClass instance to its display will also advance to animation frames based on updates to the currentState property. The following example is the custom skin that will be assigned to a Button instance:

```
package oreilly.cookbook
{
    import flash.display.MovieClip;
    import flash.events.Event;

    import mx.core.UIComponent;

    public class ButtonAnimatedSkin extends UIComponent
    {

        private var _state:String;
        private var _movieClipAsset:MovieClip;

        public function ButtonAnimatedSkin() {
            super();
        }
        //when we create the children, we actually instantiate our ButtonClass
        override protected function createChildren():void {
            super.createChildren();
            _movieClipAsset = new ButtonClass();
            _movieClipAsset.addEventListener(Event.ENTER_FRAME, enterFrameHandler);
            addChild(_movieClipAsset);
        }
        //we need to make sure that we have a solid background to hit detection
        // against. Even if we can't see it, it's there.
        override protected function updateDisplayList( unscaledWidth:Number,
                                                       unscaledHeight:Number ):void {
            graphics.clear();
            graphics.beginFill( 0x000000, 0 );
            graphics.drawRect( 0, 0, _movieClipAsset.width,
                                     _movieClipAsset.height );
            graphics.endFill();
```

```
        //make sure the clip is always at the 0, 0 point
        _movieClipAsset.x = _movieClipAsset.width/2;
        _movieClipAsset.y = _movieClipAsset.height/2;
    }
    //This method will be called when the button changes its state.
    override public function set currentState( value:String ):void {
        _state = value;
        //these are some of the values that we're not using; however
        //we certainly could create distinct animations and clips for each
        //of them if we wanted to.
        if(_state == "selectedUp")      _state = "selected";
        if(_state == "selectedDown")    _state = "down";
        if(_state == "selectedOver")    _state = "over";
        switch( _state )
        {
            case "over" :
                // for each state we simply gotoAndPlay the correct frame
                //for that state
                _movieClipAsset.gotoAndPlay("OverBegin");
                break;
            case "down":
                _movieClipAsset.gotoAndPlay("DownBegin");
                break;
            case "selected":
                _movieClipAsset.gotoAndPlay("SelectedBegin");
                break;
            case "up" :
                _movieClipAsset.gotoAndPlay("EnabledBegin");
                break;
            case "disabled" :
                _movieClipAsset.gotoAndPlay("DisabledBegin");
                break;
        }
    }
    //every time we enter a frame, we want to check to see if we're at the
    //end of one of our animations for each state. If we are, we send the
    //clip back to the beginning of the cycle.
    private function enterFrameHandler(event:Event):void {
        switch(_state){
            case "over" :
                if(_movieClipAsset.currentLabel == "OverEnd") {
                    _movieClipAsset.gotoAndPlay("OverBegin");
                }
                break;
            case "down":
                if(_movieClipAsset.currentLabel == "DownEnd") {
                    _movieClipAsset.gotoAndPlay("DownBegin");
                }
                break;
            case "up" :
                if(_movieClipAsset.currentLabel == "EnabledEnd") {
                    _movieClipAsset.gotoAndPlay("EnabledBegin");
                }
                break;
            case "selected":
```

```
                            if(_movieClipAsset.currentLabel == "SelectedEnd") {
                                _movieClipAsset.gotoAndPlay("SelectedBegin");
                            }
                            break;
                        case "disabled" :
                            // don't need to do anything since disabled has only 1 frame
                            break;
                    }
                }
            }
        }
```

Within the `createChildren` override method, a new instance of `ButtonClass` is instantiated and added to the display list. Each time the current state is updated within the `Button` class, the `ButtonAnimatedSkin` class uses the new state to tell the `ButtonClass` to go to a specified frame. In the `enterFrameHandler` method, a loop is created to check whether the button is at the end of the animation. If the animation has reached its ending frame, the movie is sent back to the beginning of that state animation.

You assign the `ButtonAnimatedSkin` just as you would assign a programmatic skin, by defining the class in the `skin` style property:

```
<mx:Button toggle="true" skin="oreilly.cookbook.ButtonAnimatedSkin"
    y="300" x="300"/>
```

See Also

Recipe 9.13, Recipe 9.14, and Recipe 9.15.

9.18 Customize the Preloader

Problem

You want to customize the preloader displayed during download and initialization of a Flex application.

Solution

Create a custom preloader display by creating a subclass of the `mx.preloaders.DownloadProgressBar` class (which is the default application preloader display) or by creating a subclass of `flash.display.Sprite` that implements the `mx.preloaders.IPreloaderDisplay` interface.

Discussion

By default, a Flex application is composed of two frames. The first frame creates a preloader that dispatches a series of events corresponding to the load and initialization of the application. The default progress bar updates its display based on those events. Upon completion of download, the system manager advances to the second frame, where application creation and initialization proceeds. Upon complete initialization of the application, the system manager is notified and removes the preloader display.

Internally, this process is handled by the system manager, which initializes an instance of the mx.preloaders.Preloader class to monitor the download and initialization of your application. The Preloader instance instantiates the assigned download progress bar, adds it to its display list, and sets the preloader property of the IPreloaderDisplay implementation to itself. The defined Preloader instance can listen to a variety of events dispatched from the preloader, as detailed in Table 9-2.

Table 9-2. Events Dispatched by the Preloader Class

Event	Description
ProgressEvent.PROGRESS	Dispatched during download of the SWF file.
Event.COMPLETE	Dispatched when the SWF file has been completely downloaded.
FlexEvent.INIT_PROGRESS	Dispatched during initialization of the application.
FlexEvent.INIT_COMPLETE	Dispatched when the application has completed initialization. The IPreloaderDisplay implementation must listen for this event in order to fire a COMPLETE event accordingly. The COMPLETE event is listened to by the passed-in Preloader instance in order to instruct the system manager that the application is ready for display.
RslEvent.RSL_ERROR	Dispatched upon load failure of a runtime shared library (RSL).
RslEvent.RSL_PROGRESS	Dispatched during download of an RSL.
RslEvent.RSL_COMPLETE	Dispatched when an RSL has been completely downloaded.

To create a custom progress bar to handle these events, you can create either a subclass of mx.preloaders.DownloadProgressBar or a subclass of mx.display.Sprite that implements mx.preloaders.IPreloaderDisplay, which is the makeup of DownloadProgress Bar itself.

The DownloadProgressBar class defines protected event handlers for the events listed in Table 9-2. By creating a subclass of DownloadProgressBar, you can override these event handlers to modify and update your custom display accordingly:

```
package oreilly.cookbook
{
    import flash.events.Event;
    import flash.events.ProgressEvent;
    import flash.geom.Rectangle;

    import mx.preloaders.DownloadProgressBar;

    public class DPBSubclass extends DownloadProgressBar
    {
        public function DPBSubclass()
        {
            super();
            // minimum display time after download.
```

```
                MINIMUM_DISPLAY_TIME = 3000;
                // set the default text during initialization
                //    progress.
                initializingLabel = "Download complete!\nInitializing...";
            }
            // override label area to display custom text.
            override protected function get labelRect():Rectangle
            {
                return new Rectangle(14, 5, 150, 30);
            }
            // override download progress handler to display
            //    custom text.
            override protected function progressHandler(
                                    event:ProgressEvent ):void
            {
                super.progressHandler(event);
                label = Math.round( event.bytesLoaded / 1000 ).toString()
                        + "k of " + Math.round( event.bytesTotal / 1000 ).toString()
                        + "k";
            }

            // override to ensure display of progress bar during init and download.
            override protected function showDisplayForInit( elapsedTime:int,
                                                    count:int):Boolean
            { return true; }
            override protected function showDisplayForDownloading( elapsedTime:int,
                                                    event:ProgressEvent):Boolean
            { return true; }
        }
    }
```

In this example, the progressHandler event handler defined by DownloadProgressBar is
overridden to display custom text in response to the PROGRESS event dispatched by the
preloader. Modifications to the display area of the label are made as well through the
override of the read-only labelRect. Internally, the label to display textual notifications
is created by the superclass. To assign the DPBSubclass class as the custom preloader
display, set the preloader property value of the <mx:Application> tag by using the fully
qualified class name, as shown:

```
<mx:Application
    xmlns:mx="http://www.adobe.com/2006/mxml"
    layout="vertical"
    preloader="oreilly.cookbook.DPBSubclass">
    <mx:Script>
        <![CDATA[
            // embed large audio file in order to see
            //    the preloader display.
            [Embed(source="assets/audio/audio.mp3")]
            private var _audio:Class;

        ]]>
    </mx:Script>
</mx:Application>
```

You can override the public `preloader` setter method in a subclass of `DownloadProgress Bar` to define your own event handlers if you prefer to handle events with more-granular control when modifying the inherited display elements. But if you want more control over the visual makeup of a custom preloader display, you can create a subclass of `Sprite` that implements the `IPreloaderDisplay` interface.

When creating an instance of `IPreloaderDisplay`, you must define implementations for various properties and methods. The property values related to visual aspects, such as `backgroundColor` and Stage dimensions, are assigned upon instantiation of the custom preloader display by the `Preloader` instance, which then invokes the `initialize` method. The `preloader` property of an `IPreloaderDisplay` instance is the `Preloader` instance for which the implementation should assign event handlers.

The following snippet implements `IPreloaderDisplay` to create a custom download progress bar:

```
package oreilly.cookbook
{
    import flash.display.Shape;
    import flash.display.Sprite;
    import flash.events.Event;
    import flash.events.ProgressEvent;
    import flash.events.TimerEvent;
    import flash.text.TextField;
    import flash.text.TextFormat;
    import flash.utils.Timer;

    import mx.events.FlexEvent;
    import mx.preloaders.IPreloaderDisplay;
    import mx.preloaders.Preloader;

    public class CustomProgress extends Sprite implements IPreloaderDisplay
    {
        private var _bgAlpha:Number;
        private var _bgColor:uint;
        private var _bgImage:Object;
        private var _bgSize:String;
        private var _stageHeight:Number;
        private var _stageWidth:Number;
        private var _preloader:Preloader;

        private var _downloadBar:Shape;
        private var _initBar:Shape;
        private var _initField:TextField;

        public function CustomProgress()
        {
            _initField = new TextField();
            _initField.defaultTextFormat =
                new TextFormat( 'Arial', 12, 0xFFFFFF, true );

            _downloadBar = new Shape();
            addChild( _downloadBar );
```

```
        _initBar = new Shape();
        addChild( _initBar );
    }

    // initialize any properties on display.
    public function initialize():void
    {
        _downloadBar.x = ( _stageWidth / 2 ) - 20;
        _initBar.x = _downloadBar.x - 2;
        _downloadBar.y = ( _stageHeight / 2 ) - 50;
        _initBar.y = _downloadBar.y;
        _initField.x = _initBar.x + 2;
        _initField.y = _initBar.y + 100 - 15;
    }
    // define event handlers of the Preloader instance
    public function set preloader( obj:Sprite ):void
    {
        _preloader = obj as Preloader;
        _preloader.addEventListener( ProgressEvent.PROGRESS,
                                     downloadProgressHandler );
        _preloader.addEventListener( FlexEvent.INIT_PROGRESS,
                                     initProgressHandler );
        _preloader.addEventListener( FlexEvent.INIT_COMPLETE,
                                     initCompleteHandler );
    }

    public function get backgroundAlpha():Number
    {
        return _bgAlpha;
    }
    public function set backgroundAlpha(value:Number):void
    {
        _bgAlpha = value;
    }

    public function get backgroundColor():uint
    {
        return _bgColor;
    }
    public function set backgroundColor(value:uint):void
    {
        _bgColor = value;
    }

    public function get backgroundImage():Object
    {
        return _bgImage;
    }
    public function set backgroundImage(value:Object):void
    {
        _bgImage = value;
    }

    public function get backgroundSize():String
```

```
{
    return _bgSize;
}
public function set backgroundSize(value:String):void
{
    _bgSize = value;
}

public function get stageHeight():Number
{
    return _stageHeight;
}
public function set stageHeight(value:Number):void
{
    _stageHeight = value;
}

public function get stageWidth():Number
{
    return _stageWidth;
}

public function set stageWidth(value:Number):void
{
    _stageWidth = value;
}

// handle SWF file download progress.
private function downloadProgressHandler( evt:ProgressEvent ):void
{
    var perc:Number = ( ( evt.bytesLoaded / evt.bytesTotal ) * 100 );
    var top:Number = 100 - perc;
    _downloadBar.graphics.clear();
    _downloadBar.graphics.beginFill( 0xFF0000, 1 );
    _downloadBar.graphics.moveTo( 0, 0 );
    _downloadBar.graphics.lineTo( 10, 0 );
    _downloadBar.graphics.lineTo( 10, perc * 0.9 );
    _downloadBar.graphics.lineTo( 0, perc * 0.9 );
    _downloadBar.graphics.lineTo( 0, 0 );
    _downloadBar.graphics.endFill();

    _initBar.graphics.clear();
    _initBar.graphics.beginFill( 0xFFFFFF, 1 );
    _initBar.graphics.moveTo( 0, 100 );
    _initBar.graphics.lineTo( 2, 100 );
    _initBar.graphics.lineTo( 2, top );
    _initBar.graphics.lineTo( 0, top );
    _initBar.graphics.lineTo( 0, 100 );
    _initBar.graphics.endFill();
}
// handle application initialization progress.
private function initProgressHandler( evt:FlexEvent ):void
{
    _initField.text = "initializing...";
    addChild( _initField );
```

```
        }
        // handle completion of download and initialization.
        private function initCompleteHandler( evt:FlexEvent ):void
        {
            var timer:Timer = new Timer( 3000, 1 );
            timer.addEventListener( TimerEvent.TIMER_COMPLETE, notifyOfComplete );
            timer.start();
        }
        // notify of completion of download and initialization.
        private function notifyOfComplete( evt:TimerEvent ):void
        {
            dispatchEvent( new Event( Event.COMPLETE ) );
        }
    }
}
```

Custom preloaders need to dispatch a COMPLETE event after receiving an INIT_COMPLETE from the Preloader instance in order to notify the system manager that all operations have been completed and the preloader can be removed from the display. As such, if you override the public preloader setter method in a subclass of DownloadProgressBar or create an implementation of IPreloaderDisplay, be sure to define a handler for the INIT_COMPLETE event and dispatch the COMPLETE event accordingly. In the preceding example, the COMPLETE event is dispatched upon completion of a timer in order for the user to view the initialization display a little longer.

You assign the CustomProgress class as the preloader property value in the <mx:Application> declaration just as you did previously in this recipe. For example:

```
<mx:Application
    xmlns:mx="http://www.adobe.com/2006/mxml"
    layout="vertical"
    preloader="oreilly.cookbook.CustomProgress">
<mx:Script>
    <![CDATA[
        // embed large audio file in order to see
        //    the preloader display.
        [Embed(source="assets/audio/audio.mp3")]
        private var _audio:Class;

    ]]>
</mx:Script>
</mx:Application>
```

You are not limited to using only the drawing API in customizing the download progress bar. You can embed graphical elements, such as an image file or a SWF, to be used in modifying the look and feel of an application preloader as well.

CHAPTER 10

Dragging and Dropping

The drag-and-drop capabilities of the Flex Framework enable you to enhance the Rich Internet Application experience by allowing a user to visually move data from one place to another. Drag-and-drop support can be added to any component that extends the `mx.core.UIComponent` class. Within a drag-and-drop operation, there is an initiator and a receiver. Any instance of a `UIComponent` can accept drop operations initiated by a drag gesture, and some Flex components that are list-based, such as `List`, `Tree` and `Data Grid`, have built-in support for managing a drag-and-drop operation to help automate the process of moving data from one source to another and within the component itself.

A drag-and-drop operation is initiated by a mouse gesture. You select a component or item by clicking the mouse and then drag the item while keeping the mouse button depressed. During the drag gesture, an image referred to as a *drag proxy* is added to the display and follows the movement of the mouse to indicate that the item is being dragged. Along with the drag proxy, built-in icons are displayed to indicate that the cursor is over a component that accepts drop operations. To enable a component to accept drop operations, you set drag-and-drop event handlers on the component. A drop-enabled component is considered a *drop target* and can inspect the drag source data object to determine whether the data is in an acceptable format for the component. The drag source object can be either copied to or moved from one component to another and within the same component—making the component both the *drag initiator* and the *drop target*.

This chapter focuses on the drag-and-drop capabilities of the Flex Framework and how they can enrich the user experience.

10.1 Use the DragManager Class

Problem

You want to move data from one place in an application to another.

Solution

Use the `mx.manager.DragManager` class to manage drag-and-drop operations and listen for drag-and-drop events on a drop target.

Discussion

The `DragManager` class is used to manage drag-and-drop operations performed in your application. When a drag-and-drop operation is initiated, a drag source object is added to the `DragManager` by using the static `doDrag` method. Components that register event listeners for events dispatched by the `DragManager` are considered *drop targets* and can accept the data source object available on the `DragManager`.

The data source object given to the `DragManager` by an initiating component can be moved or copied. The default process for a drag-and-drop operation is to move the data from one place to another, but you can implement your own copy processes as required when manually add drag-and-drop support using the `DragManager`

The following example lets you move a `Box` component within a `Canvas` container:

```
<mx:Application
    xmlns:mx="http://www.adobe.com/2006/mxml"
    layout="horizontal">

    <mx:Script>
        <![CDATA[
            import mx.core.DragSource;
            import mx.core.IUIComponent;
            import mx.events.DragEvent;
            import mx.managers.DragManager;

            private static const FORMAT:String = "box";

            private function mouseDownHandler( evt:MouseEvent ):void
            {
                var initiator:IUIComponent = evt.currentTarget as IUIComponent;
                var dragSource:DragSource = new DragSource();
                dragSource.addData( initiator, FORMAT );

                DragManager.doDrag( initiator, dragSource, evt );
            }
            private function dragEnterHandler( evt:DragEvent ):void
            {
                if( evt.dragSource.hasFormat( FORMAT ) )
                {
                    DragManager.acceptDragDrop( Canvas( evt.currentTarget ) );
                }
            }
            private function dropHandler( evt:DragEvent ):void
            {
                var box:Box = Box( evt.dragInitiator );
                box.x = evt.localX;
                box.y = evt.localY;
```

```
            }

      ]]>
   </mx:Script>

   <mx:Canvas id="canvas"
      backgroundColor="0xEEEEEE"
      width="300" height="300"
      dragEnter="dragEnterHandler(event);"
      dragDrop="dropHandler(event);">
      <mx:Box id="dragItem"
         width="20" height="20"
         backgroundColor="0x00FFCC"
         mouseDown="mouseDownHandler(event);"
         />
   </mx:Canvas>

</mx:Application>
```

When the `mouseDown` event is dispatched from the `<mx:Box>` instance, the `mouseDownHandler` method is invoked and a `DragSource` data object is added to the `DragManager`. The `DragManager.doDrag` method initiates a drag-and-drop operation and requires at least three arguments: the drag initiator item reference, an `mx.core.Drag Source` object, and the `flash.events.MouseEvent` object that invoked the event handler and contains mouse information related to the drag operation. The default image rendered during the drag operation is a rectangle with an alpha transparency. You can change the image (referred to as a *drag proxy*) and its properties within the `doDrag` method, but the default parameter values are used for this example.

By assigning event handlers to the `dragEnter` and `dragDrop` events dispatched from the `DragManager`, the `Canvas` component is considered a drop target for drag-and-drop actions initiated by the `Box` component. Within the `dragEventHandler` method, the drag source data format, originally set in the `doDrag` method, is checked to enable drop actions by using the static `acceptDragDrop` method of the `DragManager` object. The parameter for the `acceptDragDrop` method is the drop target that will respond to drag-and-drop events, such as the `dragDrop` event. The `dropHandler` method of the application responds to a drop action and positions the moved initiator (in this example, the `Box` component) based on the position of the cursor when the mouse button was released.

Though the previous example defaults to moving data from one place to another, you can easily establish processes to copy that data. The following example copies information from the drag-enabled `Box` component to the `DragSource` object, which is used to produce a new `Box` instance to be added to the display of the drop target:

```
<mx:Application
   xmlns:mx="http://www.adobe.com/2006/mxml"
   layout="horizontal">

   <mx:Script>
      <![CDATA[
         import mx.core.DragSource;
```

```
import mx.events.DragEvent;
import mx.managers.DragManager;

private static const FORMAT:String = "box";

private function mouseDownHandler( evt:MouseEvent ):void
{
    var initiator:Box = evt.currentTarget as Box;
    var boxData:Object = new Object();
    boxData.width = initiator.width;
    boxData.height= initiator.height;
    boxData.backgroundColor = initiator.getStyle( "backgroundColor" );
    var dragSource:DragSource = new DragSource();
    dragSource.addData( boxData, FORMAT );

    DragManager.doDrag( initiator, dragSource, evt );
}
private function dragEnterHandler( evt:DragEvent ):void
{
    if( evt.dragSource.hasFormat( FORMAT ) )
    {
        DragManager.acceptDragDrop( Canvas( evt.currentTarget ) );
    }
}
private function dropHandler( evt:DragEvent ):void
{
    var boxData:Object = evt.dragSource.dataForFormat( FORMAT );
    var box:Box = new Box();
    box.width = boxData.width;
    box.height = boxData.height;
    box.setStyle( "backgroundColor", boxData.backgroundColor );
    box.x = evt.localX;
    box.y = evt.localY;
    canvas.addChild( box );
}

        ]]>
    </mx:Script>

    <mx:Canvas id="canvas"
        backgroundColor="0xEEEEEE"
        width="300" height="300"
        dragEnter="dragEnterHandler(event);"
        dragDrop="dropHandler(event);">
        <mx:Box id="dragItem"
            width="20" height="20"
            backgroundColor="0x00FFCC"
            mouseDown="mouseDownHandler(event);"
            />
    </mx:Canvas>

</mx:Application>
```

In the mouseDownHandler event handler method, a custom generic object is created with properties related to the initiating Box component. This object is added to the Drag

Source object and is accessed from the `DragSource.dataForFormat` method within the `dragDrop` event handler for the application. In the `dropHandler` method, a new `Box` component is instantiated with the properties passed within the drag-and-drop operation and is added to the display list of the `Canvas` container.

10.2 Specify a Drag Proxy

Problem

You want to customize the image displayed when a drag operation is initiated.

Solution

Specify a custom image display for the optional `dragImage` parameter of the `DragManager.doDrag` method.

Discussion

By default, the image used during a drag-and-drop operation is a rectangle with alpha transparency. The display object rendered upon initializing a drag operation is referred to as a *drag proxy*. You can change this image by assigning a customized `IFlexDisplayObject` instance as the `dragImage` parameter value. Any component from the Flex Framework can be assigned as a drag proxy because they are extensions of `mx.core.UIComponent`, which implements the `IFlexDisplayObject` interface. Though adding the component as a drag proxy is an easy way to present an accurate representation of the item being dragged, doing so may prevent unnecessary overhead. The `BitmapAsset` class also implements the `IFlexDisplayObject` interface and is a convenient way to grab a bitmap data representation of the visual data you are moving from one place to another in your application.

The following example specifies a `BitmapAsset` as the drag proxy for a drag-and-drop operation:

```
<mx:Application
    xmlns:mx="http://www.adobe.com/2006/mxml"
    layout="horizontal">

    <mx:Script>
        <![CDATA[
            import mx.core.BitmapAsset;
            import mx.core.DragSource;
            import mx.events.DragEvent;
            import mx.managers.DragManager;

            private var xoffset:Number;
            private var yoffset:Number;
            private static const FORMAT:String = "box";

            private function mouseDownHandler( evt:MouseEvent ):void
```

```
        {
            xoffset = evt.localX;
            yoffset = evt.localY;
            var initiator:Box = evt.currentTarget as Box;
            var proxyBox:BitmapAsset = new BitmapAsset();
            proxyBox.bitmapData = new BitmapData( initiator.width,
                                                  initiator.height );
            proxyBox.bitmapData.draw( initiator );
            var dragSource:DragSource = new DragSource();
            dragSource.addData( initiator, FORMAT );

            DragManager.doDrag( initiator, dragSource, evt,
                                proxyBox, 0, 0, 0.5 );
        }
        private function dragEnterHandler( evt:DragEvent ):void
        {
            if( evt.dragSource.hasFormat( FORMAT ) )
            {
                DragManager.acceptDragDrop( Canvas( evt.currentTarget ) );
            }
        }
        private function dropHandler( evt:DragEvent ):void
        {
            var box:Box = Box( evt.dragInitiator );
            box.x = evt.localX - xoffset;
            box.y = evt.localY - yoffset;
        }

    ]]>
</mx:Script>

<mx:Canvas id="canvas"
    backgroundColor="0xEEEEEE"
    width="300" height="300"
    dragEnter="dragEnterHandler(event);"
    dragDrop="dropHandler(event);">
    <mx:Box id="dragItem"
        width="20" height="20"
        backgroundColor="0x00FFCC"
        mouseDown="mouseDownHandler(event);"
        />
</mx:Canvas>

</mx:Application>
```

When the drag operation is initiated and the mouseDownHandler event handler is invoked, a bitmap representation of the drag initiator is drawn to the BitmapData instance of a new BitmapAsset instance. The BitmapAsset instance is supplied as the drag proxy and is rendered as the drag display for the drag-and-drop operation with an alpha transparency of 50 percent. By keeping a class local reference to the mouse-down position when the operation is initiated, the copied Box instance is added to the drop target at an offset equivalent to the local drop position.

You are not limited to setting the drag proxy image as a bitmap representation of the drag initiator component and can also specify a custom embedded graphic to be displayed while transferring data from one part of the application to another.

See Also

Recipe 10.1.

10.3 Drag and Drop Within a List

Problem

You want to move and copy data within the same list-based component instance.

Solution

Use the built-in drag-and-drop management of a list-based component.

Discussion

You can enable drag-and-drop capability to any component by assigning event handlers for events coming from `DragManager`. Though you can manually add this support to list controls, list-based components of the Flex Framework, such as `List`, `Tree`, and `Data Grid`, have built-in support to manage drag-and-drop operations. Along with internally handling events coming from `DragManager`, list-based controls—controls extending the `mx.controls.listClasses.ListBase` class—haveinpublic methods and properties to enable operations and manage data.

The following example displays a list whose items can be moved within its collection by enabling drag-and-drop support via the `dragEnabled` and `dropEnabled` properties:

```
<mx:Application
    xmlns:mx="http://www.adobe.com/2006/mxml"
    layout="horizontal"
    creationComplete="creationHandler();">

<mx:Script>
    <![CDATA[
        import mx.collections.ArrayCollection;

        private function creationHandler():void
        {
            var collection:ArrayCollection =
                new ArrayCollection( ['Josh', 'Todd', 'Abey'] );
            contactList.dataProvider = collection;
        }

    ]]>
</mx:Script>
```

```
<mx:Panel title="Contact List:"
    width="200" height="200">
    <mx:List id="contactList"
        width="100%" height="100%"
        dragEnabled="true"
        dropEnabled="true"
        dragMoveEnabled="true"
        />
</mx:Panel>

</mx:Application>
```

The inline dragEnabled, dropEnabled, and dragMoveEnabled properties of the List control of this example are each declared as true. The dragEnabled and dropEnabled properties in essence allow the component to respond to events coming from the DragManager class. The dragMoveEnabled property is a flag that indicates whether items dragged from the list can be moved or copied into the list. By default, the value is false, enabling copies of the drag source data to be added to the list. By setting the dragMoveEnabled property to true, the item will be removed from its previous index to the index within the list that the mouse cursor was pointing to, when the drop event is completed.

If you enabled copying of data by setting or leaving the default value of the dragMoveEnabled property as false, when a drag-and-drop operation is performed within the List you may see some oddness when selecting items from this example. That is because the classes from the collections API base operations are performed on data using a unique identifier (UID) assigned to items within the collection.

When an item is instructed to be added to the dataProvider of a list-based control, the protected ListBase.copyItemWithUID method is invoked and assigns a unique identifier to the dropped item. However, when the data source is a simple list of String objects —such as the Array source for the ArrayCollection used in this example—the items do not internally qualify to be given a new ID. As such, when you perform any type of selection operation on the List control in this example, you will see that the operation selects the item at the highest index with the UID. In other words, if you were to drag-copy the first item from a list to the fifth elemental index, whenever you go to select that first item again, the list will render the item at the fifth index as the correct selection.

To ensure that copied data will be unique and given a UID when added to the collection, you can add event handlers for the drag-and-drop operations and copy the data as required by your applications. The following example modifies the previous example by assigning an event handler for the dragComplete event dispatched by the List control:

```
<mx:Application
    xmlns:mx="http://www.adobe.com/2006/mxml"
    layout="horizontal"
    creationComplete="creationHandler();">

<mx:Script>
    <![CDATA[
        import mx.utils.ObjectUtil;
```

```
import mx.events.DragEvent;
import mx.collections.ArrayCollection;

private function creationHandler():void
{
    var collection:ArrayCollection =
        new ArrayCollection( ['Josh', 'Todd', 'Abey'] );
    contactList.dataProvider = collection;
}

private function dropHandler( evt:DragEvent ):void
{
    var listItem:Object = evt.dragSource.dataForFormat( "items" );
    var index:int = contactList.calculateDropIndex( evt );
    ArrayCollection( contactList.dataProvider ).setItemAt(
                                ObjectUtil.copy( listItem ), index );
}
        ]]>
    </mx:Script>

    <mx:Panel title="Contact List:"
        width="200" height="200">
        <mx:List id="contactList"
            width="100%" height="100%"
            dragEnabled="true"
            dropEnabled="true"
            dragMoveEnabled="false"
            dragComplete="dropHandler(event);"
            />
    </mx:Panel>

</mx:Application>
```

Setting the dragMoveEnabled property to false enables copy operations, and the List
instance is available to accept new items upon completion of a drag-and-drop gesture.
The dragComplete inline event property registers the dropHandler method as an event
handler for the completion of a drop operation. Within the event handler, the current
item being dragged is retrieved from the DragSource by using the items format, which
is the internal format set when a drag-and-drop operation is initiated. The elemental
index within the list is retrieved from the List.calculateDropIndex method and used
to update the item internally added to the collection. A deep-copy of the item is made
and a new unique identifier is assigned by invoking the ObjectUtil.copy method. Because the data provider is an ArrayCollection object, any updates to elements within
the collection will trigger data binding within the List instance, and changes will be
instantly reflected in the display.

See Also

Recipe 10.1.

10.4 Drag and Drop Between Lists

Problem

You want to drag data from one List control to another List control.

Solution

Use the built-in drag-and-drop management of the List controls and enable each component to accept drag-and-drop operations.

Discussion

The built-in management of drag-and-drop operations for list-based Flex components makes it easy to transfer data from one List control to another by removing the need to manually interface with the DragManager object. By setting the dragEnabled and dropEnabled properties available on a ListBase-derived component, you default to the internal operations of moving and copying the drag source data.

When performing a two-way drag-and-drop between List controls, both controls are enabled to accept drag-and-drop operations. When the drag initiator and drop target are of the same basic type, such as two List controls, the structure of the drag source data object is unimportant in successfully completing the operations, because both controls render data by using the same item renderer type. When enabling one-way and two-way drag-and-drop between list-based controls of different types, such as a List component and a DataGrid component, you do have to take into account how the drag source data is structured because the controls have different item renderers and display data differently.

The following example allows a user to move items from a List component into a DataGrid that displays the full information for the list entry:

```
<mx:Application
    xmlns:mx="http://www.adobe.com/2006/mxml"
    layout="horizontal"
    creationComplete="creationHandler();">

<mx:Script>
    <![CDATA[
        import mx.collections.ArrayCollection;

        private function creationHandler():void
        {
            contactList.dataProvider = new ArrayCollection([
                {label:'Josh Noble', phone:'555.111.2222'},
                {label:'Todd Anderson', phone:'555.333.4444'},
                {label:'Abey George', phone:'555.777.8888'}
                ]);
        }
    ]]>
```

```
        </mx:Script>

        <mx:Panel title="Contact List:"
            width="200" height="200">
            <mx:List id="contactList"
                width="100%" height="100%"
                dragEnabled="true"
                dropEnabled="true"
                dragMoveEnabled="false"
                />
        </mx:Panel>
        <mx:Panel title="Contact Info:"
            width="300" height="200">
            <mx:DataGrid id="contactGrid"
                width="100%" height="100%"
                dragEnabled="true"
                dropEnabled="true"
                dragMoveEnabled="true">
                <mx:columns>
                    <mx:DataGridColumn dataField="label" headerText="Name"/>
                    <mx:DataGridColumn dataField="phone" headerText="Phone"/>
                </mx:columns>
            </mx:DataGrid>
        </mx:Panel>

    </mx:Application>
```

Generic objects with a `label` property and a `phone` property are added to an `ArrayCollection` object. When the `ArrayCollection` is supplied as the `dataProvider` property of the `List` instance, a list of each `label` property is displayed. As items are dragged from the `List` component and dropped onto the `DataGrid`, data is copied over, and `label` and `phone` properties of the drag source object are displayed within the grid.

Because the `dropEnabled` property of both the list-based controls is set to true, this example demonstrates a two-way drag-and-drop system.

See Also

Recipe 10.1.

10.5 Enable and Disable Drag Operations

Problem

You want to enable and disable drag-and-drop operations on list-based components at runtime.

Solution

Use drag-and-drop event properties of a list-based control to manage property values.

Discussion

The list-based components of the Flex Framework have built-in management for interacting with the `DragManager` and provide a convenient way to enable controls to respond to drag-and-drop gestures, by using the `dragEnabled` and `dropEnabled` properties. You set event handlers as you would for any other `UIComponent`-derived application, by using the `dragStart`, `dragEnter`, `dragOver`, `dragExit`, `dragDrop`, and `dragComplete` inline event properties.

To enable a list-based component to receive drag actions, you set the Boolean value of the `dragEnabled` property on the control instance. To enable a list-based component to receive drop actions, you set the Boolean value of the `dropEnabled` property on the control instance. List-based controls can have one-way or two-way drag-and-drop capabilities. In a one-way system, the control instance can either accept drop actions or allow drag actions. In a two-way system, the control allows both drag and drop actions to be performed.

By assigning event handlers for drag-and-drop events dispatched by the `DragManager`, you can manage how your application handles the event and drag source data. The following example creates an event handler for the `dragEnter` event to determine whether to enable or disable drop actions on two `List` controls:

```
<mx:Application
    xmlns:mx="http://www.adobe.com/2006/mxml"
    layout="horizontal"
    creationComplete="creationHandler();">

    <mx:Script>
        <![CDATA[
            import mx.events.DragEvent;
            import mx.collections.ArrayCollection;

            [Bindable]
            public var isEnabled:Boolean = true;
            private static const DIS_LABEL:String =
                        "disable drag and drop";
            private static const EN_LABEL:String =
                        "enable drag and drop";

            private function creationHandler():void
            {
                list1.dataProvider = new ArrayCollection([
                    'Spider Monkey', 'Orangutan',  'Gorilla'
                ]);
                list2.dataProvider = new ArrayCollection([
                    'Lion', 'Cheetah', 'Puma'
                ])
            }

            private function clickHandler():void
            {
                enableBtn.label = ( enableBtn.label == DIS_LABEL )
```

```
                        ? EN_LABEL
                        : DIS_LABEL;
            isEnabled = !isEnabled;
        }

        private function dragEnterHandler( evt:DragEvent ):void
        {
            evt.target.dropEnabled = ( evt.target != evt.dragInitiator );
        }

    ]]>
</mx:Script>

<mx:VBox width="100%" height="100%">
    <mx:Button id="enableBtn"
        label="disable drag and drop"
        click="clickHandler();"
        />
    <mx:HBox width="100%" height="100%">
        <mx:List id="list1"
            width="200" height="200"
            dragEnabled="{isEnabled}"
            dragMoveEnabled="true"
            dragEnter="dragEnterHandler(event);"
            />
        <mx:List id="list2"
            width="200" height="200"
            dragEnabled="{isEnabled}"
            dragMoveEnabled="true"
            dragEnter="dragEnterHandler(event);"
            />
    </mx:HBox>
</mx:VBox>

</mx:Application>
```

Each list allows drag actions to be initiated based on the class-local bindable isEnabled property that is updated within the click event handler for the Button instance. When the lists are enabled to allow drag actions, the dragEnter event is dispatched as an item is selected and the mouse pointer enters the bounds of the component.

By setting the dragMoveEnabled property on a list to true, you are performing a move action when the drop gesture is complete. By default, the value for the dragMoveProperty is false, meaning that when a drag-and-drop operation is complete, the drag source data object will be copied from the drag initiator to the drop target.

To ensure that data is not moved from within a List instance, the dropEnabled property value of each component is updated upon a dragEnter event. The dragEnterHandler event handler checks whether the drop target is the same as the drag initiator and updates the dropEnabled property. To disable drop operations to be performed on a component that initiated the drag gesture, the dropEnabled property is set to false.

See Also

Recipe 10.3 and Recipe 10.4.

10.6 Customize the DragImage of a List-Based Control

Problem

You want to customize the appearance of the drag image when performing drag-and-drop operations within a list-based component.

Solution

Create a custom UIComponent to be displayed during a drag-and-drop gesture and override the protected dragImage getter in a custom List control.

Discussion

The list-based controls of the Flex Framework inherently manage drag-and-drop actions. This means you are not required to set up event listeners for events dispatched by the DragManager. However, because you do not interface with the DragManager directly, the dragImage displayed when performing a drag-and-drop operation in a list-based control is defaulted to display the item renderer with an alpha transparency. You cannot set the drag image as a property of a list-based control as you would manually when using the DragManager.doDrag method.

To customize the image shown during a drag-and-drop gesture for a List control, you will need to create a custom List component that extends the targeted control and overrides the protected dragImage getter property. From that override, you can return a custom drag image that extends the UIComponent class.

The following example is a custom drag image class that extends the UIComponent class and overrides the protected createChildren method to add an image to the drag display:

```
package oreilly.cookbook
{
    import flash.display.Bitmap;
    import flash.display.Loader;
    import flash.display.LoaderInfo;
    import flash.events.Event;
    import flash.net.URLRequest;

    import mx.controls.List;
    import mx.controls.listClasses.IListItemRenderer;
    import mx.core.UIComponent;

    public class CustomDragProxy extends UIComponent
    {
        public function CustomDragProxy()
        {
```

```
        super();
    }

    override protected function createChildren():void
    {
        super.createChildren();

        var list:List = List( owner );
        var items:Array = list.selectedIndices;
        items.sort();

        for( var i:int = 0; i < items.length; i++ )
        {
            var item:Object = list.dataProvider[items[i]];
            var loader:Loader = new Loader();
            loader.contentLoaderInfo.addEventListener( Event.COMPLETE,
                                                       completeHandler );
            addChild( loader );

            loader.load( new URLRequest( item.image ) );

            var source:IListItemRenderer = list.indexToItemRenderer(items[i]);
            loader.x = source.x;
            loader.y = source.y - 20 + ( i * 45 );
        }
    }

    private function completeHandler( evt:Event ):void
    {
        var info:LoaderInfo = LoaderInfo( evt.target );
        var image:Bitmap = Bitmap( info.content );
        image.width = image.height = 40;
    }
  }
}
```

Internally, the protected createChildren method is called upon instantiation of the component. In overriding the createChildren method as this example (saved as CustomDragProxy.as) does, you can customize items to be added to the display list of the component. The component that initiated the creation of this drag image proxy is considered a List control, and the owner property is cast as an instance of the List class. By casting the owner property, properties available on the parent List instance can be accessed and used to modify the display.

Depending on the number of items selected in the List control, Loader instances are added to the display, and an image file is loaded based on the URL supplied for the image property of the item data. After the image is instructed to load, an instance of the item renderer is accessed by using the List.indexToItemRenderer method to position the parent Loader object.

To supply a custom drag image proxy to a list-based control, you need to extend the desired control and override the dragImage getter property. The following example is a custom `List` class that returns a custom drag image proxy when the `dragImage` getter is invoked:

```
package oreilly.cookbook
{
    import mx.controls.List;
    import mx.core.IUIComponent;

    public class CustomList extends List
    {
        public var dragProxy:Class;

        public function CustomList()
        {
            super();
        }

        override protected function get dragImage():IUIComponent
        {
            if( dragProxy == null )
                return super.dragImage;

            var proxy:IUIComponent = new dragProxy();
            proxy.owner = this;
            return proxy
        }
    }
}
```

In this example, when the `dragImage` getter property is accessed, a new drag image proxy is instantiated and returned. If you remember from the preceding example in this recipe, the `CustomDragProxy` class accesses the parent `List` instance by using the inherited `owner` property of the `UIComponent` class. In the `CustomList` class, that `owner` property is set in the `dragImage` override prior to returning the instance of the `dragProxy` class. Set the `dragProxy` property to the fully qualified class name of the drag proxy class that will be instantiated each time the `dragImage` property is accessed.

The following example adds the `CustomList` control to the application and sets the `CustomDragProxy` class as the `dragProxy` property for the custom `List` control:

```
<mx:Application
    xmlns:mx="http://www.adobe.com/2006/mxml"
    xmlns:flexcookbook="oreilly.cookbook.*"
    layout="horizontal"
    creationComplete="creationHandler();">

    <mx:Script>
        <![CDATA[

            import mx.collections.ArrayCollection;

            private function creationHandler():void
            {
                contactList.dataProvider = new ArrayCollection([
```

```
                    {label:'Josh', image:'assets/bigshakey.png'},
                    {label:'Todd', image:'assets/smiley.png'}
                ]);
            }

        ]]>
    </mx:Script>

    <mx:Panel title="Contact List:"
        width="200" height="200">
        <flexcookbook:CustomList id="contactList"
            width="100%" height="100%"
            allowMultipleSelection="true"
            dragEnabled="true"
            dropEnabled="true"
            dragMoveEnabled="true"
            dragProxy="com.oreilly.flexcookbook.CustomDragProxy"
            />
    </mx:Panel>

</mx:Application>
```

The `dataProvider` supplied to the `CustomList` component is an array of objects with a `label` property and an `image` property. The `CustomDragProxy` is declared inline by using the fully qualified class name as the `dragProxy` property value for the list. When a drag gesture is initiated, an instance of `CustomDragProxy` is created and the `image` property associated with the list item data object is used to load the graphic file displayed during the drag-and-drop operation.

See Also

Recipe 10.1, Recipe 10.2, and Recipe 10.3.

10.7 Customize the Drop Indicator of a List-Based Control

Problem

You want to customize the graphic display of the drop indicator in a `List` control shown during drag-and-drop operations.

Solution

Create a custom programmatic skin and set the `dropIndicatorSkin` style property for a `List` control.

Discussion

List-based components of the Flex Framework have default programmatic skins that render the indicator when you perform drag-and-drop operations. When the `List Base.showDropFeedback` method is invoked internally within a list, an instance of the indicator class is created and positions the display one pixel above or to the left of the item renderer, depending on how items are organized within the List control. You can customize the drop indicator by extending the mx.skins.ProgrammaticSkin class and setting the dropIndicatorSkin style property of a component.

The following example is a custom drop indicator that overrides the updateDisplay List method of the ProgrammaticSkin class and uses the drawing API to show an arrow graphic based on the current direction property:

```
package oreilly.cookbook
{
    import mx.skins.ProgrammaticSkin;

    public class CustomDropIndicator extends ProgrammaticSkin
    {
        public var direction:String = "horizontal";

        public function CustomDropIndicator()
        {
            super();
        }

        override protected function updateDisplayList( unscaledWidth:Number,
                                                       unscaledHeight:Number ):void
        {
            super.updateDisplayList( unscaledWidth, unscaledHeight );

            graphics.clear();
            graphics.beginFill( 0x000000 );

            if( direction == "horizontal" )
            {
                graphics.moveTo( 4, -10 );
                graphics.lineTo( 6, -10 );
                graphics.lineTo( 6, -4 );
                graphics.lineTo( 10, -4 );
                graphics.lineTo( 5, 0 );
                graphics.lineTo( 0, -4 );
                graphics.lineTo( 4, -4 );
                graphics.lineTo( 4, -10 );
            }
            else
            {
                graphics.moveTo( 10, 4 );
                graphics.lineTo( 10, 6 );
                graphics.lineTo( 5, 6 );
                graphics.lineTo( 5, 10 );
                graphics.lineTo( 0, 5 );
                graphics.lineTo( 5, 0 );
                graphics.lineTo( 5, 4 );
                graphics.lineTo( 10, 4 );
            }
            graphics.endFill();
        }
```

```
    }
}
```

The `direction` property is based on how the parent `List` control organizes collection items added to display. When the `direction` is set to `horizontal`, a downward-facing arrow is displayed above the item render. When the `direction` property value is not `horizontal`, it is considered vertically oriented and a westward-facing arrow is displayed.

The following application adds a `List` control and a `TileList` control to the display list and sets the `dropIndicatorSkin` property of each component to the custom indicator created in the previous example:

```
<mx:Application
    xmlns:mx="http://www.adobe.com/2006/mxml"
    layout="horizontal"
    creationComplete="creationHandler();">

    <mx:Script>
        <![CDATA[
            import mx.collections.ArrayCollection;

            private function creationHandler():void
            {
                contactList.dataProvider = new ArrayCollection([
                    'Josh', 'Abey', 'Todd'
                ]);
            }

        ]]>
    </mx:Script>

    <mx:List id="contactList"
        width="200" height="200"
        allowMultipleSelection="true"
        dragEnabled="true"
        dropEnabled="true"
        dropIndicatorSkin="com.oreilly.flexcookbook.CustomDropIndicator"
        />
    <mx:TileList id="tileList"
        width="180" height="200"
        dropEnabled="true"
        dropIndicatorSkin="com.oreilly.flexcookbook.CustomDropIndicator"
        />

</mx:Application>
```

When you drag an item from the `List` component over the `TileList`, you will see an arrow pointing to the item renderer instance at the index that the mouse cursor is over during the gesture. When performing a drag gesture over the `List` component, the drag indicator will be an arrow pointing down to the visual index to place the drag source object.

The `dragIndicatorSkin` property is a style property for list-based components and can be set as any other style property that accepts the fully qualified class name of a programmatic skin class to render custom displays.

See Also

Recipe 10.3 and Recipe 10.4.

CHAPTER 11

States

States are a powerful tool that encapsulate a lot of the work of creating *stateful components*, that is, components that have multiple views. These could be controls that need to operate as both an editor and a display, a dialog box with multiple screens, or a component with a menu view and detail view. These multiple views, when contained within a single component, are referred to as *states*. The Flex Framework defines a class called State, contained within the mx.state package, that lets you define the properties of a particular view within a single component. All UIComponents let you add one or more mx.state.State objects to their states array, which enables you to easily add and remove any child components, control styles, and use Effects and Transitions when a State is entered or exited. Frequently, unless there's a real need to create a separate mechanism to store distinct states and what changes those states entail, using x.states.State is a far cleaner and simpler way to implement multiple states or views within a single component.

States can add children to a component that will be removed by the component as soon as the state is exited. You also can define transitions that will play as the current State of a component is changed and apply effects to selected children any time the state property is changed. Any properties of a component that are meant to be temporary or that are relevant only to a certain state of a component can be easily and efficiently implemented in a state.

For developers coming from a Flash background, states can be a somewhat bizarre way of adding and removing children and changing effects. You may feel you need more control over when and how transitions, effects, and display list changes are made. Although sometimes you may require more control, often the judicious use of states will save you time and help you avoid simple mistakes by simplifying the process of adding and removing those components, leaving you with cleaner MXML.

11.1 Set Styles and Properties in a State

Problem

You want to set a style or a property when a certain state is current and then remove that style or property when the state is exited.

Solution

Use the `SetStyle` tag to change any style when the state is entered and automatically revert to the previous style upon exiting the state.

Discussion

The `SetStyle` and `SetProperty` tags allow you to set a style or property attribute, respectively, on any component within scope when a state is entered. When the state is exited, styles or properties set in a state, as well as any children added during that state, are reverted to the base state or all the properties outside all the states.

The `SetStyle` and `SetProperty` tags require a target that possesses the property or style to be set, along with the name and value of that property or style:

```
<mx:SetProperty target="{this}" name="height" value="500"/>
<mx:SetStyle target="{this}" name="backgroundColor" value="#ccccff"/>
```

Here the initial state of the component is set by using the `currentState` property:

```
<mx:VBox xmlns:mx="http://www.adobe.com/2006/mxml" width="400" height="300" currentStat
e="initialState">
```

Any changes made in a state will be undone when the state is exited, including the `initialState`. The following full code listing shows how changing the `currentState` of the component removes any components added in a previous state and adds any components defined in the new `State` being set as the `currentState`:

```
<mx:VBox xmlns:mx="http://www.adobe.com/2006/mxml" width="400" height="300"
currentState="initialState">
    <mx:Script>
        <![CDATA[

            private var i:int = 1;

            private function cycleStates():void
            {
                switch(i){
                    case 0:
                        currentState = "initialState";
                    break;
                    case 1:
                        currentState = "addImg";
                    break;
                    case 2:
```

```
                        currentState = "changeHolderBG";
                    break;
                }
                if(i == 2){i=0;}else{i++;}
            }

        ]]>
    </mx:Script>
    <mx:states>
        <mx:State name="initialState"/>
        <mx:State name="addImg">
            <mx:SetProperty target="{this}" name="height" value="500"/>
            <mx:SetStyle target="{this}" name="backgroundColor" value="#ccccff"/>
            <mx:AddChild relativeTo="{mainHolder}">
                <mx:Image source="../assets/image.jpg"/>
            </mx:AddChild>
        </mx:State>
        <mx:State name="changeHolderBG">
            <mx:SetProperty target="{mainHolder}" name="height" value="500"/>
            <mx:SetStyle target="{this}" name="backgroundColor" value="#ffcccc"/>
            <mx:SetProperty target="{mainHolder}" name="alpha" value="0.5"/>
        </mx:State>
    </mx:states>
    <mx:Button click="cycleStates()" label="change"/>
    <mx:HBox id="mainHolder"/>
</mx:VBox>
```

11.2 Create Transitions to Enter and Leave States

Problem

You want to create effects that play whenever a state is entered or exited.

Solution

Use the Transitions object and set the fromState and toState properties to define when the transition should play.

Discussion

A *transition* is an effect or a series of effects that play when a state is entered. The Transition object is given fromState and toState properties, during which the transition will play. The value of the fromState and toState properties can be either specific states or a wildcard (*) which represents any state.

There are several approaches to creating a Transition object, adding an effect to a component, and then binding an effect property of the Transition to that effect. In the following code snippet, a Transition is defined and its effect is bound to an effect with the id of glow.

```
<mx:Transition id="thirdTrans" fromState="edit" toState="show" effect="{glow}"/>
```

Note that like a State, a Transition object defines actions to be taken. The actions then have their targets assigned, but the targets are not part of the Tansition itself. You can also add SetPropertyStyle or SetPropertyAction to the Transition object to change a style or a property such as height or width on any child of the current component or the current component itself:

```
<mx:Transition id="firstTrans" fromState="show" toState="edit">
        <mx:SetPropertyAction target="{holder}" name="alpha" value="0"/>
    </mx:Transition>
```

Use SetStyleAction any time the Transition will set a style property of its target component:

```
<mx:Transition id="secondTrans" fromState="*" toState="upload">
        <mx:SetStyleAction target="{holder}" name="backgroundColor" value="#ff0000
"/>
    </mx:Transition>
```

The following code creates three States and defines Transition objects for switches between those states:

```
<mx:HBox xmlns:mx="http://www.adobe.com/2006/mxml" width="400" height="300"
currentState="show">
    <mx:Script>
        <![CDATA[

            [Bindable]
            private var _imgURL:String;

            [Bindable]
            private var _title:String;

        ]]>
    </mx:Script>
    <mx:Glow blurXTo="20" blurYTo="20" duration="1000" color="0xffff00" id="glow"
target="{holder}"/>
    <mx:Glow blurXTo="25" blurYTo="25" duration="1000" color="0xffffff" id="fade"
target="{holder}"/>
```

Here multiple Transition objects are defined and their fromState and toState properties set, indicating when the transition will be played. Within those Transition objects, the code defines the changes that will occur when the transition is played:

```
<mx:transitions>
        <mx:Transition id="firstTrans" fromState="show" toState="edit">
            <mx:SetPropertyAction target="{holder}" name="alpha" value="0"/>
        </mx:Transition>
        <mx:Transition id="secondTrans" fromState="*" toState="upload">
            <mx:SetStyleAction target="{holder}" name="backgroundColor" value=
"#ff0000"/>
        </mx:Transition>
        <mx:Transition id="thirdTrans" fromState="edit" toState="show" effect=
"{glow}"/>
        <mx:Transition id="fifthTrans" fromState="upload" toState="*" effect=
"{fade}"/>
```

```
        </mx:transitions>
        <mx:states>
            <mx:State/>
            <mx:State name="show">
                <mx:AddChild relativeTo="{holder}">
                    <mx:HBox>
                        <mx:Label text="{_title}"/>
                        <mx:Image source="{_imgURL}"/>
                    </mx:HBox>
                </mx:AddChild>
            </mx:State>
            <mx:State name="edit" exitState="_title = input.text;">
                <mx:AddChild relativeTo="{holder}">
                    <mx:HBox>
                        <mx:TextInput id="input" text="{_title}"/>
                    </mx:HBox>
                </mx:AddChild>
            </mx:State>
            <mx:State name="upload">
                <mx:AddChild relativeTo="{holder}">
                    <mx:HBox>
                        <mx:Button label="start upload"/>
                    </mx:HBox>
                </mx:AddChild>
            </mx:State>
        </mx:states>
        <mx:ComboBox dataProvider="{['show', 'edit', 'upload']}" change=
"{this.currentState = cb.selectedItem as String}" id="cb"/>
        <mx:Canvas id="holder"/>
    </mx:HBox>
```

11.3 Use the AddChildAction and RemoveChildAction

Problem

You want to control when the children are added and removed in a sequence of effects that play during a transition.

Solution

Use the AddChildAction and RemoveChildAction tags to control when the children are added and removed, respectively, in the Sequence.

Discussion

The AddChildAction and RemoveChildAction objects perform similar functions as the SetPropertyAction and SetPropertyStyle objects, that is, they enable you to take functionality normally encapsulated in the State object and move it to the Transition for integration with the Parallel or Sequence objects that the Transition contains.

Using an `AddChild` object in the `State` by default adds the child as soon as the state is entered. To control the timing of when the child is added or to play certain effects before the child is removed or added, we can use the `AddChildAction` within a sequence instead of the `AddChild` tag in the `State`. For example, this code snippet provides the order of execution to the `Transition` object:

```
<mx:Transition fromState="view" toState="edit">
    <mx:Sequence>
        <mx:Fade alphaFrom="1" alphaTo="0" duration="1000" target="{viewCanvas}"/>
        <mx:RemoveChildAction  target="{viewCanvas}"/>
        <mx:AddChildAction relativeTo="{this}">
            <mx:target>
                <mx:Canvas id="editCanvas" addedToStage="editCanvas.includeInLayout =
true" removedFromStage="editCanvas.includeInLayout = false">
                    <mx:TextInput text="SAMPLE"/>
                </mx:Canvas>
            </mx:target>
        </mx:AddChildAction>
    </mx:Sequence>
</mx:Transition>
```

The example executes the `Fade` effect first, then removes the child, and then adds the new child. If you used `AddChild` within a `State`, the child would be added before the `Fade` effect had finished, which wouldn't work the way the example intends. By using `AddChildAction`, you can control when the child is added.

Note that the `RemoveChild` tag controls *when* the child is removed, but it does not remove the child. The `AddChildAction` mechanism doesn't call its `remove` method automatically. To remove the child, you must add a `RemoveChild` object in the `State` as shown:

```
<mx:State name="edit">
    <mx:RemoveChild target="{viewCanvas}"/>
</mx:State>
```

The full code listing is shown here:

```
<mx:HBox xmlns:mx="http://www.adobe.com/2006/mxml" width="400" height="300"
currentState="view">
    <mx:transitions>
        <mx:Transition fromState="view" toState="edit">
            <mx:Sequence>
                <mx:Fade alphaFrom="1" alphaTo="0" duration="1000" target=
"{viewCanvas}"/>
                <mx:RemoveChildAction  target="{viewCanvas}" effectStart=
"trace('removing')"/>
                <mx:AddChildAction relativeTo="{this}">
                    <mx:target>
                        <mx:Canvas id="editCanvas" addedToStage="editCanvas.
includeInLayout = true" removedFromStage="editCanvas.includeInLayout = false">
                            <mx:TextInput text="SAMPLE"/>
                        </mx:Canvas>
                    </mx:target>
                </mx:AddChildAction>
                <mx:SetPropertyAction target="{editCanvas}" name="includeInLayout"
```

```
        value="true"/>
                        <mx:SetPropertyAction target="{editCanvas}" name="alpha" value="1"/>
                        <mx:Glow color="0xffff00" blurXTo="30" blurYTo="30" blurXFrom="0"
blurYFrom="0" duration="1000" target="{this}"/>
                        <mx:Glow color="0xffff00" blurXTo="30" blurYTo="30" blurXFrom="0"
blurYFrom="0" duration="1000" target="{editCanvas}"/>
                </mx:Sequence>
            </mx:Transition>
            <mx:Transition fromState="edit" toState="view">
                <mx:Sequence>
                        <mx:Fade alphaFrom="1" alphaTo="0" duration="1000" target=
"{editCanvas}"/>
                        <mx:RemoveChildAction target="{editCanvas}"/>
                        <mx:AddChildAction relativeTo="{this}"  effectStart=
"trace('removing')">
                            <mx:target>
                                <mx:Canvas id="viewCanvas" addedToStage="viewCanvas.
includeInLayout = true" removedFromStage="viewCanvas.includeInLayout = false">
                                    <mx:Text text="DIFFERENT TEXT"/>
                                </mx:Canvas>
                            </mx:target>
                        </mx:AddChildAction>
                        <mx:SetPropertyAction target="{viewCanvas}" name="includeInLayout"
value="true"/>
                        <mx:SetPropertyAction target="{viewCanvas}" name="alpha" value="1"/>
                        <mx:Glow color="0xffff00" blurXTo="30" blurYTo="30" blurXFrom="0"
blurYFrom="0" duration="1000" target="{this}"/>
                        <mx:Glow color="0xffff00" blurXTo="30" blurYTo="30" blurXFrom="0"
blurYFrom="0" duration="1000" target="{viewCanvas}"/>
                </mx:Sequence>
            </mx:Transition>
        </mx:transitions>
        <mx:states>
            <mx:State name="view">
                <mx:RemoveChild target="{editCanvas}"/>
            </mx:State>
            <mx:State name="edit">
                <mx:RemoveChild target="{viewCanvas}"/>
            </mx:State>
        </mx:states>
        <mx:ComboBox dataProvider="{['view', 'edit']}" change="currentState =
cb.selectedItem as String" id="cb"/>
</mx:HBox>
```

11.4 Filter Transitions to Affect Only Certain Types of Children

Problem

You want a transition to affect only certain children within the list of targets.

Solution

Use an `EffectTargetFilter` object to define a `filter` function to determine which targets a certain `Effect` within the `Transition` will affect and which it will not.

Discussion

The `EffectTargetFilter` object enables you to define filters to determine which targets the transition will play on. The `EffectTargetFilter` object requires a filter function, much like an array, that returns true or false for each object that the `Transition` is passed. Pass this filter function to the `EffectTargetFilters` `filterFunction` property as shown:

```
filter.filterFunction = func;
private function func(propChanges:Array, instanceTarget:Object):Boolean
{
    if(instanceTarget is HBox)
    {
        return true;
    }
    return false;
}
```

You could add a conditional statement here to determine whether the function will return true if `Sequence` or `Parallel` should be applied to the object. Note that it cannot be effectively applied to individual effects within a `Transition` object. (For more information, see Recipe 11.5.)

Pass the `EffectTargetFilters` object to the `Parallel` or `Sequence` as shown:

```
<mx:Sequence filter="resize" targets="{[one, two, three]}" customFilter="{filter}">
```

When the `Sequence` is invoked, the `customFilter` object returns all objects to be affected by the filter, which means that it is possible to change the filtering function multiple times in the lifetime of a component, if necessary. The full code listing is shown here:

```
<mx:VBox xmlns:mx="http://www.adobe.com/2006/mxml" width="400" height="300"
creationComplete="comp()" xmlns:cookbook="oreilly.cookbook.*">
    <mx:Script>
        <![CDATA[
            import mx.containers.HBox;
            import mx.effects.EffectTargetFilter;

            [Bindable]
            private var filter:EffectTargetFilter;

            private function comp():void {
                filter = new EffectTargetFilter();
                filter.filterFunction = func;
            }

            private function func(propChanges:Array, instanceTarget:Object):Boolean {
                if(instanceTarget is HBox) {
                    return true;
```

```
            }
            return false;
        }

    ]]>
    </mx:Script>
    <mx:transitions>
        <mx:Transition toState="closeState" fromState="openState">
            <mx:Sequence filter="resize" targets="{[one, two, three]}" customFilter=
"{filter}">
                <mx:Move xTo="200" xFrom="0"/>
                <mx:Glow color="0xffff00" blurXTo="20" blurYTo="20"/>
            </mx:Sequence>
        </mx:Transition>
    </mx:transitions>
    <mx:states>
        <mx:State name="closeState"/>
        <mx:State name="openState"/>
    </mx:states>
    <mx:HBox id="one">
        <mx:Text text="one"/>
        <mx:Text text="two"/>
    </mx:HBox>
    <mx:HBox id="two">
        <mx:Text text="one"/>
        <mx:Text text="two"/>
    </mx:HBox>
    <mx:Canvas id="three">
        <mx:Text text="one"/>
        <mx:Text text="two" y="10"/>
    </mx:Canvas>
    <mx:Button click="(currentState == 'openState') ? currentState = 'closeState' :
currentState = 'openState'"/>
</mx:VBox>
```

See Also

Recipe 11.6.

11.5 Apply Parts of a Transition to Certain Children

Problem

You want to apply certain parts of a Transition, Sequence, or Parallel object to only certain children.

Solution

Filter the targets for each effect based on a filtering function that returns an array of all children meeting the criteria.

Discussion

As mentioned in Recipe 11.4, the `EffectTargetFilter` object's filtering can be applied only to an entire sequence or an entire `Parallel Composite` effect. To filter the targets of the individual effects that make up a `Transition`, you must write a custom function to return an array that will be used to set the `targets` property for each effect. Because the effect will have its own targets set independently of the `Transition`'s targets, the filtering function must loop through all the children within the component. This can be a costly operation, and sometimes it may be better to add any children that might be affected by an effect to an independent array.

The filtering function in this example loops through all children of the component, and depending on the parameter passed into the method, returns a list of all the `HBox`es or all the `Canvas` objects that the component contains:

```
private function returnArray(state:*):Array
{
    var arr:Array = new Array();
    var i:int;
    if(state == "foo") {
        for(i = 0; i<this.numChildren; i++) {
            if(getChildAt(i) is HBox) {
                arr.push(getChildAt(i));
            }
        }
    } else {
        for(i = 0; i<this.numChildren; i++) {
            if(getChildAt(i) is Canvas) {
                arr.push(getChildAt(i));
            }
        }
    }
    return arr;
}
```

The effect that invokes this method is as follows:

```
<mx:Move xTo="200" xFrom="0" targets="{returnArray('foo')}"/>
<mx:Glow color="0xffff00" blurXTo="20" blurYTo="20" targets="{returnArray('bar')}"/>
```

Each time the effect is invoked, the array is re-created, meaning that a single `Effect` can affect different types of children based on the `currentState` of the component. This lets you create a single `Effect` and use it in different ways, based on the filtering function that returns all the targets for that `Effect`. The full code listing is shown here:

```
<mx:VBox xmlns:mx="http://www.adobe.com/2006/mxml" width="400" height="300">
    <mx:Script>
        <![CDATA[
            import mx.core.UIComponent;

            [Bindable]
            private function returnArray(state:*):Array
            {
```

```
                        var arr:Array = new Array();
                        var i:int;
                        if(state == "foo") {
                            for(i = 0; i<this.numChildren; i++) {
                                if(getChildAt(i) is HBox) {
                                    arr.push(getChildAt(i));
                                }
                            }
                        } else {
                            for(i = 0; i<this.numChildren; i++) {
                                if(getChildAt(i) is Canvas) {
                                    arr.push(getChildAt(i));
                                }
                            }
                        }
                        return arr;
                    }

                ]]>
            </mx:Script>
            <mx:transitions>
                <mx:Transition toState="closeState" fromState="openState">
                    <mx:Sequence>
                        <mx:Move xTo="200" xFrom="0" targets="{returnArray('foo')}"/>
                        <mx:Glow color="0xffff00" blurXTo="20" blurYTo="20" targets=
"{returnArray('bar')}"/>
                    </mx:Sequence>
                </mx:Transition>
            </mx:transitions>
            <mx:states>
                <mx:State name="closeState"/>
                <mx:State name="openState"/>
            </mx:states>
            <mx:HBox id="one">
                <mx:Text text="one"/>
                <mx:Text text="two"/>
            </mx:HBox>
            <mx:HBox id="two">
                <mx:Text text="one"/>
                <mx:Text text="two"/>
            </mx:HBox>
            <mx:Canvas id="three">
                <mx:Text text="one"/>
                <mx:Text text="two" y="10"/>
            </mx:Canvas>
            <mx:Canvas id="four">
                <mx:Text text="three"/>
                <mx:Text text="four" x="10" y="10"/>
            </mx:Canvas>
            <mx:Button click="(currentState == 'openState') ? currentState =
'closeState': currentState = 'openState'"/>
        </mx:VBox>
```

See Also

Recipe 11.4.

11.6 Base a State on Another State

Problem

You want to create a state that inherits all the properties of another state while overriding only certain properties.

Solution

Use the basedOn property to set a State from which the newly created State will inherit its overrides.

Discussion

Creating states that are based on other states is a convenient way of creating a sort of inheritance among states. When one state is based on another, it simply inherits all the overrides of the first state, and then any additional overrides defined in the new state are added in. This means that if a State defines an AddChild method and then another State is based on that State and defines its own AddChild method, any actions of the original State's AddChild method will be present in the new State, as well as any other overrides present in the new State.

Basing a State on another State is quite simple:

```
<mx:State name="secondaryState2" basedOn="primaryState">
```

In the following example, the secondaryState2 object adds the same child as the primaryState object, and the SetProperty of both methods fires. The SetProperty of secondaryState2 fires last; hence the title will be Third Title, not Super New Title.

```
<mx:Panel xmlns:mx="http://www.adobe.com/2006/mxml" width="400" height="500"
title="Initial Title">
    <mx:states>
        <mx:State name="primaryState">
            <mx:AddChild>
                <mx:VBox>
                    <mx:Text fontSize="18" text="NEW TEXT 1"/>
                    <mx:Text fontSize="18" text="NEW TEXT 2"/>
                </mx:VBox>
            </mx:AddChild>
            <mx:SetProperty target="{this}" name="title" value="'Super New Title'"/>
        </mx:State>
        <mx:State name="secondaryState1">
            <mx:AddChild>
                <mx:RichTextEditor height="300" width="250"/>
            </mx:AddChild>
```

```
        <mx:SetProperty target="{this}" name="title" value="'Lame Old Title'"/>
    </mx:State>
    <mx:State name="secondaryState2" basedOn="primaryState">
        <mx:SetProperty target="{this}" name="title" value="'Third Title'"/>
    </mx:State>
</mx:states>
<mx:ComboBox dataProvider="{['primaryState', 'secondaryState1', 'secondaryState2']
}" change="currentState=cb.selectedItem as String" id="cb"/>
</mx:Panel>
```

11.7 Integrate View States with HistoryManagement

Problem

You must integrate states with the `HistoryManagement` mechanism of the Flex Framework.

Solution

Create an application or component that extends the `IHistoryManagerClient` interface. Using `HistoryManagement`, register the application with the `HistoryManager` when the component is ready. Use the `HistoryManager.save` method to save the current state when changes are made.

Discussion

The `IHistoryManager` client defines the following methods:

`loadState(state:Object):void`
> Loads the state of this object.

`saveState():Object`
> Saves the state of this object.

`toString():String`
> Converts this object to a unique string.

These methods allow the component to properly save to the `State` any information that is needed to restore that `State` later. The `loadState` method loads the `State` information from the URL where it is stored. Here the `saveState` method below the `State` is saved as well as the information currently in the `TextInput`:

```
public function saveState():Object {
    trace(" save state ");
    var state:Object = {};
    state.lastSearch = lastSearch;
    state.currentState = currentState;
    return state;
}
```

The `loadState` method of the component receives and reads the `State` from an object passed from the `HistoryManager` and sets the `currentState` of the component, as shown:

```
public function loadState(state:Object):void {
        if (state) {
            trace(" last search "+state.lastSearch);
            lastSearch = searchInput.text = state.lastSearch;
            currentState = state.currentState;
        }
}
```

The full code listing is shown here:

```
<mx:Application xmlns:mx="http://www.adobe.com/2006/mxml"
    implements="mx.managers.IHistoryManagerClient"
    creationComplete=" HistoryManager.register(this)"
    currentState="search">

<mx:Script>
    <![CDATA[
    import mx.managers.HistoryManager;

    public function loadState(state:Object):void {
        if (state) {
            trace(" last search "+state.lastSearch);
            lastSearch = searchInput.text = state.lastSearch;
            currentState = state.currentState;
        }
    }

    // Save the current state and the searchString value.
    public function saveState():Object {
        trace(" save state ");
        var state:Object = {};
        state.lastSearch = lastSearch;
        state.currentState = currentState;
        return state;
    }

    // The search string value.
    [Bindable]
    public var lastSearch:String;

    public function search():void {
        currentState = "display";
        lastSearch = searchInput.text;
        HistoryManager.save();
    }

    public function reset():void {
        trace(" reset ");
        currentState = 'search';
        searchInput.text = "";
        lastSearch = "";
        HistoryManager.save();
    }
```

```
        ]]>
    </mx:Script>

    <mx:states>
        <mx:State name="display">
            <mx:SetProperty target="{panel}" name="title" value="Results"/>
            <mx:AddChild relativeTo="{panel}">
                <mx:VBox id="results">
                    <mx:Text text="Getting Results"/>
                    <mx:Button label="Reset" click="reset()"/>
                </mx:VBox>
            </mx:AddChild>
        </mx:State>
        <mx:State name="search">
            <mx:SetProperty target="{panel}" name="title" value="Search"/>
            <mx:AddChild relativeTo="{panel}">
                <mx:HBox id="searchFields" defaultButton="{btn}">
                    <mx:TextInput id="searchInput" />
                    <mx:Button id="btn" label="Find" click="search();" />
                </mx:HBox>
            </mx:AddChild>
        </mx:State>
    </mx:states>
    <mx:Panel id="panel" title="Results" resizeEffect="Resize">
    </mx:Panel>
</mx:Application>
```

11.8 Use Deferred Instance Factories with States

Problem

You need an object that can instantiate different types of objects for an AddChild object.

Solution

Create a factory class that can be set in the targetFactory property of an AddChild object.

Discussion

The targetFactory property of the AddChild object requires an object that implements the IDeferredInstance interface. The IDeferredInstance interface requires a single method: getInstance():Object. This method returns the instance of the object that has been created when the AddChild object requests a new display object to be added to the component.

The class presented here is fairly simple, but returns separate types of UIComponents based on the type property:

```
package oreilly.cookbook
{
    import mx.containers.HBox;
    import mx.containers.VBox;
```

```
import mx.controls.Button;
import mx.controls.Text;
import mx.controls.TextInput;
import mx.core.IDeferredInstance;
import mx.core.UIComponent;

public class SpecialDeferredInstance implements IDeferredInstance
{

    private var comp:UIComponent;
    private var _type:String;

    public function set type(str:String):void {
        _type = str;
    }

    public function get type():String{
        return _type;
    }

    public function getInstance():Object
    {
        var text:Object;
        if(_type == "TextVBox"){
            comp = new VBox();
            text = new Text();
            text.text = "TEXT";
            comp.addChild(text as Text);
            var btn:Button = new Button();
            btn.label = "LABEL";
            comp.addChild(btn);
            comp.height = 160;
            comp.width = 320;
        }
        else
        {
            comp = new HBox();
            text = new TextInput();
            text.text = "TEXT";
            comp.addChild(text as TextInput);
            var btn:Button = new Button();
            btn.label = "LABEL";
            comp.addChild(btn);
            comp.height = 160;
            comp.width = 320;
        }
        return comp;
    }

}
}
```

Now that targetFactory is set, the AddChild method can have different types of objects based on the type parameter of the SpecialDeferredInstance object. For example:

```
<mx:VBox xmlns:mx="http://www.adobe.com/2006/mxml" width="400" height="300"
currentState="empty">
    <mx:Script>
        <![CDATA[
            import oreilly.cookbook.SpecialDeferredInstance;
            [Bindable]
            private var defInst:SpecialDeferredInstance = new
SpecialDeferredInstance();
        ]]>
    </mx:Script>
    <mx:states>
        <mx:State name="defInst">
            <mx:AddChild relativeTo="{mainHolder}" targetFactory="{defInst}"/>
        </mx:State>
        <mx:State name="empty"/>
    </mx:states>
    <mx:Button click="currentState == 'defInst' ? currentState = 'empty' :
currentState = 'defInst'" label="change"/>
    <mx:HBox id="mainHolder"/>
</mx:VBox>
```

11.9 Use Data Binding with Objects Added in a State

Problem

You need to bind to a property on an object that will not be created until a certain state
is entered.

Solution

Use the `bindProperty` method of the `mx.binding.utils.BindingUtils` class to dynamically create binding on the property desired.

Discussion

You can create binding at compile time by using the curly-brace notation within
MXML, or you can create it at runtime by using the `bindProperty` method. The `bind
Property` method has the following signature:

```
public static function bindProperty(site:Object, prop:String, host:Object,
chain:Object, commitOnly:Boolean = false):ChangeWatcher
```

The method's parameters are as follows:

site
:   The object that defines the property to be bound to `chain`. If you want to use binding
    to change the `text` of a `TextField`, for example, the `site` would be the `TextField`.

prop
:   The name of the public property defined in the `site` object to be bound. The prop-
    erty will receive the current value of `chain`, when the value of `chain` changes. If you

want to use binding to change the text of a TextField, for example, the prop would be the text.

host

The object that hosts the property or property chain to be watched. If you were binding to the text value of a TextInput, the host would be the TextInput.

chain

A value specifying the property or chain to be watched. The values can be a string containing the name of a public bindable property of the host object. If you were binding to the text value of a TextInput, the chain would be the text.

commitOnly

Set to true if the handler should be called only on committing change events.

Data binding is discussed further in Chapter 14, "Data Binding." This recipe concentrates on using bindProperty to create binding on the newly created RichtTextEditor and binding it to the TextArea:

```
<mx:Panel xmlns:mx="http://www.adobe.com/2006/mxml" width="450" height="650"
title="Initial Title" layout="vertical">
    <mx:Script>
        <![CDATA[
            import mx.binding.utils.*;
        ]]>
    </mx:Script>
    <mx:states>
        <mx:State name="primaryState">
            <mx:AddChild>
                <mx:VBox id="vbox">
                    <mx:Text fontSize="18" text="NEW TEXT 1"/>
                    <mx:Text fontSize="18" text="NEW TEXT 2"/>
                </mx:VBox>
            </mx:AddChild>
            <mx:SetProperty target="{this}" name="title" value="'Super New Title'"/>
        </mx:State>
        <mx:State name="secondaryState1">
            <mx:AddChild>
```

Here the htmlText property of the TextArea is bound to the htmlText value of the newly created RichTextEditor by using the bindProperty method. If you were to try to bind the htmlText property of the TextArea to a control that had not yet been created, an error would be thrown. This technique allows you to bind to newly created controls when they are created:

```
                <mx:RichTextEditor id="richText" height="200" width="250"
creationComplete="BindingUtils.bindProperty(area, 'htmlText', richText, 'htmlText')"/>
            </mx:AddChild>
            <mx:SetProperty target="{this}" name="title" value="'Lame Old Title'"/>
        </mx:State>
        <mx:State name="secondaryState2" basedOn="primaryState">
            <mx:SetProperty target="{this}" name="title" value="'Third Title'"/>
        </mx:State>
    </mx:states>
```

```
    <mx:ComboBox dataProvider="{['primaryState', 'secondaryState1',
 'secondaryState2']}" change="currentState=cb.selectedItem as String" id="cb"/>
        <mx:TextArea height="100" width="450" id="area" htmlText="foo bar baz"/>
    </mx:Panel>
```

11.10 Add and Remove Event Listeners in State Changes

Problem

You need to add event listeners to components that are created and added in state changes and remove the listeners when the state changes.

Solution

Attach the event listeners on the `addedToStage` event of the component and remove them on the `removedFromStage` event. Or, use the `SetEventHandler` object to create an event listener that will be removed when the state is exited.

Discussion

Ensuring that event handlers are properly removed in ActionScript 3 is one of the best ways to ensure that your application won't cause the Flash Player to consume too much memory without releasing it properly. With this in mind, adding event handlers to components should always be accompanied by an organized way to remove those event handlers when the component is destroyed. For example, you can simply add and remove the event handler when the component is added and removed from the stage:

```
<mx:AddChild relativeTo="{holder}">
    <mx:TextInput text="TEXT" id="textInput1" width="200" addedToStage="{textInput1.
addEventListener(TextEvent.TEXT_INPUT, checkNewTextInput)}" removedFromStage="
{textInput2.addEventListener( TextEvent.TEXT_INPUT, checkNewTextInput) }" />
</mx:AddChild>
```

You can achieve the same effect by using the `SetEventHandler` object, which accepts the target that the event handler will be attached to, the name of the event listened for, and the `handlerFunction` that will handle the event when it is dispatched:

```
<mx:SetEventHandler handlerFunction="checkNewTextInput" name="{TextEvent.TEXT_INPUT}"
target="{textInput2}"/>
```

As the user changes the state, the event handler is added and removed. This can be confirmed by changing the name of the event listened to type `Event.ENTER_FRAME` to see exactly when the listener is added and removed. The complete code is listed here:

```
<mx:Canvas xmlns:mx="http://www.adobe.com/2006/mxml" width="400" height="300">
    <mx:Script>
        <![CDATA[

            private function checkNewTextInput(event:Event):void
            {
                trace(" event "+event.target);
```

```
            }

        ]]>
    </mx:Script>
    <mx:states>
        <mx:State id="openState" name="openState">
            <mx:AddChild relativeTo="{holder}">
                <mx:TextInput text="TEXT" id="textInput1" width="200" addedToStage=
"{textInput1.addEventListener(TextEvent.TEXT_INPUT, checkNewTextInput)}"
                    removedFromStage="{textInput2.addEventListener
(TextEvent.TEXT_INPUT, checkNewTextInput)}"/>
            </mx:AddChild>
        </mx:State>
        <mx:State id="closedState" name="closedState">
            <mx:SetEventHandler handlerFunction="checkNewTextInput" name=
"{TextEvent.TEXT_INPUT}" target="{textInput2}"/>
            <mx:AddChild relativeTo="{holder}">
                <mx:TextInput id="textInput2" width="200" text="MORE TEXT"/>
            </mx:AddChild>
        </mx:State>
    </mx:states>
    <mx:VBox id="holder">
        <mx:Button click="(this.currentState == 'openState') ? currentState =
'closedState' : currentState = 'openState'" label="change"/>
    </mx:VBox>
</mx:Canvas>
```

11.11 Add View States to a Flash Component

Problem

You want to use the distinct frames of a Flash component as states when you import
the component from the Flash authoring environment into your Flex application.

Solution

Provide frame labels for frames that you would like to act as states within the `UIMovie`
`Clip` or `ContainerMovieClip` instance that will be used in the Flex application.

Discussion

First, create the class that will be instantiated within your Flex application. This class
has to extend either the `UIMovieClip` class, if it will not have children added to it within
the Flex application, or the `ContainerMovieClip` class, if it will have children added to
it. For example:

```
package{

    import flash.text.TextField;
    import mx.flash.ContainerMovieClip;

    public class FlashAssetClass extends ContainerMovieClip{
```

```
            private var txt:TextField;

            public function FlashAssetClass() {
                    txt = new TextField();
                    addChild(txt);
                    txt.text = "INIT";
                    super();
            }

            override public function set currentState(value:String):void {
                trace(" set current state ");
                super.currentState = value;
                txt.text = value;
            }

            override public function gotoAndStop(frame:Object, scene:String=null):void {
                trace(" go to and stop ");
                txt.text = String(frame);
                super.gotoAndStop(frame, scene);
            }
            }
            }
    }
```

The currentState and gotoAndStop methods are overridden so that both methods will trace when they are changed and will change the TextField that is added to the component. Figure 11-1 shows several distinct Flash movie frames, labeled First, Second, and Third, that will be recognized as the states within the Flex application.

To use the frames of the Flash component, you'll need this MXML code:

```
<mx:Canvas xmlns:mx="http://www.adobe.com/2006/mxml" width="400" height="400"
creationComplete="createComp()">
    <mx:Script>
        <![CDATA[
            import mx.controls.Label;

            import FlashAssetClass;

            private var classInst:FlashAssetClass;

            private function createComp():void {
                classInst = new FlashAssetClass();
                rawChildren.addChild(classInst);
                invalidateDisplayList();
            }

        ]]>
    </mx:Script>
    <mx:Button click="classInst.currentState = 'First';" label="First" y="300"/>
    <mx:Button click="classInst.currentState = 'Second';" label="First" y="330"/>
    <mx:Button click="classInst.currentState = 'Third';" label="First" y="360"/>
</mx:Canvas>
```

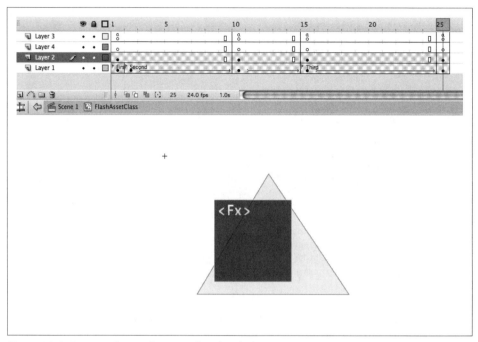

Figure 11-1. *Creating distinct frames within the Flash IDE*

Note that to change the state of the `FlashAssetClass` object, you simply set the `current State`, just as you would with any other component.

When the state is changed, the `ContainerMovieClip` class by default makes a call to the `gotoAndStop` method, stopping the playback of the distinct frames that were created in the Flash IDE. If you want to set the `currentState` to play a specific animation that you've created in the Flash IDE, you can override the `currentState` setter to call the `gotoAndPlay` method, which will not stop the playback of frames and will show the animation created in the Flash IDE. For example:

```
override public function set currentState(value:String):void {
    trace(" set current state ");
    //super.currentState = value;
    gotoAndPlay(value);
    txt.text = value;
}
```

Using the `gotoAndPlay` method requires that calls to the `stop` method of the `ContainerMovieClip` have been added in the correct places so that the playback of frames will be halted; otherwise, the movie will play back to the first frame.

11.12 Work with State Change Events

Problem

You want to understand and use the events associated with the changing of states.

Solution

Attach trace statements to the `ENTER_STATE` events and `CREATION_COMPLETE` of children to show that the children are created when the state is entered and removed from the stage, but not destroyed.

Discussion

The series of events that occur when a state is changed are somewhat complex. The states that the `State` itself broadcasts are mixed in with the `creation`, `addedToStage`, and `removedFromStage` events that the children in the state dispatch. Seeing how they all interrelate gives a very clear overview of how the Flex Framework actually changes the state of a component. The following are the different `Event` types that are dispatched while `State` objects are created, entered, and exited:

`mx.events.StateChangeEvent.CURRENT_STATE_CHANGE`
Dispatched after the view state has changed.

`mx.events.StateChangeEvent.CURRENT_STATE_CHANGING`
Dispatched after the `currentState` property changes, but before the view state changes.

The `State` events are as follows:

`mx.events.FlexEvent.ENTER_STATE`
Dispatched when the view state has been entered. This event is dispatched after the changes to the base view state have been applied.

`mx.events.FlexEvent.EXIT_STATE`
Dispatched before a view state is exited. This event is dispatched before the changes to the base view state have been removed.

The `Child` events are listed here:

`mx.events.FlexEvent.ADD`
Dispatched when the component is added to a container as a content child by using the `addChild` or `addChildAt` method.

`mx.events.FlexEvent.REMOVE`
Dispatched when the component is removed from a container as a content child by using the `removeChild` or `removeChildAt` method.

`mx.events.FlexEvent.PREINITIALIZE`
Dispatched at the beginning of the component initialization sequence.

`mx.events.FlexEvent.INITIALIZE`

Dispatched when the component has finished its construction and has all initialization properties set.

`mx.events.FlexEvent.CREATION_COMPLETE`

Dispatched when the component has finished its construction, property processing, measuring, layout, and drawing.

When a component changes from its base state (the state that the component is in when it is created) to its second state, the sequence of events and creations is as follows:

```
[child] constructor()
[component] CURRENT_STATE_CHANGING;
[child] ADD;
[child] PREINITIALIZE;
[child] createChildren();
[child] INITIALIZE;
[state] ENTER_STATE; (second state)
[component] CURRENT_STATE_CHANGE;
[child] commitProperties();
[child] updateDisplayList();
[child] CREATION_COMPLETE;
```

When a component changes from its second state back to its base state, the order of events and method calls is as follows:

```
[component] CURRENT_STATE_CHANGING;
[state] EXIT_STATE; (second state)
[child] REMOVE;
[component] CURRENT_STATE_CHANGE;
```

Not as much goes on in this change. You do get an `EXIT_STATE` event as the component leaves the second state this time, but no `ENTER_STATE` as it reenters the base state. Notice in the first sequence that although an `ENTER_STATE` event is dispatched as the component enters its second state, a corresponding `EXIT_STATE` as the component's base state is absent. As the component changes back to the second state, you see the following:

```
[component] CURRENT_STATE_CHANGING;
[child] ADD;
[state] ENTER_STATE; (second state)
[component] CURRENT_STATE_CHANGE;
[child] updateDisplayList();
```

It is important to note the differences between the first time the component enters its second state and the second time it enters its second state; the child is not re-created, simply re-added to the parent.

11.13 Dynamically Generate and Use New States and Transitions

Problem

You need to dynamically generate new states and transitions affiliated with those states.

Solution

Create new `State` and `Transition` objects, add their properties, and add them to the states and transitions array that every `UIComponent` object defines.

Discussion

Creating new states and transitions is not done frequently. However, it is useful in certain cases, such as templated components. Because every `UIComponent` object has a states array and transitions array, containing all of the `State` and `Transition` objects for that component, creating new states and transitions simply requires defining the `State` or `Transition` and pushing it into the appropriate array:

```
var state:State = new State();
var button:Button = new Button();
button.label = "LABEL";
var addChild:AddChild = new AddChild(vbox, button);
state.overrides = [addChild];
state.name = "buttonState";
states.push(state);
```

The array of overrides used here is a list of the overrides that the `State` will be using, that is, what functionality it will define. Further properties that the particular `State` object will define, such as any `SetProperty` or `SetStyle` actions, are also added to the overrides array. All the overrides that a `State` defines are objects that implement that `IOverride` interface, and normally include the following:

- `AddChild`
- `RemoveChild`
- `SetEventHandler`
- `SetProperty`
- `SetStyle`

(For more information on the `IOverride` interface, see Recipe 11.15.)

In the full code listing that follows, take note of the methods for creating `Transition` objects and adding properties, specifically the `toState` and `fromState` properties:

```
<mx:VBox xmlns:mx="http://www.adobe.com/2006/mxml" width="400" height="300">
    <mx:Script>
        <![CDATA[
```

```
import mx.controls.Button;
import mx.states.AddChild;
import mx.states.State;
import mx.states.Transition;
import mx.effects.Move;

public function addTransitions():void {
    var transition:Transition = new Transition();
    var move:Move = new Move();
    move.duration=400;
    move.target = vbox;
    transition.fromState = "buttonState";
    transition.toState = "*";
    transition.effect = move;
    transitions.push(transition);
}

public function addState():void {
    var state:State = new State();
    var button:Button = new Button();
    button.label = "LABEL";
    var addChild:AddChild = new AddChild(vbox, button);
    state.overrides = [addChild];
    state.name = "buttonState";
    states.push(state);
}

        ]]>
    </mx:Script>
    <mx:VBox id="vbox"/>
    <mx:Button click="addTransitions()" label="new transition"/>
    <mx:Button click="addState()" label="new state"/>
    <mx:Button click="currentState = 'buttonState'" label="change state"/>
</mx:VBox>
```

See Also

Recipe 11.15.

11.14 Create Custom Actions to Use in a State

Problem

You want to create a custom action to add to the list of overrides that a State object
will call when the state is entered.

Solution

Create a class that implements the IOverride interface and define all the actions that
you would like to pass to the custom action.

Discussion

To implement conditional statements in a state's action, you need to create a custom `IOverride` object that can execute your conditional logic when the state is entered. Any object that implements this interface can be added to the state's overrides array—that is, any component possessing the following methods:

`apply(parent:UIComponent):void`
> This method applies the override, performing the actual action of the override. The value of the parent parameter that will be changed should be stored in this method so that the `remove` method can undo any changes when the state is exited.

`initialize():void`
> This method initializes the override and can be blank.

`remove(parent:UIComponent):void`
> This method is called by the state mechanism when the state to which the `IOverride` has been added is exited. Any values changed in the `apply` method should have been stored so their values can be restored.

In the following example, the `IOverride` interface is implemented by a class called `CustomOverride` ("truth in advertising" always works best when naming classes), and conditional logic is applied to the `apply` statement:

```
package oreilly.cookbook
{
    import flash.display.DisplayObject;

    import mx.core.UIComponent;
    import mx.states.IOverride;

    public class CustomOverride implements IOverride {

        private var widthValue:Number;
        private var _target:DisplayObject;

        public function CustomOverride(target:DisplayObject = null) {
            _target = target;
        }

        public function get target():DisplayObject {
            return _target;
        }

        public function set target(value:DisplayObject):void {
            _target = value;
        }
        //empty
        public function initialize():void {}

        //here we make sure to store the value of the parent before we change it
        //so that we can use this value in the remove method
        public function apply(parent:UIComponent):void {
```

```
            widthValue = _target.width;
            if(_target.width > 500) {
                _target.width = 500;
            }
        }

        //here we use the stored value
        public function remove(parent:UIComponent):void {
            _target.width = widthValue;
        }
    }
}
```

Here the new CustomOverride class is used to change the size of a box. This class should be extended to use multiple targets and potentially to do something more substantial than just change the width of the target, but for demonstration purposes it's sufficient.

```
<mx:states>
    <mx:State name="openState">
        <cookbook:CustomOverride target="{box1}"/>
    </mx:State>
</mx:states>
```

CHAPTER 12

Effects

Effects are an important part of a Flex application and are one of the most important elements of the *Rich* in the popular moniker *Rich Internet Application.* Understanding effects and the effect framework in Flex is important not only for design and implementation, that is, the element effects that the user will see, but also for the aspects that the user will not notice if the effects are implemented correctly, but will certainly notice if the application lags or doesn't perform garbage collection appropriately. At the core of the effects engine is a system of timers and callbacks that are not all that much different conceptually from this:

```
var timer:Timer = new Timer(100, 0);
timer.addEventListener(TimerEvent.TIMER, performEffect);
timer.start();

private function performEffect(event:Event):void {
    //effect implementation
}
```

Of course, the reality of the effect framework is more complex than simply allowing the developer to create an instance of an `Effect` class and call a `play` method on it. In reality, the `EffectManager` class manages all instances of all effects to avoid overtaxing the processor with unnecessary timers and function calls. An effect should be thought of as two distinct elements: the `EffectInstance` (which contains information about the effect, what it should do, and what elements it will affect) and the `Effect` class (which acts as a factory, generating the effect, starting it, and deleting it when it has finished).

The playing of an effect consists of four distinct actions. First, it creates an instance of the `EffectInstance` class for each target component of the effect. That means that an effect that will affect four targets will result in the creation of four `EffectInstance` objects. Second, the framework copies all the configuration information from the factory object to the instance; the duration, number of repetitions, delay time, and so on, are all set as properties of the new instance. Third, the effect is played on the target by using the instance object. Finally, the framework, and in particular the `EffectManager` class, deletes the instance object when the effect completes.

Usually when working with the effects, you as the developer work only with the factory class that handles generating the effect. However, when you begin creating custom effects, you'll create both an `Effect` object that will act as the factory for that effect type, and an `EffectInstance` object that will actually play on the target. Using an effect, whether you're aware of it or not, consists of creating a factory that will generate your instance objects. Any configuration that you do is setting up the factory object, which will then pass those values on to the generated instance object. Look in the framework source, and you'll notice a `Glow` class and a `GlowInstance` class. To create your own effects, you'll create a similar pair of classes.

12.1 Call an Effect in MXML and in ActionScript

Problem

You want to create and call an effect instance in your application.

Solution

To define an effect in MXML, add the `Effect` tag as a top-level tag within your component. To define an effect in ActionScript, import the correct effect class, instantiate an instance of it, assign a `UIComponent` as its target, and call the `play` method to play the effect.

Discussion

The `Effect` class requires a target `UIComponent` to be set. When instantiating an `Effect` in ActionScript, the target can be passed into the `Effect` through the constructor:

```
var blur:Blur = new Blur(component);
```

The target can also be set once the `Effect` has been instantiated by using the **target** property of the `Effect` class. The target is the `UIComponent` that the `Effect` will affect when the `play` method of the `Effect` is called. When an `Effect` is defined in MXML, the target `UIComponent` must be assigned within a binding tag:

```
<mx:Glow id="glowEffect" duration="1000" color="#ff0f0f" target="{glowingTI}"/>
```

In the following example, the `Glow` effect in MXML will be instantiated when the button is clicked:

```
<mx:Button click="glowEffect.play()"/>
```

In the next example, a `Blur` effect in the `applyBlur` method assigns the `glowingTI` as its target through the constructor. After the relevant properties of the `Effect` are set, the `play` method is called.

```
<mx:VBox xmlns:mx="http://www.adobe.com/2006/mxml" width="400" height="600">
    <mx:Script>
        <![CDATA[
```

```
            import mx.effects.Blur;
            private var blur:Blur;
            private function applyBlur():void {
                blur = new Blur(glowingTI);
                blur.blurXFrom = 0;
                blur.blurXTo = 20;//the amount of blur in pixels
                blur.blurYFrom = 0;
                blur.blurYTo = 20;//the amount of blur in pixels
                blur.duration = 1000;
                blur.play();
            }
        ]]>
    </mx:Script>
    <!-- the properties of the Glow effect set here are the color of the Glow and the
length of time that the Glow will be displayed -->
    <mx:Glow id="glowEffect" duration="1000" color="#ff0f0f" target="{glowingTI}"/>
    <mx:TextInput id="glowingTI"/>
    <mx:Button click="applyBlur()" toggle="true" id="glowToggle" label="Play the
BlurEffect"/>
    <mx:Button click="glowEffect.play()" label="Play the Glow Effect"/>
</mx:VBox >
```

12.2 Build a Custom Effect

Problem

You want to build a custom effect that can be used in both MXML and ActionScript.

Solution

Create a class that extends `Effect` and create any custom getters and setters that you
would like to pass to each effect instance when it is created. Then create an instance
class that extends `EffectInstance` and that you will use to actually enact the changes
of your effect.

Discussion

Within the Flex Framework, an effect is made up of two elements: an `Effect` and an
`EffectInstance`. The `Effect` creates the `EffectInstance` and passes its properties on to
them. This division of responsibility allows you to easily create effects that can be played
on multiple targets.

To do so, first define the `TestEffect` class (the factory that will generate the
`EffectInstance` objects), set their properties, and call the `play` method of each instance:

```
package oreilly.cookbook
{
    import mx.effects.Effect;
    import mx.effects.IEffectInstance;
    import mx.events.EffectEvent;
    import oreilly.cookbook.TestInstance;
```

```
public class TestEffect extends Effect
{

    public var color:uint;
    public var alpha:Number;

    public function TestEffect(target:Object=null) {
        // call the base constructor of course
        super(target);
        // set our instance class to the desired instance type
        instanceClass = TestInstance;
    }

    override protected function initInstance(instance:IEffectInstance):void {
        trace(" instance initialized ");
        super.initInstance(instance);
        // now that we've instantiated our instance, we can set its properties
        TestInstance(instance).color = color;
        TestInstance(instance).alpha = alpha;
    }

    override public function getAffectedProperties():Array {
        trace(" return all the target properties ");
        return [];
    }

    override protected function effectEndHandler(event:EffectEvent):void {
        trace(" effect ended ");
    }

    override protected function effectStartHandler(event:EffectEvent):void {
        trace(" effect started ");
    }
    }
}
```

Note that in the preceding code, in the initInstance method, the instance of the
EffectInstance class is created. The TestInstance class is cast to the TestInstance type,
and the properties of the TestInstance are set to the values of the TestEffect factory
class. This enables you to set the properties of each instance of the TestInstance only
once through the TestEffect factory.

The TestInstance class that will be generated by the TestEffect factory is shown here:

```
package oreilly.cookbook
{
    import flash.display.DisplayObject;

    import mx.core.Container;
    import mx.core.FlexShape;
    import mx.core.UIComponent;
    import mx.effects.EffectInstance;

    public class TestInstance extends EffectInstance
```

```
        {
            public var alpha:Number;
            public var color:uint;

            public function TestInstance(target:Object) {
                super(target);
            }

            override public function play():void {
                super.play();
                (target as DisplayObject).alpha = alpha;
                var shape:FlexShape = new FlexShape();
                shape.graphics.beginFill(color, 1.0);
                shape.graphics.drawRect(0, 0, (target as DisplayObject).width, (target as
    DisplayObject).height);
                shape.graphics.endFill();
                var uiComp:UIComponent = new UIComponent();
                uiComp.addChild(shape);
                UIComponent(target).addChild(uiComp);
            }
        }
    }
```

The target property of each TestInstance is set by the TestEffect factory class when the TestInstance is created. This ensures that if multiple targets are passed into the targets property of the Effect class, TestEffect, an instance of the TestInstance, will be created and will play on each target. The color and alpha properties of the TestInstance will set when the instance is created in the initInstance method of the TestEffect.

The overridden play method of the TestInstance class contains the display logic to alter the target UIComponent assigned to the TestInstance.

12.3 Create Parallel Series or Sequences of Effects

Problem

You want to create multiple effects that either play in parallel (at the same time) or play one after another.

Solution

Use the Parallel tag to wrap multiple effects that will play at the same time or use the Sequence tag to wrap multiple effects that will play one after another.

Discussion

The Sequence tag plays the next effect in the sequence when the previous Effect object fires its effectComplete event. Sequences can of course consist of multiple Parallel effect tags, because a `Parallel` tag is treated the same as an `Effect` and possesses the `play` method that the `Sequence` will call when the previous `Effect` or `Parallel` tag has finished playing.

```
<mx:Sequence id=" sequencee" target="{this}">
    <mx:Blur duration="3000" blurXTo="10" blurYTo="10" blurXFrom="0" blurYFrom="0"/>
    <mx:Glow duration="3000" color="#ffff00"/>
</mx:Sequence>
```

The `Parallel` tag works by passing all the target objects, or the targets to each `Effect` or `Sequence` wrapped by the tag, and calling the `play` method on each `Effect` that the `Parallel` tag wraps:

```
<mx:Parallel id=" parallel" targets="{[bar, foo]}">
    <mx:Blur duration="3000" blurXTo="10" blurYTo="10" blurXFrom="0" blurYFrom="0"/>
    <mx:Glow duration="3000" color="#ffff00"/>
</mx:Parallel>
<mx:ComboBox id="bar" dataProvider="{['one', 'two', 'three']}"/>
<mx:ComboBox id="foo" dataProvider="{['one', 'two', 'three']}"/>
```

12.4 Pause, Reverse, and Restart an Effect

Problem

You need to be able to pause an effect while it is running, and then restart the effect from its current position or from the beginning.

Solution

Use the `pause` method to stop the effect so that it can be restarted and use the `resume` method to resume the effect from the location where it was stopped.

Discussion

The `stop` method of the `Effect` class produces the same behavior as the `pause` method: They both stop the effect as it is playing. The `stop` method, however, resets the underlying timer of the effect so the effect cannot be resumed. The `pause` method simply pauses the timer, and hence the effect, enabling you to restart it from the exact point where it paused. An effect can be reversed while it is paused; it cannot be reversed when it is stopped.

You can pause and resume a `Parallel` or a `Sequence` of effects as well. Here's the code you need:

```
<mx:VBoxxmlns:mx="http://www.adobe.com/2006/mxml" width="400" height="300">
    <mx:Parallel id="parallel" target="{this}">
        <mx:Blur duration="3000" blurXTo="10" blurYTo="10" blurXFrom="0" blurYFrom="0"
/>
        <mx:Glow duration="3000" color="#ffff00"/>
    </mx:Parallel>
    <mx:Button click="parallel.play();" label="play()"/>
```

```
    <mx:Button click="parallel.pause();" label="pause()"/>
    <mx:Button click="parallel.reverse()" label="reverse()"/>
    <mx:Button click="parallel.resume()" label="resume ()"/>
</mx:VBox >
```

If the reverse method is called on the Sequence, Parallel, or effect after the pause method has been called, the resume method will need to be called before the effect will begin playing in reverse.

12.5 Create Custom Effect Triggers

Problem

You want to create custom effect triggers for components.

Solution

Use the Effect metadata tag to define the name of the trigger and the event that will play the effect bound to the trigger in the component.

Discussion

A *trigger* defines an event that will play an effect. Triggers are commonly used in the Flex Framework—for instance, to define a mouseDownEffect for a ComboBox component:

```
<mx:ComboBox mouseDownEffect="{glowEffect}"/>
```

When the mouseDown event is dispatched within the ComboBox, the effect that has been bound to the mouseDownEffect property of this ComboBox instance will be played. In this case, the effect called glowEffect will be played. To define a custom trigger name, define an Event with both a name and an event type, and define an Effect with a trigger name and the name of the event that will fire the effect that is bound to the trigger:

```
[Event(name="darken", type="flash.events.Event")]
[Effect(name="darkenEffect", event="darken")]
```

In the preceding code, a trigger named darkenEffect is defined, to which an Effect can be bound. The Effect bound to this trigger will be fired when an Event with the name darken is dispatched by the component. A more complete code example is shown here:

```
<mx:HBoxxmlns:mx="http://www.adobe.com/2006/mxml" width="400" height="300">
    <mx:Metadata>
        [Event(name="darken", type="flash.events.Event")]
        [Effect(name="darkenEffect", event="darken")]

        [Event(name="lighten", type="flash.events.Event")]
        [Effect(name="lightenEffect", event="lighten")]
    </mx:Metadata>
    <mx:Script>
        <![CDATA[
```

```
            import flash.events.Event;

            private function dispatchDarken():void {
                //this will cause whatever Effect is bound
                //to the darkenEffect trigger to play
                dispatchEvent(new Event("darken"));
            }

            private function dispatchLighten():void {
                //this will cause whatever Effect is bound
                //to the lightenEffect trigger to play
                dispatchEvent(new Event("lighten"));
            }

        ]]>
    </mx:Script>
    <mx:Button click="dispatchDarken()" label="darken"/>
    <mx:Button click="dispatchLighten()" label="lighten"/>
</mx:HBox>
```

The above file will be saved as CustomTriggerExample and implemented in the example below using the `<cookbook:CustomTriggerExample>` tag. To implement this component and use the two new triggers, two **Glow** effects are bound to the two triggers:

```
<mx:HBoxxmlns:mx="http://www.adobe.com/2006/mxml" width="400" height="900"
xmlns:cookbook="oreilly.cookbook.*">
    <mx:Glow color="#000000" duration="3000" id="darkenFilter"/>
    <mx:Glow color="#ffffff" duration="3000" id="lightenFilter"/>
    <cookbook:CustomTriggerExample darkenEffect="{darkenFilter}" lightenEffect=
"{lightenFilter}"/>
</mx:HBox>
```

12.6 Create Tween Effects

Problem

You want to create a custom tweening effect that slowly changes its properties over a specified duration.

Solution

Extend the TweenEffect and TweenEffectInstance classes to create a factory object and a class that will be generated by the factory for each target that the effect is passed.

Discussion

The notable difference between an Effect and a TweenEffect is that the TweenEffect takes place over time. The beginning values and ending values of the TweenEffect are passed in to the EffectInstance, which then uses those values over time either to generate the new filter's instances that will be added to the target or to alter properties on the target. These changing values are generated over the duration of the effect by using an `mx.effects.Tween` object within the `TweenInstance` class.

The recipe that follows demonstrates how to build a simple tween effect that slowly fades out the alpha of its target over the duration assigned to the `TweenEffect` class. Tweens, like effects, are built from two classes, in this case: a factory `TweenEffect` class to generate the `TweenInstance`s for each target passed to the `TweenEffect`, and the `TweenInstance` that will create the `Tween` object and use the values that the `Tween` object generates over the duration of the effect.

First, take a look at the `TweenEffect`:

```
package oreilly.cookbook
{
    import mx.effects.TweenEffect;

    public class CustomTweenEffect extends TweenEffect
    {
        public var finalAlpha:Number = 1.0;

        public function CustomTweenEffect (target:Object=null) {
            super(target);
        }

        public function CustomDisplacementEffect(target:Object=null){
            super(target);
            this.instanceClass = CustomTweenInstance;
        }

        //create our new instance
        override protected function initInstance(instance:IEffectInstance):void {
            super.initInstance(instance);
            // now that we've instantiated our instance, we can set its properties
            CustomTweenInstance(instance).finalAlpha = this.finalAlpha;
        }

        override public function getAffectedProperties():Array {
            trace(" return all the target properties ");
            return [];
        }

    }
}
```

The `finalAlpha` property of each `CustomTweenInstance` object passed in to the `initInstance` method is set when the `TweenInstance` is instantiated.

The `CustomTweenInstance` class extends the `TweenEffectInstance` class and overrides the `play` and `onTweenUpdate` methods of that class. The overridden `play` method contains the logic for instantiating the `Tween` object that generates the changing values over the duration of the `TweenEffect`:

```
override public function play():void {
    super.play();
    this.tween = new Tween(this, 0, finalAlpha, duration);
    (target as DisplayObject).alpha = 0;
}
```

The finalAlpha property and the duration property are passed in from the CustomTweenEffect, and mx.effects.Tween will generate a value for each frame of the SWF that moves smoothly from the initial value, in this case 0, to the final value, in this case the finalAlpha variable. Multiple values can be passed to the Tween object in an array if needed, as long as the array of initial values and the array of final values have the same number of elements. The play method of the TweenEffectInstance, called here by super.play, adds an event listener to the Tween for the onTweenUpdate method. By overriding this method, you can add any custom logic to the TweenEffectInstance:

```
override public function onTweenUpdate(value:Object):void {
    (target as DisplayObject).alpha = value as Number;
}
```

Here the alpha property of the target is set to the value returned by the Tween variable, slowly bringing the alpha property of the target to the value of the finalValue variable:

```
package oreilly.cookbook
{
    import flash.display.DisplayObject;
    import mx.effects.effectClasses.TweenEffectInstance;

    public class CustomTweenInstance extends TweenEffectInstance
    {
        public var finalAlpha:Number;

        public function NewTweenInstance(target:Object) {
            super(target);
        }

        override public function play():void {
            super.play();
            this.tween = new Tween(this, 0, finalAlpha, duration);
            (target as DisplayObject).alpha = 0;
        }

        override public function onTweenUpdate(value:Object):void {
            (target as DisplayObject).alpha = value as Number;
        }

    }
}
```

Each time the onTweenUpdate method is called, the value of the alpha is recalculated and updated for the target.

12.7 Use the DisplacementMapFilter Filter in a Flex Effect

Problem

You want to create a tween effect that causes one image to transform into another.

Solution

Extend both the `TweenEffect` and `TweenEffectInstance` classes, creating a `TweenEffect` instance that can have final displacement values passed in to each `TweenEffectInstance` class that it creates. Within the custom `TweenEffectInstance`, create a `DisplacementMapFilter` object and use the Flex Framework's tweening engine to reach the desired displacement values by generating new filters on each `onTweenUpdate` event.

Discussion

The `DisplacementMapFilter` displaces or deforms the pixels of one image by using the pixels of another image to determine the location and amount of the deformation. This is often used to create the impression of an image being underneath another image, as though under a sheet.

The location and amount of displacement applied to a given pixel is determined by the color value of the displacement map image. The constructor of the `DisplacementMap Filter` is as follows:

```
public function DisplacementMapFilter(mapBitmap:BitmapData = null, mapPoint:Point =
null, componentX:uint = 0, componentY:uint = 0, scaleX:Number = 0.0, scaleY:Number
= 0.0, mode:String = "wrap", color:uint = 0, alpha:Number = 0.0)
```

Understanding such a long line of code is often easier when it's broken down piece by piece:

`BitmapData` *(default = null)*
> This is the `BitmapData` object that will be used to displace the image or component that the filter is applied to.

`mapPoint`
> This is the location on the filtered image where the top-left corner of the displacement filter will be applied. You can use this if you want to apply the filter to only part of an image.

`componentX`
> This specifies which color channel of the map image affects the x position of pixels. The `BitmapDataChannel` defines all the valid options as constants with the values `BitmapDataChannel.BLUE` or 4, `BitmapDataChannel.RED` or 1, `BitmapDataChannel.GREEN` or 2, or `BitmapDataChannel.ALPHA` or 8.

componentY

> This specifies which color channel of the map image affects the y position of pixels. The possible values are the same as the componentX values.

scaleX

> This multiplier value specifies how strong the x-axis displacement is.

scaleY

> This multiplier value specifies how strong the y-axis displacement is.

mode

> This is a string that determines what should be done in any empty spaces created by pixels being shifted away. The options, defined as constants in the Displace mentMapFilterMode class, are to display the original pixels (mode = IGNORE), wrap the pixels around from the other side of the image (mode = WRAP, which is the default), use the nearest shifted pixel (mode = CLAMP), or fill in the spaces with a color (mode = COLOR).

The CustomDisplacementEffect instantiates the CustomDisplacementInstance. It's shown here:

```
package oreilly.cookbook
{
    import mx.effects.IEffectInstance;
    import mx.effects.TweenEffect;
    import mx.events.EffectEvent;

    public class CustomDisplacementEffect extends TweenEffect
    {

        public var image:Class;
        public var yToDisplace:Number;
        public var xToDisplace:Number;

        public function CustomDisplacementEffect(target:Object=null)
        {
            super(target);
            this.instanceClass = CustomDisplacementInstance;
        }


        override protected function initInstance(instance:IEffectInstance):void {
            trace(" instance initialized ");
            super.initInstance(instance);
            // now that we've instantiated our instance, we can set its properties
            CustomDisplacementInstance(instance).image = image;
            CustomDisplacementInstance(instance).xToDisplace = this.xToDisplace;
            CustomDisplacementInstance(instance).yToDisplace = this.yToDisplace;
        }

        override public function getAffectedProperties():Array {
            trace(" return all the target properties ");
            return [];
        }
```

```
        }
    }
```

The `CustomDisplacementInstance` handles actually creating the `DisplacementEffect` object that will be applied to the target. The bitmap object, the filter used in the `DisplacementEffect`, and the x and y displacement amounts of the `CustomDisplacementTween` are applied to the instance and passed into the `Displacemen tEffect`.

The `CustomTweenEffect` generates instances of the `CustomDisplacementInstance`, shown here:

```
package oreilly.cookbook
{
    import flash.display.BitmapData;
    import flash.display.BitmapDataChannel;
    import flash.display.DisplayObject;
    import flash.filters.DisplacementMapFilter;
    import flash.filters.DisplacementMapFilterMode;
    import flash.geom.Point;

    import mx.effects.Tween;
    import mx.effects.effectClasses.TweenEffectInstance;

    public class CustomDisplacementInstance extends TweenEffectInstance
    {

        public var image:Class;
        public var xToDisplace:Number;
        public var yToDisplace:Number;
        public var filterMode:String = DisplacementMapFilterMode.WRAP;

        private var filter:DisplacementMapFilter;
        private var img:DisplayObject;
        private var bmd:BitmapData;

        public function CustomDisplacementInstance(target:Object)
        {
            super(target);
        }

        override public function play():void {
            super.play();
            //make our embedded image accessible to use
            img = new image();
            bmd = new BitmapData(img.width, img.height, true);
            //draw the actual byte data into the image
            bmd.draw(img);
```

The new filter is initially created, which will set all the values to the beginning state of the filter:

```
            filter = new DisplacementMapFilter(bmd, new Point(DisplayObject(target).wi
            dth/2 - (img.width/2), DisplayObject(target).height/2 - (img.height/2))),
            BitmapDataChannel.RED, BitmapDataChannel.RED, 0, 0, filterMode, 0.0, 1.0);
```

```
            //copy any filters already exisiting on the target so that we don't
destroy them when we add our new filter
            var targetFilters:Array = (target as DisplayObject).filters;
            targetFilters.push(filter);
            //set the actual filter onto the target
            (target as DisplayObject).filters = targetFilters;
            //create a tween that will begin to generate the next values of each frame
of our effect
                this.tween = new Tween(this, [0, 0], [xToDisplace, yToDisplace],
duration);


            }
```

Much of the heavy work for this class is done in the setDisplacementFilter method.
Because filters are cumulative (they will be applied one atop the other), the previous
DisplacementMapFilter must be removed. This is done by looping through the
filters array of the target, removing any instances of the DisplacementMapFilter. Then
a new filter is created by using the values passed in from the Tween and the filter is
applied to the target. Note that to have the filter be displayed properly, the filter's
Array must be reset. Adding the filter to the Array by using the Array.push method will
not cause the target DisplayObject to be redrawn with the new filter.

```
            private function setDisplacementFilter(displacement:Object):void {
                var filters:Array = target.filters;
            // Remove any existing Displacement filter to ensure that ours is the only one
                var n:int = filters.length;
                for (var i:int = 0; i < n; i++) {
                    if (filters[i] is DisplacementMapFilter)
                        filters.splice(i, 1);
            }
                //create the new filter with the values passed in from the tween
                filter = new DisplacementMapFilter(bmd, new Point(0, 0), BitmapDataChannel
.RED, BitmapDataChannel.RED, displacement[0] as Number, displacement[1] as
Number, filterMode, 0.0, 0);
                //add the filter to the filters on the target
                filters.push(filter);
                target.filters = filters;
            }

            //each time we're ready to update, re-create the displacement map filter
            override public function onTweenUpdate(value:Object):void
            {
                setDisplacementFilter(value);
            }

            //set the filter one last time and then dispatch the tween end event
            override public function onTweenEnd(value:Object):void
            {
                setDisplacementFilter(value);

                    super.onTweenEnd(value);
            }
```

```
        }
    }
```

When the tween is finished, the final values of the `DisplacementMapFilter` are used to set the final appearance of the target `DisplayObject`, and the `onTweenEnd` method of the `TweenEffectInstance` class is called.

12.8 Create an AnimateColor Effect

Contributed by Darron Schall

Problem

You want to smoothly transition from one color to another.

Solution

Use a custom effect, `AnimateColor`, to achieve a smooth color transition between two color values.

Discussion

Using the `AnimateProperty` effect to transition between colors results in a flicker and is problematic because of the nature of color values themselves. The `AnimateProperty` effect smoothly transitions between `fromValue` and `toValue`, but is applicable only when the values are truly numbers. For example, `AnimateProperty` works great to animate moving a component from x location 10 to x location 100.

Colors, on the other hand, aren't really numbers. They're represented by numeric values, such as 0xFFCC33 hex or 16763955 in decimal, but each number is really composed of three separate numbers (*channels*): a red value, a blue value, and a green value. Each of these channels ranges from 0 through 255 (0xFF). Solid red is represented as 0xFF0000, solid green as 0x00FF00, and solid blue as 0x0000FF. Thus, a color value such as 0x990099 is a mixture of part red and part blue.

To smoothly animate a color, you have to look at the parts of the color value individually. For example, if you're transitioning from 0x000000 to 0xFF0000, the transition should apply to only the red channel. `AnimateProperty`, however, sees this as wanting to transition from 0 to 16711680. The number 255 is between those to and from values and will likely show up during the transition, but 255 is the same as 0x0000FF, or solid blue. Thus, solid blue appears during the transition, but again, only the red channel should be animated.

Using this basic understanding, that the animation from one color to another needs to be done on a per-channel basis for the color values, I created a new effect named `AnimateColor`.

You use the `AnimateColor` effect like this:

```
<ds:AnimateColor xmlns:ds="com.darronschall.effects.*"
        id="fadeColor"
        target="{someTarget}"
        property="backgroundColor" isStyle="true"
        fromValue="0xFF0000"
        toValue="0x00FF00"
        duration="4000" />
```

The `AnimateColor` effect calculates the difference between the `fromValue` and `toValue` of each color channel. Each step of the animation, then, generates a new color that takes into account how much each individual channel needs to change. The overall result is a smooth color animation. In the preceding code example, the `backgroundColor` of `someTarget` is changed from solid red to solid blue over 4 seconds, showing a bit of purple during the transition.

12.9 Use the Convolution Filter to Create a Tween

Problem

You want to create a `TweenEffect` to use on an MXML component using the `ConvolutionFilter`.

Solution

Create a `TweenEffectInstance` class that instantiates new `ConvolutionFilter` instances in the `onTweenUpdate` event handler and assign those `ConvolutionFilter` instances to the target `DisplayObject`'s filters array.

Discussion

The `ConvolutionFilter` alters its target `DisplayObject` or `BitmapImage` in a very flexible manner, allowing the creation of effects such as blurring, edge detection, sharpening, embossing, and beveling. Each pixel in the source image is altered according to the values of its surrounding pixels. The alteration to each pixel is determined by the `Matrix` array passed in to the `ConvolutionFilter` in its constructor. The constructor of the `ConvolutionFilter` has the following signature:

```
public function ConvolutionFilter(matrixX:Number = 0, matrixY:Number = 0, matrix:Array
= null, divisor:Number = 1.0, bias:Number = 0.0, preserveAlpha:Boolean = true,
clamp:Boolean = true, color:uint = 0, alpha:Number = 0.0)
```

Take a closer look piece by piece:

matrixX:Number *(default = 0)*
    This is the number of columns in the matrix.

matrixY:Number *(default = 0)*
    This specifies the number of rows in the matrix.

`matrix:Array` *(default = null)*

    This is the array of values used to determine how each pixel will be transformed. The number of items in the array needs to be the same value as `matrixX` * `matrixY`.

`divisor:Number` *(default = 1.0)*

    This specifies the divisor used during matrix transformation and determines how even the `ConvolutionFilter` applies the matrix calculations. If you sum the matrix values, the total will be the divisor value that evenly distributes the color intensity.

`bias:Number` *(default = 0.0)*

    This is the bias to add to the result of the matrix transformation.

`preserveAlpha:Boolean` *(default = true)*

    A value of false indicates that the alpha value is not preserved and that the convolution applies to all channels, including the alpha channel. A value of true indicates that the convolution applies to only the color channels.

`clamp:Boolean` *(default = true)*

    For pixels that are off the source image, a value of true indicates that the input image is extended along each of its borders as necessary by duplicating the color values at the given edge of the input image. A value of false indicates another color should be used, as specified in the color and alpha properties. The default is true.

`color:uint` *(default = 0)*

    This is the hexadecimal color to substitute for pixels that are off the source image.

`alpha:Number` *(default = 0.0)*

    This is the alpha of the substitute color.

The `TweenEffect` class that will make use of `TweenEffectInstance`s that use the `ConvolutionFilter` is very similar to the `TweenEffect` class shown in Recipe 12.8, as you can see:

```
package oreilly.cookbook
{
    import mx.effects.IEffectInstance;
    import mx.effects.TweenEffect;

    public class ConvolutionTween extends TweenEffect
    {
```

The values that will be passed to the each new `EffectInstance` created are set here:

```
        public var toAlpha:Number;
        public var fromAlpha:Number;

        public var toColor:uint;
        public var fromColor:uint;

        public var fromMatrix:Array;
        public var toMatrix:Array;

        public var toDivisor:Number;
        public var fromDivisor:Number;
```

```
        public var toBias:Number;
        public var fromBias:Number;

        public function ConvolutionTween(target:Object=null)
        {
            super(target);
            this.instanceClass = ConvolutionTweenInstance;
        }
```

Each newly created instance of the ConvolutionTweenInstance class has its properties set here:

```
        override protected function initInstance(instance:IEffectInstance):void {
            trace(" instance initialized ");
            super.initInstance(instance);
            // now that we've instantiated our instance, we can set its properties
            ConvolutionTweenInstance(instance).toAlpha = toAlpha;
            ConvolutionTweenInstance(instance).fromAlpha = fromAlpha;

            ConvolutionTweenInstance(instance).toColor = toColor;
            ConvolutionTweenInstance(instance).fromColor = fromColor;

            ConvolutionTweenInstance(instance).fromMatrix = fromMatrix;
            ConvolutionTweenInstance(instance).toMatrix = toMatrix;

            ConvolutionTweenInstance(instance).toDivisor = toDivisor;
            ConvolutionTweenInstance(instance).fromDivisor = fromDivisor;

            ConvolutionTweenInstance(instance).toBias = toBias;
            ConvolutionTweenInstance(instance).fromBias = fromBias;

        }

        override public function getAffectedProperties():Array {
            trace(" return all the target properties ");
            return [];
        }
    }

}
```

The ConvolutionTweenInstance receives its **target** object and values from the ConvolutionTweenEffect factory class:

```
package oreilly.cookbook
{
    import flash.filters.ConvolutionFilter;

    import mx.effects.Tween;
    import mx.effects.effectClasses.TweenEffectInstance;

    public class ConvolutionTweenInstance extends TweenEffectInstance
    {

        private var convolutionFilter:ConvolutionFilter;
```

```
public var toAlpha:Number;
public var fromAlpha:Number;

public var toColor:uint;
public var fromColor:uint;

public var fromMatrix:Array;
public var toMatrix:Array;

public var toDivisor:Number;
public var fromDivisor:Number;

public var toBias:Number;
public var fromBias:Number;

public function ConvolutionTweenInstance(target:Object) {
    super(target);
}
```

In the overridden play method, each from value, representing the initial values of the ConvolutionFilter, and to values, representing the final values of the ConvolutionFilter applied to the target, are passed into a Tween instance. Because the Tween class cannot tween an Array, each value of the Array is tweened and then used to create a new Matrix array, as shown:

```
override public function play():void {

    this.tween = new Tween(this,
        [fromMatrix[0], fromMatrix[1], fromMatrix[2], fromMatrix[3],
fromMatrix[4], fromMatrix[5], fromMatrix[6], fromMatrix[7], fromDivisor,
fromBias, fromAlpha, fromColor],
        [toMatrix[0], toMatrix[1], toMatrix[2], toMatrix[3], toMatrix[4],
toMatrix[5], toMatrix[6], toMatrix[7], , toDivisor, toBias, toAlpha, toColor],
        duration);
    convolutionFilter = new ConvolutionFilter(fromMatrixX, fromMatrixY,
fromMatrix, 1.0, 0, true, true, fromAlpha, fromColor);
    }
```

Each new value from the Tween is passed into onTweenUpdate as an object. Within this object, in a zero-indexed array, is each new value to represent the transition from the initial state to the final state at a given point in time. Because the ConvolutionFilter requires an array, each value in the array is tweened, and then passed into a new array for the matrix parameter of the Convolution filter:

```
override public function onTweenUpdate(value:Object):void {
    //get the filters from the target
    var filters:Array = target.filters;
    // Remove any existing Displacement filter to ensure that ours is the
only one
    var n:int = filters.length;
    for (var i:int = 0; i < n; i++) {
        if (filters[i] is ConvolutionFilter)
            filters.splice(i, 1);
```

```
        }
        //create the new filter
        convolutionFilter = new ConvolutionFilter(3, 3, [value[0], value[1],
    value[2], value[3], value[4], value[5], value[6], value[7]], value[8], value[9]
    true, true, value[10], value[11]);
        //add the filter to the target
        filters.push(convolutionFilter);
        target.filters = filters;


        }
    }
}
```

Note that any ConvolutionFilters applied to the target are removed. If this were not done, the effects of the multiple ConvolutionFilters would cumulatively be applied to the target, producing a much different effect than desired.

CHAPTER 13

Collections

Collections are powerful extensions to ActionScript's indexed array component, the core ActionScript `Array`. Collections add functionality for sorting the contents of an array, maintaining a read position within an array, and creating views that can show a sorted version of the array. Collections also can notify any event listeners that the data they contain has been changed, as well as perform custom logic on any items added to the source array. It is this capability of the collection to notify listeners of data changes that allows data binding, and it is the collection's capability to sort its content that allows `DataGrid` and `List` components to sort and filter their contents. Collections are an integral aspect of working with data-driven controls as well as server-side services returned from a database

The two most commonly used types of collections are the `ArrayCollection` class and the `XMLListCollection` class. The `ArrayCollection` wraps an `Array` element and provides convenience methods for adding and removing items as well as the ability to create a cursor enabling the last read position in the `Array` to be stored easily. The `XMLListCollection` wraps an XML object and provides similar functionality: access to objects via an index, convenience methods for adding new objects, and cursor functionality. The `XMLListCollection` is particularly powerful when dealing with arrays of XML objects and frequently removes the need for parsing XML into arrays of data objects.

13.1 Add, Sort, and Retrieve Data from an ArrayCollection

Problem

You need to push new data into an `ArrayCollection` and retrieve certain items from the same `ArrayCollection`.

Solution

Create a new `ArrayCollection` and use the `addItemAt` or `addItem` method to insert objects into the `ArrayCollection`, the `getItemIndex` or `contains` method to determine whether an item exists in an array, and the sort property of the ArrayCollection to sort the ArrayCollection and retrieve the first or last items determined by a certain field.

Discussion

To see how the various methods of adding, testing, and sorting the items in an Array Collection work, you first need a collection. To create one, use a snippet such as this:

```
<mx:VBox xmlns:mx="http://www.adobe.com/2006/mxml" width="400"
height="300" creationComplete="init()">
    <mx:Script>
        <![CDATA[
            import mx.collections.SortField;
            import mx.collections.Sort;
            import mx.collections.ArrayCollection;

            private var coll:ArrayCollection;

            private function init():void {
                coll =
new ArrayCollection([{name:"Martin Foo", age:25}, {name:"Joe Bar", age:15},
{name:"John Baz", age:23}]);
            }
```

To insert an item into a specific location within the ArrayCollection object's source, use the addItemAt method:

```
private function addItem():void {
    coll.addItemAt({name:"James Fez", age:40}, 0);
}
```

To determine whether a complex object is present in the ArrayCollection, you need to compare the values of the object that will need to be compared. It might be tempting to try something like this:

```
private function checkExistence():void {
    trace(coll.contains({name:nameTI.text, age:Number(ageTI.text)}));
    trace(coll.getItemIndex({name:nameTI.text, age:ageTI.text})); // traces -1 if not
present
}
```

However, this will not work, because the contains and getItemIndex methods compare the pointers of the objects, not their values. Because the objects being compared are two distinct objects, that is, two distinct locations in memory with unique identifiers, the Flash Player does not recognize them as being equal. The getItemIndex method will not return the index of the item or that the ArrayCollection contains the item. To determine whether an item with the same values exists within the collection, you must compare each item in the source Array of the collection. To do so, use a function similar to this:

```
private function checkExistence():int {
    var i:int;
    var arr:Array = coll.souce;
    while(i < arr.length) {
```

```
            if(arr[i].name == nameTI.text && arr[i].age == ageTI.text) {
                return i;
            }
            i++;
        }
        return -1;
    }
```

The Sort object provides a findItem method that performs a similar and more-flexible search through all the objects of an ArrayCollection, via the source property of the ArrayCollection. The findItem method has the following signature:

```
public function findItem(items:Array, values:Object, mode:String,
returnInsertionIndex:Boolean = false, compareFunction:Function = null):int
```

The value parameter can be any object that contains all the properties and required values. The mode String can be Sort.ANY_INDEX_MODE, if you want the index of any instance; Sort.FIRST_INDEX_MODE, if you want the index of the first instance; or Sort.LAST_INDEX_MODE, if you want the index of the last instance. The returnInsertionIndex parameter indicates whether the findItem function should return the position in the sorted array where the item would be placed if an object matching the value parameter were not found. The compareFunction sets a function that the Sort should use to determine whether two items are similar.

To replace the preceding method, you can use the findItem method of the Sort object:

```
private function checkExistence():int {
    var sort:Sort = new Sort();
    return sort.findItem(coll.source, {name:nameTI.text, age:Number(ageTI.text)}, Sort
.ANY_INDEX_MODE);
}
```

To sort the ArrayCollection, create a Sort and pass it an array of SortField objects. These SortField objects contain a string representing the property within each object contained by the ArrayCollection that should be used to determine the sort. To sort on the age property of each object in the collection, create a Sort object and pass it a SortField with its field set to age:

```
private function getOldest():void {
    var sort:Sort = new Sort();
    sort.fields = [new SortField("age", false)];
    coll.sort = sort;
    coll.refresh();
    trace(coll.getItemAt(0).age+" "+coll.getItemAt(0).name);
}
```

This function sorts the ArrayCollection from the lowest age value to the highest age value.

13.2 Filter an ArrayCollection

Problem

You need to filter an `ArrayCollection`, removing any results that don't match the criteria set in the filter.

Solution

Pass a filter function with the signature `function(item:Object):Boolean` to the filter property of the `ArrayCollection`. The filter function will return true if the value should stay in the `ArrayCollection`, and false if the value should be removed.

Discussion

The `filterFunction` property is defined by the `ListCollectionView` class, which the `ArrayCollection` class extends. After a `filterFunction` is passed to any class that extends the `ListCollectionView`, in this case an `ArrayCollection` object, the `refresh` method must be called for the filter to be applied to the `ArrayCollection`.

```
import mx.collections.ArrayCollection;

private var coll:ArrayCollection;

private function init():void {
    coll = new ArrayCollection([{name:"Martin Foo", age:25}, {name:"Joe Bar", age:15},
 {name:"John Baz", age:23}, {name:"Matt Baz", age:21}]);
    coll.filterFunction = filterFunc;
    coll.refresh();
    for(var i:int =  0; i<coll.length; i++) {
        trace(coll.getItemAt(i).name);
    }
}

private function filterFunc(value:Object):Object {
    if(Number(value.age) > 21) {
        return true;
    }
    return false;
}
```

It is important to note that the source array of the `ArrayCollection` will not be altered by the `filterFunction`. In the preceding example, after the `refresh` method is called, the source array will remain 4. The source array will always remain the same, and this allows multiple `filterFunctions` to be passed, which will remove the previous filter and filter the original source array.

13.3 Determine When an Item Is Modified in an ArrayCollection

Problem

You need to determine when an item has been added or removed from an ArrayCollection by an out-of-scope process.

Solution

Listen for an event of type collectionChange or CollectionEvent.COLLECTION_CHANGE dispatched by the ArrayCollection class, which extends EventDispatcher.

Discussion

Any time an object is added to or removed from the collection, a CollectionEvent of type collectionChange is dispatched. When a control is bound to a collection, the binding is notified that the collection has changed through this event. Adding an event listener to the collection to listen for the COLLECTION_CHANGE event lets you write logic to handle any changes to the collection:

```
private var coll:ArrayCollection = new ArrayCollection();
coll.addEventListener(CollectionEvent.COLLECTION_CHANGE, collChangeHandler);
```

The CollectionEvent class defines the following additional properties:

items : Array
> When the event is dispatched in response to items being added to the ArrayCollection, the items property is an array of added items. If items have been removed from the collection, the items array is all the removed items.

kind
> This is a string that indicates the kind of event that occurred. Possible values are add, remove, replace, or move.

location
> This property is the zero-based index in the collection of the item(s) specified in the items property.

oldLocation
> When the kind value is move, this property is the zero-based index in the target collection of the previous location of the item(s) specified by the items property.

Using the CollectionEvent, the state of the ArrayCollection or XMLListCollection before and after a change can be inferred and is very useful when needing to ensure that any changes in the Flex application are updated on a server.

13.4 Create a GroupingCollection

Problem

You need to create distinct groups based on certain properties within the items contained by a collection.

Solution

Pass an `Array` to the constructor of the `GroupingCollection` or set the source of an already instantiated `GroupingCollection` object.

Discussion

Any `GroupingCollection` can have an instance of a `Grouping` object with an appropriate `GroupingField` used to define the property of the data objects that will be used to generate the group. You can use a `GroupingCollection` to group data objects by a property that they all share. To populate a `GroupingCollection` with data objects that all possess a `state` and a `region` property, you could specify the following:

```
var groupingColl:GroupingCollection = new GroupingCollection();
groupingColl.source = [{city:"Columbus", state:"Ohio", region:"East"},
{city:"Cleveland", state:"Ohio", region:"East"}, {city:"Sacramento",
state:"California", region:"West"}, {city:"Atlanta", state:"Georgia",
region:"South"}];
```

To group the objects by their `state` properties, that is, create groupings of all objects that are within the same state, create a `Grouping` instance and pass it an array of `GroupingField` objects:

```
var groupingInst:Grouping = new Grouping();
groupingInst.fields = [new GroupingField("state")];
groupingColl.grouping = groupingInst;
groupingColl.refresh(false);
```

After the `Grouping` instance has been instantiated, set the `grouping` property of the `GroupingCollection` to `groupingInst` and refresh the collection to group all the collection's data objects by the value of their `state` properties:

```
<mx:VBox xmlns:mx="http://www.adobe.com/2006/mxml"
width="400" height="300"
creationComplete="init()">
    <mx:Script>
        <![CDATA[
            import mx.collections.Grouping;
            import mx.collections.GroupingField;

            import mx.collections.GroupingCollection;

            [Bindable]
            private var groupingColl:GroupingCollection;
```

```
                private function init():void {
                    groupingColl = new GroupingCollection();

                    groupingColl.source = [{city:"Columbus", state:"Ohio",
        region:"East"}, {city:"Cleveland", state:"Ohio", region:"East"},
        {city:"Sacramento", state:"California", region:"West"}, {city:"Atlanta",
        state:"Georgia", region:"South"}];
                    var groupingInst:Grouping = new Grouping();
                    groupingInst.fields = [new GroupingField("state")];
                    groupingColl.grouping = groupingInst;
                    groupingColl.refresh(false);
                }
```

After you set the grouping of `GroupingCollection`, setting another grouping overwrites the current grouping when you call the `refresh` method :

```
                private function createRegionGrouping():void {
                    var groupingInst:Grouping = new Grouping();
                        groupingInst.fields = [new GroupingField("region")];
                    groupingColl.grouping = groupingInst;
                    groupingColl.refresh(false);
                }

            ]]>
        </mx:Script>
    <mx:AdvancedDataGrid dataProvider="{groupingColl}">
    <mx:columns>
                <mx:AdvancedDataGridColumn dataField="city"/>
    </mx:columns>
    </mx:AdvancedDataGrid>
        <mx:Button click="createRegionGrouping()"/>
    </mx:VBox>
```

To pass multiple groupings, instead pass multiple `GroupingField` objects to the `Grouping` object's `fields` property:

```
groupingInst.fields = [new GroupingField("region"), new GroupingField("state")];
```

This will group all the data objects first by their regions and then secondarily by their state. This means that for the data set shown in this example, Columbus and Cleveland will be underneath the region and then state, because they are both in the East region and the Ohio state.

13.5 Create a Hierarchical Data Provider for a Control

Problem

You want to use a *flat object* (an object without parent-to-child relationships) that represents hierarchical data as the `dataProvider` for a `DataGrid`.

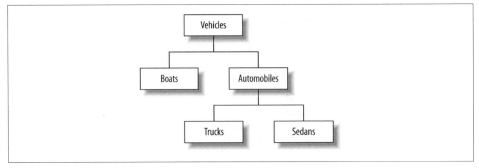

Figure 13-1. An object hierarchy

Solution

Create a custom data class that implements the `IHierarchicalData` interface and create methods to determine whether a node or object in the data has parent nodes and whether it has children nodes.

Discussion

The `IHierarchicalData` interface defines all the methods that the `DataGrid` and `AdvancedDataGrid` components need to display hierarchical data. The term *hierarchical data* refers to data that describes a series of parent-child relationships. For example, imagine a representation of different types of vehicles—cars, trucks, boats—each of which contains more-specific kinds of vehicles. The hierarchy from sedan to the very top might look like Figure 13-1.

One way to represent this data is the following:

```
private var data:Object = [{name:"Vehicles", id:1, parentId:0, type:"parent"},
{name:"Automobiles", id:2, parentId:1, type:"parent"},
{name:"Boats", id:3, parentId:0, type:"parent"},
{name:"Trucks", id:4, parentId:1, type:"parent"},
{name:"Sedans", id:5, parentId:2, type:"parent"}];
```

Here you assign each node an `id` and a `parentId` that defines the parent of that node. This type of data structure can quickly grow unwieldy and is typically quite difficult to represent. An alternative is to use the `IHierarchicaData` interface; with this approach, the `AdvancedDataGrid` can display the data as grouped data, or the `Tree` control can display it as a data tree. The `IHierarchicalData` interface requires that the following methods are defined:

`canHaveChildren(node:Object):Boolean`
> This method determines whether any given node has children.

`dispatchEvent(event:Event):Boolean`
> This method dispatches an event.

`getChildren(node:Object):Object`
> This method returns all the children of a node as an object.

`getData(node:Object):Object`

This method returns all the data of a node, including children, as an object.

`getParent(node:Object):*`

This method returns the parent of any node.

`getRoot():Object`

This method returns the root of an object with hierarchical data.

`hasChildren(node:Object):Boolean`

This method returns true if a node possesses children, and false if it does not.

The `ObjectHierarchicalData` class detailed next implements each of these methods by using the same hierarchical structure shown in Figure 13-1:

```
package oreilly.cookbook
{
    import flash.events.EventDispatcher;
    import mx.collections.IHierarchicalData;

    public class ObjectHierarchicalData extends EventDispatcher implements
IHierarchicalData
    {
        private var source:Object;

        public function ObjectHierarchicalData(value:Object)
        {
            super();
            source = value;
        }

        /* in our simple system, only parents with their type set to
        'parent' can have children; otherwise, they can't have children */
        public function canHaveChildren(node:Object):Boolean
        {
            if (node.type == "parent") {
                return true;
            }
            return false;
        }

        /* for any given node, determine whether a node has any children by
        looking through all the other nodes for that node's ID as a parentTask */
        public function hasChildren(node:Object):Boolean
        {
            trace(node.name);
            var children:Array = new Array();// = source.parentTask == parentId);
            for each(var obj in source) {
                if(obj.parentTask == node.id) {
                    children.push(obj);
                }
            }
            if (children.length > 0)
                return true;

            return false;
```

```
    }

    /* for any given node, return all the nodes that are children of that
    node in an array */
    public function getChildren(node:Object):Object
    {
        var parentId:String = node.id;
        var children:Array = new Array();
        for each(var obj in source) {
            if(obj.parentTask == parentId) {
                children.push(obj);
            }
        }
        return children;
    }

    public function getData(node:Object):Object

    {
        for each(var obj in source) {
            for(var prop in node) {
                if(obj[prop] == node[prop]) {
                    return obj;
                } else {
                    break;
                }
            }
        }
        return null;
    }
    /* we want to return every obj that is a root object
    which, in this case, is going to be all nodes that have a parent node
of '0' */
    public function getRoot():Object
    {
        var rootsArr:Array = new Array();
        for each(var obj in source) {
            if(obj.parentTask == "0") {
                rootsArr.push(obj);
            }
        }
        return rootsArr;
    }

    public function getParent(node:Object):*
    {
        for each(var obj in source) {
            if(obj.parentTask == node.parentTask) {
                return obj;
            }
        }
        return null;
    }

}
```

```
}
```

Now that all the correct methods are in place to determine the relations between all the nodes within the data object, you can set the new hierarchical data class to the `dataProvider` of an `AdvancedDataGrid`. This allows the control to display the correct relationships in hierarchical data. A data object with the relationship between the nodes described through the `parentTask` and `id` properties can be passed in to the new `ObjectHierarchicalData` object:

```
<mx:Canvas xmlns:mx="http://www.adobe.com/2006/mxml" width="400" height="300"
creationComplete="init()">
    <mx:RemoteObject>
    </mx:RemoteObject>
    <mx:Script>
        <![CDATA[

            import mx.collections.*;

            [Bindable]
            private var ohd:ObjectHierarchicalData;
            /* here's the huge object that we're going to use to populate our
ObjectHierarchicalData object */
            private var largeObject:Object =
            [
            { "id":"1", "name":"Misc", "type":"parent", "parentTask":"0"},
            {"id":"2", "name":"Clean the kitchen", "type":"parent", "parentTask":"0"},
             {"id":"3", "name":"Pay the bills", "type":"parent", "parentTask":"0"},
            {"id":"4", "name":"Paint the shed", "type":"parent", "parentTask":"1"},
            {"id":"5", "name":"Get ready for party", "type":"parent",
"parentTask":"1"},
            {"id":"6", "name":"Do the dishes", "type":"child", "parentTask":"2"},
            {"id":"7", "name":"Take out trash", "type":"child", "parentTask":"2"},
            {"id":"8", "name":"Gas Bill", "type":"child", "parentTask":"3"},
            {"id":"9", "name":"Registration", "type":"child", "parentTask":"3"},
            {"id":"10", "name":"Fix the car", "type":"parent", "parentTask":"0"},
            {"id":"11", "name":"New tires", "type":"child", "parentTask":"10"},
            {"id":"12", "name":"Emissions test", "type":"child", "parentTask":"10"},
            {"id":"13", "name":"Get new paint", "type":"child", "parentTask":"4"},
            {"id":"14", "name":"Buy brushes", "type":"child", "parentTask":"4"},
            {"id":"15", "name":"Buy Drinks", "type":"child", "parentTask":"5"},
            {"id":"16", "name":"clean living room", "type":"child", "parentTask":"5"},
            {"id":"16", "name":"finish invitations", "type":"child",
"parentTask":"5"} ];

            private function init():void {

                ohd = new ObjectHierarchicalData(largeObject);
            }

        ]]>
    </mx:Script>
    <mx:AdvancedDataGrid dataProvider="{ohd}" width="300" height="200">
<mx:columns>
            <!-- all we want to display of the object is the name, the ADG will
```

```
                    take care of displaying the parent child relationship -->
               <mx:AdvancedDataGridColumn dataField="name"/>
          </mx:columns>
      </mx:AdvancedDataGrid>
  </mx:Canvas>
```

13.6 Navigate a Collection Object and Save Your Position

Problem

You want to navigate a collection bidirectionally and save the location at which you stop processing.

Solution

Use the `createCursor` method of the `ListViewCollection` class to create a cursor that can be moved ahead and back while maintaining position in the collection so that it can be used later to determine where processing stopped.

Discussion

You use a view cursor to traverse the items in a collection's data view and access and modify data in the collection. A *cursor* is a position indicator; it points to a particular item in the collection. You can use a collection's `createCursor` method to return a view cursor. View cursor methods and properties are defined in the `IViewCursor` interface.

By using the `IViewCursor` methods, you can move the cursor backward and forward, seeking items with certain criteria within the collection, getting the item at a certain location, saving the point of last access in the collection, and adding, removing, or changing the values of items.

When you use the standard Flex collection classes, `ArrayCollection` and `XMLListCollection`, you use the `IViewCursor` interface directly, and you do not reference an object instance. For example:

```
<mx:VBox xmlns:mx="http://www.adobe.com/2006/mxml" width="400" height="300"
creationComplete="init()">
    <mx:Script>
        <![CDATA[
            import mx.collections.SortField;
            import mx.collections.Sort;
            import mx.collections.IViewCursor;
            import mx.collections.CursorBookmark;
            import mx.collections.ArrayCollection;

            [Bindable]
            private var coll:ArrayCollection;

            [Bindable]
            private var cursor:IViewCursor;
```

```
        private function init():void {
            coll = new ArrayCollection([{city:"Columbus", state:"Ohio",
    region:"East"}, {city:"Cleveland", state:"Ohio", region:"East"},
    {city:"Sacramento", state:"California", region:"West"}, {city:"Atlanta",
    state:"Georgia", region:"South"}]);
            cursor = coll.createCursor();
        }
```

In the following example, the `findFirst` method of the `IViewCursor` object is used to locate the first object in the collection that contains any property matching the input entered by the user into the `TextInput` control:

```
        private function findRegion():void {
            var sort:Sort = new Sort();
            sort.fields = [new SortField("region")];
            coll.sort = sort;
            coll.refresh();
            cursor.findFirst({region:regionInput.text});
        }

        private function findState():void {
            var sort:Sort = new Sort();
            sort.fields = [new SortField("state")];
            coll.sort = sort;
            coll.refresh();
            cursor.findFirst({region:stateInput.text});
        }

    ]]>
    </mx:Script>
    <mx:Label text="{cursor.current.city}"/>
    <mx:Button click="cursor.moveNext()" label="Next"/>
    <mx:Button click="cursor.movePrevious()" label="Previous"/>
    <mx:HBox>
        <mx:TextInput id="regionInput"/>
        <mx:Button click="findRegion()" label="find region"/>
    </mx:HBox>
    <mx:HBox>
        <mx:TextInput id="stateInput"/>
        <mx:Button click="findRegion()" label="find state"/>
    </mx:HBox>
</mx:VBox>
```

The `IViewCursor` defines three methods for searching within a collection:

`findFirst(values:Object):Boolean`
: This method sets the cursor location to the first item that meets the criteria.

`findLast(values:Object):Boolean`
: This method sets the cursor to the last item that meets the criteria.

`findAny(values:Object):Boolean`
: This method sets the cursor location to any item that meets the criteria. This is the quickest method and should be used if the first or last item is not needed.

None of these methods will work on an unsorted `ArrayCollection` or `XMLListCollection`.

13.7 Create a HierarchicalViewCollection Object

Problem

You want to create a collection that will let you work with an `IHierarchicalData` object as a collection.

Solution

Create a class that implements the `IHierarchicalData` interface to determine the parent and child nodes of each node. Create a new `HierarchicalViewCollection` object and pass the `IHierarchicalData` object to the constructor of the `HierarchicalViewCollection` class.

Discussion

By default, to work with `HierarchicalData`, the `AdvancedDataGrid` creates a `HierarchicalCollectionView`. This `HierarchicalCollectionView` allows the `AdvancedDataGrid` to retrieve an `ArrayCollection` and apply all those methods to that `HierarchicalData`. This is helpful not only when working with the `AdvancedDataGrid`, but also when working with custom components that will display hierarchical data. The `ObjectHierarchicalData` class from Recipe 13.5 implements `IHierarchicalData` and provides methods to determine the parent or child relationship between different nodes. The `HierarchicalViewCollection` class uses these methods to visually open and close nodes, as well as determine whether a data object contains a certain value. This recipe uses `ObjectHierarchicalData` to create an instance of the `HierarchicalCollectionView`.

The methods of the `HierarchicalViewCollection` are as follows:

`addChild(parent:Object, newChild:Object):Boolean`
Adds a child node to a node of the data.

`addChildAt(parent:Object, newChild:Object, index:int):Boolean`
Adds a child node to a node at the specified index.

`closeNode(node:Object):void`
Closes a node to hide its children.

`contains(item:Object):Boolean`
Checks the collection for the data item to determine whether the item exists within the collection. This means that passing in a complex object with a different location in memory than an object with the same values within the collection won't return true.

```
createCursor():IViewCursor
```
Returns a new instance of a view iterator over the items in this view.

```
getParentItem(node:Object):*
```
Returns the parent of a node.

```
openNode(node:Object):void
```
Opens a node to display its children.

```
removeChild(parent:Object, child:Object):Boolean
```
Removes the child node from the parent node.

```
removeChildAt(parent:Object, index:int):Boolean
```
Removes the child node from a node at the specified index.

Determining which node to manipulate relies on a good implementation of the get Data method of the IHierarchicalData interface. By allowing an object with a key-value pairing to be passed in to the getData method, which then returns the node that contains that same pairing, the HierarchicalViewCollection can determine which object in the source data object to manipulate. Here a large hierarchical data object is defined, passed to a HierarchicalData object, and then a HierarchicalCollectionView is created:

```
var largeObject:Object =
    [{ id:"1", name:"Misc", type:"parent", parentTask:"0"},
    {id:"2", name:"Clean the kitchen", type:"parent", parentTask:"0"},
    {id:"3", name:"Pay the bills", type:"parent", parentTask:"0"},
    {id:"4", name:"Paint the shed", type:"parent", parentTask:"1"},
    {id:"5", name:"Get ready for party", type:"parent", parentTask:"1"},
    {id:"6", name:"Do the dishes", type:"child", parentTask:"2"},
    {id:"7", name:"Take out trash", type:"child", parentTask:"2"},
    {id:"8", name:"Registration", type:"child", parentTask:"3"},
    {id:"9", name:"Fix the car", type:"parent", parentTask:"0"},
    {id:"10", name:"New tires", type:"child", parentTask:"9"},
    {id:"11", name:"Get new paint", type:"child", parentTask:"4"},
    {id:"12", name:"Buy Drinks", type:"child", parentTask:"5"},
    {id:"13", name:"finish invitations", type:"child", parentTask:"5"}];

    /* create a new class that implements the IHierarchicalData interface */
    var dataObj:ObjectHierarchicalData = new ObjectHierarchicalData(largeObject);

    /* pass that class to the HierarchicalCollectionView class*/
    var hCollView:HierarchicalCollectionView = new
HierarchicalCollectionView(dataObj);
    hCollView.openNode(largeObject[2]);

    var ac:ArrayCollection  = hCollView.getChildren( hCollView.source.getData(
    {id:"3"}));
    hCollView.closeNode(hCollView.source.getData({name:"Pay the bills"})
```

The HierarchicalViewCollection wraps the IHierarchicalData view object, providing methods to create views from the objects within the collection by using the getChil dren method.

13.8 Filter and Sort an XMLListCollection

Problem

You need to filter and then sort an XMLListCollection.

Solution

Use the filterFunction and sortFunction properties of the ListViewCollection class that the XMLListCollection extends or simply pass an object of type Sort to the XMLList Collections sort property.

Discussion

The XMLListCollection describes XML data that has multiple nodes contained within the root. For example, a collection of food items contained within a nutrition node will translate into an XMLListCollection that will allow the food nodes to be treated as a collection:

```
<nutrition>
 <food>
    <name>Avocado Dip</name>
    <calories>110</calories>
    <total-fat>11</total-fat>
    <saturated-fat>3</saturated-fat>
    <cholesterol>5</cholesterol>
    <sodium>210</sodium>
    <carb>2</carb>
    <fiber>0</fiber>
    <protein>1</protein>
</food>
...
</nutrition>
```

You filter an XMLListCollection in the same way you filter an ArrayCollection: by passing a reference to a function that accepts an object and returns a Boolean value indicating whether the object should remain in the filtered view. For example:

```
coll.filterFunction = lowCalFilter;
private function lowCalFilter(value:Object):Boolean {
    if(Number(value.calories) < 200) {
        return true;
    }
    return false;
}
```

Sorting an XMLListCollection requires a Sort object with its fields array populated with SortField objects:

```
var sort:Sort = new Sort();
   sort.fields = [new SortField("calories", false, false, true)];
```

```
coll.sort = sort;
coll.refresh();
```

A complete code listing showing an XMLListCollection being built from an HTTPService call, sorted, and then filtered, is shown here:

```
<mx:VBox xmlns:mx="http://www.adobe.com/2006/mxml" width="400" height="300"
creationComplete="xmlService.send()">
    <mx:HTTPService url="assets/data.xml" resultFormat="xml" id="xmlService" result=
"createXMLCollection(event)"/>
    <mx:Script>
        <![CDATA[
            import mx.collections.SortField;
            import mx.collections.Sort;
            import mx.rpc.events.ResultEvent;
            import mx.collections.XMLListCollection;

            [Bindable]
            private var coll:XMLListCollection;

            private function createXMLCollection(event:ResultEvent):void {
                var list:XMLList = new XMLList(event.result);
                coll = new XMLListCollection(list.food);
                var sort:Sort = new Sort();
                sort.fields = [new SortField("calories", false, false, true)];
                coll.sort = sort;
                coll.refresh();
              }

            private function applyFilter():void {
                coll.filterFunction = lowCalFilter;
                coll.refresh();
            }

            private function lowCalFilter(value:Object):Boolean {
                if(Number(value.calories) < 200) {
                    return true;
                }
                return false;
            }

        ]]>
    </mx:Script>
    <mx:DataGrid dataProvider="{coll}">
            <mx:columns>
                    <mx:DataGridColumn dataField="calories"/>
                    <mx:DataGridColumn dataField="name"/>
            </mx:columns>
    </mx:DataGrid>
    <mx:Button click="applyFilter()" label="filter"/>
</mx:VBox>
```

You can perform complex filtering by using E4X statements with various nodes in the XML collection; for example, access attributes by using the @ syntax as shown here:

```
private function lowFatFilter(value:Object):Boolean {
    if(value.calories(@fat) < Number(value.calories)/5) {
        return true;
    }
    return false;
}
```

13.9 Sort on Multiple Fields in a Collection

Problem

You need to sort a collection on multiple fields.

Solution

Pass multiple SortField objects to a Sort object and then set that object to the sort property of the collection.

Discussion

Because arrays can be sorted by multiple SortFields, the fields property of the Sort object is an array. These multiple sorts create a hierarchy of sorting, in which all objects are sorted in groups that match the first SortField object's field property, then the second, and so on. This example code sorts the collection first into regions and then into states:

```
coll = new ArrayCollection{[{city:"Cleveland", state:"Ohio", region:"East"},
{city:"Sacramento", state:"California", region:"West"}, {city:"Atlanta",
state:"Georgia", region:"South"}, {city:"Columbus", state:"Ohio", region:"East"}
]);
var sort:Sort = new Sort();
sort.fields = [new SortField("region"), new SortField("state")];
coll.sort = sort;
coll.refresh();
```

The items in the array collection will now appear as shown in Figure 13-2.

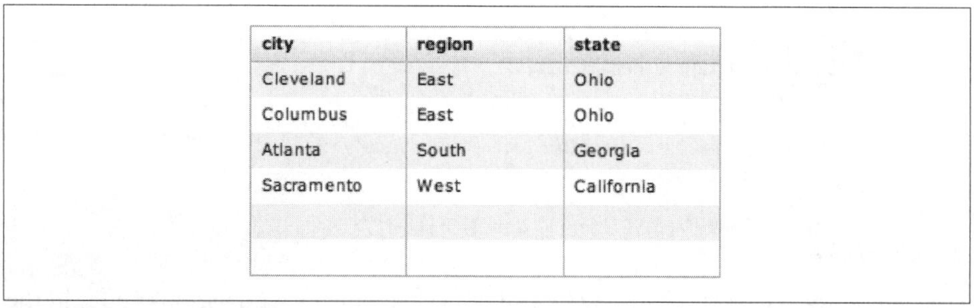

city	region	state
Cleveland	East	Ohio
Columbus	East	Ohio
Atlanta	South	Georgia
Sacramento	West	California

Figure 13-2. Data sorted on multiple fields

13.10 Sort on Dates in a Collection

Problem

You need to sort on the date values that are stored as string properties of data objects.

Solution

Create new Date objects from each date property of the object and use the dateCom pare method of the mx.utils.ObjectUtil class to compare the dates.

Discussion

The ObjectUtil class provides a dateCompare method that can determine which of two Date objects occurs earlier. You can use this to sort a collection of Date objects by creating a sortFunction that returns the result of the ObjectUtil.dateCompare method. The dateCompare method returns a 1, 0, or –1: returning a 0 if values are null or equal; a 1 if the first value is null or located before the second value in the sort; or a –1 if the second value is null or located before first value in the sort.

```
import mx.collections.Sort;
import mx.collections.ArrayCollection;

import mx.utils.ObjectUtil;

//the signature of a sort function must be
//function [name](a:Object, b:Object, fields:Array = null):int
private function sortFunction(a:Object, b:Object, fields:Array = null):int {
    var tempDateA:Date = new Date(Date.parse(a.dob));
    var tempDateB:Date = new Date(Date.parse(b.dob));
    return ObjectUtil.dateCompare(tempDateA, tempDateB);

}

private var arrColl:ArrayCollection;

private function init():void {
    arrColl = new ArrayCollection([{name:"Josh", dob:"08/17/1983"}, {name:"John",
dob:"07/30/1946"}, {name:"John", dob:"07/30/1990"}, {name:"John",
dob:"07/30/1986"}]);
    var sort:Sort = new Sort();
    sort.compareFunction = sortFunction;
    arrColl.sort = sort;
    arrColl.refresh();
    trace(arrColl);
}
```

13.11 Create a Deep Copy of an ArrayCollection

Problem

You need to copy all the items in an indexed array or an object into a new object.

Solution

Use the `mx.utils.ObjectUtil.copy` method.

Discussion

As a quick demonstration shows, copying an object simply creates a pointer to the new object, which means that any changes to the values of the first object are reflected in the second object:

```
var objOne:Object =
{name:"foo", data:{first:"1", second:"2"}};
var objTwo = objOne;
objOne.data.first = "4";
trace(objTwo.data.first);//traces 4
```

To instead copy all of an object into another object, use the `copy` method of the `mx.utils.ObjectUtil` class. The method accepts an object and returns a *deep copy* of that object in a new location in memory. This means that any properties of the object are copied over and no longer refer to the same location as the properties of the original object. To use the method:

```
var objTwo = mx.utils.ObjectUtil.copy(objOne);
```

The `copy` method works by creating a `ByteArray` from the object passed into it, and then writing that `ByteArray` back as a new object, as is shown here:

```
var ba:ByteArray = new ByteArray();
ba.writeObject(objToCopy);
ba.position = 0;
var objToCopyInto:Object = ba.readObject();
return objToCopyInto;
```

Now the original example will behave as expected:

```
var objOne:Object = {name:"foo", data:{first:"1", second:"2"}};
var objTwo = objOne;
var objThree = mx.utils.ObjectUtil.copy(objOne);
objOne.data.first = "4";
trace(objTwo.data.first);//traces 4
trace(objThree.data.first);//traces 1, which is the original value
```

To copy an object of a specific type into a new object of that type presents a special difficulty. The following code will throw an error:

```
var newFoo:Foo = ObjectUtil.copy(oldFoo) as Foo;
```

The Flash Player will not know how to convert the `ByteArray` into the type requested by the cast. By using the `ByteArray`, the object is serialized into ActionScript Message Format (AMF) binary data, the same way that serialized objects are sent in Flash Remoting. To deserialize the data object, the type must be registered with the Flash Player by using the `flash.net.registerClassAlias` method. This method registers the class so that any object of that type can be deserialized from binary data into an object of that type. The `registerClassAlias` method requires two parameters:

```
public function registerClassAlias(aliasName:String, classObject:Class):void
```

The first parameter is the fully qualified class name of the class, and the second is an object of type `Class`. The fully qualified class name will be something like `mx.containers.Canvas` or `com.oreilly.cookbook.Foo`. In the example here, neither the class name nor a reference to the class will be known when the object is copied. Fortunately, the `flash.utils.getQualifiedClass` name returns the fully qualified class name of the object passed to it, and the `flash.utils.getDefinitionByName` returns a reference to the class of the object passed in to it. By using these two methods, you can register the class of any object:

```
private function copyOverObject(objToCopy:Object, registerAlias:Boolean = false):Object
{
        if(registerAlias) {
        var className:String = flash.utils.getQualifiedClassName(objToCopy);
        flash.net.registerClassAlias(className,
(flash.utils.getDefinitionByName(className) as Class));
        }
    return mx.utils.ObjectUtil.copy(objToCopy);
}
```

Now an `ArrayCollection` of strongly typed objects can be correctly copied over by passing each object in the `ArrayCollection` to the `copyOverObject` method:

```
private function copyOverArray(arr:Array):Array {

    var newArray:Array = new Array();
    for(var i:int; i<arr.length; i++) {
    newArray.push(copyOverObject(arr[i], true));
    }
    return newArray;
}
var ac:ArrayCollection = new ArrayCollection([{name:'Joseph', id:21}, foo,
{name:'Josef', id:81}, {name:'Jose', id:214}]);
var newAC:ArrayCollection = new ArrayCollection(copyOverArray(ac.source));
```

Note that all the data contained within the objects of the original `ArrayCollection` will be present in the copied `ArrayCollection` if the two `ArrayCollections` are simply copied by using `mx.utils.ObjectUtil.copy`. However, the class information about each object will not be present, and any attempt to cast an object from the collection to a type will result in an error or a null value.

13.12 Use Data Objects with Unique IDs

Problem

You will have multiple data objects in multiple locations throughout your application, but you need to ensure that all objects are assigned unique `id` properties that can be used to test equality between objects and determine whether they represent the same piece of data.

Solution

Have your data object implement the `IUID` interface and use the `mx.core.UIDUtil.createUID` method to generate a new application-unique `id` for that object.

Discussion

This situation can be especially important when using messaging either via Adobe LiveCycle messaging or other services because objects are compared by reference when using simple equality (the == operator) or complex equality (the === operator). Determining whether two objects represent the same data is frequently done by comparing the properties of all of their fields. With large complex objects, this can drag resources unnecessarily. When you implement the `IUID` interface, however, a class is marked as containing an `id` property that can be compared to determine whether the objects represent the same data. Even if the two objects are deep copies of one another, the `uid` property will remain the same and the objects will be identifiable as representing the same data.

The `id` generated by the `createUID` property of the `UIDUtil` class is a 32-digit hexadecimal number of the following format:

```
E4509FFA-3E61-A17B-E08A-705DA2C25D1C
```

The following example uses the `createUID` method to create a new instance of a `Message` class that implements `IUID`. The get `uid` and set `uid` methods of the `IUID` interface provide access to the object's generated `id`:

```
package {
    import mx.core.IUID;
    import mx.utils.UIDUtil;

    [Bindable]
    public class Message implements IUID {
        public var messageStr:String;
        public var fromID:String;
        private var _uid:String;

        public function Message() {
            _uid = UIDUtil.createUID();
        }
```

```
        public function get uid():String {
            return _uid;
        }

        public function set uid(value:String):void {
            // Since we've already created the id, there's
                //nothing to be done here, but the method is
                //required by the IUID interface
        }
    }
}
```

CHAPTER 14

Data Binding

The Flex Framework provides a robust structure for architecting component-driven applications. Within this powerful framework is an event-based system in which objects can subscribe to updates of property values on other objects by using *data binding*.

Data binding provides a convenient way to pass data between different layers within an application, by linking a source property to a destination property. Changes to properties on a destination object occur after an event is dispatched by the source object to notify all destination objects of an update. With the property on a source object marked as bindable, other objects can subscribe to updates by using a destination property. To enable data binding on a property, you must define the `[Bindable]` metadata tag in one of three ways:

- Before a class definition:

    ```
    package com.oreilly.flexcookbook
    {
        import flash.events.EventDispatcher;

        [Bindable]
        public class DataObject extends EventDispatcher{}
    }
    ```

    Adding a `[Bindable]` tag prior to a class definition establishes a binding expression for all public attributes held on that class. Classes using binding must be an implementation of `IEventDispatcher` because data binding is an event-based notification system to copy source properties to destination properties.

- Before a public, protected, or private variable:

    ```
    [Bindable] private var _lastName:String;
    [Bindable] protected var _age:Number;
    [Bindable] public var firstName:String;
    ```

    Bindable variables marked as `private` are available for binding within that class only. Protected variables are available for data binding to the class in which the variable is declared and any subclasses of that class. Public variables are available for data binding to that class, any subclasses, and any external classes.

- Before the definition of a public, protected, or private attribute using implicit getter/setter methods:

```
private var _lastName:String;
...
[Bindable]
public function get lastName():String
{
    return _lastName;
}
public function set lastName( str:String ):void
{
    _lastName = str;
}
```

When you define implicit getter/setter methods as bindable, by adding the [Bindable] metadata tag above the getter declaration, the property can be bound to using dot-notation syntax. This allows you to use the same syntax you would use to access a non-bound variable, `Owner.property` for example, to set the source of data binding.

Internally, bindable properties held on objects within the Framework dispatch a `propertyChange` event when their values are updated. The [Bindable] metadata tag accepts an `event` attribute that you can define with a custom event type:

```
[Bindable(event="myValueChanged")]
```

By default, the `event` attribute is set as `propertyChange`. If the `event` attribute is left as the default, destination properties are notified by using that event type internally. If you assign a custom event type to notify objects of updates to a value, you must also dispatch the event explicitly within the class.

Binding, through event notification, occurs upon initialization of the source object and at any time during the application when the source property is modified. You can force data binding to execute upon a destination object that is a subclass of `mx.core.UIComponent` by using the `executeBindings` method.

Data binding provides a layer of data synchronization between multiple objects, facilitating the creation of rich applications. This chapter addresses the various techniques of incorporating data binding into the architecture of an application.

14.1 Bind to a Property

Problem

You want to bind a property of one object to that of another object.

Solution

Use either curly braces ({}) within an MXML component declaration or the `<mx:Binding>` tag.

Discussion

When you assign a property of one object (the *destination object*) to be bound to a property of another object (the *source object*), an event from the source object is dispatched to notify the destination object of an update to the value. Internally, the property value of the source is copied to the property value of the destination. To bind properties within an MXML declaration, you can use curly braces ({}) or the `<mx:Binding>` tag. To assign a binding within a component declaration, curly braces are used to wrap the source property and evaluate updates to the value. Consider an example:

```
<mx:Application
        xmlns:mx="http://www.adobe.com/2006/mxml"
        layout="vertical">

    <mx:Panel
            paddingLeft="5" paddingRight="5"
            paddingTop="5" paddingBottom="5">
            <mx:Label text="Enter name:" />
            <mx:TextInput id="nameInput" maxChars="20" />
            <mx:HRule width="100%" />
            <mx:Label text="You've typed:" />
            <mx:Text text="{nameInput.text}" />
    </mx:Panel>

</mx:Application>
```

In this example, the `text` property of a `Text` control is bound to the `text` property of the `TextInput` control. As the value of the `text` property held on the `TextInput` instance is updated, so is the value of the `text` property held on the `Text` instance. Within the curly braces, dot-notation syntax is used to evaluate the `text` attribute value held on the `TextInput` instance, which is given the `id` of `nameInput`.

You can also use the `<mx:Binding>` tag within MXML to define a data-binding expression; the result is the same as using curly braces within a component declaration. Which method should you use? The answer is based on the control. In terms of a Model-View-Controller (MVC) architecture, when you define an `<mx:Binding>` tag, you are creating a controller for your view. When using curly braces, you are not afforded the separation of view and controller because the view control acts as the controller.

Though curly braces are easy, quick to develop, and have the same end result, choosing to use the `<mx:Binding>` tag may prove beneficial in your development process because the syntax is easy to read and also lets you define more than one source property to the same destination.

To use the `<mx:Binding>` tag, you define a `source` attribute and a `destination` attribute:

```
<mx:Application
      xmlns:mx="http://www.adobe.com/2006/mxml"
      layout="vertical">

      <mx:Binding source="nameInput.text" destination="nameOutput.text" />

      <mx:Panel
          paddingLeft="5" paddingRight="5"
          paddingTop="5" paddingBottom="5">
          <mx:Label text="Enter name:" />
          <mx:TextInput id="nameInput" maxChars="20" />
          <mx:HRule width="100%" />
          <mx:Label text="You've typed:" />
          <mx:Text id="nameOutput" />
      </mx:Panel>

</mx:Application>
```

The result is the same as the previous one, but this example assigns `id` properties to both the `TextInput` and `Text` controls to be used as the source and destination properties, respectively, in the `<mx:Binding>` declaration.

You may notice that curly braces are not needed within the `source` and `destination` attributes, as opposed to how they are needed during an inline binding declaration. The reason is that the source and destination attribute values are evaluated as an ActionScript expression. This allows you to add any extra data needed in the expression. For instance, if you want the `Text` control of these examples to display the length of the input text appended with the string *'letters.'*, define the `source` attribute value as the following:

```
<mx:Binding source="nameInput.text.length + ' letters.'"
      destination="nameOutput.text" />
```

14.2 Bind to a Function

Problem

You want to use a function as the source for binding to a property value.

Solution

Use curly braces within a component declaration to pass a bound property as an argument to a function or to define a function that is invoked based on a bindable event.

Discussion

Updating a destination property value based on a source property value is a quick and easy way to ensure data syncing. When using just property values, the property of the destination must be the same type as that of the source property. There may come a time when you need the binding property to be of a different type or to display different but related values—which is where the power of using functions for binding comes into play.

You can use functions for binding in two ways: passing a bound property as the argument to a function or defining a function as bound to a property.

The following example passes a bound property of a source object into a function to update the property value on a destination object:

```
<mx:Application
        xmlns:mx="http://www.adobe.com/2006/mxml"
        layout="vertical">

    <mx:CurrencyFormatter id="formatter" precision="2" />

    <mx:Form>
            <mx:FormItem label="Enter the withdrawl amount:">
                    <mx:TextInput id="amtInput" />
            </mx:FormItem>
            <mx:FormItem label="Formatted amount:">
                    <mx:TextInput editable="false" restrict="1234567890"
                            text="{formatter.format( amtInput.text )}" />
            </mx:FormItem>
    </mx:Form>

</mx:Application>
```

The text property of the first TextInput instance is used in formatting the value to be displayed by the second TextInput instance using the <mx:CurrencyFormatter>. Through binding, the format method is called upon each update of the text property value of amtInput. Passing a bound property as an argument to a function is a convenient way to ensure data synchronization without using a one-to-one property value between a source and a destination.

To bind to a function without passing a bound property as an argument, you can use the event attribute of the [Binding] metadata tag to define a function as being bindable to an event. When the specified event is captured, the function is invoked and enforces an update to any bound properties. Consider an example:

```
<mx:Application
        xmlns:mx="http://www.adobe.com/2006/mxml"
        layout="vertical"
        creationComplete="initHandler();">

    <mx:Script>
      <![CDATA[
          private var _fruit:String;
          private var _fruits:Array = ["Apple", "Banana", "Orange"];

          private function initHandler():void
          {
```

```
                    fruitCB.dataProvider = _fruits;
                }
                [Bindable(event="fruitChanged")]
                private function isOrangeChosen():Boolean
                {
                    return _fruit == "Orange";
                }

                public function get fruit():String
                {
                    return _fruit;
                }
                public function set fruit( str:String ):void
                {
                    _fruit = str;
                    dispatchEvent( new Event( "fruitChanged" ) );
                }

            ]]>
        </mx:Script>

        <mx:Label text="select a fruit:" />
        <mx:HBox>
            <mx:ComboBox id="fruitCB"
                    change="{fruit = fruitCB.selectedLabel}" />
            <mx:Button label="Eat the orange."
                    enabled="{isOrangeChosen()}" />
        </mx:HBox>

    </mx:Application>
```

In this example, the enabled attribute of the Button instance is bound to the Boolean value returned by the isOrangeChosen method. The return value is based on the value of the _fruit variable, which is updated upon change of the ComboBox selection. Any update to the fruit attribute will dispatch the fruitChanged event and invoke the isO rangeChosen method, which in turn will enforce an update to the value of the enabled attribute of the Button instance.

Essentially, the enablement of the button is bound to the label selected in the Combo Box control. Defining a function for binding is a convenient way to update values on a destination object that may be of a different type than the properties of a source object.

See Also

Recipe 14.1.

14.3 Create a Bidirectional Binding

Problem

You want to bind the properties of two controls as the source and destination objects of each other.

Solution

Supply the property of each control as the source in a data-binding expression.

Discussion

The term *bidirectional binding* refers to two components acting as the source object for the destination properties of each other. The Flex Framework supports bidirectional binding and ensures that the property updates do not result in an infinite loop. Consider an example:

```
<mx:VBox
    xmlns:mx="http://www.adobe.com/2006/mxml"
    layout="vertical">
    <mx:Label text="From Input 2:" />
    <mx:TextInput id="input1" text="{input2.text}" />
    <mx:HRule />
    <mx:Label text="From Input 1:" />
    <mx:TextInput id="input2" text="{input1.text}" />

</mx:VBox>
```

Both `TextInput` instances act as the source and the destination, updating the `text` property on each other. As text is entered into one `TextInput`, the value is copied to the other `TextInput` field.

See Also

Recipe 14.1.

14.4 Bind to Properties by Using ActionScript

Problem

You want to create a data-binding expression by using ActionScript rather than declarative MXML.

Solution

Use the `mx.utils.binding.BindingUtils` class to create `mx.utils.binding.Change Watcher` objects.

Discussion

Creating data-binding expressions by using ActionScript affords you more control over when and how destination property values are updated. To establish a binding by using ActionScript, you use the `BindingUtils` class to create a `ChangeWatcher` object. There are two static methods on `BindingUtils` that can be used to create a data binding: `bindProperty` and `bindSetter`.

Using the `bindProperty` method of `BindingUtils` is similar to using the `<mx:Binding>` tag in MXML as you define a source and destination arguments. Unlike the comparable attributes used by the `<mx:Binding>` tag, which evaluates assignments as ActionScript expressions, the arguments for `BindingUtils.bindProperty` are separated by defining a *site* and a *host* (destination and source, respectively) and their properties. For example:

```
var watcher:ChangeWatcher =
    BindingUtils.bindProperty( destination, "property", source, "property" );
```

Using the `BindingUtils.bindSetter` method, you can assign a function to handle data-binding updates of a source property:

```
var watcher:ChangeWatcher =
    BindingUtils.bindSetter( invalidateProperty, source, "property" );
...
private function invalidateProperty( arg:* ):void
{
    // perform any necessary operations.
}
```

It isn't necessary to define a `ChangeWatcher` variable when invoking the static `bindProperty` and `bindSetter` methods. However, at times you may want to utilize the returned `ChangeWatcher` object as it exposes methods you can use during runtime that give you the capability to change the data source, change the destination property, and stop the binding operation.

The following example establishes data binding between the `text` property of a `TextInput` control and the `text` property of a `Text` control by using the `BindingU tils.bindProperty` method:

```
<mx:Application
    xmlns:mx="http://www.adobe.com/2006/mxml"
    layout="vertical"
    creationComplete="initHandler();">

    <mx:Script>
        <![CDATA[
            import mx.binding.utils.ChangeWatcher;
            import mx.binding.utils.BindingUtils;

            private var _nameWatcher:ChangeWatcher;

            private function initHandler():void
            {
                _nameWatcher = BindingUtils.bindProperty( nameField, "text",
```

```
    nameInput, "text" );
            }
            private function clickHandler():void
            {
                if( _nameWatcher.isWatching() )
                {
                    _nameWatcher.unwatch();
                    btn.label = "watch";
                }
                else
                {
                    _nameWatcher.reset( nameInput );
                    btn.label = "unwatch";
                }
            }
        }
    ]]>
</mx:Script>

<mx:Panel title="User Entry."
    paddingLeft="5" paddingRight="5"
        paddingTop="5" paddingBottom="5">
        <mx:Form>
            <mx:FormItem label="Name:">
                <mx:TextInput id="nameInput" />
            </mx:FormItem>
        </mx:Form>
        <mx:HRule width="100%" />
        <mx:Label text="You Entered:" fontWeight="bold" />
        <mx:HBox>
            <mx:Label text="First Name:" />
            <mx:Text id="nameField" />
        </mx:HBox>
        <mx:Button id="btn" label="unwatch"
            click="clickHandler();" />
    </mx:Panel>
</mx:Application>
```

Using the `BindingUtils.bindProperty` method, data binding is defined as a one-to-one relationship between the source property and the destination property. In this example, any updates made to the `text` property of the `TextInput` control instance are reflected in the `text` property of the `Text` control instance. The life cycle of the binding expression can be stopped and reset by `ChangeWatcher` on interaction with the `Button` instance.

To have more control over how a destination property value is updated or to update multiple destinations based in a single source, use the `BindingUtils.bindSetter` to assign a function to act as the marshal for data binding as shown:

```
<mx:Application
    xmlns:mx="http://www.adobe.com/2006/mxml"
    layout="vertical"
    creationComplete="initHandler();">

    <mx:Script>
        <![CDATA[
```

```
                import mx.binding.utils.ChangeWatcher;
                import mx.binding.utils.BindingUtils;

                private var _nameWatcher:ChangeWatcher;

                private function initHandler():void
                {
                    _nameWatcher = BindingUtils.bindSetter( invalidateName,
        nameInput, "text" );
                }
                private function invalidateName( arg:* ):void
                {
                    if( btn.label == "unwatch" )
                        nameField.text = nameInput.text;
                }

                private function clickHandler():void
                {

                    if( _nameWatcher.isWatching() )
                    {
                        _nameWatcher.unwatch();
                        btn.label = "watch";
                    }
                    else
                    {

                        _nameWatcher.reset( nameInput );
                        btn.label = "unwatch";
                    }

                }
            ]]>
        </mx:Script>

        <mx:Panel title="User Entry."
            paddingLeft="5" paddingRight="5"
            paddingTop="5" paddingBottom="5">
            <mx:Form>
                <mx:FormItem label="Name:">
                    <mx:TextInput id="nameInput" />
                </mx:FormItem>
            </mx:Form>
            <mx:HRule width="100%" />
            <mx:Label text="You Entered:" fontWeight="bold" />
            <mx:HBox>
                <mx:Label text="First Name:" />
                <mx:Text id="nameField" />
            </mx:HBox>
            <mx:Button id="btn" label="unwatch"
                click="clickHandler();" />
        </mx:Panel>

    </mx:Application>
```

Updates to any values within the destination are determined by the operations within the setter argument that is passed as the first parameter to the `BindingUtils.bindSet` `ter` method. This setter method acts as the event handler any time the destination object dispatches an event to notify listeners that its value has changed. In this example, the `text` property is updated based on the `label` property of the `Button` instance.

Though the `invalidateName` method will be invoked upon any change to the `text` property of the `nameInput` control, updates to the destination property value are dictated by the current activity of the `ChangeWatcher`, which is evaluated in the `if` statement based on the label of the button.

It is important that any `ChangeWatcher` objects created within an instance be directed to unwatch data-binding expressions in order to be eligible for garbage collection by the Flash Player. When creating a `Change` `Watcher` object, as is done in the previous examples using the `BindingU` `tils` class, a reference is held in memory for both the source and destination of the binding. To release those references from memory and have an object marked for garbage collection be freed appropriately, they need to be removed by using the `unwatch` method.

14.5 Use Bindable Property Chains

Problem

You want to define a source property that is part of a property chain.

Solution

Use dot notation to access the source within a property chain using either the `<mx:Bind` `ing>` tag or curly braces (`{}`), or use an array of strings for the chain argument of the static `BindingUtils.bindProperty` and `BindingUtils.bindSetter` methods.

Discussion

When a property source is defined in a data-binding expression, changes to all properties leading up to that property are monitored. If you specify a binding to the `text` property of a `TextInput` control, the `TextInput` instance is part of a bindable property chain:

```
<mx:TextInput id="myInput" />
<mx:Label text="{myInput.text}" />
```

Technically, the class hosting the `myInput` control is also part of this property chain, but the `this` directive is not necessary within the definition of a data-binding expression as it is scoped. Essentially, the value of `myInput` is first evaluated to not being null and the binding moves down the chain to the source: the `text` property of the `TextInput` instance. For updates to be triggered and the source value copied over to the destination object, only the source property has to be bindable.

You access the source property within a property chain of a model just as you would the source property from a control, as seen in the previous example in this recipe. Within MXML, you can define the bindable property chain by using dot-notation syntax:

```
<!-- property chain binding using <mx:Binding> -->
<mx:Binding source="usermodel.name.firstName" destination="fNameField.text" />
<mx:Label id="fNameField" />

<!-- property chain binding using curly braces ({}).
<mx:Label text="{usermodel.name.firstName}" />
```

To define the bindable property chain by using ActionScript 3, you specify the chain as an array of string values when you call either the BindingUtils.bindProperty or BindingUtils.bindSette method:

```
BindingUtils.bindProperty( nameField, "text",
                              usermodel, ["name", "firstName"] );
BindingUtils.bindSetter( invalidateProperties,
                              this, ["usermodel", "name", "firstName"] );
```

The chain argument for these two methods is an array of strings that defines the bindable property chain relative to the host.

The following example uses curly braces, the <mx:Binding> tag, and the BindingUtils.bindProperty method to define data-binding expressions that use property chains:

```
<mx:Application
    xmlns:mx="http://www.adobe.com/2006/mxml"
    layout="vertical"
    creationComplete="initHandler();">

    <mx:Script>
        <![CDATA[
            import mx.binding.utils.BindingUtils;
            // create data binding using BindingUtils.
            private function initHandler():void
            {
                BindingUtils.bindProperty( lastNameField, "text",
                                              usermodel, ["name", "lastName"] );
            }
            private function clickHandler():void
            {
                usermodel.name.firstName = fNameInput.text;
                usermodel.name.lastName = fNameInput.text;
                usermodel.birth.date = dateInput.text;
            }
        ]]>
    </mx:Script>

    <!-- defined model -->
    <mx:Model id="usermodel">
```

```
        <user>
            <name>
                    <firstName>Ted</firstName>
                    <lastName>Henderson</lastName>
            </name>
            <birth>
                    <date>February 29th, 1967</date>
                </birth>
        </user>
    </mx:Model>

    <!-- create data binding using <mx:Binding> -->
    <mx:Binding source="usermodel.birth.date" destination="dateField.text" />
    <mx:Form>
        <mx:FormItem label="First Name:">
            <!-- create data binding using curly braces -->
            <mx:Text text="{usermodel.name.firstName}" />
     </mx:FormItem>
        <mx:FormItem label="Last Name:">
            <mx:Text id="lastNameField" />
        </mx:FormItem>
        <mx:FormItem label="Birthday:">
            <mx:Text id="dateField" />
        </mx:FormItem>
    </mx:Form>
    <mx:HRule />

    <mx:Form>
        <mx:FormItem label="First Name:">
            <mx:TextInput id="fNameInput" />
        </mx:FormItem>
        <mx:FormItem label="Last Name:">
            <mx:TextInput id="lNameInput" />
        </mx:FormItem>
        <mx:FormItem label="Birthday:">
            <mx:TextInput id="dateInput" />
        </mx:FormItem>
        <mx:FormItem label="Submit Changes">
            <mx:Button label="ok" click="clickHandler();" />
        </mx:FormItem>
    </mx:Form>
</mx:Application>
```

See Also

Recipe 14.1 and Recipe 14.3.

14.6 Bind to Properties on XML by Using E4X

Problem

You want to bind properties of a destination object to an XML source.

Solution

Use ECMAScript for XML (E4X) when defining a data-binding expression using curly braces or the `<mx:Bindable>` tag.

Discussion

The E4X language in ActionScript 3 is used for filtering data from XML (Extensible Markup Language) via expressions that are similar to the syntax of ActionScript expressions. There is not enough room in this recipe to discuss the finer details of writing an E4X expression, but it is important to note that you can use the language to create bindings between a control and XML.

E4X expressions can be defined by using the curly braces within a component declaration and within an `<mx:Binding>` tag. You cannot use E4X with the `BindingUtils` class. To better understand how the E4X technique works, consider an example based on this XML:

```
<item>
    <name>Moe</name>
    <type>The brains.</type>
    <description>Has bowl cut.</description>
</item>
```

You can wrap an E4X expression in an attribute by using curly braces:

```
<mx:Label text="{_data..item.(name == 'Moe').description}" />
```

Or you can create the binding by using the `<mx:Binding>` tag:

```
<mx:Binding source="_data..item.(name == 'Moe').description"
    destination="desc.text" />
<mx:Label id="desc" />
```

Both of these methods produce the same result. Curly braces are not needed in the source attribute of an `<mx:Binding>` binding tag, however, because the value is evaluated as an ActionScript expression.

The following example uses E4X to create a binding for the `dataProvider` property of a `List` and a `DataGrid`:

```
<mx:Application
    xmlns:mx="http://www.adobe.com/2006/mxml"
    layout="vertical">

    <mx:Script>
        <![CDATA[
            [Bindable] private var _data:XML =
                    <items>
                        <item id='1'>
                            <name>Larry</name>
                            <type>The foil.</type>
                            <description>Has curly hair.</description>
                        </item>
```

```
                        <item id='2'>
                            <name>Moe</name>
                            <type>The brains.</type>
                            <description>Has bowl cut.</description>
                        </item>
                        <item id='3'>
                            <name>Curly</name>
                            <type>The braun.</type>
                            <description>Has bowl cut.</description>
                        </item>
                    </items>;

            ]]>
        </mx:Script>

        <mx:Binding source="{_data..item.(@id == '1').name} {_data..item.(@id ==
    '1').description.toLowerCase()}" destination="lab.text" />
        <mx:Label id="lab" />
        <mx:List width="200" dataProvider="{_data..item.name}" />
        <mx:DataGrid width="200" dataProvider="{_data..item}">
            <mx:columns>
                <mx:DataGridColumn dataField="name" />
                <mx:DataGridColumn dataField="type" />
            </mx:columns>
        </mx:DataGrid>
    </mx:Application>
```

Upon initialization of the components in the display, binding is executed and property values are updated based on the E4X expressions supplied.

See Also

Recipe 14.1.

14.7 Create Customized Bindable Properties

Problem

You want data binding to occur based on a custom event rather than relying on the default propertyChange event.

Solution

Set the event attribute of the [Bindable] metadata tag and dispatch an event by using that event string as the type argument.

Discussion

The data-binding infrastructure of the Flex Framework is an event-based system. The default event type dispatched from a binding is the propertyChange event. Internally, updates to destination property values are made without having to dispatch this event directly from the source of the binding. You can specify a custom event type to be associated with a data-binding expression by using the event property of the [Bindable] metadata tag. For example:

```
Bindable(event="myValueChanged")]
```

When you override the default event attribute within a [Bindable] tag definition, you must dispatch the specified event in order for binding to take effect.

The following example uses custom binding events to update destination property values:

```
<mx:Application
        xmlns:mx="http://www.adobe.com/2006/mxml"
        layout="vertical">

    <mx:Script>
      <![CDATA[

          private var _firstName:String;
          private var _lastName:String;
          public static const FIRST_NAME_CHANGED:String = "firstNameChanged";
          public static const LAST_NAME_CHANGED:String = "lastNameChanged";

          private function clickHandler():void
          {
              firstName = fnInput.text;
              lastName = lnInput.text;
          }

          [Bindable(event="firstNameChanged")]
          public function get firstName():String
          {
              return _firstName;
          }
          public function set firstName( str:String ):void
          {
              _firstName = str;
              dispatchEvent( new Event( FIRST_NAME_CHANGED ) );
          }

          [Bindable(event="lastNameChanged")]
          public function get lastName():String
          {
              return _lastName;
          }
          public function set lastName( str:String ):void
          {
              _lastName = str;
              dispatchEvent( new Event( LAST_NAME_CHANGED ) );
          }

      ]]>

    </mx:Script>
```

```
<mx:Panel title="User Entry."
    paddingLeft="5" paddingRight="5"
    paddingTop="5" paddingBottom="5">
    <mx:HBox>
        <mx:Label text="First Name:" />
        <mx:TextInput id="fnInput" />
    </mx:HBox>
    <mx:HBox>
        <mx:Label text="Last Name:" />
        <mx:TextInput id="lnInput" />
    </mx:HBox>
    <mx:Button label="submit" click="clickHandler();" />
    <mx:HRule width="100%" />
    <mx:Label text="You Entered:" fontWeight="bold" />
    <mx:HBox>
        <mx:Label text="First Name:" />
        <mx:Text text="{firstName}" />
    </mx:HBox>
    <mx:HBox>
        <mx:Label text="Last Name:" />
        <mx:Text text="{lastName}" />
    </mx:HBox>
</mx:Panel>
</mx:Application>
```

When a user submits entries for his first and last name, the `firstName` and `lastName` properties are updated. Within each respective setter method, the corresponding event defined in the `[Bindable]` tags is dispatched to invoke updates on destination properties.

A valuable aspect of creating customized bindable properties is dictating when a destination property within the data-binding expression is updated. Because data binding is based on an event model, using customized binding affords you control over when or if the data binding is triggered.

The following example adds a timer to defer dispatching a bindable property event:

```
<mx:Application
    xmlns:mx="http://www.adobe.com/2006/mxml"
    layout="vertical"
    creationComplete="initHandler();">

    <mx:Script>
        <![CDATA[
            private var _timer:Timer;
            private var _firstName:String;
            private var _lastName:String;
            public static const FIRST_NAME_CHANGED:String = "firstNameChanged";
            public static const LAST_NAME_CHANGED:String = "lastNameChanged";

            private function initHandler():void
            {
                _timer = new Timer( 2000, 1 );
                _timer.addEventListener( TimerEvent.TIMER_COMPLETE, timerHandler );
```

```
            }
        private function clickHandler():void
        {

            firstName = fnInput.text;
            lastName = lnInput.text;
        }
        private function timerHandler( evt:TimerEvent ):void
        {
            dispatchEvent( new Event( FIRST_NAME_CHANGED ) );
        }

    [Bindable(event="firstNameChanged")]
    public function get firstName():String
    {
            return _firstName;
    }
        public function set firstName( str:String ):void
        {
            _firstName = str;
            _timer.reset();
            _timer.start();
        }

        [Bindable(event="lastNameChanged")]
        public function get lastName():String
        {
            return _lastName;
        }
        public function set lastName( str:String ):void
        {
            _lastName = str;
            dispatchEvent( new Event( LAST_NAME_CHANGED ) );
        }

    ]]>
</mx:Script>

<mx:Panel title="User Entry."
    paddingLeft="5" paddingRight="5"
    paddingTop="5" paddingBottom="5">
    <mx:HBox>
        <mx:Label text="First Name:" />
        <mx:TextInput id="fnInput" />
    </mx:HBox>
    <mx:HBox>
        <mx:Label text="Last Name:" />
        <mx:TextInput id="lnInput" />
        </mx:HBox>
    <mx:Button label="submit" click="clickHandler();" />
    <mx:HRule width="100%" />
    <mx:Label text="You Entered:" fontWeight="bold" />
    <mx:HBox>
        <mx:Label text="First Name:" />
```

```
                <mx:Text text="{firstName}" />
            </mx:HBox>
            <mx:HBox>
                <mx:Label text="Last Name:" />
                <mx:Text text="{lastName}" />
            </mx:HBox>
        </mx:Panel>
    </mx:Application>
```

The event type is still defined on the implicit getter for the `firstName` attribute, but dispatching the event is deferred to the completion of a `Timer` instance. If you run this program, data binding to the `lastName` property would happen instantaneously as the custom event is dispatched within the setter method for that attribute. Updates on the binding destination of the `firstName` property, however, are performed after 2 seconds because a `Timer` instance is set to dispatch the custom event `firstNameChanged`.

See Also

Recipe 14.1.

14.8 Bind to a Generic Object

Problem

You want to bind properties by using a top-level `Object` instance as the source.

Solution

Use the `mx.utils.ObjectProxy` class to wrap the `Object` and dispatch binding events.

Discussion

Creating a binding to a generic `Object` directly invokes an update only upon initialization of the destination object. To update properties on the destination object as property values change on the `Object`, use the `ObjectProxy` class. To create an instance of `Object Proxy`, pass the `Object` in the constructor. For example:

```
var obj:Object = {name:'Tom Waits', album:'Rain Dogs', genre:'Rock'};
var proxy:ObjectProxy = new ObjectProxy( obj );
```

Modifications to the properties of the original object are handled by the `ObjectProxy`, which dispatches a `propertyChange` event when an update has occurred. The `property Change` event is the default event dispatched from a binding. When the default event is dispatched, the source property value is copied over to the specified destination object property. The following example passes a generic object to an instance of the `Object Proxy` class as a constructor argument:

```
<mx:Application
    xmlns:mx="http://www.adobe.com/2006/mxml"
    layout="vertical">
```

```
<mx:Script>
    <![CDATA[
        import mx.utils.ObjectProxy;

        private var obj:Object = {name:'Tom Waits',
                                  album:'Rain Dogs',
                                  genre:'Rock'};
        [Bindable]
        private var proxy:ObjectProxy = new ObjectProxy( obj );

        private function clickHandler():void
        {

            proxy.name = nameField.text;
            proxy.album = albumField.text;
            proxy.genre = genreField.text;
        }

    ]]>
</mx:Script>

<mx:Form>
    <mx:FormItem label="Name:">
        <mx:TextInput id="nameField" />
    </mx:FormItem>
    <mx:FormItem label="Album:">
        <mx:TextInput id="albumField" />
    </mx:FormItem>
    <mx:FormItem label="Genre:">
        <mx:TextInput id="genreField" />
    </mx:FormItem>
    <mx:FormItem label="Submit Changes">
        <mx:Button label="ok" click="clickHandler();" />
    </mx:FormItem>
</mx:Form>
<mx:HRule width="100%" />
<mx:Form>
    <mx:FormItem label="Name:">
        <mx:Text text="{proxy.name}" />
    </mx:FormItem>
    <mx:FormItem label="Album:">
        <mx:Text text="{proxy.album}" />
    </mx:FormItem>
    <mx:FormItem label="Genre:">
        <mx:Text text="{proxy.genre}" />
    </mx:FormItem>
</mx:Form>

</mx:Application>
```

In this example, when updates are submitted, the properties on the ObjectProxy are modified and changes are reflected in the controls that are bound to the proxy. You are not limited to updating only predefined property values on a proxy object and can define binding expressions for properties that can be assigned to the proxy at any time.

You should create a custom class and expose bindable properties instead of using generic `Objects`. However, when that is not possible within the application architecture, the use of an `ObjectProxy` is beneficial.

See Also

Recipe 14.1.

14.9 Bind to Properties on a Dynamic Class

Problem

You want to bind properties on a destination object to properties not explicitly defined on a dynamic class.

Solution

Create a subclass of `mx.utils.Proxy` that implements the `mx.events.IEventDspatcher` interface and dispatch a `propertyChange` event within the `setProperty` override of the `flash_proxy` namespace.

Discussion

The `Proxy` class lets you access and modify properties by using dot notation. To effectively work with dynamic property references, override the `getProperty` and `setProperty` methods of the `flash_proxy` namespace within your subclass implementation. With custom behaviors defined within these methods, you gain access to properties as if they were exposed directly on that class. However, dynamic property references are not enough to establish binding because data binding is an event-based system.

Because bindings are triggered by events, to create a `Proxy` class that is eligible for data binding, you must also implement the `IEventDispatcher` interface and its methods. In order for dynamic property references to be made for binding, the class is declared by using the **dynamic** keyword and defined by using the `[Bindable]` metadata tag with the event attribute set as `propertyChange`:

```
[Bindable(event="propertyChange")]
dynamic public class Properties extends Proxy implements IEventDispatcher {}
```

An excellent example of when you would want to create a custom `Proxy` class is to access data loaded from an external source by establishing behavior rules within the `setProperty` and `getProperty` override methods, as opposed to writing a parser that will fill property values on a custom object from that loaded data.

For instance, an application loads the following XML from which element properties can be accessed and modified:

```
<properties>
    <property id="name"><![CDATA[Tom Waits]]></property>
    <property id="album"><![CDATA[Rain Dogs]]></property>
    <property id="genre"><![CDATA[Rock]]></property>
</properties>
```

You can create a subclass of `mx.utils.Proxy` and use E4X in the `setProperty` and `getProperty` method overrides, allowing a client to access and modify XML data properties:

```
override flash_proxy function getProperty( name:* ):*
{
    return xml..property.(@id == String( name ) );
}

override flash_proxy function setProperty( name:*, value:* ):void
{
    var index:Number = xml..property.(@id == String( name ) ).childIndex();
    xml.replace( index, '<property id="' + name + '">' + value + '</property>' );
}
```

Data bindings are triggered by an event upon update to a property value. The `setProperty` override in this example, although it updates a property value, does not dispatch a notification of change. In order for binding to dynamic property references to be invoked, you must dispatch a `PropertyChangeEvent` from the `Proxy` subclass:

```
override flash_proxy function setProperty( name:*, value:* ):void
{
    var oldVal:String = xml..property.(@id == String( name ) );
    var index:Number = xml..property.(@id == String( name ) ).childIndex();
    xml.replace( index, '<property id="' + name + '">' + value + '</property>' );
    var evt:Event = PropertyChangeEvent.createUpdateEvent( this, name,
                                                oldVal, value );
    dispatchEvent( evt );
}
```

The static `createUpdateEvent` method of the `PropertyChangeEvent` class returns an instance of a `PropertyChangeEvent` with the `type` property set to `propertyChange`, which is the default event for bindings and the one assigned in the `[Bindable]` metadata tag for the class.

The following example is a complete implementation of a `Proxy` subclass eligible for data binding:

```
package com.oreilly.flexcookbook
{
    import flash.events.Event;
    import flash.events.EventDispatcher;
    import flash.events.IEventDispatcher;
    import flash.net.URLLoader;
    import flash.net.URLRequest;
    import flash.utils.Proxy;
    import flash.utils.flash_proxy;

    import mx.events.PropertyChangeEvent;
```

```actionscript
[Event(name="complete", type="flash.events.Event")]
[Bindable(event="propertyChange")]
dynamic public class Properties extends Proxy
    implements IEventDispatcher
{
    private var _evtDispatcher:EventDispatcher;
    private var _data:XML;
    private var _loader:URLLoader;

    public static const COMPLETE:String = "complete";

    public function Properties()
    {
        _evtDispatcher = new EventDispatcher();
    }
    // load external xml.
    public function loadProperties( fnm:String ):void
    {
        _loader = new URLLoader();
        _loader.addEventListener( Event.COMPLETE, loadHandler );
        _loader.load( new URLRequest( fnm ) );
    }
    // set data property and dispatch 'complete' notification.
    private function loadHandler( evt:Event ):void
    {
        data = XML( _loader.data );
        dispatchEvent( new Event( Properties.COMPLETE ) );
    }
    public function get data():XML
    {
        return _data;
    }
    public function set data( xml:XML ):void
    {
        _data = xml;
    }
    // use E4X to return property value held on xml.
    override flash_proxy function getProperty( name:* ):*
    {
        if( _data == null ) return "";
        else return _data..property.(@id == String( name ) );
    }
    // use E4X to modify property value on xml. Dispatch 'propertyChange'
    override flash_proxy function setProperty( name:*, value:* ):void
    {
        var oldVal:String = _data..property.(@id == String( name ) );
        var index:Number =
            _data..property.(@id == String( name ) ).childIndex();
        _data.replace( index, '<property id="' + name + '">' + value +
                              '</property>' );
        var evt:Event = PropertyChangeEvent.createUpdateEvent( this, name, oldVal,
value );
        dispatchEvent( evt );
    }
```

```
            // IEventDispatcher implementation.
            public function addEventListener( type:String,
                                              listener:Function,
                                              useCapture:Boolean = false,
                                              priority:int = 0,
                                              useWeakReference:Boolean = false):void
            {
                _evtDispatcher.addEventListener( type, listener, useCapture,
                                                 priority, useWeakReference );
            }
            // IEventDispatcher implementation.
            public function removeEventListener( type:String,
                                                 listener:Function,
                                                 useCapture:Boolean = false ):void
            {

                _evtDispatcher.removeEventListener( type, listener, useCapture );
            }
            // IEventDispatcher implementation.
            public function dispatchEvent( evt:Event ):Boolean
            {
                return _evtDispatcher.dispatchEvent( evt );
            }
            // IEventDispatcher implementation.
            public function hasEventListener( type:String ):Boolean
            {
                return _evtDispatcher.hasEventListener( type );
            }
            // IEventDispatcher implementation.
            public function willTrigger( type:String ):Boolean
            {
                return _evtDispatcher.willTrigger( type );
            }
        }
    }
```

You can access and modify elements within the loaded XML held on the Properties
proxy by using dot-notation syntax:

```
var myProxy:Properties = new Properties();
myProxy.load('properties.xml' );
..
var name:String = myProxy.name;
myProxy.album = "Blue Valentine";
```

Although you can work with dynamic property references by using dot notation, you
can not use that syntax in curly braces or the <mx:Binding> tag to create data-binding
expressions in MXML. If you were to use dot notation, you would receive a warning
when you compiled your application.

Because the XML data is loaded at runtime, it makes sense that you establish binding
after it has been loaded. To do so, the mx.utils.BindingUtils class is employed to force
an update and ensure proper data binding to the proxy.

The following snippet creates an application that uses an instance of the `Properties` proxy class to establish data binding to control properties:

```
<mx:Application
    xmlns:mx="http://www.adobe.com/2006/mxml"
    layout="vertical"
    creationComplete="initHandler();">

    <mx:Script>
        <![CDATA[
            import mx.binding.utils.BindingUtils;
            import com.oreilly.flexcookbook.Properties;

            private var _properties:Properties;
            // create proxy and load xml.
            private function initHandler():void
            {
                _properties = new Properties();
                _properties.addEventListener( Event.COMPLETE,
                                                    propertiesHandler );
                _properties.loadProperties( "data/properties.xml" );
            }
            // xml data loaded. establish data binding.
            private function propertiesHandler( evt:Event ):void
            {
                BindingUtils.bindProperty( nameOutput, "text",
                                            _properties, "name" );
                BindingUtils.bindProperty( albumOutput, "text",
                                            _properties, "album" );
                BindingUtils.bindProperty( genreOutput, "text",
                                            _properties, "genre" );
            }
            // change properties of proxied data.
            private function changeHandler():void
            {
                _properties.name = nameField.text;
                _properties.album = albumField.text;
                _properties.genre = genreField.text;
            }
        ]]>
    </mx:Script>
    <mx:Label text="Data Loaded." />
    <mx:Form>
        <mx:FormItem label="Name:">
            <mx:Text id="nameOutput" />
        </mx:FormItem>
        <mx:FormItem label="Album:">
            <mx:Text id="albumOutput" />
        </mx:FormItem>
        <mx:FormItem label="Genre:">
        <mx:Text id="genreOutput" />

        </mx:FormItem>
    </mx:Form>
    <mx:HRule width="100%" />
```

```
<mx:Form>
    <mx:FormItem label="Name:">
        <mx:TextInput id="nameField" />
    </mx:FormItem>
    <mx:FormItem label="Album:">
        <mx:TextInput id="albumField" />
    </mx:FormItem>
    <mx:FormItem label="Genre:">
        <mx:TextInput id="genreField" />
    </mx:FormItem>

    <mx:FormItem label="Submit Changes">
        <mx:Button label="ok" click="changeHandler();" />
    </mx:FormItem>
</mx:Form>
</mx:Application>
```

Within the propertiesHandler event handler, data binding is accomplished by using the BindingUtils.bindProperty method after a successful load of the XML data by the Properties instance. The text property of each respective Text control from the first Form is bound to a corresponding element within the XML based on the id attribute. Using E4X in the getProperty override method of the Properties class, a binding update is made and the values copied over.

Changes to property values are made by using dot notation in the changeHandler event handler, which in turn will invoke the setProperty method on the Properties instance and dispatch a notification to invoke binding by using a PropertyChangeEvent object.

See Also

Recipe 14.4, Recipe 14.5, and Recipe 14.6.

CHAPTER 15

Validation, Formatting, and Regular Expressions

Validation, formatting, and regular expressions may seem a somewhat strange grouping at first glance, but they tend to be used for similar things in the everyday experience of developers: parsing the format of strings to detect a certain pattern, altering the string into a certain format if specific patterns are or are not encountered, returning error messages to users if necessary properties are not encountered—things like phone numbers, capitalized first names, currency, zip codes, ISBN numbers, the sorts of data that we need from third parties or users that may not always be in the correct format required by our application. The Flex Framework provides two powerful tools to integrate this type of parsing and formatting with the UI elements of the Framework in the `Valida tor` and `Formatter` classes. Beneath both of these is the *regular expression*, a new introduction to the ActionScript language and Flash Player platform, but a venerable and powerful programming tool, used by nearly all, and loved and loathed in equal measure for its incredible power and difficult syntax.

The `Validator` is an event dispatcher object that checks a field within any Flex control to ensure that the value submitted falls within its set parameters. These parameters can indicate a certain format, whether a field is required, or a length of a field. The integration of the `Validator` with the Flex control means that displaying the result of a validation error simply requires setting the source of a `Validator` class to be the control where the user input will occur and indicating the property that the `Validator` should check. The `Validator` will dispatch the event to the control, and the control will display a custom error message that has been set in the `Validator`. There are many predefined validators in the Flex Framework for credit cards, phone numbers, email, and social security numbers, but this chapter focuses more on building custom validators and integrating validators and validation events with controls.

The `Formatter` class has a simple but highly important job: taking any value and altering it to fit a prescribed format. This can mean changing nine sequential digits into a properly formatted phone number such as (555) 555–5555, formatting a date correctly, or formatting zip codes for different countries. The `Formatter` class itself defines a single method of importance to us: `format`. This is the method that takes the input and returns the proper string.

Both of these classes, at their roots, perform the type of string manipulation that can be done with a regular expression, though they do not tend to use regular expressions in their base classes. Regular expressions are certainly one of the most powerful, elegant, and difficult tools available in most modern programming languages. They let a programmer create complex sets of rules that will be executed on any chosen string. Almost all major programming languages have a built-in regular expression engine that, while varying somewhat in features, maintains the same syntax, making the regular expression a useful tool to add to your repertoire. The ActionScript implementation of the regular expression is the `RegExp` class, which defines two primary methods: the `test` method, which returns a true or false value if the `RegExp` is matched anywhere in the string, and the `exec` method, which returns an array of all matches and an object, along with the location in the string where the first match is encountered. A regular expression can also be tested by using the `match`, `search`, and `replace` methods of the `String` class. Of these, I find that the methods in the `String` class tend to be more useful because they allow manipulation of the characters using the regular expression. Regular expressions are a vast topic, and whole books are devoted to their proper use, so this chapter covers only some of their more-specific aspects and provides solutions to common problems, rather than attempting to show a more-general set of use cases for the user.

15.1 Use Validators and Formatters with TextInput and TextArea Controls

Problem

You need to validate and then format multiple `TextInput` and `TextArea` controls.

Solution

For each type of input—date, phone, currency—use a `Validator` to ensure that the input is appropriate and then use a `Formatter` control to set the text of the `TextInput`.

Discussion

To use validators and formatters together in a component, simply create multiple validators for each of the needed types of validation. When the `focusOut` event occurs on the appropriate `TextInput`, call the `validate` method on the proper validator. To bind the validator to the correct `TextInput`, set the `TextInput` as the source of the validator and the text as the property of the `TextInput`:

```
<mx:NumberValidator id="numValidator" source="{inputCurrency}" property="text"/>
```

The formatter is called after the data has been validated. The base `Formatter` class accepts a formatting string consisting of hash marks that will be replaced by the digits or characters of the string that is being formatted. For a phone number, for example, the phone number formatting string is as follows:

```
(###) ###-####
```

The formatter for the phone number is set up as here:

```
<mx:PhoneFormatter id="phoneFormatter" formatString="(###) ###-####" validPatternChars=
"#-() "/>
```

To use this formatter, call the `format` method and pass the `text` property of the desired `TextInput`:

```
inputPhone.text = phoneFormatter.format(inputPhone.text);
```

The complete code listing follows. Note that in each of its example methods, if the result is not valid, the application clears the user-entered text and displays an error message. In practice, this probably would not be the best user experience.

```
<mx:VBox xmlns:mx="http://www.adobe.com/2006/mxml" width="600" height="400">
    <mx:Script>
        <![CDATA[

            import mx.events.ValidationResultEvent;
            private var vResult:ValidationResultEvent;
// Event handler to validate and format input.
            private function dateFormat():void
            {
                vResult = dateVal.validate();
                if (vResult.type==ValidationResultEvent.VALID) {
                    inputDate.text = dateFormatter.format(inputDate.text);
                } else {
                    inputDate.text= "";
                }
            }

            private function phoneFormat():void {
                vResult = phoneValidator.validate();
                if (vResult.type==ValidationResultEvent.VALID) {
                    inputPhone.text = phoneFormatter.format(inputPhone.text);
                } else {
                    inputPhone.text= "";
                }
            }

            private function currencyFormat():void {
                vResult = numValidator.validate();
                if (vResult.type==ValidationResultEvent.VALID) {
                    inputCurrency.text =
currencyFormatter.format(inputCurrency.text);
                } else {
                    inputCurrency.text= "";
                }
            }
```

```
        ]]>
    </mx:Script>
    <mx:DateFormatter id="dateFormatter" formatString="day: DD, month: MM, year: YYYY"/
>
        <mx:DateValidator id="dateVal" source="{inputDate}" property="text" inputFormat="m
m/dd/yyyy"/>
        <mx:PhoneNumberValidator id="phoneValidator" property="text" source="{inputPhone}"
/>
        <mx:PhoneFormatter id="phoneFormatter" formatString="(###) ###-####" validPatternC
hars="#-() "/>
        <mx:CurrencyFormatter id="currencyFormatter" currencySymbol="€" thousandsSeparator
From="." decimalSeparatorFrom=","/>
        <mx:NumberValidator id="numValidator" source="{inputCurrency}" property="text"/>
    <mx:Form>
        <mx:FormItem label="Currency Input">
            <mx:TextInput id="inputCurrency" focusOut="currencyFormat()" width="300"/>
        </mx:FormItem>
        <mx:FormItem label="Phone Number Input">
            <mx:TextInput id="inputPhone" focusOut="phoneFormat()" width="300"/>
        </mx:FormItem>
        <mx:FormItem label="Date Input">
            <mx:TextInput id="inputDate" focusOut="dateFormat();" width="300"/>
        </mx:FormItem>
    </mx:Form>
</mx:VBox>
```

15.2 Create a Custom Formatter

Problem

You want to create a custom formatter that will accept any appropriate string and return it with the correct formatting.

Solution

Extend the Formatter class and override the format method.

Discussion

Within the format method, create a SwitchSymbolFormatter instance and pass to Switch SymbolFormatter's formatValue method a string of hash marks to represent the characters you want replaced with your original string. The formatValue method, if provided the format ###-### and the source 123456, will return 123-456. Return this value from the format method of your custom formatter.

The Formatter class uses a string of hash marks that will be replaced by all the characters in the string passed to the format method. Replacing those characters is simply a matter of looping through the string and, character by character, building out the properly formatted string and then replacing it.

```
package oreilly.cookbook
{
    import mx.formatters.Formatter;
    import mx.formatters.SwitchSymbolFormatter;

    public class ISBNFormatter extends Formatter
    {

    public var formatString : String = "####-##-####";

        public function ISBNFormatter()
        {
            super();
        }

        override public function format(value:Object):String {
            // we need to check the length of the string
            // ISBN can be 10 or 13
                if( ! (value.toString().length == 10 || value.toString().length == 13) ) {
                    error="Invalid String Length";
                    return ""
                }

                // count up the number of hash marks passed into our format string
                var numCharCnt:int = 0;
                for( var i:int = 0; i<formatString.length; i++ ) {
                    if( formatString.charAt(i) == "#" ) {
                        numCharCnt++;
                    }
                }

                // if we don't have the right number of items in our format string
                // time to return an error
                if( ! (numCharCnt == 10 || numCharCnt == 13)  ) {
                    error="Invalid Format String";
                    return ""
                }

                // If the formatString and value are valid, format the number.
                var dataFormatter:SwitchSymbolFormatter = new SwitchSymbolFormatter();
                return dataFormatter.formatValue( formatString, value );
        }

    }
}
```

15.3 Create a More-International Zip Code Validator by Using Regular Expressions

Problem

You need to validate all the South American postal code formats for countries that use them.

Solution

Create a series of regular expressions using groups to represent each country that has a postal code to be validated. Create a custom `Validator` class that can be passed a country value, and using that value, use the correct `RegExp` in the `doValidation` method. If the value passed to the `doValidation` method matches the `RegExp`, or the country selected doesn't have a postal code validation, return true; otherwise, return false.

Discussion

Using regular expressions in custom validators lets you create far more versatile validation methods than would be possible without them. Without regular expressions, the `Validator` is restricted to a single string that it can validate. Using more than one regular expression in a validator enables you to create a class that can validate multiple string formats.

This code sample sets up a hash table of different countries' postal codes. When the user selects a country and passes it into the validator, the correct regular expression is chosen from the hash:

```
private var countryHash:Object = {"Argentina":/[a-zA-Z]\d{4}[a-zA-Z]{3}/, "Brazil":/\d{
5}-\d{3}/, "Mexico":/\d{5}/, "Bolivia":/\d{4}/, "Chile":/\d{7}/, "Paraguay":/\d{4}/,
"Uruguay":/\d{5}/};
```

The `country` property of the validator is used in the `doValidation` method of the `Validator` class that the example overrides:

```
//ensure that we have a country set
  if(countryHash[_country] != null) {
    //read from our hash table and get the correct RegExp
    var regEx:RegExp = countryHash[_country];
    if(regEx.test(value as String)) {
      return results;
    } else { // if the postal code doesn't validate, return an error
      var err:ValidationResult = new ValidationResult(true, "", "",
"Please Enter A Correct Postal Code");
      results.push(err);
    }
  } else {
    return results;
  }
```

The complete code listing for the validator is shown here:

```
package oreilly.cookbook
{
    import mx.validators.ValidationResult;
    import mx.validators.Validator;

    public class SouthAmericanValidator extends Validator
    {
        //store all of our countries and their postal codes in a hash table
        private var countryHash:Object = {"Argentina":/[a-zA-Z]\d{4}[a-zA-Z]{3}/,
"Brazil":/\d{5}-\d{3}/, "Mexico":/\d{5}/, "Bolivia":/\d{4}/, "Chile":/\d{7}/,
"Paraguay":/\d{
4}/, "Uruguay":/\d{5}/};

        private var results:Array;
        private var _country:String;

        public function SouthAmericanValidator() {
            super();
        }

        public function set country(str:String):void {
            _country = str;
            trace(_country);
        }

        // Define the doValidation() method.
        override protected function doValidation(value:Object):Array {
            // Clear results Array.
            results = [];

        //if we don't have a country set, we return an error
            if(_country == "") {
                var err:ValidationResult = new ValidationResult(true, "", "", "Please S
elect a Country");
                results.push(err);
                return results;
            } else {
                //if it's a country that doesn't have a zip code, we return w/o an erro
r
                if(countryHash[_country] != null) {
                    //read from our hash table and get the correct RegExp
                    var regEx:RegExp = countryHash[_country];
                    if(regEx.test(value as String)) {
                        return results;
                    } else { // if the postal code doesn't validate, return an error
                        var err:ValidationResult = new ValidationResult(true, "", "", "Pl
ease Enter  A Correct Postal Code");
                        results.push(err);
                    }
                } else {
                    return results;
                }
            }
            return results;
```

```
            }

        }
    }
```

To implement the custom validator, ensure that the country is set before calling the doValidation method of the validator. In this example, a ComboBox is used to set the country property of the SouthAmericanValidator object:

```
<mx:HBox xmlns:mx="http://www.adobe.com/2006/mxml" width="400" height="300" xmlns:cookb
ook="oreilly.cookbook.*">
    <cookbook:SouthAmericanValidator property="text" source="{zip}" required="true" id=
"validator" invalid="showInvalid(event)"/>
    <mx:Script>
        <![CDATA[
            import mx.events.ValidationResultEvent;

            private function showInvalid(event:ValidationResultEvent):void {
                trace( " event " + event.message );
                zip.errorString = event.message;
            }

        ]]>
    </mx:Script>
    <mx:Form>
        <mx:FormItem label="Select country ">
            <mx:ComboBox dataProvider="{['Argentina', 'Brazil', 'Mexico', 'Bolivia', 'Ecu
ador', 'Colombia', 'Chile','Paraguay','Uruguay']}"
                    id="cb" change="validator.country = cb.selectedItem as String"/>
        </mx:FormItem>
        <mx:FormItem label="Enter zip ">
            <mx:TextInput id="zip"/>
        </mx:FormItem>
    </mx:Form>
</mx:HBox>
```

15.4 Create a Validator to Validate UPCs

Problem

You need to validate UPCs within a form.

Solution

Create a custom validator that checks whether the checksum value of the UPC is present and correct and returns an error if it is not.

Discussion

A Universal Product Code, or UPC, consists of a 12-digit number used by cash registers and many merchants. The UPC can be checked by a seemingly mysterious checksum that is calculated by summing the multiplicand of every third number in the code and then adding every third number again to that sum. The code is far easier to understand than the explanation:

```
var sum:Number = 0;
for ( var i:Number=0; i < UPC.length; i += 2){
    sum += Number(UPC.charAt(i)) * 3;
}
for ( i = 1; i < UPC.length-1; i += 2) {
    sum += Number(UPC.charAt(i));
}
var checkSum:Number = ( 10 - (sum % 10) ) % 10;
// If checksum does not match, issue a validation error.
if ( Number(UPC.charAt(11)) != checkSum ) {
    results.push(new ValidationResult(true, null, "invalidUPC", "Invalid UPC Number."))
;
    return results;
}
```

This guarantees that the UPC code is a valid code. The rest of the code is quite straight-forward:

```
package com.passalong.utils
{
    import mx.validators.Validator;
    import mx.validators.ValidationResult;
    import mx.controls.Alert;

    public class UPCValidator extends Validator
    {
        private var results:Array;

        public function UPCValidator()
        {
            super();
        }

        override protected function doValidation(value:Object):Array
        {
            // Convert value to a String in order to inspect each digit.
            var UPC:String = String(value);
            // strip off decimal point from beginning -- added to force recognition of
leading zeros
            UPC = UPC.substring(1);
            var UPCnum:Number = Number(UPC);

            // Clear results Array.
            results = [];

            // Call base class doValidation().
            results = super.doValidation(value);
            // Return if there are errors.
            if (results.length > 0)
                return results;

            // If input value is not a number, or contains no value,
            // issue a validation error.
```

```
            if (isNaN(UPCnum) || !value )
            {
                results.push(new ValidationResult(true, null, "NaN",
                    "UPC required."));
                return results;
            }

        if ( UPC.length != 12 )
        {
            results.push(new ValidationResult(true, null, "invalidUPCLength",
                "Please enter a full 12-digit UPC."));
            return results;
        }
        else
        {
            var sum:Number = 0;

            for ( var i:Number=0; i < UPC.length; i += 2)
                sum += Number(UPC.charAt(i)) * 3;

            for ( i = 1; i < UPC.length-1; i += 2) {
                sum += Number(UPC.charAt(i));
            }
            var checkSum:Number = ( 10 - (sum % 10) ) % 10;

                // If checksum does not match, issue a validation error.
                if ( Number(UPC.charAt(11)) != checkSum )
                {
                    results.push(new ValidationResult(true, null, "invalidUPC",
                        "Invalid UPC Number."));
                    return results;
                }

            return results;
        }
    }
  }
 }
}
```

Special thanks to Mike Orth for contributing the idea and the code for this recipe.

15.5 Validate Combo Boxes and Groups of Radio Buttons

Problem

You need to validate groups of radio buttons and combo boxes to ensure that the prompt is not selected or that one of the radio buttons in a group is selected.

Solution

Use a NumberValidator to check the radio buttons, and a custom Validator to validate the combo box.

Discussion

To return a `ValidationResultEvent` for a group of radio buttons, use a `NumberValida` `tor` to check that the `selectedIndex` of the `RadioButtonGroup` is not –1, which would indicate that there is not a selected radio button. To validate a combo box, create a custom validator and check that the `selectedItem` of the `ComboBox` is not null, and is not a custom prompt or invalid value, if one is provided.

The code for the custom `ComboBox` validator is quite straightforward and is commented and shown here:

```
package oreilly.cookbook
{
    import mx.validators.ValidationResult;
    import mx.validators.Validator;

    public class ComboValidator extends Validator
    {
        //this is the error message that is returned if an item in the ComboBox
        //is not selected
        public var error:String;
        //if the developer sets a manual prompt, but pushes something into the
        //array of the ComboBox (I've seen it many times for different reasons)
        // we want to check that against what the selected item in the CB is
        public var prompt:String;

        public function ComboValidator() {
            super();
        }
        //here we check for either a null value or the possibility that
        //the developer has added a custom prompt to the comboBox, in which
        //case we want to return an error
        override protected function doValidation(value:Object):Array {
            var results:Array = [];
            if(value as String == prompt || value == null) {
                var res:ValidationResult = new ValidationResult(true, "", "", error);
                results.push(res);
            }
            return results;
        }
    }
}
```

One strategy for performing multiple validations is to use an array: Add to the array all of a component's validators that need to be called, and then use the public static `Validator.validateAll` to validate all the validators in the array. This is particularly valuable when multiple fields need to be validated at the same time. If any of the validators return an error, all those errors are joined together and displayed in an `Alert` control:

```
<mx:VBox xmlns:mx="http://www.adobe.com/2006/mxml" width="600" height="400" xmlns:cookb
ook="oreilly.cookbook.*" creationComplete="init()">
    <mx:Script>
```

```
        <![CDATA[

            import mx.events.ValidationResultEvent;
            import mx.validators.Validator;
            import mx.controls.Alert;

            [Bindable]
             private var validatorArr:Array;
        //make an array of all the validators that we'll check with one method later
             private function init():void {
                 validatorArr = new Array();
             //push all the validators into the same array
                 validatorArr.push(rbgValidator);
                 validatorArr.push(toggleValidator);
                 validatorArr.push(comboValidator);
             }
        // validate all the items in the validator array and show an alert if there
        // are any errors
             private function validateForm():void {
             // the validate all method will validate
             all the Validators in an array
             //passed to the validateAll method
                 var validatorErrorArray:Array = Validator.validateAll(validatorArr);;
                 var isValidForm:Boolean = validatorErrorArray.length == 0;
                 if (!isValidForm) {
                     var err:ValidationResultEvent;
                     var errorMessageArray:Array = [];
                     for each (err in validatorErrorArray) {
                         errorMessageArray.push(err.message);
                     }
                     Alert.show(errorMessageArray.join("\n"), "Invalid form...", Alert.
OK);
             }
         }

        ]]>
    </mx:Script>
    <mx:StringValidator id="rbgValidator" source="{rbg}" property="selectedValue"/>
    <mx:NumberValidator id="toggleValidator" source="{toggleButton}" property="selected
Index" allowNegative="false" negativeError="Please select a Radio Button"/>
    <cookbook:ComboValidator id="comboValidator" error="Please Select A State" prompt="
{stateCB.prompt}" source="{stateCB}" property="selectedItem"/>
    <mx:Form id="form">
        <mx:FormItem>
            <mx:ComboBox id="stateCB" dataProvider="{someDataProvider}" prompt="Select A
State"/>
        </mx:FormItem>
        <mx:FormItem>
            <mx:RadioButtonGroup id="rbg"/>
            <mx:RadioButton group="{rbg}" label="first" id="first"/>
            <mx:RadioButton group="{rbg}" id="second" label="second"/>
            <mx:RadioButton id="third" label="third" group="{rbg}"/>
        </mx:FormItem>
        <mx:FormItem>
```

```
<mx:ToggleButtonBar id="toggleButton">
    <mx:dataProvider>
        <mx:Array>
            <mx:String> First Option </mx:String>
            <mx:String> Second Option </mx:String>
            <mx:String> Third Option </mx:String>
            <mx:String> Fourth Option </mx:String>
            <mx:String> Fifth Option </mx:String>
        </mx:Array>
    </mx:dataProvider>
</mx:ToggleButtonBar>
        </mx:FormItem>
    </mx:Form>
    <mx:Button label="validate" click="validateForm()"/>
</mx:VBox>
```

15.6 Show Validation Errors by Using ToolTips in a Form

Problem

You want to create and display multiple validation error results regardless of whether the user has the TextInput or another control focused.

Solution

Use the ToolTipManager to create a new ToolTip class and position it over the control. Create a Style object and assign it to the ToolTip to give a red background and the correct font color.

Discussion

The error tip that displays when a validator returns an error is simply a ToolTip component. You can use a style to represent all the necessary visual information for the ToolTip: backgroundColor, fontColor, fontType, and so forth. Use the setStyle method of the ToolTip to apply this style to the new tooltips created for each validation error; for example:

```
errorTip.setStyle("styleName", "errorToolTip");
```

To display multiple tooltips, position them by using the stage position of the relevant control. For example:

```
var pt:Point = this.stage.getBounds(err.currentTarget.source);
var yPos:Number = pt.y * -1;
var xPos:Number = pt.x * -1;
//now create the error tip
var errorTip:ToolTip =
ToolTipManager.createToolTip(err.message, x
Pos + err.currentTarget.source.width, yPos) as ToolTip;
```

When the form validates, all the tooltips are removed by using the `ToolTipManager` `destroyToolTip` method and looping through each `ToolTip` added. The code you need is shown here:

```
<mx:VBox xmlns:mx="http://www.adobe.com/2006/mxml" width="500" height="400" xmlns:cookb
ook="oreilly.cookbook.*" creationComplete="init();">
    <mx:Style>
        /* here's our CSS class that we'll use to give our tooltip the appearance
            of an error message */
        .errorToolTip {
            color: #FFFFFF;
            fontSize: 9;
            fontWeight: "bold";
            shadowColor: #000000;
            borderColor: #CE2929;
            borderStyle: "errorTipRight";
            paddingBottom: 4;
            paddingLeft: 4;
            paddingRight: 4;
            paddingTop: 4;
        }

    </mx:Style>
    <mx:Script>
        <![CDATA[
            import mx.controls.ToolTip;
            import mx.managers.ToolTipManager;
            import mx.events.ValidationResultEvent;
            import mx.validators.Validator;
            import mx.controls.Alert;

            [Bindable]
             private var validatorArr:Array;

             private var allErrorTips:Array;

             private function init():void {
                 validatorArr = new Array();
                 validatorArr.push(comboValidator1);
                 validatorArr.push(comboValidator2);
             }
```

Here's where the actual validation occurs:

```
             private function validateForm():void {
                 // if we have error tips already, then we want to remove them
                 if(!allErrorTips) {
                     allErrorTips = new Array();
                 } else {
                     for(var i:int = 0; i<allErrorTips.length; i++) {
                         // remove the tooltip
                         ToolTipManager.destroyToolTip(allErrorTips[i]);
                     }
                     //empty our array
                     allErrorTips.length = 0;
                 }
```

```
            var validatorErrorArray:Array =
    Validator.validateAll(validatorArr);
```

If nothing has been pushed into the **validatorErrorArray**, you know that no validation error have been thrown; otherwise, you want to go about creating those error tips and placing them:

```
            var isValidForm:Boolean = validatorErrorArray.length == 0;
            if (!isValidForm) {
                var err:ValidationResultEvent;
                for each (err in validatorErrorArray) {
                    // Use the target's x and y positions to set position of erro
    r tip. We want their actual stage positions
                    // in case there's some layout management going on so we use
    the getBounds method
```

Because the **ErrorEvent**'s **target** property is the control or component that threw the event, use that property to place the error tip:

```
                    var pt:Rectangle =
    this.stage.getBounds(err.currentTarget.sou
    rce);
                    var yPos:Number = pt.y * -1;
                    var xPos:Number = pt.x * -1;
                    //now create the error tip
                    var errorTip:ToolTip = ToolTipManager.createToolTip(err.message, x
    Pos + err.currentTarget.source.width, yPos) as ToolTip;
                    // Apply the errorTip class selector.
                    errorTip.setStyle("styleName", "errorToolTip");
                    // store the error tip so we can remove it later on when the user
    re-validates
                    allErrorTips.push(errorTip);
                }
            }
        }
    ]]>
    </mx:Script>
    <!-- our two validators -->
    <cookbook:ComboValidator id="comboValidator1" error="Please Select A State" prompt=
"{stateCB1.prompt}" source="{stateCB1}" property="selectedItem"/>
    <cookbook:ComboValidator id="comboValidator2" error="Please Select A State" prompt=
"{stateCB2.prompt}" source="{stateCB2}" property="selectedItem"/>
    <mx:Form id="form">
        <mx:FormItem>
            <mx:ComboBox id="stateCB1" dataProvider="{someDataProvider}" prompt="Select A
    State"/>
        </mx:FormItem>
        <mx:FormItem>
            <mx:ComboBox id="stateCB2" dataProvider="{someDataProvider}" prompt="Select A
    State"/>
        </mx:FormItem>
    </mx:Form>
    <mx:Button label="validate" click="validateForm()"/>
</mx:VBox>
```

15.7 Use Regular Expressions for Locating Email Addresses

Problem

You need to identify any email addresses entered or encountered in text.

Solution

Create a regular expression to match the *name@host.com* formatted email address and use the global flag to indicate that the expression can match multiple times.

Discussion

The necessary regular expression looks like this:

```
var reg:RegExp = /\w+?@\w+?\.\w{3}/g;
```

To match all the email addresses in a large block of text, use the `String match` method, which returns an array of all matches. The `match` method accepts either a string to search for or a regular expression to search for.

15.8 Use Regular Expressions for Matching Credit Card Numbers

Problem

You need a regular expression that will match the valid major credit card types: Visa, MasterCard, American Express, and Discover.

Solution

Create a regular expression that uses the initial digits of each major credit card type and match the expected numbers of digits for each type.

Discussion

You can use the fact that each major credit card type starts with identifying digits to create a single regular expression for determining whether a card number is valid. All MasterCard cards start with 5, all Visa cards start with 4, all American Express cards start with 30, and all Discover cards start with 6011. The expression you need is as follows:

```
(5[1-5]\d{14})|(4\d{12}(\d{3})?)|(3[47]\d{13})|(6011\d{14})
```

For MasterCard, the expression `(5[1-5]\d{14})` matches only valid numbers without any spaces in them. It's generally a good idea to clear the spaces out of any credit card numbers before sending them on to a processing service. The next segment of the expression matches Visa cards, after that American Express, and finally Discover. The alternation flag (|) in between the regular expression's four parts indicates that you can match any one of the four valid card patterns to return a match.

15.9 Use Regular Expressions for Validating ISBNs

Problem

You want to create a regular expression to validate International Standard Book Numbers (ISBNs).

Solution

Create a pattern that allows for the use of hyphens, the possibility that the ISBN number is 10 or 13 digits long, and that the number may or may not end with an *X*.

Discussion

The regular expression shown here uses the caret (^) and dollar sign ($) markers to indicate that the pattern must be the only item in the line. These symbols could be removed to match all ISBN numbers within a block of text as well:

```
private var isbnReg:RegExp = /^(?=.{13}$)\d{1,5}([- ])\d{1,7}\1\d{1,6}\1(\d|X)$/;
private function testISBN():void {
    var s:String ="ISBN 1-56389-016-X";
    trace(s.match(isbnReg));
}
```

The caret indicates that the pattern must be the beginning of a line, and the dollar sign indicates that whatever directly precedes it must be the end of the line. Between these two symbols, you have groups of integers, separated optionally by hyphens (-).

15.10 Create Regular Expressions by Using Explicit Character Classes

Problem

You want to use regular expressions with explicit characters to match patterns in text —for example, words containing only vowels.

Solution

Use brackets ([and]) to hold all the characters that you would like to match the pattern —for example, [aeiou] to match all vowels.

Discussion

To match patterns in a block of text, you can use multiple character flags in your regular expression to signal the various character classes that you may wish to match. Here are a few common flags:

[ ] *(square brackets)*
> Defines a character class, which defines possible matches for a single character; for example, `/[aeiou]/` matches any one of the specified characters.

- *(hyphen)*
> Within character classes, use the hyphen to designate a range of characters; for example `/[A-Z0-9]/` matches uppercase A through Z or 0 through 9.

/ *(backslash)*
> Within character classes, insert a backslash to escape the] and - characters; for example, `/[+\-]\d+/` matches either + or - before one or more digits. Within character classes, other characters, which are normally metacharacters, are treated as normal characters (not metacharacters), without the need for a backslash: `/[$£]/` matches either $ or £. For more information, see the Flex documentation on character classes.

| *(pipe)*
> Used for alternation, to match either the part on the left side or the part on the right side; for example, `/abc|xyz/` matches either *abc* or *xyz*.

To match only odd numbers, you would write this:

```
var reg:RegExp = /[13579]/;
```

To match only vowels, you would use this:

```
var vowels:RegExp = /[aeiou]/;
```

To not match vowels, you would use this:

```
var notVowels:RegExp = /[^aeiou]/;
```

Note that the caret in the preceding example means *not* only within the square brackets. Outside the square brackets, the caret indicates that the string must occur at the beginning of a line.

15.11 Use Character Types in Regular Expressions

Problem

You want to use regular expressions to match character types (integers, characters, spaces, or the negations of these) in your patterns.

Solution

Use the character type flags.

Discussion

Using the character class is by far the easiest and most efficient way to match characters when creating patterns to test against. To perform those tests, use character type flags. These consist of a backslash to tell the regular expression engine that the following characters are a character type (as opposed to a character to be matched) and then specify the desired character class. Many of these character types also have negations, for example:

- \d matches a decimal digit. This is the equivalent of [0-9].
- \D matches any character other than a digit. This is the equivalent of [^0-9].
- \b matches at the position between a word character and a nonword character. If the first or last character in the string is a word character, \b also matches the start or end of the string.
- \B matches at the position between two word characters. Also matches the position between two nonword characters.
- \f matches a form-feed character.
- \n matches the newline character.
- \r matches the return character.
- \s matches any white-space character (a space, tab, newline, or return character).
- \S matches any character other than a white-space character.
- \t matches the tab character.
- \unnnn matches the Unicode character with the character code specified by the hexadecimal number *nnnn*. For example, \u263a is the smiley character.
- \v matches a vertical-feed character.
- \w matches a word character (A–Z, a–z, 0–9, or _). Note that \w does not match non-English characters, such as é, ñ, or ç.
- \W matches any character other than a word character.
- \xnn matches the character with the specified ASCII value, as defined by the hexadecimal number *nn*.
- \ (backslash) escapes the special metacharacter meaning of special characters.
- . (dot) matches any single character. A dot matches a newline character (\n) only if the s (dotall) flag is set. For more information, see the s (dotall) flag in the Flex documentation.

A few quick examples show the usage of these metacharacters. To match a 1 followed by two letters, use the following:

```
/1\w\w/;
```

To match a 1 followed by two nonletters, use this:

```
/1\W\W/;
```

To match five consecutive numbers, you could use

```
/\d\d\d\d\d/;
```

although a far easier way to do this is shown here:

```
/\d{5}/;
```

To match two numbers separated by a space:

```
/\d\b\d/;
```

To match three numbers separated by any character:

```
/\d.\d.\d/;
```

The metacharacters allow you to create expressions that will match certain patterns of any integer, alphabetic character, or blank space, as well as matching the negation of all of these. This lets you create much more powerful and terse regular expressions.

15.12 Match Valid IP Addresses by Using Subexpressions

Problem

You want to find multiple valid IP addresses in a block of text.

Solution

Use subexpressions to create valid matches for each three-digit number in the IP address.

Discussion

Using what you learned in Recipe 15.11, you can match between one and three numbers of an IP address by using the \d flag:

```
\d{1,3}
```

If you want to match three sets of one and four numbers, use this:

```
(\d{1,4}){3}
```

Just as /d{3} matches 333, when you create a subexpression, you can match that subexpression. The subexpression is a distinct element that can be treated like any other pattern. So for the IP address, you want to match four sets of three numbers separated by periods. Think about this as three sets of three numbers with periods and then one set of three numbers. Doing so leads to a far more efficient expression, such as the following:

```
(\d{1,3}\.){3}\d{1,3}
```

This approach will bring you closer, but it won't work completely because it also matches a string like 838.381.28.999, which is not a valid IP address. What you need is something that takes into account that the maximum value for one of the three-digit numbers in the IP address is 255. Using subexpressions, you can create that:

```
((((\d{1,2})|(1\d{2})|(2[0-4]\d)|(25[0-5]))\.){3}((\d{1,2})|(1\d{2})|(2[0-4]\d)|(25[0-5])))
```

First, take a closer look at this section:

```
((((\d{1,2})|(1\d{2})|(2[0-4]\d)|(25[0-5]))\.){3}
```

Breaking this into English, you see two digits that are either 1 or 2, (\d{1,2}) or a 1 followed by two other numbers (1\d{2}), or a 2 followed by two of anything between 0 and 4 (2[0-4]\d), or 2 and 5 followed by anything between 0 and 5 (25[0-5]). Any one of these is then followed by a period.

Finally, we wind up with something like this:

```
((\d{1,2})|(1\d{2})|(2[0-4]\d)|(25[0-5]))
```

This is exactly the same as the previous pattern, with one exception: the exclusion of the period at the end. An IP address (for example, 192.168.0.1) doesn't contain a final period.

The subexpression syntax functions as follows:

- {n} indicates at least *n* times.
- {n,m} indicates at least *n* but no more than *m* times.

15.13 Use Regular Expressions for Different Types of Matches

Problem

For various numbers of times, you want to match patterns described with regular expressions.

Solution

Use the grouping syntax, either the period (.) expression or the plus (+) expression, to match different groups various numbers of times.

Discussion

As you saw in Recipe 15.12, the braces syntax allows you to indicate the number of times that a subexpression should be matched and whether the results should be returned. Suppose, for example, you want to match all characters between 0 and 4 in two strings:

```
var firstString:String = "12430";
var secondString:String = "603323";
```

Consider all the types of matches that you could execute on these two strings. The modifiers you could use are as follows:

- ?? matches zero or one time only.
- *? matches zero or more times.
- +? matches one or more times.

Remember that matching and returning matches are quite different. If you want to find out whether the two example strings contain only characters between 0 and 4, for example, use the RegExp test method, which returns a Boolean true or false value. If you want all characters in the String that match until a nonmatch is found, use the String match method. If you want all characters in the String that match regardless of any nonmatches, use the global flag on the regular expression /[0-4]+g/ together with the String match method.

For example, /[abc]+/ matches *abbbca* or *abba* and returns abc from abcss.

\w+@\w+\.\w+ matches anything resembling an email address. Note that the period is escaped, meaning it is simply a period and not read as part of the regular expression's syntax. The use of the + symbol indicates that any number of characters can be found; these characters must be followed by the at (@) symbol, which in turn can be followed by any number of additional characters.

This code snippet demonstrates various quantifiers and comments their results:

```
var atLeastOne:RegExp = /[0-4]+/g;
var zeroOrOne:RegExp = /[0-4]*/g;
var atLeastOne2:RegExp = /[0-4]+?/g;
var zeroOrOne2:RegExp = /[0-4]*?/g;
var firstString:String = "12430";
var secondString:String = "663323";

firstString.match(atLeastOne));//returns "1243"
secondString.match(atLeastOne));//returns "3323" because we want as many characters as
 will match
firstString.match(zeroOrOne));//returns  "1243" the first few characters match
secondString.match(zeroOrOne));//returns "" because the first few characters don't mat
ch, we stop looking
firstString.match(atLeastOne2));//returns "1,2,4,3" because all we need is one match
secondString.match(atLeastOne2));//returns "3,3,2,3"
firstString.match(zeroOrOne2));//returns ""
secondString.match(zeroOrOne2));//returns ""
zeroOrOne2.test(firstString));//returns true
zeroOrOne2.test(secondString));//returns false
```

15.14 Match Ends or Beginnings of Lines with Regular Expressions

Problem

You want to match patterns that occur only at the beginning or the end of lines, or patterns that exist on their own lines with nothing in front of or behind them.

Solution

Use the caret (^) and dollar sign ($) markers in your regular expression.

Discussion

When matching patterns on discrete lines or at a line's start or end, place the caret marker at the beginning of your regular expressions to indicate that your pattern must occur at the beginning of a line, and place the dollar sign at the end of your pattern to indicate that the end of the line must follow your pattern.

For example, to match *jpg* or *jpeg* with any length of a filename, but only where the name is encountered on a line with nothing else around it, use the following:

```
/^.+?\.jpe?g$/i
```

To match only words that occur at the end of a line in a text field, use this:

```
/\w+?$/;
```

And to match words that occur at the beginning of a line only, use this:

```
/^\w+?/;
```

15.15 Use Back-References

Problem

You want to match a pattern and then use that match to check the next potential match, for example, matching pairs of HTML tags.

Solution

Use back-references in your regular expression to check the match against the most recent match.

Discussion

The Flash Player regular expression engine can store up to 99 back-references, which is simply a list of all the matches. The flag \1 always indicates the most recent match, and \2 indicates the second most recent match. Likewise, in the String replace method, which uses the matches from another regular expression, the most recent match is indicated by $1.

To ensure that pairs of HTML tags match (for example, that <h2> is followed by </h2>), this example uses the back-reference \1 to indicate the most recent match:

```
private var headerBackreference:RegExp = /<H([1-6])>.*?<\/H\1>/g;
private function init():void {
    var s:String = "<BODY> <H2>Valid Chocolate</H2> <H2>Valid Vanilla</H2> <H2>This is
not valid HTML</H3></BODY>";
    var a:Array = s.match(headerBackreference);
    if(a != null) {
        for(var i:int = 0; i<a.length; i++) {
            trace(a[i]);
        }
    }
}
```

You could also use the back-reference to replace all valid URLs with an <a> tag to make a hyperlink. The way of indicating the back-reference here is slightly different. First, consider the code and then read the explanation:

```
private var domainName:RegExp = /(ftp|http|https|file):\/\/[\S]+(\b|$)/gim;
private function matchDomain():void {
    var s:String = "Hello my domain is http://www.bar.com, but I also like http://foo.n
et as well as www.baz.org";
        var replacedString = (s.replace(domainName, '<a href="$&">$&</a>').replace(/([
^\/])(www[\S]+(\b|$))/gim,'$1<a href="http://$2">$2</a>'));
}
```

The first match is made by using the match for a valid URL:

```
/(ftp|http|https|file):\/\/[\S]+(\b|$)/gim;
```

Next, all the valid URLs are wrapped in <a> tags:

```
s.replace(domainName, '<a href="$&">$&</a>')
```

At this point you will have

```
Hello my domain is <a href="http://www.bar.com">http://www.bar.com</a>, but I also like
<a href="http://foo.net">http://foo.net</a> as well as www.baz.org
```

which is not quite right. Because the original RegExp looked for strings starting with *ftp*, *http*, *https*, or *file*, *http://www.baz.org* isn't matched. The second replace statement looks through the string for any instance of www that is not prefaced by a /, which would have already matched:

```
replace(/([^\/])(www[\S]+(\b|$))/gim,'$1<a href="http://$2">$2</a>'))
```

The $1 and $2 here indicate the first and second matches within the pattern, the second being the actual URL name that you want.

15.16 Use a Look-Ahead or Look-Behind

Problem

You want to match patterns not precede or follow certain other characters.

Solution

Use a negative look-ahead, (?!), or negative look-behind, (?<!), to indicate any characters that cannot be in front of or behind your match. Use a positive look-ahead (?=) or positive look-behind (?<=) to indicate characters that should be located in front of or behind your match.

Discussion

The positive look-behind indicates a pattern in front of an expression that you do want used to determine a match, but that you do *not* want included in a match. For example, to match all numbers that follow a dollar sign, but not the dollar sign itself, in the string

```
400 boxes at $100 per unit and 300 boxes at $50 per unit.
```

use a regular expression with a positive look-behind:

```
/(?<=\$)\d+/
```

On the other hand, if you want to match all characters that do not have a dollar sign in front of them, use a negative look-behind:

```
/\b(?<!\$)\d+\b/
```

Note that the negative look-behind replaces the = of the positive look-behind with a ! symbol to indicate that in order for the string to match, the dollar sign must not be present. To match only the prices from a string, you can use a positive look-ahead:

```
private var lookBehindPrice:RegExp = /(?<=[\$|€])[0-9.]+/g;

private function matchPrice():void {
    var s:String = "dfsf24ds: €23.45 ds2e4d: $5.31 CFMX1: $899.00 d3923: €69";
    trace(s.match(this.lookBehindPrice));
}
```

To match variable declarations in a string, you can use positive look-aheads as shown:

```
private var lookBehindVariables:RegExp = /(?<=var )[0-9_a-zA-Z]+/g;
private function matchVars():void {
    var s:String = " private var lookAheadVariables:RegExp = /blah/  private var str:St
ring = 'foo'";
        trace(s.match(lookBehindVariables));
}
```

If you want, for example, to match all strings with the value *pic* that do not have *.jpg* behind them, you can use a negative look-ahead:

```
var reg:RegExp = /pic(?!\.jpg)/;
```

CHAPTER 16

Working with Services and Server-Side Communication

One of the most important aspects of working with Flex is communicating with a server and database. The recipes in this chapter focus mainly on configuring a Flex application to communicate with servers and processing data sent to the application from a server in one of the three main ways that servers and applications communicate.

Flex provides three classes to communicate with servers: `HTTPService`, `RemoteObject`, and `WebService`. The `HTTPService` class facilitates communication with a server using the Hypertext Transfer Protocol (HTTP). A Flex application can use `GET` or `POST` requests to send data to a server and process XML or character strings that are returned from the request. With the `HTTPService` class, you can communicate with PHP pages, ColdFusion pages, JavaServer Pages (JSP), Java servlets, Ruby on Rails, and Microsoft Active Server Pages (ASP). You can use the `RemoteObject` class for communicating with a server via ActionScript Message Format objects. `RemoteObjects` also can communicate with Java or ColdFusion remoting gateways or with .NET and PHP by using open source projects such as AMFPHP, SabreAMF, or WebORB. The `WebService` class communicates with a web service that defines its interface by using the Web Services Description Language (WSDL) and uses either SOAP-based XML or XML.

To create a service component, you need to configure the properties of the service, setting the URL of the server that will be used to send requests and receive data, as well as information about the type of data expected. For the `HTTPService` object, you need to set the method for passing parameters to the server, either `GET` or `POST`, and the `resultFormat`. For the `WebService` component, you must set the URL of the WSDL document for the service, describe each operation that the `WebService` will use in the `<mx:Operation>` tag, and set result and fault handlers for that operation. For the `RemoteObject` class, the URL of the service is described in the services-config.xml file that is compiled into the SWF file. Each method that the service defines can be listed and its result and fault handlers defined.

After a call is made to an `HTTPservice`, the data returned by the service is placed in a `lastResult` object contained in the service component. The `resultFormat` property of the service components is an ActionScript `Object` by default. All data returned by the service is represented as properties of the `Object`. Any XML data returned by a `WebSer vice` or an `HTTPService` is transformed by Flex into its respective base types, `Number`, `String`, `Boolean`, and `Date`. If a strongly typed object is needed, a custom data type, then instances of that type must be created and populated by using the objects stored within the `lastResult`. The `WebService` and `RemoteObject` classes use a result event handler function that's called when the result of the service is returned. A fault event handler is used to handle any faults returned by the service. Any data processing done to the results of the service is performed in the body of the result function.

16.1 Configure an HTTPService

Problem

You need to create and configure an `HTTPService` component to allow your application to communicate with HTTP-based services.

Solution

Add an `HTTPService` component to your application and set its `url` property to the URL from which the application will request data. If the response from the service will be XML that requires custom processing, set the `xmlDecode` property to a method that accepts an XML object.

Discussion

The `HTTPService` object facilitates all communication done over HTTP. This includes any information sent via `GET` or `POST` commands, as well as information retrieved from a URL request, even static files. The `HTTPService` object can have result and fault event handlers assigned to it that accept `mx.event.ResultsEvent` objects and `mx.event.FaultEvent` objects, respectively:

```
<mx:HTTPService url="http://192.168.1.101/service.php" id="service"
result="serviceResult(event)" fault="serviceFault(event)">
```

This lets you process the results of an HTTP request. The `result` property of the `HTTPService` object can also be bound to, using the `result` property of the `HTTPSer vice` object:

```
<mx:Image source="{service.lastResult as String}"/>
```

Note that the `lastResult` of the `HTTPService` is an object and must be cast as a string.

The `HTTPService` object can also be used to send information via `GET` or `POST` variables to a script by configuring the request property of the `HTTPService` object:

```
<mx:HTTPService>
    <mx:request xmlns="">
        <id>{requestedId}</id>
```

```
            </mx:request>
        </mx:HTTPService>
```

This sends the `requestedId` property wrapped within an `<id>` tag to the URL set within the `HTTPService` object.

In the following example, an `HTTPService` object loads XML from a PHP script:

```
<mx: Application xmlns:mx="http://www.adobe.com/2006/mxml" width="400" height="300">
    <mx:HTTPService url="http://localhost/service.php" id="service"
result="serviceResult(event)" fault="serviceFault(event)"
    method="GET" contentType="application/xml" useProxy="false">
        <mx:request xmlns="">
            <id>{requestedId}</id>
        </mx:request>
    </mx:HTTPService>
    <mx:Script>
        <![CDATA[
            import mx.rpc.events.FaultEvent;
            import mx.rpc.events.ResultEvent;

            [Bindable]
            private var requestedId:Number;

            //trace the result of the service out
            private function serviceResult(event:Event):void {
                trace(service.lastResult.name);
            }

            // in the event that the service faults or times out
            private function serviceFault(event:Event):void {
                trace('broken service');
            }

            private function callService():void {
                requestedId = input.text as Number;
                service.send()
            }

        ]]>
    </mx:Script>
    <mx:TextInput id="input"/>
    <mx:Button label="get user name" click="callService()"/>
    <mx:Text text="{service.lastResult.name}"/>
    <mx:Text text="{service.lastResult.age}"/>
</mx:Application>
```

This is the PHP script that will read from the GET variables sent by the Flex application and return properly formatted XML data:

```
<?php
$id_number = $_GET["id"];
echo('<id>'.$id_number.'</id><name>Todd Anderson</name><age>30</age>')
?>
```

16.2 Use RESTful Communication Between Flex Applications

Problem

You need to integrate a Flex application with a server that uses RESTful, or Representational State Transfer–style communication, such as Rails or another server.

Solution

Create an `HTTPService` object to communicate with your server and use the appropriate paths in conjunction with `POST` and `GET` methods to call server methods.

Discussion

The term *RESTful service* is used to describe a service that uses all four possible HTTP headers: `PUT`, `POST`, `DELETE`, and `GET`. These four headers are usually mapped to the four basic data-access operations: create, read, update, and delete, commonly referred to with the charming acronym CRUD. In practice, a single overloaded server-side method performs the four basic data-access operations depending on the header sent. In a RESTful application, the method is frequently mapped to a resource, so that the four data-access methods, CRUD, allow the creation, deletion, update, or request of the resource. This resource can be a simple resource, a table in a database, or a complexly modeled object.

The Flash Player is limited to using only `GET` and `POST` methods, which means that any communication between a Flex application and a service will need to indicate the `DELETE` or `PUT` methods through a different manner, such as appending them to a `GET` or `POST` message.

To send a `PUT` command to a Rails application, you can do something like the following:

```
var request:URLRequest = new URLRequest();
var loader:URLLoader = new URLLoader();
loader.addEventListener(Event.COMPLETE, resultHandler);
loader.addEventListener(IOErrorEvent.IO_ERROR, errorHandler);
loader.addEventListener(HTTPStatusEvent.HTTP_STATUS,httpStatusHandler);
request.url = "http://rails/view/resource";

// Set the request type as POST and send the DELETE command as
// a variable in the data of the request
request.method = URLRequestMethod.POST;
request.data._method = "DELETE";

loader.load(request);
```

Ruby on Rails allows the `_method` variable to indicate the desired method even when the correct HTTP method cannot be used. For other types of RESTful services, similar approaches must be used.

To work around this with an `HTTPService` object, you can use the BlazeDS or Adobe LiveCycle servers. The `HTTPService` defines a `useProxy` property, which if set to true instructs the Flash Player to communicate only with a server defined in the services-config.xml file. A request to build and send a proxied `PUT/DELETE/OPTIONS` (and so forth) request is sent to either the Adobe LiveCycle or BlazeDS server, and then the server builds and sends the actual HTTP request and returns the response to the player. The proxy also handles fault responses in the HTTP 500 code range that represents messages for server errors and returns them to the player in a form that `HTTPService` can process usefully, because the Flash Player doesn't handle responses in the 500 range.

After you configure the `HTTPService` object to use the BlazeDS or LiveCycle proxy, you can use the full range of headers with the `HTTPService` object by setting the `method` property of the service:

```
<mx:HTTPService id="proxyService" destination="http://localhost/app/url"/>
<mx:Script>
    <![CDATA[
        private function sendPut():void {
            proxyService.method = "DELETE";
            proxyService.send("id=2");
        }

    ]]>
</mx:Script>
```

Finally there is a library called as3httpclient developed by Gabriel Handford that uses the binary Flash socket to read the HTTP stream and decode the HTTP response. This allows you to send and read GET, POST, PUT, and DELETE HTTP responses but requires that a crossdomain.xml file is created that will allow the Flash Player to connect to the server using port 80. While communicating with a server using the `Socket` is difficult, if you need to communicate with a server that uses RESTful responses and strict HTTP, this library provides a powerful alternative to the standard `HTTPService`. More information and code downloads can be found at *http://code.google.com/p/as3httpclientlib/*.

16.3 Configure and Connect to a RemoteObject

Problem

You need to configure a `RemoteObject` for a Flex application to connect to a ColdFusion, AMFPHP, or Java object that has been exposed for service communication with your Flex application.

Solution

Create a `RemoteObject` instance in your application and set an `id` for your service, as well as a URL where the services will be accessible.

Discussion

The `RemoteObject` lets you define communication between your application and actual class objects on a server. This is quite different from the `WebService` component (which relies on the WSDL file of a `WebService`) or the `HTTPService` (which simply uses the URL to send and receive HTTP information). The `RemoteObject` component can be used to call methods on a ColdFusion CFC component or Java class that has been exposed for communication. `RemoteObject`s can also be used to communicate with objects and re- sources defined by open source projects such as AMFPHP, SabreAMF, and the WebORB project. The `RemoteObject` defines the following configurable properties:

`channelSet : ChannelSet`
> Provides access to the `ChannelSet` used by the service.

`concurrency : String`
> Value indicates how to handle multiple calls to the same service.

`constructor : Object`
> Reference to the class object or constructor function for a given object instance.

`destination : String`
> Destination of the service.

`endpoint : String`
> Lets you quickly specify an endpoint for a `RemoteObject` destination without refer- ring to a services configuration file at compile time or programmatically creating a `ChannelSet`.

`makeObjectsBindable : Boolean`
> Forces returned anonymous objects to bindable objects when true.

`operations : Object`
> Specifies methods that the service defines; used when defining a `RemoteObject` in MXML. This tag is not typically used in ActionScript.

`requestTimeout : int`
> Provides access to the request time-out in seconds for sent messages.

`showBusyCursor : Boolean`
> Displays a busy cursor while a service is executing, if true.

`source : String`
> Lets you specify a source value on the client; not supported for destinations that use the `JavaAdapter` to serialize communication between a SWF file and a Java object.

Because `RemoteObject` methods can return objects that do not need to be processed or deserialized from XML, the result of a `RemoteObject` call can be cast to an `ArrayCollection` or a strongly typed value object from the `ResultEvent`. In the following code snippet, a `RemoteObject` is configured to use a Java service available at *http://local host:8400*:

```
<mx:Application xmlns:mx="http://www.adobe.com/2006/mxml" width="400" height="300">
    <mx:RemoteObject id="local_service" concurrency="single"
destination="http://localhost:8400/app"
        showBusyCursor="true" source="LocalService.Namespace.Service.ServiceName">
            <mx:method name="getNames" fault="getNamesFault(event)"
result="getNamesResult(event)"/>
            <mx:method name="getAges" fault="getAgesFault(event)"
result="getAgesResult(event)"/>
    </mx:RemoteObject>
    <mx:Script>
        <![CDATA[
            import mx.collections.ArrayCollection;
            import mx.rpc.events.ResultEvent;
            import mx.controls.Alert;
            import mx.rpc.events.FaultEvent;

            private function getNamesFault(event:FaultEvent):void {

                mx.controls.Alert.show(event.message as String, "Service Error");

            }

            private function getNamesResult(event:ResultEvent):void {

                var namesColl:ArrayCollection = event.result as ArrayCollection;
            }

            private function getAgesFault(event:FaultEvent):void {

                mx.controls.Alert.show(event.message as String, "Service Error");
            }

            private function getAgesResult(event:ResultEvent):void {

                var agesColl:ArrayCollection = event.result as ArrayCollection;
            }

        ]]>
    </mx:Script>
</mx:Application>
```

The result event of each method is bound to a different event-handling method. In ActionScript this would be done by adding an event-listening method to the RemoteObject:

```
import mx.collections.ArrayCollection;
import mx.rpc.events.ResultEvent;
import mx.controls.Alert;
import mx.rpc.events.FaultEvent;
import mx.rpc.AbstractService;
import mx.rpc.AsyncToken;
import mx.rpc.Responder;

private function init():void {
```

```
    var responder:Responder = new Responder( getNamesResult, getNamesFault );
    var call:AsyncToken = ( local_service as AbstractService).getNames();
    call.addResponder(responder);

}

private function getNamesFault(event:FaultEvent):void {

    Alert.show(event.message as String, "Service Error");

}

private function getNamesResult(event:ResultEvent):void {

    var namesColl:ArrayCollection = event.result as ArrayCollection;
}
```

In the preceding example, the `mx.rpc.Responder` class is used to store the methods that will handle the result and fault events from the server. This responder is then added to an `AsyncToken` class that will fire when the service returns either a result or a fault.

16.4 Use Flex Remoting with AMFPHP 1.9

Contributed by Sankar Paneerselvam

Problem

You need to use Flex remoting to communicate with a server with AMFPHP installed.

Solution

Create the AMFPHP installation and configure it to connect it to the data source. Use the `RemoteObject` to access the AMFPHP service and call methods on it.

Discussion

To demonstrate how to use AMFPHP with Oracle Database Express Edition (XE), this example displays the employee table from an Oracle database using remoting components. The EMPLOYEES table from the HR schema has the following structure in Oracle Database XE.

EMPLOYEE_ID	PLS_INTEGER
FIRST_NAME	VARCHAR2
LAST_NAME	VARCHAR2
EMAIL	VARCHAR2
PHONE_NUMBER	VARCHAR2
HIRE_DATE	DATE

JOB_ID	PLS_INTEGER
SALARY	NUMBER
COMMISSION_PCT	NUMBER
MANAGER_ID	PLS_INTEGER
DEPARTMENT_ID	PLS_INTEGER

To create a corresponding Employee class in PHP, you can use the following:

```php
<?php
class Employee
{
    var $EMPLOYEE_ID;
    var $FIRST_NAME;
    var $LAST_NAME;
    var $EMAIL;
    var $PHONE_NUMBER;
    var $HIRE_DATE;
    var $JOB_ID;
    var $SALARY;
    var $COMMISSION_PCT;
    var $MANAGER_ID;
    var $DEPARTMENT_ID;

    var $_explicitType = "project.Employee";
}
?>
```

The $_explicitType assumes that you will have a corresponding class in ActionScript for mapping the Employee class there.

This recipe uses the AMFPHP open source PHP framework for streaming data over PHP. AMFPHP uses services that can be called by a Flex RemoteObject to return AMF-formatted data. In this recipe, we're using a service called EmployeeService to return the employee data. The service file should be placed under the services folder of the AMFPHP installation. It assumes you'll use a top-level directory called Project and place all the services under it.

```php
<?php
require_once('./Employee.php');
class EmployeeService {
 var $myconnection=null;
    var $statement=null;
function getEmployees(){
    $myconnection = oci_connect('hr','hr', "//localhost/xe");
        # Check Oracle connection"
        if (!myconnection) {
            # Dont use die (Fatal Error), return useful info to the client
            trigger_error("AMFPHP Remoting 'EmployeeService'
class could not connect: " . oci_error());
        }
        $query="SELECT * FROM EMPLOYEES";
        # Return a list of all the employees
```

```
        $statement=oci_parse($myconnection,$query);
        if (!$statement) {
            oci_close($myconnection);
            trigger_error("AMFPHP Remoting 'EmployeeService'
class database SELECT query error: " . oci_error());
        }
        oci_execute($statement);
        while ($row = oci_fetch_array($statement,OCI_RETURN_NULLS)) {
            $data_array[] = $row;
        }
        return($data_array);
    }
}
?>
```

You can check the service by using the Service browser located at the browser folder of your AMFPHP installation for testing the services.

Remoting in Flex requires that a service-config.xml file be provided. You can add the service-config.xml file into your Flex project as shown in the following code segment. You may need to modify the location and port number of your server. Nothing else should be modified.

```
<services-config>
    <services>
        <service id="amfphp-flashremoting-service"
class="flex.messaging.services.RemotingService"
messageTypes="flex.messaging.messages.RemotingMessage">
            <destination id="amfphp">
                <channels>
                    <channel ref="my-amfphp"/>
                </channels>
                <properties>
                    <source>*</source>
                </properties>
            </destination>
        </service>
    </services>
    <channels>
        <channel-definition id="my-amfphp" class="mx.messaging.channels.AMFChannel">
            <endpoint uri="http://localhost:9999/amfphp2/amfphp/gateway.php"
class="flex.messaging.endpoints.AMFEndpoint"/>
        </channel-definition>
    </channels>
</services-config>
```

This service-config.xml file should be registered with the following steps:

1. In Flex Builder, click Project→Properties.

2. Under the Flex Compiler section, add **-services service-config.xml** after locale en_US. If you haven't already made changes to this field, it should look like this:

    ```
    -locale en_US -services service-config.xml
    ```

3. Click on Apply for the settings to take effect.

Now create an ActionScript class to hold the remote objects:

```
package project
{
    [RemoteClass(alias="project.Employee")]
    public class Employee
    {
        public var EMPLOYEE_ID:Number;
        public var FIRST_NAME:String;
        public var LAST_NAME:String;
        public var EMAIL:String;
        public var PHONE_NUMBER:Number;
        public var HIRE_DATE:Date;
        public var JOB_ID:Number;
        public var SALARY:Number;
        public var COMMISSION_PCT:Number;
        public var MANAGER_ID:Number;
        public var DEPARTMENT_ID:Number;
    }
}
```

Here's the MXML code for calling a remote method, getting results, and displaying it:

```
<mx:Application xmlns:mx="http://www.adobe.com/2006/mxml" layout="absolute">
```

Here the RemoteObject that will call the Employee service has its destination, source, and event handler methods set:

```
<mx:RemoteObject id="myservice" source="Project.EmployeeService"
destination="amfphp" fault="faultHandler(event)" showBusyCursor="true">
    <mx:method name="getEmployees" result="resultHandler(event)"
fault="faultHandler(event)">
    </mx:method>
</mx:RemoteObject>
<mx:Script>
    <![CDATA[
        import Project.Employee;
        import mx.utils.ArrayUtil;
        import mx.collections.ArrayCollection;
        import mx.rpc.events.FaultEvent;
        import mx.rpc.events.ResultEvent;
        import mx.controls.Alert;
```

When the data is returned, the dp:ArrayCollection will be set to the result property of the ResultEvent from the server:

```
        [Bindable]
        private var dp:ArrayCollection;

        private function faultHandler(event:FaultEvent):void {
            Alert.show(event.fault.faultString, event.fault.faultCode.toString());
        }
        private function resultHandler(event:ResultEvent):void {
            dp=new ArrayCollection(ArrayUtil.toArray(event.result));
        }
    ]]>
</mx:Script>
```

```
            <mx:Canvas x="0" y="0" width="100%" height="100%">
                <mx:Button x="10" y="10" label="Get data"
        click="myservice.getOperation('getEmployees').send()"/>
```

Each column correlates to a property in the data object returned from the service:

```
            <mx:DataGrid x="10" y="40" width="100%" height="100%"  dataProvider="{dp}">
                <mx:columns>
                    <mx:DataGridColumn headerText="EMPLOYEE_ID" dataField="EMPLOYEE_ID"/>
                    <mx:DataGridColumn headerText="FIRST_NAME" dataField="FIRST_NAME"/>
                    <mx:DataGridColumn headerText="LAST_NAME" dataField="LAST_NAME"/>
                    <mx:DataGridColumn headerText="EMAIL" dataField="EMAIL"/>
                    <mx:DataGridColumn headerText="PHONE_NUMBER"
        dataField="PHONE_NUMBER"/>
                    <mx:DataGridColumn headerText="HIRE_DATE" dataField="HIRE_DATE"/>
                    <mx:DataGridColumn headerText="JOB_ID" dataField="JOB_ID"/>
                    <mx:DataGridColumn headerText="SALARY" dataField="SALARY"/>
                    <mx:DataGridColumn headerText="COMMISSION_PCT"
        dataField="COMMISSION_PCT"/>
                    <mx:DataGridColumn headerText="MANAGER_ID" dataField="MANAGER_ID"/>
                    <mx:DataGridColumn headerText="DEPARTMENT_ID"
        dataField="DEPARTMENT_ID"/>
                </mx:columns>
            </mx:DataGrid>
        </mx:Canvas>
    </mx:Application>
```

When the user clicks the Get Data button, the code sends a remote request, gets the results of the data, and populates the DataGrid.

16.5 Use the IExternalizable Interface for Custom Serialization

Contributed by Peter Farland

Problem

You want to customize which properties are sent over the wire when sending strongly typed data via RemoteObject or DataService.

Solution

Use the ActionScript 3 API flash.utils.IExternalizable, which is compatible with Java's java.io.IExternalizable API.

Discussion

A common scenario for using externalizable classes is to include read-only properties in serialization. Although there are other approaches to achieve this for server code, there aren't many approaches available for client code. So for an elegant solution that works for both the client and server, you can make your classes externalizable for two-way custom serialization.

This approach is relatively straightforward. The client ActionScript class simply implements `flash.utils.IExternalizable`. This API requires two methods, `readExternal` and `writeExternal`, which take `flash.utils.IDataInput` and `flash.utils.IDataOutput` streams, respectively. The implementations of these methods mirror the server Java class, which implements `java.io.Externalizable`, which also has two methods, `readExternal` and `writeExternal`, taking `java.io.ObjectInput` and `java.io.ObjectOutput` streams, respectively.

Although the `IDataInput` and `IDataOutput` classes let you design your own protocol and write such fundamental data types as `byte`, `int`, and UTF-8-encoded `Strings`, most implementations take advantage of the `readObject` and `writeObject` methods, respectively, as these use AMF 3 to efficiently deserialize and serialize ActionScript objects. (Remember that AMF 3 has three advantages: You can send objects by reference to avoid redundant instances from being serialized, to retain object relationships. and to handle cyclical references. You can send object traits so that the description of a type is sent only once rather than repeated for each instance. You can send reoccurring strings by reference to again avoid redundant information from being sent.) You may even decide to omit property names altogether in your externalizable classes' custom serialization code and rely on a fixed order to send just the property values.

 This example focuses on serializing read-only properties, but there may be many other usages for custom serialization, such as omitting properties, avoiding redundant serialization of information, or including properties from custom namespaces.

Notice how the following Java `writeExternal` method

```
public void writeExternal(ObjectOutput out) throws IOException
{
    out.writeObject(id);
    out.writeObject(name);
    out.writeObject(description);
    out.writeInt(price);
}
```

mirrors the client `readExternal` method in ActionScript:

```
public function readExternal(input:IDataInput):void
{
    _id = input.readObject() as String;
    name = input.readObject() as String;
    description = input.readObject() as String;
    price = input.readInt();
}
```

A similar relationship exists for the reverse situation, for sending instances back from the client to the server.

16.6 Track Results from Multiple Simultaneous Service Calls

Contributed by Andrew Alderson

Problem

You need to determine which returned data belongs to which of your multiple simultaneous service calls.

Solution

Use ASyncToken to add a variable to each call to identify it.

Discussion

Because mx.rpc.ASyncToken is a dynamic class, you can add properties and methods to it at runtime. The Flex documentation states that it is "a place to set additional or token-level data for asynchronous rpc operations."

As an example, consider an application with a DateChooser control in it. Every time the user scrolls to a new month, you need to retrieve an XML file from the server for that month. Because there is no way to guarantee in which order these files will come back, you need a way to identify them. By using ASyncToken, you can add an identifying property to the result event that is returned by the service call. For example:

```
    <mx:Application xmlns:mx="http://www.adobe.com/2006/mxml"
layout="horizontal"> <mx:Script>
    <![CDATA[
    import mx.rpc.events.FaultEvent;
    import mx.rpc.events.ResultEvent;
    import mx.rpc.AsyncToken;
    import mx.events.DateChooserEvent;
    private function scrollHandler(event:DateChooserEvent):void {
        var month:int = event.currentTarget.displayedMonth;
        var monthName:String = event.currentTarget.monthNames[month];

        service.url = "xml/"+monthName+".xml";
        var token:AsyncToken = service.send();
        token.resultHandler = onResult;
        token.faultHandler = onFault;
        token.month = monthName;
    }
    private function onResult(event:ResultEvent):void {
        resultText.text = "MonthName: "+event.token.month+"\n\n";

        resultText.text += "Result: "+event.result.data.month;
    }
    private function onFault(event:FaultEvent):void {
        resultText.text = event.fault.faultString;
    }
]]> </mx:Script>
<mx:HTTPService id="service" result="event.token.resultHandler(event)"
```

```
fault="event.token.faultHandler(event)"/>
<mx:DateChooser id="dateChooser" scroll="scrollHandler(event)"/>
<mx:TextArea id="resultText" width="300" height="200"/>
</mx:Application>
```

The preceding code calls the `scrollHandler` event to retrieve an XML file from the server. If the user clicks fast enough, you could have multiple requests happening at the same time. In `HTPPService`, the `send` method returns an `ASyncToken` so you can access this and add a property to identify the month to which the returned data belongs. You can use the `ResultEvent`'s `token` property to access your `month` property through this in the result handler.

This method can also be used with `WebService` and `RemoteObject` calls. In these calls, the operation or method that is called returns the `ASyncToken`:

```
var token : AsyncToken = service.login( loginVO );
```

16.7 Use Publish/Subscribe Messaging

Problem

You want to notify the client Flex application whenever data has changed on the server side or to broadcast messages to all listeners on a messaging server.

Solution

Use the `mx.messaging.Producer` and `mx.messaging.Consumer` tags to configure the destination channel that will be used for communication and to set the event handler for the message event. Configuring these correctly requires using either the Adobe Live-Cycle or the BlazeDS servers.

Discussion

The Publish/Subscribe model uses two components: `mx.messaging.Producer` and `mx.messaging.Consumer`. The `Producer` sends messages to a *destination*, a location on the server where messages are processed. The `Consumer` subscribes to messages at a destination and processes those messages when they arrive from the destination.

Messaging in Flex allows ActionScript Messaging and Java Message Service (JMS) messaging. ActionScript Messaging supports only clients that can speak AMF and support the necessary classes to work properly. JMS messaging allows LiveCycle or BlazeDS to participate in the Java Message Service and interact with any JMS client. Any application that can talk to JMS can be called directly from a Flex client, and any Java application can publish events to Flex.

The `Consumer` receives messages via the `mx.messaging.events.MessageEvent`:

```
private function receiveChatMessage(msgEvent:MessageEvent):void
{
```

```
                var msg:AsyncMessage = AsyncMessage(msgEvent.message);
                trace("msg.body "+msg.body);
        }
```

The **Producer** sends messages by using the **send** method, which accepts
mx.messaging.AsyncMessage as a parameter. The body of the **AsyncMessage** is the value
sent to all subscribers of the channel:

```
                var msg:AsyncMessage = new AsyncMessage();
                msg.body = "test message";
                producer.send(msg);
```

The complete code listing is as follows:

```
        <mx:Application xmlns:mx="http://www.adobe.com/2006/mxml" xmlns="*"
            pageTitle="Simple Flex Chat" creationComplete="chatSubscriber.subscribe()">
            <!-- Messaging Declarations -->
            <mx:Producer id="producer" destination="http://localhost:8400/chatDestination"/>
            <mx:Consumer id="subscriber" destination="http://localhost:8400/chatDestination"
        message="receiveChatMessage(event)" />
            <mx:Script>
                <![CDATA[

                import mx.messaging.events.MessageEvent;
                import mx.messaging.messages.AsyncMessage;

                private function sendChatMessage():void
                {
                    var msg:AsyncMessage = new AsyncMessage();
                    msg.body = "test message";
                    producer.send(msg);
                }

                private function receiveChatMessage(msgEvent:MessageEvent):void
                {
                    var msg:AsyncMessage = AsyncMessage(msgEvent.message);
                    trace("msg.body "+msg.body);
                }
                ]]>
            </mx:Script>
        </mx:Application>
```

16.8 Register a Server-Side Data Type Within a Flex Application

Problem

You need to register a server-side data type in your application so that objects received
from a **RemoteObject** can be cast as instances of that remote class within your Flex
application.

Solution

Use the flash.net.RegisterClass method or mark the class as a RemoteClass in the class declaration.

Discussion

Before an object can be deserialized from AMF data into a Class object, the signature of that class must be registered with the Flash Player in order to deserialize objects into the correct types. For instance, say the following type is defined in C#:

```
using System;
using System.Collections;

namespace oreilly.cookbook.vo
{
    public class RecipeVO {
            public string title;
          public ArrayList ingredients;
        public ArrayList instructions

            public RecipeVO(){}
    }
}
```

The corresponding ActionScript type could be the following:

```
package oreilly.cookbook.vo
{
    public class RecipeVO

    public var ingredients:Array;
    public var instructions:Array;
    public var title:String;

    public function RecipeVO(){}

}
```

The service that returns the RecipeVO object can create a new object in C# and return it:

```
using System;
using System.Web;
using oreilly.cookbook.vo;
namespace oreilly.cookbook.service
{
    public class RecipeService
    {
        public RecipeService() { }

        public RecipeVO getRecipe() {
            RecipeVO rec = new RecipeVO();
            rec.title = "Apple Pie";
            string[] ingredients = {"flour", "sugar", "apples", "eggs", "water"};
            rec.ingredients = new ArrayList(ingredients);
```

```
                    string[] instructions = {"instructions are long", "baking is hard",
    "maybe I'll just buy it at the store"};
                    rec.instruction = new ArrayList(instructions);
                    return rec;
            }
        }
    }
```

Even though this service and the corresponding value object (in this case, the RecipeVO) are written in C#, the service and the corresponding serialization would be very similar in Java and many other server-side languages.

When the service returns, the resulting RecipeVO can be accessed as shown:

```
<mx:RemoteObject id="recipeService" destination="fluorine"
source="oreilly.cookbook.FlexService" showBusyCursor="true"
    result="roResult(event)" fault="roFault(event)" />

    <mx:Script>
        <![CDATA[

        private function initApp():void {
            // we have to register the object for the result to be able
to properly cast
            // as the RecipeVO
            flash.net.registerClassAlias("oreilly.cookbook.vo.RecipeVO", RecipeVO);
        }

        public function serviceResult(e:ResultEvent):void {
            var rec:RecipeVO = (e.result as RecipeVO)
        }

        public function serviceFault(e:FaultEvent):void {
            trace(" Error :: "+(e.message as String));
        }


        ]]>
    </mx:Script>
```

After the class has been registered by using the registerClassAlias method, objects with a matching signature that have been sent via remoting can be cast to the RecipeVO class.

16.9 Communicate with a WebService

Problem

You need to enable your Flex application to communicate with a server via web services that will send WSDL messages to describe their service methods and then to use that information to call methods on that web service.

Solution

Create an `mx.rpc.WebService` object and set the `wsdl` property of the `WebService` to the location of the WSDL document that defines your service.

Discussion

The `WebService` component enables an application to communicate with a web service using a defined WSDL file. The Flash Player recognizes the following properties within a WSDL file:

`<binding>`
Specifies the protocol that clients, such as Flex applications, use to communicate with a web service. Bindings exist for SOAP, HTTP `GET`, HTTP `POST`, and Multipurpose Internet Mail Extensions (MIME). Flex supports the SOAP binding only.

`<fault>`
Specifies an error value that's returned as a result of a problem processing a message.

`<input>`
Specifies a message that a client, such as a Flex application, sends to a web service.

`<message>`
Defines the data that a web service operation transfers.

`<operation>`
Defines a combination of `<input>`, `<output>`, and `<fault>` tags.

`<output>`
Specifies a message that the web service sends to a web service client, such as a Flex application.

`<port>`
Specifies a web service endpoint, which specifies an association between a binding and a network address.

`<portType>`
Defines one or more operations that a web service provides.

`<service>`
Defines a collection of `<port>` tags. Each service maps to one `<portType>` tag and specifies different ways to access the operations in that tag.

`<types>`
Defines data types that a web service's messages use.

The Flex application inspects the WSDL file to determine all the methods that the service supports and the types of data that will be returned by each service. A typical WSDL file defines the name of the service, any types used by the service, and the content of any messages that the service would expect and return.

To create a WebService object, set an id for the service as well as the location of the WSDL file that defines the service:

```
<mx:WebService id="userRequest" wsdl="http://localhost:8400/service/service?wsdl">
    <mx:operation name="getRecipes" result="getRecipeHandler()"
        fault="mx.controls.Alert.show(event.fault.faultString)"/>
</mx:WebService>
```

The WebService dispatches a LoadEvent of type load or LoadEvent.LOAD, which indicates that the WebService has loaded and parsed the WSDL file set in the wsdl property and is ready to have methods called on it. The WebService object cannot be called before this, so it is recommended that this event be used to indicate that the service can be called. The WebService component also defines a ready Boolean value that can be checked to confirm that the WSDL file has been loaded and that the WebService is ready. In the following example, a method is defined and event handlers are attached to the result and fault events of the service:

```
<mx:Application xmlns:mx="http://www.adobe.com/2006/mxml" width="400" height="300">
    <mx:WebService id="userRequest" wsdl="http://localhost:8500/service/service?wsdl"
load="callService()">
        <mx:operation name="getRecipes" resultFormat="object"
fault="createRecipeFault(event)" result="createRecipeHandler(event)"/>
    </mx:WebService>
    <mx:Script>
        <![CDATA[
            import mx.rpc.events.FaultEvent;
            import mx.collections.ArrayCollection;
            import mx.rpc.events.ResultEvent;
            import mx.controls.Alert;

            private function callService():void {
                userRequest.getRecipes();
            }

            private function createRecipeHandler(event:ResultEvent):void {
                var arrayCol:ArrayCollection = event.result as ArrayCollection;
            }

            private function createRecipeFault(event:FaultEvent):void {
                Alert.show(" error :: "+event.message);
            }

        ]]>
    </mx:Script>
</mx:Application>
```

16.10 Add a SOAP Header to a Request to a WebService

Problem

You need to send a SOAP header along with a request to a WebService component.

Solution

Create a `SOAPHeader` object and pass in the namespace that should be used with the values passed in and the content that should be appended to the header. Then use the `WebService.addHeader` method to send the header along with the request.

Discussion

SOAP headers are frequently used by web services to receive logins, user information, or other data along with a request. A `SOAPHeader` object is created with a `QName` that will define the qualified namespace of the data contained within it and an object defining the data to be sent in the header in key-value pairs:

```
SOAPHeader(qname:QName, content:Object)
```

Here is an example of creating two `SOAPHeader` objects:

```
// Create a QName that can be used with your header
var qname:QName=new QName("http://soapinterop.org/xsd", "CookbookHeaders");
var headerone:SOAPHeader = new SOAPHeader(qname, {string:"header_one",int:"1"});
var headertwo:SOAPHeader = new SOAPHeader(qname, {string:"header_two",int:"2"});
```

To add the header to all requests made through a web service, call the `addHeader` method on the `WebService` object itself:

```
// calling addHeader on the WebService
service.addHeader(headerone);
```

To add the `SOAPHeader` to only a specific method that the service defines, use the name of the method to assign the `SOAPHeader` to that method:

```
// Add the headertwo SOAP Header to the getRecipe operation.
service.getRecipes.addHeader(headertwo);
```

If the SOAP headers are no longer needed, call the `clearHeaders` method on any `Web Service` or method that has had headers added to it:

```
service.clearHeaders();
service.getRecipes.clearHeaders();
```

16.11 Parse a SOAP Response from a WebService

Problem

You need to parse a SOAP response returned in answer to a request.

Solution

Use the Flash Player's native deserialization of SOAP types to ActionScript types for the SOAP-encoded XML that is returned from a `WebService`.

Discussion

The results of a SOAP response can be parsed using E4X expressions. The most commonly used types are shown in Table 16-1, along with their correct SOAP and ActionScript representations.

Table 16-1. SOAP Types and Their Corresponding ActionScript Types

Generic Type	SOAP	ActionScript 3
String	xsd:String	String
Integer	xsd:int	Int
Float	xsd:float	Number
Boolean	xsd:Boolean	Boolean
Date	xsd:date	Date
Array	xsd:string[], xsd:int[], and so forth	ArrayCollection
Object	Element	Object
Binary	xsd:Base64Binary	flash.utils.ByteArray
Null	xsl:Nil	Null

A WSDL file that defined the following return types

```
<wsdl:types>
  <schema elementFormDefault="qualified"
targetNamespace = "http://cookbook.webservices.com"
xmlns = "http://www.w3.org/2001/XMLSchema">
   <complexType name="Recipe">
    <sequence>
     <element name="title" nillable="true" type="xsd:string"/>
     <element name="ingredients" nillable="true" type="xsd:string[]"/>
   <element name="instructions" nillable="true" type="xsd:string[]"/>
  </sequence>
   </complexType>
   </schema>
  </wsdl:types>
```

had the following response returned from a request to the WebService:

```
<soap:Envelope xmlns:soap="http://www.w3.org/2001/12/soap-envelope"
soap:encodingStyle="http://www.w3.org/2001/12/soap-encoding">
  <soap:Body xmlns:ns="http://cookbook.oreilly.com/service">
   <ns:GetRecipes>
    <ns:Recipe>
      <ns:title>"Blueberry Pie"</ns:title>
      <SOAP-ENC:Array SOAP-ENC:arrayType="xsd:string[3]">
        <ns:ingredient>"Blueberry"</ns:ingredient>
        <ns:ingredient>"Sugar"</ns:ingredient>
        <ns:ingredient>"Crust"</ns:ingredient>
      </SOAP-ENC:Array>
      <SOAP-ENC:Array SOAP-ENC:arrayType="xsd:string[3]">
        <ns:instruction>"Blueberry"</ns:instruction>
```

```
            <ns:instruction>"Sugar"</ns:instruction>
            <ns:instruction>"Crust"</ns:instruction>
        </SOAP-ENC:Array>
      </ns:Recipe>
    </ns:GetRecipes>
  </soap:Body>
</soap:Envelope>
```

This response could be parsed easily into the requisite objects by using dot notation, as would be done with any XML object. For more information on the different SOAP types and their ActionScript equivalents, see *http://www.adobe.com/go/kb402005*, which describes all the possible SOAP types.

16.12 Communicate Securely with AMF by Using SecureAMFChannel

Problem

You need to communicate over Flash remoting, using AMF data and Secure Sockets Layer (SSL).

Solution

Define your channel to be a `SecureAMFChannel` in the services-config.xml file that you use when compiling your application.

Discussion

The `SecureAMFChannel` lets you use an `AMFChannel` for communication over SSL, ensuring that any data sent over an `AMFChannel` is secure. To create a new channel that uses the secured versions of the AMF classes, simply create the services-config.xml file with a channel that uses the `mx.messaging.channels.SecureAMFChannel` as its class. The endpoint should also be configured to use the `flex.messaging.endpoints.SecureAMFEndpoint` class as shown here:

```
<channels>
    <channel ref="secure-amf"/>
</channels>

<channel-definition id="secure-amf" class="mx.messaging.channels.SecureAMFChannel">
    <endpoint uri="https://{server.name}:{server.port}/gateway/"
    class="flex.messaging.endpoints.SecureAMFEndpoint"/>
    <properties>
        <add-no-cache-headers>false</add-no-cache-headers>
        <polling-enabled>false</polling-enabled>
        <serialization>
            <instantiate-types>false</instantiate-types>
        </serialization>
```

```
        </properties>
    </channel-definition>
```

The preceding code snippet will work for ColdFusion, Adobe LiveCycle, and BlazeDS:

```
<mx:Application xmlns:mx="http://www.adobe.com/2006/mxml" width="400" height="300"
creationComplete="init()">
    <mx:RemoteObject id="channelRO"/>
    <mx:Script>
        <![CDATA[

            import mx.messaging.ChannelSet;
            import mx.messaging.channels.SecureAMFChannel;

            private var cs:ChannelSet

            private function init():void {

                cs = new ChannelSet();
                // note that the name of the channel is the same as in the
services-config.xml file
                var chan: SecureAMFChannel = new SecureAMFChannel("secure-amf",
"gateway")

                chan.pollingEnabled = true;
                chan.pollingInterval = 3000;
                cs.addChannel(chan);
                channelRO.channelSet = cs;

            }

        ]]>
    </mx:Script>
</mx:Application>
```

Now you can use the channel to call through the RemoteObject and make secured AMF polling calls.

16.13 Send and Receive Binary Data via a Binary Socket

Problem

You want to receive binary data and respond in a similar binary format after processing that data.

Solution

Use the flash.net.Socket and open a socket connection to the server and on the port number with which your application will communicate.

Discussion

The flash.net.Socket is the lowest-level tool for communication available in the Flex Framework or in ActionScript 3 and enables you to make socket connections and to read and write raw binary data. The Socket lets you send and receive messages in Post Office Protocol version 3 (POP3), Simple Mail Transfer Protocol (SMTP), and Internet Message Access Protocol (IMAP), as well as in custom binary formats. Flash Player can interface with a server by using the binary protocol of that server directly.

To create a new Socket, create the Socket instance by using the constructor, and call the connect method by passing an IP address or domain name and a port number:

```
var socket:Socket;
//create the new socket and connect to 127.0.0.1 on port 8080
private function init():void {

    socket = new Socket();
    socket.addEventListener(ProgressEvent.SOCKET_DATA, readSocketData);
    socket.connect("127.0.0.1", 8080);

}
// send data to the socket
private function sendSocketData(string:String):void {
    // send the string data and specify the encoding for the string
    // in this case iso-08859-1, standard western european encoding
    socket.writeMultiByte(string, "iso-8859-1");
}

// when data is passed to socket, read it into a new ByteArray
private function readSocketData(progressEvent:ProgressEvent):void {

    trace(progressEvent.bytesLoaded);
    var ba:ByteArray = new ByteArray();
    trace(socket.readBytes(bs));

}
```

In the preceding sendSocketData method, the writeMultiByte method sends data through the Socket to the connection. This method accepts a string value to send as binary data in the encoding specified by the second parameter. The readSocketData method reads any data sent to the Socket and reads the bytes of the data into the new ByteArray object. To read data back from the ByteArray, you can use the various read methods for reading integers, strings, and arrays. Objects sent over a Socket as binary data can be read by using the ByteArray readObject method if the class type has been registered via the flash.net.RegisterClass method.

To connect a Socket to a port number lower than 1024, you need a cross-domain.xml file at the root of the site to explicitly allow access to that port. For instance, to allow the Flash Player to communicate with a web server on port 80, use the following:

```
<?xml version="1.0"?>
<cross-domain-policy>
```

```
    <allow-access-from domain="*" to-ports="80" />
  </cross-domain-policy>
```

After the correct cross-domain.xml file is in place, the Socket can communicate with the server on the correct port.

16.14 Communicate Using an XMLSocket

Problem

To create a connection to a server that will receive XML data without requesting it.

Solution

Use the XMLSocket class to open a connection to a server that will allow the server to send information to the client and have that information be received and handled when it arrives at the client.

Discussion

The XMLSocket class implements client sockets that let the Flash Player or AIR application communicate with a server computer identified by an IP address or domain name. To use the XMLSocket class, the server computer must run a daemon that understands the protocol used by the XMLSocket class. For the protocol:

- XML messages are sent over a full-duplex Transmission Control Protocol /Internet Protocol (TCP/IP) stream socket connection.

- Each XML message is a complete XML document, terminated by a zero (0) byte.

You can send and receive an unlimited number of XML messages over a single XMLSocket connection. To connect to an XMLSocket object, create a new XMLSocket object and call the connect method using an IP address or domain name and then a port number:

```
var xmlsock:XMLSocket = new XMLSocket();
xmlsock.connect("127.0.0.1", 8080);
```

The port number is required because the XMLSocket can't communicate on ports lower than 1024. To receive data from the XMLSocket, add an event listener for the DataEvent.DATA event:

```
xmlsock.addEventListener(DataEvent.DATA, onData);
private function onData(event:DataEvent):void
{
    trace("[" + event.type + "] " + XML(event.data));
}
```

The string returned can be cast as XML and parsed by using E4X.

CHAPTER 17

Browser Communication

In many cases, you may find it necessary to communicate with the browser that contains your application. Browser communication enables you to build applications that go beyond the Flex application itself; you can link to existing sites, communicate with other applications via JavaScript, and enable interaction with your browser's history, as a start. The `ExternalInterface` class lets you call out to the browser containing the Flash application, get information about the page, and call JavaScript methods, as well as letting JavaScript methods call into the Flash application. This chapter focuses on the functionality contained within the core Flex Framework, though there are other tools to assist with integration of the browser and the Flash Player—the Adobe Flex Ajax Bridge (FABridge), and Joe Berkovitz's UrlKit among them.

17.1 Link to an External URL

Problem

You need to navigate to a separate URL.

Solution

Use the `navigateToURL` method to navigate the browser to the new URL.

Discussion

The `navigateToURL` function enables you to navigate the browser to a new URL in either the same window, a new window, or a specific window frame. This is one of the most common communications with the browser from a Flex application. To invoke the `navigateToURL` function from within your Flex 3 application, use this approach:

```
<mx:Application xmlns:mx="http://www.adobe.com/2006/mxml" layout="absolute">

    <mx:Script>
        <![CDATA[
            import flash.net.navigateToURL;
```

```
            private function goToURL() : void
            {
                navigateToURL( new URLRequest( newUrl.text ), target.selectedItem as
String );
            }
        ]]>
    </mx:Script>

    <mx:TextInput
        id="newUrl"
        top="10" left="10" right="10"
        text="http://www.oreilly.com/" />

    <mx:ComboBox
        id="target"
        top="40" left="10"
        dataProvider="{ [ '_blank', '_self' ] }" />

    <mx:Button
        label="Go"
        left="10" top="70"
        click="goToURL()" />

</mx:Application>
```

In this example, users can type in any URL and click the Go button to navigate to it. The first parameter of the navigateToURL method is a URLRequest object for the desired URL. The second parameter is the target window where that URL should be displayed. This could be any named window in the browser: _blank for a new window, _self for the current page, _top for the topmost frame container, or _parent for the parent of the current frame container.

17.2 Work with FlashVars

Problem

You need to pass data from your containing HTML page to your Flex 3 application.

Solution

Use FlashVars to add parameters directly into the HTML <embed> tag containing your Flex 3 SWF.

Discussion

You can embed data directly into the HTML that contains your Flex 3 application and easily read that data at runtime by using FlashVars variables. There are two ways to get these values into your Flex application.

You can modify the JavaScript that is used to embed your Flex application in the HTML page, as shown in the following example. Notice the last line in the snippet: It specifies four variables that are used to pass the data into the Flex application through the FlashVars parameter:

```
AC_FL_RunContent(
    "src", "${swf}",
    "width", "${width}",
    "height", "${height}",
    "align", "middle",
    "id", "${application}",
    "quality", "high",
    "bgcolor", "${bgcolor}",
    "name", "${application}",
    "allowScriptAccess","sameDomain",
    "type", "application/x-shockwave-flash",
    "pluginspage", "http://www.adobe.com/go/getflashplayer",
    "FlashVars", "param1=one&param2=2&param3=3&param4=four"
);
```

You could also modify the <object> and <embed> HTML tags directly if you are not using JavaScript to embed your Flex 3–compiled SWF file:

```
<object classid="clsid:D27CDB6E-AE6D-11cf-96B8-444553540000"
    id="${application}" width="${width}" height="${height}"

    codebase="http://fpdownload.macromedia.com/get/flashplayer/current/swflash.cab">
    <param name="movie" value="${swf}.swf" />
    <param name="quality" value="high" />
    <param name="bgcolor" value="${bgcolor}" />
    <param name="allowScriptAccess" value="sameDomain" />
    <param name="FlashVars" value="param1=one&param2=2&param3=3&param4=four" />
    <embed src="${swf}.swf" quality="high" bgcolor="${bgcolor}"
        width="${width}" height="${height}" name="${application}" align="middle"
        play="true"
        loop="false"
        quality="high"
        allowScriptAccess="sameDomain"
        type="application/x-shockwave-flash"
        pluginspage="http://www.adobe.com/go/getflashplayer"
        FlashVars="param1=one&param2=2&param3=3&param4=four"
    </embed>
</object>
```

In the Flex application, you can access FlashVars data any time through the Application.application.parameters object. This ActionScript example shows you how to access each of four FlashVars parameters as strings, as well as display them in a TextArea's text field:

```
private function onCreationComplete() : void
{
    var parameters : Object = Application.application.parameters;
    var param1 : String = parameters.param1;
    var param2 : int = parseInt( parameters.param2 );
    var param3 : int = parseInt( parameters.param3 );
```

```
        var param4 : String = parameters.param4;

        output.text = "param1: " + param1 + "\n" +
                      "param2: " + param2 + "\n" +
                      "param3: " + param3 + "\n" +
                      "param4: " + param4;
    }
```

17.3 Invoke JavaScript Functions from Flex

Problem

You need to invoke JavaScript functions from Flex.

Solution

Use `ExternalInterface` to invoke JavaScript functions from ActionScript.

Discussion

The `ExternalInterface` ActionScript class encapsulates everything that you need to communicate with JavaScript at runtime. You simply need to use the `ExternalInterface.call` method to execute a JavaScript function in the HTML page that contains your Flex application.

To invoke a simple JavaScript function in ActionScript, use the following:

```
ExternalInterface.call( "simpleJSFunction" );
```

The basic JavaScript function that would be invoked is shown next. The name of the JavaScript function is passed into the `call` method as a string value, and a JavaScript Alert window appears above your Flex application:

```
function simpleJSFunction()
{
    alert("myJavaScriptFunction invoked");
}
```

You can use this same technique to pass data from ActionScript into JavaScript with function parameters. With a line like this, you can invoke a JavaScript function with parameters passed into it:

```
ExternalInterface.call( "simpleJSFunctionWithParameters", "myParameter" );
```

Using this approach, you can pass multiple parameters, complex value objects, or simple parameters from ActionScript into JavaScript.

In JavaScript, you would handle this as you would any other function call that accepts a parameter. When invoked, this function will display the parameter value `myParameter` in a JavaScript alert above your Flex application:

```
function simpleJSFunctionWithParameters( parameter )
{
    alert( parameter);
}
```

Often, you may find it necessary to invoke a JavaScript function to return a value from JavaScript to your Flex application. To return a value from JavaScript to your Flex application, use this:

```
var result:String = ExternalInterface.call( "simpleJSFunctionWithReturn" );
```

You can see that the corresponding JavaScript function returns a string value, which will be stored in the **result** string instance within the ActionScript class:

```
function simpleJSFunctionWithReturn()
{
    return "this is a sample return value: " + Math.random();
}
```

17.4 Invoke ActionScript Functions from JavaScript

Problem

You need to invoke ActionScript functions from JavaScript in the HTML containing the Flex application.

Solution

Use `ExternalInterface` to set up callbacks from JavaScript to Flex and invoke Action-Script functions from JavaScript.

Discussion

The `ExternalInterface` ActionScript class not only encapsulates everything you need to communicate with JavaScript at runtime, but also includes everything that you need to invoke ActionScript functions from JavaScript.

Before you can invoke ActionScript functions from JavaScript, you need to register callbacks for the ActionScript functions that you want to expose to JavaScript. The callbacks are registered through the `ExternalInterface` class within ActionScript. Callbacks provide a mapping for JavaScript function calls to actual ActionScript functions.

This example shows you how to register callbacks for three ActionScript functions:

```
private function registerCallbacks() : void
{
    ExternalInterface.addCallback( "function1", callback1 );
    ExternalInterface.addCallback( "function2", callback2 );
    ExternalInterface.addCallback( "function3", callback3 );
}
```

The corresponding ActionScript functions for these are as follows:

```
private function callback1() : void
{
    Alert.show( "callback1 executed" );
}

private function callback2( parameter : * ) : void
{
    Alert.show( "callback2 executed: " + parameter.toString() );
}

private function callback3() : Number
{
    return Math.random()
}
```

Notice that `callback1` is a simple ActionScript function that can be invoked. It does not require any parameters and does not return a value. The function `callback2` accepts a single parameter, and the function `callback3` returns a randomly generated number.

When you want to invoke these functions from JavaScript, you must call a JavaScript function with the callback alias. The following JavaScript code will show you how to invoke these ActionScript functions that have been exposed:

```
function invokeFlexFunctions()
{
    var swf = "mySwf";
    var container;
    if (navigator.appName.indexOf("Microsoft") >= 0)
    {
        container = document;
    }
    else
    {
        container = window;
    }
    container[swf].function1();
    container[swf].function2( "myParameter" );
    var result = container[swf].function3();
    alert( result );
}
```

The variable `swf` contains the name of the Flex application, as it has been embedded within the HTML page (in this case, it is mySwf). The first thing that this script does is get a reference to the JavaScript DOM, based on the browser type. After the script has the proper browser DOM, it invokes the Flex functions based on the publicly exposed mappings that are specified when registering callbacks.

The ActionScript function `callback1` gets invoked simply by calling the `function1` callback on the Flex application instance within the JavaScript DOM, as shown:

```
container[swf].function1();
```

After this function is invoked, an alert message shows within the Flex application.

The ActionScript function `callback2` gets invoked simply by calling the `function2` callback and passing a value into it:

```
container[swf].function2( "myParameter" );
```

When invoked, this will display an Alert window within the Flex application that shows the parameter value specified by the JavaScript invocation.

The following example shows you how to return a value from Flex to JavaScript. The `function3` callback invokes the `callback3` ActionScript function. This function returns a randomly generated number to JavaScript.

When `callback3` is invoked, a random number is generated by Flex and returned to JavaScript. This value is then displayed in a JavaScript Alert window. For example:

```
var result = container[swf].function3();
alert( result );
```

17.5 Change the HTML Page Title via BrowserManager

Problem

You need to change the HTML page title for your Flex 3 application.

Solution

Use the `BrowserManager` class instance's `setTitle` method to change the HTML page title.

Discussion

The `BrowserManager` class in Flex 3 is used to easily interact with the HTML DOM of the HTML page that contains your Flex application. Among its features is the ability to change the title of the HTML page that contains your application. The following ActionScript code snippet sets the page title for you:

```
private function changePageTitle( newTitle : String ) : void
{
    //get an instance of the browser manager
    var bm : IBrowserManager = BrowserManager.getInstance();

    //initialize the browser manager
    bm.init();

    //set the page title
    bm.setTitle( newTitle );
}
```

17.6 Parse the URL via BrowserManager

Problem

You need to read and parse data from the browser's current URL.

Solution

Use the `BrowserManager` and `URLUtil` classes to read and parse the current page URL.

Discussion

The following example shows you how to read and parse the current page URL by using the `BrowserManager` and `URLUtil` classes, as well as write the parsed results to an `mx:TextArea` instance.

The `URLUtil` class has functions that will help you parse the different pieces of the current URL. When using deep linking within Flex 3, the URL is broken into two parts: the base and the fragment. The URL *base* is everything that is to the left of the # sign. The *fragment* is everything that is to the right of the # sign. The fragment is used to pass values into a Flex application and is also used in history management. A properly constructed fragment can be parsed by the `URLUtil.stringToObject` method into an ActionScript object that contains the values in the fragment, broken out to string values. Each name-value pair in the URL fragment should be delimited by a semicolon (;).

```
<mx:Application
    xmlns:mx="http://www.adobe.com/2006/mxml"
    layout="absolute"
    creationComplete="parseURL()">

<mx:Script>
    <![CDATA[
        import mx.utils.ObjectUtil;
        import mx.managers.IBrowserManager;
        import mx.managers.BrowserManager;
        import mx.utils.URLUtil;

        private function parseURL() : void
        {
            //get an instance of the browser manager
            var bm:IBrowserManager = BrowserManager.getInstance();

            //initialize the browser manager
            bm.init();

            //output the url parameter values
            output.text += "Full URL:\n" + bm.url + "\n\n";
            output.text += "Base URL:\n" + bm.base + "\n\n";
            output.text += "URL Fragment:\n" + bm.fragment + "\n\n";

            //convert url parameters to an actionscript object using URLUtil
```

```
                var o:Object = URLUtil.stringToObject(bm.fragment);
                output.text += "Object:\n" + ObjectUtil.toString( o ) + "\n\n";
                output.text += "name:\n" + o.name + "\n\n";
                output.text += "index:\n" + o.index + "\n\n";
                output.text += "productId:\n" + o.productId + "\n\n";

                //parse URL using URLUtil
                output.text += "URL Port:\n" + URLUtil.getPort( bm.url ) + "\n\n";
                output.text += "URL Protocol:\n" + URLUtil.getProtocol( bm.url ) +
"\n \n";
            output.text += "URL Server:\n" + URLUtil.getServerName( bm.url ) + "\n\n";
                output.text += "URL Server with Port:\n" +
URLUtil.getServerNameWithPort( bm.url );
            }

        ]]>
    </mx:Script>

    <mx:TextArea id="output" left="10" top="10" bottom="10" right="10"/>

</mx:Application>
```

If the preceding example had the URL *http://localhost:8501/flex3cookbook/ main.html#name=Andrew;index=12345;productId=987*, the result would be:

```
Full URL:
http://localhost:8501/flex3cookbook/main.html#name=Andrew;index=12345;productId=987

Base URL:
http://localhost:8501/flex3cookbook/main.html

URL Fragment:
name=Andrew%20Trice;index=12345;productId=987654

Object:
(Object)#0
  index = 12345
  name = "Andrew"
  productId = 987

name:
Andrew

index:
12345

productId:
987

URL Port:
8501

URL Protocol:
http

URL Server:
```

```
localhost

URL Server with Port:
localhost:8501
```

17.7 Deep-Link to Data via BrowserManager

Problem

You need to pass data from the browser's URL into Flex controls, and you need to update the value of the browser URL based on data within your Flex application, which should also work the browser's Forward and Back navigational buttons.

Solution

Use the `BrowserManager` class and `BrowserChangeEvents` to read and write data on the browser URL.

Discussion

Whenever the browser URL changes either by text input on the address bar, or through the usage of the navigation controls (Forward and Back buttons), a `BrowserChangeEvent.BROWSER_URL_CHANGE` event is dispatched through the `BrowserMan ager` instance. Whenever this type of event is encountered, you simply invoke the `updateValues` method to update values within the Flex controls. This lets you easily link to, and cycle through, your input values.

The following example shows you how to read data from the browser's URL and put those values into Flex `mx:TextInput` fields. When the sample application loads, it will read the data from the current URL and write the values of the `firstName` and `last Name` parameters into the text boxes. When the value of either the `firstName` or `lastName` `mx:TextInput` field is changed, the application will call the `setFragment` function on the browser manager, which will update the browser's URL with the new values for the `firstName` and `lastName` parameters. This enables you to copy and paste the URL, so that you can easily link directly into the current view, and it also adds every change to the browser history.

```
<mx:Application
    xmlns:mx="http://www.adobe.com/2006/mxml"
    layout="absolute"
    creationComplete="onCreationComplete()" >

    <mx:Script>
        <![CDATA[
            import mx.events.BrowserChangeEvent;
            import mx.managers.IBrowserManager;
            import mx.managers.BrowserManager;
            import mx.utils.URLUtil;
```

```
            private var bm:IBrowserManager

            private function onCreationComplete():void
            {
                //get an instance of the browser manager
                bm = BrowserManager.getInstance();

                //initialize the browser manager
                bm.init();

                //set initial values based on url parameters
                updateValues();

                //add event listeners to handle back/forward browser buttons
                bm.addEventListener( BrowserChangeEvent.BROWSER_URL_CHANGE,
onURLChange );
            }

            private function updateValues():void
            {
                //update text box values based on url fragment
                var o:Object = URLUtil.stringToObject(bm.fragment);
                firstName.text = o.firstName;
                lastName.text = o.lastName;
            }

            private function updateURL():void
            {
                //update URL fragment
                bm.setFragment( "firstName=" + firstName.text + ";lastName=" +
lastName.text );
            }

            private function onURLChange( event : BrowserChangeEvent ):void
            {
                //call update values based on change url
                updateValues();
            }
        ]]>
    </mx:Script>

    <mx:TextInput x="10" y="10" id="firstName" change="updateURL()" />
    <mx:TextInput x="10" y="40" id="lastName" change="updateURL()" />

</mx:Application>
```

17.8 Deep-Link Containers via BrowserManager

Problem

You need to control the visible contents of Flex 3 containers based on URL parameters.

Solution

Use the BrowserManager class and BrowserChangeEvents to control the visibility and track the history of the visible Flex components.

Discussion

In this scenario, you use the URL fragment to control and track which containers and components are visible within a Flex application. When the application loads, you initialize the BrowserManager class instance, which helps you parse and handle the browser URL. The updateContainers method (shown in the following code segment) determines which of the tabs within the mx:TabNavigator instance is visible. Any time that tab navigator's visible tab changes, you set the selectedIndex property in the URL fragment by using the following snippet:

```
bm.setFragment( "selectedIndex=" + tabNav.selectedIndex );
```

This updates the browser's URL and adds the change to the browser history. If someone were to copy and paste the current browser URL, that user would link directly to the currently selected tab navigator.

```
<mx:Application
    xmlns:mx="http://www.adobe.com/2006/mxml"
    layout="absolute"
    creationComplete="onCreationComplete()">

    <mx:Script>
        <![CDATA[
            import mx.events.BrowserChangeEvent;
            import mx.managers.IBrowserManager;
            import mx.managers.BrowserManager;
            import mx.utils.URLUtil;

            private var bm:IBrowserManager;

            private function onCreationComplete() : void
            {
                //get an instance of the browser manager
                bm = BrowserManager.getInstance();

                //initialize the browser manager
                bm.init();

                //set visible containers based on url parameters
                updateContainers();

                //add event listeners to handle back/forward browser buttons
                bm.addEventListener( BrowserChangeEvent.BROWSER_URL_CHANGE,
onURLChange );

                updateURL():
            }
```

```
            private function updateContainers():void
            {
                //convert url parameters to an actionscript object
                var o:Object = URLUtil.stringToObject(bm.fragment);

                //set the selected index
                if ( !isNaN(o.selectedIndex) )
                {
                    var newIndex : Number = o.selectedIndex;
                    if ( newIndex >= 0 && newIndex < tabNav.numChildren )
                        tabNav.selectedIndex = newIndex;
                }
            }

            private function onURLChange( event:BrowserChangeEvent ):void
            {
                //call updateContainers when url value changes
                updateContainers();
            }

            private function updateURL():void
            {
                bm.setFragment( "selectedIndex=" + tabNav.selectedIndex );
            }

        ]]>
    </mx:Script>

    <mx:TabNavigator
        bottom="10" top="10" right="10" left="10"
        id="tabNav"
        historyManagementEnabled="false">

        <mx:Canvas label="Tab 0" show="updateURL()" >
            <mx:Label text="Tab 0 Contents" />
        </mx:Canvas>

        <mx:Canvas label="Tab 1" show="updateURL()" >
            <mx:Label text="Tab 1 Contents" />
        </mx:Canvas>

        <mx:Canvas label="Tab 2" show="updateURL()" >
            <mx:Label text="Tab 2 Contents" />
        </mx:Canvas>

    </mx:TabNavigator>
</mx:Application>
```

You may also notice that the historyManagementEnabled parameter on the
TabNavigator is set to false. This is because you are using events from the BrowserMan
ager class to determine whether the browser URL has changed, and to update the tab
contents accordingly. Every change to the visible tab ends up with changes to the
browser history; users can go back and forward through the visible tabs by using the
browser's Back and Forward buttons.

17.9 Implement Custom History Management

Problem

You want actions or changes in your custom components to register with the browser's history and be navigable via the browser's Forward and Back buttons.

Solution

Implement custom history management in your Flex components by implementing the `mx.managers.IHistoryManagerClient` interface.

Discussion

For this solution to work, history management must be enabled for your Flex project. You can verify that history management is enabled by going to the Flex Project Properties dialog box, selecting the Flex Compiler screen, and verifying that the Enable Integration with Browser check box is selected.

The following code shows you how to implement the `IHistoryManagerClient` interface for a custom text box component. Any time that a change is made in this component, that change will register with the browser history. Users can go backward and forward through the inputs of this `TextInput` control by using the browser's Back and Forward buttons.

```
<mx:TextInput
    xmlns:mx="http://www.adobe.com/2006/mxml"
    text="Change Me!"
    implements="mx.managers.IHistoryManagerClient"
    creationComplete="mx.managers.HistoryManager.register(this);"
    change="textChanged(event)">

    <mx:Script>
        <![CDATA[
            import mx.managers.HistoryManager;

            public function saveState():Object
            {
                return {text:text};
            }

            public function loadState(state:Object):void
            {
                var newState:String = state ? state.text : "";

                if (newState != text)
                {
                    text = unescape( newState );
                }
            }
```

```
        private function textChanged(e:Event):void
        {
            HistoryManager.save();
        }
    ]]>
</mx:Script>

</mx:TextInput>
```

After the component has been created, you must register that class instance with the history manager. You can see this in the **creationComplete** event handler for the custom component:

```
creationComplete="mx.managers.HistoryManager.register(this);"
```

The **IHistoryManagerClient** interface requires the **saveState** and **loadState** functions to be present within your custom component.

Any time the value of the custom **TextInput** control is changed, the **textChanged** method is invoked, which calls the save function on the history manager. When state is saved by the history manager, the **saveState** method is invoked.

The **saveState** method should return an object that will be persisted in the browser's history. In this case, the method is returning an object with the property **text**, which is set to the text value of the **TextInput** component.

When the browser history is changed via the Forward and Back buttons, the **load State** method gets invoked. The **loadState** method reads the **text** property from the **State** object that is passed into it. It then sets the **text** property of the **TextInput** control based on the value passed in through the **State** object.

You can add this component to your Flex application by using code similar to the following:

```
<mx:Application
    xmlns:mx="http://www.adobe.com/2006/mxml"
    layout="absolute"
    xmlns:local="*">

    <local:MyTextInput />

</mx:Application>
```

CHAPTER 18

Modules and Runtime Shared Libraries

When building Rich Internet Applications, eventually you will have to consider file sizes and download times. The Flex Framework offers several alternatives for separating application code into separate SWF files to enrich the user experience.

Runtime shared libraries (RSLs) are files that can be downloaded and cached on a client. After an RSL is downloaded and persists on the client, multiple applications can access assets from that cached RSL. Applications can load two types of RSLs: unsigned and signed. *Unsigned RSLs*, such as standard and cross-domain SWF files, are stored in the browser cache. *Signed RSLs*, which are libraries that have been signed by Adobe and have the *.swz* extension, are stored within the Flash Player cache.

As the name suggests, an RSL is loaded at runtime and is considered a dynamically linked library. Statically linked libraries are SWC files that you compile into an application by using the `library-path` and `include-libraries` compiler options. Application SWF files using statically linked libraries generally have a larger file size and take longer to download yet have the added benefit of running quickly because all the code is available to the application. Applications employing RSLs load faster and have a smaller file size, but may take more time at start up while loading the RSLs and increase memory usage as a consequence. The power of using RSLs becomes apparent when considering multiple applications that share the same code base. Because RSLs are downloaded once, multiple applications that dynamically link to the same RSL can access assets already available from cache on the client. Though RSLs have the great benefit of being cached on a client, the entire library of an RSL is loaded by an application without consideration of which classes are actually used by that application.

Modules are similar to RSLs in that they provide another way of separating application code into SWF files to decrease download time and file size. One benefit of using modules is that, unlike with RSLs, the main application shell does not have to load modules when it starts. The application has the capability to load and unload modules as needed. The development process when using modules also provides an added benefit: You can work on modules separately from the application because they are independent of each other. As changes are needed for a module, you have to recompile only that module and not the entire application.

You can create modular applications by using ActionScript and MXML. Flex-based modules use the `<mx:Module>` root tag, while ActionScript-based modules extend either `mx.modules.Module` or `mx.modules.ModuleBase`. Module classes are similar to applications. A module is compiled by using the MXML compiler tool (mxmlc), generating a SWF file that can be dynamically loaded and unloaded by an application at runtime. You can manage the loading and unloading of modules in Flex by using `<mx:Module Loader>` and in ActionScript by using the `mx.modules.ModuleLoader` and `mx.modules.Mod uleManager` classes.

The capability to create modular applications is a great aspect of the Flex Framework, affording more control over the loading time and file size of an application. By using RSLs and modules, you can separate code from an application that can be loaded and used by other applications. Both techniques have their benefits, and this chapter addresses how each is used in the development process and in deployment.

18.1 Create a Runtime Shared Library

Problem

You want to create a *runtime shared library* (RSL) to be downloaded and cached by an application or multiple applications within the same domain.

Solution

Create a library of custom classes, components, and other assets to be compiled into a SWC file. Then extract the library.swf file from the SWC file and include it in the deploy directory for your application, to be used as an RSL.

Discussion

The SWC file format is an archive that contains a library.swf file and a catalog.xml file. The library is a set of assets compiled into a SWF file, and the catalog describes the hierarchy of dependencies found in the library. To use the library as an RSL, you need to extract the library.swf file from the generated SWC and include it within the deploy directory for your application.

Although you must have the library in the same domain as the applications that will access it during runtime, the library SWF file does not have to be present when you compile an application. However, the presence of the SWC file is needed during compile time, because it is used for dynamic linking.

The following example is an MXML component that will be packaged into a SWC archive file. The class will be included in the generated library SWF file, and an instance will be added to the display list of the main application:

```
<mx:Canvas
    xmlns:mx="http://www.adobe.com/2006/mxml"
    width="300" height="200">

    <mx:Metadata>
        [Event(name="submit", type="flash.events.Event")]
    </mx:Metadata>

    <mx:Script>
        <![CDATA[

            public static const SUBMIT:String = "submit";
            private function clickHandler():void
            {
                dispatchEvent( new Event( CustomEntryForm.SUBMIT ) );
            }
            public function get firstName():String
            {
                return firstNameField.text;
            }
            public function get lastName():String
            {
                return lastNameField.text;
            }

        ]]>
    </mx:Script>

    <mx:Form>
        <mx:FormItem label="First Name:">
            <mx:TextInput id="firstNameField" />
        </mx:FormItem>
        <mx:FormItem label="Last Name:">
            <mx:TextInput id="lastNameField" />
        </mx:FormItem>
        <mx:Button label="submit" click="clickHandler();" />
    </mx:Form>

</mx:Canvas>
```

This simple component enables a user to enter information and dispatches a submit event. To package this class into a SWC file, you invoke the compc utility with the source-path and include-classes command-line options. With a path to the /bin directory of your Flex SDK installation set in your System Paths system variable, the following command-line entry will generate a SWC file named CustomLibrary.swc:

```
> compc -source-path . -include-classes com.oreilly.flexcookbook.CustomEntryForm -outpu
t CustomLibrary.swc
```

With the MXML component saved as CustomEntryForm.mxml in the com/oreilly/flexcookbook directory of the current development directory, the supplied source path input value is the current directory (denoted as a dot). You can supply any number of classes to include by using the fully qualified class name of each, separated by a space.

The library.swf file archived in the generated SWC file is used as the RSL. To extract the library file from the generated SWC, you can use any standard unzip utility. When compiling the application, the SWC file is used for dynamic linking. You can rename the extracted library file as you see fit, but you must supply that filename as the runtime shared library value to be linked to your applications. For this example, the extracted library is renamed CustomLibrary.swf.

The following example application uses the `CustomEntryForm` component from a loaded RSL:

```
<mx:Application
    xmlns:mx="http://www.adobe.com/2006/mxml"
    xmlns:flexcookbook="com.oreilly.flexcookbook.*"
    layout="vertical">

    <mx:Script>
        <![CDATA[

            private function onFormSubmit():void
            {
                greetingField.text = "Hello " + entryForm.firstName +
                                    " " + entryForm.lastName;
            }

        ]]>
    </mx:Script>
    <mx:Panel title="Enter Name:" width="400" height="400">
        <flexcookbook:CustomEntryForm id="entryForm" submit="onFormSubmit()" />
        <mx:HRule width="100%" />
        <mx:Label id="greetingField" />
    </mx:Panel>

</mx:Application>
```

An application using assets from an RSL references classes and declares MXML components just as it would if referencing statically linked libraries and local class files from your development directory. In this example, the `flexcookbook` namespace is declared in the `<mx:Application>` tag and used to add the `CustomEntryForm` component to the display list.

To compile the application to use the RSL previously generated and renamed to CustomLibrary.swf, invoke the mxmlc utility by using the `external-library` and `runtime-shared-libraries` command-line options:

```
> mxmlc –external-library=CustomLibrary.swc –runtime-shared-libraries=CustomLibrary.swf
RSLExample.mxml
```

In this command, CustomLibrary.swc is used for compile-time link checking, and the URL for the RSL library is declared as being served from the same domain as the generated application SWF. When it is time for deployment, you will place RSLExample.swf and CustomLibrary.swf in the same directory on a server. At startup, the application loads the `CustomLibrary` RSL and has that code available to present a form for the user to enter information.

18.2 Use Cross-Domain Runtime Shared Libraries

Problem

You want to store RSLs in a separate location on a server that can be accessed by any application not within the same domain.

Solution

Use the `compute-digest` option of the compc utility when creating the RSL, which will be stored in the application during compile time when linking to the RSL. Then create a cross-domain policy file to include along with the locations of any RSLs in the `runtime-shared-library-paths` option of the mxmlc tool.

Discussion

An RSL digest is a hash used to ensure that the RSL being loaded by the Flash Player is from a trusted party. When creating an RSL with the `compute-digest` option set to true, the digest is written to the catalog.xml file of a SWC archive. When you link a cross-domain RSL to an application during compilation, that digest is stored in the application SWF and is used to verify the authenticity of a requested RSL.

With a path to the /bin directory of your Flex SDK installation set in your System Path, the following command will generate a SWC file named CustomLibrary.swc:

```
> compc –source-path . –include-classes com.oreilly.flexcookbook.CustomEntryForm -outpu
t CustomLibrary.swc –compute-digest=true
```

The default value of the `compute-digest` option is true, and you need not include it to create a digest when compiling a library. The digest is required when linking cross-domain RSLs to an application by using the `runtime-shared-library-paths` option of the MXML compiler.

In the previous section, you saw an example of a *standard* RSL that resides in the same domain as the application and was linked by using the `runtime-shared-libraries` compiler option. Standard RSLs can use digests as well, but the use of digests is not required.

The SWC file generated from this command is an archive folder containing a library.swf file and a catalog.xml file. To extract the library and catalog from the SWC file, you can use any standard unzip utility. The library is a set of assets compiled into a SWF file and will be used as the RSL. The catalog describes information found in the library along with the digest created by using the `compute-digest` option. The following shows the digest entry for the RSL written to the `<digests>` element of the catalog file:

```
<digests>
    <digest type="SHA-256" signed="false"
        value="2630d7061c913b4cea8ef65240fb295b2797bf73a0db96ceec5c319e2c00f8a5"    />
</digests>
```

The `value` is a hash generated by the compiler using the SHA-256 algorithm. When you compile an application linked to an RSL, this digest value is stored in the application and is used to verify the requested RSL from the server.

Along with a digest to ensure that the RSL is from a trusted resource, a cross-domain policy file is required on the target server where the library resides. A cross-domain policy file is an XML file listing domains that are granted access to data on a remote server. To allow multiple applications found in domains other than that in which the RSL resides, list each domain path in a separate `<allow-access-from>` element in the crossdomain.xml file. The following is an example of a crossdomain.xml file:

```
<?xml version="1.0"?>
<cross-domain-policy>
    <allow-access-from domain="*.mydomain.com" />
    <allow-access-from domain="*.myotherdomain.com" />
</cross-domain-policy>
```

The preceding cross-domain policy file allows any SWF files from the subdomains of *http://mydomain.com* and *http://myotherdomain.com* to access data on the server, including cross-domain RSLs.

To grant any SWF files held on the listed domains access to data held on the target server, you can place the cross-domain policy file on the root of the server. Although this is a viable option, you may want more control over how applications access RSLs on the target server. By using the `runtime-shared-library-path` option of the MXML compiler, you can specify the location of a cross-domain policy file that lists permitted domains that can access the libraries.

To compile an application dynamically linked to the cross-domain RSL that was previously generated by using the compc tool and renamed to CustomLibrary.swf, invoke the mxmlc utility by using the `runtime-shared-library-path` command-line option and the full URL paths to the RSL and cross-domain policy file found on the target server:

```
> mxmlc RSLExample.mxml -runtime-shared-library-path=
        CustomLibrary.swc,
        http://www.mytargetdomain.com/libraries/CustomLibrary.swf,
        http://www.mytargetdomain.com/libraries/crossdomain.xml
```

The comma-delimited argument values of the `runtime-shared-library-path` option are the location of the SWC file to compile against, the full URL path to the RSL residing on a remote server, and the full URL path to the cross-domain policy file that grants permission to an application from another domain to load the RSL. The existence of the runtime shared library SWF file is not checked during compilation, but the URL is stored in the application and is checked at runtime.

The benefit of using cross-domain RSLs, along with the decreased file size and download time, is to enable applications not residing in the same domain as the library to have access to trusted data. As more applications are deployed on other servers that use the runtime shared library, you can update the list of domains in the cross-domain policy file.

See Also

Recipe 18.1.

18.3 Use the Flex Framework as a Runtime Shared Library

Problem

You want to reduce the file size and download time of your application by linking to an RSL of the Flex Framework.

Solution

Compile the application by using the framework.swc file and either the signed or unsigned framework RSLs found in the /frameworks directory of your Flex 3 SDK installation.

Discussion

If you are familiar with building applications that utilize the Flex Framework, you are probably aware of the increased file size—and consequent increased download time—of the deployed application SWF. Even a relatively simple application such as the following example, when compiled, results in a SWF file with an unexpected byte size relative to the amount of code presented:

```
<mx:Application
    xmlns:mx="http://www.adobe.com/2006/mxml"
    layout="vertical">

    <mx:Label text="Hello World" />

</mx:Application>
```

With not much code other than adding a label to the display list to print the text *Hello World*, this application, when compiled using the mxmlc tool, generates a SWF with a file size close to 149KB. The reason for this is that the Flex components and libraries are compiled into the application as well. That makes sense: After all, you need those resources to effectively run a stand-alone SWF in the Flash Player. For such a simple application, however, the file size is quite an expense when you consider that it will be loaded by a browser. In thinking of the benefits that runtime shared libraries provide, not only in file size and download time, but also in allowing multiple applications access to the same resources from a single library, a good case can be made to compile applications that dynamically link to the Flex Framework stored in an RSL.

One of the features included with the Flex 3 SDK and Flash Player release 3 (Flash Player 9.0.60 and later) is the ability to separate the Flex Framework from the application code. Included in the /frameworks/libs directory of your Flex 3 SDK is an archive of the Flex Framework: the framework.swc file. Within the /frameworks/rsl directory of your Flex 3 SDK is the signed RSL of the Flex Framework; at the time of this writing, that file is named framework_3.0.189825.swz.

Unsigned RSLs, such as those created in the previous recipes for this chapter, are stored within the browser cache and can be loaded by any application within the same domain as the RSL or any domain specified within a cross-domain policy file. Signed RSLs (with the extension of .swz) are stored within the Flash Player cache. Signed RSLs that are cached in the Flash Player can be removed by using the Settings Manager. Only Adobe can sign RSLs to be cached in the Flash Player, providing security from a third party to inject and execute code.

To compile an application against the framework.swc included in the Flex 3 SDK and dynamically link to the signed Flex Framework RSL, you use the `runtime-shared-library-path` option of the mxmlc tool:

```
> mxmlc HelloWorldApplication.mxml –target-player=9.0.60
    -runtime-shared-library-path=
    /<sdk-installation>/frameworks/framework.swc,
    framework_3.0.1.189825.swz
```

The first argument value of the `runtime-shared-library-path` option is the location of the framework.swc file in the /frameworks folder of your Flex 3 SDK installation. The second argument, delimited by a comma, is the name of the signed RSL of the Flex Framework. At the time of this writing, that is the framework_3.0.1.189825.swz file found in the /rsls folder of the Flex 3 SDK installation.

By placing the SWZ file in the same domain as the generated application SWF file on a remote server, the signed RSL is loaded into the cache of the Flash Player when that application is first downloaded. Any other applications that you compile by using the same `runtime-shared-library-path` option arguments will draw from that cached file. This also means that any Flex application created by another developer with the same argument values will benefit from an application that has already loaded and cached the RSL in the Flash Player.

If you take a look at the generated application SWF file that was once approximately 149KB in size prior to compiling against the framework.swc, you will notice that the file size has dropped significantly and is about 49KB as a result of dynamically linking to the signed Flex Framework RSL.

See Also

Recipe 18.1 and Recipe 18.2.

18.4 Optimize a Runtime Shared Library

Problem

You want to reduce the file size of a runtime shared library that is loaded by an application.

Solution

Use the optimizer command-line tool included in the Flex 3 SDK to remove debugging code and unnecessary metadata included in the library of the SWC file.

Discussion

As a default, the library.swf file generated when creating a SWC file contains debugging and metadata code. This may provide an unnecessary overhead when an application loads an RSL from a remote server or from the browser cache. To create an optimized RSL, you first create the SWC archive file by using the compc tool from the Flex 3 SDK, and then extract the library file by using any standard unzip utility. The library.swf file is the RSL that will be loaded by an application that is compiled against the generated SWC. You can then recompile the RSL by using the optimizer command-line tool.

The generated library within a SWC archive file will vary in size depending on class libraries included during compilation. However, to gain a better understanding of the power that the optimizer tool affords, create the following MXML component and save the file as MyCustomComponent.mxml:

```
<mx:Canvas
    xmlns:mx="http://www.adobe.com/2006/mxml">

    <mx:TextArea text="Lorem ipsum dolor sit amet" />

</mx:Canvas>
```

This simple component will display an `<mx:TextArea>` component with some text.

With a path to the /bin directory of your Flex SDK installation, the following command using the compc utility generates a SWC file named library.swc within the root of your development directory:

```
> compc –source-path . –include-classes MyCustomComponent -output library.swc
```

Using any standard unzip utility, extract the library.swf file from the generated SWC file. With this example, the extracted library is approximately 320KB in size.

Using the optimizer command-line tool, you can reduce the file size of the target runtime shared library by removing any unnecessary debugging and metadata code within the generated SWF file:

```
> optimizer –keep-as3-metadata=
    "Bindable,Managed,ChangeEvent,NonCommittingChangeEvent,Transient"
    –input library.swf -output optimized.swf
```

The file size of the optimized RSL is now less than half that of the original library, approximately 135KB.

It is recommended that you include at least the `Bindable`, `Managed`, `ChangeEvent`, `NonCom``mittingChangeEvent`, and `Transient` metadata names in the argument value for the `keep-``as3-metadata` option because these are common metadata tags associated with components from the Flex Framework. Other metadata, such as `RemoteClass`, can be added to the comma-delimited argument list based on the class dependencies of the RSL library.

See Also

Recipe 18.1 and Recipe 18.2.

18.5 Create an MXML-Based Module

Problem

You want to create an MXML-based module to be loaded by an application during runtime.

Solution

Create an MXML class that extends the `mx.modules.Module` class by using the `<mx:Mod``ule>` root tag, and compile the module by using the mxmlc command-line tool.

Discussion

A *module* is similar to an application and is compiled by using the mxmlc utility to generate a SWF file that can be loaded into an application or another module at runtime. To create an MXML-based module, you extend the `mx.modules.Module` class by using the `<mx:Module>` as the root tag of the MXML file.

The following example is a module that displays a list of contacts within a data grid:

```
<mx:Module
    xmlns:mx="http://www.adobe.com/2006/mxml"
```

```
        width="100%" height="100%">

        <mx:XMLList id="contacts">
            <contact>
                <name>Josh Noble</name>
                <phone>555.111.2222</phone>
                <address>227 Jackee Lane</address>
            </contact>
            <contact>
                <name>Todd Anderson</name>
                <phone>555.333.4444</phone>
                <address>1642 Ocean Blvd</address>
            </contact>
            <contact>
                <name>Abey George</name>
                <phone>555.777.8888</phone>
                <address>1984 Winston Road</address>
            </contact>
        </mx:XMLList>

        <mx:DataGrid id="contactGrid"
            width="100%" height="100%"
            rowCount="4"
            dataProvider="{contacts}">
            <mx:columns>
                <mx:DataGridColumn dataField="name" headerText="Name"/>
                <mx:DataGridColumn dataField="phone" headerText="Phone"/>
                <mx:DataGridColumn dataField="address" headerText="Address"/>
            </mx:columns>
        </mx:DataGrid>

    </mx:Module>
```

The structure of this module is similar to an application or custom component. When an application is required to display a list of contacts, it can load this module and add it to the display list.

To compile this example into a SWF file to be loaded by an application, use the mxmlc tool just as you would when compiling a simple application with the file argument being that of the Module class:

```
> mxmlc ContactList.mxml
```

This command generates a SWF file named ContactList.swf, though you can use the output option to specify a different name as long as the application knows the correct name when it is time to be loaded. The generated file size of the SWF is approximately 245KB—a substantial size, if you think about its contents being included within a compiled application. By separating this code into a module, you are saving download time and reducing the file size of any application that may require loading this module.

18.6 Create an ActionScript-Based Module

Problem

You want to create an ActionScript-based module to be loaded by an application at runtime.

Solution

Create an ActionScript class that extends either the `mx.modules.Module` or `mx.mod ules.ModuleBase` classes and compile the module by using the mxmlc command-line tool.

Discussion

You can create ActionScript-based modules by extending the `Module` and `ModuleBase` classes of the module API. Depending on the role the module plays within the application, the choice to extend either `Module` or `ModuleBase` is based on the necessity of a display list. The `Module` class is a display container that is an extension of `FlexSprite` and will include some framework code. The `ModuleBase` class extends `EventDis patcher` and can be used to separate logic code from an application that does not depend on visual elements.

MXML-based modules are an extension of `mx.modules.Module` and use the `<mx:Mod ule>` root tag. If you are creating a module that contains visual elements, you extend the `Module` class and override protected methods as you see fit, such as the `createChil dren` method inherited from `UIComponent`. The following example shows a module that adds input elements to the display to enable a user to enter information:

```
package
{
    import mx.containers.Form;
    import mx.containers.FormItem;
    import mx.controls.TextInput;
    import mx.modules.Module;

    public class ASContactList extends Module
    {
        private var _form:Form;
        private var _firstNameItem:FormItem;
        private var _lastNameItem:FormItem;
        public function ASContactList()
        {
            super();
            this.percentWidth = 100;
            this.percentHeight = 100;
        }

        override protected function createChildren():void
        {
```

```
            super.createChildren();
            _form = new Form();
            _firstNameItem = createInputItem( "First Name:" );
            _lastNameItem = createInputItem( "Last Name:" );
            _form.addChild( _firstNameItem );
            _form.addChild( _lastNameItem );
            addChild( _form );
        }

        private function createInputItem( label:String ):FormItem
        {
            var item:FormItem = new FormItem();
            item.label = label;
            item.addChild( new TextInput() );
            return item;
        }
    }
}
```

You compile an ActionScript-based module as you would an MXML-based module, by using the mxmlc utility with the file input value being that of the ActionScript file:

```
> mxmlc ASContactList.as
```

This command generates a SWF file named ASContactList.swf, though you can use the output option to specify a different name as long as the application knows the correct name when it is time to be loaded. The Module class is an extension of mx.core.Con tainer, and as such internally casts children to be added to the display list as being of type mx.core.IUIComponent. You can add components from the Flex Framework to the display list of an ActionScript-based module by using the addChild method. To add components from the ActionScript API, such as flash.text.TextField and mx.media.Video, you need to wrap them in an instance of UIComponent.

The Module class contains framework code in order to interact with and display user interface objects. If your module does not rely on framework code, you can create a class that extends ModuleBase. The mx.modules.ModuleBase class extends EventDis patcher and provides a convenient way to separate logic code from your modular application.

The following is an example of a module that extends the ModuleBase class:

```
package
{
    import mx.modules.ModuleBase;

    public class EntryStateModule extends ModuleBase
    {
        public function EntryStateModule() {}

        public function greet( first:String, last:String ):String
        {
            return "Hello, " + first + " " + last + ".";
        }
        public function welcomBack( first:String, last:String ):String
```

```
        {
            return "Nice to see you again, " + first + ".";
        }
    }
}
```

When loaded by an application, this simple module provides a way to structure salutations through the public `greet` and `welcomeBack` methods. This module contains no framework code and as a consequence is significantly smaller in file size compared to that of a module created by using the `Module` class.

Compilation of a module extending the `ModuleBase` class is the same as that of a file extending `Module`:

```
> mxmlc EntryStateModule.as
```

This command generates a SWF file named EntryStateModule.swf. To access the public methods available on the module in this example, the parent application or parent module references the `child` property of the `ModuleLoader` instance or the `factory` property of an `IModuleInfo` implementation, which is discussed in Recipe 18.8.

See Also

Recipe 18.5 and Recipe 18.8.

18.7 Load a Module by Using ModuleLoader

Problem

You want to load modules into your Flex application.

Solution

Use the `<mx:ModuleLoader>` container to load modules into your application.

Discussion

The `mx.modules.ModuleLoader` class is a container that acts similarly to the `mx.controls.SWFLoader` component. It loads SWF files and adds modules to the display list of an application. `ModuleLoader` differs from `SWFLoader` in that it has a contract that dictates that the SWF file that is loaded implements `IFlexModuleFactory`. Compiled modules contain the `IFlexModuleFactory` class factory, which allows an application to dynamically load the modular SWF files at runtime without requiring the class implementations within the main application shell.

Though the `ModuleLoader` object is a display container, it can load modules that extend `Module` and `ModuleBase` and does not rely on the module to contain framework code or display visual objects. The `url` property of the `ModuleLoader` class is a reference to the location of a module expressed as a URL. Setting the `url` property internally calls the public `loadModule` method of the `ModuleLoader` class and begins the download process of the module.

The following example loads a module from the same domain as the application:

```
<mx:Application
    xmlns:mx="http://www.adobe.com/2006/mxml"
    layout="vertical">

    <mx:Panel title="Contacts:" width="350" height="180"
        horizontalAlign="center" verticalAlign="middle">
        <mx:ModuleLoader url="ContactList.swf" />
    </mx:Panel>

</mx:Application>
```

When this application starts up, the `ModuleLoader` is instructed to load a module titled ContactList.swf from the same domain. After the module has loaded successfully, it is added to the display list of the application.

The `ModuleLoader` component also allows you to unload and load different modules dynamically. Setting the `url` property of a `ModuleLoader` instance internally calls the public `loadModule` method of `ModuleLoader` and adds the module as a child. To remove the module from the display, you call the public `unloadModule` method of the `Module Loader` class. Calling `unloadModule` sets the module reference to `null`, but does not change the `url` property value.

The following example is an application that loads and unloads modules based on user interaction:

```
<mx:Application
    xmlns:mx="http://www.adobe.com/2006/mxml"
    layout="vertical">

    <mx:Script>
        <![CDATA[

            private function displayModule( moduleUrl:String ):void
            {
                var url:String = moduleLoader.url;
                if( url == moduleUrl ) return;
                if( url != null ) moduleLoader.unloadModule();
                moduleLoader.url = moduleUrl;
            }

            private function showHandler():void
            {
                displayModule( "ContactList.swf" );
            }
            private function enterHandler():void
            {
                displayModule( "ContactEntry.swf" );
            }
```

```
        ]]>
    </mx:Script>

    <mx:Panel title="Contacts:" width="350" height="210"
        horizontalAlign="center" verticalAlign="middle">
        <mx:ModuleLoader id="moduleLoader" height="110" />
        <mx:HRule width="100%" />
        <mx:HBox width="100%">
            <mx:Button label="show list" click="showHandler();" />
            <mx:Button label="enter contact" click="enterHandler();" />
        </mx:HBox>
    </mx:Panel>

</mx:Application>
```

The `click` event handlers of the `Button` controls update the module to be loaded into the `ModuleLoader`. This application alternates between displaying a list of contact information and displaying a form to enter new contacts, by loading the ContactList.swf module and the ContactEntry.swf module, respectively.

When a module is loaded into an application, it is added to the module list of the `mx.modules.ModuleManager` object. When removed, the reference is turned to `null` to free memory and resources. Using the `ModuleLoader` is a convenient way to manage the loading and unloading of modules in a Flex-based application.

See Also

Recipe 18.5, Recipe 18.6, and Recipe 18.8.

18.8 Use ModuleManager to Load Modules

Problem

You want more-granular control over the loading and unloading of modules in your Flex- and ActionScript-based applications.

Solution

Access methods of the `ModuleManager` class directly to listen for status events of loading modules.

Discussion

The `ModuleManager` class manages loaded modules. The `<mx:ModuleLoader>` component internally communicates with this manager when the public `ModuleLoader.loadMod ule` and `ModuleLoader.unloadModule` methods are invoked. You can directly access the modules managed by the `ModuleManager` by using ActionScript. When a module URL is passed into the public `ModuleManager.getModule` method, the location is added to the managed list of modules and an instance of `mx.modules.IModuleInfo` is returned.

Modules are essentially instances of the private ModuleInfo class of ModuleManager. ModuleInfo objects load the SWF file and are wrapped in a proxy class implementing IModuleInfo, which is returned from the ModuleManager.getModule method. You can listen for status events on this proxy to have more control on how your application interacts with loaded modules.

The following example shows how an application uses the ModuleManager to control how a module is added to the display:

```
<mx:Application
    xmlns:mx="http://www.adobe.com/2006/mxml"
    layout="vertical"
    creationComplete="creationHandler();">

    <mx:Script>
        <![CDATA[
            import mx.events.ModuleEvent;
            import mx.modules.ModuleManager;
            import mx.modules.IModuleInfo;

            private var _moduleInfo:IModuleInfo;

            private function creationHandler():void
            {
                _moduleInfo = ModuleManager.getModule( 'ContactList.swf' );
                _moduleInfo.addEventListener( ModuleEvent.READY,
                                                moduleLoadHandler );
                _moduleInfo.load();
            }

            private function moduleLoadHandler( evt:ModuleEvent ):void
            {
                canvas.addChild( _moduleInfo.factory.create() as DisplayObject );
            }

        ]]>
    </mx:Script>

    <mx:Canvas id="canvas" width="500" height="500" />

</mx:Application>
```

When this application has completed its initial layout operations, the ContactList module is instructed to be loaded by using the IModuleInfo object returned from the ModuleManager.getModule method. The IModuleInfo implementation acts as a proxy to the Loader instance, which is instructed to download the module.

After the module is successfully downloaded, it is added to the display list by using the IFlexModuleFactory.create method. This method returns the instance of the module that is cast as a DisplayObject to be added to the display of the Canvas container.

You can listen to events related to the download status of a module by using the IModuleInfo object proxy returned from the getModule method. In this example, the application waits until the module is completely loaded before adding it to the display list. The events are dispatched as instances of the `ModuleEvent` class and range from progress to error states related to the download status of a SWF module (Table 18-1). You can also assign event SETUP constant variable (ModuleEvent class)andlers for these events inline by using the `<mx:ModuleLoader>` class.

Table 18-1. The mx.events.ModuleEvent Class

Constant Variable	String Value	Description
PROGRESS	`"progress"`	Dispatched while the module is loading. From this event, you can access the bytesLoaded and bytesTotal properties of the module being loaded.
SETUP	`"setup"`	Dispatched when enough information about the loading module is available.
READY	`"ready"`	Dispatched when the module has finished loading.
UNLOAD	`"unload"`	Dispatched when the module has been unloaded.
ERROR	`"error"`	Dispatched when an error has occurred while downloading the module.

The `unload` method of the `IModuleInfo` implementation will remove references to the module from the `ModuleManager` but will not unload the SWF file from the display. To remove the module from the display, you must explicitly call the `removeChild` method of the parent display.

In comparison to the `ModuleLoader` class that internally begins loading a module based on an update to its `url` property, using the `IModuleInfo` implementation returned from the `getModule` method affords you the capability to defer the loading and subsequent display of a module in your applications. This allows you to preload modules and have them immediately available for display to reduce the time in requesting and rendering modules upon user interaction.

See Also

Recipe 18.5, Recipe 18.6, and Recipe 18.7.

18.9 Load Modules from Different Servers

Problem

You want to store modules on a server that is separate from the server you use to deploy applications.

Solution

Use the `flash.system.Security` class to establish trust between the main application SWF file and the loaded module SWF file.

Discussion

The Flash Player security is domain based, allowing a SWF file from a specific domain to access data from that same domain without restriction. When a SWF file is loaded into the Flash Player, a security sandbox is set up for that domain and grants access to any assets within that sandbox. This model is in place to ensure that a SWF file is accessing external resources and communicating with other SWF files from a trusted source.

In order to allow a SWF file in a specific domain to access assets, including modules, from another domain, you will need to have a cross-domain policy file available on the remote server and to use the `Security.allowDomain` method in your main application. To allow a loaded module to interact with the parent SWF file—a communication known as *cross-scripting*—the module needs to call the `allowDomain` method as well.

Consider the following module that is available from a remote server:

```
<mx:Module
    xmlns:mx="http://www.adobe.com/2006/mxml"
    layout="absolute"
    initialize="initHandler();">

    <mx:Script>
        <![CDATA[
            private function initHandler():void
            {
                Security.allowDomain( "appserver" );
            }
        ]]>
    </mx:Script>

    <mx:Text width="100%" text="{loaderInfo.url}" />

</mx:Module>
```

When a parent SWF loads this module and the `initialize` event is fired, the module grants communication access to the loading SWF file and displays the URL from which the module was loaded.

When this module is compiled and placed on a remote server (for the sake of this example, that domain name is `moduleserver`), a cross-domain policy file is added to the root of that domain, allowing the parent SWF file, residing on `appserver`, to load the module:

```
<?xml version="1.0"?>
<cross-domain-policy>
    <allow-access-from domain="appserver" to-ports="*" />
</cross-domain-policy>
```

In order for the parent-loading SWF to load and establish cross-scripting communication with the loaded module, you call the `Security.allowDomain` method by using the domain name of the remote server and load the crossdomain.xml file, shown here:

```
<mx:Application
    xmlns:mx="http://www.adobe.com/2006/mxml"
    layout="vertical"
    preinitialize="initHandler();">

    <mx:Script>
        <![CDATA[
            private function initHandler():void
            {
                Security.allowDomain( "moduleserver" );
                Security.loadPolicyFile( "http://moduleserver/crossdomain.xml" );
                var loader:URLLoader = new URLLoader();
                loader.addEventListener( Event.COMPLETE, loadHandler );
                loader.load(new URLRequest("http://moduleserver/crossdomain.xml"));
            }
            private function loadHandler( evt:Event ):void
            {
                moduleLoader.url = "http://moduleserver/modules/MyModule.swf";
            }
        ]]>
    </mx:Script>

    <mx:ModuleLoader id="moduleLoader" />

</mx:Application>
```

The `preinitialize` event handler for the main application establishes communication with any loaded resources from the `moduleserver` server by calling the `SecurityDomain.allowDomain` method. The application also invokes the `Security.loadPolicyFile` method with the location of the cross-domain policy file found on the remote server. The Flash Player retrieves the policy file and ensures that the application SWF file from `appserver` can be trusted. The `loadPolicyFile` method needs to be called prior to loading the cross-domain policy file by using an instance of `URLLoader`; otherwise, security exceptions will be thrown.

After the policy file has finished loading, the application SWF assigns the `url` property of an `<mx:ModuleLoader>` instance to that of the desired module available on the remote server. With the application and module granting access to each other's specified server, cross-scripting is permitted and the communication lines are open.

See Also

Recipe 18.7 and Recipe 18.8.

18.10 Communicate with a Module

Problem

You want to access and pass data between the parent SWF and a loaded module.

Solution

Use the `child` property of `mx.modules.ModuleLoader` and the `factory` property of an `mx.modules.IModuleInfo` instance to listen for events, invoke public methods, and access public properties available from the parent SWF and the loaded module.

Discussion

An application shell can communicate with a loaded module by using properties of `ModuleLoader` and `ModuleManager`. Communication is not limited to an `<mx:Applica tion>` instance, because modules can load other modules as well, making the loading module a parent to the loaded module with access points being the same as an application.

To access data from a loaded module, you can typecast the returned properties of the specified loader instance to that of the loaded module class. When using an `<mx:Modu leLoader>` object, the module instance is available from the `child` property:

```
<mx:Script>
    <![CDATA[
        private var myModule:MyModule;

        private function moduleReadyHandler():void
        {
            myModule = moduleLoader.child as MyModule;
            myModule.doSomething();
        }
    ]]>
</mx:Script>

<mx:ModuleLoader id="moduleLoader"
    url="MyModule.swf"
    ready="moduleReadyHandler();" />
```

When access to data of the loaded module is made available to the parent application, the `moduleReadyHandler` event handler of the application is invoked. By typecasting the `child` property of the `<mx:ModuleLoader>` to that of the module's class, you can access data and call public methods available on the module.

When using the `ModuleManager` class in a parent application, the module instance is returned from the public `create` method of the `IFlexModuleFactory` instance held on the `IModuleInfo` implementation:

```
private var _moduleInfo:IModuleInfo;

private function creationHandler():void
{
    _moduleInfo = ModuleManager.getModule( 'MyModule.swf' );
    _moduleInfo.addEventListener( ModuleEvent.READY, moduleLoadHandler );
    _moduleInfo.load();
}
```

```
private function moduleLoadHandler( evt:ModuleEvent ):void
{
    var myModule:MyModule = _moduleInfo.factory.create() as MyModule;
    myModule.doSomething();
}
```

When you typecast the values returned from the child property of ModuleLoader or the Object returned from the IFlexModuleFactory.create method to that of the loaded module, you introduce a tight coupling between the module and the loading application. To diminish the dependency created by typecasting the module to its class instance, as a general rule you should use interfaces. By typing to an interface, you introduce flexibility into your code and allow the parent application to interface with more than one instance of a particular class.

To exemplify the flexibility that typing to an interface affords you when developing modular applications, consider a situation where you have created a module that is loaded and used as a form to input user information. As requirements in the application progress and change, you may find that you need more than one type of form to display. Though they may appear different visually, and perhaps perform different operations related to user data, access to the data of modules remains the same in their method signatures. Having different modules implement an interface introduces flexibility in your application as they can be typed to a common API.

The following example is an interface exposing properties related to user information that separate modules can implement:

```
package
{
    import flash.events.IEventDispatcher;

    public interface IUserEntry extends IEventDispatcher
    {
        function getFullName():String;
        function get firstName():String;
        function set firstName( str:String ):void;
        function get lastName():String;
        function set lastName( str:String ):void;
    }
}
```

To create a module that implements this interface, declare the implements property value of the <mx:Module> node to that of the IUserEntry interface:

```
<mx:Module
    xmlns:mx="http://www.adobe.com/2006/mxml"
    implements="IUserEntry"
    layout="vertical"
    width="100%" height="100%">

    <mx:Metadata>
        [Event(name="submit", type="flash.events.Event")]
    </mx:Metadata>
```

```
<mx:Script>
    <![CDATA[
        private var _firstName:String;
        private var _lastName:String;
        public static const SUBMIT:String = "submit";

        private function submitHandler():void
        {
            firstName = firstNameInput.text;
            lastName = lastNameInput.text;
            dispatchEvent( new Event( SUBMIT ) );
        }

        public function getFullName():String
        {
            return _firstName + " " + _lastName;
        }

        [Bindable]
        public function get firstName():String
        {
            return _firstName;
        }
        public function set firstName( str:String ):void
        {
            _firstName = str;
        }
        [Bindable]
        public function get lastName():String
        {
            return _lastName;
        }
        public function set lastName( str:String ):void
        {
            _lastName = str;
        }
    ]]>
</mx:Script>

<mx:Form>
    <mx:FormItem label="First Name:">
        <mx:TextInput id="firstNameInput" width="100%" />
    </mx:FormItem>
    <mx:FormItem label="Last Name:">
        <mx:TextInput id="lastNameInput" width="100%" />
    </mx:FormItem>
    <mx:Button label="submit" click="submitHandler();" />
</mx:Form>

</mx:Module>
```

This module presents display controls for entering and submitting information regarding the first and last name of a user. The getter/setter properties and the public getFullName method are implemented in the <mx:Script> tag of the module. Data binding to the firstName and lastName attributes is established by the IUserEntry interface extending the `IEventDispatcher` interface, of which the `mx.modules.Module` and `mx.mod ules.ModuleBase` classes are both implementations.

To access data from this or any module that implements the `IUserEntry` interface, the parent application can typecast the corresponding property value based on the module loader instance.

The following example uses the `child` property of an `<mx:ModuleLoader>` instance to access data from the `IUserEntry` module implementation:

```
<mx:Application
    xmlns:mx="http://www.adobe.com/2006/mxml"
    layout="vertical">

    <mx:Script>
        <![CDATA[
            private var myModule:IUserEntry;

            private function moduleReadyHandler():void
            {
                myModule = moduleLoader.child as IUserEntry;
                myModule.addEventListener( "submit", submitHandler );
            }
            private function submitHandler( evt:Event ):void
            {
                welcomeField.text = 'Hello, ' + myModule.getFullName();
                trace( myModule.firstName + " " + myModule.lastName );
            }
        ]]>
    </mx:Script>

    <mx:ModuleLoader id="moduleLoader"
        url="ContactEntry.swf"
        ready="moduleReadyHandler();" />
    <mx:Label id="welcomeField" />
</mx:Application>
```

The **ready** event handler for the `<mx:ModuleLoader>` instance establishes an event handler for user information submission. When the `submitHandler` method is invoked, it prints the return string from the `getFullName` implementation of the loaded module. By typing the `child` property of the `ModuleLoader` instance to the `IUserEntry` interface, you ensure a loose coupling design in communication from the parent application to the module. This allows you to dynamically interface with modules of different class types that have the same implementation.

Communication is not limited to the parent SWF accessing data on the module. Modules can also access data from their parent-loading application by using the `parentAp plication` property:

```
<mx:Module
    xmlns:mx="http://www.adobe.com/2006/mxml"
    layout="absolute"
    creationComplete="creationHandler();">
```

```
<mx:Script>
    <![CDATA[
        private function creationHandler():void
        {
            infoField.text = parentApplication.getInformation();
        }
    ]]>
</mx:Script>

<mx:Text id="infoField" />
```
```
</mx:Module>
```

When the module has finished its initial layout, the `creationHandler` method is invoked, and the returned data from the `getInformation` method of the parent-loading application is displayed in the child `Text` component.

The `parentApplication` property of a `Module` instance is inherited from the `UICompo nent` superclass and is an `Object` type. The dynamic `Object` class is at the root of the ActionScript runtime class hierarchy. As such, you can access data on the `parentAppli cation` instance by using dot notation without respect to the parent class implementation, meaning that modules call properties held on the parent application regardless of the property being available and without throwing a runtime exception.

As a general rule, a module should not access data of a parent application by using the `parentApplication` property because that creates a tightly coupled relationship between the module and the loading parent. To reduce this coupling, you can type applications that will load a specific module to an interface—as has been done with modules in the previous examples of this recipe. To ensure that different applications have the same communication with a singular module, however, it is recommended to supply data to the module directly from the parent application as opposed to accessing data from the dynamic `parentApplication` property. Doing so will enable you to develop modular applications without constrictions as to a module being knowledgeable about its loading parent.

See Also

Recipe 18.7, Recipe 18.8, and Recipe 18.9.

18.11 Pass Data to Modules by Using Query Strings

Problem

You want to pass data to a module during the loading phase.

Solution

Append a query string to the URL of a module SWF to be loaded. After the module has loaded, parse the URL string by using the `loaderInfo` property of the module.

Discussion

You can append query string parameters to the URL used to load a module. When the module is loaded, you can access the URL by using the `loaderInfo` property of the `mx.modules.Module` class. Using ActionScript, you can parse parameters available on the URL of the module loaded into a parent application. A query string is assembled by following the location of a module with a question mark (?) and having parameters delimited by an ampersand (&) symbol.

The following example application appends a query string to the URL of a module:

```
<mx:Application
    xmlns:mx="http://www.adobe.com/2006/mxml"
    layout="vertical"
    creationComplete="creationHandler();">

    <mx:Script>
        <![CDATA[
            private static const F_NAME:String = "Ted";
            private static const L_NAME:String = "Henderson";

            private function creationHandler():void
            {
                var params:String = "firstName=" + F_NAME +
                                    "&lastName=" + L_NAME;
                moduleLoader.url = "NameModule.swf?" + params;
            }
        ]]>
    </mx:Script>

    <mx:ModuleLoader id="moduleLoader" />

</mx:Application>
```

After the creation of the `<mx:ModuleLoader>` instance and the completion of the initial layout of the parent application, the `url` property value is supplied by using a query string construct of property-value pairs. The `firstName` and `lastName` property values are passed into the loaded module by using constant variables in this example, but could very well be values received from a service.

A loaded module can parse the appending URL query by using the `loaderInfo` property:

```
<mx:Module
    xmlns:mx="http://www.adobe.com/2006/mxml"
    layout="absolute"
    width="100%" height="100%"
    creationComplete="creationHandler();">
```

```
<mx:Script>
    <![CDATA[
        import mx.utils.ObjectProxy;

        [Bindable] private var _proxy:ObjectProxy;

        private function creationHandler():void
        {
            _proxy = new ObjectProxy();

            var pattern:RegExp = /.*\?/;
            var query:String = loaderInfo.url.toString();
            query = query.replace( pattern, "" );

            var params:Array = query.split( "&" );

            for( var i:int = 0; i < params.length; i++ )
            {
                var keyVal:Array = ( params[i] ).toString().split("=");
                _proxy[keyVal[0]] = keyVal[1];
            }
        }

    ]]>
</mx:Script>

<mx:Text text="{'Hello, ' + _proxy.firstName + ' ' + _proxy.lastName}" />

</mx:Module>
```

The loaded module parses the query string parameters on the appended URL and adds them as properties to the `ObjectProxy` class. Using the inherent data-binding capability of the `ObjectProxy` class, the `firstName` and `lastName` parameter values are displayed in the `Text` control as those properties are updated.

Passing data by using a query string is a convenient way for a loaded module to receive and operate on data upon initialization. Using query strings does not enforce a tightly coupled relationship between the parent application and a module in execution because it is the responsibility of the module to handle the data as it sees fit and ensure that it does not throw runtime errors. However, this technique for supplying data to a module is prone to human development error; misspelling in the query string can lead to miscommunication between the parent-loading application and the module.

See Also

Recipe 18.10.

18.12 Optimize Modules by Using Linker Reports

Problem

You want to reduce the file size and subsequent download time of a module.

Solution

Use the `link-report` command-line option of the mxmlc utility when compiling the application to generate a linker report file. Then use that report file as the input value for the `load-externs` command-line option when compiling a module to ensure that only classes that the module requires are compiled.

Discussion

When you compile a module, all custom and framework code that the module depends on is included in the generated SWF file. Some of this code, especially that of the Framework, may be common to both a module and a loading parent application. You can remove redundancies and reduce the file size of a module by compiling the module against a linker report file.

A *linker report file* is an externalized list of classes that the application is dependent on and that can be generated by using the `link-report` command-line option when compiling an application. The following command will generate a linker report named report.xml in the current directory:

```
>mxmlc -link-report=report.xml MyApplication.mxml
```

This generated linker report file can then be used to compile a module against, to remove code redundancy, and to reduce the file size of a module. Use the `link-externs` command-line option with the report input value as that of the generated file:

```
>mxmlc -link-externs=report.xml MyModule.mxml
```

The result is a generated module SWF file that does not contain any code that both the application and module depend on. This is a great optimization tool when you take into account the framework code that may be compiled into both the application and the module. Externalizing code and compiling modules against linker reports does create a development dependency between the application and the module, however. If changes are made to the application, you may need to regenerate a linker report and recompile the module to ensure that code is available.

If your application uses more than one module, this optimization technique can also be used to compile code that may not necessarily be used in the parent application, but is common to more than one module. In fact, it is a general rule that you should compile any manager classes, such as `mx.managers.DragManager` and `mx.managers.PopUpMan ager`, that modules may depend on into the main application. This is because modules cannot access code resources from other modules, and runtime exceptions will be thrown if, for instance, one module is trying to reference the `DragManager` from another module.

To ensure that modules can access the same manager within an application, you need to import and declare a class local variable in the main application file:

```
import mx.managers.PopUpManager;
var popUpManager:PopUpManager;
```

You can then generate the linker report to compile the modules against, ensure that the modules are using the same manager reference, and reduce code redundancy and module file size.

See Also

Recipe 18.5 and Recipe 18.6.

CHAPTER 19

The Adobe Integrated Runtime API

Included in the Flex SDK are classes that can be used to develop applications for the desktop targeting the *Adobe Integrated Runtime* (AIR). Adobe AIR is a cross-platform runtime that lets developers leverage existing web technologies to bring the Rich Internet Application experience to the desktop. The AIR runtime provides a consistent cross–operating system environment that enables developers to create applications targeting the Adobe AIR platform and eliminates the need to build and deploy separate applications for different operating systems. While the AIR framework affords you the capability to create HTML and Ajax-based desktop applications, the examples in this chapter focus on leveraging the Flex Framework.

To run applications targeting the AIR platform, you first need to install the runtime, which can be found on the Adobe website at *http://labs.adobe.com/technologies/air/*. Applications that are run within the Adobe AIR runtime can be installed and accessed like any other native desktop application.

Creating AIR applications leveraging the Flex Framework is similar to creating Flex applications targeting the web browser. Included in the Flex 3 SDK are classes that let you interact with the file system, the operating system clipboard, and a local database, to name just a few of the capabilities available from the AIR API. To package AIR applications into an installer file, you need an application SWF file and an application descriptor file, as well as to sign the application against an encrypted keystore certificate. To sign your applications—ensuring end users that they are installing an uncorrupted version of your application—you can generate self-signed certificates or can use certificates from a trusted certificate vendor such as VeriSign or Thawte. AIR installer files have the extension of .air, and when installed run within the Adobe AIR runtime.

Covering all the features available in the AIR API is a book unto itself. This chapter addresses some main features to get you on your way to developing desktop applications targeting the Adobe AIR runtime.

19.1 Create an AIR Application Leveraging the Flex Framework

Problem

You want to create a desktop application using the Flex and AIR APIs.

Solution

Create a main application file in MXML with the `<mx:WindowedApplication>` root tag and an application descriptor file that specifies properties for installing, accessing, and launching your AIR application.

Discussion

Developing an AIR-based application leveraging the Flex Framework is similar to developing a Flex application for the Web and provides you with the capability to communicate with the operating system. When developing web-based Flex applications, the main application file contains the `<mx:Application>` root tag. For AIR applications that will run on the desktop by using native operating system windows, the root of the main application file is the `<mx:WindowedApplication>` tag.

The `mx.core.WindowedApplication` class is an extension of `mx.core.Application` that has properties and methods relating to native operating system windows. The `WindowedApplication` is the main window for an AIR application. From it you can spawn other native windows, access the file system, and interact with the operating system—most operations you expect from a desktop application.

The following is an example of a simple main file for an AIR application:

```
<mx:WindowedApplication
    xmlns:mx="http://www.adobe.com/2006/mxml"
    layout="vertical"
    title="Hello World">

    <mx:Label text="Welcome to AIR" />

</mx:WindowedApplication>
```

When this application is launched, the title *Hello World* will be displayed in the application window title bar and in the system taskbar. The text *Welcome to AIR* is printed on the display.

To compile an AIR application, you use the amxmlc command-line tool included in the /bin directory of your Flex 3 SDK installation. You may be familiar with using the mxmlc tool also found in the /bin directory to compile Flex- and ActionScript-based applications. When you run the mxmlc utility, it uses the default flex-config.xml configuration file found in the /frameworks directory of the SDK installation. The amxmlc tool uses the air-config.xml configuration file found in the /frameworks directory and compiles against the airglobal.swc archive file found in the /libs/air folder.

With the /bin folder set within your system paths, you can compile an AIR application by opening a command prompt and entering the following command:

```
>amxmlc HelloWorld.mxml
```

This generates a HelloWorld.swf file in the directory pointed to in the command prompt. If you click and launch the SWF file, you will not see anything except the default background color. This is because you are running the application in the Flash Player. To see the AIR application, you need to run it within the Adobe AIR runtime. The generated SWF file is a necessary file when deploying and packaging your AIR application, as is another file known as the application descriptor.

An *application descriptor* is an XML file that specifies properties used to install, launch, and identify an AIR application on an operating system. This file is required to deploy an AIR application during development and to package an application into an installer file for distribution. Along with parameters such as the directory to install the application within the Program Files directory of the operating system, and associated icon files, the application descriptor file lets you set window properties for your main application window that become read-only after it is launched.

The following is a basic application descriptor file for the AIR application created in the previous example:

```
<application xmlns="http://ns.adobe.com/air/application/1.0">

    <id>com.oreilly.flexcookbook.HelloWorld</id>
    <filename>HelloWorld</filename>
    <name>Hello World</name>
    <version>0.1</version>
    <description>A Hello World Application</description>

    <initialWindow>
        <content>HelloWorld.swf</content>
        <systemChrome>standard</systemChrome>
        <transparent>false</transparent>
        <visible>true</visible>
        <width>400</width>
        <height>400</height>
    </initialWindow>

</application>
```

The parameters set in this example are only a subset of the properties available, but may be common configurations to most AIR applications you will build. The <application> tag is the root tag for the descriptor file and has an attribute referencing the URI for the AIR namespace. The last segment of the namespace (1.0) is the AIR runtime version that the application is targeting.

The required parameters of an application descriptor file are <id>, <filename>, <version>, and the <initialWindow> parent and <content> child nodes. The id element is the application identifier and must be unique to the application. As such, it is recommended to use a dot-delimited reverse-DNS string as the value. This ID is used for installation of and access to the application storage directory. The `filename` element is used as a reference to the application in the operating system, including the name for the application executable and installation folder. The `version` element is the developer-specified version number of the application, and does not require any standard format but is necessary when distributing updates to your application. The `content` element of the `<initialWindow>` node is the main application SWF file to be loaded into AIR when the application is launched. The SWF file is generated by using the amxmlc command-line tool included in the Flex 3 SDK with the file input argument pointing to the main AIR application file.

Aside from the required parameters set in this application descriptor file, the `<name>`, `<description>`, and window settings have also been added to this example. The `name` and `description` element values will be displayed in the installation window. The `sys temChrome`, `transparent`, and `visible` properties of the `<initialWindow>` node relate to the visual appearance of the main application window. These properties can be set here in the descriptor file or in the root `<mx:WindowedApplication>` tag declaration of the main file, but will become read-only after the application is running. The `width` and `height` properties are the dimensions of the application upon launch. These parameters are optional, as are other parameters of the `initialWindow` that relate to size constraints and position, but have been added in this example because they may be common values you will configure for your applications.

19.2 Understand the AIR Command-Line Tools

Problem

You want to use the command-line tools included in the Flex 3 SDK to deploy, debug, and package AIR applications.

Solution

Use the amxmlc, adl, and adt utilities found in the /bin folder of your Flex 3 SDK installation directory.

Discussion

Included in the Flex 3 SDK are command-line tools that compile, launch, and package AIR applications into installer files. To compile an AIR application, you use the amxmlc command-line tool with the file input argument pointing to the main application file. The main file can be an HTML file, an ActionScript file, or an MXML file. The examples in this chapter focus on leveraging the Flex Framework to develop AIR applications, and the main application will have the .mxml file extension. The adl utility is used to launch an AIR application within the Adobe AIR runtime during development and prior to packaging for installation. The adt tool is used to create and sign certificates as well as package the AIR application into an installer file.

The amxmlc tool used to generate the main AIR application SWF file is similar to the mxmlc command-line tool used to compile Flex applications. In fact, the amxmlc command invokes the MXML compiler and instructs the compiler to use the air-config.xml configuration file found in the /frameworks folder of the SDK installation directory. All command-line options available when using the mxmlc utility, such as specifying a default or additional configuration file, are available when running the amxmlc, but for the examples in this chapter you will use the basic options to generate an application SWF.

The file input argument for the amxmlc tool is a main application file leveraging the Flex Framework with the `<mx:WindowedApplication>` root tag. The following is an example of a simple main file for an AIR application:

```
<mx:WindowedApplication
    xmlns:mx="http://www.adobe.com/2006/mxml"
    layout="vertical"
    title="Hello World">

    <mx:Label text="Welcome to AIR" />

</mx:WindowedApplication>
```

The `mx.core.WindowedApplication` class is the application container for Flex-based AIR applications. The `WindowedApplication` class extends the `mx.core.Application` class and is the main native desktop window for an AIR application.

To compile this application to be run within the AIR environment, you use the amxmlc tool just as you would use the mxmlc tool to compile a web-based Flex application:

```
>amxmlc –output HelloWorld.swf HelloWorld.mxml
```

This generates a SWF file named HelloWorld.swf in the directory that the command prompt is pointing to. The **output** option is optional, and you can achieve the same result by leaving it out of the command. If the **output** option is not included, the compiler will name the generated SWF file after the filename of the file input argument. You may want to specify a different name for the application SWF file, so the **output** option has been included in the example, but the correct filename must be present in the application descriptor file that is used to deploy and package the AIR application.

As stated earlier in this chapter, an *application descriptor* is an XML file that specifies properties used to install, launch, and identify an AIR application on an operating system. If you were to launch the SWF file generated by the amxmlc compiler in the Flash Player, you would see only the default background because the application can be run only within the Adobe AIR runtime. To run an application compiled by using the amxmlc tool, you will need an application descriptor file that points to the compiled application SWF file.

The following is an example of a simple application descriptor file, saved as Hello-World-app.xml, that specifies the previously generated SWF file as the application content file:

```
<application xmlns="http://ns.adobe.com/air/application/1.0">

    <id>com.oreilly.flexcookbook.HelloWorld</id>
    <filename>HelloWorld</filename>
    <name>Hello World</name>
    <version>0.1</version>
    <description>A Hello World Application</description>

    <initialWindow>
        <content>HelloWorld.swf</content>
        <systemChrome>standard</systemChrome>
        <transparent>false</transparent>
        <visible>true</visible>
        <width>400</width>
        <height>400</height>
    </initialWindow>

</application>
```

Within the descriptor file are property values for the initial application window (the WindowedApplication instance of the main file) and parameters to install and identify the application on the operating system. You will notice that the content element value is the location of the application SWF file generated by the amxmlc tool.

While developing an AIR application, you can use the Adobe Debug Launcher (adl) tool to launch the application and preview how it will run prior to packaging and installing. The adl tool also provides support for printing out trace statements to the console while the Flash Debugger (FDB) is running. To run the AIR application prior to packaging by using the adl utility, enter the following command with the descriptor file input value being the location of the previously created application descriptor file:

```
>adl HelloWorld-app.xml
```

If this command is run successfully and the application is launched, you will see something similar to Figure 19-1.

With the application performing as intended, you can package the AIR application into an installer file by using the AIR Developer Tool (adt). AIR installer files need to be signed by using a digital certificate to verify the authenticity of the application. To generate an installer file, you can use a certificate from a trusted certificate authority, such as VeriSign or Thawte, or you can use a self-signed certificate. Code-signing a certificate from a certificate authority when packaging an application is used to verify the identity of the signer during installation and provides an assurance to an end user that the application has not been maliciously altered. Though self-signed certificates created by using the adt utility also verify that the application has not been altered after signing, they cannot be used to verify the identity of the signer and display the Publisher property within the installation window as being unknown.

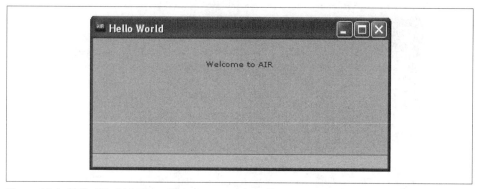

Figure 19-1. Hello World AIR application

It is recommended to code-sign AIR applications by using a certificate from a trusted certificate authority, but for the examples in this chapter, you will be using a self-signed certificate to generate the installer files.

To create a self-signed certificate by using the adt tool, enter the following command:

```
>adt -certificate -cn HelloWorld 1024-RSA certificate.pfx password
```

This command generates a file named certificate.pfx in the directory that the command prompt is pointing to. Along with the generation of the certificate and associated private key, the common name of the certificate is specified as HelloWorld, and the key type to use for the certificate is specified as 1024-RSA. Valid key types are 1024-RSA and 2048-RSA and describe the encryption type for the key. Valid file extensions for the certificate file are .pfx and .p12, which are Personal Information Exchange file types.

The certificate and private key created via the adt tool are stored in a PKCS12-type keystore file. The certificate and key are then used to sign and package the AIR application by using the package command of the adt tool. To package the application into an installer file, enter the following command:

```
>adt –package –storetype pkcs12 -keystore certificate.pfx HelloWorld.air HelloWorld-app
.xml HelloWorld.swf
```

The storetype parameter refers to the version of the Public-Key Cryptography Standards (PKCS) keystore used to the store the private key and certificate. The keystore is the certificate created via the certificate command of the adt tool previously. The last three input values are the name specified for the installer file, the application descriptor file, and the application SWF file, respectively. You can add more file paths to the end of this command to be packaged and installed as they are required by the application. The locations are relative to the current directory, but you can use the -C option to change directories to include files.

Running the package command of the adt tool prompts you to enter the password you used to generate the certificate; for this example, that is *password*. If this command is run successfully and the password accepted, a file named HelloWorld.air is generated

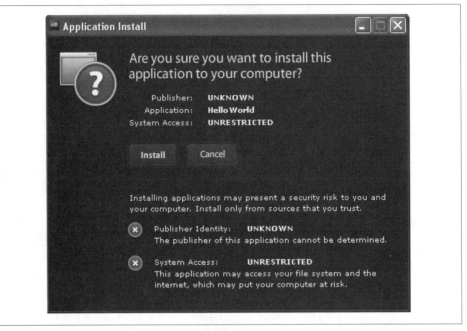

Figure 19-2. Initial installer window for the Hello World application

within the directory that the command prompt pointed to when executing the command. This file is the installer file for the Hello World application. To install the application, navigate to the directory you targeted by using this command and double-click on the HelloWorld.air file. You will be presented with a window that looks similar to Figure 19-2.

Figure 19-2 is the initial installer window that will be presented to an end user when installing your AIR applications. The application name is presented as the element value given to the <name> property within the descriptor file, and the publisher identity is considered unknown because you used a self-signed certificate when packaging the AIR application. If you click the Install button, you will be presented with another window similar to that of Figure 19-3.

Clicking the Continue button from the second installation window seen in Figure 19-3 will install the application and add a shortcut icon to the desktop. You can specify the directory in which you wish to install the application, but if you left the field as the default directory for your operating system, you can find the application on Windows at C:\Program Files\HelloWorld and on Mac OS X at HD/Applications/HelloWorld. The directory into which the application is installed is known as the *application directory*. A directory for storage files, referred to as the *application storage directory*, is also created during installation and can be located on Windows at C:\Documents and Settings\<*username*>\Application Data\com.oreilly.flexcookbook.HelloWorld and on Mac OS X at /Users/<*username*>/Library/Preferences/

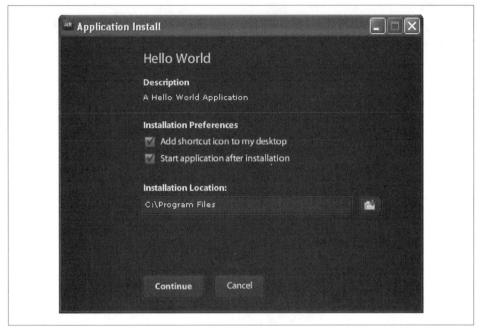

Figure 19-3. Second installation window for the Hello World application

com.oreilly.flexcookbook.HelloWorld. The folder name is the dot-delimited reverse-DNS name you specified as the ID for the application in the application descriptor file. Both the application directory and the application storage directory created during installation can be accessed by using the file system API of AIR. You can read and write files to the storage directory, but the application directory is read-only.

You can remove an AIR application just as you would any other desktop application: by using the Add and Remove Programs window on Windows and by dragging the application directory to the trash on Mac OS X. Doing so will remove any files created during installation but will not remove any ancillary files created after installation, including the application storage directory.

See Also

Recipe 19.1.

19.3 Open and Manage Native Windows

Problem

You want to spawn native windows from your AIR application.

Solution

Use the `flash.display.NativeWindow` and `mx.core.Window` classes from the AIR windowing API.

Discussion

You can create native windows in AIR that conform to the operating system conventions in not only their functionality but also their look and feel. Though you can easily create native windows that have the same window chrome and rectangular shape as other desktop application windows, you can also create and apply custom skins by using the style properties and custom graphics. Along with customizing the window chrome that holds controls for manipulating a window, you can also listen for events dispatched by the native window for those controls.

The root tag for a main MXML application targeting the AIR runtime is the `<mx:Win dowedApplication>` tag. This is the initial window for an application when the application is launched. Custom settings can be set within the application descriptor file and declared in the `<mx:WindowedApplication>` tag. The `WindowedApplication` window acts as a container for an instance of the `flash.display.NativeWindow` class and lets you add Flex components directly to the display list within the MXML markup. You can access the `NativeWindow` instance of the `WindowedApplication` class through the `nativeWindow` property.

The `NativeWindow` class acts as an interface for controlling native desktop windows. To spawn native windows in an AIR application leveraging the Flex Framework, you create instances of the `mx.core.Window` class. Like the `WindowedApplication` class, the `Window` class acts as a container to the underlying `NativeWindow` instance, which can be accessed through the `nativeWindow` property. Initialization properties for the window can be set in the root `<mx:Window>` tag of the custom window component.

The following example is a custom native window that extends the `Window` class:

```
<mx:Window
    xmlns:mx="http://www.adobe.com/2006/mxml"
    title="Hello"
    width="200" height="200">

    <mx:Label text="I am a Window!" />

</mx:Window>
```

When instructed to open, this window will be placed on the desktop with the dimensions of 200 width and 200 height and display the text *Hello* in the title bar of the window chrome. Other window chrome and transparency properties can be set within the `<mx:Window>` root tag, as well as handlers for events dispatched by the `Native Window` instance. The following example removes the standard system chrome, restricts the controls for maximizing and minimizing the window, and adds event listeners for the window controls:

```
<mx:Window
    xmlns:mx="http://www.adobe.com/2006/mxml"
    title="Hello"
    systemChrome="none" transparent="true"
    maximizable="false" minimizable="false"
    width="200" height="200"
    windowComplete="completeHandler();"
    closing="closingHandler(event);">

    <mx:Script>
        <![CDATA[
            private function completeHandler():void
            {
                nativeWindow.addEventListener( NativeWindowBoundsEvent.RESIZING,
                                                resizeHandler );
            }
            private function resizeHandler( evt:NativeWindowBoundsEvent ):void
            {
                trace( evt.beforeBounds + " : " + evt.afterBounds );
            }
            private function closingHandler( evt:Event ):void
            {
                trace( "goodbye!" );
            }
        ]]>
    </mx:Script>

    <mx:Label text="I am a Window!" />

</mx:Window>
```

When this window is opened, the window chrome will be styled with the standard Flex chrome and disable the minimize and maximize controls for the window. Handlers responding to events dispatched by the `NativeWindow` instance are established for the creation, resizing, and closing of the window.

Included in the windowing API is the option to set the native window type. When setting the `type` property to a value from the enumeration of types found in the `Native WindowTypes` class, the window is treated with a combination of the custom chrome and control presence. By default, the `type` property of a `Window` is `normal`. Windows with the `utility` and `lightweight` type do not show up in the Windows operating system taskbar or the Mac OS X window menu. Utility windows are considered pared-down normal windows that have a slimmer visual chrome and present only a Close button. Lightweight windows need to have the `systemChrome` property set to false and act more as notification windows, such as a toaster-style alert window common in other desktop applications.

The appearance of the title bar, status bar, and resizing handle can also be configured by using the `showTitleBar`, `showStatusBar`, and `showGripper` properties of the `<mx:Win dow>` component. To remove the standard Flex chrome, you can set the `showflex Chrome` property of the `<mx:Window>` tag to false and have a window that displays only the contents of its stage without any standard system chrome controls; for this example, that will result in the text *I am a Window!* being printed on the screen without any background or window chrome.

To display an `<mx:Window>` component, you first create an instance of the window and then call the open method:

```
<mx:WindowedApplication
    xmlns:mx="http://www.adobe.com/2006/mxml"
    layout="vertical"
    windowComplete="initHandler();"
    closing="closeHandler();">

    <mx:Script>
        <![CDATA[
            import com.oreilly.flexcookbook.CustomWindow;

            private var window:CustomWindow;
            private function initHanlder():void
            {
                window = new CustomWindow();
                window.alwaysInFront = true;
                window.open();
            }

            private function closeHandler():void
            {
                if( !window.closed ) window.close();
            }
        ]]>
    </mx:Script>

</mx:WindowedApplication>
```

When the application has finished its initial layout and opened the underlying Native Window instance, the windowComplete event is dispatched and the initHandler method is invoked. Within the initHandler method, an instance of the CustomWindow class is created and opened. The window is also instructed to always remain at the top of the z-order of windows on the screen by setting the alwaysInFront property to true. You can also manually position windows based on the z-order of other windows—including the WindowedApplication instance—by using the orderInFrontOf, orderInBackOf, order ToFront, and orderToBack methods of the Window class.

It is important to note that closing a main application window prior to closing any opened custom window objects will not cause the application to exit. As such, a clos ing event listener is established to check that all other windows have been closed properly in order to quit the application.

See Also

Recipe 19.1 and Recipe 19.2.

19.4 Create Native Menus

Problem

You want to provide a native menu to allow users to perform specified commands.

Solution

Use the native menu API to create application and window menus.

Discussion

The classes of the native menu API let you interface with the native menu features of the operating system. You can add menu items and listen for events dispatched upon selection. There are many types of native menus, and how you create and interact with them is dependent on the operating system that the AIR application is running under. As such, you should be sure to add support for all targeted operating systems when adding native menus to your applications.

The Mac OS X operating system supports application menus. An *application menu* is a global menu that can be accessed from the application toolbar and is independent of the currently focused native window. The application menu is automatically created by the Mac OS X operating system, and you can add items and submenus, as well as event handlers, to the standard menus.

The native menus supported by the Windows operating system are considered *window menus*. Window menus appear in a native window object, just below the title bar, and are supported only in native windows that have system chrome. As such, window menus cannot be added to an `<mx:Window>` instance that has the `systemChrome` property set to `none`.

To determine the operating system that the AIR application is running under, you use the `NativeWindow.supportsMenu` and `NativeApplication.supportsMenu` properties during runtime:

```
if( NativeWindow.supportsMenu )
{
    // Windows
}
else if( NativeApplication.supportsMenu )
{
    // Mac OS X
}
```

If the `NativeWindow.supportsMenu` property value is true, native window menus are supported and the application is currently running under the Windows operating system. The `flash.desktop.NativeApplication` class, which provides application-wide information and functions, also has a static `supportsMenu` property. If the `NativeApplica`

tion object supports application-wide menus, the application is currently running under the Mac OS X environment.

To add a native menu object to act as the root of the menu, you instantiate a new `NativeMenu` instance and set it as the `menu` property for either the `NativeWindow` or `NativeApplication` instance:

```
if( NativeWindow.supportsMenu )
{
    stage.nativeWindow.menu = new NativeMenu();
}
else if( NativeApplication.supportsMenu )
{
    NativeApplication.nativeApplication.menu = new NativeMenu();
}
```

With the root menu set, you can add menu and submenu items to the `NativeMenu` object. The following example creates an application menu or a window menu for the main `<mx:WindowedApplication>` object, depending on the operating system the application is running in:

```
<mx:WindowedApplication
    xmlns:mx="http://www.adobe.com/2006/mxml"
    layout="vertical"
    windowComplete="initHandler();">

    <mx:Script>
        <![CDATA[

            private function initHandler():void
            {
                var fItem:NativeMenuItem = new NativeMenuItem( "File" );
                var fileMenu:NativeMenuItem;
                if( NativeWindow.supportsMenu )
                {
                    stage.nativeWindow.menu = new NativeMenu();
                    fileMenu = stage.nativeWindow.menu.addItem( fItem );
                }
                else if( NativeApplication.supportsMenu )
                {
                    NativeApplication.nativeApplication.menu = new NativeMenu();
                    fileMenu =
                        NativeApplication.nativeApplication.menu.addItem( fItem );
                }
                fileMenu.submenu = createFileMenu();
            }

            private function createFileMenu():NativeMenu
            {
                var menu:NativeMenu = new NativeMenu();

                var openItem:NativeMenuItem = new NativeMenuItem( "Open" );
                var openCmd:NativeMenuItem = menu.addItem( openItem );
                openCmd.addEventListener( Event.SELECT, openHandler );
```

```
                var saveItem:NativeMenuItem = new NativeMenuItem( "Save" );
                var saveCmd:NativeMenuItem = menu.addItem( saveItem );
                saveCmd.addEventListener( Event.SELECT, saveHandler );

                return menu;
            }
            private function openHandler( evt:Event ):void
            {
                printOut.text += "You selected open.\n";
            }
            private function saveHandler( evt:Event ):void
            {
                printOut.text += "You selected save.\n";
            }

        ]]>
    </mx:Script>

    <mx:TextArea id="printOut"
        width="100%" height="100%"
        />

</mx:WindowedApplication>
```

When the application is created and the initial layout complete, the `initHandler` method is invoked and a new File menu is added to the `menu` instance of either the `WindowedApplication` instance or the `NativeApplication` object, depending on the operating system (Windows or Mac OS X, respectively). Submenu items are added to the File menu within the `createFileMenu` method, and event listeners are added to respond the `select` event from each command item.

When this application is run in the Windows operating system, the main application window will present the File menu item just below the title bar. When run in the Mac OS X operating system, the File menu item will appear on the application toolbar. Selecting the File menu will open a context menu with submenu items. Clicking on either item will invoke the registered event listener and print text out to the `<mx:TextArea>` object.

The `NativeMenuItem` class also provides support for adding a separator line. The default value for the `isSeperator` argument of the constructor is false, but if set to true will render a horizontal rule within the native menu:

```
var rule:NativeMenuItem = new NativeMenuItem( "Line", true );
```

You can also enable and disable menu items at runtime by using the `enabled` property of the `NativeMenuItem` class:

```
var saveItem:NativeMenuItem = new NativeMenuItem( "Save" );
saveItem.enabled = false;
```

By enabling and disabling menu items at runtime, you can dictate what menu commands are available, depending on application requirements.

The concept of a native menu does not apply only to application menus and window menus. *Context menus*—opened in response to a right-click or Command-click within windows and system tray and dock icons—are also considered native menus as well. In fact, the `flash.ui.ContextMenu` and `flash.ui.ContextMenuItem` classes are extensions of the classes found in the AIR native menu API.

See Also

Recipe 19.3.

19.5 Read and Write to a File

Problem

You want to access, create, and write to files on the file system.

Solution

Use the `File`, `FileStream`, and `FileMode` classes of the AIR file system API.

Discussion

A `File` object acts as a pointer to and is a representation of a file or directory. To read and write files to the hard drive, you use `FileStream` to place the `File` object into a buffer. You can open files to read in and write to by using synchronous and asynchronous methods of the `FileStream` class. When using the synchronous `FileStream.open` method, the file is treated similar to that of a `ByteArray` object, and any other operations will be paused until the file has been read in or written to. The asynchronous `File Stream.openAsync` method acts more like a `URLStream` object, and data is placed on the buffer as it becomes available. The decision to use either the synchronous or asynchronous method to read and write to files is one based on the requirements of your application, but it is important to note that you should close the stream after the operation has completed.

You can specify the action you intend to perform on the file when placed on the buffer by using the string constants of the `FileMode` class when you invoke the `File Stream.open` and `FileStream.openAsync` methods. The `FileMode.WRITE` constant, when opening a file stream, will create and write data to a file if not previously existent and will overwrite any data in a file if it exists. The `FileMode.APPEND` constant will write any data placed on the buffer to the end of a file, and the `FileMode.UPDATE` constant gives read/write access to the file. All writing directives will create a new file if one does not exist. When using `FileMode.READ`, data from the file is placed on the buffer and the file must previously exist.

In order to read and write to a file, you need to point the `File` object to a file in a directory found on the user's computer. The `File` class has a number of static properties and methods to point to standard directories of the operating system's file system and to the application directory and application storage directory.

The following example uses the synchronous `FileStream.open` method to write a file to the desktop:

```
var file:File = File.desktopDirectory.resolvePath( "test.txt" );
var stream:FileStream = new FileStream();
stream.open( file, FileMode.WRITE );
stream.writeUTFBytes( "Hello World" );
stream.close();
```

A file named `test.txt` is either created or opened and placed on the buffer of a `File Stream` object. The text *Hello World* is written to the file by using the `FileStream.write UTFBytes` method. To open and read the data from this file, use the `FileStream.read UTFBytes` method:

```
var file:File = File.desktopDirectory.resolvePath( "test.txt" );
var stream:FileStream = new FileStream();
stream.open( file, FileMode.READ );
trace( stream.readUTFBytes( stream.bytesAvailable ) );
stream.close();
```

When you open a file to be read by using the `FileMode.READ` argument, the `File Stream` object immediately begins to read data into the buffer. To access data on the buffer, you use the `FileStream.bytesAvailable` property. When the synchronous `File Stream.open` method is used, all operations are paused until all the data is placed on the buffer, because this is the operation that is running within the main application thread. You can use the asynchronous `FileStream.openAsync` method to asynchronously open a file and listen for progress and complete events to read data that is continuously added to the read buffer.

If you were to place the file on the write buffer again by using the `FileMode.WRITE` argument when opening the stream, you would overwrite any data held in the file. To check whether a file is already available at the specified path, you can use the `exists` property of the `File` class:

```
var file:File = File.desktopDirectory.resolvePath( "test.txt" );
if( file.exists )
{
    trace( "File created: " + file.creationDate );
    file = File.desktopDirectory.resolvePath( "test2.txt" );
}
var stream:FileStream = new FileStream();
stream.open( file, FileMode.WRITE );
stream.writeUTFBytes( "Hello World" );
stream.close();
```

The `FileStream.writeUTFBytes` and `FileStream.readUTFByte` methods in these examples are just a small subset of methods on the `FileStream` class used to read from and write to the buffer of a file stream.

When discussing reading and writing to files, it is important to note the read and write permissions of directories created on the file system when an AIR application is installed. Two primary directories are created for an application during installation: the application directory and the application storage directory. File paths to these directories can be resolved by using `File.applicationDirectory` and `File.applicationStorageDirectory`, respectively. The application directory has read-only permission, allowing files from the directory to be put on only a read buffer. The application storage directory has read and write access, and you can write files to this directory that your application requires after installation.

19.6 Serialize Objects

Problem

You want to serialize custom objects in your application to files on the hard drive.

Solution

Register custom classes with a class-alias and use the `FileStream.writeObject` method to serialize objects to a file by using the ActionScript Message Format (AMF) encoding.

Discussion

Using the AIR file system API, you can write objects to the buffer of a file stream to be serialized via AMF encoding. Most built-in object types of the ActionScript language, such as `String` and `Boolean`, are automatically supported when serializing objects. These types can be encoded to a binary format by using AMF and will retain their value when deserialized. Custom types, however, are not serialized automatically. To enable custom objects to be eligible for serialization, you register the class with a *class-alias* either by using the `registerClassAlias` method or by declaring the `[RemoteClass]` metadata tag before a class definition.

Consider that your application would like to output user information as an object that can be loaded at a later time by either the same application or another application that knows how to handle that object. The custom class you would create to represent information about a user may look something like the following:

```
package com.oreilly.flexcookbook
{
    [RemoteClass]
    [Bindable]
    public class UserData
    {
        public var firstName:String;
        public var lastName:String;
        public var age:Number;
        public var sessionLength:Number;
```

```
        public function UserData( firstName:String = "",
                                     lastName:String = "" )
        {
            this.firstName = firstName;
            this.lastName = lastName;
        }


    }
}
```

Each time your application is first opened by a user, a new UserData object is created
and information is entered by the user. You could save this information in a formatted
string to a text file if you prefer, but you can also serialize the object to file so you can
easily load it back into your application as the object itself without having to parse a
string and reset the properties onto a new instance of the UserData class. To serialize
the object and retain its property values upon deserialization, register it by using the
[RemoteClass] metadata tag.

By inserting the [RemoteClass] metadata tag prior to the class definition, you are enabling the class to preserve the type information and property values when serialized
and deserialized using AMF. You can also add the [Transient] metadata tag before a
variable definition to exclude that property during serialization. Because the session
Length property of the previous example is updated while the application is running
and does not need to be saved from session to session, you can exclude the property
from serialization by marking it as a transient property:

```
package com.oreilly.flexcookbook
{
    [RemoteClass]
    public class UserData
    {
        public var firstName:String;
        public var lastName:String;
        public var age:Number;
        [Transient]
        public var sessionLength:Number;

        public function UserData( firstName:String = "",
                                     lastName:String = "" )
        {
            this.firstName = firstName;
            this.lastName = lastName;
        }


    }
}
```

To serialize custom objects to a file, you use the FileStream.writeObject method. The
default encoding format when writing and reading binary data via writeObject and
readObject is the AMF 3 specification. By setting the FileStream.objectEncoding property, you can use the AMF 0 format as well. The following example is an application
that will save user information to a file with the extension .user:

```
<mx:WindowedApplication
    xmlns:mx="http://www.adobe.com/2006/mxml"
    layout="vertical">

    <mx:Script>
        <![CDATA[
            import com.oreilly.flexcookbook.UserData;

            private var userData:UserData = new UserData();
            private static const EXT:String = ".user";
            private function submitHandler():void
            {
                userData.firstName = firstField.text;
                userData.lastName = lastField.text;
                userData.age = ageField.value;

                saveUserData();
            }
            private function saveUserData():void
            {
                var fnm:String = userData.firstName + "_" +
                                 userData.lastName + EXT;
                var file:File = File.desktopDirectory.resolvePath( fnm );
                var stream:FileStream = new FileStream();
                stream.open( file, FileMode.WRITE );
                stream.writeObject( userData );
                stream.close();
            }

        ]]>
    </mx:Script>

    <mx:Form>
        <mx:FormItem label="First Name:">
            <mx:TextInput id="firstField"
                change="{submitBtn.enabled = firstField.text != ''}"
                />
        </mx:FormItem>
        <mx:FormItem label="Last Name:">
            <mx:TextInput id="lastField"
                change="{submitBtn.enabled = lastField.text != ''}"
                />
        </mx:FormItem>
        <mx:FormItem label="Age:">
            <mx:NumericStepper id="ageField"
                minimum="18" maximum="110"
                />
        </mx:FormItem>
        <mx:Button id="submitBtn" label="submit"
            enabled="false"
            click="submitHandler();"
            />
    </mx:Form>

</mx:WindowedApplication>
```

After a user has entered and opted to submit information, the submitHandler event handler is invoked, the UserData object is updated, and a call to the saveUserData method is made. Within the saveUserData method, the file path is resolved by using the firstName and lastName properties of the UserData instance, and the file is written to the desktop with the .user extension. When this file is opened and written to the read buffer of a file stream, the property values will be retained during deserialization. The following example extends the application to offer support for opening a .user file and populating the form fields:

```
<mx:WindowedApplication
    xmlns:mx="http://www.adobe.com/2006/mxml"
    layout="vertical">

    <mx:Script>
        <![CDATA[
            import com.oreilly.flexcookbook.UserData;

            [Bindable]
            private var userData:UserData = new UserData();
            private var file:File = File.desktopDirectory;
            private var filter:FileFilter = new FileFilter("User File", "*.user");
            private static const EXT:String = ".user";

            private function submitHandler():void
            {
                userData.firstName = firstField.text;
                userData.lastName = lastField.text;
                userData.age = ageField.value;

                saveUserData();
            }
            private function saveUserData():void
            {
                var fnm:String = userData.firstName + "_" +
                                 userData.lastName + EXT;
                var file:File = File.desktopDirectory.resolvePath( fnm );
                var stream:FileStream = new FileStream();
                stream.open( file, FileMode.WRITE );
                stream.writeObject( userData );
                stream.close();
            }

            private function openHandler():void
            {
                file.browseForOpen( "Open User", [filter] );
                file.addEventListener( Event.SELECT, selectHandler );
            }
            private function selectHandler( evt:Event ):void
            {
                var stream:FileStream = new FileStream();
                stream.open( file, FileMode.READ );
                userData = stream.readObject();
            }
        ]]>
```

```
        </mx:Script>

        <mx:Form>
            <mx:FormItem label="First Name:">
                <mx:TextInput id="firstField"
                    text="{userData.firstName}"
                    change="{submitBtn.enabled = firstField.text != ''}"
                    />
            </mx:FormItem>
            <mx:FormItem label="Last Name:">
                <mx:TextInput id="lastField"
                    text="{userData.lastName}"
                    change="{submitBtn.enabled = lastField.text != ''}"
                    />
            </mx:FormItem>
            <mx:FormItem label="Age:">
                <mx:NumericStepper id="ageField"
                    value="{userData.age}"
                    minimum="18" maximum="110"
                    />
            </mx:FormItem>
            <mx:Button id="submitBtn" label="submit"
                enabled="false"
                click="submitHandler();"
                />
        </mx:Form>
        <mx:HRule width="100%" />
        <mx:Button label="open" click="openHandler();" />

    </mx:WindowedApplication>
```

When a user chooses to open their profile, a dialog box is created by using the `File.browseForOpen` method with a filter to show only files with the extension of .user. When a file is selected to be opened, the `selectHandler` method is invoked and the file is placed on the read buffer of a `FileStream` object by using the `FileStream.readOb ject` method. The `readObject` method will deserialize the `UserData` object and through data binding will populate the form fields with the saved property values.

The `FileStream.writeObject` and `FileStream.readObject` methods provide a huge benefit in serializing custom data objects to the file system. By registering a class by using the `[RemoteClass]` metadata tag, you make the class eligible for encoding to a binary format using AMF. Being able to serialize custom objects greatly reduces the overhead that may be introduced in your application if you were to load and parse text files with key-value pairs into custom objects.

See Also

Recipe 19.5.

19.7 Use the Encrypted Local Store

Problem

You want to store data on a user's hard drive that cannot be read or written to by another application.

Solution

Use the encrypted local store of an AIR application to securely store information.

Discussion

When an AIR application is installed, an encrypted local store is made available for the application to store information that needs to be kept secure. Using the Data Protection API (DPAPI) for AIR applications on Windows and Keychain for those on Mac OS X, data is encrypted and available to only content that resides within the same security sandbox. The maximum amount of space allotted to an encrypted local store is 10MB.

Data is stored in a hash table, and you use a key string to set and receive data stored in the encrypted local store. The data is serialized `ByteArray` objects, which allows you to store most built-in object types and any custom objects with a registered class-alias. Access to the encrypted local store is available through the static methods of the `flash.data.EncryptedLocalStore` class. The `getItem` and `setItem` methods take a key string value to receive and associate data with. You can also remove any data by using the key string and clear the entire storage by using methods of the `EncryptedLocal Store` class.

The following example uses the `EncryptedLocalStore` to store user data:

```
<mx:WindowedApplication
    xmlns:mx="http://www.adobe.com/2006/mxml"
    layout="vertical"
    windowComplete="completeHandler();">

    <mx:Script>
        <![CDATA[
            import com.oreilly.flexcookbook.UserData;

            [Bindable]
            public var userData:UserData;

            private function submitHandler():void
            {
                userData = new UserData( firstField.text, lastField.text );

                var bytes:ByteArray = new ByteArray();
                bytes.writeObject( userData );
                EncryptedLocalStore.setItem( "user", bytes );

                views.selectedChild = userCanvas;
```

```
        }
        private function completeHandler():void
        {
            var user:ByteArray = EncryptedLocalStore.getItem( "user" );
            if( user != null )
            {
                userData = user.readObject() as UserData;
                views.selectedChild = userCanvas;
            }
        }

    ]]>
</mx:Script>

<mx:ViewStack id="views"
    width="300" height="300"
    backgroundColor="0xEEEEEE">
    <!-- Entry Form -->
    <mx:Form id="inputForm">
        <mx:FormItem label="First Name:">
            <mx:TextInput id="firstField" />
        </mx:FormItem>
        <mx:FormItem label="Last Name:">
            <mx:TextInput id="lastField" />
        </mx:FormItem>
        <mx:Button label="submit" click="submitHandler();" />
    </mx:Form>
    <!-- Welcom Display -->
    <mx:VBox id="userCanvas">
        <mx:Label text="Hello," />
        <mx:HBox>
            <mx:Label text="{userData.firstName}" />
            <mx:Label text="{userData.lastName}" />
        </mx:HBox>
    </mx:VBox>
</mx:ViewStack>

</mx:WindowedApplication>
```

When the application is launched and has finished its initial layout, the `completeHan
dler` method is invoked and checks for any data stored in the encrypted local store with
an associated key value of `user`. If available, a `ByteArray` object is returned, deserialized,
and cast as a `UserData` object. If the data is not available, the user can enter information
and submit the data to be stored. In the `submitHandler` method, user data is serialized
to a `ByteArray` object by using the `ByteArray.writeObject` method and stored with the
`user` key string. Anything you can serialize by using the `ByteArray` methods, such as
UTF-encoded strings, Boolean values, and numbers, can be stored in the encrypted
local store.

See Also

Recipe 19.6.

19.8 Browse for Files

Problem

You want to present Open File and Save File dialog boxes to open or save files to a directory.

Solution

Use the browsing methods of the `flash.filesystem.File` class.

Discussion

The `File` class offers the capability to open a dialog box for selecting single and multiple files to open. When using the `File.browseForOpen` method, a `select` event is dispatched upon selection of a file from the dialog box. When a user selects files from the dialog box by using `File.browseForOpenMultiple`, a `selecteMutiple` event is dispatched.

The following example opens a dialog box to select a single file with a specified file extension:

```
private var file:File = new File();
private var filter:FileFilter = new FileFilter( "Text", "*.txt; *.xml; *.html" );

private function initHandler():void
{
    file.browseForOpen( "Open File", [filter] );
    file.addEventListener( Event.SELECT, selectHandler );
    file.addEventListener( Event.CANCEL, cancelHandler );
}

private function selectHandler( evt:Event ):void
{
    var stream:FileStream = new FileStream();
    stream.open( file, FileMode.READ );
    trace( stream.readUTFBytes( stream.bytesAvailable ) );
    stream.close();
}
private function cancelHandler( evt:Event ):void
{
    trace( "Browse cancelled." );
}
```

A new `File` object is created and the `File.browseForOpen` method is called to display an Open File dialog box. Using the `FileFilter` class, you can specify which type of files are displayed within the dialog box, to restrict a user to selecting only files with a particular extension. You can listen for a `select` event dispatched from the `File` object upon selection of a file from the dialog box. In the `selectHandler` event handler, a new `FileStream` object is opened and the `File` instance is placed on the read buffer.

Calling the `File.browseForOpenMultiple` method will open a dialog box that enables a user to select multiple files. Upon selection of files, a `selectMultiple` event is dispatched and the `File` objects are held on the `files` property of the `FileListEvent` object:

```
private var file:File;
private var filter:FileFilter = new FileFilter( "Text", "*.txt; *.xml; *.html" );

private function initHandler():void
{
    file = File.desktopDirectory;
    file.browseForOpenMultiple( "Open File", [filter] );
    file.addEventListener( FileListEvent.SELECT_MULTIPLE, selectHandler );
}

private function selectHandler( evt:FileListEvent ):void
{
    trace( "Selected files from:  " + file.url + "\n" );
    var files:Array = evt.files;
    for( var i:int = 0; i < files.length; i++ )
    {
        trace( ( files[i] as File ).name + "\n" );
    }
}
```

In this example, an Open File dialog box is opened and points to the user's desktop directory. After the selected files have been instructed to be opened, the `selectHandler` method is invoked and prints the `name` property of each selected `File` object to the debug console.

The `File` class also has support for presenting a Save File dialog box. From the Save File dialog box, a user chooses a directory to save a file and has an input field for the filename. You listen for the `select` event just as you would for the `File.browseForOpen` method to handle a user selection. The following example opens a Save File dialog box and writes the text *Hello World* to the target file:

```
private var file:File;

private function initHandler():void
{
    file = File.desktopDirectory;
    file.browseForSave( "Save As" );
    file.addEventListener( Event.SELECT, selectHandler );
}

private function selectHandler( evt:Event ):void
{
    var stream:FileStream = new FileStream();
    stream.open( evt.target as File, FileMode.WRITE );
    stream.writeUTFBytes( "Hello World." );
    stream.close();
}
```

The browsing methods of the `File` class provide a convenient way to present a user interface for file selection that conforms to the operating system dialog box. Providing a graphic representation of files and directories is not limited to the dialog boxes spawned via methods of the `File` class, however. There are also several display classes available in the SDK that you can use in your AIR applications.

See Also

Recipe 19.5, and Recipe 19.6.

19.9 Use the AIR File System Controls

Problem

You want to add controls for navigating through and displaying contents of a specific directory in the file system.

Solution

Use the file system controls included in the SDK.

Discussion

The AIR API of the Flex 3 SDK includes controls to facilitate browsing directories of the computer's file system. The controls available for AIR applications combine the functionality of list-based components from the Framework, such as `Tree`, `List`, and `DataGrid`, with the awareness of the file system. Though the presentation and user interaction of the file system controls is the same as their Flex component counterparts, file system data is handed to the controls via the `directory` property rather than the `dataProvider` property.

The following example uses the `FileSystemComboBox` and `FileSystemList` components to navigate within the computer file system and display contents of a directory:

```
<mx:WindowedApplication
    xmlns:mx="http://www.adobe.com/2006/mxml"
    layout="vertical"
    windowComplete="initHandler();">

    <mx:Script>
        <![CDATA[
            import mx.events.FileEvent;

            private function initHandler():void
            {
                fileCB.directory = File.documentsDirectory;
            }

            private function changeHandler( evt:FileEvent ):void
            {
                trace( evt.file.nativePath );
            }
```

```
        ]]>
    </mx:Script>

    <mx:FileSystemComboBox id="fileCB"
        directory="{fileList.directory}"
        directoryChange="changeHandler(event);"
        />
    <mx:FileSystemList id="fileList"
        directory="{fileCB.directory}"
        />

</mx:WindowedApplication>
```

The mx.controls.FileSystemComboBox displays a hierarchy of directories within a drop-down control. When the application has loaded and the initial layout is complete, the initial directory for the combo box is set to the user's Documents directory. If you access the drop-down of the combo box control, you will see the hierarchical directory structure that leads to that directory. Subdirectories of the Documents directory will not be available from the FileSystemComboBox and, upon selection of another directory item within the drop-down, previously available directories lower in the selected directory hierarchy will no longer be available for selection.

In this example, when a selection is made from the FileSystemComboBox control, the directory displayed in the FileSystemList control is updated and the changeHandler method is invoked. The event object passed from the directoryChange event is a FileE vent object. The current directory selected is accessed via the file property of the FileEvent object, and the native path is printed to the debug console. By using two-way binding for the directory properties of the FileSystemComboBox and FileSystem List, each component is updated with the current directory selected by the user.

Along with displaying hidden files or files with a specific file extension, the FileSystem List class also has properties that relate to browsing history. You can use instances of the FileSystemHistoryButton class to enable a user to navigate through the browsing history while selecting directories to view.

The following example uses FileSystemHistoryButton components to facilitate navigating to previously selected directories of a FileSystemList component:

```
<mx:WindowedApplication
    xmlns:mx="http://www.adobe.com/2006/mxml"
    layout="vertical">

    <mx:HBox width="100%">
        <mx:FileSystemHistoryButton label="Back"
            dataProvider="{fileList.backHistory}"
            enabled="{fileList.canNavigateBack}"
            click="fileList.navigateBack();"
            itemClick="fileList.navigateBack(event.index)"
            />
        <mx:FileSystemHistoryButton label="Forward"
            dataProvider="{fileList.forwardHistory}"
```

```
                enabled="{fileList.canNavigateForward}"
                click="fileList.navigateForward();"
                itemClick="fileList.navigateForward(event.index)"
                />
        </mx:HBox>

        <mx:FileSystemList id="fileList"
            width="100%" height="250"
            directory="{File.documentsDirectory}"
            />

    </mx:WindowedApplication>
```

The data provider for each history button is the array of `File` objects previously selected from the directories displayed in the `FileSystemList`. The `FileSystemList` has internal management to update the `backHistory`, `forwardHistory`, `canNavigateBack`, and `canNa vigateForward` properties. You can access particular directory items held on the `File SystemList` control from the drop-down context menu of the `FileSystemHistoryBut ton` components. The object dispatched from the `itemClick` event of a `FileSystemHis toryButton` instance is a `MenuEvent`. You can use the `index` property of the event object to target a specific point in browsing history and update the directory listing displayed in the `FileSystemList` component.

Though the `FileSystemList` control displays the current files and directories within a specified directory, it does not show a hierarchical view of directories found on the file system. You can display directories in a tree structure by using the `FileSystemTree` control. The `FileSystemTree` class lets you specify whether to show hidden files, files of a certain extension, `File` objects considered only as directories, as well as other filtering options. Along with customizing how a user views and navigates through a directory, the `FileSystemTree` component dispatches a `directoryClosing` event, a `direc toryOpening` event, and a `directoryChange` event. You can assign event listeners for these events that dispatch a `FileEvent` object.

The following example uses an instance of the `FileSystemTree` class to display the root directory of the file system upon instantiation:

```
    <mx:WindowedApplication
        xmlns:mx="http://www.adobe.com/2006/mxml"
        layout="vertical">

        <mx:FileSystemTree id="fileTree"
            width="100%" height="100%"
            directory="{FileSystemTree.COMPUTER}"
            />

    </mx:WindowedApplication>
```

The `FileSystemTree` control is a convenient way to enable a user to browse through the hierarchy of a targeted directory. The items of the `FileSystemTree` component are la-beled by using the name of the file or folder. To display more information about the file and folder objects, you can use the `FileSystemDataGrid` class. The

`FileSystemDataGrid` control automatically displays instances of the `DataGridColumn` to show the filename, type, size, creation date, and modification date. You can navigate through directories by using the `FileSystemDataGrid` control and double-clicking on an item. The following example uses a `FileSystemDataGrid` control to navigate the Desktop directory of a the file system:

```
<mx:WindowedApplication
    xmlns:mx="http://www.adobe.com/2006/mxml"
    layout="vertical">

    <mx:FileSystemDataGrid id="fileGrid"
        width="100%" height="100%"
        directory="{File.desktopDirectory}"
        />

</mx:WindowedApplication>
```

Double-clicking on an item from the data grid will refresh the display to show files and folders within the selected directory. This action will dive into the directory and display its contents, but the component does not have any controls that enable a user to navigate back up the file system hierarchy. Similar to the `FileSystemList`, the `FileSystem DataGrid` internally manages a browsing history, and you can use instances of the `Fil eSystemHistoryButton` class to interact with that history.

Using the file system controls included in the AIR API is a convenient way to enable users to navigate through the computer's file system. It is important to note that AIR does not respond to file system notifications, so if a file or directory is deleted while using the file system controls, the display will not be refreshed. To ensure that operations are not performed on files that are considered out-of-date, you can call the `refresh` method available on the `FileSystemList`, `FileSystemTree`, and `FileSystemData Grid` controls.

See Also

Recipe 19.5 and Recipe 19.8.

19.10 Use the Native Drag-and-Drop API

Problem

You want to drag data into and out of your application.

Solution

Add data to a `Clipboard` object and manage drag-and-drop operations by using the `NativeDragManager` class.

Discussion

You can add support for data transfer to and from the file system and between AIR applications by using the native drag-and-drop API. When a drag-and-drop gesture is initiated, data of a specified format is added to a `Clipboard` object and passed to the `NativeDragManager` through the `doDrag` method. You can register event listeners to events dispatched by the `NativeDragManager` during and at completion of the drag-and-drop operation. Instances of the `NativeDragEvent` class are dispatched, and you access the `Clipboard` data via the `NativeDragEvent.clipboard` property within an event handler.

A drag-and-drop gesture is initiated when a user selects an element of the application with the mouse. While the user keeps the mouse button depressed, the operation enters the *dragging* phase, from which any registered component extending the `flash.dis` `play.InteractiveObject` class can accept drag-and-drop actions. The drag-and-drop gesture is completed when the user releases the mouse. A component that initiates the drag-and-drop gesture is considered a *drag initiator*. An `InteractiveObject` instance that accepts the drop action is considered a *drop target*.

While the Flex Framework offers drag-and-drop support within an application, the native drag-and-drop API enables a user to drag and drop data between the file system and other AIR applications. When dragging and dropping data within an AIR application, it is recommended that you still use the drag-and-drop API of the Flex Framework. If you are familiar with working with the `mx.managers.DragManager` class for transferring data within a Flex application, you will find that the `flash.desktop.Nati` `veDragManager` class is very similar. An important aspect to note between these classes is that `DragSource` objects are added to the `DragManager` instance, while `Clipboard` objects are added to the `NativeDragManager` instance.

The following example uses the `NativeDragManager` to add an image file to a `Clip` `board` object that will be transferred to a directory on the file system by using a drag-and-drop gesture:

```
<mx:WindowedApplication
    xmlns:mx="http://www.adobe.com/2006/mxml"
    layout="vertical"
    windowComplete="initHandler();"
    closing="closeHandler();">

    <mx:Script>
        <![CDATA[
            import mx.graphics.codec.PNGEncoder;

            private var tempDir:File = File.createTempDirectory();
            private var imageData:BitmapData;

            private function initHandler():void
            {
                imageData = new BitmapData( image.width, image.height );
                imageData.draw( image );
            }
```

```
private function closeHandler():void
{
    tempDir.deleteDirectory();
}

private function clickHandler():void
{
    var transfer:Clipboard = new Clipboard();
    transfer.setData( ClipboardFormats.FILE_LIST_FORMAT,
                                    [getImageFile()], false );

    NativeDragManager.dropAction = NativeDragActions.COPY;
    NativeDragManager.doDrag( this, transfer, imageData );
}

private function getImageFile():File
{
    var tempFile:File = tempDir.resolvePath( "img.png" );

    var png:ByteArray = new PNGEncoder().encode( imageData );
    var stream:FileStream = new FileStream();
    stream.open( tempFile, FileMode.WRITE );
    stream.writeBytes( png );
    stream.close();

    return tempFile
}

    ]]>
</mx:Script>

<mx:Image id="image"
    source="@Embed(source='assets/bigshakey.png')"
    buttonMode="true" useHandCursor="true"
    mouseDown="clickHandler();"
    />

</mx:WindowedApplication>
```

When the mouseDown event is dispatched by the Image control, the clickHandler method is invoked and a new Clipboard object is created. A representation of the data to be transferred is created by using the Clipboard.setData method. The data format for the Clipboard object is a file list array with a single file: an image file held in a temporary directory of the file system. When a user drags the image out of the application into any directory on the file system and releases the mouse button, the image file will be transferred to that location.

You can also drag data into an application from the file system and from another AIR application. To enable your application to accept native drag-and-drop operations, you listen for the drag-and-drop action events dispatched by the NativeDragManager class. The following example is an application that accepts image files from a drag-and-drop gesture:

```
<mx:WindowedApplication
    xmlns:mx="http://www.adobe.com/2006/mxml"
    layout="absolute"
    windowComplete="initHandler();">

    <mx:Script>
        <![CDATA[
            import mx.controls.Image;

            private var loader:Loader;
            private var xposition:Number;
            private var yposition:Number;

            private function initHandler():void
            {
                addEventListener( NativeDragEvent.NATIVE_DRAG_ENTER,
                                  dragEnterHandler );
                addEventListener( NativeDragEvent.NATIVE_DRAG_DROP,
                                  dragDropHandler );
            }

            private function dragEnterHandler( evt:NativeDragEvent ):void
            {
                if( evt.clipboard.hasFormat( ClipboardFormats.FILE_LIST_FORMAT ) )
                    NativeDragManager.acceptDragDrop( this );
            }

            private function dragDropHandler( evt:NativeDragEvent ):void
            {
                var pt:Point = globalToLocal(new Point( evt.localX, evt.localY ));
                xposition = pt.x;
                yposition = pt.y;
                var files:Array = evt.clipboard.getData(
                                    ClipboardFormats.FILE_LIST_FORMAT ) as Array;
                loader = new Loader();
                loader.contentLoaderInfo.addEventListener( Event.COMPLETE,
                                                           completeHandler );
                loader.load( new URLRequest( files[0].url ) );
            }

            private function completeHandler( evt:Event ):void
            {
                var bmp:Bitmap = loader.content as Bitmap;
                var image:Image = new Image();
                image.source = bmp;
                image.x = xposition;
                image.y = yposition;
                addChild( image );
            }

        ]]>
    </mx:Script>

</mx:WindowedApplication>
```

When the application is loaded and has completed its initial layout, event listeners for the `nativeDragEnterEvent` and `nativeDragDropEvent` events are assigned. When a file is dragged into the application, the application is given permission to listen for drop events by calling the `NativeDragManager.acceptDragDrop` method with the argument value of the application itself. When a `dragDropEvent` action is performed, the transferred data is considered a list of `File` objects and the first item in the array is loaded into an `Image` control.

Though the examples of this recipe demonstrate the interaction between an AIR application and the file system when transferring data by using the `NativeDragManager`, you are not limited to working only with `File` objects. You can also pass bitmap data and strings formatted in HTML, URL, or plain text by using a drag-and-drop gesture.

See Also

Recipe 19.5.

19.11 Interact with the Operating System Clipboard

Problem

You want to place data on and access data from the operating system clipboard.

Solution

Use the static `generalClipboard` property of the `Clipboard` class.

Discussion

You can transfer data and objects not only through drag-and-drop operations but by interacting with the operating system clipboard through the static `generalClipboard` property of the `flash.desktop.Clipboard` class. Supported standard formats to be copied from and to an AIR application are bitmap data, file list data, and text data in standard, HTML, and URL format. When this data is available, it is translated into a `BitmapData` object, an array of `File` objects, and a `String` object, respectively. You can also add custom data formats to be transferred on a `Clipboard` object, but that data will be available only to other AIR applications that know how to handle data of that format.

In the following example, you can add data to, access data from, and remove data held on the operating system clipboard:

```
<mx:WindowedApplication
    xmlns:mx="http://www.adobe.com/2006/mxml"
    layout="vertical">

    <mx:Script>
        <![CDATA[
```

```
        private function addHandler():void
        {
            Clipboard.generalClipboard.setData( ClipboardFormats.TEXT_FORMAT,
                                                textField.text );
        }
        private function removeHandler():void
        {
            Clipboard.generalClipboard.clear();
        }

        private function pasteHandler():void
        {
            if( Clipboard.generalClipboard.hasFormat(
                                ClipboardFormats.TEXT_FORMAT ) )
            {
                textField.text =
                    Clipboard.generalClipboard.getData(
                                ClipboardFormats.TEXT_FORMAT ) as String;
            }
        }
    ]]>
    </mx:Script>

    <mx:TextArea id="textField"
        width="100%" height="100%"
        />
    <mx:Button label="add to clipboard"
        click="addHandler();"
        />
    <mx:Button label="remove from clipboard"
        click="removeHandler();"
        />
    <mx:Button label="past from clipboard"
        click="pasteHandler();"
        />

</mx:WindowedApplication>
```

The addHandler event handler places the text string currently displayed in the <mx:Tex
tArea> control on the operating system clipboard. You can paste that data into any
other application regardless of whether it is running within the Adobe AIR runtime.
String data transferred to the operating system clipboard by any application can also
be pasted into the <mx:TextArea> control. Within the pasteHandler method, the format
of the data currently on the system clipboard is checked by using the hasFormat method.
If it is string data, it is converted to an ActionScript String object and pasted into the
component. You can also clear data from the clipboard by using the clear method as
is done in the removeHandler method.

The type of data format is not limited to the constant values enumerated in the Clip
boardFormats class. You can specify any string value that multiple AIR applications
recognize. Take, for instance, the possibility that two or more applications handle user
information. To share this information between the applications using the operating

system clipboard, you could place data on the clipboard similar to the following code snippet:

```
Clipboard.generalClipboard.setData( "userObject",
                              new UserObject( 'Ted', 'Henderson' ) );
```

Any AIR application that knows how to handle data of `userObject` format can access and handle the `UserObject` instance placed on the operating system clipboard.

See Also

Recipe 19.10.

19.12 Add HTML Content

Problem

You want to display HTML content in your application.

Solution

Use the `<mx:HTML>` control to load and display HTML content in a scrollable container.

Discussion

The Adobe AIR runtime provides support for rendering HTML in SWF-based applications. The rendering engine is built on WebKit technology and supports content that can be run in any WebKit-based browser, such as Safari. At the heart of this engine is the `flash.html.HTMLLoader` class of the AIR HTML API. As an extension of the `flash.display.Sprite` class, an `HTMLLoader` object can be added to ActionScript-based and Flex-based applications targeting the Adobe AIR runtime.

Also included in the API is the `<mx:HTML>` control, which lets you conveniently add HTML content within a scrollable container to applications leveraging the Flex Framework. The `mx.controls.HTML` class internally interfaces with an instance of the `HTMLLoader` class and provides access to objects of the HTML Document Object Model (DOM). This provides you with the capability to interact with JavaScript objects available on the DOM and any CSS applied to the HTML page. You are not limited to loading HTML pages served from a server, and can load HTML pages from the local sandbox and even by supplying an HTML-formatted string.

To load an HTML page into the `<mx:HTML>` control, you assign a `location` property value. The location string is passed to the internal `HTMLLoader` instance, which loads and renders the requested page. The following example loads a web page into an `<mx:HTML>` control and has other controls on the display to enable a user to navigate to other pages:

```
<mx:WindowedApplication
    xmlns:mx="http://www.adobe.com/2006/mxml"
    layout="vertical">

    <mx:Script>
        <![CDATA[

            [Bindable]
            public var urlLocation:String = "http://www.adobe.com";

        ]]>
    </mx:Script>

    <mx:Form width="100%">
        <mx:FormItem width="100%">
            <mx:HBox width="100%">
                <mx:TextInput id="urlField"
                    width="100%"
                    text="{html.location}"/>
                <mx:Button label="go"
                    click="{urlLocation = urlField.text}"
                    />
            </mx:HBox>
        </mx:FormItem>
    </mx:Form>
    <mx:HTML id="html"
        width="100%" height="100%"
        location="{urlLocation}"
        />

</mx:WindowedApplication>
```

The application loads the web page at *http://www.adobe.com* upon startup and provides controls to navigate to and load other HTML pages by changing the location property of the <mx:HTML> control. After the page is loaded, you can interact with the HTML content just as you would within a web browser. The HTMLLoader instance also internally manages a browsing history and provides a convenient way for the application to navigate to locations previously requested. The following example adds controls to navigate forward and back within the history of the HTMLLoader object via methods of the <mx:HTML> control:

```
<mx:WindowedApplication
    xmlns:mx="http://www.adobe.com/2006/mxml"
    layout="vertical">

    <mx:Script>
        <![CDATA[

            [Bindable]
            public var urlLocation:String = "http://www.adobe.com";

        ]]>
    </mx:Script>
```

```
<mx:Form width="100%">
    <mx:FormItem width="100%">
        <mx:HBox width="100%">
            <mx:Button label="back"
                click="html.historyBack();"
                />
            <mx:Button label="forward"
                click="html.historyForward();"
                />
            <mx:TextInput id="urlField"
                width="100%"
                text="{html.location}"/>
            <mx:Button label="go"
                click="{urlLocation = urlField.text}"
                />
        </mx:HBox>
    </mx:FormItem>
</mx:Form>
<mx:HTML id="html"
    width="100%" height="100%"
    location="{urlLocation}"
    />

</mx:WindowedApplication>
```

The `HTML.historyBack` and `HTML.historyForward` methods navigate within the history of locations passed to the `HTMLLoader` object. If you are familiar with building Ajax applications, the history managed by the `HTMLLoader` class is similar to the `window.his tory` JavaScript object. Along with methods to navigate forward and back within the history, you can access the length of history, access the current position, and load a specific page within the history by using the `historyGo` method. From this example, you may notice how quick you can be on your way developing a SWF-based custom web browser.

There are several events dispatched by the `HTMLLoader` instance during the load and rendering phases when the `location` property is updated. You can listen for these events and assign handlers inline within the declaration of an `<mx:HTML>` control. It is important to note the order of these events and when interaction with the loaded HTML DOM is available.

```
<mx:HTML id="html"
    width="100%" height="100%"
    location="http://www.adobe.com"
    htmlDOMInitialize="initHandler();"
    locationChange="changeHandler();"
    complete="completeHandler();"
    htmlRender="renderHandler();"
    />
```

The `locationChange` event is dispatched when the `location` property has been updated on the internal `HTMLLoader` instance. The `htmlDOMInitialized` event is dispatched when the document is created and before you can interact with objects on the HTML DOM.

You can interact with the HTML DOM after the `complete` event is dispatched. The `htmlRender` event is dispatched upon initial rendering and any subsequent re-rendering of the HTML content.

19.13 Cross-Script Between ActionScript and JavaScript

Problem

You want to access HTML element nodes, access JavaScript variables and functions, and manipulate CSS styles of a loaded HTML page.

Solution

Listen for the complete event and access the HTML DOM by using the `domWindow` property of an `<mx:HTML>` control.

Discussion

The `HTMLLoader` class provides access to objects in the DOM of a loaded HTML document. You can access node elements of the HTML window and also interact with JavaScript in the page, accessing variables and methods and also calling ActionScript methods from JavaScript. This interaction between JavaScript and ActionScript is referred to as *cross-scripting*.

You access the global JavaScript object of an HTML document loaded into an `<mx:HTML>` control through the `domWindow` property. The `domWindow` property is a generic `Object` type, and properties of the HTML DOM can be accessed by using the same dot notation as you would on other ActionScript objects. By using the `domWindow` property, you can access HTML node elements, variables, and functions on the JavaScript object and any CSS style sheets available on the loaded document. Consider the following HTML document that will be loaded into an HTML control of an application:

```
<html>
    <body>
        <p id="helloField">Hello World</p>
    </body>
</html>
```

This simple page will display the text *Hello World* when loaded into a web browser or the `<mx:HTML>` control of an AIR application. You can access the `helloField` element of this page after the content has finished loading by using the `getElementId` method, just as you would in JavaScript:

```
<mx:WindowedApplication
    xmlns:mx="http://www.adobe.com/2006/mxml"
    layout="vertical">

    <mx:Script>
        <![CDATA[
```

```
        private function completeHandler():void
        {
            var p1:String =
                html.domWindow.document.getElementById('helloField').innerHTML;
            trace( p1 );
        }

    ]]>
    </mx:Script>

    <mx:HTML id="html"
        width="100%" height="100%"
        location="test.html"
        complete="completeHandler();"
        />

</mx:WindowedApplication>
```

The complete event is dispatched from the internal HTMLLoader instance of the
<mx:HTML> control when the content has finished loading and the DOM is available.
Within the completeHandler method, the application accesses the node value of the
helloField element of the loaded test.html document and prints the string in the debug
console. The domWindow property of the <mx:HTML> control is an ActionScript representation of the HTML DOM window. Access to data held on a loaded HTML document
is not limited to read-only permissions, and you can change the text value displayed in
the helloField element as well:

```
html.domWindow.document.getElementById('helloField').innerHTML = "Hola!";
```

You can access and manipulate CSS style sheets by using the styleSheets property. The
styleSheets property is an array object created based on the declaration order of cascading style sheets added to the document. In the following snippet, the HTML
document has been updated to provide a style to the helloField element:

```
<html>
    <style>
        #helloField {
            font-size: 24px;
            color: #FF0000;
        }
    </style>
    <body>
        <p id="helloField">Hello World</p>
    </body>
</html>
```

To access and manipulate the style applied to the helloField element, you access the
style sheet from the styleSheets property:

```
var styleSheets:Object = html.domWindow.document.styleSheets;
trace( styleSheets[0].cssRules[0].style.fontSize );
styleSheets[0].cssRules[0].style.color = "#FFCCFF";
```

Each style declaration within a CSS style sheet is placed into an object array and is accessed via the `cssRules` property. You can access and update style properties supported by a CSS declaration though the `style` object.

 Modifications to styles are not kept within the history of the `HTMLLoader` instance. If the `location` property of the `<mx:HTML>` control is updated, any change made to styling of the HTML document will not be retained if the same HTML document was reloaded by using the `HTML.historyBack` method.

You can also access JavaScript variables and functions of the HTML document by using the `domWindow` property. The HTML document has been updated to hold an `age` property and a method to change the property value:

```
<html>
    <script>
        var age = 18;
        function setAge( num )
        {
            age = num;
            handleAgeChange( age );
        }

        function sayHello()
        {
            return "Hello";
        }
    </script>
    <body>
        <p id="helloField">Hello World</p>
    </body>
</html>
```

You may notice that within the `setAge` method, a call to a nonexistent `handleAge Change` function is made. Though ActionScript methods can be assigned as delegates for JavaScript function calls made in the HTML DOM, if the `setAge` method is invoked and there is neither a JavaScript function nor a delegated ActionScript handler, a `Ref erenceError` will be thrown. Likewise, if a call is made on the `domWindow` property that does not exist on the `JavaScript` object, an error is thrown. This creates a large dependency with script bridging between ActionScript and JavaScript, but because the properties are a generic `Object` type, a loose coupling is introduced and an application does not depend on a specific HTML document or vice versa.

The following example loads the `test.html` document, updates the `age` property, and invokes the `sayHello` method on the `JavaScript` object:

```
<mx:WindowedApplication
    xmlns:mx="http://www.adobe.com/2006/mxml"
    layout="vertical">
```

```
<mx:Script>
    <![CDATA[

        private function completeHandler():void
        {
            trace( html.domWindow.sayHello() );

            html.domWindow.handleAgeChange = ageHandler;
            trace( "Current Age: " + html.domWindow.age );
            html.domWindow.setAge( 30 );
        }

        private function ageHandler( value:Object ):void
        {
            trace( "Age changed = " + value );
        }

    ]]>
</mx:Script>

<mx:HTML id="html"
    width="100%" height="100%"
    location="test.html"
    complete="completeHandler();"
    />

</mx:WindowedApplication>
```

An error is not thrown by the application when the setAge JavaScript method is invoked because the handleAgeChange function is delegated to the ageHandler method in the ActionScript code. You can send any type of data between JavaScript and ActionScript, but data not of a simple type (such as a Date object) must by converted to appropriate type.

See Also

Recipe 19.12.

19.14 Work with Local SQL Databases

Problem

You want to save and retrieve data locally that will be used by your application.

Solution

Create a database file on the user's hard drive and execute statements by using standard Structured Query Language (SQL) syntax .

Discussion

Included in the Adobe AIR runtime is an SQL database engine enabling you to create local databases for information storage. A database is saved as a file and is not restricted to reside within a specific directory on the file system, allowing any application access to data within the database. The SQL engine of AIR lets you create relational databases to store and retrieve complex data via standard SQL statements.

Included in the SQL database API are several classes that let you create and open database files, make statements, listen for operational events, and retrieve schema information about a database. A database file is created by using the `flash.filesystem.File` class with any valid file extension. A connection to the database is opened by passing the file path to the `open` or `openAsync` methods of the `flash.dataSQLConnection` class. If you do not pass a file reference to the `open` and `openAsync` methods, an in-memory database is created and opened to allow statement executions. Statements can be executed synchronously and asynchronously. Success and failure events can be listened to during the execution of a statement, but asynchronous execution runs database operations outside the main application thread, allowing other code to be run while the statement is executed.

The following example creates a new database file if not previously existent and opens a connection to the database:

```
var db:File = File.applicationStorageDirectory.resolvePath( "Authors.db" );

var sqlConn:SQLConnection = new SQLConnection();
sqlConn.addEventListener( SQLEvent.OPEN, openHandler );
sqlConn.addEventListener( SQLErrorEvent.ERROR, errorHandler );
sqlConn.openAsync( db );

private function openHandler( evt:SQLEvent ):void
{
    trace( "Database created." );
}
private function errorHandler( evt:SQLErrorEvent ):void
{
    trace( "Error " + evt.error.message + " :: " + evt.error.details );
}
```

A file named Authors.db, if not previously existent, is created by the `SQLConnection` instance in the application storage directory and is opened by using the `openAsync` method. If the operation is successful, a `SQLEvent` object is dispatched and the `openHandler` method is invoked. If an error occurred during the operation, a `SQLErrorEvent` is dispatched. The `error` property of an `SQLErrorEvent` object is an `SQLError` object with inherited properties of the `flash.errors.Error` class—such as `message`—and properties that detail the failed operation.

To execute SQL statements, you assign a declarative string value to the `text` property of an `SQLStatement` object and call the `execute` method. The following example uses the `CREATE TABLE` statement of the SQL language to create a new table in a database:

```
var db:File = File.applicationStorageDirectory.resolvePath( "Authors.db" );

var sqlConn:SQLConnection = new SQLConnection();
sqlConn.addEventListener( SQLEvent.OPEN, openHandler );
sqlConn.addEventListener( SQLErrorEvent.ERROR, errorHandler );
sqlConn.openAsync( db );

private function openHandler( evt:SQLEvent ):void
{
    var sql:String = "CREATE TABLE IF NOT EXISTS authors (" +
                     "authorId    INTEGER    PRIMARY KEY," +
                     "firstName   TEXT       NOT NULL," +
                     "lastName    TEXT       NOT NULL" +
                     ");";

    var statement:SQLStatement = new SQLStatement();
    statement.sqlConnection = sqlConn;
    statement.text = sql;
    statement.addEventListener( SQLEvent.RESULT, resultHandler );
    statement.addEventListener( SQLErrorEvent.ERROR, errorHandler );

    statement.execute();
}
private function resultHandler( evt:SQLEvent ):void
{
    trace( "Table created." );
}
private function errorHandler( evt:SQLErrorEvent ):void
{
    trace( "Error " + evt.error.message +
           ":: " + evt.error.details );
}
```

When the database connection is opened, an SQL statement is executed to create a new authors table with the column (property) names of authorId, firstName, and last Name. To execute an SQL statement, you provide a declarative statement string to the text property of an SQLStatement object. The SQLConnection instance is passed to the SQLStatement object by using the sqlConnection property, and event listeners are created prior to execution. Because the connection has been opened asynchronously by using the SQLConnection.openAsync method, the table creation statement will be run asynchronously as well and allow other code to be run during the operation.

You execute queries by using the SQL declarative language. Along with the CREATE TABLE command, some other common statements you may execute on a database are the INSERT, SELECT, UPDATE, and DELETE queries. The following snippet is an example of performing an INSERT query to add data to a database table:

```
private var insertQuery:SQLStatement = new SQLStatement();

private function addAuthor( fName:String, lName:String ):void
{
    var sql:String = "INSERT INTO authors VALUES (" +
                     "null," +
```

```
                               "'" + fName + "','" +
                               "'" + lName + "'" +
                               ");";

        insertQuery.sqlConnection = sqlConn;
        insertQuery.text = sql;
        insertQuery.addEventListener( SQLEvent.RESULT, insertHandler );
        insertQuery.addEventListener( SQLErrorEvent.ERROR, errorHandler );

        insertQuery.execute();
    }
    private function insertHandler( evt:SQLEvent ):void
    {
        var result:SQLResult = insertQuery.getResult();
        trace( "Row ID : " + result.lastInsertRowID + " / " +
               "# Rows Affected : " + result.rowsAffected );
    }
```

Author data is added to the `authors` database table by using the `INSERT INTO` SQL statement. If the operation is executed successfully, the `insertHandler` method is invoked and a `SQLResult` object is retrieved from the `getResult` method of the `SQLStatement` instance used in the query.

To facilitate and enhance the performance when executing queries, the `SQLStatement` class has a `parameters` property and an `itemClass` property. In cases like this one, where the same statement may be called a number of times that only replaces values, you can use the `parameters` property of the `SQLStatement` to declare a single statement string and update values when statements are executed. The `parameters` property is an associative array that can store key value pairs by using named and unnamed parameters.

The following snippet updates the previous code example by using named parameters:

```
    var insertSql:String = "INSERT INTO authors VALUES (" +
                    "null,:firstName,:lastName);";

    insertQuery.sqlConnection = sqlConn;
    insertQuery.text = insertSql;
    insertQuery.parameters[":firstName"] = fName;
    insertQuery.parameters[":lastName"] = lName;
```

The values are replaced when the statement is executed, and you can use either the : or @ character before the property name. As an alternative, you can store values by using numeric indices with property names in the SQL statement represented as the ? character:

```
    var insertSql:String = "INSERT INTO authors VALUES (" +
                    "null,?,?);";

    insertQuery.sqlConnection = sqlConn;
    insertQuery.text = insertSql;
    insertQuery.parameters[0] = fName;
    insertQuery.parameters[1] = lName;
```

Values are replaced at the elemental index for each ? character during execution of the statement. The benefit of using parameters within an SQL statement is not only the improved performance during execution, but also the security that using substitute values provides against any malicious attacks known as *SQL injection*.

If your application has data objects that relate to table data held in a local database, the `itemClass` property of the `SQLStatement` class is a convenient way to map row results retrieved during a `SELECT` query. The following snippet is an example of using the `itemClass` property to map returned author data to the `com.oreilly.flexcook book.Author` class:

```
import com.oreilly.flexcookbook.Author;

private var selectQuery:SQLStatement = new SQLStatement();

private function getAuthors():void
{
    var sql:String = "SELECT authorId, firstName, lastName FROM authors";
    selectQuery.sqlConnection = sqlConn;
    selectQuery.text = sql;
    selectQuery.itemClass = Author;
    selectQuery.addEventListener( SQLEvent.RESULT, selectHandler );
    selectQuery.addEventListener( SQLErrorEvent.ERROR, errorHandler );

    selectQuery.execute();
}

private function selectHandler( evt:SQLEvent ):void
{
    var authors:Array = selectQuery.getResult().data;
    for( var i:int = 0; i < authors.length; i++ )
    {
        var author:Author = authors[i] as Author;
        trace( author.firstName + " " + author.lastName );
    }
}
```

When the query is successfully executed, the `selectHandler` method is invoked and the `SQLResult` object is retrieved by calling the `getResult` method of the `SQLStatement` instance. The `data` property on the `SQLResult` object is the array of rows retrieved from the database—in this case, an array of authors. Each element in the array can be mapped to an `Author` object because the `Author` class was provided as the `itemClass` property prior to executing the statement.

It is too much for this book to cover the SQL language and statements supported in Adobe AIR, but this recipe has introduced some important techniques in executing statements on a local database.

See Also

Recipe 19.5, Recipe 19.6, and Recipe 19.7.

19.15 Detect and Monitor a Network Connection

Problem

You want to detect a connection to the Internet and monitor the availability of a service.

Solution

Use the `ServiceMonitor`, `SocketMonitor`, and `URLMonitor` classes from the AIR monitoring API.

Discussion

Adobe AIR includes classes that can detect the availability of a connection to a network resource. Along with providing the capability to alert users to a change in connection, these classes also enable developers to create applications that support *occasional connectivity*: a seamless work environment in which an online service is used while a resource is available, and local data can be saved and retrieved while a resource is unavailable. Local data could include serialized objects held in individual files or in the encrypted local store and data entered into a local database.

You can listen for the `networkChange` event dispatched by the `NativeApplication` instance to detect a change in a network connection. The event is dispatched when the connection is made available and when it is made unavailable. The event does not hold information related to the availability of a connection. As such, you should make requests by using event handlers to detect whether the application can work with a desired service.

The following example creates an event listener for the `networkChange` event:

```
<mx:WindowedApplication
    xmlns:mx="http://www.adobe.com/2006/mxml"
    layout="vertical"
    networkChange="networkChangeHandler();">

    <mx:Script>
        <![CDATA[

            private function networkChangeHandler( evt:Event ):void
            {
                // check connection
            }

        ]]>
    </mx:Script>

</mx:WindowedApplication>
```

The `networkChange` event handler in this example is declared within the `<mx:Windowe dApplication>` root tag and is invoked whenever the `NativeApplication` has detected a change to the network connection. A check for network resources is not made upon startup of the application, so if the availability is required, you will need to perform the desired operations when the application has finished loading to check whether a connection exists.

The networkChange event alerts the application only that a change to the network has occurred and not whether a desired service is available or unavailable. Depending on the requirements for your application, you can use the SocketMonitor and URLMonitor classes within the monitoring API to detect whether a required service is available. The ServiceMonitor class is the base class for the all monitoring classes and provides a convenient way to continually poll for the availability of a service. To detect changes to an HTTP connection, you use a URLMonitor object, which is a subclass of the ServiceMonitor class. The following snippet detects the availability of a website by using an HTTP header request:

```
private var monitor:URLMonitor;

private function startMonitor():void
{
    var req:URLRequest = new URLRequest( "http://www.adobe.com" );
    req.method = URLRequestMethod.HEAD;

    monitor = new URLMonitor( req );
    monitor.pollInterval = 30000;
    monitor.addEventListener( StatusEvent.STATUS, statusHandler );
    monitor.start();
}

private function statusHandler( evt:StatusEvent ):void
{
    trace( "Available: " + monitor.available );
    trace( "Event code: " + evt.code );
}
```

The value for the pollInterval property of a URLMonitor object is in milliseconds. In this example, an HTTP header request is made to the service at intervals of 30 seconds. The service will continually poll the connection, but will dispatch the StatusEvent only upon the initial poll request and only when a change in the service availability is made. In this example, the statusHandler method will first be invoked after 30 seconds from when the startMonitor method was called. Afterwards, the statusHandler method will be invoked again only if the available property of the URLMonitor instance changes, such as when a change to a network connection is made.

Using a SocketMonitor instance to check the connection to a socket is very similar to checking HTTP status by using a URLMonitor instance, and takes a host and port argument during instantiation:

```
socketMonitor = new SocketMonitor( "www.adobe.com", 1025 );
socketMonitor.addEventListener( StatusEvent.STATUS, statusHandler );
socketMonitor.start();
```

19.16 Detect User Presence

Problem

You want to detect when the presence of a user has become idle.

Solution

Set the `idleThreshold` property of the `NativeApplication` instance and listen for `userIdle` and `userPresent` events.

Discussion

Detection of user presence is based on keyboard and mouse activity, and idleness is determined by a period of elapsed time without such activity. You can set the time limit within an *inactive* period to consider the user idle within your application. The `NativeApplication` instance created upon startup of an application provides properties and methods that are application specific and can be accessed anywhere within the application. Along with events for a change in network connection, application activation, and invocation, are events dispatched based on user presence.

The following example uses the `NativeApplication` instance to detect the presence of a user:

```
<mx:WindowedApplication
    xmlns:mx="http://www.adobe.com/2006/mxml"
    layout="vertical"
    windowComplete="completeHandler();">

<mx:Script>
    <![CDATA[

        private function completeHandler():void
        {
            NativeApplication.nativeApplication.idleThreshold = 10;
            NativeApplication.nativeApplication.addEventListener(
                Event.USER_IDLE, idleHandler );
            NativeApplication.nativeApplication.addEventListener(
                Event.USER_PRESENT, presenceHandler );
        }

        private function idleHandler( evt:Event ):void
        {
            trace( "Hello?!?!" );
        }
        private function presenceHandler( evt:Event ):void
        {
            trace( "Welcome Back!" );
        }

    ]]>
</mx:Script>
```

```
    </mx:WindowedApplication>
```

When the application is launched and has finished its initial layout, the `completeHan dler` method is invoked, which sets an idle threshold amount and creates event listeners for presence events dispatched by the `NativeApplication` instance. The `idleThreshold` property is indicated in seconds, and after 10 seconds of inactivity from the user, the `idleHandler` method is invoked. When a mouse gesture or keyboard event is detected by the operating system after being considered idle, the `presenceHandler` is invoked to welcome the user back. Using the user presence events can prove beneficial in applications that run operations only while the user is presently at her computer.

19.17 Create System Tray and Dock Applications

Problem

Your application is intended to run in the background and is not required to have a main interface.

Solution

Set the visibility of the application to false in the `<mx:WindowedApplication>` root tag and application descriptor file and use the `DockIcon` and `SystemTrayIcon` classes to add custom application icons.

Discussion

You can create applications that do not have a main user interface and are intended to run in the background. These applications are represented and accessed through the system tray or dock. Both the Mac OS X and Windows operating systems support application icons but differ in their user conventions. As such, AIR provides classes to represent application icons specific to the operating system: the `DockIcon` class for applications running under Mac OS X and the `SystemTrayIcon` class for those in Windows. To detect which icon is supported by the operating system that the application is running in, you use the `supportsDockIcon` and `supportsSystemTrayIcon` properties of the `NativeApplication` class.

The `DockIcon` and `SystemTrayIcon` classes are extensions of the `flash.desktop.Interac tiveIcon` abstract base class. The `icon` property of the `NativeApplication` instance is a reference to the application icon supported by the operating system. You can assign graphics for the icon by using the `bitmaps` property. The elements within the `bitmaps` array are `BitmapData` objects with the common dimension sizes used for the application icon of the operating system. If the `bitmaps` property is empty, a default icon will be used in the dock on Mac OS X and no icon will appear for the application in the system tray on Windows.

Along with customizing the application icon graphics, you can add native context menus to be presented when the icon is clicked. From the context menu, you can listen for select events and run commands as required by the application. The following example is an application that will run in the system tray and dock and provides a command to quit the application:

```
<mx:WindowedApplication
    xmlns:mx="http://www.adobe.com/2006/mxml"
    layout="vertical"
    visible="false"
    windowComplete="completeHandler();">

    <mx:Script>
        <![CDATA[
            [Embed(source='assets/AIRApp_16.png')]
            private var icon16:Class;
            [Embed(source='assets/AIRApp_32.png')]
            private var icon32:Class;
            [Embed(source='assets/AIRApp_48.png')]
            private var icon48:Class;
            [Embed(source='assets/AIRApp_128.png')]
            private var icon128:Class;

            private function completeHandler():void
            {
                var shellMenu:NativeMenu = createShellMenu();

                var icon:InteractiveIcon =
                        NativeApplication.nativeApplication.icon;
                if( NativeApplication.supportsDockIcon )
                {
                    ( icon as DockIcon ).menu = shellMenu;
                }
                else
                {
                    ( icon as SystemTrayIcon ).menu = shellMenu;
                    ( icon as SystemTrayIcon ).tooltip = "My App";
                }

                var bitmaps:Array = [new icon16(), new icon32(),
                                new icon48(), new icon128()];
                icon.bitmaps = bitmaps;
            }

            private function createShellMenu():NativeMenu
            {
                var menu:NativeMenu = new NativeMenu();
                var quitCmd:NativeMenuItem = new NativeMenuItem( "Quit" );
                quitCmd.addEventListener( Event.SELECT, quitHandler );
                menu.addItem( quitCmd );
                return menu;
            }

            private function quitHandler( evt:Event ):void
```

```
    {
        NativeApplication.nativeApplication.exit();
    }

    ]]>
    </mx:Script>

</mx:WindowedApplication>
```

When the application is started and the initial layout complete, the current operating system is determined by using the `NativeApplication.supportsDockIcon` property. If the value is true, the operating system is Mac OS X and the `InteractiveIcon` type accessed from the `icon` property of the `NativeApplication` is a `DockIcon` object. A native context menu is created and returned from the `createShellMenu` method and added as the `menu` property for the application icon. The sole item added to the menu is a `quit` command that will invoke the `quitHandler` method when selected by the user.

One important property to set within the `<mx:WindowedApplication>` root tag is the `visible` property. By setting this property to false, you are hiding the main native window for the application and restricting all user access to the application to the system tray or dock icon. You will have to set the same `visible` property to false in the application descriptor file as well to hide the interface displayed during the initialization phase of the application. The following is a simple example of the descriptor file used by a system tray and dock application:

```
<application xmlns="http://ns.adobe.com/air/application/1.0">

    <id>SystTrayApp</id>
    <name>SystTrayApp</name>
    <filename>SystTrayApp</filename>
    <version>0.1</version>
    <initialWindow>
        <content>SystTrayApp.swf</content>
        <systemChrome>none</systemChrome>
        <transparent>true</transparent>
        <visible>true</visible>
    </initialWindow>

</application>
```

CHAPTER 20

Unit Testing with FlexUnit

Unit testing is a practice and concept that has been slowly gaining in popularity and acceptance in the Flex community as Flex applications have grown larger and more complex. *Unit testing*, the process of ensuring that new additions or changes to a project do not introduce bugs or modify expected behavior, enables large teams to work in tandem without introducing bugs and confirm that small individual parts of a program, down to specific methods, all return the expected results. This lets bugs and errors be pinpointed much more quickly, because a properly written unit test will test the behavior of a single method or a very small piece of functionality.

The core of unit testing is the *test case*, an evaluation that passes a value into a method of an application and reports the test as passing if the correct value is returned. These can be as simple as checking whether a method returns the correct integer value for an operation or as complex as ensuring that some display logic is appropriately performed or that a service has returned the correct object type. Many test cases taken together are referred to as a *test suite*, a group of test cases that can test an entire application or a specific aspect of a very large application. The test suite will show all test cases that have passed or failed. As a developer adds new code to the application, new test cases are written to provide coverage for that new code and are added to the test suite, and then the entire test suite is run. This ensures that any added code does not interfere with previously functional code and that the new code integrates as expected with the application.

The FlexUnit Framework allows you to create test cases and asynchronous tests and evaluate test suites in a test harness application that provides a visual display of all the tests in that test suite. The recipes in this chapter, all of which were written and developed by Daniel Rinehart, show how to develop meaningful test cases and integrate them into coherent test suites, as well as how to use more-advanced tools like the Antennae library that assist in automatically generating tests as you develop your applications.

20.1 Create an Application That Uses the FlexUnit Framework

Problem

You want to create an application that uses the FlexUnit Framework classes to create and run tests.

Solution

Download and unpack the FlexUnit Framework and include the flexunit.swc file in the application's compilation path.

Discussion

The FlexUnit Framework includes a graphical test runner and base classes that can be used to create custom tests. You can download it from Google Code at *http://code.goo gle.com/p/as3flexunitlib/*. Be sure you download the most recent version.

After you unpack the ZIP file into a location of your choice, you simply include flexunit.swc in your application's compilation path to use the FlexUnit Framework. If you're using Flex Builder, choose Project → Properties → Flex Build Path → Library Path → Add SWC, and then navigate to the file flexunit/bin/flexunit.swc. If you prefer the command line, modify the mxmlc arguments to include `-library-path+=flexunit/bin/flexunit.swc`, adjusting the path as needed.

20.2 Create an Application to Run FlexUnit Tests

Problem

You need to create an application to run FlexUnit tests and graphically view the results.

Solution

Use a `TestSuite` instance and `TestRunnerBase` component to run the tests.

Discussion

`TestRunnerBase` is the default graphical test runner included with the FlexUnit Framework. To create an application that includes `TestRunnerBase`, edit the main application MXML file's contents to read as follows:

```
<mx:Application xmlns:mx="http://www.adobe.com/2006/mxml" xmlns:flexui="flexunit.flexu
i.*">
    <flexui:TestRunnerBase id="testRunner" width="100%" height="100%"/>
</mx:Application>
```

After you compile and run the application, the output will look like Figure 20-1.

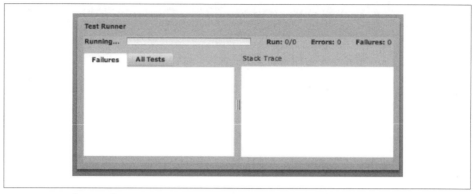

Figure 20-1. The initial appearance of a FlexUnit test application

Next, create a `TestSuite` to hold the collection of tests to be run. In the same MXML file, add the `<mx:Script>` block:

```
<mx:Script>
    <![CDATA[
        import flexunit.framework.TestSuite;

        private function createTestSuite():TestSuite
        {
            var testSuite:TestSuite = new TestSuite();
            return testSuite;
        }
    ]]>
</mx:Script>
```

Note that this example does not add any tests to the `TestSuite` instance; it just creates the object to which you can add `TestCase` instances.

Finally, assign the `TestSuite` instance to the `TestRunnerBase` instance by adding a `handleCreationComplete` function:

```
private function handleCreationComplete():void
{
    testRunner.test = createTestSuite();
    testRunner.startTest();
}
```

This function will start the tests automatically after the application loads. To call it, add a `creationComplete` handler to the application:

```
<mx:Application xmlns:mx="http://www.adobe.com/2006/mxml" xmlns:flexui="flexunit.flexu
i.*" creationComplete="handleCreationComplete();">
```

After you compile and run the application, the output will still look like Figure 20-1, but now you can add `TestCase` instances to the `TestSuite` instance, and they will run when the application starts.

Here's the final MXML file:

```
<mx:Application xmlns:mx="http://www.adobe.com/2006/mxml" xmlns:flexui=
"flexunit.flexui.*" creationComplete="handleCreationComplete();">
    <mx:Script>
        <![CDATA[
            import flexunit.framework.TestSuite;

            private function createTestSuite():TestSuite
            {
                var testSuite:TestSuite = new TestSuite();
                return testSuite;
            }

            private function handleCreationComplete():void
            {
                testRunner.test = createTestSuite();
                testRunner.startTest();
            }
        ]]>
    </mx:Script>
    <flexui:TestRunnerBase id="testRunner" width="100%" height="100%"/>
</mx:Application>
```

20.3 Create a FlexUnit Test Case

Problem

You need to create a FlexUnit TestCase class for testing code.

Solution

Create a class that extends TestCase and include one or more public methods whose
name starts with *test*.

Discussion

When creating an ActionScript class that extends TestCase, the standard convention is
to name it after the class being tested and to add *Test* as a suffix. For example, if the
class to be tested is called RegExp, the TestCase class would be called RegExpTest. Additionally, by convention the TestCase class is placed in the same package as the class
under test. For a class called mx.core.UITextFormat, you would make the TestCase class
mx.core.UITextFormatTest.

For example, to create a new ActionScript class called RegExpTest that extends Test
Case, use the following:

```
package
{
    import flexunit.framework.TestCase;

    public class RegExpTest extends TestCase
    {
```

```
        }
    }
```

The FlexUnit Framework uses reflection to determine the methods in a `TestCase` that should be run. Starting function names with *test* indicates to FlexUnit that the function should be included in those that are run. For this recipe's example, add the method `testRegExp` to `RegExpTest`:

```
public function testRegExp():void
{
}
```

The next phase of the process is to make one or more assertions. An *assertion* is a programmatic way of verifying a statement of fact. The most common form is comparing an expected value to the actual value returned by some operation. FlexUnit includes a number of assertion types that can be used to test different situations. The most common assertions and their functions are as follows:

`assertEquals`
> Compare with `==`.

`assertTrue`
> Check that the condition is true.

`assertNull`
> Check that the condition is null.

`assertStrictlyEquals`
> Compare with `===`.

FlexUnit also provides various convenience assertions that test for the opposite condition, such as `assertFalse` and `assertNotNull`. (See the Assert API documentation included with FlexUnit for a complete list of assertions.)

Each assertion function can take an optional string as the first argument. If the assertion fails, the string will be prefixed before the default "expected X but was Y" failure message that the assertion outputs. When writing assertions, keep in mind that if an assertion fails, the rest of the test method will not be executed.

`TestCase` extends `Assert`, which defines all the assertion functions. This allows subclasses of `TestCase` to directly call the assertion functions. The following code demonstrates the various assertion methods and should be added to the `testRegExp` function:

```
var regExp:RegExp = new RegExp("a", "i");
assertFalse(regExp.test("b"));
assertFalse("regExp doesn't match", regExp.test("b"));

assertNull(regExp.exec("b"));
assertNull("regExp doesn't match", regExp.exec("b"));

assertNotNull(regExp.exec("Apple"));
assertNotNull("regExp matches", regExp.exec("Apple"));
```

```
                 assertTrue(regExp.exec("Apple") is Array);
                 assertTrue("regExp exec returned an Array",
    regExp.exec("Apple") is Array);

                 assertEquals("A", regExp.exec("Apple")[0]);
                 assertEquals("regExp matched A in Apple", "A", regExp.exec("Apple")[0]);

                 assertStrictlyEquals(regExp, regExp);
                 assertStrictlyEquals("regExp object identity", regExp, regExp);
```

You can add new test methods to the `TestCase` to test other logical groups of operations.
It is convention that each test method focus on testing a specific operation or task. For
example, when testing create, retrieve, update, and delete operations, each one should
be put into its own `test` method such as `testCreate`, `testRetrieve`, and so forth. This
way, should assertions start to fail, multiple failures will be reported, which will help
you diagnosis the issue.

Keep in mind, however, that the order that the test methods in a `TestCase` are run is
random. Each test should create its own data and make no assumptions about another
test having already run. The complete ActionScript file follows:

```
package
{
    import flexunit.framework.TestCase;

    public class RegExpTest extends TestCase
    {
        public function testRegExp():void
        {
            var regExp:RegExp = new RegExp("a", "i");
            assertFalse(regExp.test("b"));
            assertFalse("regExp doesn't match", regExp.test("b"));

            assertNull(regExp.exec("b"));
            assertNull("regExp doesn't match", regExp.exec("b"));

            assertNotNull(regExp.exec("Apple"));
            assertNotNull("regExp matches", regExp.exec("Apple"));

            assertTrue(regExp.exec("Apple") is Array);
            assertTrue("regExp exec returned an Array", regExp.exec("Apple")
    is Array);

            assertEquals("A", regExp.exec("Apple")[0]);
            assertEquals("regExp matched A in Apple", "A", regExp.exec("Apple")[0]);

            assertStrictlyEquals(regExp, regExp);
            assertStrictlyEquals("regExp object identity", regExp, regExp);
        }
    }
}
```

The final step is to add the newly created `TestCase` to the `TestSuite`, which is described
in the next recipe.

See Also

Recipe 20.2 and Recipe 20.4.

20.4 Add a Test Case to a Test Suite

Problem

You need to add a test case to an existing test suite.

Solution

Use the `TestSuite addTestSuite` method.

Discussion

To add your test case to the test suite, use the `addTestSuite` method, which takes in a reference to the `TestCase` class. Behind the scenes, FlexUnit uses reflection to find all methods that start with *test* and add them to be executed.

The following example is an update of Recipe 20.2's `createTestSuite` method and adds `RegExpTest` to the set of tests to be executed:

```
private function createTestSuite():TestSuite
{
    var testSuite:TestSuite = new TestSuite();
    testSuite.addTestSuite(RegExpTest);
    return testSuite;
}
```

If the `TestCase` is not in the default package, be sure to add an import for the class. For example:

```
import mx.core.UITextFormatTest;

private function createTestSuite():TestSuite
{
    var testSuite:TestSuite = new TestSuite();
    testSuite.addTestSuite(RegExpTest);
    testSuite.addTestSuite(UITextFormatTest);
    return testSuite;
}
```

When you add multiple test cases to a test suite, they run in the order they're added.

See Also

Recipe 20.2 and Recipe 20.3.

20.5 Run Code Before and After Every Test

Problem

You need to run specific code before and after every test in a test case.

Solution

Override the `setUp` and `tearDown` methods in `TestCase`.

Discussion

By default, every `test` method defined in a `TestCase` runs in its own instance of the `TestCase`. Should multiple `test` methods require the same system state or data, you can use the `setUp` method to centralize setting up the test without having to explicitly call a method at the start of every test. Likewise, if after every test you need to clean up certain objects or test assertions, the `tearDown` method is guaranteed to run, regardless of any assertion failures or errors. Remember that a `test` method stops executing as soon as the first assertion fails or an error is generated. This last point is a key benefit of the `tearDown` method if tests use external resources or objects that should always be freed up.

The `setUp` method is most often used to put the system into a known good state. For complex tests, this may require hooking up multiple objects or connecting to external resources. To create code that runs before every test in a `TestCase`, override the `setUp` method as follows:

```
override public function setUp():void
{
}
```

You can place any code, including assertions, in the `setUp` method. The ability to use assertions in `setUp` allows quick canceling of a test if some resource or object isn't available. Note that if the `setUp` method fails an assertion or throws an error, neither the intended `test` method or the `tearDown` method will be called. This is the only case when `tearDown` isn't called.

Analogous to `setUp` is the `tearDown` method, which is run after every test in the `Test Case`, regardless of failed assertions or errors. Think of it as the `finally` part of a `try...catch...finally` block that is wrapped around the `test` method call. With that said, a `tearDown` method is not usually needed. Remember that by default every `test` method runs in its own instance of the `TestCase`. This means that class-level variables will be set to instantiation values, negating any changes a previous test method may have made. Common situations in which a `tearDown` method is handy include executing shared assertions that should be made after every `test` method or releasing resources that are external to the system, such as disconnecting a `Socket`. To create code that runs after every `test` method in a `TestCase`, override the `tearDown` method as follows:

```
            override public function tearDown():void
            {
            }
```

The following code demonstrates how each **test** method, when run, calls the **setUp**, **test** code, and **tearDown** methods:

```
    package
    {
        import flexunit.framework.TestCase;

        public class SetUpTearDownTest extends TestCase
        {
            private var _phase:String = "instance";

            override public function setUp():void
            {
                updatePhase("setUp()");
            }

            override public function tearDown():void
            {
                updatePhase("tearDown()");
            }

            public function testOne():void
            {
                updatePhase("testOne()");
            }

            public function testFail():void
            {
                updatePhase("testFail()");
                fail("testFail() always fails");
            }

            public function testError():void
            {
                updatePhase("testError()");
                this["badPropertyName"] = "newValue";
            }

            private function updatePhase(phase:String):void
            {
                trace("Running test", methodName, "old phase", _phase,
    "new phase", phase);
                _phase = phase;
            }
        }
    }
```

Sample output from running **SetUpTearDownTest** is as follows:

```
    Running test testFail old phase instance new phase setUp()
    Running test testFail old phase setUp() new phase testFail()
    Running test testFail old phase testFail() new phase tearDown()
```

```
Running test testError old phase instance new phase setUp()
Running test testError old phase setUp() new phase testError()
Running test testError old phase testError() new phase tearDown()
Running test testOne old phase instance new phase setUp()
Running test testOne old phase setUp() new phase testOne()
Running test testOne old phase testOne() new phase tearDown()
```

Notice that each test starts with a _phase value of `instance` and that regardless of an assertion failure or error, the `setUp` and `tearDown` methods are executed.

See Also

Recipe 20.2.

20.6 Share Test Data Between Test Cases

Problem

You want to share simple and complex test data instances between multiple test cases.

Solution

Create a factory class that can generate required test data instances.

Discussion

A common unit-testing need is to have multiple test cases share the same or similar test data. This data may be simple, such as an object that represents an address, or it may be complex, such as an order that has many interrelated entities that must be set up in a particular manner. Instead of cutting and pasting code or trying to load data from an external resource to create and initialize such objects in each `TestCase`, the creation can be centralized into a factory. This type of test data centralization is referred to as the `ObjectMother` pattern.

In its simplest form, the `ObjectMother` is a single utility class with a static method for creating each type of object that is needed. Typically, the creation methods will come in two forms. The first form requires passing in values for each property that needs to be set, and the method just assembles the object. The second form requires few or no arguments, and the method provides realistic, intelligent defaults for each field. As additional object types are needed, they can use the lower-level creation methods to build more and more complex objects.

Another benefit of the `ObjectMother` class is to provide testing constants or other magic values that many tests will reference.

The following is an example of what a simple `ObjectMother` implementation could look like:

```
package
{
    public class ObjectMother
    {
        public static const SHIPPING_ZIP_CODE:String = "0123";

        public static function createAddress(line:String, city:String, state:String,
    zip:String):Address
        {
            var address:Address = new Address();
            address.line = line;
            address.city = city;
            address.state = state;
            address.zip = zip;
            return address;
        }

        public static function createAddressShipping():Address
        {
            return createAddress("123 A Street", "Boston", "MA", SHIPPING_ZIP_CODE);
        }

        public static function createAddressBilling():Address
        {
            return createAddress("321 B Street", "Cambridge", "MA", "02138");
        }

        public static function createOrder(lineItems:Array = null):Order
        {
            var order:Order = new Order();
            order.shippingAddress = createAddressShipping();
            order.billingAddress = createAddressBilling();
            for each (var lineItem:LineItem in lineItems)
            {
                addLineItemToOrder(order, lineItem);
            }
            return order;
        }

        public static function addLineItemToOrder(order:Order, lineItem:LineItem):void
        {
            order.addLineItem(lineItem);
        }
    }
}
```

Starting with a simple `Address` object, the standardized parameter-creation method
`createAddress` is defined. Two helper functions, `createAddressShipping` and `createAd
dressBilling`, are added to provide a quick way for `TestCase` methods to get access to
fully fleshed-out `Address` instances. The helper functions build on the generic `createAd
dress` function by using any creation logic already written in that method. This tiered
creation policy becomes handy when the types of objects being created become more
complex, as shown in the `createOrder` example, or when there are many steps to creating a single object.

Because new instances of objects are created each time a method is called, changes made by one TestCase won't have unintended side effects on other TestCases. At the same time, because the test data objects are centralized, changing the data in the ObjectMother to support a new test may break existing brittle tests. This is usually a minor concern compared to the benefit of having readily accessible test data.

20.7 Handle Events in a Test Case

Problem

You need to wait for an event in a TestCase.

Solution

Use the addAsync FlexUnit method.

Discussion

Testing behavior in a TestCase often involves waiting for asynchronous events. If the TestCase methods concern only synchronous events, such as property change events fired immediately when the property is set, no special handling is required. When asynchronous events are involved, however, you need to take extra care in testing. A common example requiring listening for asynchronous events in a test is waiting for a URLLoad to finish or a UIComponent to finish creation. This recipe discusses the syntax and gotchas of handling events in a sample TestCase using the URLLoad class and a fictitious Configuration object.

Events need to be treated specially in TestCases because unless FlexUnit is informed that it should be waiting for an event, as soon as the test method ends, FlexUnit will think that the method passed and start running the next test method. This can lead to false-positive tests, where FlexUnit displays a green bar but behind the scenes a test silently failed, or worse, displayed an error message.

To inform FlexUnit that it should wait for an event to fire before marking a test as passed or failed, the listener passed to addEventListener must be replaced by a call to addAsync. The first two arguments to addAsync are required, whereas the remaining two are optional. The required first argument is the listener that should be called when the event is fired. This is the method that would have been used as the listener before introducing addAsync. The required second argument is the time-out in milliseconds for waiting for the event to fire. Should the event not fire by the time-out, FlexUnit will mark the test as failed and continue running the other test methods.

A typical usage of addAsync can be seen in the following example:

```
package
{
    import flash.events.Event;
```

```
import flash.net.URLLoader;
import flash.net.URLRequest;

import flexunit.framework.TestCase;

public class ConfigurationTest extends TestCase
{
    public function testParse():void
    {
        var urlLoader:URLLoader = new URLLoader();
        urlLoader.addEventListener(Event.COMPLETE, addAsync(verifyParse, 1000));
        urlLoader.load(new URLRequest("sample.xml"));
    }

    private function verifyParse(event:Event):void
    {
        var configuration:Configuration = new Configuration();
        assertFalse(configuration.complete);
        configuration.parse(new XML(event.target.data));
        assertTrue(configuration.complete);
    }
}
```

The testing of the parse method on the Configuration object has been broken into two methods. The first method constructs the objects and initiates the action that requires waiting for the event. The verify method then uses the result of the event to perform its processing and make assertions. In normal execution, the verifyParse method would have been directly used as the listener argument to addEventListener, but here it was wrapped with addAsync and given a 1000-millisecond time-out. Note that the name of the listener function doesn't start with *test*; if it did, FlexUnit would attempt to run that method as an additional test, which is not desirable.

The type of the event is honored by FlexUnit, and the target listener can cast its argument as such. If instead of a generic Event being dispatched in the preceding example, a FlexEvent or some other Event subclass was used, the listener could safely define its parameter to be that type. Should a mismatch of event types occur, a Type Coercion failure would be reported at runtime.

At this point, there are two important caveats about addAsync that need to be mentioned. First, never have more than one addAsync waiting at a time. The FlexUnit Framework doesn't correctly handle detecting and failing a test if more than one addAsync is defined. It is possible to chain addAsync calls, so that in the listener called by one addAsync, a new addAsync can be created as shown in the following code segment.. Second, don't register an addAsync for an event that will be fired multiple times during a test. Because the addAsync mechanism is used as a rendezvous point for the FlexUnit Framework to know when a test has finished or failed, having the same addAsync called multiple times can produce false positives and odd behavior.

When using addAsync instead of having to use a closure or to create an instance variable, such information can instead be passed along to the listener by using the optional third argument of addAsync. The pass-through data can be anything, providing flexibility in what data can be passed. For example, the test defined previously could be written to create and verify the complete flag of the Configuration object prior to initiating the XML load. Such an approach follows the fail-fast pattern of unit tests, helping to keep the running time of the entire test suite as short as possible. The modified test method using pass-through data is written like this:

```
public function testComplete():void
{
    var configuration:Configuration = new Configuration();
    assertFalse(configuration.complete);

    var urlLoader:URLLoader = new URLLoader();
    urlLoader.addEventListener(Event.COMPLETE, addAsync(verifyComplete, 1000,
configuration));
    urlLoader.load(new URLRequest("sample.xml"));
}

private function verifyComplete(event:Event, configuration:Configuration):void
{
    configuration.parse(new XML(event.target.data));
    assertTrue(configuration.complete);
}
```

Here the object that was created in the test method is passed along to verifyComplete as the second argument. Generic objects or primitive types like ints can also be passed by using this mechanism.

By default, if the event is not dispatched by the time-out specified, a failure will be generated by FlexUnit. If instead some custom handling should occur if the event doesn't fire, use the optional fourth argument to addAsync to specify the function that should be called. Defining a custom failure handler is helpful when testing that an event didn't fire or to perform cleanup specific to the objects involved in the test. The custom failure handler will always be passed the pass-through data even if it is null. To test that the Configuration object never fires a complete event, try this approach:

```
public function testCompleteEvent():void
{
    var configuration:Configuration = new Configuration();
    assertFalse(configuration.complete);
    configuration.addEventListener(Event.COMPLETE, addAsync(verifyEvent, 250,
configuration, verifyNoEvent));
}

private function verifyEvent(event:Event, configuration:Configuration):void
{
    fail("Unexpected Event.COMPLETE from Configuration instance");
}

private function verifyNoEvent(configuration:Configuration):void
{
    assertFalse(configuration.complete);
}
```

It is still necessary to define a listener for the event, but as shown in this example, should that event fire, it represents an error condition. The custom failure handler verifies that the Configuration is still in the proper state given that the event didn't fire.

If multiple asynchronous events will fire in order to set up or test an object, it is important that only one addAsync be active at a time, as already mentioned. To get around this limitation in the handling of one event, you can create another addAsync. Extending the preceding example, if the parsing of a configuration requires loading additional files, the complete status may not immediately change. A sample of how these two events could be chained is shown here:

```
public function testComplexComplete():void
{
    var configuration:Configuration = new Configuration();
    assertFalse(configuration.complete);

    var urlLoader:URLLoader = new URLLoader();
    urlLoader.addEventListener(Event.COMPLETE, addAsync(verifyComplexParse, 10
00, configuration));
    urlLoader.load(new URLRequest("complex.xml"));
}

private function verifyComplexParse(event:Event, configuration:Configuration):
void
{
    configuration.addEventListener(Event.COMPLETE,
addAsync(verifyComplexComplete, 1000, configuration));
    configuration.parse(new XML(event.target.data));
    assertFalse(configuration.complete);
}

private function verifyComplexComplete(event:Event,
configuration:Configuration):void
{
    assertTrue(configuration.complete);
}
```

In the verifyComplexParse function that is configured in the first addAsync, a second call to addAsync is made to set up the next event in the chain to listen for. Chaining can be done as many levels deep as needed.

See Also

Recipe 20.8.

20.8 Test Visual Components with FlexUnit

Problem

You need to test a visual component.

Solution

Temporarily place the component on the display hierarchy and then test it.

Discussion

Some may argue that testing the behavior of visual components strays from the goal of unit testing because it is hard to isolate the class being tested to allow for controlled test conditions. The testing of components is complicated by the richness of the Flex Framework in how it determines when certain methods such as measure get called. The influence of styles and parent containers can also impact how a component behaves. As such, you're better off thinking of the testing of visual components as automated functional testing.

Before you can test the behavior of a visual component, the component must go through the various life-cycle steps. The Flex Framework automatically handles this when a component is added to the display hierarchy. TestCases are not visual components, however, which means that the component must be associated with an object external to the TestCase. This external association means that you must take extra care to clean up after both failed and successful tests; otherwise, stray components could inadvertently impact other tests.

Component testing pattern

The simplest way to get a reference to a display object to which you can add the component being tested is to use Application.application. Because the TestCase is running within a Flex application, this singleton instance is available. The creation and activation of a visual component is not a synchronous activity; before it can be tested, the TestCase needs to wait for the component to get into a known state. Waiting for the FlexEvent.CREATION_COMPLETE event by using addAsync is the easiest way to reach that known state for a newly created component. To ensure that one TestCase method doesn't impact the running of another TestCase method, the component created needs to be cleaned up and any external references to it removed. Using the tearDown method and a class instance variable is the best way to accomplish these two tasks. The following sample code shows the creation, attachment, activation, and cleanup pattern for an instance of Tile:

```
package mx.containers
{
    import flexunit.framework.TestCase;

    import mx.core.Application;
    import mx.events.FlexEvent;

    public class TileTest extends TestCase
    {
        // class variable allows tearDown() to access the instance
        private var _tile:Tile;
```

```
override public function tearDown():void
{
    try
    {
        Application.application.removeChild(_tile);
    }
    catch (argumentError:ArgumentError)
    {
        // safe to ignore, just means component was never added
    }
    _tile = null;
}

public function testTile():void
{
    _tile = new Tile();
    _tile.addEventListener(FlexEvent.CREATION_COMPLETE, addAsync(verifyTile,
1000));
    Application.application.addChild(_tile);
}

private function verifyTile(flexEvent:FlexEvent):void
{
    // component now ready for testing
    assertTrue(_tile.initialized);
}
    }
}
```

The key points to note are that a class variable is defined to allow the `tearDown` method to reference the instance that was created and added to `Application.application`. The addition of the component to `Application.application` may not have succeeded, which is why the `tearDown` method wraps the `removeChild` call in a `try...catch` block to prevent any erroneous errors from being reported. The `test` method uses `addAsync` to wait for the component to be in a stable state before running tests against it.

Component creation testing

Although you can manually call `measure` and the various other Flex Framework methods on a component instance by having it be part of the display hierarchy, the `test` better simulate the environment that the object will run in. Unlike a unit test, the environment external to the component isn't tightly controlled, which means extra care must be taken to focus the testing on the component and not the surrounding environment. As an example, the layout logic of the `Tile` container created earlier can be tested by adding children to it:

```
public function testTileLayout():void
{
    _tile = new Tile();
    var canvas:Canvas = new Canvas();
    canvas.width = 100;
    canvas.height = 100;
```

```
        _tile.addChild(canvas);
        canvas = new Canvas();
        canvas.width = 50;
        canvas.height = 50;
        _tile.addChild(canvas);
        canvas = new Canvas();
        canvas.width = 150;
        canvas.height = 50;
        _tile.addChild(canvas);
        _tile.addEventListener(FlexEvent.CREATION_COMPLETE, addAsync
(verifyTileLayout, 1000));
        Application.application.addChild(_tile);
    }

    private function verifyTileLayout(flexEvent:FlexEvent):void
    {
        var horizontalGap:int = int(_tile.getStyle("horizontalGap"));
        var verticalGap:int = int(_tile.getStyle("verticalGap"));
        assertEquals(300 + horizontalGap, _tile.width);
        assertEquals(200 + verticalGap, _tile.height);
        assertEquals(3, _tile.numChildren);
        assertEquals(0, _tile.getChildAt(0).x);
        assertEquals(0, _tile.getChildAt(0).y);
        assertEquals(150 + horizontalGap, _tile.getChildAt(1).x);
        assertEquals(0, _tile.getChildAt(1).y);
        assertEquals(0, _tile.getChildAt(2).x);
        assertEquals(100 + verticalGap, _tile.getChildAt(2).y);
    }
```

In this example, three children of various sizes are added to the Tile. Based on the
Tile layout logic, this example should create a 2 × 2 grid and make each tile within the
grid the maximum width and height found among the children. The verify method
asserts that the default logic does in fact produce this result. It is important to note that
the test is focusing only on the logic used by the component. This isn't testing whether
the layout looks good, just that its behavior matches the documentation. Another important point to note about testing components at this level is the effect that styles can
have on a component. The dynamic lookup of the horizontalGap and verticalGap in
the verify method is one way to make the test less brittle in case the default values
change. This test method could have instead set the style values when it created the
instance to ensure the values being used.

Postcreation testing

After the component is created, additional changes made to it can be tricky to test. The
generic FlexEvent.UPDATE_COMPLETE event is tempting to use but can fire multiple times
as a result of a single change made to a component. Although its possible to set up logic
that correctly handles these multiple events, the TestCase ends up inadvertently testing
the Flex Framework's event and UI update logic instead of the logic just within the
component. As such, designing the test to focus just on the component's logic becomes

something of an art. This is another reason why most consider component testing at this level to be functional testing instead of unit testing.

The following is an example of adding another child to the `Tile` created previously and detecting that the change has been made:

```
// class variable to track the last addAsync() Function instance
private var _async:Function;

public function testTileLayoutChangeAfterCreate():void
{
    _tile = new Tile();
    var canvas:Canvas = new Canvas();
    canvas.width = 100;
    canvas.height = 100;
    _tile.addChild(canvas);
    canvas = new Canvas();
    canvas.width = 50;
    canvas.height = 50;
    _tile.addChild(canvas);
    canvas = new Canvas();
    canvas.width = 150;
    canvas.height = 50;
    _tile.addChild(canvas);
    _tile.addEventListener(FlexEvent.CREATION_COMPLETE,
addAsync(verifyTileLayoutAfterCreate, 1000));
    Application.application.addChild(_tile);
}

private function verifyTileLayoutAfterCreate(flexEvent:FlexEvent):void
{
    var horizontalGap:int = int(_tile.getStyle("horizontalGap"));
    var verticalGap:int = int(_tile.getStyle("verticalGap"));
    assertEquals(300 + horizontalGap, _tile.width);
    assertEquals(200 + verticalGap, _tile.height);
    assertEquals(3, _tile.numChildren);
    assertEquals(0, _tile.getChildAt(0).x);
    assertEquals(0, _tile.getChildAt(0).y);
    assertEquals(150 + horizontalGap, _tile.getChildAt(1).x);
    assertEquals(0, _tile.getChildAt(1).y);
    assertEquals(0, _tile.getChildAt(2).x);
    assertEquals(100 + verticalGap, _tile.getChildAt(2).y);

    var canvas:Canvas = new Canvas();
    canvas.width = 200;
    canvas.height = 100;
    _tile.addChild(canvas);
    _async = addAsync(verifyTileLayoutChanging, 1000);
    _tile.addEventListener(FlexEvent.UPDATE_COMPLETE, _async);
}

private function verifyTileLayoutChanging(flexEvent:FlexEvent):void
{
    _tile.removeEventListener(FlexEvent.UPDATE_COMPLETE, _async);
    _tile.addEventListener(FlexEvent.UPDATE_COMPLETE, addAsync
```

```
        (verifyTileLayoutChangeAfterCreate, 1000));
        }

    private function verifyTileLayoutChangeAfterCreate(flexEvent:FlexEvent):void
    {
        var horizontalGap:int = int(_tile.getStyle("horizontalGap"));
        var verticalGap:int = int(_tile.getStyle("verticalGap"));
        assertEquals(400 + horizontalGap, _tile.width);
        assertEquals(200 + verticalGap, _tile.height);
        assertEquals(4, _tile.numChildren);
        assertEquals(0, _tile.getChildAt(0).x);
        assertEquals(0, _tile.getChildAt(0).y);

        assertEquals(200 + horizontalGap, _tile.getChildAt(1).x);
        assertEquals(0, _tile.getChildAt(1).y);

        assertEquals(0, _tile.getChildAt(2).x);
        assertEquals(100 + verticalGap, _tile.getChildAt(2).y);

        assertEquals(200 + horizontalGap, _tile.getChildAt(3).x);
        assertEquals(100 + verticalGap, _tile.getChildAt(3).y);
    }
```

The event-handling logic now uses a `class` variable to track the last added asynchronous function created by `addAsync` in order to allow it to be removed and a different listener added to handle the second time the same event type is fired. If an additional change was going to be made that would fire another `FlexEvent.UPDATE_COMPLETE`, the `verify TileLayoutChanging` method would also have to store its `addAsync` function to allow it to be removed. This chained event handling is brittle in that if the Flex Framework logic changes how such events are fired, the code might fail. The test doesn't care that two `FlexEvent.UPDATE_COMPLETE` events fire in order for the component to complete its task of laying out its children; it is an unintended effect of trying to capture component logic at this level. If the intermediate state captured in `verifyTileLayoutChanging` is vital to the logic of the component, the assertions made in that method would have merit and a change in the number of events should warrant this test failing if the events are not fired correctly.

Although a component may dispatch additional events, such as `Event.RESIZE`, the component state at the point the event is dispatched is usually unstable. In the case of a `Tile` when `Event.RESIZE` is dispatched, the component's width has changed but the position of the children has not. Additionally, there may be actions queued via `call Later` such that removing the component from the display hierarchy will cause errors when the queued actions attempt to execute. You can avoid some of these issues when testing a component whose update logic is synchronous, removing the need for any event handling. Alternatively, the component being tested may dispatch an event that clearly defines when a change has been fully realized. Whichever method you choose to handle such cases, keep in mind how brittle these approaches are and how much they inadvertently test behavior outside the component.

Testing with timers

If many complex changes are being made to a component at once, the number and order of events dispatched may be too cumbersome to maintain. Instead of waiting for a specific event, another approach is to wait for a period of time. This approach makes it easy to handle multiple objects that are being updated or a component that uses Effect instances that take a known amount of time to play. The primary drawback is that testing based on time can produce false positives if the speed or resources of the testing environment change. Waiting for a fixed amount of time also means that the runtime of the entire TestSuite increases more rapidly than just adding another synchronous or event-driven test.

The preceding Tile example can be written by using timer-based triggers as shown here:

```
private function waitToTest(listener:Function, waitTime:int):void
{
    var timer:Timer = new Timer(waitTime, 1);
    timer.addEventListener(TimerEvent.TIMER_COMPLETE, addAsync(listener,
waitTime + 250));
    timer.start();
}

public function testTileLayoutWithTimer():void
{
    _tile = new Tile();
    var canvas:Canvas = new Canvas();
    canvas.width = 100;
    canvas.height = 100;
    _tile.addChild(canvas);
    canvas = new Canvas();
    canvas.width = 50;
    canvas.height = 50;
    _tile.addChild(canvas);
    canvas = new Canvas();
    canvas.width = 150;
    canvas.height = 50;
    _tile.addChild(canvas);
    Application.application.addChild(_tile);
    waitToTest(verifyTileLayoutCreateWithTimer, 500);
}

private function verifyTileLayoutCreateWithTimer(timerEvent:TimerEvent):void
{
    var horizontalGap:int = int(_tile.getStyle("horizontalGap"));
    var verticalGap:int = int(_tile.getStyle("verticalGap"));
    assertEquals(300 + horizontalGap, _tile.width);
    assertEquals(200 + verticalGap, _tile.height);
    assertEquals(3, _tile.numChildren);
    assertEquals(0, _tile.getChildAt(0).x);
    assertEquals(0, _tile.getChildAt(0).y);
    assertEquals(150 + horizontalGap, _tile.getChildAt(1).x);
    assertEquals(0, _tile.getChildAt(1).y);
    assertEquals(0, _tile.getChildAt(2).x);
    assertEquals(100 + verticalGap, _tile.getChildAt(2).y);
```

```
                var canvas:Canvas = new Canvas();
                canvas.width = 200;
                canvas.height = 100;
                _tile.addChild(canvas);
                waitToTest(verifyTileLayoutChangeWithTimer, 500);
            }

        private function verifyTileLayoutChangeWithTimer(timerEvent:TimerEvent):void
            {
                var horizontalGap:int = int(_tile.getStyle("horizontalGap"));
                var verticalGap:int = int(_tile.getStyle("verticalGap"));
                assertEquals(400 + horizontalGap, _tile.width);
                assertEquals(200 + verticalGap, _tile.height);
                assertEquals(4, _tile.numChildren);
                assertEquals(0, _tile.getChildAt(0).x);
                assertEquals(0, _tile.getChildAt(0).y);
                assertEquals(200 + horizontalGap, _tile.getChildAt(1).x);
                assertEquals(0, _tile.getChildAt(1).y);
                assertEquals(0, _tile.getChildAt(2).x);
                assertEquals(100 + verticalGap, _tile.getChildAt(2).y);
                assertEquals(200 + horizontalGap, _tile.getChildAt(3).x);
                assertEquals(100 + verticalGap, _tile.getChildAt(3).y);
            }
```

Unlike the previous test examples that could complete as fast as the events fire, this version of the test has a minimum runtime of 1 second. The additional time added to the timer delay when calling addAsync is to handle small variances in when the timer will fire. The intermediate method to swap FlexEvent.UPDATE_COMPLETE listeners from the preceding example is removed, but otherwise the test code remains the same.

Using programmatic visual assertions

The ability to capture the raw bitmap data of a rendered component can make it easy to programmatically verify certain visual aspects of a component. An example would be to test that changing the background and border styles of a component changes how it is drawn. After creating an instance of the component, the bitmap data can be captured and examined. The following is a sample test to verify that adding a border to a Canvas produces the intended results:

```
package mx.containers
{
    import flash.display.BitmapData;

    import flexunit.framework.TestCase;

    import mx.core.Application;
    import mx.events.FlexEvent;

    public class CanvasTest extends TestCase
    {
        // class variable allows tearDown() to access the instance
        private var _canvas:Canvas;
```

```
override public function tearDown():void
{
    try
    {
        Application.application.removeChild(_canvas);
    }
    catch (argumentError:ArgumentError)
    {
        // safe to ignore, just means component was never added
    }
    _canvas = null;
}

private function captureBitmapData():BitmapData
{
    var bitmapData:BitmapData = new BitmapData(_canvas.width, _canvas.height);
    bitmapData.draw(_canvas);
    return bitmapData;
}

public function testBackgroundColor():void
{
    _canvas = new Canvas();
    _canvas.width = 10;
    _canvas.height = 10;
    _canvas.setStyle("backgroundColor", 0xFF0000);
    _canvas.addEventListener(FlexEvent.CREATION_COMPLETE, addAsync
(verifyBackgroundColor, 1000));
    Application.application.addChild(_canvas);
}

private function verifyBackgroundColor(flexEvent:FlexEvent):void
{
    var bitmapData:BitmapData = captureBitmapData();
    for (var x:int = 0; x < bitmapData.width; x++)
    {
        for (var y:int = 0; y < bitmapData.height; y++)
        {
            assertEquals("Pixel (" + x + ", " + y + ")", 0xFF0000, bitmapData.
getPixel(x, y));
        }
    }
}

public function testBorder():void
{
    _canvas = new Canvas();
    _canvas.width = 10;
    _canvas.height = 10;
    _canvas.setStyle("backgroundColor", 0xFF0000);
    _canvas.setStyle("borderColor", 0x00FF00);
    _canvas.setStyle("borderStyle", "solid");
    _canvas.setStyle("borderThickness", 1);
    _canvas.addEventListener(FlexEvent.CREATION_COMPLETE, addAsync
```

```
            (verifyBorder, 1000));
                    Application.application.addChild(_canvas);
            }

            private function verifyBorder(flexEvent:FlexEvent):void
            {
                var bitmapData:BitmapData = captureBitmapData();
                for (var x:int = 0; x < bitmapData.width; x++)
                {
                    for (var y:int = 0; y < bitmapData.height; y++)
                    {
                        if ((x == 0) || (y == 0) || (x == bitmapData.width - 1) ||
(y == bitmapData.height - 1))
                        {
                            assertEquals("Pixel (" + x + ", " + y + ")", 0x00FF00,
bitmapData.getPixel(x, y));
                        }
                        else
                        {
                            assertEquals("Pixel (" + x + ", " + y + ")", 0xFF0000,
bitmapData.getPixel(x, y));
                        }
                    }
                }
            }
        }
    }
```

The `testBackgroundColor` method verifies that all pixels in the `Canvas` are assigned the background color correctly. The `testBorder` method verifies that when a border is added to the `Canvas`, the outside pixels switch to the border color while all other pixels remain the background color. The capturing of the bitmap data is handled in the `captureBitmapData` method and makes use of the ability to `draw` any Flex component into a `BitmapData` instance. This is a powerful technique that can be used to verify programmatic skins and other visual components that may otherwise be hard to unit-test.

For an alternative approach to testing the visual appearance of a component, look at the Visual FlexUnit package available at *http://code.google.com/p/visualflexunit/*.

Hiding the component being tested

One side effect of adding the component to be tested to `Application.application` is that it will be rendered. This can cause the FlexUnit testing harness to resize and re-position as the tests are running and components are being added and removed to the display hierarchy. To suppress this behavior, you can hide the component being tested by setting its `visible` and `includeInLayout` properties to false prior to being added to the display hierarchy. For example, if the `Canvas` should be hidden while being tested in the preceding code, the addition of it to the display hierarchy would be rewritten as follows:

```
        _canvas.visible = false;
        _canvas.includeInLayout = false;
        Application.application.addChild(_canvas);
```

See Also

Recipe 20.3 and Recipe 20.7.

20.9 Install and Configure Antennae

Problem

You want to automate the building and testing of Flex applications.

Solution

Download and unpack the open source Antennae templates and configure them for a particular system.

Discussion

Antennae is an open source project designed to automate the building and testing of Flex applications. It uses Ant and Java to provide cross-platform utilities to compile Flex libraries and Flex applications, generate FlexUnit test suites, and run FlexUnit tests in an automated manner. Antennae also defines a framework for building complex projects with multiple dependencies and for intelligently handling recompilation. You can download Antennae from *http://code.google.com/p/antennae/*. Be sure to grab the most recent version of Antennae-*.zip. When you unpack it, the Antennae ZIP packages everything under a subdirectory called Antennae.

Antennae is divided into multiple pieces to make inclusion in a project as straightforward as possible. The major pieces are as follows:

lib
> Includes compiled Java and Flex utilities for `TestSuite` generation, command-line FlexUnit running and reporting, the FlexUnit library, and a FlexUnit application template.

src
> Source for the Java and Flex utilities included in the lib directory, excluding FlexUnit (which is available elsewhere).

templates
> Antennae templates for building Flex libraries, Flex applications, FlexUnit applications, and Flex projects with complex dependencies.

tools
> Generic Ant target, task, and property definitions used to automate building and testing.

tutorial

Step-by-step examples of how to use basic Ant features and Antennae templates.

Additionally, the base directory includes documentation and sample files used to configure Antennae for use on various platforms.

To run and experiment with all templates and tutorial information included with Antennae, it first needs to be configured. To provide easy cross-platform and multiple-developer support, Antennae centralizes all the properties most likely to change into a single file that you can customize on an as-needed basis. The two files in the base directory, build-user.properties.mac and build-user.properties.win, are starting points for configuring Antennae. Linux users should use the build-user.properties.mac file as an example but note that certain features may not be available because of limitations of the Flex Framework.

Copy the appropriate starting file and name it build-user.properties (this name is the same regardless of the platform). The next step will be to customize the file for your system. You can edit the file in any text editor.

The key property that you must set is `flex2.dir`: Change it to point to the location of a Flex 2 or Flex 3 distribution (a base directory that has bin, lib, and player as subdirectories). You can use either the Flex SDK included with Flex Builder or the stand-alone Flex SDK.

If you plan to use the command-line FlexUnit automation tools, you must set the `flex2.standalone.player` property. It is recommended that the debug version of the stand-alone player be used. Using the debug version allows stack traces to be captured, which helps in determining how a test failed.

The `tomcat.webapps.dir` property needs to be set only if you're running the deploy target for the tutorial/multi/app/ sample.

Finally, the various properties prefixed with `air` are for compiling, running, and packaging Flex-based AIR applications. For additional information on the configuration of these properties, please see the Antennae wiki documentation available at *http://code.google.com/p/antennae/w/list*.

To quickly see how Antennae builds and tests projects, explore the tutorial directory. Running Ant with a target of `build` or `test` will walk through all projects in the tutorial directory, calling the correct target on each. In particular, the `test` target demonstrates both a successful and unsuccessful FlexUnit run.

The base directory includes a README.txt file that gives an overview of how Antennae is set up and the philosophy behind building and testing projects with Antennae. The tutorial and template directories each include a README.txt file that explains the intent and usage of each of the projects included in those directories.

20.10 Generate Automated Test Suites

Problem

You want to automatically include all test cases in a test suite.

Solution

Use the Antennae `TestSuite`-generation tool.

Discussion

To run a `TestCase`, you must include it in a `TestSuite`. The process of creating a new `TestCase` and then adding it to a `TestSuite` can become habit, but if multiple developers are working on the same code base, the chance that a `TestCase` gets overlooked increases. Instead of manually adding each `TestCase` to the `TestSuite`, you can have the `TestSuite` automatically generated. The open source Antennae project includes a utility to automate the creation of a `TestSuite` by examining a source folder and adding tests contained within it.

The Antennae package includes a JAR file in the lib subdirectory called arc-flexunit2.jar, which contains the class `com.allurent.flexunit2.framework.AllTestsFileGenerator`. When the `AllTestsFileGenerator` is run against a source directory, it will find all classes named Test*.as or *Test.as and create a `TestSuite` with them included. The utility creates the `TestSuite` on standard output that can be redirected to any location. The generated `TestSuite` file is part of the root package and is called `FlexUnitAllTests`. Assuming Antennae was unpacked into ~/Antennae and C:\Antennae, you can invoke the utility with the following:

```
java -cp ~/Antennae/lib/arc-flexunit2.jar
com.allurent.flexunit2.framework.AllTestsFileGenerator
~/FlexCookbook/src/ > ~/FlexCookbook/src/FlexUnitAllTests.as

java -cp C:\Antennae\lib\arc-flexunit2.jar
com.allurent.flexunit2.framework.AllTestsFileGenerator
C:\FlexCookbook\src\ > C:\FlexCookbook\src\FlexUnitAllTests.as
```

In the first example, ~/Antennae/lib/arc-flexunit2.jar is the location of the JAR file. The name of the class to run is `com.allurent.flexunit2.framework.AllTestsFileGenerator`, ~/FlexCookbook/src/ is the root of the source tree that should be examined for files, and ~/FlexCookbook/src/FlexUnitAllTests.as is the location of the generated file.

The format of the generated `TestSuite` file looks like this:

```
package
{
    import flexunit.framework.*;
    import mx.containers.CanvasTest;
    import mx.containers.TileTest;
```

```
public class FlexUnitAllTests
{
    public static function suite() : TestSuite
    {
        var testSuite:TestSuite = new TestSuite();
        testSuite.addTestSuite(mx.containers.CanvasTest);
        testSuite.addTestSuite(mx.containers.TileTest);
        return testSuite;
    }
}
}
```

The generation of the FlexUnitAllTests file can be automated such that it is always created before the FlexUnit application is compiled. (See the Antennae documentation for additional details including the use of the AllTestsFileGenerator utility from within Flex Builder.)

Instead of manually constructing the `TestSuite` in the main application, the `FlexUni tAllTests` class is specified as the `TestSuite` to run. Each time the `FlexUnitAllTests` class is regenerated, all included tests will be compiled and run. The modified FlexUnit application that uses the `FlexUnitAllTests` looks like this:

```
<mx:Application xmlns:mx="http://www.adobe.com/2006/mxml" xmlns:flexui=
"flexunit.flexui.*" creationComplete="handleCreationComplete();">
    <mx:Script>
        <![CDATA[
            import flexunit.framework.TestSuite;

            private function handleCreationComplete():void
            {
                testRunner.test = FlexUnitAllTests.suite();
                testRunner.startTest();
            }
        ]]>
    </mx:Script>
    <flexui:TestRunnerBase id="testRunner" width="100%" height="100%"/>
</mx:Application>
```

By convention all files that are named Test*.as or *Test.as are included in the generated `TestSuite`. You can overwrite this behavior by creating a filters file that specifies via regular expressions which files should be included. Each line of the filters file specifies a single regular expression that each filename will be matched against. If the filename matches any of the regular expressions specified, that filename will be included. The regular expression is run against the complete path of the filename that allows for the inclusion of `TestCase`s based on package or other criteria. A sample filters file looks like this:

```
/mx/containers/.*Test.as
RegExpTest.as
```

The first line includes all tests in any directory under /mx/containers/. The second line includes a specific test called RegExpTest.as wherever it occurs. It is important to note that the AllTestsFileGenerator utility operates at the file-system level only. As such it is important to specify Test.as in any rule to avoid picking up non-TestCase files.

If the preceding rules were stored in a file called filters.txt, the utility would be called as follows:

```
java -cp ~/Antennae/lib/arc-flexunit2.jar
com.allurent.flexunit2.framework.AllTestsFileGenerator
~/FlexCookbook/src/ filters.txt >
~/FlexCookbook/src/FlexUnitAllTests.as

java -cp C:\Antennae\lib\arc-flexunit2.jar
com.allurent.flexunit2.framework.AllTestsFileGenerator
C:\FlexCookbook\src\ filters.txt >
C:\FlexCookbook\src\FlexUnitAllTests.as
```

When a filters file is in use, a test that always fails is automatically added to the Test Suite. This is done as a reminder that certain TestCases may have been excluded and the TestSuite doesn't represent the full set of tests that could be run.

CHAPTER 21

Compiling and Debugging

Compiling Flex applications is most often done through Flex Builder or through invoking the MXML compiler (mxmlc) on the command line, but there are many other tools that let you compile an application, move files, or invoke applications. Tools such as make, Ant, or Rake, for example, enable you to simplify an entire compilation and deployment routine so that you can invoke it from a single command.

Debugging in Flex is done through the debug version of the Flash Player, which enables you to see the results of **trace** statements. With Flex Builder 3, you can step through code line by line and inspect the properties of variables. Flex Builder 3 also introduces a new profiling view that lets you examine memory usage and the creation and deletion of objects. Outside of Flex Builder, numerous open source tools expand your options. With Xray and Console.as for Firebug, for example, you can inspect the values of objects, or you can view the output of **trace** statements with FlashTracer or the Output Panel utility instead of using the Flex Builder IDE. The recipes in this chapter cover debugging with both the tools provided in Flex Builder as well as tracing values and inspecting objects by using Xray and FlashTracer.

21.1 Use Trace Statements Without Flex Builder

Problem

You want to create **trace** statements that will assist you in debugging your application, but you do not have Flex Builder 3.

Solution

Download and use one of the many open source tracing tools available.

Discussion

Since Adobe made the Flex 3 library and compiler freely available, developers have gained more options for viewing **trace** statements output by the Flash Player. No longer

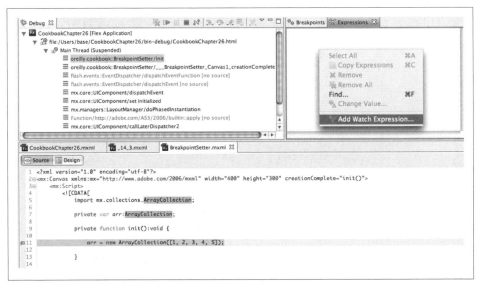

Figure 21-1. Viewing output with Xray

are you limited to using the Flash IDE or Flex Builder IDE; now you can choose from several tools. For example, Xray (developed by John Grden) creates `trace` statement viewers within Flash. Xray allows for not only the viewing of `trace` statements during application execution, but also the basic inspection of objects during execution (Figure 21-1).

A third option is the FlashTrace utility (developed by Alessandro Crugnola). Installing this plug-in in the Firefox browser enables you to receive any `trace` statements that are executed within the application. If you like, you can also log the results of the trace to a file.

You can download Xray from *http://osflash.org/xray#downloads* and FlashTrace from *http://www.sephiroth.it/firefox*.

21.2 Use the Component Compiler

Problem

You want to compile a Flex component into a SWC file that can be used as a runtime shared library (RSL).

Solution

Use the Component compiler (compc) and either pass command-line arguments to the compiler or pass a configuration XML file as the `load-config` argument.

Discussion

To invoke the Component compiler, compc, use this syntax:

```
compc -source-path . -include-classes oreilly.cookbook.foo -output example.swc
```

Some of the most important options for the compc are as follows:

-benchmark
> Indicates that the compiler should benchmark the amount of time needed to compile the SWC.

-compiler.debug
> Indicates whether the generated SWC should have debugging information and functionality included with it.

-compiler.external-library-path [path-element] [...]
> Indicates SWC files or directories to compile against but to omit from linking.

-compiler.include-libraries [library] [...]
> Indicates libraries (SWCs) to completely include in the SWF.

-compiler.library-path [path-element] [...]
> Indicates SWC files or directories that contain SWC files that should be used in compiling.

-compiler.locale [locale-element] [...]
> Specifies the locale for internationalization.

-compiler.optimize
> Enables postlink SWF optimization.

-compiler.services <filename>
> Specifies the path to the Flex Data Services configuration file.

-compiler.theme [filename] [...]
> Lists all CSS or SWC files to apply as themes within the application.

-compiler.use-resource-bundle-metadata
> Determines whether resources bundles are included in the application.

-include-classes [class] [...]
> Indicates all the classes that should be included in the RSL; can be repeated multiple times or have a wildcard path listed.

-include-file <name><path>
> Indicates all the files that should be included in the RSL; can be repeated multiple times or have a wildcard path listed.

-include-resource-bundles [bundle] [...]
> Sets whether a localization resource bundle should be included.

-load-config <filename>
> Loads a file containing configuration options.

`-output <filename>`
Determines the name and location of the file that is generated by compc.

`-runtime-shared-libraries [url] [...]`
Indicates any external RSLs that should be bundled into the RSL generated by compc in this compilation.

`-runtime-shared-library-path [path-element] [rsl-url] [policy-file-url] [rsl-url] [policy-file-url]`
Sets the location and other information about an RSL that the application will use.

`-use-network`
Toggles whether the SWC is flagged for access to network resources.

Compiling many classes into a runtime shared library can result in a very long command. To simplify this, you can use either configuration files or manifest files.

As with the MXML compiler (mxmlc), you can use configuration files with compc by specifying a `load-config` option. Also like mxmlc, compc automatically loads a default configuration file called flex-config.xml. Unless you want to duplicate the entire contents of flex-config.xml (much of which is required), specify a configuration file in addition to the default by using the `+=` operator:

```
compc -load-config+=configuration.xml
```

Any flags passed to the compiler can be described in XML and passed to compc in the `-load-config` option:

```
<include-sources>src/.</include-sources>
```

21.3 Install the Flex Ant Tasks

Problem

You want to use the Flex Ant tasks included with the Flex 3 SDK.

Solution

Copy the flex_ant/lib/flexTasks.jar file to Ant's lib directory ({ANT_root}/lib).

Discussion

To ensure that Ant always has access to all tasks included in the Flex Ant tasks library provided with the Flex 3 SDK, you must copy the tasks into the lib directory of the Ant installation. If you do not copy this file to the lib directory, you must specify it by using Ant's `-lib` option on the command line when you make a project XML file.

21.4 Use the compc and mxmlc Tasks in the Flex Ant Tasks

Problem

You want to use the mxmlc or compc tasks that are included with the Flex Ant tasks to simplify compiling Flex applications and working with Ant.

Solution

Install the Flex Ant tasks into your Ant libraries and then use either the `<mxmlc>` or `<compc>` tags, with the compile options passed to the tags as XML arguments.

Discussion

The Flex Ant tasks greatly simplify working with Ant for compiling Flex applications by providing prebuilt common tasks for developers to use. All the options you can set for the command-line use of mxmlc or compc can be passed to the Flex Ant task. For example, after you declare the mxmlc task, you can declare the file output options as shown:

```
<mxmlc file="C:/Flex/projects/app/App.mxml" output="C:/Flex/projects/bin/App.swf">
```

Instead of needing to specify the location of mxmlc and set all the options as arguments to the executable, the mxmlc Ant task can be used, saving configuration time and making your build files far easier to read. Further options can be set as shown here:

```
<!-- Get default compiler options. -->
<load-config filename="${FLEX_HOME}/frameworks/flex-config.xml"/>
<!-- List of path elements that form the roots of ActionScript class hierarchies.
-->
<source-path path-element="${FLEX_HOME}/frameworks"/>
<!-- List of SWC files or directories that contain SWC files. -->
<compiler.library-path dir="${FLEX_HOME}/frameworks" append="true">
    <include name="libs" />
    <include name="../bundles/{locale}" />
</compiler.library-path>
</mxmlc>
```

The `<compc>` task for the Flex Ant tasks works similarly; all of the options for compc are passed through to the `<compc>` task:

```
<compc output="${output}/mylib.swc" locale="en_US">
```

21.5 Compile and Deploy Flex Applications That Use RSLs

Problem

You need to deploy a Flex application that uses one or more runtime shared libraries (RSLs).

Solution

Use the `external-library-path` compiler option to indicate the location of the RSL or RSLs after the application is compiled.

Discussion

When it initializes, a Flex application needs to know the location of any necessary runtime shared libraries. The `external-library-path` compiler option contains this information; passing it to the compiler enables the Flash Player to begin loading the bytes for the RSL right away, without needing to load a separate SWF file before instantiating components or classes.

In order to use an RSL file, you need to first create an RSL. RSLs are stored within SWC files that are then accessed by the application at runtime. The SWC RSL file is compiled by using compc, and the application SWF file is compiled by using the mxmlc compiler. In order for the application to use the RSL, a reference to the location of the RSL must be passed to mxmlc by using the `runtime-shared-libraries` option. In this example, Ant is used to compile both the SWC file and the application that will access it, meaning that we'll need to use both compc and mxmlc. In the build.xml file that Ant will use, both of the compilers will need to be declared as variables:

```
<property name="mxmlc" value="C:\FlexSDK\bin\mxmlc.exe"/>
<property name="compc" value="C:\FlexSDK\bin\compc.exe"/>
```

Next, use compc to compile the RSL that the application will access and use the move task to place it in the application/rsl directory:

```
<target name="compileRSL">
    <exec executable="${compc}">
      <arg line="-load-config+=rsl/configuration.xml" />
    </exec>
    <mkdir dir="application/rsl" />
    <move file="example.swc" todir="application/rsl" />
    <unzip src="application/rsl/example.swc" dest="application/rsl/" />
</target>
```

Then compile the application SWF by using mxmlc. Note that we're passing an XML file called configuration.xml to the compiler by using `-load-config`. This file will contain all the information about how we want our application compiled, including, in this case, the location of the RSL:

```
<target name="compileApplication">
    <exec executable="${mxmlc}">
      <arg line="-load-config+=application/configuration.xml" />
    </exec>
</target>

<target name="compileAll" depends="compileRSL,compileApplication">
</target>
```

Note that both actual command-line calls to the compilers use a configuration.xml file containing information about the location of the runtime shared libraries that will be passed to mxmlc:

```
<flex-config>
  <compiler>
    <external-library-path>
      <path-element>example.swc</path-element>
    </external-library-path>
  </compiler>
  <file-specs>
    <path-element>RSLClientTest.mxml</path-element>
  </file-specs>
  <runtime-shared-libraries>
    <url>example.swf</url>
  </runtime-shared-libraries>
</flex-config>
```

In place of adding the `external-library-path` flag to the command-line invocation of mxmlc as shown here

```
mxmlc -external-library-path=example.swc
```

the configuration.xml file is passed as the `load-config` flag in the call to the compiler, and each option is read from the XML file.

A similar file can be passed to compc:

```
<flex-config>
  <compiler>
    <source-path>
      <path-element>.</path-element>
    </source-path>
  </compiler>
  <output>example.swc</output>
  <include-classes>
    <class>oreilly.cookbook.shared.*</class>
  </include-classes>
</flex-config>
```

The complete Ant file for this recipe is shown here:

```
<?xml version="1.0"?>
<project name="useRSL" basedir="./">

  <property name="mxmlc" value="C:\FlexSDK\bin\mxmlc.exe"/>
  <property name="compc" value="C:\FlexSDK\bin\compc.exe"/>

  <target name="compileRSL">
    <exec executable="${compc}">
      <arg line="-load-config+=rsl/configuration.xml" />
    </exec>
    <mkdir dir="application/rsl" />
    <move file="example.swc" todir="application/rsl" />
    <unzip src="application/rsl/example.swc" dest="application/rsl/" />
  </target>
```

```
<target name="compileApplication">
  <exec executable="${mxmlc}">
    <arg line="-load-config+=application/configuration.xml" />
  </exec>
</target>

<target name="compileAll" depends="compileRSL,compileApplication">
</target>

</project>
```

21.6 Create and Monitor Expressions in Flex Builder Debugging

Problem

You want to track the changes to a value in your Flex application as the application executes.

Solution

Use the Flex Builder Debugger to run your application and set a breakpoint where the variable that you would like to inspect is within scope. In the Expressions window of the Flex Builder Debugger, create a new expression.

Discussion

The use of expressions is a powerful debugging tool that lets you see the value of any variable within scope. Any object within the scope where the breakpoint is set can be evaluated by creating an expression, as shown in Figure 21-2.

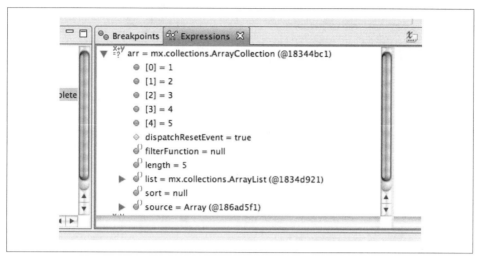

Figure 21-2. Creating an expression

For example, if you place a breakpoint at the line where the array is instantiated, marked here with *breakpoint here*

```
<mx:Canvas xmlns:mx="http://www.adobe.com/2006/mxml" width="400" height="300" creationC
omplete="init()">
    <mx:Script>
        <![CDATA[
            import mx.collections.ArrayCollection;

            private var arr:ArrayCollection;

            private function init():void {
                arr = new ArrayCollection([1, 2, 3, 4, 5]);//breakpoint here
            }

            private function newFunc():void {
                var newArr:ArrayCollection = new ArrayCollection([3, 4, 5, 6]);
            }

        ]]>
    </mx:Script>
</mx:Canvas>
```

the expression arr will evaluate to null. When you advance the application by pressing the F6 key, the expression will evaluate to an ArrayCollection wrapping an Array of five integers (Figure 21-3).

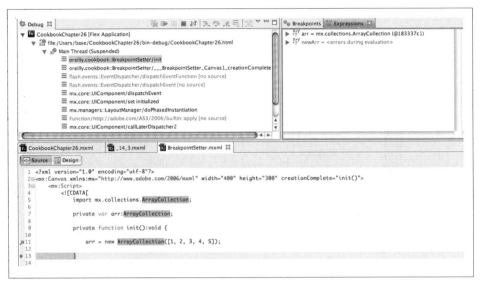

Figure 21-3. The expression showing the variable evaluated

The expression `newArr` evaluates to `null`, however, because the variable `newArr` will not be in scope (Figure 21-4).

Figure 21-4. Only variables in scope can be evaluated.

If you instead place a breakpoint at line 17, the expressions `newArr` and `arr` both evaluate to `ArrayCollections`, because both variables will be in the current scope.

21.7 Install the Ant View in the Stand-Alone Version of Flex Builder

Contributed by Ryan Taylor

Problem

You can't find the Ant view in the stand-alone version of Flex Builder.

Solution

Install the Eclipse Java Development Tools.

Discussion

To access Ant in Flex Builder's stand-alone version, you must install the Eclipse Java Development Tools. To do so:

1. In the Flex Builder menu bar, choose Help → Software Updates → Find and Install.
2. Select the Search for New Features to Install option and then click Next.
3. Choose The Eclipse Project Updates in the dialog box and then click Finish.
4. A menu appears, asking you to select a location from which to download the files. Select any location, preferably one that is geographically near you for faster download times, and then click OK.
5. Browse the various SDK versions in the Eclipse Project Updates tree until you find Eclipse Java Development Tools. Select the check box next to it and then click Next.
6. After the Update Manager finishes downloading the necessary files, you will be prompted with a feature verification dialog box. Click Install All.
7. After installation is completed, restart Flex Builder.

You can now find the Ant view in Flex Builder by browsing to Window → Other Views → Ant.

21.8 Create an Ant Build File for Automating Common Tasks

Contributed by Ryan Taylor

Problem

You want to leverage the capabilities of Ant to help automate common tasks such as compiling and generating documentation.

Solution

Create an Ant build file in which tasks can be added for automating your processes.

Discussion

Creating an Ant build file is easy and the first step toward using Ant to automate common tasks. Simply create a new XML document named build.xml and save it in a directory named build in the root of your project directory. Saving the file in this directory is not mandatory, but a common convention.

The root node in your build file should look something like this:

```
<project name="MyAntTasks" basedir="..">
</project>
```

You will want to set the name attribute to something unique for your project. This is the name that will show up inside the Ant view in Eclipse. For the basedir attribute, make sure it is set to the root of your project directory. You will use the basedir property frequently when defining other properties that point toward files and directories inside your project folder.

Next, you will likely want to create some additional properties for use throughout the various tasks that you may add later. For instance, to create a property that points toward your project's source folder, you could do something like this:

```
<project name="MyAntTasks" basedir="..">
    <property name="src" value="${basedir}/src" />
</project>
```

The preceding example also demonstrates how to use a property after it has been defined, with the syntax ${property}.

If you find that you are defining a lot of properties and you would like to keep your build file as clean as possible, you can declare properties in a separate file instead. To do this, create a new text file named build.properties and save it in the same directory as your build.xml file. Inside this file, declaring properties is as simple as this:

```
src="${basedir}/src"
```

That's all there is to it. Some examples of useful properties to define are paths to your source folder(s), your bin folder, and the Flex 3 SDK directory. You'll catch on pretty quickly to what you need. From here, you are ready to start adding tasks to your build file.

See Also

Recipe 21.3.

21.9 Compile a Flex Application by Using mxmlc and Ant

Contributed by Ryan Taylor

Problem

You want to add tasks to your Ant build file for compiling your application.

Solution

Add executable tasks to your Ant build file that use the MXML compiler to compile your files.

Discussion

Compiling targets are by far the most common and useful types of targets you will add to your Ant build files. Flex applications are compiled by using mxmlc, which is the free command-line compiler included with the Flex 3 SDK. By adding targets for compiling to your build file, you can automate the build process: Ant will compile all your files without you ever having to open up the command prompt or terminal.

The MXML compiler (mxmlc) included in multiple formats. You can use the executable version of it by creating a target similar to this:

```
<!-- COMPILE MAIN -->
<target name="compileMain" description="Compiles the main application files.">
    <echo>Compiling '${bin.dir}/main.swf'...</echo>
    <exec executable="${FLEX_HOME}/bin/mxmlc.exe" spawn="false">
        <arg line="-source-path '${src.dir}'" />
        <arg line="-library-path '${FLEX_HOME}/frameworks'" />
        <arg line="'${src.dir}/main.mxml'" />
        <arg line="-output '${bin.dir}/main.swf'" />
    </exec>
</target>
```

Alternatively, you can use the Java version by writing a task such as this one:

```
<!-- COMPILE MAIN -->
<target name="compileMain" description="Compiles the main application files.">
    <echo>Compiling '${bin.dir}/main.swf'...</echo>
    <java jar="${FLEX_HOME}/lib/mxmlc.jar" fork="true" failonerror="true">
        <arg value="+flexlib=${FLEX_HOME}/frameworks" />
        <arg value="-file-specs='${src.dir}/main.mxml'" />
        <arg value="-output='${bin.dir}/main.swf'" />
    </java>
</target>
```

The final (and perhaps best) approach is to use the optional mxmlc tasks that are included with the Flex 3 SDK. Installing these is described in Recipe 21.3. To access them in your build file, first you will need to add a task definition:

```
<!-- TASK DEFINITIONS -->
<taskdef resource="flexTasks.tasks" classpath="${FLEX_HOME}/ant/lib/flexTasks.jar" />
```

By importing the optional Flex tasks, you can now compile by using an even more intuitive syntax, plus leverage error detection in a tool such as Eclipse as you write out the task. For example:

```
<!-- COMPILE MAIN -->
<target name="compileMain" description="Compiles the main application files.">
    <echo>Compiling '${bin.dir}/main.swf'...</echo>
    <mxmlc file="${src.dir}/main.mxml" output="${bin.dir}/main.swf">
            <source-path path-element="${src.dir}" />
    </mxmlc>
</target>
```

In all of these examples, the same basic rules apply. You need to define properties that point toward your project's src and bin directories, as well as the Flex 3 SDK. All of the properties in the examples use suggested names, except for FLEX_HOME, which is a mandatory name. The FLEX_HOME property *must* be set to the root of the Flex 3 SDK before using the mxmlc task. If you're using the EXE or JAR versions of mxmlc, you can use a property name other than FLEX_HOME.

The true power of compiling your project via Ant lies in the ability to chain targets together. For instance, you could create a compileAll target that calls each individual compile target one by one:

```
<!-- COMPILE ALL -->
<target name="compileAll" description="Compiles all application files." depends="compi
leMain, compileNavigation, compileGallery, compileLibrary">
    <echo>Finishing compile process...</echo>
</target>
```

All of this may seem a little intimidating at first; however, after you spend a little bit of time using Ant and configuration files, you will find that they can greatly improve your workflow. By letting a third-party tool such as Ant automate your compile process, you are no longer tied to using one particular development tool. You will easily be able to call on Ant to build your project from the development tool of your choice, that is, Flex Builder, FDT, TextMate, or FlashDevelop.

See Also

Recipe 21.3.

21.10 Generate Documentation by Using ASDoc and Ant

Contributed by Ryan Taylor

Problem

You want to easily generate documentation for your application.

Solution

Add an executable task to your Ant build file that uses ASDoc (included with the Flex 3 SDK) to generate the documentation for you.

Discussion

ASDoc is a free command-line utility that is included with the Flex 3 SDK. If you have ever used Adobe's LiveDocs, you are already familiar with the style of documentation that ASDoc produces. Though opening up the command prompt or terminal and using it isn't terribly difficult, a better solution is to add a target to your Ant build file for automating the process even further.

Before creating a target for generating your documentation, it is a good idea to create an additional target that cleans out your docs directory. When you define the `docs.dir` property, simply point it toward your project's docs directory:

```
<!-- CLEAN DOCS -->
<target name="cleanDocs" description="Cleans out the documentation directory.">
    <echo>Cleaning '${docs.dir}'...</echo>
    <delete includeemptydirs="true">
        <fileset dir="${docs.dir}" includes="**/*" />
    </delete>
</target>
```

With the target for cleaning out the docs directory in place, you are ready to create the target that actually generates the documentation. Notice in the sample code that the `depends` attribute mandates that the `cleanDocs` target is executed before the instructions for generating the documentation:

```
<!-- GENERATE DOCUMENTATION -->
<target name="generateDocs" description="Generates application documentation using ASD
oc." depends="cleanDocs">
    <echo>Generating documentation...</echo>
    <exec executable="${FLEX_HOME}/bin/asdoc.exe" failOnError="true">
        <arg line="-source-path ${src.dir}" />
        <arg line="-doc-sources ${src.dir}" />
        <arg line="-main-title ${docs.title}" />
        <arg line="-window-title ${docs.title}" />
        <arg line="-footer ${docs.footer}" />
        <arg line="-output ${docs.dir}" />
    </exec>
</target>
```

The `FLEX_HOME` property needs to point toward the root directory of the Flex 3 SDK on your machine. The `src.dir` and `docs.dir` properties represent your project's src and docs directories, respectively. Last but not least are the `docs.title` and `docs.footer` properties, which set the title and footer text that appears in the documentation. A common convention for the documentation title is Your Project Reference, where *Your Project* is the name of the project you are working on. The footer is a good place to put a copyright and URL.

ASDoc will successfully generate documentation from your code even if you haven't written a single comment. It is, of course, highly recommended that you thoroughly document your code by using Javadoc commenting. Not only will this produce much more in-depth documentation, but programmers unfamiliar with your code can also follow along inside the code itself.

21.11 Compile Flex Applications by Using Rake

Problem

You want to compile Flex applications by using Rake, the Ruby make tool.

Solution

Download and install Ruby 1.9 if you have not already, and then download and install Rake.

Discussion

Although written completely in Ruby, Rake functions very similarly to the classic make utility used by C++ and C programmers. After you've downloaded and installed both Ruby and Rake, you can write a simple Rake file like so:

```
task :default do
  DEV_ROOT = "/Users/base/flex_development"
  PUBLIC = "#{DEV_ROOT}/bin"
  FLEX_ROOT = "#{DEV_ROOT}/src"
  system "/Developer/SDKs/Flex/bin/mxmlc --show-actionscript-warnings=true --strict=tr
ue -file-specs #{FLEX_ROOT}/App.mxml"
  system "cp #{FLEX_ROOT}/App.swf #{PUBLIC}/App.swf"
end
```

All tasks in Rake are similar to targets in Ant, that is, they define an action to be done. The default action is always performed, and any extra actions can be optionally called within a different task. Within the task itself, variables can be declared, and system arguments can be called, as shown here:

```
system "/Developer/SDKs/Flex/bin/mxmlc --show-actionscript-warnings=true --strict=true
-file-specs #{FLEX_ROOT}/App.mxml"
```

This is the actual call to the MXML compiler that will generate the SWF file. Because an item in the Rake task won't be run until the previous task returns, the next line can assume that the SWF has been generated and can be copied to a new location:

```
system "cp #{FLEX_ROOT}/App.swf #{PUBLIC}/App.swf"
```

The rest of the Rake file declares variables that will be used to place files in the appropriate folders. The file can now be saved with any name and run at the command line by using the rake command. If you save the file as Rakefile, you can now run it by entering the following:

```
rake Rakefile
```

21.12 Use ExpressInstall for Your Application

Problem

You want to ensure that if a user does not have the correct version of Flash Player installed to view a Flex application, the correct version can be installed.

Solution

Use the ExpressInstall option when compiling to let the SWF file redirect the user to the Adobe website where the most current version of Flash Player can be installed.

Discussion

To use the Express Install, you can set the Use Express Install option in Flex Builder, in the application options (Figure 21-5).

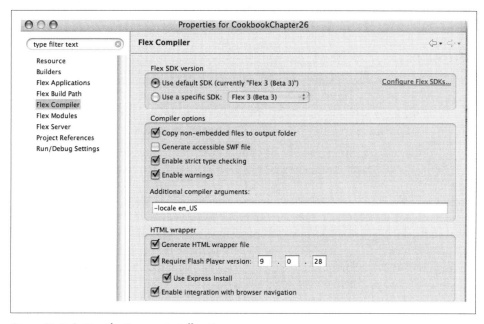

Figure 21-5. Setting the Express Install option

If you are not using Flex Builder for development, then simply set the pluginspage variable in the Object tag on the embed tag of the HTML page that the SWF file is embedded within the ExpressInstall:

```
pluginspage="http://www.adobe.com/go/getflashplayer"
```

A sample <embed> statement for a Netscape-based browser such as Firefox is shown here:

```
<embed src="CookbookChapter26.swf" id="CookbookChapter26" quality="high" bgcolor="#869c
a7" name="CookbookChapter26" allowscriptaccess="sameDomain" pluginspage="http:
//www.adobe.com/go/getflashplayer" type="application/x-shockwave-flash" align="middle"
height="100%" width="100%">
```

21.13 Use Memory Profiling with Flex Builder 3 to View Memory Snapshots

Problem

You want to view all the objects allocated in the Flash Player's memory at runtime.

Solution

Use the Memory Profiler view in Flex Builder 3 to run your application and observe the objects being created and destroyed.

Discussion

The Flex Profiler is a new addition to Flex Builder 3 and is a powerful tool that enables you to watch an application as it allocates and clears memory and objects. It connects to your application with a local socket connection. You might have to disable antivirus software to use it, however, if your antivirus software prevents socket communication.

As the Profiler runs, it takes a snapshot of data every few milliseconds and records the state of the Flash Player at that snapshot, a process referred to as *sampling*. By parsing the data from sampling, the Profiler can show every operation in your application. The Profiler records the execution time of those operations, as well as the total memory usage of objects in the Flash Player at the time of the snapshot. When an application is run in the Profiler, you'll see the Connection Established dialog box (Figure 21-6). Here you can enable memory profiling to help identify areas of an application where memory allocation problems are occurring, as well as enable performance profiling to help improve the performance of an application.

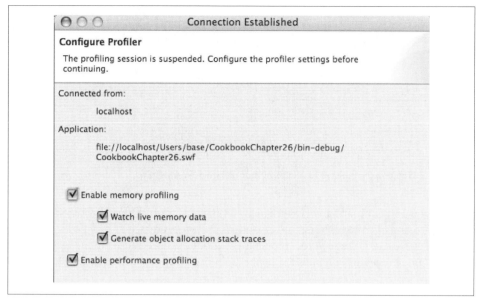

Figure 21-6. Selecting a profiling type

If you turn on the Watch Live Memory Data check box, the Profiling view displays live graphs of the objects allocated in the Flash Player (Figure 21-7).

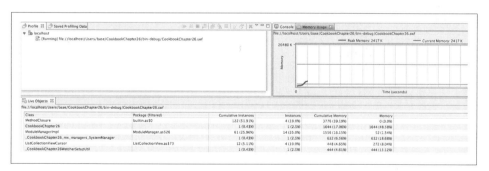

Figure 21-7. Live object and memory allocation data in the Flex Profiling view

The Profiler provides memory snapshots that can be taken at any time and provide in-depth data about the number of instances of any object and the amount of memory that they require (Figure 21-8).

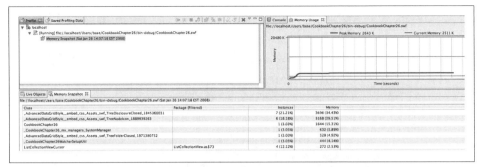

Figure 21-8. Viewing the number of instances and memory consumption in a memory snapshot

Finally, you can compare any two memory snapshots from different times in the application to find *loitering objects*, that is, objects that were created after the first memory snapshot and exist in the second. Information about the class name, memory size, and number of instances are all included in the Loitering Objects view (Figure 21-9).

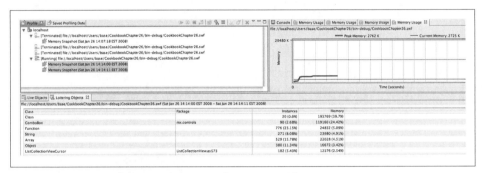

Figure 21-9. Viewing all generated objects in the Loitering Objects screen

CHAPTER 22

Configuration, Internationalization, and Printing

To ensure that your applications are usable to the widest range of users, Flex 3 provides many accessibility, internationalization, and printing options. For example, if your project must comply with accessibility standards, you'll find screen-reader detection and keyboard tab orders to help visually impaired users or users for whom the use of a pointing device is difficult or impossible. Flex's tool set for internationalization and localization was much improved in Flex 3. New localization features include a built-in internationalization resource manager, runtime locale determination, runtime locale switching, and resource modules that can be requested at runtime. If your challenge is closer to home—you need printed deliverables—the latest version of Flex has that covered too. Flex 3 enables you to print Flex components and includes a data grid component specifically for printing repetitive, multipage output.

This chapter contains recipes that will walk you through formatting many kinds of output for printing, including a solution for formatting collections of components for printing across multiple pages by using `PrintDataGrid` with a custom item renderer. Recipes for displaying non-Western characters, detecting screen readers, and defining tab orders help make your applications more accessible to visually impaired users. Finally, several techniques for localizing applications are presented.

22.1 Add an International Character Set to an Application

Problem

You need to display text from an ideogram-based language, such as Chinese or Korean, in your application.

Solution

Use embedded fonts to ensure that the appropriate font is available to the Flash Player.

Discussion

Flex applications are capable of rendering text using non-Western characters, including Unicode-encoded text such as Chinese or Korean characters, provided that a font including those characters is available to the Flash Player. Developers can ensure that the appropriate font is available to embed into your application the same way as you would any Western font. Be aware, however, that the ease of this method comes at a price: The large number of characters in most ideogram-based languages means a bulkier SWF file. When considering this approach, you must weigh the trade-off between the increased size of your SWF file and the proper rendering of your text.

The following example, ChineseFonts.mxml, illustrates both approaches.

 When you open ChineseFonts.mxml from the accompanying disc, you will see the Chinese text next to System Font only if your system's font contains the required characters. The Embedded Font line will be displayed on all systems.

```
<mx:Application xmlns:mx="http://www.adobe.com/2006/mxml" layout="absolute">
  <mx:Style>
      @font-face
      {
        src: local("LiSong Pro");
        fontFamily: EmbeddedChinese;
        fontStyle: normal;
        fontWeight: normal;
      }
  </mx:Style>
  <mx:Form>
   <mx:FormItem label="System Font">
      <mx:Label text="快的棕色狐狸慢慢地跳過了懶惰灰色灰鼠" />
   </mx:FormItem>
   <mx:FormItem label="Embedded Font">
    <mx:Label fontFamily="EmbeddedChinese" text="快的棕色狐狸慢慢地跳過了懶惰灰色灰鼠" />
   </mx:FormItem>
  </mx:Form>
</mx:Application>
```

Although the MXML source for the Unicode-encoded method is unremarkable, the XML data it loads contains text in simplified Chinese:

```
<mx:Application xmlns:mx="http://www.adobe.com/2006/mxml" layout="absolute">
    <mx:Style>
        @font-face
        {
            src: local("LiSong Pro");
            fontFamily: EmbeddedChinese;
            fontStyle: normal;
            fontWeight: normal;
        }
    </mx:Style>
```

```
<mx:XML source="books.xml" id="booksData" />
<mx:VBox fontFamily="EmbeddedChinese">
    <mx:Repeater id="iterator" dataProvider="{booksData.book}">
        <mx:VBox backgroundColor="0xffffff">
            <mx:Label text="{iterator.currentItem.@title}" />
            <mx:Text width="200" text="{iterator.currentItem.toString()}" />
            <mx:HRule width="200" />
        </mx:VBox>
    </mx:Repeater>
</mx:VBox>
</mx:Application>
```

The following is the document loaded by the example:

```
<books>
    <book title="阿波罗为 Adobe 导电线开发商口袋指南">
        现在您能建立和部署基于闪光的富有的互联网应用(RIAs) 对桌面使用 Adobe 的导电线框架。
由阿波罗产品队的成员写，这是正式指南对于 Adobe 阿波罗，新发怒平台桌面运行时间阿尔法发行从
Adobe 实验室。众多的例子说明怎么阿波罗工作因此您可能立即开始大厦 RIAs 为桌面。
    </book>
    <book title="编程的导电线 2">
        编程的导电线 2 谈论导电线框架在上下文。作者介绍特点以告诉读者不仅怎样，而且原因为什么
使用一个特殊特点，何时使用它，和何时不是的实用和有用的例子。这本书被写为发展专家。
当书不假设观众早先工作了以一刹那技术，读者最将受益于书如果他们早先建立了基于互联网，n
tiered 应用。
    </book>
    <book title="ActionScript 3.0 设计样式">
        如果您是老练的闪光或屈曲开发商准备好应付老练编程技术与 ActionScript 3.0,
这实践介绍逐步设计样式作为您通过过程。您得知各种各样的类型设计样式和修建小抽象例子在尝试
您的手之前在大厦完全的运作的应用被概述在书。
    </book>
</books>
```

22.2 Use a Resource Bundle to Localize an Application

Problem

You need to support a small number of alternate languages in your application.

Solution

Use compiled-in resource bundles to provide localized assets.

Discussion

For basic localization of Flex applications, you can use resource bundles. *Resource bundles* are ActionScript objects that provide an interface to access localized content defined in a properties file through data binding or ActionScript code. Each bundle your application uses represents a single localization properties file. The *properties file* is a text file containing a list of localization property keys and their associated values.

The key and value pairs are listed in the file in the format `key=value`, and properties files are saved with a .properties extension.

Localized values for text strings, embedded assets such as images, and references to ActionScript class definitions can all be defined in a properties file. When localizing an application, you define an entry in a properties file for each item in your application that would need to be updated in order for the application to fully support an alternate language. The following example properties file defines the values of several properties in American English:

```
#Localization resources in American English
pageTitle=Internationalization Demo
language=American English
flag=Embed("assets/usa.png")
borderSkin=ClassReference("skins.en_US.LocalizedSkin")
```

When localizing an application, you need to create a copy of the properties file that contains values appropriate to the target language for each language supported. If your application must support American English and French, for example, you must create a second properties file containing translated text, a reference to an image of the French flag instead of the American flag, and a reference to the appropriate border skin for the French-language version of the application:

```
#Localization resources, En Francais
pageTitle=Demo d'internationalisation
language=Francais
flag=Embed("assets/france.png")
borderSkin=ClassReference("skins.fr_FR.LocalizedSkin")
```

When setting up your properties files, be sure to consider several factors, most importantly the size and complexity of your application. You may wish to create a properties file for each custom component in your application, for example, or for packages of related components that share resources. You may want to define properties files that are useful on a global scale, such as a file containing custom application-error messages, or commonly used labels like the ones used on buttons.

No matter how you decide to break up your localization properties, you will need to create a directory structure to organize the files. Illustrated in Figure 22-1, a best practice is to create a directory named locale or localization that contains subdirectories named after the locale identifiers. These subdirectories house all the properties files for a given locale. Adhering to this practice will make it easy to instruct the compiler how to find the properties files.

When you build your application, the compiler creates subclasses of the `ResourceBun dle` class for each properties file you define. The easiest way to access items defined in your properties file is through the `@Resource` directive. Using this method, the compiler substitutes the appropriate property values for the `@Resource` directive. With `@Resource` directives, you never actually write code that uses a `ResourceBundle` instance; the compiler does all the work for you. `@Resource` directives take two arguments, a

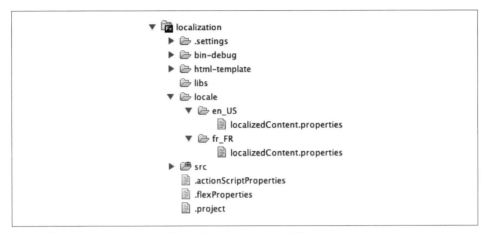

Figure 22-1. Directory structure for localization properties files

bundle identifier and a key, which it uses to look up the appropriate property value in the appropriate properties file. For example, to reference the property name `applica tionTitle` in a localization properties file named localizationProperties.properties, use the following:

```
@Resource(key='applicationTitle', bundle='localizationProperties')
```

A more-complete example, LocalizationResource.mxml, defines a small application that consumes the localization properties files defined in the first two code snippets:

```
<mx:Application xmlns:mx="http://www.adobe.com/2006/mxml" layout="absolute">
    <mx:Metadata>
        [ResourceBundle("localizedContent")]
    </mx:Metadata>
    <mx:VBox     horizontalCenter="0"
                 verticalCenter="0"
                 horizontalAlign="center"
                 borderSkin="@Resource(key='borderSkin', bundle='localizedContent')">
        <mx:Label fontSize="24" text="@Resource(key='pageTitle', bundle='localizedCont
ent')" />
        <mx:Label fontSize="24" text="@Resource(key='language', bundle='localizedConte
nt')" />
        <mx:Image source="@Resource(key='flag', bundle='localizedContent')" />
    </mx:VBox>
</mx:Application>
```

Note that the [`ResourceBundle`] metadata tells the compiler which bundles are required for a given component. This is important because resource bundles are built at compile time, and all required resources for the supported languages must be compiled into the application SWF.

The compiler must also be configured to build in localization support for the required locales. In Flex Builder 3, you set these options in the Project Properties dialog box for the Flex project. In the Flex Build Path panel, you define a source path that points to your localization files. If you followed the best practice of using a locale directory, your

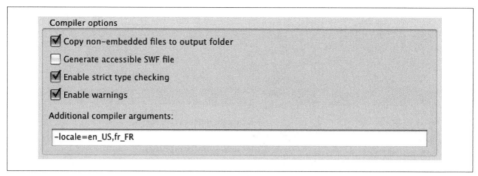

Figure 22-2. Localization build path entry

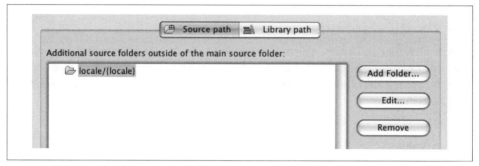

Figure 22-3. Localization compiler arguments

source path entry will be `locale/{locale}`, as shown in Figure 22-2. In addition, you need to identify the locales you wish to support in the Flex Compiler panel's Additional Compiler Arguments field. For example, to support American English and French, enter **-locale en_US,fr_FR** (Figure 22-3). When the compiler builds your application and is looking for properties files, it substitutes each of the locale identifiers into your source path expression, specifically `locale/en_US` for American English properties files and `locale/fr_FR` for French properties files.

The step you need to perform before building a localized application is to localize relevant Flex Framework content, such as error messages. To do so, use the Adobe-provided command-line utility called copylocale to copy these files to a new locale. You will have to perform this step once for every locale, but that copy is available for use in any project built against that installation of the Flex Framework. You will not have to repeat this step in each project. Note that copylocale will not actually make localized copies of the files for you, but it will let you compile your application. You can find copylocale in the bin subdirectory of the Flex 3 SDK installation. To run it, simply pass in the default locale identifier and the identifier of the locale you want to make a copy for:

```
Copylocale.exe en_US fr_FR
```

Figure 22-4. LocalizationResource.mxml with compiler argument "-locale=en_US"

Figure 22-5. LocalizationResource.mxml with compiler argument "-locale=fr_FR"

Prior to Flex 3, you could not change locales at runtime. This meant your only approach to building localized applications by using resource bundles was to compile a separate copy of an application for each supported locale. This approach may still be valid in certain cases—for example, when minimal localization is required and the smallest SWF file size is desired. To use this technique, set the -locale compiler argument to the desired target locale and build your application. The two main advantages to this option are simplicity and small SWF file size due to the compiler including only one set of localization properties files. To see this technique in action, you can try compiling the LocalizationResource.mxml example application for American English (en_US), Figure 22-4, or for French (fr_FR), Figure 22-5, by setting the locale compiler argument appropriately.

22.3 Use the ResourceManager for Localization

Problem

You want to support a small number of locales and either determine the locale programmatically at runtime or allow the user to choose the locale.

Solution

Use the ResourceManager class to support multiple locales and allow the application to change locales at runtime.

Discussion

The `ResourceManager` class is the Flex programmer's main ActionScript interface into the resource bundles created by the compiler from localization properties files. It enables you to retrieve various types of resources from resource bundles and provides a mechanism to set the desired locale at runtime. The resource manager is a singleton that manages localization for an entire application. Every class that derives from `UICom` `ponent` has a protected property named `resourceManager` that provides a reference to the resource manager singleton.

Although the `@Resource` directive is convenient for binding localized content into MXML tags, it is much less useful for pure ActionScript components or ActionScript methods that rely on localized resources. In these situations, you're better off using the resource manager, which provides methods used to access localized data or used as the target of a data-binding expression in ActionScript or MXML. The following example, excerpted from LocalizationManager.mxml, substitutes `ResourceManager` methods for the `@Resource` directives used in Recipe 22.2's LocalizationResource.mxml:

```
<mx:VBox      horizontalCenter="0"
       verticalCenter="0"
       horizontalAlign="center"
       borderSkin="{resourceManager.getClass('localizedContent', 'borderSkin')}">
     <mx:Label fontSize="24" text="{resourceManager.getString('localizedContent', 'page
Title')}" />
     <mx:Label fontSize="24" text="{resourceManager.getString('localizedContent', 'lang
uage')}" />
     <mx:Image source="{resourceManager.getClass('localizedContent', 'flag')}" />
</mx:VBox>
```

Although the method names vary according to the type of resource you're retrieving, the arguments here are all similar to the arguments required by an `@Resource` directive, namely the resource bundle name and the key value for the desired property.

Using the resource manager to bind localization property values to their targets has an additional benefit: Flex 3 gives you the ability to change the desired locale at runtime; no longer are you forced to build separate localized SWF files for each supported locale. Binding properties to resource methods enables the application to update itself for the desired locale. In the LocalizationManager.mxml example, buttons are provided to let the user switch between English and French:

```
<mx:HBox>
     <mx:Button label="In English" click="resourceManager.localeChain = ['en_US']" />
     <mx:Button label="En Francais" click="resourceManager.localeChain = ['fr_FR']" />
</mx:HBox>
```

In the example, the `localeChain` property is reset depending on the button the user selects. The `localeChain` property is an array of strings, representing an ordered list of desired locales. This is useful if, for example, the application is going to receive information about the user's language preferences from the browser through either the Accept-Language HTTP header or the host operating system's language preferences.

For a user from the United Kingdom, the preferred locale is en_GB, but the user can also accept en_US. When a method call is invoked on the resource manager, it will search for a resource bundle with the specified name in one of the locales defined in the locale chain, in the order they appear. Therefore, an application localized for en_US would be delivered to the user from the United Kingdom if you set localeChain as follows:

```
resourceManager.localeChain = ["en_GB", "en_US"];
```

It is a good practice to ensure that the American English locale appears in the property chain somewhere. Many of the Flex Framework components assume that framework localization resources exist, and they will throw an error if they are unable to locate their localized content. Appending en_US to the end of your property chain will help to ensure that the framework classes themselves do not fail because they could not locate localized resources.

When building an application that utilizes the resource manager simply for binding, you do not need to do anything differently compared to @Resource. However, if your application is going to support multiple locales from which one is selected at runtime, resources for every supported locale must be compiled into the application. You can supply a comma-delimited list of supported locales to the compiler in place of the single locale used in Recipe 22.2.

22.4 Use Resource Modules for Localization

Problem

You need to support a large number of locales in your application.

Solution

Use resource modules to load only the localization support required by your application at runtime.

Discussion

Localization using resource bundles that are compiled into your application will cause the size of your SWF file to grow with each additional locale you need to support. The overwhelming majority of users will require resources for just one locale, adding up to a lot of dead weight in the download size of your application. Flex 3 adds the ability to compile the resource bundles for a given locale into SWF files called *resource modules*, which your application can then load dynamically at runtime. You then can prompt for or determine programmatically which locale the user prefers, and load only the resource module required to support that user's locale.

To build resource modules from your localization properties files, you must first determine which resources your application requires. This includes not only resources you define, but also resources required by the Flex Framework. You can use the mxmlc compiler to analyze your application and output a list of required resources. You can do this from Flex Builder 3 by modifying the Additional Compiler Arguments field in the Project Properties dialog box, but it's easy enough to do from the command line. This will also save you from having to navigate back to the applicable panel in the Project Properties dialog box each time you need to update the list. When you invoke the compiler, you specify no locale and a file where the compiler writes the results of the analysis in addition to the name of the application MXML file:

```
mxmlc -locale= -resource-bundle-list=resources.txt ResourceModules.mxml
```

When the command completes, the contents of the resources.txt output file looks like this:

```
bundles = containers controls core effects localizedContent skins styles
```

You will use this output to tell the compiler which resource bundles to build into your resource module. To compile an application that uses resource modules, you must use the command-line compiler. You specify the source path for your localization properties files, the resource bundles list from the previous step, and the name of the resulting SWF file. The compiler then builds resource bundles from your localization properties files and packages them into a SWF file. For example, to build resource bundles for Recipe 22.4's ResourceModules.mxml example, use this:

```
mxmlc -locale=en_US -source-path=.,locale/{locale}
-include-resource-bundles=containers,controls,core,effects,localizedContent,skins,styl
es
-output en_US_resources.swf
```

To compile resource modules in French, use this command:

```
mxmlc -locale=fr_FR -source-path=.,locale/{locale}
-include-resource-bundles=containers,controls,core,effects,localizedContent,skins,styl
es
-output fr_FR_resources.swf
```

There are several items of interest in these commands. First, you define the locale you want to build by using the -locale argument just as you do when compiling resource bundles into your application. Second, although the source path argument may look familiar, including the current directory (.) in your source path is important in this case. The example includes an embedded class reference in the localizedContent properties file, and the compiler may not be able to resolve the reference to the class without the root of the application in the source path. Note that this assumes you invoke mxmlc from your project's source root. Next, the include-resource-bundles argument is filled in based on the list generated in the previous example. This list is comma-delimited and cannot contain spaces between the delimiter and the bundle name. Finally, the example asks the compiler to name the output en_US_resources.swf. You can name the output SWF anything you like, but it's good practice to come up with a naming convention that includes the locale identifier in the filename. This way, you can programmatically determine the name of the resource module your application should load based on a locale identifier.

When you compile resource modules using mxmlc, references to embedded assets such as images will be resolved relative to the location of the localization properties file into which that reference is embedded. Therefore, if your application used compiled-in resource bundles that had embedded assets defined relative to the project's source root, these will have to be updated to work as resource modules.

In your application code, you use the resource manager's `loadResourceModule` method. You pass a URL to the method, identifying the resource module SWF file you want to use. This method works in a similar fashion to other mechanisms for loading Action-Script objects at runtime, such as `SWFLoader` or conventional modules. A request is made to the server for the required SWF, which is then downloaded by the browser. Requests for resources from other domains require a cross-domain policy file. You must wait until the resource module has been loaded into your application before you can make use of it. When the resource module is ready for use, a `ResourceEvent` will be dispatched. You can listen for these events by defining a listener for `ResourceEvent.COMPLETE` events. The `loadResourceModule` method returns a reference to an object that implements the `IEventDispatcher` interface that you use to register listeners for the complete event. The following code is excerpted from the ResourceModules.mxml example and demonstrates how a resource module is loaded and utilized:

```
import mx.events.ResourceEvent;
import mx.resources.ResourceManager;

private var selectedLocale:String;

private function setAppLocale(locale:String):void
{
    this.selectedLocale = locale;
    if (resourceManager.getLocales().indexOf(locale) == -1)
    {
        var dispatcher:IEventDispatcher = resourceManager.loadResourceModule(locale +
"_resources.swf");
        dispatcher.addEventListener(ResourceEvent.COMPLETE, onResourceLoaded);
    }
    else
    {
        onResourceLoaded(null);
    }
}

private function onResourceLoaded(e:ResourceEvent):void
{
    resourceManager.localeChain = [this.selectedLocale];
    views.selectedIndex = 1;

    contentBackground.setStyle("borderSkin", resourceManager.getClass('localizedConten
t', 'borderSkin'));
    contentBackground.invalidateDisplayList();
```

```
            contentBackground.validateNow();
    }
```

In this example, a user is prompted to choose between American English and French languages. When the user selects a language, the setAppLocale function is called to load the required resource module. This method first checks whether resources for the requested locale have already been loaded by searching the result of the resource manager's getLocales method. It is a good practice to test whether you already have the resources required in order to save the overhead of requesting and loading resources you may already have. If the requested locale isn't already loaded, a call is made to the loadResourceModule method to retrieve it, and a listener for the complete event is registered so you know when the resource module has been loaded and is ready for use.

In response to the complete event, the application then sets the localeChain property to make use of the newly loaded resource module. Of note in this method are the three method calls on the contentBackground object. Style settings are not bound in Flex, so objects referencing style properties from resource modules must be updated programmatically in order to pick up changes to their styling properties.

The loadResourceModule method can take several optional parameters in addition to the resource module URL. If your application loads multiple resource modules, you will want to load all but the last with the update parameter set to false. This will save overhead by not running the resource manager's update routines repeatedly.

22.5 Support IME Devices

Problem

You need to distribute your application in a language that uses multibyte characters, such as Japanese, Chinese, or Korean.

Solution

Use the Capabilities class to detect an input method editor and the IME class to control how it interacts with your Flex application.

Discussion

Far Eastern languages such as Chinese represent words with single ideograms, rather than with combinations of letters as in Latin languages. In Latin languages, the number of individual characters is limited and can be easily mapped onto a keyboard with a limited number of keys. It would be impossible to do the same for Far Eastern languages, which would require thousands of keys. Input method editors (IMEs) are software tools that allow characters to be composed with multiple keystrokes. An IME runs at the operating system level, external to the Flash Player.

The `Capabilities` class has a property called `hasIME` that you can use to determine whether the user has an IME installed. You can use the `flash.system.IME` object to test whether the IME is enabled and what conversion mode it is set to. The following example tests for an IME and, if it finds one, starts the IME and sets the required conversion mode:

```
private function detectIME():void
{
    if (Capabilities.hasIME == true)
    {
        output.text = "Your system has an IME installed.\n";
        if (flash.system.IME.enabled == true)
        {
            output.text += "Your IME is enabled. and set to " +
                        flash.system.IME.conversionMode;
        }
        else
        {
            output.text += "Your IME is disabled\n";
            try
            {
                flash.system.IME.enabled = true;
                flash.system.IME.conversionMode =
                    IMEConversionMode.JAPANESE_HIRAGANA;
                output.text += "Your IME has been enabled successfully";
            }
            catch (e:Error)
            {
                output.text +="Your IME could not be enabled.\n"
            }
        }
    }
    else
        output.text = "You do not have an IME installed.\n";
}
```

When trying to manipulate the IME settings, you should always use a `try...catch` block. If the IME in use by the user does not support the specified settings, the call will fail.

You may wish to disable the IME in some cases, such as for a text field that expects numeric input. You can trigger a function to disable the IME when a component gets focus and re-enable the IME after the component loses focus, if the IME is inappropriate for a given data entry component:

```
<mx:Script>
    <[[
        private function enableIME(enable:Boolean):void
        {
            if (Capabilities.hasIME)
            {
                try
                {
                    flash.system.IME.enabled = enable;
```

```
                    trace("IME " + (enable ? "enable" : "disable"));
                }
                catch (e:Error)
                {
                    Alert.show("Could not " (enable ? "enable" : "disable") + " IME");
                }
            }
        }
    ]]>
</mx:Script>
<mx:VBox horizontalCenter="0" verticalCenter="0" >
    <mx:TextInput id="numericInput" focusIn="enableIME(false)" focusOut="enableIME(tru
e)" />
    <mx:TextInput id="textInput" />
</mx:VBox>
```

If you want to know when a user has composed a character, you can listen for events on the System.ime object:

```
System.ime.addEventListener(IMEEvent.IME_COMPOSITION, onComposition);
```

22.6 Detect a Screen Reader

Problem

You must provide support for visually impaired users and would like to customize your application for screen-reader users.

Solution

Use the active static property of the Accessibility class to detect a screen reader.

Discussion

Rich media capabilities and a cinematic user experience are hallmarks of a Rich Internet Application. Unfortunately, these capabilities can make using a Flex application difficult for visually impaired users. Screen-reader support is important for visually impaired users and may in fact be their only method of interacting with your application. If accommodating visually impaired users is a requirement, you may wish to alter the user experience specifically for screen-reader users. The active property of the Accessibility class can be used to test whether a user is using a screen reader. The following code block, excerpted from ScreenReader.mxml, uses Accessibility.active to determine whether an animation should play:

```
private function showNextPage():void
{
    if (Accessibility.active == false)
    {
        page2.visible = true;
        pageChangeAnimation.play();
    }
```

```
        else
        {
            page1.visible = false;
            page2.alpha = 1;
        }
    }
}
```

22.7 Create a Tabbing Reading Order for Accessibility

Problem

You must support users who may have difficulty using a pointing device.

Solution

Define a tab order for components in your application so that the user may navigate the application without using a pointing device.

Discussion

Tab order is an important usability concern in an application. It enables users to ef-fectively navigate through an application without having to switch between the key-board and a pointing device unnecessarily. For users with impairments that make using a pointing device difficult or impossible, tab order is a necessity. You can specify the tab order in your components by setting the `tabIndex` property of each object in your component. The following example, saved as TabOrder.mxml, sets a tab order so a user can easily navigate through an address form without using a mouse:

```
<mx:Application xmlns:mx="http://www.adobe.com/2006/mxml" layout="absolute" creationCo
mplete="firstName.setFocus()">
    <mx:Canvas width="228" height="215" x="50" y="50" backgroundColor="#FFFFFF">
        <mx:Label x="10" y="10" text="First Name" tabIndex="1" />
        <mx:TextInput x="10" y="36" width="100" id="firstName" tabIndex="2"/>
        <mx:Label x="118" y="10" text="Last Name" tabIndex="3" />
        <mx:TextInput x="118" y="36" width="100" id="lastName" tabIndex="4"/>
        <mx:Label x="10" y="69" text="Address" tabIndex="5" />
        <mx:TextInput x="10" y="95" width="208" id="address" tabIndex="6"/>
        <mx:Label x="10" y="125" text="City" tabIndex="7"/>
        <mx:TextInput x="10" y="151" width="100" id="city" tabIndex="8"/>
        <mx:Label x="118" y="125" text="State" tabIndex="9"/>
        <mx:TextInput x="118" y="151" width="34" id="state" tabIndex="10"/>
        <mx:Label x="160" y="125" text="Zip" tabIndex="11"/>
        <mx:TextInput x="160" y="151" width="58" id="zip" tabIndex="12"/>
        <mx:Button x="153" y="181" label="Submit" id="submit" tabIndex="13"/>
    </mx:Canvas>
</mx:Application>
```

Note that in the example, the `tabIndex` property is set for all labels as well as the text inputs and buttons, even though the labels cannot receive focus. For users who require a screen reader, the tab order also dictates the order in which the screen reader will describe items on the page. When considering screen-reader users, it is important that you set the `tabIndex` property for all accessible components, not just those that can receive focus. Any items that do not have their `tabIndex` set will be placed at the end of the tab order, which could confuse screen-reader users when those items are read out of order compared to the visual layout.

22.8 Print Selected Items in an Application

Problem

You need to create printed output from an application.

Solution

Use the classes in the `mx.printing` package to define, format, and produce printed output.

Discussion

The `mx.printing` package implements several classes used to produce printed output. For example, the `FlexPrintJob` class defines a print job, adds items to the job, and sends the job to the printer. The following example, saved in BasicPrintJob.mxml, creates a print job, adds two pages of output, and sends the job to the printer:

```
<mx:Canvas xmlns:mx="http://www.adobe.com/2006/mxml" width="400" height="300">
    <mx:Script>
        <![CDATA[
            import mx.printing.FlexPrintJob;

            public function print():void
            {
                var printJob:FlexPrintJob = new FlexPrintJob();
                if (printJob.start())
                {
                    printJob.addObject(pageContainer1);
                    printJob.addObject(pageContainer2);
                    printJob.send();
                }
            }
        ]]>
    </mx:Script>
    <mx:VBox width="380" height="260" verticalCenter="-20" horizontalCenter="0">
        <mx:VBox id="pageContainer1">
            <mx:Label text="Page 1" />
            <mx:TextArea id="page1" width="100%" height="100%" />
        </mx:VBox>
        <mx:VBox id="pageContainer2">
            <mx:Label text="page 2" />
            <mx:TextArea id="page2" width="100%" height="100%" />
        </mx:VBox>
```

```
</mx:VBox>
<mx:Button bottom="5" right="10" label="Print" click="print();" />
```

When the **start** method is called, the operating system displays the Print dialog box. Execution is suspended until the user has finished configuring the print job. If the user decides to cancel the print job, the **start** method returns false. Otherwise, the function calls the **addObject** method to add the text area to the print job, and calls the **send** method to send the job to the printer.

Each time you call **addObject**, the item and all of its children are placed on a new page. In the printed output generated by the example, the page labels and text inputs contained in **pageContainer1** and **pageContainer2** are sent to the printer on separate pages.

The **addObject** method also accepts an optional parameter that tells the print job how to scale the added item. If an item is too big to fit, the print job will render it on multiple pages. By default, the item will be scaled to the width of the page, but several other options are available. These options are defined as static constants on the **FlexPrint JobScaleType** class. You may, for example, want to scale a column chart so that it fits vertically within a single page, ensuring that the value of each column can be read on a single page:

```
Public function print():void
{
    if (printJob.start())
    {
        printJob.addObject(columnChart, FlexPrintJobScaleType.MATCH_HEIGHT);
        printJob.send();
    }
}
```

If the chart is too wide to fit within a single page, the excess will be printed on a new page. An example, called ScaleExample.mxml, has been provided to demonstrate the effects of the various scale types.

22.9 Format Application Content for Printing

Problem

You want your application to produce output specifically formatted for printing.

Solution

Build custom print renderer components to format output specifically for printing.

Discussion

Often, the output you want to create is different from what is displayed to the user in the application. You may wish to create printable versions of application objects, or generate reports of data not shown to the user through the application. This is accomplished by using a print renderer, a component you create specifically for generating printed output.

In the BasicPrintJob.mxml example from Recipe 22.8, you may not want to print the page label or the text input control's border. Also, you probably want the entered text printed as if it were created in a word processor, filling the width of the page without scaling the text, and continuing on to the next page when the end of the page is reached. To format a text block for printing, use a component such as BasicTextRenderer.mxml:

```
<mx:Canvas xmlns:mx="http://www.adobe.com/2006/mxml" backgroundColor="0xffffff">
    <mx:String id="textToPrint" />
    <mx:Text width="100%" text="{textToPrint}" />
</mx:Canvas>
```

When you use a print renderer to format output, you must first add the renderer to a display list in order for Flex to lay out the visual aspects of the component. Take care when considering where to add the component. Unintended consequences, such as shifts in layout or unintended scroll bars, can occur in some cases. In the following code, taken from BasicPrintRenderer.mxml, the renderer is added to the parent application's display list in order to avoid the appearance of scroll bars:

```
public function print():void
{
    var printJob:FlexPrintJob = new FlexPrintJob();
    if (printJob.start())
    {
        var printRenderer:BasicTextRenderer = new BasicTextRenderer();
        printRenderer.width = printJob.pageWidth;
        printRenderer.textToPrint = page1.text;
        printRenderer.visible = false;
        Application.application.addChild(printRenderer);
        printJob.addObject(printRenderer);
        printJob.send();
        Application.application.removeChild(printRenderer);
    }
}
```

Also of note in this example is the use of the pageWidth property on the print job object. Both the pageWidth and pageHeight properties are set when the start method has returned. When writing a print renderer component, it is important to pay attention to these properties when sizing their components. By using these properties, you can ensure that your renderer will work in both portrait and landscape mode, and with varying paper sizes and types of printers.

22.10 Control Printing of Unknown Length Content over Multiple Pages

Problem

You need to control the layout of printed output over multiple pages, but you don't know how much data you will be printing or the sizes of the components you need to lay out.

Solution

If you are printing tabular data, you can use the `PrintDataGrid` component to control how data is printed over multiple pages. Used creatively, the `PrintDataGrid` component can be used to control a variety of repetitive multipage output.

Discussion

If you have tabular data, such as a spreadsheet-style report, you can use the `PrintData Grid` component to format that data for multipage output. The `PrintDataGrid` component is a specialized data grid that is designed to format printed data across multiple pages. The following example, from MultipageDataGrid.mxml, utilizes a `PrintData Grid` to format a report for printing:

```
public function print():void
{
    var printJob:FlexPrintJob = new FlexPrintJob();
    if (printJob.start())
    {
        var printGrid:PrintDataGrid = new PrintDataGrid();
        printGrid.width = printJob.pageWidth;
        printGrid.height = printJob.pageHeight;
        printGrid.columns = populationGrid.columns;
        printGrid.dataProvider = populationData.state;
        printGrid.visible = false;
        Application.application.addChild(printGrid);
        printJob.addObject(printGrid);
        while (printGrid.validNextPage)
        {
            printGrid.nextPage();
            printJob.addObject(printGrid);
        }
        printJob.send();
        Application.application.removeChild(printGrid);
    }
}
```

When using a `PrintDataGrid`, you set its size to match your page size. Adding the grid to the print job will add the first page. You can test whether additional pages of data exist by using the `validNextPage` property, and you can advance to the next page of output by using the `nextPage` method.

Used creatively, the PrintDataGrid component can help format many kinds of output. PrintDataGrid isn't restricted to printing only tabular text. PrintDataGrid can be used in combination with an item renderer to produce repetitive layouts of things like charts, images, or complex components. In the following example, GridSquares.mxml, the PrintDataGrid is used in combination with an item renderer to produce a collection of red squares identical to the ManualMultiPage.mxml example:

```
public function print(itemSize:int, itemCount:int):void
{
    var printData:Array = new Array();
    for (var i:int = 0;  i < itemCount;  i++)
    {
        printData.push(itemSize);
    }

    var column:DataGridColumn = new DataGridColumn();
    column.headerText = "";
    column.itemRenderer = new ClassFactory(SquareRenderer);

    var printGrid:PrintDataGrid = new PrintDataGrid();
    printGrid.showHeaders = false;
    printGrid.visible = false;
    printGrid.setStyle("horizontalGridLines", false);
    printGrid.setStyle("verticalGridLines", false);
    printGrid.setStyle("borderStyle", "none");
    printGrid.columns = [column];
    printGrid.dataProvider = printData;
    Application.application.addChild(printGrid);

    var printJob:FlexPrintJob = new FlexPrintJob();
    if (printJob.start())
    {
        printGrid.width = printJob.pageWidth;
        printGrid.height = printJob.pageHeight;
        printJob.addObject(printGrid);
        while (printGrid.validNextPage)
        {
            printGrid.nextPage();
            printJob.addObject(printGrid);
        }
        printJob.send();
    }

    Application.application.removeChild(printGrid);
}
```

22.11 Add a Header and a Footer When Printing

Problem

You need to produce printed output with headers and footers.

Solution

Create a print renderer component to control the page layout.

Discussion

Combining a print renderer with a `PrintDataGrid` enables much finer control over your printed layouts than the `PrintDataGrid` can provide itself. A common task is to add headers and footers to printed pages. This technique involves manipulating whether the header and footer are included in the layout and testing the results by using the `validNextPage` property of the `PrintDataGrid`. The following code, HeaderFooterPrintRenderer.mxml, defines a print renderer that produces multipage output with header and footer areas included where appropriate:

```
<?xml version="1.0"?>
<mx:VBox xmlns:mx="http://www.adobe.com/2006/mxml"
        backgroundColor="#ffffff" horizontalAlign="center">

    <mx:Script>
        <![CDATA[

            public function startJob():void
            {
                //Try to print this on a single page
                header.visible = true;
                header.includeInLayout = true;
                footer.visible = true;
                footer.includeInLayout = true;

                this.validateNow();

                if (printGrid.validNextPage)
                {
                    //The grid is too big to fit on a single page
                    footer.visible = false;
                    footer.visible = false;

                    this.validateNow();
                }
            }

            public function nextPage():Boolean
            {
                header.visible = false;
                header.includeInLayout = false;

                printGrid.nextPage();

                footer.visible = !printGrid.validNextPage;
                footer.includeInLayout = !printGrid.validNextPage;

                this.validateNow();
```

```
                    return printGrid.validNextPage;
                }
            ]]>
        </mx:Script>
        <mx:DateFormatter id="formatter" formatString="M/D/YYYY" />
        <mx:Canvas id="header" height="80" width="100%">
            <mx:Label     text="Population by State"
                          fontSize="24"
                          color="0x666666"
                          horizontalCenter="0"
                          verticalCenter="0"
                          width="100%"
                          textAlign="center" />
        </mx:Canvas>
        <mx:VBox height="100%" width="80%">
            <mx:PrintDataGrid id="printGrid" width="100%" height="100%">
                <mx:columns>
                    <mx:DataGridColumn    dataField="@name"
                                          headerText="State" />
                    <mx:DataGridColumn    dataField="@population"
                                          headerText="Population"/>
                </mx:columns>
            </mx:PrintDataGrid>
        </mx:VBox>
        <mx:DateFormatter id="format" formatString="m/d/yyyy" />
        <mx:Canvas id="footer" height="80" width="100%">
            <mx:Label     text="{formatter.format(new Date())}"
                          left="20" bottom="5" />
        </mx:Canvas>
    </mx:VBox>
```

This component defines a header containing the report title and a footer that displays the date the report was printed. The `startJob` method initializes the print layout to the appropriate first-page layout. It first tries to lay out the page as if all data will fit on a single page. After a call to the `validateNow` method forces the layout of the component to occur, you can test whether the report will fit within one page by testing the `Print DataGrid`'s `validNextPage` property. If the value is false, the report will fit. If not, the layout is adjusted to hide the footer and the layout is updated again. At this point, whether the report is a single page or multiple pages, the first page is ready to be added to the print job. If the report does require multiple pages, the `nextPage` method will prepare the layout appropriately. It hides the header (it will never be used except on the first page) and enables the footer when appropriate.

Building the page-layout intelligence into the renderer greatly simplifies the actual print routine. The following code block, taken from HeaderFooter.mxml, demonstrates the use of the example print renderer in an application:

```
public function print():void
{
    var printJob:FlexPrintJob = new FlexPrintJob();
    if (printJob.start())
    {
        var printRenderer:HeaderFooterPrintRenderer =
```

```
            new HeaderFooterPrintRenderer();

    printRenderer.visible = false;
    this.addChild(printRenderer);
    printRenderer.width = printJob.pageWidth;
    printRenderer.height = printJob.pageHeight;
    printRenderer. .dataProvider = populationData.state;
    printRenderer.startJob()

    do
    {
        printJob.addObject(printRenderer);
    }
    while (printRenderer.nextPage());

    //Send the last page
    printJob.addObject(printRenderer);
    printJob.send();

    this.removeChild(printRenderer);
    }
}
```

The print method begins a print job and sets up a print renderer in a similar fashion to previous examples. This portion of the code finishes by calling the startJob method on the print renderer, which lays out the renderer for the first page. In the next section of the method, the do...while block continues to add pages to the print job until the nextPage method returns false, indicating there are no more pages to lay out. However, because the do...while block invokes the nextPage method at the end of the block, the last page will not yet be added to the print job when the loop completes. The function queues the last page manually, sends the print job, and removes the renderer from the display list.

Index

Symbols

\# (pound) sign, setting symbol attribute values, 292

\$ (dollar sign), matching the ending of a line, 447, 453

& (ampersand), passing data with query strings, 524

* (wildcard), getting values from fromState/ toState properties, 335

+ (plus) expression, 451

- (hyphen), designating ranges of characters, 448

- (hyphen), using compiler arguments, 11

. (dot)
    grouping syntax, 451
    matching characters, 449

/ (backslash) escape, 448

; (semicolon), setting the Path system variable, 14

== operator, 402

=== operator, 402

?! (negative look-aheads), 455

?<! (negative look-behind), 455

?<= (positive look-behind), 455

?= (positive look-ahead), 455

[ ] (square brackets) character class, 448

^ (caret), matching the beginning of a line, 447, 453

{ } (curly braces)
    assigning skin classes inline, 298
    bindable property chains, using, 415
    binding properties and, 406
    objects, creating, 21
    writing event handlers with, 18

| (pipe) in regular expressions, 448

A

acceptDragDrop method (DragManager), 315

Accessibility class, 644

ActionScript
    arrays and objects, creating, 20
    children, setting properties, 18
    code-behind model and, 28
    components, creating, 24–26
    cross-scripting with JavaScript, 567–570
    custom effects, building, 363–365
    data binding and, 411–415
    JavaScript, invoking, 487–489
    modules, creating, 510–512
    MXML, integrating, 1
    projects, creating, 9
    scope, setting, 21–24

ActionScript Message Format (AMF), 401, 546
    SecureAMFChannel, using, 479

ActivityEvent.ACTIVITY events, 243

activityLevel property (Microphone), 243

ADD property (BlendMode), 250

addAsync (FlexUnit), 592

addChild method, 25
    containers, adding/removing from, 68
    TabControls, creating/enabling/disabling, 85

addChild method (HierachicalViewCollection), 394

AddChild method (State), 344, 347

AddChildAction tag, 337–339

addChildAt method
    containers, adding/removing from, 68

We'd like to hear your suggestions for improving our indexes. Send email to *index@oreilly.com*.

L

label attribute (menuitem), 49
Label component, 265
Label control (mx.text), 111
label property (TreeItemRenderer), 142
labelField property, 140
labelFunction property, 47
LAYER property (BlendMode), 250
layout flow for text, 73
layout management, positioning children, 63
left constraint property, 69
library-path (compiler option), 12, 499
library.swf file, 500
LIGHTEN property (BlendMode), 251
LinkBar class, 80
LinkButton control, 57
linker report files, 526
Linux
    compiling MXML files, 16
List control
    calculateDropIndex method, 321
    defaultChangeEffect property, 219
    editable property and, 133
    iconFunction property, 135
    item editor, editing, 151
    itemChangeEffect property, 136
    list renderers, creating, 193–196
list renderers
    ClassFactory object, using, 196–200
ListBase control, 133
    copyItemWithUID method, 320
    drawSelectionIndicator method, 159
    itemsChangeEffect property and, 137
    makeRowsAndColumns method, 217
    showDropFeedback method, 329
listData property (IDropInItemRenderer), 214
lists, 133–159
    drag-and-drop
        between, 322–323
        within, 319–322
    editable, creating, 133–135
    effects, adding to indicate changes, 136–138
    formatting/validating data, 151–153
    icons, setting for, 135
    right-click menus, creating for, 157–159
    selectable items, allowing, 148
    TileList class, setting basic item renderers, 138

ListViewCollection class, 392, 396
LiveCycle server (Adobe), 461, 480
LiveDocs, 624
-load-config option (compc), 613, 616
loaderInfo property, 524
LoadEvent.LOAD event, 476
loadModule (ModuleLoader), 514
loadPolicyFile (Security), 518
loadState function, 497
loadState method (IHistoryManager), 345
loadStyleDeclarations method (StyleMangaer), 272
local function, 285, 286
locale (compiler option), 12
localeChain property, 638
localization, 637–639
    resource modules, using, 639–642
localToGlobal method, 58
localX property (MouseEvent class), 66
localY property (MouseEvent class), 66
location property (CollectionEvent class), 385
look-aheads (regular expressions), 455

M

Mac OS X
    compiling MXML files, 16
make, 611
makeObjectsBindable property (RemoteObject), 462
makeRowsAndColumns method (ListBase), 217
match method (String), 432
match( ) method (String)
    email addresses, locating, 446
Matrix object, 238
matrix parameter (ConvolutionFilter), 238
matrixY parameter (ConvolutionFilter), 238
maxHeight property, 70
maxWidth property, 70
measure method, 597
Memory Profiler view, 628
MenuBar control, 48
    dynamically populating menus, 50
    event handlers, creating, 52
menuitem nodes, 49
menus, 39
    alert messages, displaying, 53
    dynamically populating, 50–52
    event handlers, creating, 52–53

OVERLAY property (BlendMode), 251
override keyword, 25
owner property, 200
    DataGrid, 173
    mx.controls.listClasses.BaseListData, 201

P

paddingBottom style, 64
paddingLeft style, 64
paddingRight style, 64
paddingTop style, 64
PanelSkin class, 59
Parallel object, applying transitions children, 341
Parallel tag, 365
parent argument (Alert class), 55
parents, sizing children using percentage positioning, 65
parse method, 593
parseStyle method (StyleSheet), 126
pasteHandler method, 563
Path systems variable, compiling MXML files, 14
path-element (compiler option), 11
pause method, 366
pausing effects, 366
percentage positioning, 65
PHP, 457
pipe (|) in regular expressions, 448
pixel-level collisions, 245–248
pixilated videos, smoothing, 244
PKCS (Public-Key Cryptography Standards), 535
play method (Sound), 232
    seed controls, creating for sound files, 234
plus (+) expression, 451
PNG files, 230
    applying custom, 289
pop-up windows
    borders, creating custom, 59–60
    multiple, displaying and positioning, 56–59
PopUp control, 91
PopUpManager class, 56–59
    focusIn/focusOut events, handling, 60
    multiple dialog boxes, managing, 91
    TitleWindow components, creating, 79
<port> property (WSDL), 475
<portType> property (WSDL), 475

position property, 21
    SoundChannel, 232
positive look-ahead (?=), 455
positive look-behind (?<=), 455
POST requests, 457
pound (#) sign, setting symbol attribute values, 292
preinitialize event handler, 78, 518
presenceHandler method, 578
preserveAlpha parameter (ConvolutionFilter), 239
preventDefault method, 152
print method, 653
print renderers, 647
PrintDataGrid component, 649
private variables, 21
programmatic skinning, 295–299
PROGRESS constant variable (ModuleEvent class), 516
ProgressEvent.PROGRESS event
    Image, 257
    Preloader Class, 307
Project Properties dialog box
    custom history management, implementing, 496
projects (Flex), creating, 2–7
prop parameter (binProperty method), 349
properties files, 633
Properties panel (Flash IDE library(, applying skins from SWF files, 291
property chains, 415–417
protected variables, 22
public variables, 21
Public-Key Cyptography Standards (PKCS), 535
publish method (NetStream), 240
PUT requests
    RESTful communication, 460

Q

query strings, 524
question mark (?), passing data with query strings, 524
quitHandler method, 580

R

\r (return character), 449
radio buttons, 440

Adobe

ADD CODE, THEN SIMMER

x x x x x x x x x x x x x x x x x x x x x x x x x x x x x x x x x x x x x x x x x x x x x x x x x x x x x x x x x x x x x x x x x x x x x x x x x

ADOBE® FLEX® COOKBOOK

Created in partnership with O'Reilly Media, the online Adobe Flex Cookbook site is where Flex developers come together to find and share code recipes for common RIA development tasks. In fact, some of the recipes you'll find in this book came from the online site. So visit the Adobe Flex Cookbook website today to find solutions and share your own. Bask in the glow of helping fellow developers and start building better RIAs, faster. Who knows, some of your recipes could end up in these pages!

GET COOKING TODAY > www.adobe.com/go/flex_cookbook

The Premier Community Site for all that is RIA!

InsideRIA.com brings some of the sharpest minds—and opinions— in the Rich Internet Application community together, creating the leading resource of its kind. Check in daily for all the news on topics including Flex and ActionScript 3, User Experience, Standards, Adobe® AIR™, Microsoft Silverlight, JavaFX, Google Gears, and other open source topics. InsideRIA also features monthly articles, screencasts, tutorial series and more. If you're a part of the RIA development and design community, you belong here.

InsideRIA.com